THE ULTIMATE WORLD WAR II CALENDAR

VOLUME I: JANUARY TO JUNE

PATRICK WATSON

Copyright © 2023 Patrick Watson.

All rights reserved. No part of this book may be reproduced, stored, or transmitted by any means—whether auditory, graphic, mechanical, or electronic—without written permission of both publisher and author, except in the case of brief excerpts used in critical articles and reviews. Unauthorized reproduction of any part of this work is illegal and is punishable by law.

ISBN: 979-8-89031-558-8 (sc)
ISBN: 979-8-89031-559-5 (hc)
ISBN: 979-8-89031-560-1 (e)

Because of the dynamic nature of the Internet, any web addresses or links contained in this book may have changed since publication and may no longer be valid. The views expressed in this work are solely those of the author and do not necessarily reflect the views of the publisher, and the publisher hereby disclaims any responsibility for them.

One Galleria Blvd., Suite 1900, Metairie, LA 70001
(504) 702-6708
1-888-421-2397

CONTENTS

Chapter 1	The Month of January	1
Chapter 2	The Month of February	121
Chapter 3	The Month of March	223
Chapter 4	The Month of April	331
Chapter 5	The Month of May	442
Chapter 6	The Month of June	568

CHAPTER 1

THE MONTH OF JANUARY

January 1st

Western Europe
- 1872 Czech statesman Emil Hacha was born this year. He died in 1945.
- 1887 Wilhelm Canaris, Chief of the Abwehr (the German intelligence service), was born in Adlersbeck.
- 1888 British Admiral Tom Phillips was born this year. He died on December 10, 1941 when the battleship PRINCE OF WALES was sunk off Malaya by Japanese aircraft.
- 1894 British General Frederick Morgan was born this year and he died in 1967. He had served as COSSAC (Chief of Staff Supreme Allied Commander) and overseen preliminary planning for the D-Day invasion in Normandy.
- 1895 British aircraft designer Reginald Mitchell was born this year. He died in 1937. His most famous design was the Supermarine "Spitfire".
- 1914 British actor Sir Alec Guiness was born this year. He served as a lieutenant in the Royal Navy during the war.
- 1916 British actor Peter Finch was born this year. He served as a gunner with the Australian Army in the Middle East. British actor Trevor Howard was born this year. He served with the 6th Airborne Division and was discharged as a captain.
- 1922 British actor Christopher Lee was born this year. He flew with the Royal Air Force during the war.
- 1924 British author James Clavell ("Shogun", "King Rat" and "Noble House") was born this year. He was captured by the Japanese while serving as a Captain in the Royal Artillery.
- 1934 The German government ordered more than 4,000 aircraft for the new Luftwaffe.
- 1935 Wilhelm Canaris was appointed as Chief of the Abwehr (German intelligence organization).
- 1937 The keel of the Royal Navy battleship PRINCE OF WALES was laid at the Cammell Laird Shipyard in Birkenhead. She would be launched on May 3, 1939. The keel of the Royal Navy battleship KING GEORGE V was laid at the Vickers Armstrong Shipyard in Walker-on-Tyne. She would be launched on February 21, 1939.

1940 The transport ORMANDE arrived at the River Clyde in Scotland. Aboard were troops of the Canadian 1st Division. They were the first Canadian Army forces to be sent to the British Isles. The purchase of "blockade mutton" (dog meat) was legalized in Germany.

1941 The Luftwaffe attacked targets in Northern Ireland. 141 Royal Air Force bombers attacked Bremen, Germany and lost four aircraft. Eleven people were killed in the raid.

1942 The Luftwaffe sent reinforcements to Norway to assist in attacks on Allied convoys bound for Russia. At this time the number of German U-boats based in Norway was increased from three to nine. The Germans executed twenty-three Czechoslovakian workers for sabotage.

1943 British General Archibald Wavell was promoted to Field Marshal. He had commanded the British forces in North Africa from February 15, 1940 until June 22, 1942. He had also commanded the ABDA (American-British-Dutch-Australian) forces in the Southwest Pacific during its brief existence in early 1942.

1944 German Field Marshal Erwin Rommel was appointed as commander of Army Group "B" which was charged with defending the Atlantic coast from Brittany to the Netherlands. The USAAF's Strategic Air Force was activated in Europe under the command of General Carl Spaatz. 421 Royal Air Force bombers attacked Berlin and lost twenty-eight "Lancasters". Seventy-nine people were killed in the raid.

1945 The Luftwaffe destroyed 156 Allied aircraft during an attack in support of their "Ardennes Offensive", commonly referred to on the Allied side as "The Battle of the Bulge". 732 8th Air Force bombers dropped 1,820 tons of bombs on oil and rail targets in Germany and lost seven B17s and one B24. 651 8th Air Force fighters provided support for the bombers and claimed seventeen victories for the loss of two P51s. Stalag XII-A, a prisoner of war camp outside of Limburg, Germany was bombed in error by the USAAF. Sixty American officers were killed in the raid. 104 Royal Air Force bombers attacked the Dortmund-Ems Canal and lost two "Lancasters". Flight/Sergeant George Thompson, of the Royal Air Force's No.9 Squadron, won a posthumous Victoria Cross while serving aboard one of the lost aircraft. Seventeen Royal Air Force "Mosquitoes" attacked fourteen different railroad tunnels near the Ardennes in Belgium and lost one aircraft. Sergeant Charles MacGillivary, of the 44th Division, won a Medal of Honor near Woelfling, France. 157 Royal Air Force bombers attacked the Mittelland Canal. 146 Royal Air Force bombers attacked Vohwinkel, Germany and lost one "Lancaster". 139 Royal Air Force bombers attacked Dortmund, Germany. The first action by the German two-man "Seehund" submarine took place when seventeen of them attacked Allied shipping in the English Channel. Only two returned safely to port. They sank the British trawler HAYBURN WYKE.

1988   Emil Fuchs (British scientist who had given British and American atomic secrets to the Soviets) died this year.
1989   Nazi official Werner Best died this year. He had served as Reich Commissioner of Denmark.
1993   Luftwaffe ace Major Erich Hartmann died this year. He is the highest scoring in history with his 352 aerial victories.

Eastern Europe

1892   Yugoslavian resistance leader Josip Broz ("Tito") was born this year. He died on May 4, 1981.
1942   German forces counter-attacked near Kerch in the Crimea.
1943   The Germans controlled an area of approximately twenty-five by forty miles in Stalingrad. The German 4th Panzer Army (commanded by Hoth) evacuated Yelista.
1944   The Soviet government rejected a request by the Yugoslavian government-in-exile for a treaty of friendship.
1945   The Soviet destroyer DEIATELNYI was sunk by the U596.
1946   Ion Antonescu, Rumanian Premier during the war, was executed this year.

Mediterranean

1892   Abyssinian Emperor Haile Selassie was born this year and died in 1975.
1935   Cyreneca, Tripoli, and Fezzan were merged to form Libya.
1941   The Royal Navy and the Royal Air Force bombarded Bardia, Libya. Five Royal Navy destroyers stopped a French convoy off Oran. Two Frenchmen were killed and four were wounded during the incident.
1942   Axis aircraft attacked the British island of Malta. The British attacked Bardia, Libya.
1943   The American freighter ARTHUR MIDDLETON (7,176 tons) was sunk off Oran by the U73. Seventy-eight of her crew died. U73 survived until December 16, 1943. Fifteen USAAFs 98th Bombardment Group B24s attacked Tunis, Tunisia. The USAAF's 17th Bombardment Group (B26) also attacked Tunis and lost one aircraft.
1944   General George Patton turned command of the American 7th Army over to Mark Clark, who also retained command of the American 5th Army.
1950   Field Marshal Jan Smuts, the South African Prime Minister, died this year.

Atlantic

1940   The U58 sank the Swedish freighter LARS MAGNUS TROZELLI (1,951 tons). Between this date and the end of March the Germans would sink 750,000 tons of shipping and would lose six submarines. During the same period, the Allies would build 350,000 tons of new shipping.

1941 Between this date and the end of March the Germans would sink 1,300,000 tons of shipping and would lose five submarines. During the same period, the Allies would build 400,000 tons.

1942 Between this date and the end of March the Germans would sink 2,100,000 tons of shipping and would lose eleven submarines. During the same period, the Allies would build 800,000 tons.

1943 The British cruiser SCYLLA sank the German blockade runner RHAKOTIS (6,753 tons) 200 miles northwest of Cape Finisterre. The U464 sank the Swedish freighter BRAGELAND (2,608 tons). Between this date and the end of March the Germans would sink 1,500,000 tons of shipping and would lose forty submarines. During the same period, the Allies would build 2,750,000 tons.

1944 Between this date and the end of March the Germans would sink 520,000 tons of shipping and would lose sixty submarines. During the same period, the Allies would build 3,100,000 tons.

1945 Between this date and the end of May the Germans would sink 460,000 tons of shipping and would lose 153 submarines. During the same period, the Allies would build 3,800,000 tons.

North America

1874 US Secretary of the Navy William Frank Knox was born in Boston. He served with Teddy Roosevelt in Cuba during the Spanish-American War. During WWI he enlisted at the age of forty-three and rose to the rank of colonel. After the war he became a journalist and became publisher of the Chicago Daily News. He became Secretary of the Navy on July 11, 1941 becoming one of two Republicans in Roosevelt's cabinet. The other was Secretary of War Stimson. Knox died on April 23, 1944 and was replaced by his deputy Forrestal.

1880 Chicago Tribune publisher Robert McCormick was born this year. He died in 1995.

1882 American rocket scientist Robert Goddard was born this year and died in 1945.

1883 General William Donovan was born in Buffalo, New York. During WWI he won a Medal of Honor, Distinguished Service Cross, Distinguished Service Medal and three Purple Hearts. In July 1941, FDR appointed him as Coordinator of Information. That was a cover name for a secret intelligence gathering organization. During the summer of 1942, it was renamed the Office of Strategic Services which would eventually evolve into the Central Intelligence Agency. He returned to private law practice in 1946 and was named as ambassador to Thailand 1953-54. He died in 1959.

1885 USMC General Julian Smith was born this year and died in 1975.

The Month of January

1887   US naval historian Admiral Samuel Morison was born this year and died on May 15, 1976.

1893   Army General Ralph Smith was born this year.

1894   General John O'Daniel was born this year and died in 1975.

1903   Canadian Charles Foulkes was born this year. He had been a leading member of what is known as "The Great Escape".

1904   American band leader Alton Glenn Miller was born this year. He died in 1944. American nuclear physicist Julius Robert Oppenheimer was born this year. He died on February 18, 1967.

1908   Actor Gene Autry was born this year. He would fly C-47s in the China-Burma-India Theater during the war. Actor Buddy Ebsen was born this year. He served in the Coast Guard in the Aleutians.

1909   Actor Tom Ewell was born this year. He served in a USN gunnery unit in the Atlantic. Actor Burgess Meredith was born this year. He served as a captain in the USAAF.

1916   Actor Kirk Douglas was born this year. He served in a special anti-submarine unit in the Pacific until he suffered internal injuries from a depth-charge explosion.

1917   Future Vice-President Spiro Agnew was born this year. He would win a Bronze Star while serving as a company commander with the 10th Armored Division in Europe. Actor Ernest Borgnine was born this year. He would serve as serve as a Gunner's Mate aboard USN escorts during the war. Actor Richard Boone was born this year. He would serve aboard the carriers INTREPID, HANCOCK and ENTERPRISE as a TBM gunner. Actor Raymond Burr was born this year. He served in the Navy during the war.

1918   Actor Art Carney was born this year. He would be wounded in Normandy while serving with the Army. Actor Cameron Mitchell was born this year. He served as a bombardier during the war.

1919   Actor Robert Stack was born this year. He served as a gunnery officer in the Navy.

1920   Actor Neville Brand was born this year. He was best known for the movie "Stalag 17" and the television Western "Laredo". He would serve in the Army and would be its 4th most decorated soldier.

1921   Hollywood director Robert Altman (directed 1970's "M.A.S.H") was born this year. He would fly forty-six missions as a bomber pilot in the Southwest Pacific. Actor Charles Bronson was born this year. He spent the war driving an Army supply truck at Kingman, Arizona.

1922   Comedian Dan Rowan was born this year. He would serve as a pilot with the 5th Air Force.

1924   Audie Murphy was born this year and died in 1971 a plane crash. Actor Charleton Heston was born this year. He would serve as a radio operator in 11th Air Force B25s in the Aleutians. Actor Carroll O'Connor was born this year. He served aboard fourteen different merchant ships in the North Atlantic. Actor Tony Randall was born this year. He served as lieutenant in the Army. Actor Aristotle "Telly" Savalas was born this year. He was critically wounded in action with the Army. Astronaut Donald "Deke" Slayton was born this year. He flew fifty-six missions over Europe as a pilot and a further seven over Japan.

1925 US Senator Howard Baker was born this year. He would serve as an officer aboard PT boats in the Pacific. Actor Paul Newman was born this year. He served as a gunner aboard torpedo planes in the Pacific.

1926 Actor Mel Brooks was born this year. He served as a combat engineer in the ETO.

1942 Twenty-six countries signed the United Nations Charter in Washington D.C. The US Office of Price Administration banned the retail sale of automobiles and trucks. The battleship PENNSYLVANIA arrived in San Francisco to repair damage she had suffered in the December 7th attack by the IJN on Pearl Harbor.

1943 The light carrier INDEPENDENCE was commissioned. She would be expended in the Bikini A-bomb tests after the war.

1944 The 3rd Army headquarters at Fort Sam Houston, Texas, was alerted for over-seas movement. Its present commander, Courtney Hodges, would be replaced by George Patton when it arrived in the European Theater of Operations. Hodges had replaced Walter Kreuger in 1943. Kreuger would command the 6th Army in the Pacific and Hodges go on to command the 1st Army in Europe. The movie "Arsenic and Old Lace" premiered this year. The star of the movie, Cary Grant, donated his $100,000 salary to the US War Relief Fund.

1945 The submarine STICKLEBACK was launched. She was lost in an accident on May 29, 1958. President Franklin Roosevelt and General Alexander Patch (Commander of the 7th Army in the ETO) died this year.

1946 General Joseph Stilwell (commander of American troops in Southeast Asia) and Presidential advisor Harry Hopkins died this year. The destroyer-transport TATNALL was sold for scrap.

1947 John Winant (US Ambassador to Britain during the war), Admiral Marc Andrew Mitscher (carrier force commander of the 5th Fleet), USMC Generals Evans Carlson (commander of the Marine Raiders on Guadalcanal) and Roy Geiger (air commander on Guadalcanal) and US Army Major General William Sharp (commanded Allied forces on Mindanao in the Philippines in 1942) and Lieutenant General Daniel Sultan (US forces commander in India-Burma), died this year.

1948 Admirals Adolphus Andrews (Commander of the Eastern Sea Frontier) and John Newton (Nimitz' deputy in the Pacific and Commander Southern Pacific from June 1944) died this year.

THE MONTH OF JANUARY

1949 Generals John Porter Lucas (the original commander at Anzio), Walter Short (US Army commander at Pearl Harbor on December 7th) and Under Secretary of State Edward Stettinius died this year.

1950 Canadian Prime Minister MacKenzie King, US Secretary of War Henry Stimson, USAAF Chief of Staff General Henry Arnold, General Walton Walker (commanded the XX Corps in the ETO) and Donald Roebling (builder of the Brooklyn Bridge and inventor of the "Alligator" amphibious tank) died this year.

1951 Admiral Forrest Sherman (commander of the carrier WASP at the time of her loss in 1942 and later served as Chief of Naval Operations), Fritz Kuhn the self-appointed leader of the German-American Bund (he had been sentenced in prison in November 1940 for forgery and embezzlement) and 8th Air Force ace Don Gentile died this year. Also dying this year was Brigadier General Bryant Moore who had commanded the 164th Infantry Regiment on Guadalcanal in 1942. He died in action in Korea.

1952 Secretary of the Interior Harold Ickes, Andrew Higgins (landing craft designer) and Admiral Jonas Ingram (Commander Atlantic Fleet) died this year.

1953 General Jonathan Wainwright (the Allied commander in the Philippines in 1942) and Rear Admiral William Parsons (had armed the Hiroshima bomb) died this year.

1954 Admirals William Blandy (had commanded the Bikini A-bomb tests after the war) and Charles "Soc" McMorris (Chief of Staff for the Pacific Fleet), USN Captain Miles Browning (had served as Chief of Staff for both Admirals Halsey and Spruance in the Pacific), General Raymond McLain (commanded the 90th Division and the XIX Corps in the ETO), Robert Jackson (US prosecutor at the "Nuremburg Trials"), Joseph Keenan (chief prosecutor at the Tokyo war crimes trials) and atomic scientist Enrico Fermi died this year.

1955 Secretary of State Cordell Hull, US Army Major General Frank Merrill (Commander of "Merrill's Marauders" in Burma), Admiral Clifton Sprague (Commander of "Taffy 3" during the "Battle of Leyte Gulf"), USAAF General John Cannon (Commander of the 12th Air Force), USMC Major General "Red" Mike Edson (Commander of the Raiders on Guadalcanal, US Army General Stafford Irwin (commanded the 9th and 5th Divisions in Europe), Owen Roberts (Associate Supreme Court Justice and head of the first of eight official investigations into the December 7th attack on Pearl Harbor) and scientist Albert Einstein died this year.

1956 Former Chief of Naval Operations Admiral Ernest Joseph King, Admiral George Murray (commanded the carrier ENTERPRISE in 1941 and a carrier task force off the Santa Cruz Islands in October 1942), General Lewis Pick and Secretary of Commerce Jesse Jones died this year.

1957   Admiral Frederick Sherman (commanded the carrier LEXINGTON at the time of her loss in 1942 and Carrier Division 2 later in the war) and Paul "Pappy" Gunn (helped develop an air transport service in the Southwest Pacific and had been instrumental in devising increased offensive firepower for USAAF medium bombers in the area) died this year.

1958   USAAF General Claire Chennault (Commander of the American Volunteer Group and the 14th Air Force), US Army Generals John Lee (commanded "Com Z"-Services of Supply in the ETO) and Edward King (commanded the Allied forces on Bataan in 1942), 8th Air Force ace John Godfrey (18 aerial victories), Admiral Robert Ghormley (South Pacific Area Commander), Elmer Davis (Director of the Office of War Information) and Ernest Lawrence (atomic bomb physicist) died this year.

1959   USN Admirals William Halsey (Commander of the 3rd Fleet), William Daniel Leahy (Presidential advisor and former Chief of Naval Operations) and William Pye (temporarily commanded the Pacific Fleet after December 7, 1941), General George Marshall (Army Chief of Staff), and William Donovan (organizer and head of the O.S.S-Office of Strategic Services) died this year.

1960   Admirals Walden Ainsworth (had commanded USN forces at Kula Gulf and Kolombangara) and Arthur Carpender (Commander of the naval forces in the South Western Pacific) and US Army General Charles Ryder (commander of the 34th Division in Italy) died this year.

1961   American diplomats Sumner Welles and Anthony Biddle, Generals Robert Eichelberger (Commander of the 8th Army) and Bedell Smith (Eisenhower's Chief of Staff), and Admirals Aaron "Tip" Merrill (commanded cruiser and destroyer forces in the Southwest Pacific) and Richmond Kelly Turner (amphibious force commander in the Pacific) died this year. USMC ace Colonel John Smith (19 aerial victories) retired from active duty this year and would commit suicide in 1972.

1962   General John DeWitt (Commander of the Western Defense Command), Admirals Patrick Bellinger (Commander of PatWing 2 at Pearl Harbor on December 7th and Admiral Ernest Kings Chief of Staff), Robert Giffen (had commanded USN forces in the Mediterranean, the Pacific, and the Caribbean) and Richard Conolly (had commanded amphibious operations at Sicily, the Marshalls, and the Philippines) and First Lady Eleanor Roosevelt died this year.

1963   Generals Jacob Devers (Commander of the 6th Army Group), Lloyd Fredendall (Commander of the American forces at their defeat at the Kasserine Pass in North Africa) and Lawton Collins (Commander of the V Corps in Europe), USAAF General George Brett (Allied Air Force Commander in Southwest Pacific 1941-42) and Admirals Alan Kirk

(Commander of Amphibious Force-Atlantic Fleet) and William Calhoun (Commander of the Service Force-Pacific Fleet) died this year.

1964 Generals Douglas MacArthur and Ennis Whitehead (Deputy Commander of the 5th Air Force) and Admiral Francis Low (had served as Chief of Staff for the USN anti-submarine force in the Atlantic and had commanded a cruiser division off Okinawa) died this year.

1965 US Army Lieutenant General Lucian King Truscott (had replaced Lucas as Commander of the Allied Forces at Anzio and commanded the entire 5th Army in 1944), William Arnold (Chief of the Army Chaplains), USAAF General Delos Emmons (had replaced Short as commander of the Hawaiian Department), Henry Wallace (Vice-President from 1941 until 1945), Joseph Grew (had been Ambassador to Japan in 1941 and had later served as Under Secretary of State), bombsight inventor Carl Norden, Edward R. Murrow (American radio broadcaster), Quentin Reynolds (American journalist) and Canadian General Henry Crerar (Commander of the 1st Canadian Army in the ETO) died this year.

1966 Pacific Fleet Commander Admiral Chester Nimitz and Generals Richard Sutherland (MacArthur's Chief of Staff) and Courtney Hicks Hodges (Commander of the 1st Army in the ETO) died this year.

1967 Colonel Richard Cole retired from active duty. He had flown on the "Doolittle Raid". The following persons died this year: Admirals Husband Kimmel (Pacific Fleet Commander at Pearl Harbor on December 7th), Charles Lockwood (commander of the USN submarine force operating out of Pearl Harbor), John Reeves (commanded the carrier WASP until 1942 and a carrier division 1943-44) and Claude Bloch (Commander of the naval defenses at Pearl Harbor on December 7th), USAAF Lieutenant General Lewis Brereton (Commander of the Far East Air Force, the 9th Air Force and the 1st Allied Airborne Army), Lieutenant General Walter Krueger (Commander of the 6th Army in the PTO-Krueger had been born in Flatow, east Prussia and had come to America at the age of 8), Major General Albert Jones (commanded the 1st Filipino Corps in 1942), USMC General Holland McTyeire Smith (senior USMC officer in the Pacific), Henry Morgenthau (Secretary of the Treasury), J. Robert Oppenheimer (director of the Los Alamos laboratory that built the A-bomb), "Liberty" ship designer William Gibbs and ship-builder Henry Kaiser.

1968 USMC General Harry Schmidt (commander of the 4th Division) and US Army Major General George Parker (commanded the II Philippine Corps on Bataan in 1942) died this year.

1969 General Dwight Eisenhower, 5th Fleet Commander Admiral Raymond Spruance, General Terry Allen (Commander of the 1st and 104th Divisions), Admiral Daniel Barbey (Commander of the 7th Fleet Amphibious Force),

USAAF General George Stratemeyer (commanded USAAF forces in the CBI), Kentucky Senator Alben Barkley (Majority Leader until 1944), American cryptologist William Friedman (had led the team which broke the Japanese "Purple" codes in 1940) and Allen Dulles (head of O.S.S in Bern, Switzerland), died this year.

1970 USMC General Clifton Cates (Commander of the 4th Division), US Army Major General Leslie Groves (commander of "The Manhattan Project" the development of the atomic bomb) and Brigadier General Benjamin O. Davis (first black general in the US armed forces-his son Benjamin Jr. would become the first black Major General in 1959), Admiral John Hoover (commanded all land-based aerial support for the invasions of the Gilberts, Marshalls and Marianas) and USN Captain Charles Cooke (Commander of the battleship PENNSYLVANIA at Pearl Harbor on December 7th) died this year. The destroyer HOPEWELL was sold for scrap.

1971 Medal of Honor winner Audie Murphy, Generals Wade Haislip (Commander of XV Corps in the ETO), Emmett O'Donnell (commanded various USAAF units in the Pacific) and Norman Cota (Commander of the 28th Division in the ETO), Admiral Emory Land (Head of the War Shipping Administration), Thomas Dewey (Presidential candidate in 1944 and 1948), diplomat Dean Acheson (Assistant Secretary of State) and Admirals Thomas Hart (Commander of the Asiatic Fleet early in the war) and Joseph "Jocko" Clark (carrier task force commander in the Pacific) died this year.

1972 President Harry Truman, Admirals Harold Stark (Chief of Naval Operations at the beginning of the war), Thomas Cassin Kinkaid (Commander of the 7th Fleet), Louis Denfield (Commander of BatDiv-9), Ralph Davison (task group commander in the Pacific), Kent Hewitt (USN commander in the Mediterranean), Felix Stump (Commander of "Taffy 2" during the "Battle of Leyte Gulf) and Thomas Sprague (escort carrier group commander during the "Battle of Leyte Gulf"), USMC ace John Smith (Medal of Honor and nineteen aerial victories), USAAF General Clayton Bissel (Commander of the 10th Air Force in the CBI), Generals Joseph McNarney (US Army Deputy Chief of Staff) and Clarence Huebner (commanded the 1st Division in Europe), and General Leonard Gerow (Commander of 5th Corps, 1st Army) died this year.

1973 Admirals Frank Fletcher (carrier force commander at Midway and Guadalcanal), Arthur Radford (Commander of CarDiv-6), USMC General Archer Vandergrift (the USMC force commander on Guadalcanal), Major General Alvan Gillem (XIII Corps commander in Europe), General Archibald Arnold (commander of the 7th Infantry Division), Richard Tregaskis (author of "Guadalcanal Diary"), Eddie Rickenbacker (leading

American ace during WWI) and actor John Banner died this year. Banner was best known for his part as Sergeant Schultz in the television comedy "Hogan's Heroes", but was a Jew that had escaped from Austria after the German "Anschluss" of 1938. Another actor from the same series, Robert Clarey also a Jew, had spent three years in a German concentration camp.

1974 USAAF General Carl Spaatz (Strategic Air Force Commander in the ETO), USN Admiral James O. Richardson (Kimmel's predecessor as Commander-in-Chief of the Pacific Fleet), rifle designer John Garand, aircraft designer Alexander Seversky, Charles Lindbergh, Lieutenant Colonel Creighton Abrams (had commanded the first relief column into Bastogne during the "Battle of the Bulge" and would later become US Army Chief of Staff), American diplomat Charles Bohlen (FDR's interpreter at the Teheran Conference), aircraft designer Alexander Seversky and Canadian Lieutenant General Guy Simonds (commanded the 1st Canadian Army) died this year. Admiral John Bulkeley retired from active duty. He had commanded the PT boat unit that had evacuated General Douglas MacArthur from the Philippines in 1942.

1975 Generals Anthony "Nuts" McAuliffe (Commander of the 101st Airborne Division at Bastogne during the "Battle of the Bulge") and John O'Daniel (commanded the 3rd Division in the ETO), USMC General Julian Smith (commanded the 2nd Division), 8th Air Force ace John Meyer (24 victories) and cartoonist George Baker (creator of the cartoon character "Sad Sack") died this year.

1976 Admiral Royal Eason Ingersoll (Commander of the Atlantic Fleet), Samuel Eliot Morison (official historian for USN naval operations during WWII), USN Lieutenant Commander Wade McClusky (had commanded the carrier ENTERPRISE air group during the "Battle of Midway", General Harold Bull (had served on the staff of SHAEF), USN Captain Joseph Rochefort (had headed the Navy's code-breaking team at Pearl Harbor) and General Troy Middleton (commanded the VIII Corps in Europe), General William Arnold (commander of the Americal Division in the Pacific) died this year.

1977 Former German rocket scientist Werner von Braun, USAAF Generals George Kenney (5th Air Force Commander) and Westside Larson (3rd Air Force Commander) and Army General Lewis B. Hershey (Director of the Selective Service Committee from July 31, 1941 until 1969) died this year.

1978 General Lucius Clay (had been military Governor of Germany after the war), Admiral John Hall (had commanded USN forces off Normandy and Okinawa) and Robert Murphy (diplomat that had played a major part in the Mediterranean) died this year.

1980 General William Simpson (Commander of the 9th Army) died this year.

1984   US Army General Mark Clark (commanded the 15th Army Group in Italy) and USN Captain Edwin Layton (Head of USN Intelligence for the Pacific Fleet) died this year.

1985   USAAF Lieutenant General Nathan F. Twining died this year. He had commanded the 13th Air Force in the South Pacific, the 15th Air Force in the Mediterranean and the 20th Air Force in the Central Pacific.

1986   Averell Harriman died this year. He had served as ambassador to Russia from October 1943 until 1946. Leon Henderson died this year. He had been Chief of the Office of Price Administration.

1987   USAAF Lieutenant General Ira C. Eaker (commanded the Allied Air Forces in the Mediterranean) died this year.

1990   Major General James M. Gavin died this year. He had commanded the 82nd Airborne Division. Robert Laws died. He had won a Medal of Honor in the Philippines during WWII. USAAF General Curtis LeMay died this year. He had commanded the 20th Air Force in the Pacific during the war. Elliot Roosevelt died this year. He had been FDR's second-oldest son and had commanded a USAAF photo-recon wing in Europe.

1993   Lieutenant General Matthew B. Ridgeway died this year. He had been the US Army Airborne Force's leading commander during the war.

1996   USN Admiral Arleigh Albert "31-Knot" Burke died at the Naval Hospital at Bethesda, Maryland. He was the only officer to serve three terms as Chief of Naval Operations. He had been offered a fourth, but declined. During World War II, he had commanded Destroyer Divisions 43 and 44 and the Destroyer Squadrons 12 and 23 in the South Pacific. He would then serve as Admiral Marc Mitscher's Chief of Staff during operations off the Philippines, Guam, Iwo Jima and Okinawa. He had been awarded the Navy Cross, Legion of Merit, Distinguished Service Medal, Silver Star and Purple Heart. Also buried at Arlington on this day was Admiral Julian Becton. He had commanded the destroyer LAFFEY off Normandy and Okinawa and had been awarded the Navy Cross for the latter action.

1999   8th Air Force ace Robert Johnson (28 victories) died this month.

2003   Medal of Honor recipient Joe Foss died at the age of 87. He had scored twenty-six confirmed and sixteen probables over the Pacific.

Pacific

1877   Japanese Admiral and envoy Kichisaburo Nomura was born this year and died in 1964.

1886   Japanese Admiral Jisaburo Ozawa was born this year and died in 1966.

1889   Australian General Leslie Morshead was born this year and died in 1952.

1891   Japanese Admiral Takijiro Onishi was born this year and died in 1945.

1892   Japanese Admiral Takeo Takagi was born this year and died in 1944. Japanese Admiral Raizo Tanaka was born this year and died in 1969.

The Month of January

1941 The Commander-in-Chief of the Japanese Combined Fleet, Admiral Isoroku Yamamoto, ordered Rear Admiral Takajiro Onishi and his assistant Commander Minoru Genda to study the possibility of attacking the USN base at Pearl Harbor, Hawaii.

1942 The American freighter MALAMA (3,275 tons) was sunk by aircraft launched from the IJN armed merchant cruisers HOKUKU MARU and AIKOKU MARU. Her thirty-eight survivors were later picked up by the two Japanese ships. Two of them died in captivity. Allied forces retreated across the Pampanga River on Luzon. Sarawak was abandoned by British forces. The inter-island steamer MACTAN (2,300 tons) left Manila Bay en route to Australia. Aboard her were 224 wounded Allied troops. The Japanese freighter TEIUN MARU was sunk by a mine in the Lingayen Gulf.

1943 The USN submarine NAUTILUS rescued twenty-nine civilians from Teop, Bougainville. The USN submarine PORPOISE sank the RENZAN MARU (4,999 tons). PORPOISE was scrapped in 1957. American 5th Air Force B17s attacked Rabaul, New Britain. The German armed merchant cruiser MICHEL arrived in Yokohama, Japan. The USN salvage tug RESCUER was lost while trying to save the Soviet freighter TURKSIB off Scotch Cape in the Aleutians (See November 21, 1942). USAAF B26 "Marauders" attacked Munda, New Georgia. The Japanese High Command decided to evacuate their forces from Guadalcanal.

1944 USN Task Group 37.2 (commanded by Sherman and consisting of the carrier BUNKER HILL and the light carrier MONTEREY) attacked Japanese shipping off Kavieng, New Ireland. They damaged the light cruisers OYODO and NOSHIRO. The American 13th Air Force attacked Rabaul, New Britain and lost one B24. PBYs sank the Japanese freighter KANAIYAMA MARU in the Admiraties. The USN destroyers SMITH and HUTCHINS were damaged in a collision off New Guinea. USN LST-446 was damaged off Bougainville by an explosion. The USN submarine HERRING sank the NAGOYA MARU (6,071 tons). The HERRING was lost on June 1, 1944. The USN submarine PUFFER sank the RYUYO MARU (6,707 tons). The PUFFER was scrapped in 1961. The USN submarine RAY sank the OKUYO MARU (2,904 tons). The RAY was discarded in 1960.

1945 The IJN light cruiser KASHNII was sunk in the South China Sea by USN aircraft. The KYOKKO MARU (593 tons) was sunk by a mine. Three American 13th Air Force B25s crashed into mountains while on shipping strikes near Ceram Island. USAAF ace Colonel Charles MacDonald shot down a Japanese "Dinah" and a "Tojo" over Luzon. The American 8th Army began a 4-month "mopping-up" campaign on Leyte. The US Army's 81st Division landed on Fais Island, southeast of Ulithi. Japanese Field

Marshal Hajime Sugiyama and his wife committed suicide this year. General Korechika Anami, he had commanded the Japanese forces in China, Indo-China, and New Guinea, committed suicide on August 15th of this year.

1946 Twenty Japanese soldiers surrendered on Corregidor in Manila Bay.

1947 Admiral Osami Nagano (Chief of the IJN General Staff), General Hatazo Adachi (suicide-had been commander of the 18th Army in New Guinea) and General Haruyoshi Hyakutake (commander on Guadalcanal) died this year.

1948 Hidecki Tojo (Japan's war-time leader) died this year.

1949 IJN Admiral Hiroaki Abe (had been relieved of his command after he failed to bombard Guadalcanal on December 20, 1942) died this year.

1954 Japanese diplomat Saburo Kurusu died this year. He had assisted Ambassador Kichisaburo Nomura in his negotiations with US Secretary of State Cordell Hull prior to December 7, 1941. Australian General Leslie Morshead (commanded the 9th Division in North Africa and the 1st Corps in the southeast Pacific) and Jose Laurel died this year. Laurel had served as the Philippine President under the Japanese during the war.

1961 General Kiyotake Kawaguchi (commanded forces on Guadalcanal) died this year.

1964 Kichisaburo Nomura (Japanese Ambassador to the US) died this year.

1966 IJN Admiral Jisaburo Ozawa died this year. He had commanded the Northern Force at the "Battle of Leyte Gulf".

1969 IJN Admiral and Raizo Tanaka (commanded naval forces in the Southwest Pacific) died this year.

1974 This year, a 52-year-old Japanese Army 2nd Lieutenant, Hiru Onada, surrendered on Lubang in the Philippines.

1975 Hiroshi Oshima (Japan's ambassador to Germany) died this year. Japanese Army Private Teruo Nakamura surrendered in Indonesia this year, having been in hiding since the war.

1976 Mitsuo Fuchida (had commanded the Japanese aerial force that attacked Pearl Harbor in 1941) died this year. He had become an American citizen in 1966.

1977 IJN Admiral Takeo Kurita (had commanded the Center Force during the "Battle of Leyte Gulf") and Koichi Kido (the Emperors Lord Keeper of the Privy Seal) died this year.

1978 Australian Prime Minister Sir Robert Menzies died this year.

1989 IJN Captain Minoru Genda died this year. He had been one of the primary planners for the Japanese attack on Pearl Harbor on December 7, 1941.

China-Burma-India
1947 Burmese insurgent leader Aung San died this year.
1975 Chinese Nationalist leader Chiang Kai-Shek died this year.
1976 Chinese Communist leader Mao Tse-tung died this year.
1977 Burmese revolutionary Ba Maw died this year.

January 2nd

Western Europe
1886 German General Carl-Heinrich von Stulpnagel was born in Berlin. He would serve as Military Governor of Occupied France and would be executed in connection with the July 20, 1944 attempt on Hitler's life.
1895 Swedish Count Bernadotte was born. During the war he was vice-president of the Swedish Red Cross.
1899 German General Hermann von Oppeln-Bronikowski was born.
1941 The Luftwaffe attacked Cardiff in Wales. Forty-seven Royal Air Force bombers attacked Bremen, Germany and lost one "Whitley". Eight people were killed in the raid. German submarine force commander Admiral Karl Doenitz flew to Berlin to attempt to procure the use of German Air Force long-range aircraft to assist his U-boats in their campaign against Allied shipping. His previous requests had been ignored by the Air Force.
1942 Thirty-one Royal Air Force bombers attacked German U-boat installations at Brest, France. Twenty-seven Royal Air Force bombers attacked the same type of targets at St. Nazaire later in the day.
1943 Forty-two Royal Air Force bombers dropped mines off the Biscay ports. Twenty "Spitfires" from the USAAF's 4th Fighter Group flew patrols over the Channel.
1944 Seventy-three American 42nd Bomb Wing B26 "Marauders" attacked railways outside Nice, France. Five B17s from the USAAF's 422nd Bomb Squadron dropped 1,200,000 leaflets on Rennes, Nantes, Paris and Brest. Royal Air Force night-fighter ace John "Cat Eyes" Cunningham scored the last of his twenty aerial victories (a Me410 over Britain). 383 Royal Air Force bombers attacked Berlin and lost twenty-seven "Lancasters". Thirty-six people were killed in the raid.
1945 The American 3rd Army took Bonnerue, Hubertmont and Remagne in the Ardennes area of Belgium and repelled attacks along its relief corridor to the American-held town of Bastogne. The Germans counter-attacked in the Alsace-Lorraine Province of France. Royal Navy Admiral Bertram Ramsey, commander of the Allied Naval Forces in Europe, died in a plane crash outside of Paris. Ramsey had also commanded the Allied evacuation of Dunkirk in 1940. 962 8th Air Force bombers dropped 2,802 tons of

bombs on rail and communication targets in Germany and lost four B17s. 492 8th Air Force fighters provided escort for the bombers and lost three P51s. 521 Royal Air Force bombers attacked Nuremburg, Germany and lost six aircraft. 1,838 people were killed in the raid. 389 Royal Air Force bombers attacked Ludwigshafen, Germany and lost one "Halifax". Danish Resistance forces destroyed a V-2 rocket parts factory in Copenhagen.

1950 Emil Jannings, Nazi film star, died in Strobelhof, Austria.
1975 Luftwaffe ace Theo Osterkamp (thirty-two victories in WWI and six in WWII) died in Baden at the age of eighty-three.

Eastern Europe
1942 The British freighter WAZIRISTAN (5,135 tons) became the first ship to be sunk on the Murmansk convoy route when she was attacked by U134. She had been the first British ship to load military supplies in the US destined for Russia, 47 of her crew went down with her. The Soviets attacked near Vyama.
1943 The Soviet Air Force destroyed seventy-four Luftwaffe aircraft at Salsk, a staging field used for resupplying the surrounded German forces in Stalingrad.
1944 German forces counter-attacked towards Budapest, Hungary. Soviet forces took Radoval, which was eighteen miles from the 1939 Polish border.
1945 German forces drove Soviets back twenty miles near Komarno.

Mediterranean
1941 British naval and air forces attacked Bardia, Libya.
1942 Royal Air Force bombers attacked Naples, Italy. Axis aircraft attacked the island of Malta. The Axis garrison of 7,000 men at Bardia, Libya surrendered to Allied forces. They had been surrounded since the middle of December.
1943 The USAAF's 376th Bombardment Group (B24) and the 12th Bombardment Group (B25) attacked Heraklion Airfield on Crete and lost two B25s. USAAF 12th Air Force B17s, escorted by P38s, attacked La Goulette, Tunisia damaging two freighters. The Royal Navy minesweeper ALARM was a constructive loss after an air-attack at Bone, Italy.
1944 Forty-three American 57th Bomb Wing B25s attacked Terni, Italy.
1945 The Canadians took Conventelli, Italy.

Atlantic
1941 The U65 sank the British freighter NALGORA (6,597 tons). U65 survived until April 28, 1941.

1944   The USN destroyer SOMERS sank the German blockade runner WESTERLAND off Recife, Brazil.

North America

1941   FDR announced a plan to build 200 "Liberty"-type cargo ships.

1942   The USAAF Chief of Staff, General Henry Arnold, ordered the establishment of the 8th Air Force. The headquarters for the unit would be activated twenty-six days later in Savannah, Georgia. The US War Department announced that American troops would be sent to Northern Ireland. The Swedish liner KUNGSHOLM (20,067 tons) was purchased by the American government. She would carry more than 170,000 troops while serving as the transport JOHN ERICSSON. Jimmy Doolittle was promoted to the rank of Lieutenant Colonel.

1944   The battleship IOWA left America en route to the Pacific Theater of Operations. The RMS EMPRESS OF SCOTLAND unloaded Axis prisoners of war at Norfolk, Virginia.

1971   The destroyers METCALFE and CHAMPLIN were stricken.

1994   Benjamin L. Bosworth, age 76, died. He had been one of the prisoners of war that the 1953 movie "Stalag 17" was based on.

Pacific

1942   Japanese forces occupied Manila and the naval base at Cavite on Luzon in the Philippines. American forces on Corregidor in Manila Bay came under daily air-attack by the Japanese.

1943   US Army General Robert Eichelberger's 1st Corps took Buna and Papua on New Guinea. The US Army's 132nd Infantry Regiment attacked Japanese positions on Mount Austin, Guadalcanal. USN PT-boats attacked IJN destroyers that were attempting to deliver supplies to Japanese forces still fighting on Guadalcanal. The USN submarine GRAYBACK sank the IJN submarine I-18. GRAYBACK would be lost on February 27, 1944. The American freighter THOMAS A. EDISON was lost by grounding in the Fijis. USAAF B17s and P38s attacked IJN destroyers south of the Shortland Islands.

1944   The US Army's 32nd Division landed at Saidor, New Guinea. The USMC 7th Regiment tried to expand its bridgehead at Cape Gloucester, New Britain meeting fierce resistance. The submarine FINBACK sank the ISSHIN MARU (10,044 tons).

1945   The American tanker COWANESQUE was hit by a kamikaze. The Japanese Air Force destroyed twenty-two American aircraft on Mindoro in the Philippines. The USAAF sank the IJN escort No.138 off Luzon.

China-Burma-India

1942 Chinese forces began arriving in Burma. The Japanese Air Force attacked Singapore.

1944 The American freighter ALBERT GALLATAN (7,176 tons) was sunk by the IJN submarine I-26 in the Arabian Sea.

1945 British forces occupied Rathduang and Akyab in Burma.

January 3rd

Western Europe

1883 Clement Attlee was born in London. He would serve as Churchill's deputy Prime Minister during the war.

1940 The American steamer MORMACSUN was brought into Kirkwall by blockading Royal Navy forces. She had been en route to Bergen, Norway. An uproar in the American press forced Churchill to issue orders that no more American merchant ships be interfered with by the Royal Navy.

1941 The Luftwaffe attacked Dublin, Eire in error. Seventy-one Royal Air Force bombers attacked the port of Bremen, Germany and lost one "Whitley".

1942 Eighteen Royal Air Force bombers attacked German U-boat installations at Brest, France and lost one "Wellington". Ten Royal Air Force "Hampdens" dropped mines off Brest and lost one aircraft.

1943 Sixty-eight B17s and B24s from the American 91st, 303rd, 305th, 306th and 44th Bomb Groups attacked the German U-boat installations at St. Nazaire, France and lost seven B17s. It was the first time the 8th Air Force had used formation rather than individual bomb dropping. In the newer method all aircraft dropped on signal from the lead bomber. It was also the first time the Germans had used a "predicted barrage" (anti/aircraft fired on the attacking formations predicted route). Twenty-two Royal Air Force bombers attacked Essen, Germany and lost three "Lancasters". Six people were killed in the raid.

1944 Eight Royal Air Force "Mosquitoes" attacked various targets in Germany.

1945 The American 1st Army attacked the northern flank of the "Bulge" in the Ardennes. 1,099 8th Air Force bombers dropped 3,044 tons of bombs on rail and communication targets in Germany. 571 8th Air Force fighters provided escort for the bombers and claimed four victories for the loss of four P51s. An 8th Air Force B24 was lost while on a leaflet operation over Germany. Ninety-nine Royal Air Force "Lancasters" attacked oil targets in Germany and lost one "Lancaster". Major F. Tilston, of the Essex-Scottish Regiment (Canadian), won a Victoria Cross in Germany. German forces penetrated the US-captured city of Aachen, but were driven back out. Four German V-1 rockets impacted near the USAAF's 4th Fighter Groups base at Debden, Britain. Private First-Class George Turner, of the 14th Armored Division, won a Medal of Honor at Phillipsbourg, France. Eight German "Seehund" two-man submarines attempted to attack Allied shipping in the English Channel but are forced to turn back because of bad weather. The German destroyers Z-31 and Z-33 laid a minefield of Hammerfest, Norway.

Eastern Europe
1941   The Italians began a counter-offensive in Albania. Luftwaffe units began arriving in Albania.
1943   Soviet forces took Mozdok and Malgobek near Korosten. German forces began withdrawing from the Caucasus.
1944   Soviet forces took Novograd-Volynsky and Olevsk and crossed the 1939 Polish frontier.

Mediterranean
1925   Benito Mussolini assumed dictatorial powers in Italy.
1941   The Australian 6th Division captured Bardia, Libya. Italian losses were 10,000 casualties and 30,000 prisoners, while Allied casualties totaled less than 500.
1942   Axis aircraft attacked the island of Malta.
1943   The Italian light cruiser ULPIO TRAIANO and the transport VIMINALE were severely damaged at Palermo, Sicily by British "Chariots" (human torpedoes) launched by the Royal Navy submarines TROOPER and THUNDERBOLT.
1944   Major General Nathan F. Twining replaced James Doolittle as commander of the American 15th Air Force. Doolittle was to assume command of the 8th Air Force in Britain. Fifty-three 15th Air Force B17s dropped 171 tons of bombs on the Villar-Perosa ball-bearing factory. Fifty 15th Air Force B17s attacked the Turin railyards.
1945   The American freighter HENRY MILLER (7,207 tons) was a constructive loss after an attack by the U870 off Morocco. U870 survived until March 30, 1945.

Atlantic
1940   The U58 sank the Swedish freighter SVARTON (2,475 tons). U58 was scuttled at the end of the war.
1943   The German armed merchant cruiser MICHEL took the British freighter EMPIRE MARCH (7,040 tons). The U507 sank the British freighter BARON DECHMONT (3,675 tons). U507 survived until January 13, 1943. The USN seaplane tender HUMBOLDT rescued ten survivors from the

Philippine vessel DONA AURORA which had been sunk on December 25th by the Italian submarine ENRICO TAZZOL.

1944 The U744 sank the British freighter EMPIRE HOUSMAN (7,359 tons). U744 survived until March 6, 1944. At 0615, the USN destroyer TURNER suffered an ammunition explosion off Ambrose Light. She sank at 0827 with the loss of 153 of her crew. She had sunk in only forty-five feet of water and due to this fact her hulk was blown up on July 4, 1944 after being declared an obstruction to navigation.

North America

1940 FDR requested $1.8 billion for national defense.

1942 Admiral Ernest King, commander of the USN's Atlantic Fleet, was named as Commander-in-Chief of the entire USN Fleet. He would also be named as Chief of Naval Operations on March 18th. The five Sullivan brothers (George, Francis, Joseph, Madison, and Albert) enlisted in the USN. George and Francis had been in the Navy since 1937 and when they reenlisted, their younger brothers had joined to avenge a friend who had been killed aboard the battleship ARIZONA at Pearl Harbor. On February 3rd, they all reported aboard the light cruiser HELENA at the Brooklyn Navy Yard. They would all die on November 13th when the IJN submarine I-26 sank their ship in the South Pacific. On April 13, 1943 their mother, Mrs. Thomas F. Sullivan, would christen a destroyer named in their honor at the Bethlehem shipyard in San Francisco. The ship (THE SULLIVANS) would go on to win nine battle stars during the war and would be preserved as a memorial.

1944 The escort carrier NEHENTA BAY was commissioned. She was scrapped in 1960. The carrier RANGER was redesignated as a training carrier and aircraft transport. She was scrapped in 1947. The destroyer TURNER was destroyed near the Ambrose lightship off New York by an internal explosion.

1946 The seaplane tender CHILDS, the destroyer-minesweeper STANSBURY, and the destroyer-minelayer PREBLE were sold for scrap.

1956 The US Coast Guard cutter VIGILANT was sold.

1961 The battleship WEST VIRGINIA was scrapped at Todd Shipyard in Seattle.

Pacific

1942 A unified Allied command was established in the Southwest Pacific under the command of British General Alexander Wavell, with USAAF General George Brett as his deputy. The new force was to be designated ABDA (for **A**merican-**B**ritish-**D**utch-**A**ustralian). The Royal Navy destroyer

ENCOUNTER was sunk by the IJN. Japanese forces invaded Labuan Island in Brunei Bay. After the evacuation of General Douglas MacArthur, General Jonathan Wainwright assumed command of the Allied forces on Bataan and Corregidor in the Philippines. The USN destroyer PEARY arrived at Darwin, Australia from the Philippines. She was declared unfit for combat operations and was detailed to act as a harbor escort vessel. Two Royal Australian Air Force "Hudsons" arrived at Townsville, Australia. The aircraft, the "Tit Willow" and the "Greens Yum Yum", were to be the first Allied planes to fly over the IJN base at Truk since well before the war began (See January 4th, 6th and 9th). The IJN submarine I-158 sank the Dutch freighter LANGKOEAS (7,395 tons).

1943 The USN submarine GRAYBACK sank the IJN submarine I-18. The GRAYBACK was lost on February 27, 1944. The USN submarine BLUEFISH laid mines off Malaya.

1944 Fighting continued on New Britain near Borgen Bay. USMC ace Major Gregory Boyington was shot down by Masajiro Kawato and captured. USAAF ace Colonel Neel Kearby shot down a "Sally" and a "Zeke" near Wewak, New Guinea. USN forces attacked the Ryukyus and Formosa. The USN submarine TAUTOG sank the SAISHU MARU (2,073 tons). TAUTOG was scrapped in 1960. The USN submarine KINGFISH sank the RYUEI MARU (5,144 tons) and the BOKUEI MARU (5,135 tons). KINGFISH was discarded in 1960. The IJN tanker AKEBONO MARU was damaged by the USN submarine RATON. RATON was still commissioned in 1960.

1945 USN Task Force 38 aircraft attacked Japanese installations on Formosa and in the Ryukyus. Ninety-seven B29s attacked Nagoya, Japan and lost five aircraft. A Japanese aircraft strafed Tacloban Airfield on Leyte and destroyed nine USN TBFs and nine PV-1s. The USN escort carrier OMMANEY BAY was crashed by a Japanese "Francis" and ninety-three of her crew died. She was scuttled later in the day by a torpedo from the USN destroyer BURNS. The USN submarine KINGFISH sank the YAEI MARU (1,941 tons) and the SHOTO MARU (572 tons). The KINGFISH was discarded in 1960. The Royal Navy submarine STRATAGEM was sunk by the IJN. The USN escort carrier SARGENT BAY and the destroyer escort ROBERT F. KELLER were damaged in a collision in the Philippines.

China-Burma-India

1932 Japanese forces occupied Chinchow, Manchuria.

1942 Chiang Kai-shek was named as Commander-in-Chief of Allied Forces in China. Lieutenant Colonel A. Cumming, of the 12th Frontier Force Regiment, won a Victoria Cross in Malaya. Fifty-one crated "Hurricane"

fighters arrived in Singapore as reinforcements for the British Commonwealth forces stationed there.
1945 British forces took Yeu, Burma. American 14th Air Force P51s attacked the Japanese Air Force Base at Tsinan, China, destroying thirteen aircraft. American 20th Bomber Command B29s attacked Bangkok, Thailand.

January 4th

Western Europe
1940 Reich Marshal Hermann Goering was given control of German War Industry. The German cruiser KARLSRUHE and the minelayer SCHIFF No.23 intercepted the Swedish steamer KONG OSCAR that was carrying forty-two Polish refugees. The ship was confiscated and sent to Germany.
1941 Fifty-three Royal Air Force bombers attacked the port of Brest, France.
1943 Thirty-three Royal Air Force bombers attacked Essen, Germany and lost two "Lancasters". Fourteen people were killed in the raid. Twenty "Spitfires" from the USAAF's 4th Fighter Group flew patrols over the Channel.
1944 486 8th Air Force B17s and B24s dropped 1,069 tons of bombs on Kiel, Germany and lost eleven B17s and six B24s. 112 8th Air Force P38s and P51s provided support for the bombers and claimed one victory for the loss of one P38 and one P51. Sixty-eight 8th Air Force B17s dropped 192 tons of bombs on Munster, Germany and lost two aircraft. 430 8th Air Force P47s provided support for the bombers. The Allies "Operation Carpetbagger" took place when Royal Air Force and USAAF dropped arms and supplies to Belgian, Italian, and French partisans. Eighty Royal Air Force bombers attacked German V-1 rocket launching sites in France. Four B17s from the USAAF's 422nd Bomb Squadron dropped 800,000 leaflets on Orleans, Lorient, Tours, and Rouen in France.
1945 Staff Sergeant Isadore Jachman, of the 513th Parachute Regiment, won a posthumous Medal of Honor at Flamierge, Belgium. An 8th Air Force B24 "Carpetbagger" was shot down by British anti/aircraft fire over Namur, Belgium. The "Carpetbagger" aircraft were employed in dropping supplies to Resistance forces on the Continent. 354 Royal Air Force bombers attacked the French city of Royan, which was still occupied by German troops, and lost six aircraft.
1949 British General William Slim was promoted to Field Marshal. He had commanded the British forces in Burma.
1962 Hans Lammers, Chief of the Reich Chancellory, died in Dusseldorf.
1963 German General Fridolin von Senger und Etterlin died. He had commanded forces in Russia and in Italy including the defenses at Cassino.

2015   The last known British survivor of the notorious Death Railway in Burma, Harry Wiliams, died at the age of 96. The railway and its story was the basis for the movie "The Bridge on the River Kwai".

Eastern Europe
1942   German forces took Borovsk.
1943   The Soviets took Nalchik in the Caucasus.
1944   Tito's Partisans took Banja Luca, Yugoslavia. The Soviets took Belaya Tserkov near Kiev. A force of 108 American 15th Air Force B17s attempting to attack Sofia, Bulgaria was thwarted by weather.
1945   German forces attempted to break out of Budapest, Hungary. A KG200 Bl7 delivered German agents to the Odessa area. KG200 was a Luftwaffe unit organized to utilize captured Allied aircraft in special operations. They were also responsible for the testing of new aircraft.

Mediterranean
1941   The Greeks began an offensive against the Italians. General Archibald Wavell ordered the British forces in Libya to attack Italian forces.
1943   USAAF B26 "Marauders" attacked Kairoun, Tunisia.
1945   The British 8th Army attacked Senio, Italy.

Atlantic
1943   The American submarine SHAD sank the German minesweeper M-4242 in the Bay of Biscay.
1945   The U1232 sank the Norwegian freighter POLARLAND (1,591 tons) and damaged the Canadian tanker NIPIWAN PARK (2,373 tons).

North America
1943   The USN escort carrier TRIPOLI was damaged by a fire in San Diego.
1945   A Japanese balloon-bomb exploded near Medford, Oregon, another was found near Sebastopol, California.
2010   USN ace Captain Donald Gordon died at the age of 89. He had scored 5 aerial victories while flying the F6F "Hellcat" in the Pacific.

Pacific
1939   Prince Konoye resigned as Japan's Premier.
1942   Japanese aircraft attacked Rabaul, New Britain for the first time. The number of Allied aircraft at Rabaul totaled ten "Wirraway" trainers and four "Hudson" patrol bombers. The Royal Australian Air Force "Hudsons" "Tit Willow" and "Greens Yum Yum" (See January 3rd) arrived at Lae, New Guinea. The

first Allied civilian prisoners arrived at Santo Tomas Concentration Camp, Leyte. An aircraft launched from the IJN submarine I-19 flew over Pearl Harbor to record damages inflicted during the December 7th attack.

1943 USN forces (commanded by Ainsworth) bombarded Munda, New Georgia. The first use of the proximity fuse took place when the USN light cruiser HELENA fired on a torpedo bomber during the attack. The Japanese High Command ordered the evacuation of Guadalcanal. A Japanese counter-attack rescued part of their Buna garrison on New Guinea. The USN submarine SHAD sank the IJN minelayer M-4242 (212 tons). SHAD was discarded in 1960. USN Admiral Thomas C. Kinkaid relieved Admiral Thomas A. "Fuzzy" Theobald as Commander-North Pacific.

1944 Fighting continued on New Britain. USN Task Group 37.2 (commanded by Sherman) attacked Kavieng, New Ireland and damaged the IJN destroyers SATSUKI and FUMITSUKI. 5th Air Force B25s attacked Japanese shipping off Timor and sank the freighter HEIMEI MARU. The Japanese freighter KATSURAGISAN MARU (2,427 tons) was sunk at Truk by a mine. The USN submarine BLUEFISH sank the HAKKO MARU (6,046 tons). BLUEFISH was discarded in 1959. The USN submarine TAUTOG sank the USA MARU (3,943 tons). TAUTOG was scrapped in 1960. The USN PT-145 was scuttled at Mindiri, New Guinea. The USN submarine CABRILLA sank the TAMON No.3 (2,704 tons). The CABRILLA was still in commission in 1962.

1945 Royal Navy Task Force 63 (commanded by Vian) attacked refineries on Sumatra. The American freighter LEWIS DYCHE was sunk with all hands by a kamikaze. The IJN minesweeper W-41 was sunk off Formosa by USN carrier aircraft.

China-Burma-India

1932 Japanese forces entered Shanhaikuan, completing their occupation of Southern Manchuria.

1942 A member of Sorge's spy ring, Hisao Funakoshi, was arrested in Peiping by Japanese police. Indian leaders said they would support the Allies if they were granted dominion status after the war.

1945 British forces occupied Akyab Island off the Arakan Coast.

January 5th

Western Europe

1919 The Germans Worker's Party (the future Nazi Party) was founded by Anton Drexler in Munich. The Spartacist (Communist) uprising began in Germany and would last until the 11th.

1938	Austria tried and convicted twenty-seven Nazis for anti-government activities.
1940	Leslie Hore-Belisha was dismissed as Britain's Minister of War and replaced by Oliver Stanley. Hore-Belisha died in 1957.
1941	USN Admiral William D. Leahy became US Ambassador to Vichy France. Twelve Royal Air Force "Hampdens" attacked the Channel ports and lost one aircraft.
1942	154 Royal Air Force bombers attacked the port of Brest, France.
1943	French Premier Philip Petain announced the formation of the "Milice", the Vichy militia.
1944	General Carl Spaatz was appointed as Commander-in-Chief of the USAAF in Europe and the Mediterranean. 225 8th Air Force B17s and B24s dropped 602 tons of bombs on Kiel, Germany and lost five B17s and five B24s. 111 8th Air Force P38s and P51s provided support for the bombers and claimed twenty-two victories for the loss of seven P38s. 112 8th Air Force B17s dropped 266 tons of bombs on the Bordeaux/Meriganc airfield in France and lost eleven aircraft. Seventy-six 8th Air Force P47s provided support for the bombers and claimed two victories for the loss of five aircraft. Seventy-eight 8th Air Force B17s dropped 177 tons on Tours, France and lost one aircraft. 149 8th Air Force P47s provided support for the bombers and claimed three victories. Seventy-three 8th Air Force B17s dropped 194 tons of bombs on Neuss, Geilenkirchen, Dusseldorf and Wassenburg in Germany and lost two aircraft. 243 8th Air Force fighters provided support for the bombers and claimed six victories. The 91st Bombardment Group (B17) became the first 8th Air Force Bomb Group to complete 100 missions. 358 Royal Air Force bombers attacked Stettin, Germany and lost sixteen aircraft. 524 buildings were destroyed and 244 people were killed in the raid.
1945	German forces attacked north of Strasbourg, France. 893 8th Air Force bombers dropped 2,153 tons of bombs on rail and airfield targets in Germany and lost one B17. 537 8th Air Force fighters provided escort for the bombers and claimed five victories for the loss of one P51. 160 Royal Air Force bombers attacked Ludwigshafen, Germany and lost two "Lancasters". 267 people were killed in the raid. 664 Royal Air Force bombers attacked Hannover, Germany and lost thirty-one aircraft. 250 people were killed in the raid. 140 Royal Air Force bombers attacked Houffalize, Belgium and lost two "Lancasters". Sixty-nine Royal Air Force "Mosquitoes" attacked Berlin and lost two aircraft. Anti-Hitler conspirator Julius Leber was hung at Ploetzensee prison.
1946	The Royal Navy escort carrier ATTACKER was transferred back to the USN. The German heavy cruiser PRINZ EUGEN was transferred to the USN at Bremerhaven, Germany.

1950 Erich Ludendorff's wife, Malthilde, was tried by a De-Nazification court in Munich and sentenced to two years as a "Major Offender".
1975 German S.S. General Gottlob Berger, Chief of Staff Military S.S., died.

Eastern Europe
1942 Soviet forces landed reinforcements on the Crimean Coast; Stalin ordered a major offensive that was to begin on the 7th.
1943 Soviet forces took Morozousk, a major German airfield outside Stalingrad, and Chinliansk.
1944 The Soviets took Berdichev and Tarascha, southwest of Kiev.
1945 America and Britain refused to recognize the "Lublin Committee" as the legitimate government of Poland. Luftwaffe ace Gerd Barkhorn scored his 300th victory.

Mediterranean
1941 The Australian 6th Division took 20,000 Italians, 460 guns, 131 tanks and 700 trucks at Bardia, Libya.
1942 Axis aircraft attacked Malta. The Royal Navy submarine UPHOLDER sank the Italian submarine ST.BON off Sicily. British forces attacked the Axis at Halfaya Pass in Libya. A German convoy delivered fifty-four MkIII and MkIV tanks to the DAK at Tripoli, Libya. American 12th Air Force B17s attacked Sfax, Tunisia, destroying its power station.
1943 US General Mark Clark's 5th Army became operational in Tunisia. USAAF Sergeant Paul Leonard was killed in a Luftwaffe raid on Youks-Les-Bains, Algeria while serving as General James Doolittle's crew chief on a B26 "Marauder". He had been Doolittle's crew chief on the Tokyo raid in 1942. USAAF B26s attacked Kairoun, Tunisia.
1944 The American 5th Army began its final assault on the Germans "Gustav Line" in Italy.
1945 Fighting between British forces and Greek communists ended near Athens.
1955 Marcel Deat, Vichy Minister of Labor, died in an Italian monastery.

Atlantic
1941 The Italian submarine CAPPELLINI sank the British freighter SHAKESPEARE (5,029 tons). The CAPPELLINI was seized by the Germans in September 1943 and recommissioned as the German UIT.24. The German patrol boat V-306 was sunk by a mine off Holland.
1944 The American freighters MARTIN JOHNSON and FRANK C. EMERSON were damaged in a collision off Bermuda.

North America

1887 General Courtney Hicks Hodges, commander of the 1st Army in Europe, was born in Perry, Georgia. He entered West Point in June 1904. He was "found deficient' in mathematics and sent home. He enlisted as a private in 1906 and was commissioned in 1909. During WWI he would command a battalion and win a Silver Star and a Distinguished Service Cross. From 1938 he was assistant commandant of the Infantry School at Fort Benning, Georgia. He was commandant from October 7, 1940 until March 31, 1941. He was then named as Chief of Infantry and held that post March 9, 1942. On May 12th he assumed command of the 10th Corps in San Antonio, Texas. He then commanded the 3rd Army and the Southern Defense Command. In the spring of 1943, he went to Britain to become Omar Bradley's deputy in command of the 1st Army. He took command of the 1st Army on August 1, 1944. He was promoted to four-star rank on April 15, 1945. He retired in 1949 and died in San Antonio on January 16, 1966.

1936 The first flight of the USN's "Vindicator" dive-bomber took place.

1942 Rubber was rationed in the U.S. Curtis LeMay was promoted to Lieutenant Colonel. He would become the Air Force Chief of Staff during the 1960's.

2012 USAAF Colonel Frank Hill died in Birnamwood, Wisconsin at the age of 92. He had been credited with 7 aerial victories while flying Spitfires in the Mediterranean.

2014 USAAF Colonel William Shaeffer died in Colorado Springs, Colorado at the age of 96. He had been credited with 2 aerial victories while flying P47s over Europe and scored 3 more over Korea in 1952.

Pacific

1939 Baron Hiranamu was named as Japan's Prime Minister.

1942 The IJN submarine I-156 sank the British freighter KWANTUNG (2,626 tons). The Allies established the "Layac Line" near the Bataan Peninsula on Luzon. The USN light cruiser HELENA left Pearl Harbor for the Mare Island Naval Yard in California to repair damages suffered in the December 7th attack.

1943 The US Army's 25th Division relieved the 132nd Infantry Regiment in the attack on Mount Austin on Guadalcanal. The Japanese began evacuating their forces from Guadalcanal. The Australian 18th Brigade took Soputa, New Guinea. Japanese Air Force aircraft were encountered for the first time in the Solomons when they intercepted USAAF B17s over Rabaul, New Britain. Up to this time all the Japanese aircraft in the area had been from the IJN. Brigadier General Kenneth Walker, the commander of the American 5th Bomber Command, won a posthumous Medal of Honor during the action. Three American 11th Air Force B25s sank the freighter MONTREAL MARU. An 11th Air Force B24 sank the KOTONHIRO MARU (6,500 tons) off Attu in the Aleutians. USAAF B17s and P38s attacked IJN forces off New Georgia and lost two P38s.

1944 Fighting continued on New Britain. The USN submarine RASHER sank the KIYO MARU (7,251 tons). The RASHER was still in commission in 1960. The Japanese government increased taxes to help cover the cost of the war.

1945 A force of three USN cruisers and nine destroyers (commanded by McCrea) bombarded the Kuriles, north of the Japanese Home Islands. Another unit consisting of three cruisers and six destroyers (commanded by Smith) bombarded Iwo Jima, Haha Jima and Chichi Jima in the Central Pacific. The USN heavy cruiser LOUISVILLE (one dead), the escort carrier MANILA BAY (15 dead), the destroyer STAFFORD (2 dead) and the Royal Australian Navy heavy cruiser AUSTRALIA (25 dead) were hit by Japanese kamikazes. The IJN destroyer escort MOMI was sunk off Manila by USN escort carrier aircraft. The USN submarine CAVALLA sank the KANKO MARU (909 tons) and SHUNSEN MARU (971 tons). CAVALLA was still in commission in 1963. The USN destroyer escorts EDWIN A. HOWARD and LELAND E. THOMAS were damaged in a collision off Mindanao. The USN minelayer MONADNOCK was damaged when she ran aground off Luzon.

China-Burma-India
1933 Japan declared that it had no territorial demands south of the Great Wall of China.
1942 Japanese reinforcements landed on the Malayan Coast.

January 6th

Western Europe
1940 The U30 mined Liverpool Bay in western Britain.
1941 Three Royal Air Force "Blenheims" attacked German shipping off Holland.
1942 Thirty-one Royal Air Force "Wellingtons" attacked the port of Brest, France and damaged the German battle cruiser GNEISENAU.
1943 German Navy Commander Grossadmiral Erich Raeder reported to Hitler's headquarters at Rastenburg. After Hitler had lectured him on the various failures of the Navy, he was informed that the surface fleet was to be paid off and scrapped.

1944 USAAF General James Doolittle relieved Ira Eaker as commander of the 8th Air Force in Britain. Eaker was transferred to the command of all USAAF forces in the Mediterranean Theater. One hundred and twenty Royal Air Force "Mosquitoes" attacked targets in Germany. Fifty-seven Royal Air Force bombers dropped mines off the Biscay ports. Five B17s from the USAAF's 422nd Bomb Squadron dropped 984,000 leaflets on Amiens, Lille, Valenciennes, Cambrai, and Reims in France.

1945 788 8th Air Force bombers dropped 2,223 tons of bombs on rail targets in Germany and lost one B17. 567 8th Air Force fighters provided support for the bombers and claimed fourteen victories for the loss of two P51s. 482 Royal Air Force bombers attacked Hanau, Germany and lost six aircraft. Ninety people were killed in the raid. 147 Royal Air Force bombers attacked Neuss, Germany and lost one aircraft. Thirty-nine people were killed in the raid. The US Military Police broke up a gang of AWOL GIs and French civilians that had been dealing in stolen US Army supplies (one gang member was killed in the operation). The Royal Navy destroyer escort WALPOLE was a constructive loss after hitting a mine off Flushing. Two of her crew died. Two German "Seehund" two-man submarines attempt to attack Allied shipping in the English Channel, but fail due to engine trouble. Hitler refused Rundstedt's request to withdraw German forces to positions east of the Rhine.

1984 British General Brian Horrocks, the commander of the British Army's XXX Corps, died in a Fishbourne nursing home.

Eastern Europe
1940 Finnish ace Jorma Sarvanto (17 victories) shot down six Soviet bombers in less than four minutes.
1944 Soviet forces took Rakitino, Poland.
1945 The Germans recaptured Esztergom outside of Budapest, Hungary. The Soviet submarine S-4 was sunk by the German torpedo boat T-33.

Mediterranean
1941 The Italian submarine MARCELLO was sunk by the Royal Air Force. A British convoy consisting of four freighters left Gibraltar en route to Malta. At this time, there were only fifteen "Hurricane" fighters on Malta to defend the island.
1942 A British offensive was stopped at El Agheila, Libya.
1944 The American freighter WILLIAM S. ROSECRANS was damaged off Naples, Italy by a mine and was later scuttled by the Royal Navy. American forces took San Vittore, Italy.
1945 The American freighter ISSAC SHELBY was a constructive loss after hitting a mine off Italy.

Atlantic

1940 The Royal Navy submarine UNDINE was forced to surrender off Heligoland by German surface forces. Her crew of twenty-nine was captured, but the submarine sank while under tow en route to Germany.

1941 The U124 sank the British freighter EMPIRE THUNDER (5,965 tons). U124 survived until April 2, 1943. The German armed merchant cruiser KORMORAN took the Greek collier ANTONIS (3,729 tons).

1942 The U701 sank the British freighter BARON ERSKINE (3,657 tons). U701 survived until July 7, 1942.

1943 The U164 was sunk off Brazil by USN VP-83.

1944 The USN gunboat ST. AUGUSTINE was rammed and sunk off Norfolk, Virginia by the freighter CAMAS MEADOWS, 115 of her crew died.

North America

1941 FDR recommended his idea of "Lend-Lease" to the Congress (See January 10th). The battleship MISSOURI's keel was laid in New York.

1942 FDR asked Congress for an appropriation to build, by the end of 1943, 125,000 aircraft, 75,000 tanks, 35,000 cannon and 8 million tons of shipping.

1947 George Marshall was recalled from his post as Ambassador to China. He had served as US Army's Chief of Staff during the war.

1948 The destroyer FLUSSER was sold for scrap.

1994 The USN upheld the convictions of 50 black sailors convicted of mutiny in 1944. They had refused to load ammunition ships after two such ships had exploded at Port Chicago in Suisun Bay, California.

Pacific

1940 Admiral James O. Richardson relieved Admiral Claude C. Bloch as Commander-in-Chief US Fleet aboard the PENNSYLVANIA at Pearl Harbor. Admiral Charles P. Snyder became Commander Battle Force aboard the battleship CALIFORNIA at Pearl Harbor.

1942 Philippine President Quezon's yacht CASIANA was sunk off Corregidor by Japanese aircraft. The Allies retreated towards the Bataan Peninsula from the "Layac Line" on Luzon. Rations for the Allied troops on Bataan were halved. The steamer MACTAN arrived at Makassar in the Dutch East Indies from the Philippines (See January 1st). Japanese forces took Brunei Bay, Borneo. Japanese aircraft flying from Truk attacked Rabaul, New Britain. The two Royal Australian Air Force "Hudsons" (See January 3rd) that were to overfly the IJN anchorage at Truk landed at Rabaul, New Britain. One of the aircraft, "Greens Yum Yum", developed engine trouble and was dropped from the operation. Later in the day, the other aircraft, the "Tit Willow", was moved to Kavieng, New Ireland to escape detection by Japanese patrol planes. The IJN submarine I-156 damaged the Dutch freighter TANIMBAR (8,169 tons). A convoy consisting of the USN heavy cruiser PENSACOLA and the transports HOLBROOK and CHAUMONT (See December 28, 1941) arrived at Darwin after it had been decided that it couldn't reach the Philippines as planned.

1943 The American 5th Air Force attacked installations at Lae, New Guinea, and Japanese shipping off the Shortland Islands. A Royal Australian Air Force PBY sank the NICHIRYU MARU off New Guinea. The American 11th Air Force attacked Kiska in the Aleutians.

1944 General Millard F. Harmon assumed command of the American 13th Air Force. Sixteen USAAF P38s and eight USMC F4Us attacked Rabaul, New Britain downing nine Japanese aircraft and losing two P38s. American forces expanded their bridgehead at Cape Gloucester, New Britain.

1945 USN Task Force 38 attacked Luzon in the Philippines. The USN destroyer-transport BROOKS was hit by a Japanese kamikaze and declared a constructive loss. Three of her crew died. The USN destroyer-minesweeper LONG was hit by a kamikaze and foundered the next day (one died). The Royal Australian Navy heavy cruiser AUSTRALIA, the USN heavy cruisers LOUISVILLE and MINNEAPOLIS, the battleship NEW MEXICO (30 dead, including her commander, Captain R.W. Fleming), the light cruiser COLUMBIA, the destroyers SUMNER, WALKE (her Commanding Officer Commander George Davis won a Medal of Honor) and O'BRIEN and the destroyer-minesweeper SOUTHARD were hit by kamikazes. The USN battleship CALIFORNIA was hit by a kamikaze; among her 44 dead was Winston Churchill's personal representative to MacArthur's headquarters, Lieutenant General Herbert Lumsden. The USN submarine SEA ROBIN sank the TARAKAN MARU (5,135 tons). The USN submarine BESUGO sank the NICHIEI MARU (10,020 tons). The USN battleship MISSOURI arrived at Ulithi for combat operations. USAAF B29s attacked Omura on Kyushu. The American 13th Air Force attacked Nichols and Nielsen Airfields on Luzon.

1949 The last two Japanese soldiers on Iwo Jima surrendered to authorities. They had been hiding in caves since the battle in 1945.

1989 Japan's Emperor Hirohito died of cancer.

China-Burma-India

1941 Thai forces attacked Cambodia.

1945 14th Air Force B24s attacked Japanese shipping off Indochina and sank the IJN sub chaser Cha-64 and the tanker IYASAKA MARU.

January 7th

Western Europe

1925   The German light cruiser EMDEN was launched. She was scrapped in 1947.

1937   Germany and Italy rejected a proposal by Britain and France that would limit the number of volunteers allowed into Spain to fight in the Civil War.

1942   Ninety-five Royal Air Force bombers attacked the ports of Brest and St. Nazaire in France.

1943   Twenty-two Royal Air Force bombers attacked Essen, Germany. Ten people were killed in the raid.

1944   Allied aircraft attacked ninety-six V-1 rocket launching sites in France. The American 9th Air Force attacked Cherbourg, France. The Luftwaffe shot down a Royal Air Force "Mosquito" and recovered its secret "Oboe" navigational system intact. 420 8th Air Force B17s and B24s dropped 1,001 tons of bombs on Ludwigshafen, Germany and lost five B17s and seven B24s. USAAF Major James Stewart, the actor, was air commander for the 445th Bombardment Group (B24) on the mission. Actor Walter Mathau was also a member of the same Group. One B24 landed in Switzerland. 571 8th Air Force P38s, P47s and P51s provided support for the bombers and claimed seven victories for the loss of one P38 and five P47s. Eleven Royal Air Force "Mosquitoes" attacked targets in Germany. A Royal Air Force "Halifax", involved in dropping agents in the occupied territories, crashed on take-off killing all ten aboard. Five B17s from the USAAF's 422nd Bomb Squadron dropped 1,080,000 leaflets on Paris, Chartres, Caen, and Evreux in France.

1945   985 8th Air Force bombers dropped 2,907 tons of bombs on oil and rail targets in Germany and lost two B17s and one B24. 674 8th Air Force fighters provided support for the bombers and lost one P51. An American 9th Air Force P38 was shot down by German anti/aircraft fire over Jersey Island and the pilot was captured. German forces began a counter-offensive on the southern flank of the Western Front in an attempt to draw American forces out of the Ardennes. Staff Sergeant Curtis Shoup, of the 87th Division, won a posthumous Medal of Honor near Tillet, Belgium. 654 Royal Air Force bombers attacked Munich and lost fifteen "Lancasters". Eighty-four Royal Air Force "Mosquitoes" attacked targets in Germany.

1958   Gunter D'Alquen, Chief Editor of the S.S. weekly "Das Schwarz Korps", was fined 2,800 marks by a De-Nazification court.

Eastern Europe

1940 The Soviets formed the Northwestern Front to fight the Finns. It was to be commanded by General Semion Konstantinovich Timoshenko (died in 1970).

1944 Soviet forces surrounded Kirovograd. Forty-eight American 15th Air Force B17s attacked the aircraft factory in Maribor, Yugoslavia.

1945 Luftwaffe ace Erich Barkhorn scored his 300th aerial victory. He would score one more by the end of the war. The only man who would score more was Luftwaffe ace Erich Hartmann (352 victories).

Mediterranean

1935 France made concessions to Italy in Africa.

1938 Italy announced a fleet expansion program.

1941 The Free French submarine NARVAL was sunk off Tobruk by the Italian torpedo boat CLIO. The Italian submarine NANI was sunk by the Royal Navy escort ANEMONE.

1942 British forces entered Agedabia, Libya.

1943 The U371 sank the Royal Navy trawler JURA (545 tons) and damaged the British freighter VILLE DE STRASBOURG (7,159 tons). At 1625, the Italian destroyer BERSAGLIERE was sunk in a Palermo air-raid.

1944 The Allies took Monte Chiaia and Monte Porchia and the village of San Vittore. Sergeant Joe Specker, of the 48th Engineer Battalion, won a posthumous Medal of Honor on Mount Pozchi in Italy. Forty-eight American 12th Air Force B25s attacked the Luftwaffe base at Perugia, Italy.

Atlantic

1940 German surface forces sank the Royal Navy submarine SEAHORSE. The German freighter KONSUL HORN evaded British forces off Aruba in her attempt to return to Germany.

1944 The Italian submarine NANI was sunk by the Royal Navy corvette ANEMONE. At 1615, the Royal Navy frigate TWEED was sunk off Ireland by the U305. Her fifty-two survivors were rescued by the Royal Navy vessel NENE. U305 survived until January 17, 1944. The US Coast Guard cutter ARGO rescued twenty-three survivors from the USN gunboat ST. AUGUSTINE. The USN destroyer DAVIS rescued twenty-one survivors from the German blockade runner BURGENLAND which had been sunk on January 5th.

1945 The U650 was lost due to unknown causes.

North America

1893   Major General Willis Hale, commander of the 7th Air Force, was born in Pittsburgh, Kansas.
1942   The Navy's authorized aircraft strength was increased from 15,000 to 27,500.
1944   Four German prisoners of war escaped from Camp Phillips, Kansas.
2010   USAAF ace Colonel Walter Starck died in Ocean Pines, Maryland at the age of 89. He had scored 7 aerial victories in Europe while flying the P47 and P51.

Pacific

1941   IJN Admiral Isoroku Yamamoto submitted his plan for an attack on Pearl Harbor to Navy Minister Koshiro Oikawa.
1942   Japanese forces prepared for a major offensive on Bataan Peninsula in the Philippines. The Japanese in Sarawak reached the border of Dutch West Borneo. The USN submarine POLLACK sank the UNKAI MARU (2,225 tons) south of Honshu.
1943   The Japanese landed reinforcements at Lae, New Guinea. A Royal Australian Air Force PBY "Catalina" sank the NICHIRYU MARU off Lae, New Guinea. American forces attacked Japanese-held Mount Austin on Guadalcanal. The American 5th Air Force attacked installations at Lae, New Guinea. USAAF B17s attacked Bougainville. USAAF B26s and P39s attacked Rekata Bay and lost two aircraft.
1944   The USN submarine KINGFISH sank the FUSHIMI MARU No.3 (4,289 tons). The Japanese freighter KATSURAGISAN MARU was sunk by a Japanese-laid mine at Truk. USN Commander-in-Chief Pacific Admiral Chester Nimitz ordered Vice Admiral Frank Fletcher, Commander of USN North Pacific Forces, to attack the Kurile Islands. The USN light carrier BELLEAU WOOD and the destroyer DUNLAP were damaged in a collision off Oahu.
1945   The USN destroyer-minesweepers PALMER (twenty-eight of her crew died) and HOVEY (forty-six died) were sunk by Japanese aircraft and the transport CALLAWAY and LST 912 were damaged by kamikazes in Lingayen Gulf. American 13th Air Force B24s attacked Nichols and Nielsen Airfields on Luzon. The IJN destroyer escort HINOKI was sunk off Manila Bay by the USN destroyers AUSBURNE, SHAW, BRAINE, and RUSSELL. It was the last surface engagement between the two navies during the war. The USN submarine PICUDA damaged the MUNAKATA MARU (10,045 tons), which was later sunk by aircraft at Keelung. The USN submarine SPOT sank the NICHIEI MARU No.2 (78 tons).

China-Burma-India

1942 Japanese forces broke through the main British defensive line in Malaya.
1944 USAAF B25s sank the Vichy French freighter KAI PING at Ben Thuy, Indochina.
1945 14th Air Force B24s sank the Japanese steamer SHINSEI MARU in the Formosa Straits.

January 8th

Western Europe

1889 German General Erhard Raus was born. He died in 1956.
1916 The Royal Navy battlecruiser REPULSE was launched. She would be sunk by Japanese aircraft in January 1942 while in company with the Royal Navy battleship PRINCE OF WALES off Malaya.
1933 An uprising took place in Barcelona, Spain, but was put down by government troops. Other incidents would occur around the country until 1935 when civil war broke out.
1940 Food rationing began in Britain.
1941 The German torpedo boat WOLF was sunk off Dunkirk, France by a mine. Thirteen of her crew died. The U30 became a training boat at Flensburg on the Baltic. She had sunk eighteen ships, including the liner ATHENA on the first day of the war. Forty-eight Royal Air Force bombers attacked Wilhelmshaven and Emden in Germany. Twelve people were killed in the raid on Wilhelmshaven.
1942 Royal Air Force Air Marshal Sir Richard Peirse was relieved of his position as Commander-in-Chief of the Royal Air Force's Bomber Command. His temporary replacement would be Air Vice Marshal J.E.A. Baldwin. Baldwin served at this post until February 21st. 151 Royal Air Force bombers attacked the port of Brest, France and lost one "Manchester". One of thirty-one Royal Air Force "Wellingtons" that attacked Cherbourg, France was lost.
1943 The German minesweeper M-489 was sunk by an explosion at Rotterdam, Holland. Forty-one Royal Air Force bombers attacked Duisburg, Germany and lost three "Lancasters". Seventy-three Royal Air Force bombers dropped mines off the German and Danish coasts and lost two "Lancasters". Twelve "Spitfires" from the USAAF's 4th Fighter Group flew patrols over the Channel.
1944 Five B17s from the USAAF's 422nd Bomb Squadron dropped 2,292,000 leaflets on Antwerp, Brussels, Rennes, Brest and Nantes. Twenty-three Royal Air Force "Mosquitoes" attacked targets in Germany and lost two aircraft.

1945   604 8th Air Force bombers dropped 1,553 tons of bombs on rail and communication targets in Germany and lost two B17s. 256 8th Air Force fighters provided support for the bombers. Hitler authorized a withdrawal to Houffalize, Belgium. Houffalize came under Allied artillery fire. Technical/Sergeant Russel Dunham, of the 3rd Division, won a Medal of Honor near Kayserberg, France. Sergeant Day Turner, of the 80th Division, won a posthumous Medal of Honor at Dahl, Luxembourg. He is buried in the same military cemetery as General George Patton near Hamm, Luxembourg. The American freighter BLENHEIM was sunk by a German V-2 rocket in Antwerp, Belgium.

Eastern Europe

1940   Finnish forces destroyed the Soviet 44th Division.

1942   The Soviets relieved the surrounded city of Sevastopol. The Soviet freighters CHAPAYEV, NOGIN and ZIRYANIN were sunk by the Luftwaffe.

1943   Soviet forces took Zimovniki, located between Stalingrad and Novorossiysk. The Soviet commander, Rokossovski, issued a surrender ultimatum to the German commander at Stalingrad, Friedrich von Paulus. Erich Manstein threatened to resign as commander of German Army Group "Don".

1944   Soviet forces took Kirovograd. American 15th Air Force B24s attacked the airfield at Mostar, Yugoslavia.

Mediterranean

1941   Royal Air Force "Wellingtons" damaged the Italian battleship GIULIO CESARE at Naples, causing her to be moved to La Spezia further to the north in Italy.

1943   Eleven USAAF 97th Bombardment Group B17s attacked Ferryville, Tunisia. The British destroyers NUBIAN and KELVIN sank three Italian schooners near Kuriat.

1944   Count Ciano was put on trial by a Fascist court in Verona, Italy. Ciano had served as Mussolini's Foreign Minister. 109 American 15th Air Force B17s and twenty-three Royal Air Force "Wellingtons" attacked Reggio Emilia, Italy. Royal Air Force "Wellingtons" attacked the Luftwaffe base at Villaorba, Italy. Royal Air Force Air Marshal John Slessor was named as Deputy Commander-in-Chief of the Mediterranean Allied Air Forces under USAAF General Ira Eaker. Slessor had commanded Coastal Command since November 1942. He died in 1975. British forces took Monte Cedro, Italy.

Atlantic

1943 The U507 sank the British freighter YORKWOOD (5,401 tons). U507 survived until January 13th. The U436 sank the British tanker OLTENIA II (6,394 tons). U436 survived until May 26, 1943.

1944 The U753 was sunk off Ireland by the Royal Navy frigate BAYNTUN and the Royal Canadian Navy corvette CAMROSE. The USN light cruiser MARBLEHEAD rescued 72 survivors from the German blockade runner RIO GRANDE which had been sunk on January 4th. The USN destroyer WINSLOW rescued 35 survivors from the German blockade runner BURGENLAND which had been sunk on January 5th.

North America

1896 Admiral Clifton Sprague was born in Boston. He graduated 43rd in his 1918 Annapolis class of 199. On December 7, 1941 he was in command of the seaplane tender TANGIER at Pearl Harbor. He commissioned the carrier WASP in November 1943. He commanded her until June 1944 when he took over Escort Carrier Division 25. He was in command of "Taffy 3" during the "Battle of Leyte Gulf". That unit would turn back the Japanese fleet commanded by Kurita. He would command Carrier Division 2 from February 1945 until the end of the war. He retired on November 1, 1955 as a vice-admiral. He died on April 1, 1955 in San Diego.

1941 FDR ordered that the compliments of USN ships be brought up to wartime standards. He also requested a $10,811,000,000 defense appropriation for 1942. The US War Department announced the formation of USAFBI (Headquarters for US Forces in the British Isles). The establishment of a Headquarters for a US Air Force in Britain was announced. Brigadier General Ira C. Eaker was ordered to assist in the formation of that headquarters.

1946 The destroyer-minesweepers ZANE and HOPKINS were sold for scrap.

1974 The destroyer DOUGLAS H. FOX was sold to Chile.

Pacific

1885 Australian Prime Minister John Curtin was born. He served from 1941 until his death on July 5, 1945.

1936 Japan threatened to withdraw from the London Naval Conference unless it got parity with the other nations in numbers of ships.

1942 Japanese forces took Kota Kinabalu, North Borneo. Nine USAAF B17s left Java for Kendari, Celebes. From there, five of them attacked Japanese forces in Davao in the Philippines the next day. The IJN submarine I-156 sank the Dutch freighters VAN REES (3,000 tons) and VAN RIEBEECK (2,263 tons). A small seaplane from the Japanese submarine I-19 flew reconnaissance over Pearl Harbor.

1943   The US Army's 127th Infantry Regiment took Tarakena, New Guinea. The "Battle of Guadalcanal" officially ended. The American 5th Air Force lost its first P38 (a 39th Fighter Squadron aircraft over Lae, New Guinea). American 5th Air Force ace Dick Bong scored his 5th victory, a Japanese "Oscar" over Lae, New Guinea. He would end the war with a total of forty.
1944   USN cruisers and destroyers (commanded by Ainsworth) bombarded Faisi and Poporan in the Shortland Islands.
1945   The USN escort carriers KITKUN BAY and KADASHAN BAY and the Royal Australian Navy heavy cruiser AUSTRALIA and the LSI WESTRALIA were hit by kamikazes off Leyte. The USN escort carrier KITKUN BAY was hit by a USN 5" shell. Thirteen of her crew died. The USN submarine BALLAO sank the DAIGO MARU (5,244 tons) off Korea. The USN submarine BARB sank the SHINYO MARU (5,892 tons), ANYO MARU (9,256 tons) and SANYO MARU (2,854 tons). The USN submarines QUEENFISH, BARB and PICUDA were credited with destroying the HIKOSHIMA MARU (2,854 tons), after she had evaded twenty-six torpedoes and then ran aground. The USN submarine QUEENFISH sank the MANJU MARU (6,516 tons). The MALAY MARU (4,556 tons) was sunk by a mine. The Japanese Air Force J8M1 rocket fighter made its first flight.

China-Burma-India
1942   Japanese forces penetrated Kuala Lumpur's outer defenses in Malaya.
1943   Chiang Kai-shek refused a request by FDR to mount a spring offensive. The British returned administrative control of Madagascar to the French.

January 9th

Western Europe
1932   Germany defaulted on its WWI reparations payments to the Allies.
1940   Luftwaffe Major Hellmuth Reinberger, a member of the Airborne Operations Staff of Luftflotte 2, landed in error in Belgium while carrying the plans for the invasion of the West. He was a passenger in a Me108 "Taifun" flown by a Major Hoenmanns. They landed near Mechelen-sur-Meuse, twelve miles north of Maastricht, and were captured.
1941   The first flight of the Royal Air Force's "Lancaster" bomber took place. It would become the primary strategic bomber for the Royal Air Force during the war. 135 Royal Air Force bombers attacked synthetic oil plants in Gelsenkirchen, Germany and lost one "Whitley". One person was killed in the raid.

1942   At 1415, the Royal Navy destroyer escort VIMIERA was sunk in the Thames estuary by a mine. Eighty-two Royal Air Force bombers attacked Brest, France. Five Royal Air Force "Hampdens" dropped mines off Brest and lost one aircraft.

1943   Seven Royal Air Force "Mosquitoes" attacked targets in France and lost one aircraft. Fifty-two Royal Air Force bombers attacked Essen, Germany and lost three "Lancasters". Twenty-eight people were killed in the raid. 121 Royal Air Force bombers dropped mines in the Baltic and lost four "Halifaxes". Six "Spitfires" from the USAAF's 4th Fighter Group flew patrols over the Channel.

1944   Two German soldiers were killed at the train station in Lyons. Twenty-two French hostages were killed by the German occupation forces in retaliation.

1945   German forces began to retreat along the Ardennes front after the "Battle of the Bulge". Technical/Sergeant Charles Carey, of the 100th Division, won a posthumous Medal of Honor at Rimling, France. Two American officers and 182 enlisted personnel were accused of large-scale black-market cigarette sales in Paris (estimated $200,000 worth). USAAF 352nd Fighter Group ace Lieutenant John C. Meyer (24 victories) was badly injured in a car wreck in Belgium and was returned to America. He would retire as a Lieutenant General. The German minesweeper M-3145 was sunk in the Baltic by a mine.

Eastern Europe

1892   Soviet General Mikhail Kirponos was born.

1942   Soviet forces re-entered the Smolensk Province. The Soviet Kalinin Front (commanded by Marshal Koniev) and West Front (commanded by Marshal Zhukov) began an offensive between Minsk and Moscow. Ivan Koniev would die in 1973 and Georgi Zhukov would die in 1974.

1943   The Soviet Air Force destroyed seventy Luftwaffe aircraft at Salsk, a staging field used for resupplying the surrounded German 6th Army in Stalingrad.

1944   Soviet forces took the towns of Polonnoye and Aleksandrovka. The headquarters of the German XLVII Panzer Corps was over-run by the Soviets.

Mediterranean

1941   Hitler decided to send a panzer force to help the Italians in North Africa. This unit would grow into the famous Deutsches Afrika Korps commanded by Field Marshal Erwin Rommel. The Royal Navy submarine PANDORA sank two Italian freighters off Sardinia. The Royal Navy submarine PARTHIAN sank an Italian freighter off Calabria.

1943 At 2015, the Italian destroyer CORSARO was sunk by two mines. She had been attempting to assist the destroyer MAESTRALE which had also hit a mine. USAAF B26 bombers attacked Kairouan, Tunisia.
1944 British Prime Minister Winston Churchill and Free French leader Charles de Gaulle met at Marrakech, Morocco. The Italian submarine NAULILO was sunk at Pola, Italy by the Royal Air Force. The US Army's 10th and 34th Divisions took Cervara and Monte Trocchio respectively. Countess Ciano escaped to Switzerland. She was the wife of the former Italian Foreign Minister. The American 15th Air Force B17s attacked Pola.

Atlantic
1940 The Royal Navy submarine STARFISH was sunk by German surface craft. The U19 (commanded by Schepke) sank the Norwegian freighter MANX (1,343 tons). U19 survived until September 10, 1944.
1941 The U105 sank the British freighter BASSANO (4,843 tons). U105 survived until January 2, 1943.
1942 The U577 was sunk by Royal Air Force No.230 Squadron.
1943 The U124 sank the American freighters BIRMINGHAM CITY (6,194 tons-ten dead), MINOTAUR (4,554 tons-six dead) and COLLINGSWORTH (5,101 tons-twelve dead) and tanker BROAD ARROW (7,718 tons-twenty-three dead). U124 survived until April 3, 1943. The U441 sank the British freighter KING JAMES (5,122 tons). U441 would survive until February 12th. The U522 sank the Panamanian tanker NORBIK (10,034 tons) and the Norwegian tanker MINISTER WEDEL (6,833 tons). U522 would survive until February 23rd. The U442 sank the British tanker EMPIRE LYTTON (9,807 tons). U442 would survive until February 12th. The U436 sank the Norwegian tanker ALBERT L. ELLSWORTH (8,309 tons). U436 would survive until May 26th. The U384 sank the American freighter LOUISE LYKES (6,155 tons) with all hands. U384 would survive until March 20th. The U511 sank the British freighter WILLIAM WILBURFORCE (5,004 tons). U511 would survive the war.
1945 The U81 was sunk by the USAAF. The American freighter JONAS LIE (7,198 tons-two dead) was sunk in Bristol Channel by the U1005. The U870 sank the French patrol craft L'ENJOUE.

North America
1890 General John Lesene DeWitt, commander of the Western Defense Command, was born in Fort Sidney, Nebraska.
1895 General Lucian King Truscott, commander of the VI Corps and Lucas' replacement at Anzio, was born in Chatfield, Texas.
1935 The destroyer MONAGHAN was launched. She foundered off Samar on December 18, 1944.

1936 The M-1 Garand .30 caliber rifle was adopted as the standard US Army weapon. More than 5.5 million would be produced.
1943 The submarine SEAHORSE was launched at Mare Island in California. She was scrapped in 1968.
1944 The destroyer DEHAVEN was launched. She was transferred to the Republic of Korea in 1973. The submarine HAWKBILL was launched at Manitowoc. She was transferred to the Dutch Navy in 1953.
1947 The battleship ALABAMA was decommissioned at Seattle. She would eventually become a memorial in her namesake state.
1951 The light cruisers NASHVILLE and PHILADELPHIA were sold to Brazil and renamed CAPTAIN PRAT and BARROSO respectively.
1952 The American freighter PENNSYLVANIA (the ex-LUXEMBOURG VICTORY) was wrecked off British Columbia. Forty-six of her crew died.
2010 USAAF ace Lieutenant Colonel Sammy Pierce died in Ayden, North Carolina at the age of 88. He had scored 7 aerial victories in the Pacific while flying the P40 and P38.

Pacific

1932 A Korean nationalist attempted to assassinate Japan's Emperor Hirohito.
1942 The Japanese 65th Brigade attacked down Route 110 on Bataan, towards Abucay, Luzon. General Douglas MacArthur made his one and only trip to Bataan from his headquarters on Corregidor during the battle. At 0544, the Royal Australian Air Force Hudson "Tit Willow" (See January 3rd) took off from Kavieng, New Ireland for a recon flight over the IJN base at Truk. The "Tit Willow" returned safely to her base at Kavieng. The information acquired during the flight confirmed Allied suspicions that the Japanese intended to invade New Britain. The steamer MACTAN (See January 1st and 6th) received orders to proceed to Darwin, Australia from Makassar in the Dutch East Indies. The USN submarine POLLACK sank the TEIAN MARU (5,387 tons). The IJN submarine I-158 sank the Dutch freighter CAMPHUIJS (2,380 tons). The IJN submarine I-165 sank the Dutch freighter BENKOELEN (1,003 tons). The Australian destroyer ARUNTA evacuated 282 troops and thirty-one civilians from Japanese-held Timor Island to Darwin, Australia.
1943 The USN submarine NAUTILUS sank the YOSHINOGAWA MARU (1,422 tons). The Australian 17th Brigade was air-lifted to Wau, New Guinea. The USAAF's 475th Fighter Group P38s attacked Wewak, New Guinea. The USN battleship NEW MEXICO arrived at Fiji for operations in the Pacific Theater of Operations.
1944 USN SBDs and TBFs attacked Japanese installations and shipping at Rabaul, New Britain. Reconnaissance flights by American aircraft over

Kwajalein Atoll revealed that twenty-four Japanese ships were anchored there. Those ships would be the targets of several attacks by American aircraft over the next two months. The fighting continued on Cape Gloucester on New Britain. The US Army completed a second airfield at Piva, Bougainville. The last USAAF B26 "Marauder" mission was flown in the South Pacific. USAAF ace Colonel Neel Kearby shot down two Japanese "Tonys" over Wewak, New Guinea.

1945 At 0930, 67,000 men of the American 6th Army landed at Lingayen, Luzon. Defending the island were 262,000 men of the Japanese 14th Army. The USN battleship MISSISSIPPI, the light cruiser COLUMBIA (twenty-four dead), the destroyer escort HODGES and the Royal Australian Navy heavy cruiser AUSTRALIA were hit by kamikazes in Lingayen Gulf. Between this date and the 19th of the month, eleven B29s were lost on missions over Japan. USN Task Force 38 attacked Japanese installations on Formosa and Okinawa. The IJN escort No.3 was sunk off Formosa by USN carrier aircraft. The Dutch submarine 0-19 sank the SHINKO MARU No.1 (935 tons).

China-Burma-India

1942 Japanese submarines began operating in the Indian Ocean. Japanese forces took Port Swettenham on the Straits of Malacca. British forces were ordered to retreat to Johore for the final defense of Singapore. The American Volunteer Group strafed airfields near Meshod, Thailand, destroying eight Japanese aircraft and losing one of their own.
1943 The puppet Chinese government in Nanking declared war on America and Britain.
1944 British forces took Maungdaw, Burma.
1972 The RMS QUEEN ELIZABETH caught fire in Hong Kong Harbor and capsized the next day. She had served as a troopship during the war.

January 10th

Western Europe

1934 Dutchman Marinus Van De Lubbe was guillotined. He had been convicted of setting the fire which destroyed the German Reichstag.
1937 The British government prohibited any British citizen from serving as a volunteer in the Spanish Civil War.
1940 Hitler advised his commanders that he intended to attack in the West on January 17th. General Albert Kesselring (died in 1960) replaced Hellmuth Felmy as commander of the German Luftflotte 2 after one of the latter's aircraft landed in Belgium with invasion plans aboard (See January 9th).

	Felmy was retired to civilian life. He would return to active duty in May 1941 and serve in Iraq, Greece and Russia.
1941	Six Royal Air Force "Blenheims", escorted by seventy-two fighters, attacked an ammunition depot south of Calais in France.
1942	124 Royal Air Force bombers attacked Wilhelmshaven, Germany and lost five aircraft. Six people were injured in the raid.
1944	General Fritz Bayerlein assumed command of the German Panzer Lehr Division in Normandy (he died in 1970). Twenty Royal Air Force "Mosquitoes" attacked targets in Germany. Five B17s from the USAAF's 422nd Bomb Squadron dropped 4,800,000 leaflets on Orleans, Chateauroux, Rouen, Le Mans and Tours in France.
1945	912 8th Air Force bombers dropped 2,196 tons of bombs on airfields and rail targets in Germany and lost ten B17s. 307 8th Air Force fighters provided support for the bombers and claimed three victories for the loss of one P47 and one P51. The American 1st Army began an offensive through Houffalize towards St. Vith in Belgium. German forces counter-attacked near Strasbourg. Master/Sergeant Vito Bertoldi, of the 42nd Division, won a Medal of Honor near Hatten. Two American soldiers were sentenced in Paris to fifty years hard labor and two more received forty-five years for stealing and selling cigarettes bound for American troops at the front. Sixty-two Royal Air Force "Mosquitoes" attacked targets in Germany. Five German "Seehund" two-man submarines failed in an attempt to attack Margate on the Kentish coast of Britain. The German minesweeper M-322 was lost off Lepsoey, Norway.
1993	A secret room was discovered at the former prisoner of war prison at Colditz in Germany. It had been used by Allied POWs in their escape attempts.
2010	Royal Air Force Air Commodore Charles Widdows died at the age of 100. He had commanded a night-fighter squadron during the Battle of Britain and was that conflicts oldest surviving pilot.

Eastern Europe

1936	Soviet Foreign Minister Molotov suggested that Russia would like to improve relations with Germany.
1941	The Nazi/Soviet Pact was renewed. It increased trade between the two countries and established new borders in Lithuania. Greek forces took Klisura, Albania.
1942	The Soviet submarine M-175 was sunk off North Cape by the U584.
1943	The German 6th Army Commander, Friedrich von Paulus, refused to surrender and the Soviets began their final assault on Stalingrad with 281,000 men.

1944   American 15th Air Force B24s attacked Skoplje, Yugoslavia, while B17s hit Sofia, Bulgaria.

Mediterranean
1939   British Prime Minister Neville Chamberlain and Lord Halifax met with Mussolini in Rome.
1941   The Royal Navy carrier ILLUSTRIOUS (200 dead) and the heavy cruiser SOUTHAMPTON were damaged by forty Luftwaffe Ju87s and Ju88s off Sicily. At 0830, the Italian torpedo boat VEGA (2 of her crew survived) was sunk by the Royal Navy light cruiser BONAVENTURE and destroyer HEREWARD off Pantelleria Island. At 0835, the Royal Navy destroyer GALLANT (60 dead) was damaged by a mine. She was towed to Malta where she was declared a constructive loss on the 20th (See February 5, 1942).
1944   The American freighter DANIEL WEBSTER was a constructive loss after a Luftwaffe attack off Oran. The German S-55 was sunk by an air-attack in the Adriatic.
1945   German "Linsen" explosive boats failed in an attack against the French destroyer LE FORTUNE off San Remo.

Atlantic
1940   The German blockade runner BAHIA BLANCA sank in the Denmark Strait after striking an iceberg.
1943   The American tanker C.J. BARKDULL (6,773 tons-fifty-eight of her crew died) was sunk by the U632. U632 survived until April 6, 1943. The American freighter NORWALK was sunk in a collision with the Norwegian freighter NIDAREID north of Cuba. One of her crew was killed. The Norwegian freighter DALVANGER rescued twenty-one survivors from the American freighter COLLINGSWORTH which had been sunk the previous day by U124.
1945   The U870 sank the British freighter BLACKHEATH (4,637 tons). U870 survived until March 30, 1945. The U679 was sunk by a mine.

North America
1941   The Lend-Lease Bill was introduced into Congress. It would allow the American government to "loan" military goods and supplies to countries fighting the Axis.
1942   USN Captain Francis S. Low presented his idea for the "Doolittle Raid" to the Commander-in-Chief of the USN Fleet Admiral Ernest King. The US Army announced the delivery of its first troop-carrying gliders.

1943   The destroyers WADSWORTH, MCCORD, HOWORTH and KILLEN were launched. The WADSWORTH was transferred to Germany in 1959, the HOWORTH was sunk as a target in 1962 and the KILLEN was discarded in 1963 and the MCCORD in 1970.
1945   A USAAF P38 shot down a Japanese balloon-bomb near Alturas, California.
1970   The destroyer PRICHETT was sold to Italy.

Pacific
1942   Japanese forces landed at Tarakan Bay, Borneo. Japanese aircraft began dropping leaflets on the Allied forces fighting on Bataan calling for them to surrender. The USN submarine PICKEREL sank the KANKO MARU (2,929 tons). The USN submarine STINGRAY sank the HARBIN MARU (5,167 tons). The Dutch submarine O-19 sank the AKITA MARU (3,817 tons). The Panamanian freighter DAYLITE (1,976 tons) was sunk by a mine in Manila Bay. The USN destroyer PAUL JONES rescued survivors from the Dutch steamers CAMPHUIJS and BENKOELEN that were sunk on the 9th of January by IJN submarines I-158 and I-165 respectively.
1943   USAAF B26s attacked Munda, New Georgia and lost one aircraft. The US Army's 25th Division began the final offensive to clear Guadalcanal, when it attacked Japanese positions on Mount Austin. Sergeant William Fourniew and Technician/5th Class Lewis Hall, of the 25th Division, won posthumous Medals of Honor on Mount Austin, Guadalcanal. USN PT-boats attacked IJN destroyers that were attempting to deliver supplies to Japanese forces still fighting on Guadalcanal and lost PTs-43 and 112. The US Army's 127th Infantry Regiment established a bridgehead over the Konombi River on New Guinea. The IJN destroyer OKIKAZE was sunk southeast of Yokosuka by the USN submarine TRIGGER. The USN submarine ARGONAUT was sunk by the IJN destroyers MAIKAZE and ISOKAZE off New Britain. The USN destroyer SHAW was damaged when she ran aground in Bulari Passage, New Caledonia. USAAF B26s attacked shipping off Lae, New Guinea.
1944   Twenty American 13th Air Force B24s attacked Rabaul, New Britain. USAAF ace Lieutenant Colonel Charles MacDonald shot down a "Tony" over Wewak, New Guinea. Allied reinforcements arrived at Arawe, New Britain. The USN submarine STEELHEAD sank the YAMABIKO MARU (6,799 tons). The USN submarine THRESHER sank the HORAI MARU (91 tons). The USN submarine SEAWOLF sank the ASUKA MARU (7,523 tons) and the YAHIKO MARU (5,747 tons). The USN minesweeper YMS-127 was lost when she ran aground off the Aleutian Islands.

1945 American forces on Luzon began advancing towards the city of Manila. The USN destroyer escort LERAY WILSON was hit by a Japanese kamikaze in Lingayen Gulf. The USN attack-transport DU PAGE was crashed by a Japanese "Nick" (thirty-five of her crew died). IJN suicide boats sank the USN LCIs 365, 674 and 974 in Lingayen Gulf. The IJN escort CD-42 was sunk west of Okinawa by the USN submarine PUFFER. USN F6F fighters accidentally shot down a USAAF P47 fighter over Luzon. A USAAF P61 "Black Widow" night-fighter crashed into Mount Cyclops near Sentani, New Guinea. It was returned to America in 1991 with the intention of making it airworthy. American 13th Air Force B25s attacked Kendari Airfield on Celebes.

China-Burma-India
1938 Japanese forces occupied Tsingtao, China.
1942 The American 10th Air Force attacked the Myitgne River Bridge in Burma. Japanese aircraft attacked Singapore's airfields.
1944 The RAF began mining the Salween River near Moullmein, Burma. The American 10th Air Force mined Bangkok Harbor.
1945 British forces took Shwebo and Budalin in Burma.

January 11th

Western Europe
1915 British Army Lieutenant Colonel Robert "Paddy" Mayne was born near Belfast, Ireland. He would command the Special Air Service after its original commander, Captain David Sterling, was captured in North Africa.
1923 The forces of France and Belgium occupied the industrial Ruhr area in retaliation for Germany defaulting on its World War I reparations.
1940 France asked America for twenty-five P40 fighters. The British tanker EL OSO (7,267 tons) was sunk in Liverpool by a mine that had been laid by the U30. Eighteen Royal Air Force "Wellingtons" failed to locate any targets on a North Sea shipping search.
1941 The Royal Air Force suffered its first fatalities in Eire when a No.224 Squadron "Blenheim" crashed near Kildaire. Hitler announced that Germany would send military forces to Libya. Thirty-five Royal Air Force bombers attacked Wilhelmshaven, Germany. One person was killed in the raid. Hitler ordered the Wehrmacht High Command to prepare for the possibility of sending troops to North Africa.
1942 Twenty-six Royal Air Force bombers attacked the port of Brest, France.

1943 The USAAF's 56th Fighter Group (P47) arrived in Scotland. Seventy-six Royal Air Force bombers attacked Essen, Germany and lost one "Lancaster". Two "Spitfires" from the USAAF's 4th Fighter Group flew patrols over the Channel.

1944 "Operation Pointblank" (designed to cripple the German aircraft industry and the Luftwaffe) began when 663 8th Air Force bombers dropped 1,264 tons of bombs on Halberstadt, Brunswick, Magdeburg and Oscherleben in Germany and lost fifty-eight B17s and two B24s and four P47s and one P38. USAAF Lieutenant Colonel James Howard (six Luftwaffe and six and a half Japanese aircraft) became the only 8th Air Force fighter pilot to win a Medal of Honor. He single-handedly saved a bomber formation over Oscherleben from Luftwaffe fighters while flying a P51 "Mustang".

1945 152 Royal Air Force "Lancasters" attacked Krefeld, Germany. German forces began retreating southeast of Bastogne in Belgium. Staff Sergeant Archer Gammon, of the 6th Armored Division, won a posthumous Medal of Honor near Bastogne, Belgium. The British Army's 2nd Division took St. Hubert, Belgium. The US Army's VIII Corps took Bommerne, Pironpre and Vesqueville in Belgium. A British force consisting of the cruisers NORFOLK and BELLONA and the destroyers ONSLOW, ORWELL and ONSLAUGHT attacked a German convoy off Egersund, Norway. They sank the freighters BAHIA CAMARONES (8,551 tons) and CHARLOTTE (4,404 tons) and the minesweeper M-273.

Eastern Europe

1940 Finland asked America for forty P35 fighters to be used in its fight against Russia.

1942 Soviet forces cut the railway between Rzhev and Bryansk.

1943 The Soviets began offensive to relieve Leningrad.

1944 Soviet forces attacked Mozyr.

Mediterranean

1941 At 1520, the Royal Navy heavy cruiser SOUTHAMPTON (eighty of her crew died) was damaged 180 miles east of Malta by the Luftwaffe. She was scuttled later in the day. The Royal Navy heavy cruiser GLOUCESTER was damaged in the same action. Eleven Royal Air Force "Wellingtons" attacked Turin, Italy and lost one aircraft.

1943 Allied aircraft attacked Naples, Italy. The American 12th Air Force attacked rail and aircraft targets in North Africa.

1944 The former Italian Fascists Ciano, De Bono, Gottardi, Pareshi and Marinelli were executed at Verona, Italy. They had been sentenced by a Fascist court. American 15th Air Force B17s attacked Piraeus, Greece. The German trawler UJ-2143 and the minesweeper M-1226 (ex-Italian RD-9) were sunk in an air-attack off Greece.

Atlantic

1940 The U23 (commanded by Kretschmer) sank the Norwegian freighter FREDVILLE (1,150 tons). U23 survived until September 10, 1944.

1941 The first British convoy rescue ship, the Dutch freighter HONTESTROOM (1,875 tons), went on her first assignment. The purpose of the rescue ships was to pick up survivors of sunken ships and thus relieve escorts and other merchant ships of the danger and distraction of stopping in hostile waters while under attack by U-boats or aircraft. By the end of the war, twenty-eight more ships would be fitted out as rescue ships and would save 4,190 survivors from lost merchant ships as well as four crewmen from sunken U-boats.

1943 The U186 sank the British freighter OCEAN VAGABOND (7,174 tons). U186 survived until May 12th. The U620 sank the British tanker BRITISH DOMINION (6,983 tons). U620 survived until February 14th. The U105 sank the British sailing ship C.S. FLIGHT (67 tons). U105 survived until June 2nd.

1944 The American freighter JOSEPH SMITH (a "Liberty" ship) was scuttled in mid-Atlantic after developing hull cracks. The type would continue to have such problems until they were modified.

1945 The U1005 sank the US Army transport ROANOKE (2,606 tons-four died) and the British freighter NORMANDY COAST (1,428 tons).

North America

1919 The destroyer COLE was launched in New York. She was scrapped in 1947.

1928 USN Lieutenant Commander Marc Mitscher made the first landing on the carrier SARATOGA while flying a Chance-Vought UO-1. He would command USN carrier forces in the Pacific during the war as an Admiral.

1936 The destroyer REID was launched. She was sunk off Ormoc on December 11, 1944.

1941 The USAAF contracted for two XP-61 "Black Widow" proto-types.

1945 The USN YMS-14 was lost in a collision with the destroyer HERNDON in Boston harbor.

1951 The light cruiser BOISE was sold to Brazil and renamed NUEVE DE JULIO. She was stricken in 1979.

1985 US Army Corporal Charles "Commando" Kelly died. He had won a Medal of Honor in Italy.

1988 Medal of Honor winner USMC Major Gregory "Pappy" Boyington died of cancer in Fresno, California at the age of 75.

1994 John Bradley, age 70, died of a stroke. He was the last survivor of the group that had raised the flag on Iwo Jima on February 23, 1945. When Joe Rosenthal took the famous photo, Bradley was a USN Pharmacist

Mate 2nd Class. Three of the six were killed in action on the island, while Ira Hayes had died in 1955 and Rene Gagnon died in 1979.

Pacific

1942 The American freighter CLEVEDON exploded and sank at Yakutat, Alaska. The USN carrier SARATOGA (33,000 tons) was torpedoed 500 miles southeast of Oahu by the IJN submarine 1-6 and spent four months undergoing repairs. Japan declared war on the Netherlands and invaded the Dutch East Indies and Dutch Borneo. Fifteen Allied blockade runners were sunk while trying to resupply the Philippines. A Japanese offensive on the Bataan Peninsula failed. The American tanker MANATAWNEY sank in Manila Bay. She had been damaged in an air-raid on December 13th. The Japanese occupied Kema and Menado on Celebes. The attack on Menado involved the first use of paratroops by the Japanese. Japanese forces secured Tarakan Island, off Borneo. Three USAAF B17s flying from Malang, Java attacked Tarakan Island. The Dutch minelayer PRINS VAN ORANJE was sunk by the IJN destroyer YAMAKAZE and patrol boat No.38, off Tarakan. The US Army transport LIBERTY GLO was a total loss after being torpedoed by IJN submarine I-166 off Bali.

1943 The US Army's 25th Division took continued its assault on Mt. Austin, Guadalcanal. USN PTs 43 and 112 were sunk off Guadalcanal by the IJN. Thirty-six "Alaska Scouts" landed on Amchitka, in the Aleutians.

1944 Fighting continued on New Britain. At 0913, the IJN light cruiser KUMA was sunk by the Royal Navy submarine TALLYHO off Penang. The USN submarine SEAWOLF sank the GETSUYO MARU (6,440 tons). The USN submarine STURGEON sank the ERIE MARU (5,493 tons). The USN submarine TAUTOG sank the KOGYO MARU (6,353 tons). Ten USN PB4Y "Liberators" flying from the Gilbert and Ellice Islands attacked shipping in the Kwajalein Atoll, sinking the IJN gunboat IKUTA MARU. USMC Major Gregory Boyington, commander of VMF 214, won a Medal of Honor for actions over the Central Solomons (See North America-1988). The US airfield at Saidor, New Guinea became operational.

1945 The USN destroyer-transport BELKNAP was a constructive loss after a kamikaze attack off Luzon. Major William Shomo, of the 82nd Tactical Recon (P51) Squadron, won a Medal of Honor over Luzon. The US Army's 25th Division landed at Lingayen, Luzon. American forces took Santa Barbara and Manoag on Luzon.

1982 Jiro Horikoshi, age 78, died. He had been chief designer of the Japanese A6M "Zero" fighter.

China-Burma-India

1942   Japanese forces took Kuala Lumper, Malaya.

1944   The American 10th Air Force mined Bangkok harbor. The U532 damaged the British freighter TRIONA (7,283 tons).

1945   British forces took Gangaw, Burma. USAAF B29s attacked Singapore, losing two aircraft.

January 12th

Western Europe

1893   German Luftwaffe commander Hermann Goering was born in Rosenheim. During WWI, he would score twenty aerial victories and command the Richthofen Squadron. After the war, he took various aviation related jobs in Scandinavia. He married Swedish Karin von Fock-Kantzow on February 3, 1922. In November, the Goering's first heard Hitler speak at a Party function. During the Beer Hall Putsch of 1923, he served as the S.A. commander. During the shooting, he was hit by two granite splinters in the groin. To avoid arrest, he and his wife fled to Sweden by way of Austria and Italy. After reaching Sweden, Karin became a near invalid and Hermann an overweight hypochondriac that was addicted to morphine. By 1927, he had regained his health and had been pardoned by President Hindenburg. He returned to Germany and was elected to the Reichstag on May 20, 1928. Karin became ill and returned to Sweden where she died on October 17, 1931. On August 30, 1932, he was elected President of the Reichstag. After Hitler became chancellor, he named Goering as Prussian Minister of Interior and Commissioner for Air. By March 1935, he was in command of the Luftwaffe. On April 10, 1935, he married actress Emmy Sonnemann. By June 29, 1941, when he was named as Hitler's successor, his weight had ballooned to 280 pounds and was again addicted to morphine. He spent most of the war increasing his own fortune and disrupting the operations of his beloved Luftwaffe. In April 1945, he moved to his residence in Berchtesgaden. On the 23rd of the month, he sent a message to Hitler in Berlin asking if he was to assume leadership of Germany. Hitler, after being influenced by Martin Bormann, ordered Goering's arrest. He surrendered to the US 36th Infantry Division on May 8, 1945 near Mauterndorf. At the Nuremburg trials, he was found guilty of war crimes and on October 1, 1946 was sentenced to death. On October 15th he cheated the hangman by swallowing cyanide.

1941   Six Royal Air Force "Blenheims" attacked Flushing, Belgium. Forty-seven Royal Air Force bombers attacked targets in France.

The Month of January

1943   The French Resistance killed its first German soldier in Lyon. Fifty-nine Royal Air Force bombers attacked Essen, Germany and lost one "Lancaster". Only nine people were killed in Essen as most of the bombs fell in surrounding towns. Two "Spitfires" from the USAAF's 4th Fighter Group flew patrols over the Channel.

1944   Royal Air Force ace Wing Commander L. Wade (25 aerial victories and an American citizen), was killed in a flying accident.

1945   The American 1st and 3rd Armies met near Houffalize, Belgium. German "Biber" midget submarines attacked the bridge over the Rhine River at Nijmegen. Five American soldiers received sentences of forty to forty-five years for black-marketing cigarettes that were destined for front-line troops. American forces took Amberloup, Lavacherie, Fosset, Sprimont and Wardin in Belgium. Thirty-three Royal Air Force bombers attacked Bergen, Norway and lost three aircraft. The German minesweepers M-1 and M-273 were sunk in the raid.

Eastern Europe

1893   Alfred Rosenberg was born in Tallin, Estonia. He would become the Nazi Party's unofficial philosopher and Head of the Foreign Affairs Department. He would be sentenced to death at the Nuremburg War Crimes Trials in 1946.

1942   The Soviet battleship PARIZHSKAYA KOMMUNA and the destroyers BODRY and ZHELEZNYAKOV bombarded German positions near the Black Sea.

1943   Soviet forces launched an offensive against the Hungarian 2nd Army and the Italian 8th Army. German fighter support for Stalingrad was lost when the Soviets took Pitomnik Airfield.

1944   Soviet forces took Sarny, Poland.

1945   The Soviets began an offensive along the entire front.

Mediterranean

1941   Nine Royal Air Force "Wellingtons" flying from Britain attacked targets in Italy and lost one aircraft.

1942   The U77 damaged the Royal Navy destroyer KIMBERLEY. The U374 was sunk by the Royal Navy submarine UNBEATEN.

1943   Twelve American 12th Air Force B17s and fifteen P38s attacked Tripoli, Libya. At 0400, the Italian torpedo boat ARDENTE was lost in a collision with the destroyer GRECALE north of Sicily.

1944   The US Army's 34th Division took Cervera, Italy. French forces penetrated the Germans "Gustav Line" in Italy. The German escort SG-20 (ex-Italian torpedo boat PAPA) was a constructive loss after an air-raid on Genoa.

1945   The Royal Navy minesweeper REGULUS was sunk by a mine in the southern Corfu Channel.

Atlantic

1940   The U23 (commanded by Kretschmer) sank the Danish tanker DANMARK (10,517 tons). U23 survived until September 10, 1944.

1942   The U43 sank the Swedish freighter YNGAREN (5,246 tons). U43 survived until July 30, 1943.

1948   The American freighter JOSEPH CONNOLLY caught fire and would sink on the 24th, 900 miles east of New York. Aboard were 4,500 coffins intended to transport American war dead home from Europe.

North America

1937   The destroyer HENLEY was launched at Mare Island in California. She was sunk by the IJN submarine Ro-108 off Finschafen, New Guinea on October 3, 1943.

1942   The authorized enlisted strength of the Navy was increased to 500,000.

1944   The American 3rd Army advance party of thirteen officers and twenty-six enlisted men left the port of embarkation at Fort Hamilton, New York aboard the QUEEN MARY. They would arrive in Europe on the 29th.

1945   A Japanese balloon-bomb was found near Minton, Saskatchewan.

1950   The light cruiser PASADENA was decommissioned. She was scrapped in 1971.

1954   USN Admiral William Blandy, commander of Task Force 32 in the Pacific, died.

1967   USMC General Holland M. Smith died in San Diego. He had commanded many of the Marines amphibious landings in the Pacific during the war.

1994   The carrier BENNINGTON was sold for scrap.

2007   USN ace Hayden Gregory died on his 92nd birthday. During the war he had been credited with 5 aerial victories while flying F6F Hellcats.

2012   Frank Hill died at the age of 92. He was credited with shooting down 7 Axis aircraft over the Mediterranean.

2013   USAAF ace Wiliam J. Cullerton died in Chicago, Illinois at the age of 89. He had been credited with 5 aerial victories while flying P51s with the 357th Fighter Group based in Britain.

Pacific

1942   Second Lieutenant Alexander Nininger, of the Philippine Scouts, won a posthumous Medal of Honor near Abucay on Bataan Peninsula. His was the first US Army Medal of Honor awarded during the war. The USN submarine TROUT left Pearl Harbor for Corregidor with 3,517 3-inch shells aboard. Six Royal Australian Air Force PBY "Catalinas" failed in an attempt to attack Japanese shipping at Truk. The Australians were trying to prevent an expected Japanese assault on Rabaul, New Britain. The Australian High Command then requested a raid by USAAF B17s on Truk. The request was refused by USAAF General Lewis Brereton as he expected the Japanese to head for the Fijis and the island of Samoa instead of New Britain. The Japanese began loading American prisoners of war aboard the NITTA MARU at Wake Island. The IJN minesweepers W-13 and W-14 were sunk by Dutch artillery off Tarakan, Borneo.

1943   2,100 American troops landed on Amchitka in the Aleutians. At 0730, the USN destroyer WORDEN (fourteen of her crew died) was lost by grounding in Constantine Harbor, Amchitka. The transport ARTHUR MIDDLETON ran aground while rescuing her survivors and would be stuck for eighty-four days. The USN submarine GUARDFISH sank the IJN frigate P-1. The USN PT28 was wrecked at Dora Harbor, Alaska. The US Armys 25th Division continued its assault on Japanese-held Mount Austin, Guadalcanal. Captain Charles Davis, of the 25th Division, won a Medal of Honor during the action. He would retire as a Colonel in 1972. Australian troops attacked northwest of Gona, New Guinea. USAAF B26s attacked Munda, New Georgia and lost two aircraft.

1944   Fighting continued on New Britain. USN PB4Ys (naval version of the B24) attacked Japanese shipping at Kwajalein sinking the IJN gunboat IKUTA MARU. American 13th Air Force B25s began operations from Stirling Island in the Treasury Islands. The Japanese Army landing ship NIGITSU MARU was sunk by the USN submarine HAKE. The USN submarine ALBACORE sank the CHOKO MARU (2,629 tons) and the patrol boat H-4 (25 tons). The USN battleship ALABAMA arrived at Pearl Harbor for repairs.

1945   Fighting continued on Mindoro in the Philippines. The US Army's 40th Division took Port Saul, Luzon. The USN submarine SWORDFISH was lost off Okinawa. Staff Sergeant Robert Laws, of the 43rd Division, won a Medal of Honor on Luzon. The USN destroyer-transport BELKNAP was sunk and the destroyer escorts SUESENS and GILLIGAN, the freighters FIELD, SKINNER, JOHNSON, WESTCOTT, and WAR HAWK and the LSTs 700 and 778 were damaged in Lingayan Gulf by Japanese kamikazes.

1964   The freighter DEMETER (the ex-LST 1121) was lost.

China-Burma-India

1945   The 19th Indian Division crossed the Irrawaddy River. The USN attacked the Indo-China coast sinking fourteen warships, including the IJN light cruiser KASHII and gunboat CHIBURI and the French light cruiser

LAMOTTE PICQUET (7,249 tons and launched in 1926) and thirty-three merchantmen. Three USMC F4U fighters shot down a USAAF B24 bomber in error during the operation. The British Task Force 64 (commanded by Martin) landed troops near Myebon on the coast of Burma.

January 13th

Western Europe

1935   The residents of the Saar region voted in a plebiscite to rejoin Germany. The Saar had been removed from the German Reich as a result of its losing the First World War.

1939   Spanish Nationalists crossed the Ebro River in their assault on Barcelona.

1940   Hitler postponed his attack on the West until January 20th. The Belgian government ordered mobilization of its armed forces and Holland cancelled all military leaves.

1941   One Royal Air Force "Blenheim" attacked the Nordhorn Airfield in Germany and was lost. The Luftwaffe attacked Plymouth, Britain. Twenty-four Royal Air Force bombers attacked French ports as well as the German port of Wilhelmshaven.

1942   Royal Air Force bombers attacked Lille, France. The first use of an ejection seat in an aircraft occurred when a Luftwaffe pilot escaped from a He-280V1 jet fighter. At a meeting in London the representatives of the Allied governments pledged to prosecute Axis "war criminals" after the war.

1943   Sixty-four B17s from the USAAF's 91st, 303rd, 305th and 306th Bomb Groups attacked Lille, France and lost three aircraft. Sixty-nine Royal Air Force bombers attacked Essen, Germany and lost four "Lancasters". Fifty-two buildings were destroyed and sixty-three people were killed in the raid.

1944   Twenty-five Royal Air Force "Mosquitoes" attacked targets in Germany and lost one aircraft.

1945   909 American 8th Air Force bombers dropped 2,439 tons of bombs on rail targets in Germany and lost seven B17s and one B24. 441 8th Air Force fighters provided support for the bombers and claimed six victories for the loss of two P51s. 158 Royal Air Force bombers attacked Saarbrucken, Germany and lost one "Lancaster". The US Army's 30th Division reached the Ambleve River in Belgium. American forces cut the Houffalize-St. Vith road in Belgium. In the second raid of the day on Saarbrucken, 274 Royal Air Force bombers attacked the city and lost one "Halifax". 225 Royal Air Force bombers attacked Politz and lost two aircraft.

Eastern Europe

1942 The Soviets forced a major break in the German lines near Volokolamsk. Soviet forces took Kirov.
1943 The Soviets took Karpovka Airfield outside of Stalingrad.
1944 Soviet forces took Korets.
1945 The Soviets attacked the German 4th Panzer Army near Konigsberg, East Prussia.

Mediterranean

1941 Greece rejected a British offer of troops to help fight the Italians. Ugo Cavellero relieved Soddu as Italian commander in Albania.
1943 The U224 was sunk off Algiers by the Royal Canadian Navy destroyer VILLE DE QUEBEC. American 12th Air Force B26s attacked bridges in North Africa.
1944 240 American 12th and 15th Air Force aircraft attacked airfields near Rome. Thirty-five Royal Air Force "Baltimores" and 119 P40s attacked tank repair facilities at Loreto, Italy.

Atlantic

1940 The U20 sank the Swedish freighter SYLVIA (1,524 tons). U20 survived until September 10, 1944.
1942 The German Operation "Paukenschlag" ("Kettle Drum Roll") began when U-boats began attacking shipping off the American coast. The U130 sank the Panamanian freighter FRIAR ROCK (5,427 tons) and the Norwegian freighter FRISCO (1,582 tons). U130 survived until March 12, 1943.
1943 The U507 was sunk northwest of Natal by USN VP-83.
1944 The Brazilian minelayer CAMOCIM rescued 34 survivors from 3 German blockade runners that were sunk on January 3rd, 4th and 5th.

North America

1942 The first flight of the Sikorsky XR-4, the first USAAF helicopter, took place at Bridgeport, Connecticut. Charles Lindbergh met with USAAC Chief of Staff Henry "Hap" Arnold and Assistant Secretary of War Robert Lovett to discuss his return to USAAC. He had resigned his commission as a result of his activities with the "America First Committee" during the 1930's. The results of the meeting were negative. The American freighter CLEVEDON was lost in an explosion at Yakutat, Alaska.
1944 The light cruiser DULUTH (awarded two battle stars during the war) was launched. She was scrapped in 1961.
1945 A Japanese balloon-bomb was found near Lame Deer, Montana.

1969 Brigadier General Orrin L. Grover, age 64, died. He had commanded the USAAF pursuit squadrons in the Philippines in 1941-42.
1983 USMC General David Shoup died. He had won a Medal of Honor on Tarawa and had served as USMC Commandant from 1960-64.
1997 Vernon Baker, a 77-year-old Army veteran, was awarded a Medal of Honor for actions in Italy during April 1945. He was one of seven Blacks who had been recommended for the medal during the war, but it had been denied for a variety of reasons. Unfortunately, the other six received their medals posthumously on this date. Of the others, Staff Sergeant Ruben Rivers, First Lieutenant John Fox, Private First-Class Willy James, and Private George Watson died in action, Staff Sergeant Edward Carter died in 1963 and First Lieutenant Charles Thomas died in 1980.
2006 USN Captain Richard Devine, age 89, died in College Place, Washington. During the war he had flown F6F Hellcats off the carrier ENTERPRISE and had benn sredited with 8 aerial victories.

Pacific

1942 The steamer MACTAN (See January 1st, 6th and 9th) arrived at Darwin, Australia. The IJN submarine I-156 damaged the Dutch freighter PATRAS (2,065 tons), southwest of Bali.
1943 The USN submarine WHALE sank the IWASHIRO MARU (3,559 tons) off Kwajalein. The IJN patrol boat No.1 was sunk southwest of Kavieng, New Ireland by the USN submarine GUARDFISH. The USMC 2nd Division began an offensive along the Guadalcanal coast in support of an attack on Mount Austin. US Army General Robert Eichelberger assumed command of Advanced Allied Forces on New Guinea. General Nathan Twining became commander of the American 13th Air Force when it was activated in Noumea, New Caledonia. USAAF B26s, P38s and P39s attacked Japanese installations at Rekata Bay.
1944 Fighting continued on New Britain. The USN submarine SWORDFISH sank the YAMAKUNI MARU. A 5th Air Force B24 sank the Japanese transport HAGURO MARU off New Hanover.
1945 The USN escort carrier SALAMAUA (fifteen of her crew died) and the transport ZEILEN were hit by kamikazes in Lingayan Gulf. The US Army's XIV Corps took Guagua, Luzon.
1988 Local fishermen discovered the wreckage of a USN TBM torpedo bomber on a small island in the Palaus. The remains of the three-man crew were buried in Arlington National Cemetery on April 26th.

China-Burma-India

1942 Supplies, including anti/aircraft guns and fifty "Hurricanes", arrived in Singapore.

January 14th

Western Europe

1892 German clergyman and resistance leader Martin Niemoeller was born. He died in 1984.

1897 German General Hasso von Manteuffel was born in Potsdam. He would command the 5th Panzer Army during the "Battle of the Bulge" in 1944. He died in Diessen in 1978.

1899 German General Fritz Bayerlein was born in Wurzburg. He would serve as Chief of Staff of the Afrika Korps and would command an army corps before the end of the war. He died in 1970.

1909 Luftwaffe ace Emil Lang (173 aerial victories during the war) was born in Thalheim. He died on the Western Front.

1915 The Royal Navy battleship RESOLUTION was launched. She was scrapped in 1948.

1942 The German battleship TIRPITZ left Wilhelmshaven, Germany for Norway. Ninety-five Royal Air Force bombers attacked Hamburg, Germany and lost four aircraft. Six people were killed in the raid.

1943 122 Royal Air Force bombers attacked German U-boat installations at the port of Lorient, France and lost two "Wellingtons". 120 buildings were destroyed and twelve people were killed in the raid. Forty-one Royal Air Force bombers dropped mines off the Biscay ports and lost one "Wellington". Eight USAAF 4th Fighter Group "Spitfires" fought the Luftwaffe west of Ostend, Belgium and claimed two Fw190s. The German trawler UJ-107 was lost in a collision off Rotvaer, Norway.

1944 The US Army's 2nd Airborne Brigade (the 507th and 508th Regiments) joined the 82nd Airborne Division in Northern Ireland. 531 8th Air Force B17s and B24s dropped 1,553 tons of bombs on German V-1 rocket sites in the Pas de Calais and lost two B17s and one B24. 645 8th Air Force P38s, P47s and P51s provided support for the bombers and claimed fourteen victories for the loss of one P38, one P47 and one P51. Don Gentile shot down two Luftwaffe aircraft to become an USAAF 8th Air Force ace. American 9th Air Force B26s attacked V-1 rocket sites near Cormette in France and lost two aircraft. The Belgium Resistance leader Walthere Dewe was killed in Ixelles. The European Advisory Commission held its first meeting. The three members of the Commission were Soviet representative F.T. Gusev, Sir William Strang from Britain and John G. Winant from America. Their purpose was to devise a partitioning plan for post-war Germany. It was decided that the Soviets occupation zone was to extend 200 miles west of Berlin. This should be taken into account when criticizing Allied Supreme Commander General Dwight Eisenhower for failing to attempt capturing Berlin from the west at the end of the war. Any territory taken within the Soviet zone would have been returned to them no matter what the cost in casualties to the Western Allies. Coincidentally, this was the same day that Eisenhower arrived in London to assume command of SHAEF (Supreme Headquarters Allied Expeditionary Force). 498 Royal Air Force bombers attacked Brunswick, Germany and lost thirty-eight "Lancasters". Ten buildings were destroyed and fourteen people were killed in the raid. Eighty-two Royal Air Force bombers attacked V-1 launching sites in France. Four B17s from the USAAF's 422nd Bomb Squadron dropped 840,000 leaflets on Amiens, Lille, Cambrai and St.Omer in France.

1945 The last He111-launched V-1 impacted near Hornsea; in Yorkshire (nearly 1,200 had been launched in this manner). The American freighter MICHAEL DE KOVATS was damaged by a German V-2 rocket at Antwerp, Belgium. 847 8th Air Force bombers dropped 2,326 tons of bombs on oil targets in Germany and lost seven B17s. 761 8th Air Force fighters provided support for the bombers and claimed 158 victories for the loss of nine P51s and two P47s. 134 Royal Air Force "Lancasters" attacked Saarbrucken, Germany. Thirty-one Royal Air Force "Typhoons" and thirty-five "Spitfires" attacked V-2 launching sites in Holland. American forces took Nadrin, Wilbrin, Wilogue, Dinez, Mont-le-Bon and Henumont in Belgium. 587 Royal Air Force bombers attacked Leuna and lost ten "Lancasters". 151 Royal Air Force bombers attacked Grevenbroich. 115 Royal Air Force bombers attacked Dulmen and lost one "Halifax". Eighty-three Royal Air Force "Mosquitoes" attacked Berlin and lost three aircraft.

Eastern Europe

1941 General Georgi Zhukov replaced General Kiril Meretsov as Chief of Staff of the Red Army.

1944 The Soviet Shock Army broke out of the Oranianburg bridgehead. Soviet forces took Mozyr and Kalinkovichi. The American 15th Air Force attacked Mostar, Yugoslavia.

1945 The Soviets attacked the German 2nd Army in East Prussia.

Mediterranean

1942 The Royal Navy submarine TRIUMPH was sunk by a mine.

1943 The "Casablanca Conference" began. At the Conference, British Prime Minister Winston Churchill and President Franklin Roosevelt agreed on a policy of "unconditional surrender", to give priority to the campaign against the U-boats and to begin a combined bombing offensive against Germany. Stalin had been invited to attend, but refused. The Italian submarine NARVELLO was sunk by the Royal Navy destroyers PAKENHAM and HURSLEY. Twenty-six American 12th Air Force B17s and seventeen P38s attacked Sfax, Tunisia.

1944 USAAF Lieutenant General Ira C. Eaker arrived to assume command of the Mediterranean Area Air Forces-MAAF. Eaker had previously commanded the 8th Air Force in Britain and would die in 1987.

1945 A cease-fire was called between British and Communist troops in Greece.

Atlantic

1941 The German armed merchant cruiser PINGUIN took the Norwegian whalers OLE WEGGER (12,201 tons) and SOLGIMT (12,246 tons) and the catchers POL VIII (298 tons), POL IX (354 tons), POL X (354 tons) and TORLYN (247 tons) off Antarctica. The Italian submarine CAPPELLINI sank the British freighter EUNAEUS (7,472 tons). The CAPPELLINI was seized by the Germans in September 1943 and recommissioned as UIT.24 in the German Navy.

1942 The Panamanian tanker NORNESS (9,577 tons) was sunk off Long Island by the U123. U123 survived the war. The U43 sank the Greek freighter MARO (3,838 tons), the British freighter EMPIRE SURF (6,641 tons) and the Panamanian freighter CHEPO (5,582 tons). U43 survived until July 30, 1943. The American freighter BRAZOS was lost in a collision with the British freighter ARCHER. The US Coast Guard cutter ARGO rescued six survivors from the tanker NORNESS.

1945 The U1232 sank the British tankers BRITISH FREEDOM (6,985 tons) and ATHELVIKING (8,779 tons) and damaged the American freighter MARTIN VAN BUREN (7,176 tons-three dead) off Halifax.

2013 The wreckage of USCG Grumman "Duck" was located Near Koge Bay in Greenland. It had crashed on November 29, 1942 killing all three men aboard. The remains were to be returned to the US for burial.

North America

1890 General John Porter Lucas, the Allied commander at Anzio, was born in Kearnysville, West Virginia. He graduated 55th in his 1911 West Point class of 82. He was promoted to major general on August 5, 1941 and assumed command of the 3rd Infantry Division. In March 1942 General Truscott replaced him. One year later Lucas was named as Eisenhower's deputy ground commander in the Mediterranean. He replaced General Dawley as commander of the 6th Corps after the Salerno landings. He and his staff immediately began planning the upcoming landings at Anzio. After achieving tactical surprise at Anzio, Lucas waited to consolidate his position before moving off the coastal plain, thus giving the Germans time to recover and seal off the beach-head. He was again replaced by Truscott. He would spend the rest of the war as commander of the 4th Army, a training unit based in San Antonio, Texas. He served as chief of the Army Advisory Group in Nanking, China 1946-48. He died on December 24, 1949.

1911 The USN battleship ARKANSAS was launched at Camden, New Jersey. She was expended in 1946.
1919 The destroyer BELKNAP was launched. She was lost on January 11, 1945.
1942 The Combined Chiefs of Staff was established in Washington D.C. It would facilitate operations involving British and American forces. The American freighter MAPELE (two dead) ran aground and was lost off Alaska.
1964 The USN transport FELAND was scrapped.
1965 The USN destroyer escort FROST was stricken. She had participated in the sinking of three U-boats during the war.
1966 A Japanese balloon-bomb was found near Nehalem, Oregon.
1967 The destroyer CLARENCE K. BRONSON was sold to Turkey.
1970 The destroyer RENSHAW was sold for scrap.
1988 The US Defense Department granted Veterans Benefits to the merchant seamen of WWII.

Pacific
1901 Philippine politician Carlos Romulo was born in Manila.
1940 Premier Abe and Admiral Mitsumasa Yonai formed a new Japanese government.
1943 600 Japanese troops landed on Cape Esperance to cover the evacuation of Guadalcanal. USAAF B26s attacked Japanese floatplane installations at Rekata Bay. USAAF B17s attacked Buka Island airfield. The USN submarine GUDGEON landed six Filipino guerillas on Negros. The USN submarine SEARAVEN sank the GANJITSU MARU No.1 (216 tons) and the SHIRAHA MARU (5,682 tons).
1944 Fighting continued around Cape Gloucester, New Britain. USAAF B25s attacked Wotje in the Marshalls and sank the IJN gunboat TAMA

MARU. "Dauntless'" and "Avengers" attacked Rabaul and damaged the destroyer MATSUKAZE and the tanker NARUTO. The USN submarine SWORDFISH sank the Japanese Q-ship DELHI MARU. The USN submarine ALBACORE sank the IJN destroyer SAZANAMI southeast of Yap. The USN submarine SWORDFISH sank the YAMAKUNI MARU (6,925 tons). The USN submarine SCAMP sank the NIPPON MARU (9,974 tons). The USN submarine GUARDFISH sank the KENYO MARU (10,024 tons). The USN submarine SEAWOLF sank the YAMAZURA MARU (3,651 tons).

1945 The IJN minelayer YURIJIMA was sunk by the USN submarine COBIA. USAAF B29s attacked Nagoya, Japan and the island of Formosa. The US Army's XIV Corps took Bautista, Luzon. The USN PT-73 was lost when she ran aground off Mindoro.

China-Burma-India

1939 Japanese cavalry forces crossed the Mongolian border on a raid.
1942 Japanese aircraft attacked Singapore and Rangoon. Japanese forces landed on Sumatra and took Malacca in Malaya.
1944 14th Air Force B24s sank the Japanese GYOEI MARU.
1945 14th Air Force P51s sank the Japanese freighter AKATSUKI MARU in the Yangtze River.

January 15th

Western Europe

1937 The Austrian government granted amnesty to imprisoned Nazis in order to placate Germany.
1940 German citizens in Holland and Belgium were told by the German government to return home. Belgium refused the Allies transit rights in the event of war. The freighter GRACIA (5,642 tons) was damaged by a mine in Liverpool Harbor that had been laid by the U30.
1941 Ninety-six Royal Air Force bombers attacked Wilhelmshaven, Germany and lost one "Whitley". Twenty-one people were killed in the raid.
1942 Ninety-six Royal Air Force bombers attacked Hamburg, Germany and lost four aircraft. Eight more bombers crashed in Britain upon returning from the mission. Fifty Royal Air Force bombers attacked Emden, Germany and lost two aircraft.
1943 A B17E carrying US Army Lieutenant General Jacob Devers and his staff crashlanded in neutral Eire. All were released and Devers would later command the 6th Army Group in Southern France. 157 Royal Air Force

bombers attacked German U-boat installations at Lorient, France and lost two aircraft. 800 buildings were destroyed and twelve people were killed in the raid. Twelve "Spitfires" from the USAAF's 4th Fighter Group flew patrols over the Channel.

1944   US Army General Dwight Eisenhower arrived in Britain to assume command of SHAEF (Supreme Headquarters Allied Expeditionary Force). German Field Marshal Erwin Rommel assumed command of Army Group B which consisted of the 7th and 15th Armies and defended the French coast nearest to Britain and would be the site of the upcoming Allied invasion which would be commanded by Eisenhower. The Belgian Resistance destroyed fifty electrical towers.

1945   Sixteen Royal Air Force "Mosquitos" attacked Leirvik harbor in Norway, sinking two freighters and lost six aircraft. 619 8th Air Force bombers dropped 1,546 tons of bombs on rail targets in Germany. 729 8th Air Force fighters provided support for the bombers and claimed fourteen victories for the loss of two P51s. Eighty-two Royal Air Force bombers attacked Recklinghausen, Germany. Sixty-three Royal Air Force "Lancasters" attacked Bochum, Germany. Corporal Arthur Beyer, of the 603rd Tank Destroyer Battalion, won a Medal of Honor near Arlincourt, Belgium. American troops began fighting in Houffalize, Belgium. British forces took Bakenhoven, Holland. American forces took Achouffe, Tavernaux, Mont, Beaumont and Francheville in Belgium. The Royal Navy escort carrier THANE was a constructive loss after an attack by the U482 in the Firth of Clyde. The German patrol boat V-5304 was sunk off Lervik, Norway by Allied aircraft.

1970   The French battleship JEAN BART was sold for scrap.

1971   Luftwaffe ace Gunther Rall (275 aerial victories during the war) became Inspector of the German Air Force.

Eastern Europe

1940   Soviet forces began shelling Finnish positions near Summa and continued to do so until the end of the month.

1942   The Germans pulled back to their winter positions in front of Moscow.

1943   Soviet forces broke through the Hungarian 2nd Army, creating a 175-mile gap in the Axis front south of Voronezh. The Soviet freighter PARTIZAN was sunk by the U354.

1944   Heavy fighting took place south of Leningrad.

1945   Soviet forces attacked German positions near Krakow and Kielce in Poland.

Mediterranean

1935   Eritrea and Somaliland were merged to form Italian East Africa.
1941   The Royal Navy submarine REGENT sank the Italian steamer CITTA DI MESSINA (2,472 tons). A Luftwaffe recon aircraft flew over Valletta Harbor, Malta in order to locate the Royal Navy carrier ILLUSTRIOUS which had been damaged on January 10th by German bombers.
1942   German torpedo boats laid a minefield east of Malta.
1943   The U617 sank the Greek freighter ANNITSA (4,312 tons) and the Norwegian freighter HARBOE JENSEN (1,862 tons). The British destroyers NUBIAN and KELVIN sank the Italian steamer D'ANNUNZIO (4,537 tons) south of Lampedusa. The British destroyers PAKENHAM and JAVELIN sank an Italian auxiliary ship.
1944   The American 5th Army took Monte Trocchio in Italy. The American 15th Air Force attacked Prato, Certaldo, Arrezo, Bucine and Fano in Italy.
1945   An Italian naval squadron consisting of one cruiser, three destroyers, one torpedo boat and three barges left Port Mahon, Spain, where they had been interned since September 8, 1943, for Malta. The French cruisers MONTCALM and GEORGES LEYGUES bombarded German positions near San Remo. The Royal Navy carrier FORMIDABLE left Gibraltar en route to operations in the Far East.

Atlantic

1940   The U44 sank the Norwegian freighter FAGERHEIM (1,590 tons) and the Dutch freighter ARENDSKERK (7,906 tons). U44 survived until March 20th.
1941   The German armed merchant cruiser PINGUIN took the Norwegian whaler PELAGOS (12,803 tons) and the catchers STAR XIV (247 tons), STAR XIX (249 tons), STAR XX (249 tons), STAR XXI (298 tons), STAR XXII (303 tons), STAR XXIII (357 tons) and STAR XXIV (361 tons). The Italian submarine TORICELLI sank the Greek freighter NEMEA (5,101 tons) and the Norwegian freighter BRASK (4,079 tons). TORICELLI was lost on June 23, 1940.
1942   The U552 sank the British freighter DAYROSE (4,113 tons). U552 survived the war. The U123 sank the British tanker COIMBRA (6,768 tons). U123 survived the war. The U553 sank the British tanker DIALA (8,106 tons). U553 survived until January 28, 1943. The U203 sank the Portuguese trawler CATALINA (632 tons). U203 survived until April 25, 1943. The USN heavy cruiser WICHITA was damaged in a collision with two freighters off Iceland.
1943   The U182 sank the British freighter OCEAN COURAGE (7,173 tons). U182 survived until May 16th. The U337 was sunk by the Royal Air Force's No.206 Squadron.

1945   The U482 damaged the Royal Navy escort carrier THANE (8,300 tons) and the Norwegian tanker SPINANGER (7,429 tons). U482 survived until the 16th. The U1055 sank the British tanker MAJA (8,181 tons).

1946   The American freighter WILLIAM WEBB was wrecked on Kilden Island.

North America

1883   General Lloyd Fredendall was born in Wyoming. He failed to graduate with his 1905 class at West Point, but was commissioned in 1907. In 1940, he was promoted to major general and given command of the 4th Infantry Division. He succeeded Mark Clark as commander of the 2nd Corps in Britain on October 10, 1942. He commanded the American troops that made up the Central Task Force on November 8th during "Operation Torch". After the fiasco at Kasserine Pass, he was relived of his command. On June 1, 1943, he was promoted to lieutenant general and given command of the 2nd Army. It was a training command based in Memphis, Tennessee. He retired on March 31, 1946 and died in La Jolla, California on October 4, 1963.

1931   The heavy cruiser LOUISVILLE was commissioned. She was scrapped in 1960.

1942   The 34th Heavy Bombardment Group (B17) was activated at Langley Field, Virginia. It was to have been the first unit assigned to the new 8th Bomber Command in Britain, but it was decided to keep it in America to train other groups. It would not make it to Britain until March 1944. The Alaskan Air Force headquarters was activated at Elmendorf Airfield. The escort carrier BOGUE was launched in Tacoma, Washington. The destroyer CALDWELL was launched; she was stricken May 1, 1965. The submarine HERRING was launched. She was lost on June 1, 1944. FDR, in an official reply to baseball Commissioner Kennesaw Landis, stated that major league baseball should continue to be played during the war as it contributed to civilian morale.

1945   A Japanese balloon-bomb exploded near Ventura, California.

1950   USAAF General Henry "Hap" Arnold died in Sonoma, California. He had commanded the USAAF during the war.

1971   The destroyer-minesweeper DAVISON was stricken.

1972   The destroyer-minesweepers QUICK, DORAN and MCCOOK were stricken.

1990   8th Air Force ace Chesley Peterson (9 victories), age 69, died in Riverside, California of heart and lung disease. He had been promoted to Colonel at the age of 23 and had retired as a Major General.

2014   USN ace Franklin Troop died at the age of 92 in Decatur, Alabama. He had been credited with 7 aerial victories while flying F6Fs in the Pacific.

Pacific

1942   The Japanese ground forces attacked on Allied positions on Bataan. A Royal Australian Air Force "Catalina" dropped sixteen bombs over the Japanese anchorage at Truk but caused no damage to the shipping located there. The USN submarine S-36 was damaged by an IJN destroyer.

1943   The American assault on Mount Austin, Guadalcanal continued. The "Cactus Air Force" attacked the IJN in the Solomons and lost six aircraft. The pilot of one of those aircraft that was lost was USMC Captain Jack Moore. He was rescued five days later by the Coastwatcher Geoffrey Kuper. Kuper would rescue more than twenty American airmen before the aerial action moved farther to the north. USAAF B17s and PBYs attacked Kahili, Bougainville.

1944   Fighting continued on New Britain. The USN submarine THRESHER sank the TOHO MARU 4,092 tons) and the TATSUNO MARU (6,960 tons). The Royal Navy submarine TALLY HO sank the RYUKO MARU (2,962 tons). The USN destroyer BLACK rescued twenty-two survivors from two downed American aircraft south of Jaluit Island.

1945   The American beach-head on Luzon was lengthened to forty-five miles. USN PT73 was scuttled in Baliquias Bay, Mindoro. A TBM "Avenger" exploded aboard the escort carrier HOGGATT BAY, killing eleven and wounding fourteen. The IJN destroyer HATAKAZE and transport T-14 were sunk off Formosa by USN carriers. The IJN destroyer TSUGA was sunk off the Pescadores by USN carriers. The KYO MARU No.1 (340 tons) was sunk by a mine.

1988   The remains of three USN aviators, who had been missing since March 30, 1944 when their TBF was shot down over Palau, were recovered (See January 13th).

China-Burma-India

1942   The IJN submarine I-165 sank the Indian freighter JALARAJAN (5,102 tons). Chinese forces stopped a Japanese offensive near Changsha in Hunan Province. The Japan's Southern Army invaded Burma from the Isthmus of Kra in Thailand.

1944   The USN submarine CREVALLE laid mines off Saigon. A USAAF B25 sank the Vichy French patrol boat PING SUNG off Indochina.

1945   The Japanese began offensive against Suichwan Airfield in China. The Chinese 30th Division took Namhkam, Burma.

January 16th

Western Europe

1908   German U-boat ace Gunther Prien was born in Osterfeld.

1910   Nazi intelligence official Walter Schellenberg was born. He died on March 31, 1952 in Italy.

1940   Hitler postponed his attack in the West until the spring.

1941   The Luftwaffe attacked Bristol, Britain. Eighty-one Royal Air Force bombers attacked Wilhelmshaven, Germany and lost two "Wellingtons", two "Whitleys" and one "Hampden.

1943   201 Royal Air Force bombers attacked Berlin and lost one "Lancaster". 198 people were killed in the raid including fifty-three Allied prisoners of war.

1944   The USAAF's 4th Fighter Group received its first "Thunderbolt" fighters. The American 15th Air Force attacked the Me109 factory at Klagenfurt, Austria.

1945   Adolf Hitler moved his headquarters into the Reich Chancellory Bunker. He would remain there until his suicide at the end of the war. 578 8th Air Force bombers dropped 1,455 tons of bombs on oil and industrial targets in Germany. 654 8th Air Force fighters provided support for the bombers and lost one P51. 371 Royal Air Force bombers attacked Magdeburg, Germany and lost seventeen "Halifaxes". 328 Royal Air Force bombers attacked Zeitz, Germany and lost ten "Lancasters". 237 Royal Air Force bombers attacked Brux, Czechoslovakia. 138 Royal Air Force "Lancasters" attacked Wanne-Eickel and lost one aircraft.

Eastern Europe

1942   Georg von Kuchler relieved Wilhelm von Leeb as commander of German Army Group "North".

1943   German forces controlled 200 square miles of Stalingrad. Soviet forces routed the Italians west of the Don River.

1944   The Soviets broke through north of Velikiye Luki.

1945   The Soviet destroyer DYEYATELNY (the ex-Royal Navy CHURCHILL and ex-USN HERNDON) was sunk by the U997.

Mediterranean

1941   The Luftwaffe attacked Malta damaging the Royal Navy carrier ILLUSTRIOUS and light cruiser PERTH and lost ten aircraft.

1943   Iraq declared war on the Axis.

1944   The American 15th Air Force attacked airfields at Villaroba and Osoppo.

1945   The German MTB S-33 was sunk off Unije in the Adriatic by the British MTB-698.

1949   The French battleship JEAN BART ran her acceptance trials after being launched in 1940. She had not been completed due to the war and was commissioned in 1950 and scrapped in 1969.

Atlantic
1940   The U44 sank the Greek freighter PANACHANDROS (4,661 tons). U44 survived until March 20th. The British tanker INVERDARGLE (9,456 tons) was sunk by a mine laid by the U33.
1941   The U106 sank the British freighter ZEALANDIC (10,578 tons). U106 survived until August 2, 1943. The Italian submarine TORICELLI sank the Greek freighter FILINIS (3,111 tons). The U96 sank the British freighter OROPESA (14,118 tons). U96 survived until March 30, 1945.
1944   The American freighter SUMNER I. KIMBALL (7,176 tons), was sunk with all hands by the U960. The U544 was sunk by the USN escort carrier GUADALCANAL.
1945   The U248 was sunk by the USN destroyer escorts HAYTER, OTTER, VARIAN, and HUBBARD. The U482 was sunk by the Royal Navy sloops AMETHYST, HART, PEACOCK and STARLING and frigate LOCH CRAGGIE. The American freighter JAMES HARROD was a constructive loss after colliding with the American freighter RAYMOND STEVENS off Deal in Kent.

North America
1892   General Charles Ryder was born in Kansas. He graduated 39th in his 1915 West Point class of 164. During WWI, he was awarded two Distinguished Service Crosses, a Silver Star and a Purple Heart. He took command of the 34th Infantry Division in May 1942. The 34th was the first US Army division to be sent to Europe. The unit distinguished itself in the Mediterranean Theater and was commanded by Ryder until he was sent back to the States to take over the Ninth Corps. He retired on February 28, 1950 as a major general. He died on August 17, 1960 in Vineyard Haven, Massachusetts.
1930   The carrier LEXINGTON ended a 30-day tour of supplying electricity to Tacoma, Washington after that city suffered a municipal power failure.
1941   FDR requested $350 million for the construction off 200 merchant ships.
1942   FDR asked his cabinet to study the idea of an Alaska-Canadian Highway. Actress Carole Lombard died in a plane crash near Las Vegas, Nevada while returning to Hollywood from a bond tour. Donald Nelson was appointed head of the US War Production Board. Four B26s crashlanded near Watson Lake in Canada and another went down at White Horse.
1944   The destroyers MOALE (sold to Greece in 1972) and INGRAHAM (sold to Greece in 1971) were launched.

1966   General Courtney Hodges, commander of the 1st Army in Europe, died in San Antonio, Texas.
1969   The US Coast Guard cutter TRITON was sold.
1977   Admiral Daniel V. Gallery (captor of the U505) died in Bethesda, Maryland.

Pacific
1942   Three USAAF LB30s (an export version of the B24) and two B17s attacked Kendari, Celebes. Sergeant Jose Calugas, of the Philippine Scouts, won a Medal of Honor on the Bataan Peninsula. He would retire from the US Army as a Captain in 1957. Japanese forces broke through the Allies right flank on Bataan. Japanese paratroops landed on Sumatra. The USN submarine SEAWOLF left Darwin with thirty-six tons of ammunition for Corregidor.
1943   The American offensive on Guadalcanal continued. The USN submarine GROWLER sank the CHIFUKI MARU (5,857 tons). The USN submarine GREENLING sank the KINPOSAN MARU (3,261 tons). USAAF B17s attacked Ballale Island.
1944   Japanese forces made their last counter-attack on Cape Gloucester, New Britain and were defeated. The USN submarine SWORDFISH sank the DELHI MARU (2,205 tons). The USN submarine STURGEON damaged the IJN destroyer SUZUTSUKI. The USN submarine BLACKFISH sank the KAIKA MARU (2,087 tons). The USN submarine WHALE sank the DENMARK MARU (5,869 tons). The USN submarine REDFIN damaged the IJN destroyer AMATSUKAZE. The USN submarine SEAHORSE sank the NIKKO MARU (784 tons). The USN submarine SEAWOLF sank the TARUSHIMA MARU (4,865 tons). The IJN submarine I-181 was lost off New Guinea.
1945   USN Task Force 38 continued its attacks on Japanese shipping in the East China Sea. Fighting continued on Mindoro, Leyte and Luzon. The Royal Navy submarine PORPOISE was sunk by Japanese aircraft. The USN LSM-318 was sunk and LST-700 was damaged by kamikazes in Lingayen Gulf. USAAF B29s attacked Shinchiku.
1989   The wreckage of a Dutch Air Force C47 was found near Mossman, Australia. It had been missing since its flight from New Guinea on September 7, 1944.

China-Burma-India
1942   The Royal Air Force moved their remaining aircraft from Singapore to Sumatra. In Malaya the British try to hold the Muar River against advancing Japanese forces.

1944	The IJN submarine I-165 sank the British freighter PERSEUS (10,286 tons). The Chinese 112th Regiment took Gum Ga, Burma. Chiang Kai-shek threatened to cut off supplies to American forces in China and kick them out of their quarters by March 1st, unless the American government granted China $1 billion in credit.
1945	Chinese forces took Namhkam, Burma.

January 17th

Western Europe

1885	General Nikolaus von Falkenhorst, commander of the German Forces in Norway, was born in Breslau.
1935	The League of Nations awarded the Saar Basin to Germany. This was a result of a vote take among the population prior to the decision.
1939	The French battleship RICHELIEU was launched at Brest, France.
1940	The freighter CAIRNROSE (5,494 tons) was sunk in Liverpool Harbor by a mine laid by the U30.
1942	Eighty-three Royal Air Force bombers attacked Bremen, Germany and lost four aircraft. Five people were killed in the raid.
1943	London had its first air-raid since May 1941. 187 Royal Air Force bombers attacked Berlin and lost twenty-two aircraft. Eight people were killed in the raid. Four "Spitfires" from the USAAF's 4th Fighter Group flew patrols over the Channel.
1945	The American 3rd Army took Diekirch, Belgium. British forces took Echt and Susteren in Holland. 665 8th Air Force bombers dropped 1,031 tons of bombs on marshalling yards at Paderborn and oil refineries at Hamburg and Harburg in Germany and lost five B17s and four B24s. The U2523 was sunk during the raid on Hamburg. Ninety-two Royal Air Force "Mosquitoes" attacked targets in Germany. 320 8th Air Force fighters provided support for the bombers. The German minesweeper M-305 sank in a gale off Brusterort in the Baltic. The German patrol boat V-1417 was sunk off Terschelling by Allied aircraft.

Eastern Europe

1942	Field Marshal Walter von Reichenau died of a heart attack while returning to Germany from the Eastern Front. He was commander of Army Group "South". At 2327, the U454 sank the Royal Navy destroyer MATABELE in the Barents Sea.
1943	Soviet forces took Millerovo.
1944	The Soviets took Slavuta.
1945	The Soviets took Warsaw, Ciechagow and Czestochowa in Poland.

Mediterranean

1941 Italian aircraft attacked Malta.

1942 British forces took Halfaya, Egypt and 5,500 prisoners. The South African Parliament rejected a motion for independence from Britain. At 0735, the Royal Navy destroyer GURKHA was torpedoed north of Bardia by the U133. She sank at 0913.

1943 At 1725, the Italian destroyer BOMBARDIERE was sunk west of Sicily by the Royal Navy submarine UNITED.

1944 The Allies attacked the German "Gustav Line" in Italy. The British Army's X Corps crossed the Garigliano River. The operations by the Allies convinced the German Commander in Southern Italy to reinforce his defenses with reserves that were stationed near Rome. The American 15th Air Force attacked Arezzo, Pontassieve and Prato in Italy.

1945 Thirty German "Linsen" explosive boats failed in their attempt to attack Allied shipping off La Spezia. The German MTBs S-58 and S-60 were scuttled at Unije in the Adriatic. They had been damaged in action against British MTBs on the 10th.

Atlantic

1940 The U25 sank the British freighter POLZELLA (4,751 tons) and the Norwegian freighter ENID (1,140 tons). U25 survived until August 3rd.

1941 The U96 sank the British freighter ALMEDA STAR (14,935 tons). U96 survived until November 28th.

1942 The U87 sank the Norwegian tanker NYHOLT (8,087 tons). U87 survived until March 4, 1943. The U203 sank the Norwegian freighter OCTAVIAN (1,345 tons). U203 survived until April 25, 1943. The U123 sank the American freighter SAN JOSE (1,932 tons). U123 survived the war. The American freighter SAN JOSE was lost in a collision with the freighter SANTA ELISA.

1943 The U268 sank the Panamanian whaler VESTHOLD (14,547 tons) and the Royal Navy LCTs 2239, 2267 and 2344, which were being carried as deck cargo. U268 survived until February 19th.

1944 The U305 was sunk southwest of Ireland by the Royal Navy destroyer WANDERER and frigate GLENARM.

North America

1888 Lieutenant General Delos Emmons, commander of the Western Defense Command, was born in Huntington, West Virginia.

1936 Boeing Aircraft was awarded a contract for thirteen Model 299s, to be designated YB-17s.

1942 Chief of Naval Operations Admiral Ernest King sent Captains Francis S. Low and Donald B. Duncan, members of his staff, to USAAF

Chief-of-Staff General Henry Arnold with plans for a joint Army/Navy air attack on the Japanese Home Islands. After this meeting, Arnold assigned Lieutenant Colonel James Doolittle to plan the action. Eventually Doolittle would wrangle his way into actually commanding the attack. British Prime Minister Winston Churchill left America aboard the Royal Navy battleship DUKE OF YORK en route back to Britain. He and his advisors had been the America since the 22nd of December convincing FDR to adopt a "Germany First" policy.

1943 The light carrier COWPENS was launched at New York. She was scrapped in 1962.

1945 A Japanese balloon-bomb exploded near Moorpark, California. USAAF Chief-of-Staff Henry Arnold suffered his 4th major heart attack since the beginning of the war.

1960 The USN escort carrier GUADALCANAL was scrapped. She had participated in the sinking of three U-boats and the capture of the U505.

2007 Flying Tiger ace C. Joseph Rosbert died at the age of 89. He had been credited with shooting down 6 Japanese aircraft while flying in China.

Pacific

1942 The IJN submarine I-60 was sunk in Sunda Strait by the Royal Navy destroyer JUPITER. The Soviet freighter KOLKHOZNIK was stranded on Sambro Shoal off the Washington Coast. Filipino forces failed in an attempt to restore the western flank on Bataan.

1943 The American offensive continued on Guadalcanal. Twenty-nine USN SBDs, eighteen TBFs and seventy fighters attacked Rabaul, New Britain. They shot down seventeen Japanese aircraft, while losing twelve of their own and sinking the HAKKAI MARU, KENSHIN MARU, KOSEI MARU, LYONS MARU and TENSHIN MARU. Japanese aircraft attacked Milne Bay, New Guinea and destroyed six aircraft. Australian forces broke through Japanese defenses at Sanananda, New Guinea. The USN submarine WHALE sank the HEIYO MARU (9,816 tons). Naval Base and Naval Air Station, Brisbane Australia was established.

1944 American forces continued operations around the Arawe beach-head on New Britain. USN TBFs and SBDs, escorted by USAAF P38s, attacked Rabaul, New Britain. They sank the repair ship HAKKAI MARU, the transport KENSHIN MARU and the freighter KOSEI MARU. 5th Air Force B24s sank the freighters CHIBURI MARU and FUKEIU MARU NO.9 off Manus. Meat rationing began in Australia.

1945 The American 6th Army continued to make slow progress on Luzon. The American 13th Air Force's 18th Fighter Group (P38) became the first USAAF fighter group to be stationed on Luzon since 1942. The IJN destroyer-transport T-15 (1,500 tons) was sunk by the USN submarine

TAUTOG. The USN escort carrier NEHENTA BAY was damaged in a storm off Luzon.

China-Burma-India
1941 The Siamese torpedo boats CHONBURI, SONGHKLA and TRAT the and coastal defense vessels DOMBURI and AHIDEA were sunk in the Koh-Chang estuary in Cambodia by the French light cruiser LAMOTTE-PICQUET and corvettes AMIRAL CHARNER, DUMONT D'URVILLE and TAHURE. The action effectively wiped out the tiny Thai Navy.
1942 The American Volunteer Group shot down three Japanese bombers near Kunming, China. The British retreated from their defensive positions along the Muar River in Malaya.
1944 The Royal Air Force attacked Kyauchaw, Burma.

January 18th

Western Europe
1879 French General Henri Giraud was born in Paris. He died on March 13, 1949.
1943 The last five survivors of the November 19th British commando raid on the Norwegian heavy water plant were executed by the Germans. Twenty-nine Royal Air Force bombers dropped mines in the Baltic.
1945 Eight American soldiers received sentences of from 10 years to life for stealing and selling American Army gasoline in Paris. 120 8th Air Force B17s dropped 322 tons of bombs on Kaiserslautern. 109 8th Air Force fighters provided support for the bombers and lost one P51. 111 Royal Air Force "Mosquitoes" attacked targets in Germany and lost one aircraft. Private D. Donnini, of the Royal Scots Fusiliers, won a posthumous Victoria Cross in Germany. British forces took Schliberg and Heide in Holland.
1946 Royal Air Force Group Captain A. Hards died while test-flying a captured Luftwaffe Do335 at Royal Air Force Farnborough.

Eastern Europe
1940 The Soviet Air Force attacked the port of Kotka, Finland and severely damaged the icebreaker TARMO.
1942 Soviet forces began offensive on the south and central fronts. 95,000 Germans were surrounded at Demyansk. German forces recaptured Feodosia.
1943 The Soviets announced the lifting of the 900-day siege of Leningrad. The inhabitants had been dying at the rate of 20,000 per day. Soviet forces

took Cherkessk and Divnoye. Armed resistance took place in the Warsaw Ghetto for the first time.
1944   The Germans took 40,000 prisoners, 349 cannon and 1,203 tanks at Vitebsk.
1945   Soviet forces took Modlin, Poland and Pest, Hungary. The last German resistance ended in Warsaw. The Soviet-backed "Lublin Committee" arrived in Warsaw to assume control of liberated Poland.
1988   Andrija Artukovic, age 88, died in a Yugoslavian jail. He had ordered the executions of thousands of prisoners during WWII and was known as "Butcher of the Balkans".

Mediterranean
1941   The Luftwaffe attacked airfields on Malta, destroying six aircraft.
1943   Allied fighter-bombers destroyed twenty-three Luftwaffe Ju52s on the ground in Tunisia. "Shoot Luke" became the first USAAF B24 "Liberator" to land on Malta. The German MkVI "Tiger" tank was used operationally for the first time at Bou Arada. The American 12th Air Force attacked Tripoli, Tunisia. The British destroyers PAKENHAM and NUBIAN and the Greek destroyer VASILISSA OLGA sank the Italian transport STROMBOLI (475 tons).
1944   The American 15th Air Force attacked Pisa, Certaldo, Pontedera, Patois and Poggibonsi in Italy. A rehearsal for "Operation Shingle" (the Allied invasion of Anzio) took place near Naples. Forty-three landing craft, nineteen 105mm howitzers and nine anti-tank guns were lost.

Atlantic
1940   The Swedish freighter FOXEN (1,304 tons) was sunk by a British mine. The U44 sank the Danish freighter CANADIAN REEFER (1,831 tons). U44 survived until March 20th. The U25 sank the Swedish freighter PAJALA (6,873 tons). U25 survived until August 3rd. The U9 sank the Swedish freighter FLANDRIA (1,179 tons). U9 survived until August 20, 1944.
1941   The German armed merchant cruiser KORMORAN took the American tanker BRITISH UNION (6,987 tons).
1942   The U333 sank the British freighter CALEDONIAN MONARCH (5,851 tons). U333 survived until July 31, 1944. The U552 sank the American freighter FRANCES SALMAN (2,609 tons) with all hands. U552 survived the war. The U66 sank the American tanker ALLEN JACKSON (6,635 tons-22 dead). U66 survived until May 6, 1944. The U86 sank the Greek freighter DIMITRIOS G. THERMIOTIS (4,271 tons). U86 survived until November 29, 1943.

North America

1884 Lieutenant General Barton Yount, commander of the USAAF Training Command, was born in Troy, Ohio.

1941 The German Consul General in San Francisco displayed the Reich flag in honor of a German national holiday. It was torn down and destroyed by a mob of local citizens.

1944 The escort carrier KADASHAN BAY was commissioned. She was scrapped in 1960.

1950 The B17D "Swoose" was placed in storage at Pyote, Texas. She had served in the Southwest Pacific during 1941-42. As the oldest surviving aircraft of her type, she is currently in storage at the Smithsonian Institute in Washington D.C.

Pacific

1942 The USN submarine PLUNGER sank the EIZAN MARU (4,702 tons). The IJN submarine I-121 sank the Dutch freighter BANTAM (9,312 tons).

1943 The USN Task Group 8.6 (commanded by McMorris) consisting of the heavy cruiser INDIANAPOLIS, the light cruiser RICHMOND and the destroyers BANCROFT, CALDWELL, COGHLAN and GILLESPIE bombarded Attu in the Aleutians. Four American 11th Air Force B24s attacked Kiska in the Aleutians. USAAF B26s flew the type's last mission in the Aleutians. USAAF B17s attacked Japanese shipping off Shortland Island. The USN submarine SILVERSIDES sank the TOEI MARU (10,022 tons). The IJN submarine I-21 sank the Australian freighter KALINGO (2,051 tons) and damaged the American tanker MOBILUBE (10,222 tons-3 dead). The American freighter LIPSCOMB LYKES ran aground and was lost off New Caledonia.

1944 Fighting continued on New Britain. The USN submarine BOWFIN sank the SHOYO MARU (4,408 tons). The USN submarine FLASHER sank the YOSHIDA MARU (2,920 tons). USAAF ace Lieutenant Colonel Charles MacDonald shot down a Japanese "Hamp" over Wewak, New Guinea. American 13th Air Force ace Cotesworth Head (12 victories) was killed in action over Rabaul, New Britain. American 13th Air Force B25s attacked Rabaul.

1945 The IJN submarine Ro-47 was sunk by the USN destroyer escort FLEMING. The US Army's 6th Division took Urdaneta, Luzon. Two Japanese raiding parties landed on Peleliu and were wiped out. An 11th Air Force B24 was interned in Russia.

China-Burma-India

1932 Five Japanese civilians were killed in an anti-Japanese demonstration in Shanghai.

1942 British forces completed their withdrawal into their Johore Line in Malaya.
1944 The Royal Air Force attacked Wuntho, Burma.

January 19th

Western Europe
1888 British Admiral Henry Harwood was born in London. In 1936 he assumed command of the South American Division. On December 13, 1939 his command cornered the German pocket battleship ADMIRAL GRAF SPEE off the coast of Uruguay. After the battle the German vessel was scuttled. A year later, he became assistant chief of the naval staff in London. In 1942, he was named as C-in-C of the Mediterranean. In 1943 he had to leave the Mediterranean due to ill health. He retired in 1945 and died on June 9, 1950.
1901 German General Henning von Tresckow was born. He was one of the most persevering and dedicated anti-Hitler conspirators. He began as a lieutenant colonel in 1939 and committed suicide after the July 20, 1944 attempt on Hitler's life.
1915 The Royal Navy battleship QUEEN ELIZABETH was commissioned. She was scrapped in 1948.
1939 The German heavy cruiser SEYDLITZ was launched. She was scuttled in 1945.
1941 Hitler and Mussolini met at Obersalzburg to discuss the Greek situation.
1942 Soviet submarines K-22 and K-23 attacked shipping off Norway's northern coast sinking two small ships.
1943 The German trawler V-703 was lost in a gale off Alderney.
1945 Fighting continued between the Meuse River and the Ruhr. The US Army's 4th and 5th Divisions took Bettendorf, Germany. The US Army's 3rd Armored Division took Rettigny, Renglez and Brisy in Belgium.

Eastern Europe
1884 The Soviet Ambassador to London, Ivan Maisky, was born in Kiriloff.
1941 A civil war began in Rumania.
1942 Fedor von Bock succeeded Walter von Reichenau as commander of Army Group "South". Reichenau had died of a heart attack. Soviet forces took Mozhaisk near Moscow. The Germans took Feodosiya in the Crimea.
1943 The Soviets took Novgorod, Valuyki and Kamensk.
1944 Soviet forces took Popsha, Peterhof and Krasnoye Selo.
1945 The Soviets took Lodz, Krakow, Tarnow and Gorlice in Poland and Schlossburg in East Prussia.

Mediterranean

1941 British forces began an offensive in Ethiopia. The Luftwaffe damaged the Royal Navy carrier ILLUSTRIOUS at Malta. The Italian submarine NEGHELLI damaged the British freighter CLAN CUMMING (7,264 tons). NEGHELLI was then sunk by the Royal Navy destroyer GREYHOUND.

1942 British forces took Misurta and Tarhuna, Libya. The British began a counter-offensive in eastern Africa.

1943 The Italian submarine TRITONE was sunk by the Royal Canadian Navy escort PORT ARTHUR. The Italian minesweeper ESO (the ex-Yugoslavian SOKOL) was sunk east of Djerba by Royal Navy aircraft.

1944 The 15th Air Force attacked airfields near Rome. The British Army's 5th Division took Minturno.

1947 A Greek liner was sunk by a WWII mine, 393 died.

Atlantic

1940 The U9 sank the Swedish freighter PATRIA (1,188 tons). U9 survived until August 20, 1944. The U59 sank the French freighter QUIBERON (1,296 tons). U59 survived the war. The Royal Navy destroyer GRENVILLE was sunk in the North Sea by a mine.

1942 The U109 sank the British freighter EMPIRE KINGFISHER (6,082 tons). U109 survived until May 4, 1943. The U66 sank the Canadian tanker LADY HAWKINS (7,988 tons-204 died). U66 survived until May 6, 1944. The U123 sank the American freighters BRAZOS (4,497 tons) and CITY OF ATLANTA (5,269 tons-43 died) and the Latvian freighter CILTVAIRA (3,779 tons). U123 was scrapped in 1957. USAAF forces arrived in Aruba and Curacao in the Dutch West Indies.

1944 The U641 was sunk southwest of Ireland by the Royal Navy corvette VIOLET.

North America

1888 General Millard F. Harmon was born in San Francisco, California. He graduated 74th in his 1912 West Point class of 95. He commanded the 2nd Air Force from April 9th until December 19, 1941. He became Air Force Chief of Staff on January 26, 1942. He was sent to the South Pacific in July 1942 and arrived in New Caledonia on the 26th. Once there, he assumed command of all Air Force units in the area. In 1944, he would assume command of all Air Force units in the entire Pacific area. On February 26, 1945 he was declared missing and presumed lost on a flight to Hawaii.

1892 Admiral Allan Smith was born in Detroit. He graduated 130th in his 1915 Annapolis class of 179. He was promoted to rear admiral in March 1944 and given command of Cruiser Division 1. In July he took over the 17th Naval District (Alaska and the Aleutians). The next month he assumed command of Cruiser Division 5. He retired on February 1, 1954 as a vice admiral. He died on July 2, 1987.

1905 US Women's Army Corps commander Oveta Hobby was born in Killeen, Texas. As a colonel she would command 100,000 Wacs during the war. She resigned on July 12, 1945 and died on August 16, 1995.

1941 Secretary of State Cordell Hull assured the German government that there would be a full investigation of the previous day's flag incident in San Francisco.

1943 The Liberty ship JOHN HARVEY was completed. She would be sunk in a Luftwaffe raid on Bari harbor in Italy on December 2nd. Among her cargo was 100 tons of mustard gas. Over 600 casualties occurred because of the gas, 100 of which were fatalities.

1945 A Japanese balloon-bomb was found near Fort Simpson, Northwest Territory in Canada.

1948 The destroyer HUTCHINS was sold for scrap.

1977 Iva D'Aquino "Tokyo Rose" was pardoned by President Gerald Ford.

1992 Ted Lawson, pilot on the "Doolittle Raid" and author of the book "Thirty Seconds over Tokyo", died in Chico, California.

2012 USN Captain Warren Skon died at the age of 92 in McLean, Virginia. He had scored 7 aerial victories in the Pacific and had been awarded the Navy Cross.

Pacific

1895 Royal Air Force General Arthur "Mary" Coningham was born in Brisbane, Australia. During WWI, he served as a Royal Flying Corps on the Western Front and was awarded the Military Cross and the Distinguished Flying Cross. When WWII began, he was commanding No.4 Bomb Group in Yorkshire. In July 1941, he became commander of the Western Desert Air Force in North Africa. On February 17, 1943 he established the 1st Tactical Air Force. In January 1944, he went to Britain to command the 2nd Tactical Air Force. He retired as an Air Marshal in 1947. On January 30, 1948, he died in an air crash between the Azores and Bermuda.

1942 The British forces in North Borneo surrendered. An American counter-attack on Bataan was repulsed.

1943 Japanese forces landed reinforcements at Wewak, New Guinea. American reinforcements landed on Point Cruz, Guadalcanal. The USN submarine POLLACK sank the SEIKAI MARU (3,109 tons). The USN submarine SWORDFISH sank the MYOHO MARU (4,122 tons).

1944 Fighting continued on New Britain. The USN submarine HADDOCK damaged the IJN escort carrier UNYO. A 5th Air Force B24 sank the freighter KAISHU MARU at Manus in the Admiralties.

1945	The American 6th Army began advancing towards Clark Field on Luzon. Fighting continued on Mindoro. The USN submarine SPOT sank the USA MARU (184 tons).
2012	Navy Cross recipient Warren Skon died at the age of 92.

China-Burma-India

1942	Japanese forces were within eighty miles of Singapore. The Japanese took the Royal Air Force airfield at Tavoy, Burma.
1943	Parkash Singh, of the 8th Punjab Regiment, won a Victoria Cross in Burma. Four American 10th Air Force B24s attacked Thazi, Burma.
1944	The Royal Air Force attacked Mawku, Burma.
1945	The 25th Indian Division took Kantha, Burma. Sher Shah, of the 7/6 Punjab Regiment, won a posthumous Victoria Cross at Arakan, Burma.

January 20th

Western Europe

1883	British Admiral Bertram Ramsey was born. He died on January 2, 1945 in a plane crash in France.
1936	Edward VIII became King of England.
1939	Hjalmar Schacht was dismissed by Adolf Hitler as President of the German Reichsbank.
1940	Hitler postponed his invasion of the West until at least March.
1942	The idea of a "Final Solution" to the Jewish problem was examined at the "Wannsee Conference", in Berlin. Twenty-five Royal Air Force bombers attacked Emden, Germany and lost four aircraft.
1943	The Luftwaffe attacked southeast Britain. Thirty-nine children were killed when their school in Lewisham, Britain was bombed. Eight Royal Air Force "Wellingtons" dropped mines in the Baltic. Twenty-two USAAF 4th Fighter Group "Spitfires" flew missions over France
1944	Sholto Douglas succeeded John Slessor as commander of the Royal Air Force's Coastal Command. Four B17s from the USAAF's 42nd Bomb Squadron dropped 960,000 leaflets on Lille, Brest, Caen, and Chartres in France. 769 Royal Air Force bombers attacked Berlin and lost thirty-five aircraft.
1945	684 8th Air Force bombers dropped 1,769 tons of bombs on rail targets in Germany and the synthetic oil plant at Sterkrade, Germany. 426 8th Air Force fighters provided support for the bombers and claimed one victory for the loss of three P51s. The US Army's 5th Division took Kippenhoff and Brandenburg in Belgium.

1988 The Royal Navy submarine P556 (the ex-USN S29) was sold to a Spanish scrapyard. She had been at Portsmouth since being transferred to Britain under American Lend-Lease.

Eastern Europe

1881 American General Walter Krueger was born in Flatow, Prussia. He moved with his parents to America when he was eight years old and grew up in Madison, Indiana. During the Spanish-American War he rose to the rank of sergeant major. After seeing action in the Philippine Insurrection, he was commissioned as a second lieutenant. During WWI he was promoted to colonel and was named a chief of the American Expeditionary Forces Tank Corps. On February 31, 1939 he assumed command of the 2nd Infantry Division and was promoted to major general. He commanded the 8th Corps from October 1940 until he took over the 3rd Army on May 16, 1941. On January 25, 1943 he assumed command of the 6th Army in Australia. The 6th was parceled out on various assignments and it was not until the invasion of the Philippines in October of 1944 that Krueger actually commanded the whole unit in action. On March 5, 1945 he was promoted to four-star rank. He retired in January 1946 and died in 1967.

1939 Count Ciano visited Yugoslavia to urge improved relations Italy, Hungary, and Yugoslavia.

1944 Soviet forces took Mega and Novgorod.

1945 The Germans tried to break out of Budapest, Hungary. Soviet forces took Pest in Hungary, Nowy and Sacz in Poland and Bardjov, Presov and Kosice in Czechoslovakia and continued their advance into East Prussia. The Hungarian government signed an armistice with the Soviets.

Mediterranean

1936 Ethiopia requested financial aid from the League of Nations.

1940 The American government protested British imposed delays of American shipping at Gibraltar.

1942 British forces took Homs, Libya.

1943 The Italian submarine SANTAROSA was sunk off Tripoli by the British MTB260. The U453 sank the Belgian freighter JEAN JADOT (5,859 tons). The Italian minesweepers RD31, RD36, RD37 and RD39 were sunk off Zara by the Royal Navy destroyers JAVELIN and KELVIN. The American 12th Air Force sank the Italian tanker SATURNO.

1944 The US Army's 36th Division was repulsed in an attack across the Rapido River, with the loss of 518 killed in action, 663 wounded in action and 500 prisoners of war. The few American soldiers that succeeded in reaching the opposite shore were finally withdrawn two days later. The British Army's X Corps took Tufo. The American 15th Air Force attacked Rome airfields. US Army Major General John P. Lucas, the Commander of the upcoming "Operation Shingle" (the invasion of Anzio) was informed that his prime mission was to secure the beach-head and not to advance into the Alban Hills behind Anzio unless conditions warranted it. He would later be relieved of his command for following those orders.

Atlantic
1940 The U44 sank the Greek EKATONTARCHOS DRACOULIS (5,329 tons). U44 survived until March 20th.
1941 The U94 sank the British freighter FLORIAN (3,174 tons). U94 survived until August 28, 1942. The Italian submarine MARCELLO sank the Belgian freighter PORTUGAL (1,550 tons). MARCELLO was lost on February 22nd.
1944 The USN LST-228 was lost when she ran aground in the Azores.

North America
1919 The battleship IDAHO's keel was laid at Camden, New Jersey.
1941 FDR began his third term as President. Henry Wallace would serve as his Vice-President.
1942 The submarine GUARDFISH was launched. She was expended as a target in 1961.
1943 The USN Drydock YFD No.20 (6,000 tons) foundered off Bolinas, California. It had been built just a few months before in Eureka, California. The submarine CAPELIN was launched at Portsmouth. She was lost in December 1943. The first destroyer escort type, the BRENNAN, was commissioned at Mare Island, California. She was scrapped in 1946.
1945 FDR began his fourth term as President.
1970 The destroyer INGERSOLL was sold for scrap.
1976 The destroyer GURKE was stricken.
2007 USMC Colonel Robert McClurg, age 87, died in Skaneateles, New York. During the war he had flown F4U Corsairs and had been credited with 7 aerial victories.
2010 USAAF ace Colonel John Loisel died at the age of 89. He had scored He had scored 11 aerial victories while flying the P39 and P38 in the Pacific.

South America
1943 Chile broke relations with the Axis governments.

Pacific
1942 More than 100 Japanese carrier aircraft attacked Rabaul, New Britain. The USN submarine S-36 ran aground in Makassar Strait. The Dutch steamer SIBEROET rescued the crew and landed them at Surabaya, Java,

on February 25th. The USN PT31 ran aground in Subic Bay and was lost. The IJN submarine I-124 was sunk off Darwin by the USN destroyer EDSALL and the Australian minesweeper DELORAINE.

1943   The American assault on Mount Austin, Guadalcanal continued. The USN submarine SILVERSIDES sank the SURABAYA MARU (4,391 tons), SOMEDONO MARU (5,154 tons) and MEIU MARU (8,230 tons). USAAF B17s attacked Japanese shipping off Shortland Island and lost one escorting fighter. The American 11th Air Force attacked Kiska in the Aleutians.

1944   Fighting continued on New Britain. The USN submarine TINOSA landed agents on northeast Borneo. USAAF B25s sank the transport OGASHIMA MARU at Namu in the Marshalls. The USN submarine BATFISH sank the HIDAKA MARU (5,486 tons). The USN submarine GAR sank the KOYO MARU (5,324 tons).

1945   USAAF General Curtis LeMay assumed command of the B29s operating from the Marianas. The US Army's 37th Division took Victoria, Luzon. The US Army's 43rd Division took Mount Alava on Luzon. The USN submarine SPOT sank the TOKIWA MARU (221 tons). The USN submarine TAUTOG sank the SHURI MARU (1,857 tons).

China-Burma-India

1932   Japan demanded an apology and concessions for the January 18th attacks on Japanese nationals in Shanghai.

1942   The Royal Air Force shot down eight Japanese Air Force aircraft over Singapore. The American Volunteer Group and Royal Air Force attacked targets in Burma and lost one P40. The Japanese 15th Army which was commanded by Lieutenant General Shojiro Iida invaded Burma. The IJN submarine I-159 sank the Norwegian freighter EIDSVOLD (4,184 tons) off Christmas Island.

1944   Lieutenant A. Horwood, of the Queen's Regiment, won a posthumous Victoria Cross at Arakan, Burma. The U188 sank the British freighter FORT BUCKINGHAM (7,122 tons). 14th Air Force B24s sank the transports MENADO MARU and KUZAN MARU off Swatow, China.

1945   The Chinese 9th Division took Wanting, Burma.

January 21st

Western Europe

1942   Fifty-four Royal Air Force bombers attacked Bremen, Germany and lost three aircraft. Thirty-eight Royal Air Force bombers attacked Emden, Germany and lost four aircraft.

1943　Fifty-one Royal Air Force bombers attacked targets in France and Belgium. Eighty-two Royal Air Force bombers attacked Essen, Germany and lost four "Lancasters". Seventy Royal Air Force bombers dropped mines in the Baltic and lost six aircraft. Forty-nine "Spitfires" from the USAAF's 4th Fighter Group flew missions near Caen, France.

1944　Luftwaffe aircraft attacked Britain. 394 8th Air Force B17s and B24s dropped 1,141 tons of bombs on V-1 sites near Cherbourg and Pas de Calais in France and lost one B17 and five B24s. 8th Air Force P38s, P47s and P51s provided support for the bombers and claimed six victories for the loss of one P47. The USAAFs 354th Fighter Group (P51) scored its 100th victory. The USAAF's 361st Fighter Group (P47 then P51) flew its first 8th Air Force mission. It was also the last P47-equipped group to arrive in the European Theater Operations. USAAF 56th Fighter Group ace Robert S. Johnson (28 victories) shot down a Luftwaffe Fw190 over Rouen, France. General Eisenhower held his first meeting with his staff and commanders at SHAEF. The American 15th Air Force attacked airfields in Southern France. 648 Royal Air Force bombers attacked Magdeburg, Germany and lost fifty-seven aircraft. Most of the bombs fell outside the city. Luftwaffe night-fighter ace Manfred Meurer (65 victories) died when his He219 collided with a Royal Air Force "Lancaster" over Magdeburg. Thirty-four Royal Air Force bombers attacked Berlin and lost one "Lancaster". 111 Royal Air Force bombers attacked V-1 launching sites in France. Five B17s from the USAAF's 422nd Bomb Squadron dropped 1,200,000 leaflets on Reims, Nantes, Le Mans, Tours, and Orleans in France.

1945　The US Army's III Corps took Wiltz in the Ardennes. 753 8th Air Force bombers dropped 2,092 tons of bombs on industrial and rail targets in Germany and lost eight B17s. 469 8th Air Force fighters provided support for the bombers and claimed eight victories. A German V-1 rocket hit Antwerp, Belgium killing seventy-six. Eighty Royal Air Force "Mosquitoes" attacked targets in Germany and lost one aircraft. The German minesweeper M-305 capsized in the Baltic. The German gun ferry AF-30 sank after running aground off Hela in the Baltic. She was later salvaged.

Eastern Europe

1932　Finland and Russia signed a non-aggression pact.

1940　The site for the Auschwitz Concentration Camp was chosen.

1943　Soviet forces took Gumrak. It was the German force's last airfield at Stalingrad. The Soviets took Voroshilovsk.

1944　Field Marshal Georg von Kuchler was replaced as commander of German Army Group "North" by Walter Model. Kuchler died in 1986 and Model committed suicide in 1945. The Soviets took Mga.

1945　The Soviets took Tannenberg in East Prussia.

Mediterranean

1940 Italian liner ORAZIO caught fire and exploded in Marseilles, France.
1941 The Australian 6th Division began its attack on Tobruk, Libya. British forces took Kassala, Sudan.
1942 German Field Marshal Erwin Rommel began his last offensive in North Africa. A Luftwaffe He111 flew 1,500 miles into French Central Africa and attacked Fort Lamy, destroying ten aircraft and 400 tons of aircraft fuel. It was forced down on its return flight by lack of fuel and its crew was rescued seven days later. British forces took El Azizia, Libya.
1944 The Allied Anzio invasion force set sail from Naples. The naval forces consisted of five cruisers, twenty-four destroyers and more than 300 support ships. The American 15th Air Force attacked rail targets in Italy.
1945 The American 15th Air Force sent 189 B17s against Vienna, Austria.

Atlantic

1940 The U22 sank the Royal Navy destroyer EXMOUTH (lost with all hands) and the Norwegian freighter MIRANDA (1,328 tons) off Scotland. The U55 sank the Danish freighter TEKLA (1,496 tons). U55 survived until the 30th. The British freighter PROTESILAUS (9,577 tons) was sunk by a mine that had been laid by the U28. The British freighter FERRYHILL (1,086 tons) was sunk by a mine laid by the U61. The German supply ship ALTMARK began its return trip to Germany with the pocket battleship GRAF SPEE's prisoners.
1941 The German armed merchant cruiser ATLANTIS took the steamer MANDASOR (5,144 tons).
1942 The U754 sank the Norwegian freighters BELIZE (2,153 tons) and WILLIAM HANSEN (1,344 tons). U754 survived until July 31st. The U130 sank the steamer ALEXANDRA HOEGH (8,248 tons). U130 survived until March 12, 1943.
1943 The U301 was sunk by the Royal Navy submarine SAHIB.
1945 The U1199 damaged the American freighter GEORGE HAWLEY ((7,176 tons-two dead) and was then sunk by the Royal Navy destroyer ICARUS and the corvette MIGNONETTE. The U1172 sank the Norwegian freighter GALATEA (1,152 tons). U1172 survived until the 26th.

North America

1941 The American government discontinued its prohibition of exports to the Soviet Union.
1943 The carrier YORKTOWN (CV-10) was launched at Newport News. She was decommissioned in 1973 and was eventually preserved as a memorial at Patriot's Point, South Carolina. The "Philippine Clipper" crashed near

Ukiah, California. Among the nineteen dead was Admiral Robert English, commander of the USN Submarine Force at Pearl Harbor.
1966 The destroyer MCDERMUT arrived at Terminal Island for scrapping.
1989 USN Rear Admiral John Fredrick Davidson died. He had been commander of the submarine BLACKFISH.
2011 Medal of Honor recipient Barney Hajiro died in Hawaii at the age of 94. He had been awarded the Medal in 2000 for actions in France during October 1944.

Pacific
1940 The Royal Navy heavy cruiser LIVERPOOL stopped the Japanese transport ASAMU off Honshu, Japan and removed twenty-one German citizens.
1941 The Japanese government warned America not to interfere with Japanese foreign policy.
1942 5,000 Japanese troops landed at Rabaul, New Britain. Within 24 hours, they had destroyed the Australian Armys 22nd Battalion which was defending the port. Japanese aircraft attacked Allied positions on New Guinea. The 47 crewmen of the USN submarine S-36 were rescued by the Dutch steamer ATTLA. The commander, John McKnight, would later command the submarine PORPOISE.
1943 The USN submarine GATO sank the KENKON MARU (4,575 tons). The USN submarine POLLACK sank the ASAMA MARU (4,891 tons). American forces on Guadalcanal began preparing for a new offensive. The Allies began mopping up around Sanananda, New Guinea. Secretary of the Navy Frank Knox and Admiral Chester Nimitz arrived at Espiritu Santo. The USN SC-709 ran aground off Cape Breton and was lost.
1944 Fighting continued on New Britain. The USN submarine SEAHORSE sank the IKOMA MARU (3,156 tons) and the YASUKUNI MARU (3,021 tons).
1945 The US Army's 40th Division took Tarlac, Luzon. USN Task Force 38 attacked Formosa and the Ryukyus. The USN carrier TICONDEROGA was hit by two kamikazes. The USN carrier HANCOCK and light carrier LANGLEY were also hit.

China-Burma-India
1942 US Army General Joseph Stilwell was nominated as Chiang Kai-shek's Chief of Staff. The Japanese Air Force shot down five Royal Air Force "Hurricanes" over Singapore. British forces began retreating towards Singapore. Japanese forces moved towards Moulmein, Burma. The IJN submarine I-166 sank the British freighter CHAK SANG (2,358 tons) and the Panamanian freighter NORD (3,193 tons).
1944 The Royal Air Force attacked Pinebu, Burma.

1945   British forces landed on Ramree Island. 14th Air Force B24s sank the Japanese salvage vessel HARUTA MARU at Hong Kong.

January 22nd

Western Europe
1887   Hjalmar Schacht, Nazi Finance Minister until November 1937, was born. He died on August 8, 1970.
1936   Pierre Laval's government fell in France.
1940   Pope Pius XII condemned German rule in Poland.
1941   Twelve Royal Air Force "Blenheims" attacked targets in Germany and Holland. One of the aircraft was accidentally shot down by British anti-aircraft fire over Lowestoft. Forty Royal Air Force bombers attacked Dusseldorf, Germany.
1942   Forty-seven Royal Air Force bombers attacked Munster, Germany and lost one "Wellington". Five people were killed in the raid. One Royal Air Force "Hampden" was lost on a minelaying mission. Belgian ace Jean Offenberg (7 victories) was killed when his "Spitfire" was involved in a mid-air collision.
1943   Fifty-three Royal Air Force bombers attacked targets in France and Holland and lost five aircraft. Two Royal Air Force "Mosquitoes" attacked Köln, Germany and killed five people. Twenty-five "Spitfires" from the USAAF's 4th Fighter Group escorted Royal Air Force "Bostons" over France and claimed four Luftwaffe fighters for the loss of one of their own.
1944   Ninety-five Luftwaffe bombers dropped 268 tons of bombs on Britain and lost sixteen aircraft. The German minesweeper R-75 was lost in a collision with the U350 in the Baltic.
1945   American forces reached the outskirts of St. Vith, Belgium. Royal Air Force "Spitfires" destroyed V-2 rocket fuel factories near Dordrecht, Holland. 9th Air Force B26 "Marauders" bombed the Dasburg Bridge, stranding nearly 3,000 German vehicles, which were then destroyed by Allied fighter bombers. 167 8th Air Force B17s dropped 473 tons of bombs on the synthetic oil plant at Sterkrade and lost five aircraft. 223 8th Air Force fighters provided support for the bombers and claimed three victories for the loss of one P51. The US Army's 84th Division took Gouvy and Beho in Belgium. 302 Royal Air Force bombers attacked Duisburg in Germany and lost two "Lancasters". 152 people were killed in the raid. 152 Royal Air Force bombers attacked Gelsenkirchen, Germany.
1978   British General Oliver Leese died in Wales.

Eastern Europe

1942 A Soviet cruiser and two destroyers were damaged during a storm in the Black Sea.

1943 The final phase of the Soviet assault on Stalingrad began. Soviet forces took the city of Salsk in the Caucasus and began an assault on a German salient at Voronezh to the north of Stalingrad.

1945 Soviets forces took Insterberg and Allenstein in East Prussia, Gniezno in Poland, and Kronstadt in Upper Silesia.

Mediterranean

1941 The British Mid-East Commander-in-Chief, General Archibald Wavell, was ordered to make arrangements to support the Greeks from North Africa. British forces took Tobruk, Libya along with 30,000 prisoners, 200 guns and 70 tanks. The Italians had blown up the coastal defense ship SAN GIORGIO as well as the port installations. British forces took Jalib in Italian East Africa.

1942 The DAK took Agedabia, Cyrenica.

1943 The Germans evacuated Tripoli. The American 12th Air Force attacked El Aouina Airfield. USAAF Captain Richard E. Miller died of wounds in North Africa. He had been a bombardier on the "Doolittle Raid".

1944 "Operation Shingle" (the invasion of Anzio) involving 36,000 men of the US Army's 3rd and 45th Infantry Divisions and 1st Armored Division and the British Army's 1st Division began. The commander of the 3rd Division, Major General Lucian Truscott, would later assume overall command of the Allied forces when the present commander, Major General John P. Lucas, was relieved for failure to achieve the operations objectives. At 0400, the Commander of the German Forces in Southern Italy, Field Marshal Albert Kesselring, was informed of the invasion. At 0500, he ordered his 4th Parachute Division and units of the Hermann Goering Division to reinforce the weak defenses around Anzio. By the end of the day, the Allies had suffered only thirteen dead and ninety-seven wounded, but there were elements of five German divisions headed towards the beach-head. The USN minesweeper PORTENT was sunk off Anzio by a mine. Staff Sergeant Thomas McCall, of the 36th Division, won a Medal of Honor near San Angelo, Italy. Allied aircraft dropped two million leaflets on Rome.

Atlantic

1940 The U51 sank the Swedish freighter GOTHIA (1,640 tons). U51 survived until August 20th. The U25 sank the Norwegian freighter SONGA (2,589 tons). U25 survived until August 3rd. The U61 sank the Norwegian freighter SYDVOLD (2,434 tons). U61 survived the war.

1942   The U66 sank the American freighter NORVANA (2,677 tons) with all hands. U66 survived until May 6, 1944. The U333 sank the Greek freighter VISSILIOS A. POLEMIS (3,429 tons). U333 survived until July 31, 1944. The U82 sank the British tanker ATHELCROWN (11,999 tons). U82 survived until February 6th. The U135 sank the Belgian freighter GANDIA (9,626 tons). U135 survived until July 15, 1943. The U130 sank the Panamanian tanker OLYMPIC (5,335 tons). U130 survived until March 12, 1943. The U203 sank the Royal Navy trawler ROSEMONDE (364 tons). U203 survived until April 25, 1943.

1943   The U358 sank the Swedish freighter NEVA (1,456 tons). U358 survived until March 1, 1944. The U413 sank the Greek freighter MOUNT MYCALE (3,556 tons). U413 survived until August 20, 1944.

1944   The USN LCT-582 was lost when she ran aground in the Azores.

1945   The American freighter GEORGE HAWLEY was a constructive loss after an attack by the U1199. U1199 survived until the 21st.

North America

1920   The destroyer BULMER was launched. She was scrapped in 1947.

1941   The heavy cruiser LOUISVILLE arrived in New York with a cargo of $148,342,212.55 in British gold aboard. It had been loaded in Simonstown, South Africa.

1942   Lieutenant Colonel James Doolittle requested that twenty-four B25Bs be sent to Mid-Continental Airlines in Minneapolis, Minnesota for modifications that would be required for the attack on the Japanese Home Islands which he was in the process of planning.

1944   The advance party for American 3rd Army left New York for the ETO aboard the RMS QUEEN MARY.

1960   The light cruiser MONTPELIER was sold for scrap.

Pacific

1942   The USN destroyer STEWART tipped over in a civilian drydock at Surabaya, Java. She was further damaged by a near-miss bomb. The Japanese later salvaged her and recommissioned her into their navy. She survived the war and was recovered by the USN. The Japanese Naval Air Force attacked Batavia and Semplak Airfields on Java, destroying six aircraft. The Allies began retreating on Bataan. Japanese forces took Mussau Island, north of New Ireland and began landing on New Ireland and New Britain. The Allies evacuated Lae and Salamaua on New Guinea as well as Rabaul, New Britain. The Dutch began destroying their oil fields on Celebes. The USN's Task Force 11 (commanded by Brown), including the carrier LEXINGTON, left Pearl Harbor en route to attacking Japanese-held Wake Island. The USN destroyers GRIDLEY and FANNING were damaged in a collision off American Samoa.

1943 The US Army's XIV Corps began an offensive on Guadalcanal. Secretary of the Navy Frank Knox and Admiral Chester Nimitz arrived at Guadalcanal for an inspection tour. USAAF B17s attacked Rekata Bay. The American freighter PETER H. BURNETT (7,176 tons-one dead) was damaged by the IJN submarine I-21. The USN submarine TAUTOG sank the YASHIMA MARU (1,873 tons). 5th Air Force B17s attacked Rabaul, New Britain and sank the freighter TETSUZAN MARU.

1944 The Marshall Islands invasion force set sail. Reinforcements raised the total of defending Japanese aircraft at Rabaul to ninety-two. The USN submarine TINOSA sank the SEINAN MARU (5,401 tons) and the KOSHIN MARU (5,485 tons). The IJN submarine Ro-37 was sunk by the USN destroyer BUCHANAN.

1945 The US Army's XIV Corps (commanded by Griswold) took Bamban, Luzon. The USN battleship IOWA joined the 5th Fleet at Ulithi.

China-Burma-India

1942 Lieutenant Colonel C. Anderson, of the 2/9th Australian Infantry, won a Victoria Cross in Malaya. The IJN submarine I-164 sank the Dutch freighter VAN OVERSTRATEN (4,482 tons).

1945 The Burma Road was reopened. The 20th Indian Division took Myinmu, Burma.

January 23rd

Western Europe

1936 The Royal Navy light cruiser NEWCASTLE was launched. She was scrapped in 1959.

1943 Four Royal Air Force "Mosquitoes" attacked Osnabruck, Germany and lost one aircraft. Fifty-four B17s from the USAAF's 306th, 91st, 303rd and 305th Bomb Groups attacked the ports of Lorient and Brest in France and lost five bombers, all from the 303rd. 121 more Royal Air Force bombers attacked Lorient again later in the day and lost one "Stirling". Eighty-three Royal Air Force bombers attacked Dusseldorf, Germany and lost two "Lancasters".

1944 Supreme Allied Commander US Army General Dwight Eisenhower approved British General Bernard Montgomery's plan for the invasion of Normandy. American 9th Air Force B26s attacked V-1 sites near Calais, France. Thirty-seven Royal Air Force "Mosquitoes" attacked various targets on the Continent. Five B17s from the USAAF's 422nd Bomb

Squadron dropped 1,200,000 leaflets on Rouen, Amiens, Lille, Cambrai, and Valenciennes in France.

1945   The US Army's 7th Armored Division took St. Vith, Belgium. Master Sergeant Nicholas Oresko, of the 94th Division, won a Medal of Honor near Tettington. The light cruiser EMDEN removed the bodies of former German President Paul von Hindenburg and his wife from their burial site at Tannenberg, East Prussia. They were re-interred in the Elisabeth Church in Marburg. 181 8th Air Force B17s dropped 312 tons of bombs on the railyard at Neuss, Germany and lost one bomber.

1972   The French government donated the former USAAF 91st Bomb Group B17 "Shoo Shoo Shoo Baby" to the USAF Museum at Wright-Patterson, Ohio.

Eastern Europe

1942   Soviet forces broke through the German lines near Smolensk.

1943   The Soviets took Amavir. The last Luftwaffe aircraft to leave Stalingrad was a He111 loaded with wounded. The daily ration a German soldier in Stalingrad was 1.75 ounces of bread and 1.75 pints of soup.

1945   The Soviets took Wehlau and Kalise in East Prussia and Brodnica and Lipno in Poland.

Mediterranean

1941   The Royal Navy carrier ILLUSTRIOUS left Malta for Alexandria, Egypt.

1943   The British 8th Army entered Tripoli. The U431 sank the Egyptian sailing ship ALEXANDRIA (100 tons). The Italian liner VICTORIA was sunk by Royal Air Force "Beauforts". The "Casablanca Conference" ended. The American 12th Air Force attacked Bizerte and Ben Gardane in Tunisia. Colonel David Sterling, commander of the British Special Air Service, was captured in Tunisia by the Germans. He was replaced by Lieutenant Colonel Robert "Paddy" Mayne.

1944   The American 15th Air Force attacked airfields at Rieti and Aviano in Italy. The Allies had 50,000 men ashore at Anzio. At 1815, the Royal Navy destroyer JANUS (launched in 1939) and the hospital ship ST. DAVID were sunk and the destroyer JERVIS was damaged off Anzio by the Luftwaffe. USAAF A36 "Apache" fighter-bombers attacked the German headquarters near Franscati, fifteen miles south of Rome. Private G. Mitchell, of the London Scottish, won a posthumous Victoria Cross in Italy. The American 15th Air Force attacked rail targets in Italy.

Atlantic

1940   The U18 sank the Norwegian freighter VARILD (1,085 tons). U18 was scuttled on September 10, 1944. The U19 sank the British freighter

BALTANGLIA (1,523 tons) and the Norwegian freighter PLUTO (1,598 tons). U19 was scuttled on September 10, 1944. The U56 sank the Finnish freighter ONTO (1,333 tons). U56 survived until April 28, 1945. The Allies announced that they would not honor a Pan-American neutral zone and would attack any German ships found in such an area.

1941   The German battlecruisers SCHARNHORST and GNEISENAU left the Kattegat for the Atlantic.

1942   The Italian submarine BARBARIGO sank the Spanish freighter NAVEMAR (5,473 tons). BARBARIGO was lost on June 19, 1943. The U109 sank the British freighter THIRLBY (4,887 tons). U109 survived until May 4, 1943. The U82 sank the Norwegian tanker LEIESTEN (6,118 tons). U82 survived until February 6th.

1943   The U175 sank the American freighter BENJAMIN SMITH (7,176 tons). U175 survived until April 17, 1943.

1945   The U1172 sank the Norwegian freighter VIGSNES (1,599 tons).

North America

1928   The new carriers LEXINGTON and SARATOGA participated in USN fleet exercises for the first time.

1929   The heavy cruiser SALT LAKE CITY (awarded eleven battle stars during the war) was launched in New York. She was scuttled in 1948 after having served as a Bikini target ship.

1935   The destroyer DALE was launched in New York. She was scrapped in 1946.

1941   Charles Lindbergh stated in testimony before the House Foreign Affairs Committee of Congress that negotiations for peace with Germany should begin.

1942   US Army Task Force 6814 left New York for New Caledonia. It had been formed with National Guard troops from Massachusetts, Illinois and North Dakota for the purpose of defending New Caledonia. It would later become basis for the Americal Division.

1943   The USN YP-577 exploded at Great Lakes, Illinois.

1947   USMC General Roy Geiger, commander of the "Cactus Air Force" on Guadalcanal and the American Ground Forces on Okinawa, died in Bethesda, Maryland two days before his 62nd birthday.

1948   The destroyer THATCHER was sold for scrap.

1961   The destroyer HALE was sold to Colombia.

1971   The destroyer FRANK KNOX was sold to Greece.

2010   Lieutenant Colonel Kermit Tyler, age 86, died of pneumonia at his home in San Diego, California. He had been the officer in charge of the aircraft tracking center at Wheeler Field on Oahu on December 7, 1941. He was notified that a large radar "blip" had been detected to the northwest. He told the two privates working the radar station to "forget it", it was probably a flight of B17s due in from California. It was not.

2013 USN ace Stanley "Swede" Vejtasa died in Escondido, California at the age of 98. He had been credited with 10.5 aerial victories. The fascinating part of his score is that 3 of his victims were Japanese Zeros which he shot down while flying an SBD "Dauntless" dive-bomber, an aircraft not renowned for its abilities as a fighter. He later transferred to fighters were he claimed the remainder of his tally. He finished the war with 3 Navy Crosses and the Legion of Merit.

Pacific

1942 More Japanese troops landed on New Britain, New Ireland, Borneo and Bougainville. Australian resistance at Rabaul, New Britain ended. Japanese forces landed at Balikpapan. Dutch bombers sank the Japanese NANA MARU and JUKKA MARU off Borneo. The USN destroyer EDSALL was damaged by the explosion of one of her own depth charges off Darwin. The USN submarine SEADRAGON damaged the Japanese freighter FUKUYO MARU off Indochina. The American tanker NECHES (fifty-seven dead-7,383 tons) was sunk south-southeast of Niihau in Hawaii by the IJN submarine I-72. The loss forced the cancellation of a raid on Wake Island by Task Force 11 (commanded by Brown).

1943 The American offensive on Guadalcanal continued. USMC Captain Joseph Foss, of VMF 121, won a Medal of Honor for actions over Guadalcanal. The USN light cruisers ST. LOUIS and HONOLULU and four destroyers bombarded the Villa-Stanmore Plantation on the island of Kolombangara. Japanese aircraft attacked Milne Bay, New Guinea and damaged the freighter STEPHEN JOHNSON. The American 11th Air Force attacked Kiska in the Aleutians. Two 11th Air Force B25s crashlanded on Attu Island in the Aleutians. The IJN destroyer HAKAZE was sunk west of Kavieng, New Ireland by the USN submarine GUARDFISH.

1944 The Royal Australian Air Force attacked Kesawai, New Guinea. Australian forces took Maukiryo, New Guinea. The USN submarine GAR sank the TAIAN MARU (3,670 tons). The USN submarine SNOOK sank the MAGANE MARU (3,120 tons). The IJN submarine Ro-37 damaged the American tanker CACHE (12,000 tons).

1945 The IJN submarine I-48 was sunk by the USN destroyers RABY, CONKLIN and CORBESIER. Twenty-eight B29s attacked Nagoya and lost two aircraft. The USN submarine BARB sank the TAIKYO MARU (5,244 tons). The USN submarine SENNET sank the KAINAN MARU (84 tons). The HOZAN MARU No.1 (868 tons) and the NIKKAKU MARU (1,946 tons) were sunk by mines. The USN submarine GUARDFISH sank the USN salvage ship EXTRACTOR killing four of her crew. Serving aboard the GUARDFISH was American author Clay Blair Jr. The American 13th Air Force attacked Corregidor Island in Manila Bay. An 11th Air Force B24 was shot down over Shimushu.

China-Burma-India

1942 American prisoners of war captured on Wake Island arrived in Shanghai. General Joseph Stilwell was appointed as commander of the US Army Forces in the CBI and as Chiang Kai-shek's Chief of Staff. The American Volunteer Group and the Royal Air Force shot down fifteen Japanese aircraft over Rangoon, Burma and lost two of their own. The British evacuated the Merjui Airfield in Burma.

1944 14th Air Force B25s sank the Japanese freighter PANAMA MARU off Foochow, China. The American 10th Air Force attacked Merjui Harbor on the Malay Peninsula.

1945 Three RAF B24s were accidentally shot down by American 14th Air Force fighters over Burma.

January 24th

Western Europe

1888 German aircraft designer Ernest Heinkel was born. He died on January 30, 1958.

1889 German General Hermann Ramcke was born. He died on July 5, 1968 at the age of 79.

1891 German Field Marshal Walther Model was born in Genthin, near Magdeburg. He would command Army Groups "North", "North Ukraine" and "Center" on the Eastern Front and Army Group "B" on the Western Front. He committed suicide on April 21, 1945 rather than be captured.

1898 Karl Frank was born. He would become a leader in Czechoslovakia's Sudeten Nazi Party. He was hung on May 22, 1946 for war crimes.

1917 The Royal Navy light cruiser CALYPSO was launched. She was sunk on June 12, 1940.

1936 The Ju87V1 ("Stuka" dive-bomber proto-type) crashed, killing both crewmen.

1940 Britain renewed its pledge to help Belgium if it was attacked by Germany.

1944 Fifty-eight 8th Air Force B17s dropped 143 tons of bombs on Eschweiler, Germany and lost two B17s. 678 8th Air Force P38s, P47s and P51s provided

support for the bombers and claimed nineteen victories for the loss of four P38s, three P47s and two P51s.
1965   British Prime Minister Winston Churchill died at age 91.

Eastern Europe
1937   A Yugoslavian-Bulgarian treaty was signed.
1942   Soviet forces took Barvenkovo.
1943   Friedrich Paulus, the commander of the German 6th Army in Stalingrad, requested the authority to breakout of Stalingrad. It was refused by Hitler.
1944   The American 15th Air Force attacked rail targets in Bulgaria. The Soviets took Pushkin and Pashovsk.
1945   The U763 was sunk at Konigsberg by Soviet aircraft. Heinrich Himmler was appointed as the commander of German Army Group "Vistula". The Soviets took Gleiwitz and Oppeln in Poland. Soviet forces resumed their offensive in Latvia.
1955   German Field Marshal Ferdinand Schorner was released by the Soviets.

Mediterranean
1941   The Italians lost nine tanks in a battle with British 4th Armored Brigade at Mechili, Libya. The British lost seven tanks in the action. Australian forces attacked Italian positions at Derna, Libya.
1944   The Luftwaffe attacked Allied shipping off Anzio.

Atlantic
1940   The U44 sank the French freighter ALSACIEN (3,819 tons). U44 survived until March 20th. The U23 sank the Norwegian freighter BISP (1,000 tons). U23 was scuttled on September 19, 1944.
1941   The U123 sank the Norwegian freighter VESPASIAN (1,570 tons). U123 survived the war.
1942   The U66 sank the British tanker EMPIRE GEM (8,139 tons) and the American collier VENORE (8,017 tons-seventeen dead). U66 survived until May 6, 1944. The U106 sank the British freighter EMPIRE WILDEBEESTE (5,631 tons). U106 survived until August 2, 1943. The U333 sank the Norwegian freighter RINGSTAD (4,765 tons). U333 survived until July 31, 1944.
1943   The U105 sank the British tanker BRITISH VIGILANCE (8,093 tons). U105 survived until June 2nd. The USN sub chaser PC-576 rescued three survivors from the Dutch steamer ZAANDAM which had been sunk on November 2, 1942 by U174. They had spent 83 days on a small life raft.
1944   The American freighter SAMUEL DEXTER (a "Liberty") was abandoned after developing hull cracks and later drifted ashore in the Hebrides.

North America

1899 USAAF Major General Hoyt Vandenberg was born in Milwaukee, Wisconsin. He graduated 239th in his 1923 West Point class of 262. After several staff assignments, he replaced Brereton as commander of the Ninth Air Force. Post-war positions included Chief of Army Intelligence and Director of the Central Intelligence Agency. In May 1947 he returned to active duty with the Air Force and was promoted to four-star rank at the age of forty-nine. This made him the youngest full general since Grant in 1864. In 1948 he was named as Chief of Staff of the USAF. On June 30, 1953 he retired for physical reasons and died on April 2, 1954 of cancer.

1941 The heavy cruiser LOUISVILLE arrived in New York with $148,342,212.55 in South African gold aboard. This was intended as payment for supplies to be sent to Britain.

1942 A court of inquiry headed by Justice Owen J. Roberts submitted its report on the Pearl Harbor attack. It placed most of the blame on the military commanders Admiral Husband Kimmel and General Walter Short.

1943 The submarines PARGO and RATON were launched. PARGO was scrapped in 1961. RATON was expended in 1969.

1944 The carrier HANCOCK (CV-19) was launched at Quincy. She was stricken in 1976.

1946 General Carl Spaatz was named as USAAF Chief of Staff.

1955 Ira Hayes died of exposure on the Sacaton Indian Reservation in Arizona. He had been one of three surviving members of the group that had raised the US flag on Mount Suribachi on Iwo Jima. The scene had been preserved and made famous by photographer Joe Rosenthal.

1967 354th Fighter Group (P51) ace Kenneth Dahlberg (14 victories) was awarded a Distinguished Service Cross for actions over Trier, Germany on December 19, 1944.

1990 A P51D "Mustang" crashed off Galveston, Texas.

2014 USN ace John T. Crosby died in Palo Alto, California. He had been credited with 5 aerial victories while flying from the carrier Hornet in 1945.

Pacific

1884 Australian General Thomas Blamey, Commander-in-Chief of the Australian Army, was born in Wagga Wagga, Australia. He died in 1951.

1942 Japanese aircraft attacked the Moluccas and sank the Dutch destroyer BANCKERT at Surabaya, Java. Japanese forces took Kendari, Celebes. Japanese aircraft began operating from the Menado airfield in Northern Celebes. The Japanese also landed at Rabaul, New Britain. The USN submarine S-26 was lost in a collision with the USN PC-460 off Panama, there were three survivors. The USN submarine SWORDFISH sank the IJN patrol gunboat MYOKEN MARU (4,124 tons). Japanese forces took Balikpapan, Borneo. The IJN patrol boat No.37 was sunk off Balikpapan by the USN destroyers POPE and PARROT and the Dutch submarine K-XVIII. The Dutch submarine K-XVIII sank the TSURUGA MARU (6,987 tons).

1943   Japanese resistance ended on Mount Austin on Guadalcanal. USAAF B26 "Marauders" attacked Munda, New Georgia. USN forces (Ainsworth and Ramsey) bombarded Vila-Stanmore, Kolombangara. The USN submarine WAHOO damaged the IJN destroyer HARUSAME.

1944   USMC 1st Lieutenant Robert Hanson, of VMF215, won a posthumous Medal of Honor over Bougainville. Eighteen USMC TBFs attacked Rabaul, New Britain sinking the KOAN MARU, OGASHIMA MARU, the tanker NARUTO, TAISHO MARU and YAMAYURI MARU. USMC VMF-422 lost twenty-two F4Us and six pilots on a flight from Tarawa to Nanomea, New Caledonia during which they became lost. USAAF B25s attacked Japanese shipping off Manus and sank the transport HEIWA MARU and the IJN minelayer TATSU MARU. Japanese aircraft attacked Dreger Bay, New Guinea and damaged the American freighter JOHN MUIR. The USN submarine STURGEON sank the CHOSEN MARU (3,110 tons). The USN destroyer-minesweeper ZANE rescued survivors from the freighter PETER H. Burnett which had been sunk on January 22nd by the I-21.

1945   Japanese forces put up heavy resistance on a series of hills on Luzon. Tech/4 Laverne Parrish, of the 25th Division, won a posthumous Medal of Honor at Binalonan, Luzon. A VMF-22 F4U crashed on take-off at Guiuan Airfield on Samar, killing fourteen. The IJN destroyer SHIGURE was sunk by the USN submarine BLACKFIN. The USN submarine ATULE sank the TAIMAN MARU No.1 (6,888 tons). The American 5th Air Force attacked Corregidor. The American 13th Air Force attacked Cavite Naval Base in the Philippines. A USN task force (commanded by Badger) bombarded Iwo Jima.

1972   Sergeant Schoichi Yokoi, of the Imperial Japanese Army, surrendered near Talofofo, Guam, where he had been hiding since WWII.

China-Burma-India

1932   The IJN sent one carrier, four heavy cruisers and seven destroyers to Shanghai.

1945   Royal Navy carriers attacked oil refineries on Sumatra. The USAAF base at Suichuan, China was abandoned by the 14th Air Force. Negotiations between Nationalist and Communist forces in China were resumed after they were broken off on December 6, 1944.

January 25th

Western Europe

1939   The Spanish Nationalist Forces reached the suburbs of Barcelona. German Foreign Minister Ribbentrop attempted to persuade Poland to join the Anti-Comintern.

1942   At 2113, the German destroyer HEINEMANN was sunk off Ostend, Belgium by a mine, ninety-four died. Sixty-one Royal Air Force bombers attacked Brest, France.

1943   Twelve Royal Air Force "Bostons" attacked Flushing, Belgium and lost one aircraft. Seventeen "Spitfires" from the USAAF's 4th Fighter Group escorted them.

1944   218 8th Air Force P47s attacked the Leeuwarden airfield in Holland. Seventy-six Royal Air Force bombers attacked V-1 launching sites in France. Five B17s from the USAAF's 422nd Bomb Squadron dropped 1,200,000 leaflets on Caen, Reims, Chartres, Chateauroux, and Brest in France.

1945   Private First Class Jose Valdez, of the 3rd Division, won a posthumous Medal of Honor near Rosenkratz, France. Nikolaus Gross, a Trade Union Secretary, was executed for his part in the July 20th conspiracy.

1946   British Field Marshal Alan Brooke resigned as Chief of the Imperial General Staff.

1955   French Admiral Paul Auphan was released from prison. He had been sentenced to life in prison for collaboration. During the war he had served as Vichy's Secretary of the Navy.

1972   Luftwaffe Field Marshal Erhard Milch died in Wuppertal-Barmen. He had served as Armaments Chief of the Luftwaffe.

Eastern Europe

1943   Soviet forces split the German 6th Army in Stalingrad, leaving the Germans in control of thirty-six square miles of the city. The Soviets took Voronezh and 52,000 prisoners.

1944   The Soviets took Gatchina, southwest of Leningrad.

1945   The Soviets took Ostrow, Poland.

Mediterranean

1942   The British Army's 1st Armored Division was routed by the DAK in Libya. South Africa declared war on Thailand.

1943   Italian General Giovanni Messe was appointed to relieve Rommel as commander of Axis forces in North Africa. The U431 sank the Syrian sailing ships MOUYASSAR (47 tons), OMAR EL KATTAB (38 tons) and HASSAN (80 tons).

1944   The US Army's 36th Division crossed the Rapido River. The American 15th Air Force attacked rail targets in Italy. The USN YMS-30 was sunk off Anzio by a mine.

Atlantic
1940   The U14 sank the Norwegian freighter BIARRITZ (1,752 tons). U14 survived the war. The U44 sank the French freighter TOURNY (2,796 tons). U44 survived until March 20th. The U19 (commanded by Schepke) sank the Belgian freighter LOUVAIN (4,434 tons) and the Norwegian freighter GUDVEIG (1,300 tons). U19 was scuttled on September 10, 1944.
1942   The U754 sank the Greek freighter MOUNT KITHERON (3,876 tons). U754 survived until July 31st. The U130 sank the Norwegian tanker VARANGER (9,305 tons). U130 survived until March 12, 1943. The U123 sank the British freighter CULEBRA (3,044 tons). U123 survived the war. The American steamer TENNESSEE rescued twenty-one survivors from the American collier VENORE which had been sunk on January 25th by U66. The American tanker AUSTRALIA rescued the only other survivor the same day. The other seventeen men aboard the VENORE were lost.
1943   The U624 sank the British freighter LACKENBY (5,112 tons). U624 survived until February 7th. The U575 sank the American freighter CITY OF FLINT (4,963 tons-7 dead). U575 survived until March 14, 1944.
1944   The American freighter ANDREW CURTIN (7,176 tons-three dead) was sunk by the U716. U176 survived the war. The American freighter PENELOPE BARKER (7,177 tons-sixteen dead) was sunk by the U278. U278 survived the war.

North America
1885   USMC General Roy Stanley Geiger was born in Middleburg, Florida. He would command the "Cactus Air Force" on Guadalcanal in 1942 and would command the American ground forces on Okinawa in 1945.
1887   Canadian General Robert McNaughton was born in Moosomin, Saskatchewan. In December 1939 Major General McNaughton led the first contingent of Canadian troops to Britain. He retired in December 1943 and returned to Canada where he became Minister of National Defense on November 2, 1944. He died in 1966.
1894   Admiral Robert "Fuzzy" Theobald was born in San Francisco. He graduated 9th in his 1907 Annapolis class of 209. After Pearl Harbor he commanded the North Pacific Fleet. He held that position until he was replaced by Kinkaid on January 4, 1943. He retired on February 1, 1945 and died in Boston on May 13, 1957.
1917   The battleship MISSISSIPPI was launched at Newport News. She was scrapped in 1956.

1940   The Canadian Parliament was dissolved due to charges of unpreparedness for war.
1941   The battleship WISCONSIN's keel was laid at the Philadelphia Navy Yard. The submarine GUDGEON was launched at Mare Island. She was lost in April 1944.
1943   The American 6th Army was activated at Fort Sam Houston, Texas. It would serve in the Pacific under the command of Lieutenant General Walter Krueger.
1944   The destroyer TAUSSIG was launched. She was sold to Taiwan on May 6, 1974. Actor Rod Steiger served aboard her during the invasions of Iwo Jima and Okinawa. The anti/aircraft light cruiser FLINT (awarded four battle stars during the war) was launched in San Francisco. She was stricken in 1965.
1949   The trial of Mildred Gillars, alias "Axis Sally", began in Washington D.C.
1966   The light cruiser SAVANNAH was sold for scrap.
2014   USN ace John Stokes died in Alexandria, Virginia at the age of 94. He had been credited with 6.5 aerial victories while flying F6Fs over the Pacific.

South America
1942   Uruguay broke relations with the Axis.

Pacific
1942   The USN destroyers FORD, POPE, PARROTT, and JONES sank three Japanese freighters and a patrol boat off Balikpapan, Borneo. Japanese forces landed at Lae, New Guinea. The Australian Government ordered full mobilization. New Zealand declared war on Thailand. The IJN submarine I-73 shelled American defensive positions on Midway. She would survive until the 27th when she was sunk by the American submarine GUDGEON. The IJN destroyer HATSUHARA was damaged by aircraft off Celebes. The USN carriers ENTERPRISE and YORKTOWN met off Samoa en route to a raid on the Mandates. Japanese finally unhinge the Allied line on Bataan.
1943   American forces reached the Poha River on Guadalcanal. US Army General Horace Fuller assumed command of Allied forces around Gona and Oro Bay on New Guinea. USAAF B26s "Marauders" attacked Kolombangara. The USN submarine SHAD damaged the German blockade runner freighter NORDFELS (1,214 tons). The American 11th Air Force attacked Kiska in the Aleutians.
1945   The USN submarine SILVERSIDES sank the MALAY MARU (4,556 tons). Iwo Jima was shelled by the USN battleship INDIANA and bombed by USAAF B24s and B29s. The American 13th Air Force attacked Cavite near Manila.

1946   A battle between 120 Japanese troops and Allied forces was fought 150 miles south of Manila. Seventy-two Japanese were killed.

China-Burma-India

1893   General Geoffrey Scoones, commander of the British Army's IV Corps in Burma, was born in Quetta, India. He died in 1975.
1942   Thailand declared war on America and Britain. The Japanese Air Force attacked Rangoon, Burma. The British defenses along the Johore Line in Malaya began to give way.
1944   The U188 sank the British freighter FORT LA MAUNE (7,130 tons).
1945   The 81st East African Division took Mychaung, Burma. The Japanese High Command directed its forces in China to concentrate on defending the coast, rather than on offensive operations in the interior. America aircraft mined Singapore, Saigon, Penang and Camranh Bay.

January 26th

Western Europe

1918   The Royal Navy light cruiser DANAE was launched. She was scrapped in 1948.
1934   A 10-year German-Polish non-aggression pact was signed.
1938   German General Werner von Fritsch, Army Chief of Staff, was relieved due to false charges of homosexuality.
1939   Spanish Nationalists took Barcelona.
1941   Seventeen Royal Air Force bombers attacked Hannover, Germany.
1942   The first American troops (the 34th Infantry Division) landed in Northern Ireland. Seventy-one Royal Air Force bombers attacked Hannover, Germany. Thirty-one RAF bombers attacked Emden, Germany and lost two "Whitleys". Twenty-five Royal Air Force bombers attacked the port of Brest, France. A Royal Air Force "Whitley" was lost while on a leaflet raid over Germany.
1943   157 Royal Air Force bombers attacked the port of Lorient, France and lost three aircraft. Twenty-two "Spitfires" from the USAAF's 4th Fighter Group escorted twelve Royal Air Force "Venturas" over France.
1944   US Army General George Patton arrived at Cheddington Air Base in Britain from the Mediterranean Theater of Operations. The USAAF's 4th Fighter Group, formerly the Royal Air Force's "Eagle Squadrons", received its first US-trained pilots.
1945   Thirteen German V-2 rockets hit London. Second Lieutenant Audie Murphy, of the 3rd Division, won a Medal of Honor near Holtzwihr, France. Eight Royal Air Force "Mosquitoes" attacked the synthetic oil plant at Castrop-Rauxel.

1993   Baron Axel von dem Bussche, age 73, died in Bonn. He had been involved in a plot to assassinate Hitler. He was to have blown himself up with hand grenades hidden in the pockets of an overcoat he was modeling.

Eastern Europe
1881   US Army General Walter Krueger, commander of the American 6th Army, was born in Flatow, East Prussia (now Zlotow, Poland).
1943   The U255 sank the Soviet freighter UFA (1,892 tons).
1944   The U957 sank the British freighter FORT BELLINGHAM (7,153 tons).
1945   German forces halted their "Operation Konrad III" after losing nearly 300 tanks. It was to be their last major offensive. Soviet forces reached the Baltic coast north of Elbing, surrounding the German forces in East Prussia. The Soviets took Bromberg and Marienburg in East Prussia. Soviet forces were within 120 miles of Berlin. The Soviets liberated the Auschwitz Concentration Camp.

Mediterranean
1941   British forces began an offensive in Somalia. The Italians attempted to retake Klisura, Albania.
1942   Axis aircraft attacked Malta.
1943   The Italian High Command threatened to relieve Rommel in North Africa.
1944   The Algerian 3rd Division took Monte Abate in Italy. The Luftwaffe attacked Allied shipping off Anzio.

Atlantic
1940   The British freighter DURHAM CASTLE (8,240 tons) was sunk by a mine laid by the U57.
1941   The U105 sank the Dutch freighter HEEMSKERCK (6,516 tons). U105 survived until June 2, 1943.
1942   The U106 sank the British freighter TRAVELER (3,963 tons). U106 survived until August 2, 1943. The U125 sank the American freighter WEST IVIS (5,666 tons) with all hands. U125 survived until May 6, 1943. The U754 sank the Greek freighter ICARION (4,013 tons). U754 survived until July 31st. The U582 sank the British freighter REFAST (5,189 tons). U582 survived until October 5th. The U123 sank the Norwegian tanker PAN NORWAY (9,231 tons). U123 survived the war.
1943   The U358 sank the Norwegian tanker NORTIND (8,221 tons). U358 survived until March 1, 1944. The U607 and U594 sank the Norwegian tanker KOLLBJORG (8,259 tons), which had been damaged in a storm. U607 survived until July 13th and U594 until June 4th. The American

freighter LEWIS CASS was wrecked on Guadalupe Island off Mexico. Eleven of the crew were rescued by the US Coast Guard cutter HERMES.

1945 The U1172 was sunk in the Irish Sea by the Royal Navy frigates AYLMER, CALDER, BENTINCK, and MANNERS. The MANNERS was a constructive loss after being torpedoed by U1172 during the battle, thirty-six of her crew died.

North America

1880 General Douglas MacArthur was born near Little Rock, Arkansas. He was a sixth cousin of FDR and an eighth cousin of Winston Churchill.

1887 Admiral Marc Mitscher was born in Hillsboro, Virginia. After failing to qualify for West Point, he graduated 106th in his 1910 Annapolis class of 130. In 1916, he became Naval Aviator No.33. He took command of the carrier HORNET in October 1941. He was promoted to rear admiral on June 15, 1942 and given command of Task Force 17. He commanded the fleet air wing at Noumea, New Caledonia from December 1942 until April 1943 when he became naval air commander in the Solomons. In August 1943 he returned to the US to command the naval air on the West Coast and to regain his health. Five months later he returned to action as commander of the 3rd Carrier Division in Spruance's 5th Fleet. He was later promoted and named as commander of Task Force 58. On March 1, 1946 he declined appointment as Chief of Naval Operations so that he could take a seagoing assignment. He assumed command of the 8th Fleet in the Atlantic as a full admiral. In September, he became commander of the Atlantic Fleet. He died on February 3, 1947 while at that post.

1940 The US-Japanese Trade Treaty of 1911 expired. Japan was informed that trade would take place on a day-to-day basis.

1942 A B26 "Marauder" crashed in Canada while en route to Alaska. It was recovered in 1971 and actually flew again at Chino, California.

1944 The escort carrier MARCUS ISLAND was commissioned. She was scrapped in 1960.

Pacific

1941 Japan announced its intention of establishing a "new order" in Asia.

1942 Japanese forces landed in the Northern Solomons. The Allies completed their final withdrawal into the southern tip of the Bataan Peninsula. The Japanese took Rabaul, New Britain.

1943 USAAF B17s attacked Ballale Island Airfield. The USN submarine GRAYLING sank the USHIO MARU (749 tons) off Mindoro in the Philippines.

1944 The USN submarine SKIPJACK sank the IJN aircraft tender OKITSU MARU (6,666 tons) and the destroyer SUZUKAZE northwest of Ponape.

The USN submarine HAKE sank the SHUKO MARU (889 tons). The USN submarine CREVALLE sank the BUSHO MARU (2,569 tons). The Royal Navy submarine TEMPLAR damaged the IJN light cruiser KITAKAMI. USN PT110 was lost in a collision in Ablingi Harbor, New Britain with PT114, which was not seriously damaged. USN CVEs SUWANEE and SANGAMON were damaged in a collision in the Marshalls. USAAF B25 "Mitchells" attacked Maloelap in the Marshalls. Twelve P40s shot down eleven Japanese Naval Air Force aircraft near Taroa in the Marshalls. The Royal Australian Air Force attacked Ngada, New Guinea. A Royal Australian Air Force PBY rescued ten survivors of a USAAF B24 that had ditched off Ontong, Java. The USN Task Group 74.2 (commanded by Berkey) comprised of the cruisers PHOENIX and BOISE and the destroyers AMMEN, MULLANY and BUSH bombarded Madang and Alexishafen on New Guinea.

1945 The US Army's 37th Division reached the edge of Clark Field on Luzon. The American 13th Air Force attacked Cavite Naval Base on Luzon. The USN submarine TAUTOG sank the NAGA MARU No.11 (43 tons). The TAMON MARU No.15 (6,925 tons) was sunk by a mine.

China-Burma-India

1942 The American Volunteer Group shot down three Japanese aircraft over Rangoon, Burma and lost one (the AVGs oldest pilot Louis Hoffman, age 43, was killed in the action). Japanese forces landed at Endau, 100 miles north of Singapore. The Royal Navy carrier INDOMITABLE launched twenty-eight "Hurricanes" fighters to reinforce Allied forces at Palembang, Sumatra.

1943 Seven American 10th Air Force B24s attacked Rangoon, Burma.

1944 The U532 sank the American freighter WALTER CAMP (7,176 tons). The U188 sank the British freighters SAMOURI (7,219 tons) and SURADA (5,427 tons).

1945 The 7th Indian Division took Pauk, Burma.

January 27th

Western Europe

1934 Rightist mobs in Paris toppled the French government.

1938 German General Werner von Blomberg, War Minister, was relieved of his post since his new wife had been a prostitute.

1941 Meetings began between the British and the Americans that by March 27th, would establish provisions for the war against Germany. One of the results of these meetings was the activation of the US Army Observer

	Group, under the command of Major General James Chaney on May 19th. One of the unit's missions was to locate possible sites for future USAAF installations in Britain.
1943	Nine Royal Air Force "Mosquitoes" attacked Copenhagen, Denmark and lost one aircraft. In the first USAAF raid on a German target (Wilhelmshaven), the 91st, 303rd, 305th and 306th Bomb Groups lost one of fifty-five B17s and dropped 109 tons of bombs. Twenty-seven "B24s of the USAAF's 44th and 93rd Bomb Groups failed to find the target, but still lost two aircraft. 162 Royal Air Force bombers attacked Dusseldorf, Germany and lost six aircraft. Sixty-six people were killed in the raid. Fifty-four Royal Air Force bombers dropped mines in the Baltic and lost one "Stirling".
1944	The American 15th Air Force attacked Salon, Montpelier, and Istres in Southern France, dropping 470 tons of bombs and lost two bombers and two fighters. 530 Royal Air Force bombers attacked Berlin and lost thirty-three "Lancasters". 567 people were killed in Berlin and another twenty-eight were killed in the sixty-one other towns and villages around the city that were also hit. Five B17s from the USAAF's 422nd Bomb Squadron dropped 1,440,000 leaflets on Paris, Rennes, Le Mans, and Orleans in France.
1945	The American Third Army crossed the Our River and took Oberhausen. The Germans evacuated Stalag Luft III, a prisoner of war camp at Sagan, and force-marched the POWs to Spremberg and loaded them onto trains. Twelve Royal Air Force "Mosquitoes" attacked Berlin.
1989	The Dutch government pardoned two Nazi War Criminals (Franz Fischer, age 87, and Ferdinand Fuentern, age 79) who had been imprisoned since 1945 for deporting Dutch civilians to Germany.

Eastern Europe

1942	The Soviets took Lozovaya on the Donets Front.
1943	Soviet forces cleared the Moscow-Leningrad Railway.
1944	The Soviets announced the relief of Leningrad.
1945	Soviet forces took Memel, Lithuania.

Mediterranean

1941	The 4th Indian Division reached Agordat in Eritrea.
1944	The US Army's 34th Division took Caira, Italy and Monte Mailoa. The 3rd Algerian Division was driven off Monte Abate in Italy by a German counter-attack.

Atlantic

1940	The U20 sank the Norwegian freighters FARO (844 tons) and HOSANGER (1,591 tons) and the Danish freighters FREDENSBORG (2,094 tons) and ENGLAND (2,319 tons). U20 was sunk on September 10, 1944.

1942   The U130 sank the American tanker FRANCIS E. POWELL (7,096 tons-4 dead) off the Virginia Capes. U130 survived until March 12, 1943. The American steamer COAMO rescued seventy-one survivors from the Canadian steamer LADY HAWKINS which had been sunk on January 19th by U66.

1943   The American freighter JULIA WARD HOWE (7,176 tons-4 dead) was sunk south of the Azores by the U442. U442 was sunk on February 12, 1943. The U105 sank the American freighter CAPE DECISION (5,106 tons). U105 survived until June 2, 1943. The U514 sank the American freighter CHARLES C. PINCKNEY (7,177 tons-58 dead). U514 survived until July 8, 1943.

1945   The U825 damaged the Norwegian tanker SOLOR (8,262 tons) and the American freighter RUBEN DARIO (7,198 tons). U825 survived the war. The U1051 was sunk in St. Georges Channel by the Royal Navy frigates TYLER, KEATS and BLIGH.

North America

1939   FDR approved the sale of military aircraft to Spain.

1940   The submarine TAUTOG was launched. She was scrapped in 1960.

1943   The first woman to win a Soldier's Medal was Nurse Edith Greenwood. She had saved patients under her care from a fire in Arizona.

1947   The destroyers PHELPS and MCCALL were stricken.

1957   The last operational P51 "Mustang" was retired to the USAF museum at Wright-Patterson, Ohio.

1972   Richard Courant, Director of Mathematics at Gottingen University until he was dismissed by the Nazis, died in New York City.

1987   USN Rear Admiral Samuel G. Fuqua, died at the age of 87 in Decatur, Georgia. He had won a Medal of Honor while serving as a Lieutenant Commander aboard the battleship ARIZONA during the Pearl Harbor attack on December 7, 1941. Ralph Neppel died of cancer. He had won a Medal of Honor in Europe in 1944.

Pacific

1917   The IJN battleship HYUGA was launched. She was sunk on July 24, 1945.

1941   Joseph Grew, US Ambassador to Japan, informed Washington of rumors in Tokyo of a Japanese attack on Pearl Harbor.

1942   The HMS INDOMITABLE launched 48 aircraft to reinforce the defenses of Java. The USN submarine GUDGEON sank the IJN submarine I-73 west of Midway. The USN submarine SEAWOLF arrived at Corregidor with supplies. Japanese forces are held to minimal gains on Bataan. USAAF B17s damaged the Japanese seaplane carrier SANUKI MARU off Borneo. The Royal Navy destroyer THANET was sunk off Malaya by the IJN destroyers AMAGIRI, HATSUYUKI and SHIRAYUKI, fifty-seven survived. The Free French agreed to open French possessions in the Pacific to Allied military bases.

1943 A B17 carrying General Nathan Twining, commander of the American 13th Air Force, and fifteen others ditched off the New Hebrides. They were rescued six days later by a USN PBY. USAAF B26s and P39s attacked Kolombangara. USAAF Captain John Mitchell became the first 13th Air Force ace when he shot down two Japanese "Oscars" over Guadalcanal. Six Japanese floatplanes attacked Amchitka in the Aleutians. The IJN gunboat No.2 CHOKO MARU rescued nearly 1,000 survivors from the freighter BUYO MARU which had been sunk the previous day by the USN submarine WAHOO.

1944 The USMC took Natoma, New Britain. American authorities released a report on Japanese atrocities in the Philippines. The USN submarine SWORDFISH sank the KASAGI MARU (3,140 tons). The USN submarine THRESHER sank the KOSEI MARU (2,205 tons) and the KITAKUZI MARU (1,266 tons). The USN submarine DACE sank the KEIKAI MARU (2,827 tons).

1945 The USN submarine BERGALL sank the IJN minelayer Wa-102. The US Army's 32nd Division was landed as reinforcements at Lingayen, Luzon. Heavy fighting took place at San Miguel, Luzon. The American Iwo Jima invasion force left Hawaii for its staging area in the Marianas. Thirty-four B29s attacked Tokyo and lost nine aircraft. The American 13th Air Force attacked Cavite naval base on Luzon.

China-Burma-India

1932 Japan informed China of a January 28th deadline for an apology for attacks made on Japanese civilians in Shanghai on the 18th.

1937 Nationalist and Communist forces joined together to fight the Japanese in China.

1942 British forces began pulling back onto Singapore Island.

1942 The Japanese took Mergui, Burma.

1944 The Royal Air Force attacked Malays, Burma.

1945 The Ledo Road was finally secured, effectively breaking the Japanese blockade. It had been declared secure on the 22nd. Two Japanese freighters were sunk on the Yangtze by B24-laid mines. USAAF B29s began moving from China to India.

January 28th

Western Europe

1930　Spanish Premier de Rivera resigned and was replaced by General Damaso Berenguer. Widespread rioting took place among Germanys two million unemployed.

1933　Kurt von Schleicher resigned as German Chancellor amidst growing violence in Germany.

1935　The British Committee for the Scientific Survey of Air Defense held its first meeting. It was originally formed to study the feasibility of a "death ray" to be used against aircraft. They soon discarded that idea, but would go on to develop radar.

1938　Austrian Nazi Leopold Taus was charged with high treason for attempting to overthrow the Austrian government.

1942　Eighty-four Royal Air Force bombers attacked Munster, Germany and lost four aircraft. No bombs fell within the city. Forty-eight Royal Air Force bombers attacked Boulogne, France. No aircraft were lost to enemy fire but one was shot down by a Royal Navy ship at sea. Sixteen Royal Air Force "Blenheims" attacked French and Dutch airfields and lost one aircraft. Royal Air Force ace Wing Commander Robert Stanford Tuck (29 victories) was shot down by ground fire near Boulogne, France and was captured.

1943　Hitler ordered full mobilization of Germany's labor force.

1944　Royal Air Force ace Flying Officer C. Weaver (13 victories and a US citizen) was killed in action. Forty-three American 8th Air Force B24s dropped 123 tons of bombs on V-1 sites near Bonnieres in France. 122 8th Air Force P47s provided support for the bombers. 158 8th Air Force P47s attacked the Leeuwarden airfield in Holland. 677 Royal Air Force bombers attacked Berlin and lost forty-six aircraft. Sixty-seven Royal Air Force bombers dropped mines in Kiel Bay and lost two "Stirlings". Five B17s from the USAAF's 422nd Bomb Squadron dropped 1,360,000 leaflets on Amiens, Rouen, Bambrai, Reims and Caen in France.

1945　855 8th Air Force bombers dropped 2,201 tons of bombs on rail targets in Central Germany and the oil plants at Dortmund in Germany. 225 8th Air Force fighters provided support for the bombers. 153 Royal Air Force bombers attacked Köln and lost four "Lancasters". The last German forces in "The Bulge" were eliminated. 602 Royal Air Force bombers attacked targets around Stuttgart, Germany and lost eleven aircraft. Sixty-seven Royal Air Force "Mosquitoes" attacked Berlin. The German minesweeper R-57 was lost in a collision with the U1163 in Trondheim Fjord, Norway.

1987　Gerhard Klopfer, German S.S. General and the last survivor of the "Wannsee Conference", died at the age of 81.

Eastern Europe

1940 The Finnish 9th Division attacked the Soviet 5th Division at Kuhmo.
1941 Marshal Timoshenko's Soviet troops advanced in the Ukraine.
1943 Soviet forces took Kasternoye and Kropotkins.
1944 German General Georg von Kuchler ordered the 18th Army to retreat to the Luga River. The Soviets surrounded 60,000 Germans near Korsun. Soviet forces took Lyuban.
1945 Captured Soviet General Andrei A. Vlasov took command of anti-Soviet Russians fighting in the Waffen S.S. Soviet forces entered German Pomerania. The Soviets took Sensburg and Bischofsburg in East Prussia and Sepolno, Czarnkow and Leszno in Poland and Memel in Lithuania.

Mediterranean

1941 The Royal Navy submarine UPHOLDER sank the German freighter DUISBURG.
1942 The Germans re-occupied Benghazi, Libya.
1944 Technician/5th Class Eric Gibson, of the 3rd Division, won a posthumous Medal of Honor near Isola Bella, Italy. The American 15th Air Force attacked Aviano and Ferrara in Italy.

Atlantic

1940 A mine laid by the U22 sank the British freighter ESTON (1,478 tons). U22 survived until April 25th. The U34 sank the Greek freighter ELENI STATHATOS (5,625 tons). U34 was declared a constructive loss after a collision on August 5, 1943. The U44 sank the Greek freighter FLORA (2,980 tons). U44 survived until March 20th.
1941 The Italian submarine TORICELLI sank the British freighter URLA (5,198 tons).
1943 The U553 was lost due to unknown causes. The Portuguese destroyer LIMA and the Royal Navy destroyer QUADRANT rescued 58 survivors from the American freighter CITY OF FLINT which had been sunk on January 25th by U575.
1944 The U271 was sunk by USN VB103. The U571 was sunk by the Royal Australian Air Force's No.461 Squadron.

North America

1938 Ernest King was promoted to Vice-Admiral. He would serve as Chief of Naval Operations during the war. FDR called for massive American rearmament.
1942 The American 8th Air Force was activated at Hunter Field near Savannah, Georgia.

1943	The first XB29 was grounded for three weeks while repairs and modifications were made. The second XB29 would be used for flight tests until the repairs were completed.
1945	The USN carrier ANTIETAM was commissioned. She would appear in the 1949 film "Task Force" and was stricken in 1973.
1947	The carrier RANGER was sold for scrap and the destroyers HATFIELD, SOMERS and MOFFETT were stricken.
1951	4th Fighter Group ace Don Gentile (30 victories) died in a plane crash near Andrews Air Force Base, Maryland.
1980	The US Coast Guard cutter BLACKTHORN sank, she had been commissioned on March 27, 1944.

South America

1942	Paraguay and Brazil broke diplomatic relations with the Axis.

Pacific

1942	The US Army transport ROYAL T. FRANK (244 tons-21 dead) was sunk between Maui and Hawaii by the IJN submarine I-171. The Japanese took Rossel Island, off Papua.
1943	American forces continue their advance towards Cape Esperance on Guadalcanal. USAAF B17s attacked Kahili Airfield.
1944	Twenty American 7th Air Force B24s attacked Wotje and Kwajalein.
1945	American forces secured Mindoro in the Philippines. The USN battlecruiser ALASKA left Pearl Harbor for combat operations. The American 13th Air Force attacked Cavite, Luzon. USAAF B24s attacked Corregidor. The SANUKI MARU (7,158 tons) and the IJN escort KUME were sunk by the USN submarine SPADEFISH.

China-Burma-India

1932	Shanghai Municipal Council accepted Japanese demands of January 20th.
1942	The American Volunteer Group and the Royal Air Force shot down seventeen Japanese aircraft over Rangoon. The IJN submarine I-164 damaged the British freighter IDAR (391 tons).

January 29th

Western Europe

1928	A German-Lithuanian treaty was signed. It confirmed borders between the two countries.
1940	Luftwaffe aircraft sank four ships and damaged four more off the east coast of Britain.

1941 Thirty-four Royal Air Force bombers attacked Wilhelmshaven, Germany. Eighteen people were killed in the raid.
1942 Nine Royal Air Force "Halifaxes" and seven "Stirlings" attacked the German battleship TIRPITZ in Trondheim Fjord, Norway and lost one "Stirling".
1943 Twelve Royal Air Force "Bostons" attacked targets in France and lost one aircraft. 116 Royal Air Force bombers attacked the port of Lorient, France and lost four aircraft. Twenty-two Royal Air Force bombers dropped mines off the Biscay ports and attacked targets in France and lost two aircraft. Six "Spitfires" from the USAAF's 4th Fighter Group flew patrols over the Channel.
1944 The Luftwaffe attacked targets in Britain. 806 American 8th Air Force B17s and B24s dropped 1,895 tons of bombs on Frankfurt, Germany and lost twenty-four B17s and five B24s. 632 8th Air Force P38s, P47s and P51s provided support for the bombers and claimed forty-seven victories for the loss of five P38s and ten P47s. Five B17s from the USAAF's 422nd Bomb Squadron dropped 1,200,000 leaflets on Lille, Tours, Lorient, Nantes, and Valenciennes in France. The advance party of the American Third Army arrived in Glasgow and was greeted by its designated commander, General George Patton. Twelve Royal Air Force "Mosquitoes" attacked Duisburg, Germany.
1945 1,094 8th Air Force bombers dropped 3,113 tons of bombs on rail targets in Central Germany and factories at Kassel and lost one B24. 638 8th Air Force fighters provided support for the bombers and claimed six victories for the loss of two P51s. 148 Royal Air Force "Lancasters" attacked Krefeld, Germany. First Sergeant Leonard Funk, of the 82nd Airborne Division, won a Medal of Honor at Holzheim, Belgium. The US Army's 90th Division took Walchenhausen and Staupbach in Germany. The German escort F-5 was sunk in the Baltic by a mine. Fifty-nine Royal Air Force "Mosquitoes" attacked Berlin.

Eastern Europe
1940 Russia asked Sweden to mediate a peace with Finland.
1942 A Soviet-Iranian-Anglo treaty was signed.
1943 The Soviets took Kropotkin. The U255 sank the Soviet freighter KRANYJ PARTIZAN (2,418 tons).
1944 Georg von Kuchler was relieved by Walter Model as commander of German Army Group "North". The Soviets took Chudovo.
1945 German forces counter-attacked from East Prussia. The Soviets took Bischofsburg, Schoenlake and Woldenberg in East Prussia.

Mediterranean

1941 Greek Prime Minister Metaxas died and was replaced by Alexandros Korizis. British forces crossed into Italian Somaliland from Kenya. The Italians evacuated Derna in Cyrenaica. Seven Luftwaffe He-111s dropped mines in the Suez Canal.

1942 The U431 sank the British whaler SOTRA (313 tons).

1943 At 1950, the Royal Navy anti/aircraft auxiliary POZARICA was damaged by Luftwaffe and later sank on February 13th, after being towed to Bougie by the Royal Navy CADMUS. At 2100, the Italian minesweeper ESO was sunk by Royal Navy aircraft.

1944 The Allies had 69,000 men, 508 cannon and 237 tanks ashore at Anzio. At 1820, the Royal Navy light cruiser SPARTAN and the American freighter SAMUEL HUNTINGTON (five dead) were sunk off Anzio by Luftwaffe Hs293 glide-bombs. The American 15th Air Force attacked rail targets in Italy.

Atlantic

1940 The U51 sank the Norwegian freighter EIKA (1,503 tons). U51 survived until August 20th.

1941 The U93 sank the British freighter KING ROBERT (5,886 tons) and tanker W.B. WALKER (10,468 tons) and the Greek freighter AIKATERINI (4,929 tons). U93 survived until January 15, 1942. The U94 sank the British freighter WEST WALES (4,354 tons). U94 survived until August 28, 1942. The U106 sank the Egyptian freighter SESOSTRIS (2,962 tons). U106 survived until August 2, 1943. The German armed merchant cruiser KORMORAN took the British freighters AFRIC STAR (11,900 tons) and EURYLOCHUS (5,723 tons).

1942 The US Coast Guard cutter ALEXANDER HAMILTON was torpedoed by the U132 17 miles off Reykjavik, Iceland, 26 died. She capsized and sank the next day. U132 survived until November 5th. The British freighter DEBRETT was mistakenly attacked by USN PBYs based in Natal, Brazil.

1943 The Portuguese destroyer LIMA rescued survivors from the American freighter JULIA WARD HOWE, which had been sunk on January 28th by U442.

North America

1941 British and American military staffs held talks (code-named ABC-1) in Washington D.C. American troops arrived in St. John's, Newfoundland.

1942 The USN successfully test-fired the new 5" proximity fuse. The fuse did not require a direct hit to destroy its target. Millard Harmon replaced

Carl Spaatz as Chief of Air Staff USAAF, with Spaatz becoming USAAF Combat Commander.

1944   The battleship MISSOURI was launched at the New York Navy Yard. MISSOURI would eventually be preserved as a memorial in Pearl Harbor, Hawaii. The destroyers MANSFIELD and WREN were launched. The MANSFIELD was sold to Argentina in 1974 and the WREN was stricken in December 1974.

1945   The destroyer-minesweeper ELLIOT was sold for scrap.

1946   Harry Hopkins, FDR's personal advisor, died.

1951   The light cruiser ST. LOUIS was transferred to Brazil and renamed TAMANDARE. She was stricken in 1975.

1972   The destroyer GLEAVES was sold for scrap. It had been planned to save her as a memorial, but the project failed.

2002   Disabled World War II veteran and actor Harold Russell, age 88, died. He had won two Oscars for his portrayal of Homer Parrish in the 1946 classic film "The Best Years of Our Lives".

2015   USN ace Alex Vraciu died at the age of 96 in West Sacramento, California. He had been credited with 19 aerial victories while flying F6Fs in the Pacific.

Pacific

1942   Japanese forces landed at Bandoeng and Mampawan on Celebes. American forces arrived in Fiji. The USN minesweeper QUAIL bombarded Japanese positions on Luzon.

1943   At 1940, the USN heavy cruiser CHICAGO and the destroyer LAVALLETTE were damaged by aerial torpedoes while escorting reinforcements to Guadalcanal. The CHICAGO was sunk the next day, while under tow by the tug NAVAJO near Rennel Island. The IJN submarine I-1 was damaged by the His New Zealand ships KIWI and MOA and drifted ashore off Guadalcanal. The IJN submarine I-10 sank the American freighter SAMUEL GOMPERS (7,176 tons) off New Caledonia. Ralph Christie, USN Submarine Force commander in Australia, became the first USN admiral to go on a submarine combat patrol (aboard the BOWFIN). The IJN submarine Ro-39 was sunk by the USN destroyer WALKER. The USN submarine GATO sank the NICHIUN MARU (2,723 tons) off Buin. USAAF B26s attacked Kolombangara.

1944   USN Task Group 58.3 (commanded by Sherman), consisting of the carrier BUNKER HILL and the light carriers COWPENS and MONTEREY, attacked Kwajalein. USN Task Group 58.2 (commanded by Montgomery), consisting of the carriers INTREPID and ESSEX and the light carrier CABOT attacked Roi-Namur in the Marshalls. Task Group 58.1

(commanded by Reeves), consisting of the carriers ENTERPRISE and YORKTOWN and the light carrier BELLEAU WOOD, attacked Maloelap. USN Task Group 58.4 (commanded by Ginder), consisting of the carrier SARATOGA and the light carriers PRINCETON and LANGLEY, attacked Wotje. The AKIBASAN MARU and the net tender UJI MARU were sunk at Kwajalein and the IJN sub chasers Nos.18 and 21 during the action. The USN submarine TAMBOR sank the SHUNTAI MARU (2,254 tons). The USN submarine ANGLER sank the SHUKO MARU (889 tons), off Iwo Jima. The Royal Australian Air Force attacked Orgoruna, New Guinea.

1945 30,000 men of the US Army's XI Corps (commanded by Hall) landed at San Antonio, Luzon. The USN freighter SERPENS exploded off Guadalcanal, 196 died. The USN submarine PICUDA sank the CLYDE MARU (5,497 tons). The USN attack-transport CAVALIER (7,800 tons) was damaged by the IJN submarine Ro-46. USAAF B24s attacked Corregidor and Cavite in the Philippines.

China-Burma-India

1932 The Japanese Air Force attacked the Chapei District of Shanghai, killing approximately 12,000.

1942 The American Volunteer Group and the Royal Air Force shot down sixteen Japanese aircraft over Rangoon, Burma. The evacuation of civilians from Singapore began. The IJN submarine I-164 sank the American freighter FLORENCE LUCKENBACH (5,049 tons) in the Indian Ocean. I-164 survived until May 17, 1942.

1944 The U188 sank the Greek freighter OLGA E. EMBIRICOS (4,677 tons).

1945 Japanese forces took the USAAF base at Suichuan.

January 30th

Western Europe

1890 Stewart Graham Menzies, Chief of Britain's MI-6 during WWII, was born.

1915 German S.S. officer Joachim Peiper was born. He was killed on "Bastille Day" (July 14th) in 1976.

1933 Hitler became Chancellor of Germany, replacing Kurt von Schleicher.

1937 Hitler demanded the return of all former German colonies.

1940 Thirty-five Luftwaffe He111s attacked shipping off the east coast of Britain. They sank two ships and damaged eight more.

1941 Germany announced that all ships sailing for Britain would be attacked.

1942 The Irish government protested the arrival of American troops in Northern Ireland.

1943 Six Royal Air Force "Mosquitos" of Nos.105 and 139 Squadrons attacked Berlin and lost one aircraft. This was the first daylight raid on the German capital. Thirty-six Royal Air Force bombers attacked targets in Germany and Holland and lost four "Wellingtons". Admiral Karl Doenitz assumed command of the German Navy, replacing Erich Raeder. Vichy named Joseph Darnard as chief of their militia (the "Milice"). 148 Royal Air Force bombers attacked Hamburg, Germany and lost five "Lancasters". Fifty-eight people were killed in the raid. This was the first operation for the new H2S bombing radar.

1944 742 8th Air Force B17s and B24s dropped 1,747 tons of bombs on Brunswick and Hannover in Germany and lost eighteen B17s and two B24s. 635 8th Air Force P38s, P47s and P51s provided support for the bombers and claimed forty-five victories for the loss of two P38s and two P47s. The German minesweeper M-451 ran aground in the Baltic and was lost. The American 15th Air Force attacked Undine, Austria and lost six bombers and three escorting fighters. 534 Royal Air Force bombers attacked Berlin and lost thirty-three aircraft. More than 1,000 people were killed in Berlin and another seventeen were killed in the seventy-nine outlying towns and villages that were hit by stray bombs. Five B17s from the USAAF's 422nd Bomb Squadron dropped 1,200,000 leaflets on Chateauroux, Brest, Caen, Chartres, and Le Mans in France. The German destroyer Z-37 was a constructive loss after colliding with the Z-32 in the Bay of Biscay.

1945 The US Army's XII Corps took Rodgen, Auel and Steinkopf in Germany. Aircraft from the British escort carriers CAMPANIA and NAIRANA attacked the area around Stadlandet in Norway.

1983 British General Alan Cunningham died. He had commanded the 8th Army in North Africa for two months until he was relieved.

2015 Wehrmacht tank ace Otto Carius died at the age of 92. He had been credited with destroying more than 150 tanks during the war, mostly on the Eastern Front.

Eastern Europe

1943 Soviet forces attacked Paulus' headquarters in Stalingrad. Friedrich Paulus was promoted to Field Marshal. The Soviets took Maikop and Tikhretsk. The Soviet Navy bombarded German positions at Novorossisk on the Black Sea.

1944 The U278 sank the Royal Navy destroyer HARDY (40 of her crew died).

1945 The German liner WILHELM GUSTOFF was sunk in the Baltic by the Soviet submarine S-13 (8,000 refugees died). The Soviets established a bridgehead on the west bank of the Oder River. Soviet forces took Stolzenburg, seventy miles from Berlin.

Mediterranean

1941 British forces took Derna, Libya.

1942 The Italian submarine MEDUSA was sunk by the Royal Navy submarine THORN.

1943 At 0020, the Royal Navy corvette SAMPHIRE was sunk by the U596. Her four survivors were rescued by the Royal Navy ZETLAND. The American 12th Air Force attacked Ferryville, Tunisia. At 1405, the Italian minesweeper UNIE (the ex-Yugoslavian KOBAC) and the freighter NOTO were sunk at Ferryville, Tunisia by the 12th Air Force B17s. General Vittorio Ambrosio became Chief of the Italian Comando Supremo (died 1958). The French battleship RICHELIEU left Dakar en route to America to repair damage suffered in action with the Royal Navy in September 1940.

1944 The Allied commander at Anzio, American General John Porter Lucas, launched his first offensive at Anzio. It was stopped by the Germans on February 1st. 767 US Army Rangers attacked towards Cisterna, near Anzio, and all but six were killed or captured. Private First-Class Lloyd Hawks, of the 3rd Division, won a Medal of Honor near Carano, Italy. The American 15th Air Force attacked aircraft targets in Italy. The American 5th Army attacked the Germans "Gustav Line". The British Army's 5th Division took Monte Natale in Italy.

Atlantic

1940 The U55 sank the British tanker VACLITE (5,026 tons) and the Greek freighter KERAMIAI (5,085 tons). U55 was sunk later in the day, southwest of the Scillies, by the Royal Navy destroyer WHITSHED, the sloop FOWEY and aircraft.

1941 The U94 sank the British freighter WESTPOOL (5,125 tons). U94 survived until August 28, 1942.

1942 The U106 sank the American tanker ROCHESTER (6,836 tons-4 dead). U106 survived until August 2, 1943.

1943 The German trawler V-1102 ran aground on the Bremanger reef and was lost.

1944 At 0408, the Royal Navy destroyer HARDY (40 dead) was sunk south of Bear Island by the U278. U278 survived the war. The U314 was sunk south of Bear Island by the Royal Navy destroyers WHITEHALL and METEOR. The U367 was sunk by Royal Air Force No.172 Squadron.

1946 The American freighter ANTIETAM was sunk by a mine off Blaye, France. She suffered one dead and four wounded.

North America
1882 Franklin Roosevelt was born in Hyde Park, New York.
1946 The destroyer BROOKS was sold for scrap.
1970 The destroyers NICHOLAS, O'BANNON and HAYNESWORTH were sold for scrap. The carrier PRINCETON was stricken.

Pacific
1942 Japanese forces took Amboina Island, which was between New Guinea and Celebes.
1943 The US Army's 147th Regiment continued its advance on Cape Esperance, Guadalcanal. The USN heavy cruiser CHICAGO was sunk while under tow off Rennel Island by six aircraft torpedoes (150 dead). She had been damaged the previous day by Japanese aircraft.
1944 The IJN submarine I-175 disappeared while en route from Truk to Wotje. Eighteen USN TBFs attacked Rabaul, New Britain sinking the IWATE MARU. The USN heavy cruiser LOUISVILLE, the light cruisers SANTA FE, MOBILE, BILOXI and six destroyers bombarded Otdia Island in the Marshalls with 250 8", 1,813 6", and 4,567 5" shells. The USN destroyer ANDERSON was hit by counter-fire which killed five of her crew, including her Captain, and wounded fourteen. The USN battleships MASSACHUSETTS, INDIANA and WASHINGTON bombarded Kwajalein. The PARAN MARU and another small freighter were sunk by the USN destroyer BURNS off Ujae Atoll in the Marshalls. The USN submarine SEAHORSE sank the TOKO MARU (2,747 tons). The IJN minelayer NASAMI was sunk west of Truk by the USN submarine TRIGGER. The USN submarine SPEARFISH sank the TAMASHIMA MARU (3,560 tons). Staff Sergeant Jesse Drowley, of the Americal Division, won a Medal of Honor on Bougainville.
1945 The US Army's XI Corps took Olangopo, Luzon. The USN submarine THREADFIN sank the ISSEI MARU (1,864 tons). The American 13th Air Force attacked Cavite, Luzon. US Army troops landed on Gamble Island in the Philippines.
1951 The USN light carrier INDEPENDENCE was expended after the Bikini tests.

China-Burma-India
1941 An armistice between Thailand and Indo-China was signed.
1942 British forces withdrew onto Singapore Island. Japanese forces took Moulmein, Burma. The IJN submarine I-164 sank the Indian freighter JALATARANG (2,498 tons).
1944 The Royal Navy battleships VALIANT and QUEEN ELIZABETH, the battlecruiser RENOWN and the carriers ILLUSTRIOUS and UNICORN arrived at Colombo, from Europe.

January 31st

Western Europe

1929 The Royal Navy heavy cruiser LONDON was launched. She was scrapped in 1950.

1933 Edouard Daladier became French Premier. The Royal Navy light cruiser NEPTUNE was launched. She was sunk on December 19, 1941.

1942 Seventy-two Royal Air Force bombers attacked the port of Brest, France and lost five aircraft.

1943 48% of all American 8th Air Force aircraft entering enemy air-space during this month suffered battle-damage.

1944 Seventy-four 8th Air Force B24s dropped 217 tons of bombs on V-1 rocket sites near St. Pol/Siracourt in France. 114 8th Air Force P47s provided support for the bombers. 209 8th Air Force P38s and P47s attacked the Gilze-Rijen airfield in Belgium and claimed thirteen victories for the loss of six P38s. The American 15th Air Force attacked Klagenfurt, Austria.

1945 The American 8th Air Force had a daily average of 2,799 bombers and 1,484 fighters on strength during the month. The US Army's XVIII Corps entered Germany, east of St. Vith, Belgium. US Army Private Eddie Slovik was executed for desertion at Ste-Marie-aux-Mines. He was the only one of forty-nine sentenced to death to actually be executed. His remains were returned to America in the summer of 1987. Staff Sergeant Jonah Kelley, of the 78th Division, won a posthumous Medal of Honor at Kesternich. The German minesweeper M-382 was sunk off Norway by the Norwegian MTB-715. Fourteen Royal Air Force "Mosquitoes" attacked targets in Germany and lost one aircraft. The British government awarded seven Victoria Crosses in the month of January during the war.

1947 Wehrmacht General Franz von Epp died in an American internment camp.

1966 British General Arthur Percival, commander of the Commonwealth forces in Singapore in 1942, died.

1967 Friedrich Dibelius, a protestant leader in Nazi Germany, died in Berlin.

Eastern Europe

1941 The Turkish government received a request from Britain seeking to station ten Royal Air Force squadrons in their country. Ankara refused, stating that such an action would violate its neutrality.

1943 In Stalingrad the German 6th Army Commander Field Marshal Friedrich Paulus surrendered to the Soviet 38th Motor Rifle Brigade. The Germans in the northern pocket still held out.

1944 The Soviets reached Kingisepp west of Leningrad. The German minesweeper M-451 was lost by grounding off Finland.

1945   The Soviets took Helsberg and Freeland in East Prussia. The Soviets reached the Oder at Zehden, a point at which they were less than fifty miles from Berlin.

Mediterranean

1941   The Royal Navy minesweeper HUNTLEY (18 dead) and the Egyptian transport SOLLOUM (1,290 tons) were sunk thirty miles west of Mersa Matruh, Egypt by the Luftwaffe. Aboard the SOLLOUM were 250 Italian prisoners of war.

1942   The Royal Air Force attacked Tripoli, Libya.

1943   At 1120, the Italian corvette PROCELLARIA hit a mine in the Sicilian Channel. She sank at 1430. At 1730, the Italian torpedo boat GENERALE MARCELLO PRESTINARI hit a mine in the same area. She sank at 1825. 12th Air Force B17s attacked Bizerte, Tunisia and sank the ex-French submarines CALYPSO and NAUTILUS.

1944   The US Army's II Corps took Caira, Italy. Sergeant Truman Olsen, of the 3rd Division, won a posthumous Medal of Honor near Cisterna Di Littoria, Italy. French troops took Monte Abate in Italy. The American 15th Air Force attacked aircraft targets in Italy.

Atlantic

1940   Axis forces sank 214,506 tons of Allied and neutral shipping during January and lost one U-boat. The U13 sank the Norwegian freighter START (1,168 tons). The U21 sank the Danish freighter VIDAR (1,353 tons).

1941   Axis forces sank 320,048 tons of Allied and neutral shipping during January and lost no U-boats. The Italian submarine DANDOLO sank the British freighter PIZZARO (1,397 tons). The German armed merchant cruiser ATLANTIS took the freighter SPEYBANK (5,154 tons).

1942   Axis forces sank 419,907 tons of Allied and neutral shipping in January and lost three U-boats. At 2210, the Royal Navy destroyer BELMONT (the ex-USN SATTERLEE) was sunk off Halifax by the U82. U82 survived until February 6th. At 2230, the Royal Navy escort CULVER (ex-US Coast Guard) was sunk southwest of Ireland by the U105 survived until June 2, 1943. The German blockade runner SPREEWALD (5,083 tons) was sunk in error by the U333. U333 survived until July 31, 1944. The U107 sank the British tanker SAN ARCADIO (7,419 tons). U107 survived until August 18, 1944.

1943   Axis forces sank 261,359 tons of Allied and neutral shipping in January and lost six U-boats. The German armed merchant cruiser CORONEL failed in an attempt to break into the Atlantic.

1944 Axis forces sank 130,635 tons of Allied and neutral shipping in January and lost sixteen U-boats. The U592 was sunk west of Ireland by the Royal Navy sloops STARLING, WILD GOOSE and MAGPIE. The American freighter GEORGE S. WASSON was a constructive loss after hitting a mine off Britain. She was later scuttled as a breakwater off Normandy.

1945 Axis forces sank 82,897 tons of Allied and neutral shipping in January and lost thirteen U-boats. The U3519 was sunk by a mine.

1948 The British freighter SAMKEY was reported as missing between Cuba and London. SAMKEY was an American-built "Liberty" ship.

North America

1880 General George Marshall was born in Uniontown, Pennsylvania. He graduated from Virginia Military Institute in 1901. He was commissioned as a second lieutenant in the Army the next year. His commission was made retroactive to February 2, 1901. His first assignment was to the Philippines. After a tour in Oklahoma, he went to the Army Staff College at Fort Leavenworth where he excelled. He would remain there for two years as an instructor. He was promoted to captain on August 14, 1916. During WWI he served on several staff assignments and was promoted to lieutenant colonel. On October 1, 1936 he was promoted to brigadier general. In August 1938 he became Chief of the War Plans Division. Three months later he was named as deputy to Army's Chief of Staff Malin Craigs. Marshall took over as Chief of Staff on September 1, 1939 after Craig retired. He would serve in the position November 25, 1945. He was Secretary of State from January 21, 1947 until early 1949 when he was replaced by Dean Acheson. In September 1950 he became Secretary of Defense. He retired on September 1, 1951. After suffering a crippling stroke in early 1959, he died on October 16th of that year. He was buried at Arlington National Cemetery.

1934 The destroyer HULL was launched in New York. She foundered east of Samar on December 18, 1944 during a typhoon.

1942 The destroyer BARTON was launched. She was lost on November 13, 1942.

1943 The destroyer WALKER was launched. She was sold to Italy in 1964.

1944 The USN carrier FRANKLIN was commissioned. She was stricken in 1964. The battleship CALIFORNIA completed her repairs at Bremerton, Washington. She had been damaged during the Japanese attack at Pearl Harbor on December 7, 1941.

1945 A Japanese balloon-bomb was found near Julian, California. A Navy PBY crashed near Brookings, Oregon. All eight aboard died. The American government awarded thirty-five Medals of Honor in the month of January during the war.

1951 An F6C (recon "Mustang") set a speed record of 7 hours and 48 minutes from New York to London.
1970 Brigadier General Richard Knobloch retired. He had flown on the "Doolittle Raid".
1971 Major Waldo Bither retired from the Civil Service. He had flown as bombardier on Plane No.12 on the "Doolittle Raid".
1976 The carriers HANCOCK and BENNINGTON were stricken.
2002 USAAF ace Francis "Gabby" Gabreski, age 83, died. During World War II he shot down 28 German aircraft. He was the leading American ace in the European Theater of Operations even though he spent the last eight months of the war as a prisoner of war. During the Korean War, he commanded the 51st Fighter Group and scored a further 6.5 aerial victories. He had retired from the Air Force in 1967.
2014 USAAF ace James Tapp died at the age of 94 in Fort Collins, Colorado. He had been credited with 8 aerial victories while flying P51s in the Pacific.

Pacific

1941 IJN Admiral Kichisaburo Nomura arrived in Honolulu aboard the KAMAKURA MARU en route to Washington D.C. He was to assist in peace negotiations with the American government. Vice Admiral William S. Pye relieved Admiral Charles P. Snyder as Commander Battle Force at Pearl Harbor. Vice Admiral Walter S. Anderson became Commander Battleships Battle Force at Pearl Harbor.
1942 Allied forces sank 73,795 tons of Japanese shipping (17 ships) in January.
1943 Allied forces sank 122,590 tons of Japanese shipping (28 ships) in January. USN aircraft attacked the Japanese shipping in Vella Gulf and lost two F4Fs. They sank the transport TOA MARU. The US Army's 147th Regiment was repulsed in its attempt to cross the Bonegi River on Guadalcanal. USMC Captain Jefferson DeBlanc, of VMF-112, won a Medal of Honor near Kolombangara. A USN force consisting of the carrier SARATOGA, the heavy cruiser LOUISVILLE, the light cruisers SANTA FE, MOBILE and BILOXI and six destroyers attacked Otadi Island in the Wotje Atoll. The destroyer ANDERSON was damaged during the action and suffered six dead, including her Captain. In the month of January, the American 11th Air Force lost eleven aircraft in accidents in the Aleutians.
1944 An Australian commission was formed to investigate Japanese war crimes. Allied forces sank 339,651 tons of Japanese shipping (87 ships) in January. The USN battleships PENNSYLVANIA, MISSISSIPPI, NEW MEXICO and IDAHO and the heavy cruisers MINNEAPOLIS, SAN FRANCISCO, and NEW ORLEANS shelled Kwajalein in a pre-invasion bombardment. American forces landed on the Kwajalein and Majuro

Atolls in the Marshalls. They were the first pre-war Japanese territory to be invaded. The Japanese freighter EIKO MARU was sunk during the actual invasion. The IJN submarine I-171 was sunk by the USN destroyers GUEST and HUDSON. The USN submarine TRIGGER damaged the IJN destroyer MICHISHIO and sank the IJN minelayer NASAMI and the YASUKUNI MARU (11,933 tons) off Rabaul, New Britain. The USN submarine TULLIBEE sank the HIRO MARU (549 tons). The Japanese freighter KIYOSUMI MARU (8,614 tons) was damaged by the USN submarine BALAO. This was the third time that ship had been damaged (See November 4th and December 25th 1943). She would survive until February 16th when she was finally sunk by USN carrier aircraft at Truk. The Royal Australian Air Force attacked Bogadjim, New Guinea.

1945 Allied forces sank 425,505 tons of Japanese shipping (125 ships) in January. The US Army's 11th Airborne Division landed by sea southwest of Manila on the island of Luzon. The American 8th Army took Guagua-Nasugbu and Lian on Luzon. USN PT338 was lost by grounding on Semizara Island in the Philippines. The USN PC-1129 was sunk off Luzon by a Japanese suicide boat. The American 13th Air Force attacked Cavite, Luzon. The IJN escort UME was sunk off Formosa by the American 14th Air Force. The USN submarine BOARFISH sank the ENKI MARU (6,968 tons) and the DAIETSU MARU (6,890 tons).

China-Burma-India

1942 The last British troops withdrew onto Singapore Island. The Japanese 15th Army captured Moulmein in Burma. It would remain under Japanese control until the end of the war. The IJN submarine I-164 sank the Indian freighter JALAPALAKA (4,215 tons). The IJN submarine I-162 damaged the British tanker LONGWOOD (9,463 tons).

1943 The IJN I-8 bombarded Canton Island, China.

1945 Lieutenant G. Knowland, of the Royal Norfolk Regiment, won a posthumous Victoria Cross in Arakan, Burma.

CHAPTER 2

THE MONTH OF FEBRUARY

February 1st

Western Europe
1936   The French battleship DUNKERQUE was commissioned. She was scrapped in 1958.
1937   The He118V4 dive-bomber left Hamburg, Germany aboard the KAGU MARU. It was en route to Japan for evaluation.
1940   The U15 was lost in a collision with the German torpedo boat ILTUS in the Baltic.
1941   Thirteen Royal Air Force "Wellingtons" attacked Boulogne, France. The German heavy cruiser ADMIRAL HIPPER left Brest, France for her second combat operation in the Atlantic. She would score 6 victories on the cruise.
1942   Vidkun Quisling was named as Minister President of Norway.
1943   Twenty "Spitfires" from the USAAF's 4th Fighter Group flew patrols over the Channel.
1944   Sixteen Royal Air Force "Mosquitoes" attacked targets in Germany and lost one aircraft. The German trawler UJ-1702 was sunk in an air-attack west of Stadlandet, Norway. SHAEF issued its Initial Joint Plan which dealt with Neptune (naval) portion of Overlord. It would eventually be nicknamed "the book" by those granted access to it.
1945   616 8th Air Force bombers dropped 1,780 tons of bombs on rail targets and bridges in Germany. 298 8th Air Force fighters provided support for the bombers. 160 Royal Air Force bombers attacked Munchengladbach and lost one "Lancaster". The US Army's VI Corps crossed the Moder River. Corporal Edward Bennett, of the 90th Division, won a Medal of Honor at Heckhusscheid, Germany. 396 Royal Air Force bombers attacked Ludwigshafen, Germany and lost six "Lancasters". Twenty-five people were killed in the raid. 340 Royal Air Force bombers attacked Mainz, Germany. Thirty-three people were killed in the raid. 282 Royal Air Force bombers attacked Siegen, Germany and lost four aircraft. 128 people were killed in the raid. 122 Royal Air Force "Mosquitoes" attacked Berlin.
1994   Luftwaffe ace Johannes "Macky" Steinhoff (176 victories) died this month.

Eastern Europe

1940   Soviet General Semion Timoshenko, the Commander of the Northwestern Front, began his offensive against the Karelian Peninsula. Within two weeks they would break through the Finnish lines.

1941   This month German forces began moving Polish Jews into the Warsaw Ghetto. The Italians began counter-offensive in Albania.

1943   The Soviets took Svatova.

1944   The German Gestapo chief in Poland was assassinated. Soviet forces were within one mile of the Estonian border.

1945   The Soviets took Torun, Poland.

Mediterranean

1941   Second Lieutenant Primindra Singh Bhaget, of the Indian Engineers, won a Victoria Cross in Abyssinia. British forces took Agordat, Eritrea. Italian forces evacuated Benghazi and officially asked for German reinforcements in North Africa.

1942   The American 12th Air Force lost one B25 and two P38s over Sfax, Tunisia. The British pulled back to Gazala and Bir Hacheim.

1943   The U118 laid a minefield in the Straits of Gibraltar. It would sink the British corvette WEYBURN and three merchant ships totaling 14,064 tons and would damage the British destroyer WIVERN and two merchant ships totaling 11,269 tons. At 1840, the Royal Navy minelayer WELSHMAN (152 dead) was torpedoed by the U617 and sank at 2035.

1944   The American 135th Infantry Regiment attacked German positions near Cassino, Italy. Private First Class Alton Knappenberger, of the 3rd Division, won a Medal of Honor near Cisterna Di Littoria, Italy. The American freighter EDWARD BATES (one dead) was sunk by the Luftwaffe. The U453 sank the Lebanese sailing ship SALEM (81 tons) and the Syrian sailing ship YAHIA (64 tons).

Atlantic

1940   The U13 sank the Swedish freighter FRAM (2,491 tons). U13 survived until May 31st. The U59 sank the British freighter ELLEN M. (498 tons).

1941   The U48 sank the Greek freighter ANGELOS (4,351 tons). U48 survived the war.

1942   The U109 sank the British freighter TACOMA STAR (7,924 tons). U109 survived until May 4, 1943.

1943   The U66 sank the French trawler JOSEPH ELISE (113 tons). U66 survived until May 6, 1944.

North America

1930 The heavy cruiser AUGUSTA (awarded three battle stars during the war) was launched. She was scrapped in 1960.

1940 The battleship ALABAMA's keel was laid at Norfolk, Virginia.

1941 The USN was divided into three separate fleets-Pacific, Atlantic and Asiatic. Kimmel replaced Richardson as commander of the Pacific Fleet; King took command of the Atlantic, while Hart took the Asiatic. This made for an awkward situation at Pearl Harbor, the base for the Pacific Fleet. Neither Kimmel nor his Army counterpart General Walter Short was appointed as overall commander of the Hawaiian Islands. This divided command prevented any attempt to centralize decisions on defensive measures taken in the theater. In fact, Kimmel was not even the senior Admiral in the area. Claude Bloch, a former Fleet Commander, was Commandant of the Hawaiian 14th Naval District and was actually senior in rank to Kimmel and had preceded him as Fleet Commander. The Marine Corps began its expansion when the First and Second Brigades were brought up to division strength.

1945 A Japanese balloon-bomb was found near Red Bluff, California and another exploded near Hayfork, California.

1965 General Curtis LeMay retired as USAF Chief of Staff.

1974 The destroyers WATTS, ALFRED A. CUNNINGHAM and BLUE were stricken. BLUE and CUNNINGHAM were later expended as targets. The destroyer KENNETH P. BAILEY was sold to Iran.

1979 Major General Hugo Rush, who had commanded a 15th Air Force B24 Wing, died in Clearwater, Florida at the age of 78.

1981 Aircraft designer Donald Douglas died.

Pacific

1940 A record budget, half of which was devoted to the military, was presented to Japan's Diet.

1941 Japan announced rice rationing. Admiral Husband Kimmel, commander of the USN Pacific Fleet, was informed of rumors of a possible Japanese attack on Pearl Harbor.

1942 At 0500, the carrier YORKTOWN, the heavy cruiser LOUISVILLE, the light cruiser ST. LOUIS and four destroyers attacked targets at Jaluit, Mili and Makin. The USN carrier ENTERPRISE attacked the islands of Kwajalein, Wotje and Maloelap sinking the BORDEAUX MARU, the net tender KASHIMA MARU, the sub chaser SHONAN MARU No.10 and the gunboat TOYOTSU MARU and damaging the minelayer TOKIWA, the netlayer KASHIMA MARU, the light cruiser KATORI, the explosives cargo ship KANTO MARU and the transport NAGATA MARU and losing five SBDs and F4Fs. They also destroyed 18 Japanese aircraft during the operation. The USN submarine SEADRAGON sank the TAMAGAWA MARU in Lingayan Gulf in the Philippines. USN PT-boats and USAAF P-40s repulsed a Japanese landing on Bataan. USN PT-32 damaged the Japanese minelayer YAEYAMA off Subic Bay.

1943 American forces were repulsed by Japanese forces in an attempt to cross the Bonegi River on Guadalcanal. The USN PTs 37 and 111 were sunk off Guadalcanal by IJN destroyers. At 1500, the USN destroyer DEHAVEN (167 died) and PT-123 were sunk off Guadalcanal by the Japanese Naval Air Force. The "Cactus Air Force" lost three SBDs, while damaging the IJN destroyer MAKIGUMO which was later sunk southwest of Savo Island by a USN PT-boat. 5,424 Japanese troops were evacuated from Guadalcanal. This was the beginning of the total evacuation of the island planned by the Japanese High Command. The USN submarine TARPON sank the FUSHIMI MARU (10,935 tons). Nine Japanese floatplanes attacked Amchitka in the Aleutians.

1944 American forces landed on Roi and Namur in the Kwajalein Atoll. USMC Private First-Class Richard Anderson, of the 4th Division, won a posthumous Medal of Honor on Roi. USMC 1st Lieutenant John Power, of the 4th Division, won a posthumous Medal of Honor on Namur. The USMC Raider units in the Pacific were disbanded and incorporated into the 4th Marine Regiment. The USN submarine GUARDFISH sank the IJN destroyer UMIKAZE south of Truk. The USN submarine HAKE sank the TACOMA MARU (5,772 tons) and the NANKA MARU (4,065 tons). The USN submarine SEAHORSE sank the TOEI MARU (4,004 tons). The USN battleships WASHINGTON (3 dead) and INDIANA (3 dead) collided off Majuro. The INDIANA's commander was later court-martialed.

1945 USAAF B24s and B29s attacked Iwo Jima for the next fifteen days. USN PTs 77 and 79 were sunk in error off Talin Point, Luzon by American forces. The US Army's XIV Corps took Gapan and Santa Rosa on Luzon. The IJN submarine Ro-115 was sunk by the USN destroyers BELL, JENKINS and O'BANNION and the destroyer escort MOORE. The American 13th Air Force attacked Cavite and Corregidor in the Philippines. 20th Air Force B29s attacked Singapore.

2010 The wreck of the USN submarine FLIER was located off the Philippines in the Balabac Strait. She struck a mine on August 13, 1944 and sank with the loss of seventy of the seventy-eighty crewmen aboard. The last survivor, Ensign Al Jacobson, died in 2008.

China-Burma-India

1931 The IJN bombarded Nanking, China.

1943 The 55th Indian Brigade failed in its attack on Donbaik, Burma. 10th Air Force B24s attacked Rangoon, Burma and damaged the IJN torpedo boat KARI.
1945 The IJN tanker SHIRETOKO was lost when USAAF B29s sank the British Admiralty Drydock No. IX in Singapore Harbor.
1995 Twenty-four survivors of "Merrill's Marauders" finished a 10-day tour of their WWII battlefields in Burma.

February 2nd

Western Europe
1873 German politician Constantin von Neurath was born. He died in 1956.
1889 French General Jean-Marie Lattre de Tassigny was born.
1914 Luftwaffe ace Wilhelm Balthasar (40 victories) was born in Fulda. He was killed in action on July 3, 1941.
1941 Rudolf Hilferding, a Social Democrat and twice Finance Minister of the Weimar Republic, died in a Gestapo prison in Paris. Twelve Royal Air Force "Hampdens" attacked Brest, France.
1943 Thirty-six Royal Air Force "Venturas" attacked targets in France and Belgium. They were escorted by twenty-five "Spitfires" from the USAAF's 4th Fighter Group. 161 Royal Air Force bombers attacked Cologne, Germany and lost five aircraft. Sixty-five buildings were destroyed and fourteen people were killed in the raid. Sixty-three American 8th Air Force B17s and B24s attempted to attack Hamm, Germany but had to abort due to bad weather.
1944 Ninety-five 8th Air Force B24s dropped 315 tons of bombs on V-1 rocket sites near Watten and St. Pol/Siracourt in France and lost two aircraft. 183 8th Air Force P47s provided support for the bombers. Thirty-four 8th Air Force P38s escorted 9th Air Force B26s that attacked the airfield at Tricqueville, France. Thirteen Royal Air Force "Mosquitoes" attacked targets in Germany.
1945 The US Army's 82nd Airborne Division attacked the Siegfried Line and took Udenbreth and Neuhof. Sergeant Emile Deleau, of the 36th Division, won a posthumous Medal of Honor at Oberhofen. Carl Goerdeler, the Mayor of Leipzig, and Alfred Delp, a Jesuit Priest, were hung at the Prinz Albrecht-Strasse Prison in Berlin for their part in the July 20th conspiracy. The German patrol boat V-1702 was lost in a collision with the U987 in the Baltic. 507 Royal Air Force bombers attacked Wiesbaden, Germany and lost three "Lancasters". 1,000 people were killed in the raid. 323 Royal Air Force bombers attacked Wanne-Eickel, Germany and lost four "Halifaxes". Sixty-eight people were killed in the raid. 261 Royal Air Force

bombers attacked Karlsruhe, Germany and lost fourteen "Lancasters". There were no casualties in the target area.

1980 The Köln County Court in Germany convicted Kurt Lischka, the wartime Chief of Police in Paris, of war crimes and sentenced him to 10-years in prison.

1989 Britain's William Stephenson ("The Man Called Intrepid") died at the age of 93.

Eastern Europe

1942 The Soviets took Feodosiya on the Black Sea.

1943 The last German forces in Stalingrad surrendered. Germany had lost 226,000 men, 24 generals and 488 Ju52 transport planes in the battle.

1944 Soviet forces attacked Latvia. The Soviets took Vanakula, Estonia. Stalin agreed to supply six bases for USAAF shuttle missions. The American 15th Air Force attacked Budapest, Hungary.

Mediterranean

1941 Aircraft from the Royal Navy carrier FORMIDABLE attacked Mogadishu in Italian Somaliland. The Luftwaffe laid mines off Tobruk.

1943 The Royal Navy submarine TURBULENT sank the Italian tanker URILITAS off Palermo, Sicily. She was carrying the entire 5,000 tons of fuel for the Italian naval squadron in Sicily.

1944 The American 15th Air Force attacked Durrazzo, Italy.

1945 Winston Churchill and FDR met at Malta en route to the Yalta Conference. They discussed the postwar occupation of Austria and the territory under Soviet control.

Atlantic

1940 The U59 sank the British tanker CREOFIELD (838 tons) and the freighter PORTELET (1,064 tons). U59 survived the war.

1941 The German armed merchant cruiser ATLANTIS took the freighter KETTY BROVIG (7,031 tons).

1942 The U581 was sunk southwest of the Azores by the Royal Navy destroyer WESTCOTT. The U103 sank the
American tanker W.L. STEED (6,182 tons-34 of her crew died). U103 survived until April 15, 1945.

1943 The American freighter JEREMIAH VAN RENSSELAER (7,177 tons-46 dead) was sunk off Cape Farewell, Greenland by the U456. U456 survived until May 13th.

1946 The former German U977 was expended in USN torpedo tests.

North America

1902 George C. Marshall was commissioned as a 2nd Lieutenant. He would serve as US Army Chief of Staff during the war.

1942 The carrier HORNET took aboard two B25s at Norfolk, Virginia. Her mission was to verify the feasibility of the upcoming "Doolittle Raid" on the Japanese Home Islands. Civilian cars were rationed in America. The destroyer HERNDON was launched. She was stricken in 1971. The battlecruiser GUAM's keel was laid.

1944 The heavy cruiser PITTSBURGH was launched. She was stricken in 1973.

1945 Japanese balloon-bombs were found near Laurens in Iowa, Schuley in Nebraska, and Ontario in Oregon.

1956 Lloyd McCarter committed suicide. He had won a Medal of Honor on Corregidor in 1945.

1969 The destroyer WALLER was expended as a target.

1972 The destroyer PHILIP sank in a storm while en route to be scrapped.

Pacific

1942 The USN submarine SEADRAGON sank the TAMAGAWA MARU (6,441 tons) off Luzon. The Japanese occupied Amboina. The Allies counter-attacked on Bataan. The IJN minesweeper W-9 was sunk and the minesweepers W-11 and W-12 were damaged off Ambon by mines.

1943 American forces finally succeeded in crossing the Bonegi River on Guadalcanal. USAAF B26s attacked Munda, New Georgia and Kolombangara. 13th Air Force B17s and P39s attacked Japanese shipping off Shortland Island in the Solomons and sank the freighter KEIYO MARU. 5th Air Force B24s sank the Japanese freighter KENKOKU MARU off New Britain.

1944 The islands of Roi and Namur in the Kwajalein Atoll were secured by American forces with the loss of 3,742 Japanese and 737 Americans. One of the American dead was Harry Hopkins's son, USMC Private First-Class Stephen Hopkins. USMC Lieutenant Colonel Aquilla Dyess (posthumous) and Private Richard Sorenson, of the 4th Division, won Medals of Honor on Namur. The American 6th Army's headquarters moved from Australia to Cape Cretin, New Guinea. USMC ace Robert M. Hanson (25 victories) was killed in action over Cape St. George. A 5" mount aboard the USN battleship ALABAMA accidentally fired into another mount, killing five and wounding eleven. The USN battleships WASHINGTON and INDIANA began temporary repairs for collision damage at Majuro. The USN submarine PLUNGER sank the TOYO MARU No.5 (2,193 tons) and TOYO MARU No.8 (2,191 tons). The American 7th Air Force attacked Eniwetok.

1945　Fighting ended on Leyte. The US Army's 77th Division was withdrawn from Leyte to prepare for the Okinawa invasion. The first B29 runway was completed on Guam. USAAF B24s attacked Cavite and Corregidor in the Philippines. The IJN escort CD-144 was sunk by the USN submarine BESUGO. The USN submarine HARDHEAD sank the NANSHIN MARU No.19 (834 tons). A USAAF P38 crashed in the Aleutians. The wreck would be recovered in 1994.

China-Burma-India
1942　US Army General Joseph Stilwell was named as Chiang Kai-shek's Chief of Staff. The HMS INDOMITABLE arrived at Trincomlee, Ceylon.
1944　The Chinese freighter CHUNG CHENG (7,176 tons) was sunk in the Arabian Sea by the U188.
1945　1st Lieutenant Jack Knight, of the 124th Cavalry Regiment, won a posthumous Medal of Honor near Loi-Kang, Burma.

February 3rd

Western Europe
1873　Hugh "Father of the Royal Air Force" Trenchard was born. He died on February 10, 1956.
1935　German aircraft manufacturer Hugo Junkers died.
1939　The Royal Navy anti/aircraft light cruiser NAIAD was launched. She was sunk on March 11, 1942.
1940　The Royal Air Force's No.43 Squadron shot down three Luftwaffe He111s that attacked a British convoy off the Yorkshire coast. The Royal Navy minesweeper SPHINX was damaged off the east coast of Scotland by the Luftwaffe and foundered the next day. Forty of her crew died. The British Air Ministry issued a contract to Gloster Aircraft for a jet interceptor. The first Royal Air Force officer to be decorated by the French government during the war, Flight/Lieutenant Robert Jeffe, was awarded the Croix de Guerre for shooting down a He111 on November 2nd.
1941　Eighteen Royal Air Force bombers dropped mines off the ports of Brest and Lorient in France.
1943　Sixty Royal Air Force "Venturas" attacked targets in France, Belgium and Holland and lost two aircraft. They were escorted by twenty-two "Spitfires" from the USAAF's 4th Fighter Group. Berlin announced the loss of Stalingrad and the beginning of three days of national mourning. Luftwaffe ace Reinhold Knacke (44 victories) was killed in action over Holland. 263 Royal Air Force bombers attacked Hamburg and lost sixteen aircraft. Fifty-five people were killed in the raid. Eight Royal Air Force

"Wellingtons" dropped mines off the Biscay ports and lost one aircraft. Twenty-five "Spitfires" from the USAAF's 4th Fighter Group attacked ground targets in France.

1944 609 8th Air Force B17s dropped 1,414 tons of bombs on Emden and Wilhelmshaven in Germany losing four bombers. The accommodation ship MONTE PASQUAL (13,870 tons) was sunk at Wilhelmshaven and the minesweepers M-18 and M-29 were severely damaged. 632 8th Air Force P38s, P47s and P51s provided support for the bombers and claimed eight victories for the loss of eight P47s and one P51. Fourteen Royal Air Force "Mosquitoes" attacked targets in Germany. Thirty-five Royal Air Force bombers dropped mines off the Atlantic coast. Seven B17s from the USAAF's 422nd Bomb Squadron dropped 420 bundles of leaflets near Paris, Rouen, Amiens, Reims, Orleans, and Rennes in France.

1945 1,370 8th Air Force bombers dropped 3,279 tons of bombs on Magdeburg and Berlin and lost twenty-three B17s and two B24s. Two of the lost bombers landed in Sweden. 885 8th Air Force fighters provided support for the bombers and claimed thirty-eight victories for the loss of seven P51s and one P47. Dr. Roland Freisler, who had presided over the trials of the July 20th conspirators, died when his courtroom was hit by a USAAF bomb. Thirty-six Royal Air Force "Lancasters" attacked installations in Holland that were suspected of harboring German midget submarines. French and American forces took Colmar. The US Army's 78th Division took Debdenborn. Technician/5th Class Forrest Peden, of the 3rd Division, won a posthumous Medal of Honor near Biesheim, Germany. 210 Royal Air Force bombers attacked Bottrop, Germany and lost eight "Lancasters". 149 Royal Air Force bombers attacked Dortmund, Germany and lost four "Lancasters". Sixty-two Royal Air Force "Mosquitoes" attacked targets in Germany.

1951 German industrialist Alfried Krupp was released from Landsberg Prison.

Eastern Europe

1943 The Soviets took Kushchevskaya and Kupyansk. The U255 sank the American freighter GREYLOCK (7,460 tons). U255 survived the war.

1944 Ten German divisions were surrounded south of Korsun.

1945 The Soviets took Landsberg and Bartenstein. The German torpedo recovery boat TFA-4 was sunk off Pillau by Soviet shore-fire.

Mediterranean

1941 The Italian 10th Army was destroyed at Beda-Fomm, Libya. British forces surrounded Benghazi, Libya.

1942 The American 12th Air Force lost one B26 and three P38s in an attack on Gabes, Tunisia. The DAK attacked Derna, Libya.

1943 At 0938, the Italian torpedo boat URAGANO hit a mine and sank at 1335. At 0950, the Italian destroyer SAETTA was sunk by a mine while attempting to assist the URAGANO.

1944 Private First Class Leo Powers, of the 34th Division, won a Medal of Honor northwest of Cassino. German forces attacked the British Army's 1st Division at Anzio. The American 15th Air Force attacked rail targets in Italy.

Atlantic

1940 The U58 sank the Estonian freighter REET (815 tons). U58 survived the war. The U25 sank the British freighter ARMINISTAN (6,805 tons). U25 was sunk on August 3, 1940.

1941 The German battlecruisers SCHARNHORST and GNEISENAU left the Skagerrak for the North Sea. The U107 sank the British freighters EMPIRE CITIZEN (4,683 tons) and CRISPIN (5,051 tons). U107 was sunk on August 18, 1944.

1942 The U106 sank the Swedish freighter AMERIKALAND (15,355 tons-27 died). U106 was sunk on August 2, 1943.

1943 The U456 sank the British tanker INVERILEN (9,456 tons). U456 was sunk on May 13, 1943. The U223 sank the American transport DORCHESTER (5,649 tons-675 dead). U223 survived until March 30, 1944. Four of the dead were Chaplains George Fox, Alexander Goode, Clark Poling and John Washington, who had given up their life jackets. The US Coast Guard cutter COMMANCHE rescued 132 survivors from the DORCHESTER, while the US Coast Guard cutter ESCANABE rescued another 132. The U217 sank the British freighter RHEXENOR (7,957 tons). U217 was sunk on June 5, 1943. The U632 sank the British tanker CORDELIA (8,190 tons). U632 was sunk on April 6, 1943. The U265 was sunk by the Royal Air Force's No.220 Squadron.

1944 The USN destroyer escort J.R.Y. BLAKELEY was damaged in a collision with the American freighter FRANKIN P. MALL.

1945 The U1279 was sunk by the Royal Navy frigates BAYNTUN, LOCH ECK and BRAITHWAITE.

North America

1884 Lieutenant General Frank Maxwell Andrews was born in Nashville, Tennessee. He would die in an accident while en route to assume command of the US Army Forces in Europe.

1942 The Soviet freighter DVINOLYES was lost in a collision off Cape Race. B25 "Mitchells" of the 17th Bombardment Group, located at Pendleton, Oregon, left for Eglin Field, Florida to begin training for the "Doolittle

	Raid". The 97th, 301st, and 303rd Heavy Bombardment Groups (B17) were activated. They would be among the first units of the new 8th Bomber Command in Britain. USN Chief of Naval Operations Admiral Ernest King rejected British suggestions that a unified command be set up for the Atlantic convoys.
1943	The first flight of the P51A "Mustang" took place.
1944	The escort carrier SAVO ISLAND was commissioned. She was scrapped in 1960.
1947	Admiral Marc Mitscher died in Norfolk, Virginia. He had commanded the USN carrier forces in the Pacific during the war.
1951	President Harry Truman dedicated a memorial to the 4 chaplains who had died aboard the transport DORCHESTER (See Atlantic-1943).

Pacific

1941	During exercises off Oahu, the destroyers DALE and HULL detect a suspected submarine. It was speculated that it may have landed agents. The area around Diamond Head was searched by the destroyer LAMSON.
1942	Japanese aircraft attacked Malang and Madioen on Java and Port Moresby on New Guinea. Based on a reconnaissance report by an Allied aircraft of a Japanese landing force off Balikpapan, an ABDA naval force commanded by Dutch Admiral Doorman left Madoera en route to the Makassar Strait. It consisted of the cruisers DE RUYTER (Dutch), HOUSTON (American), MARBLEHEAD (American), TROMP (Dutch), the American destroyers BARKER, BULMER, EDWARDS and STEWART and the Dutch destroyers BANCKERT, PIET HEIN and VAN GHENT. 1st Lieutenant Willibald Bianchi, of the Philippine Scouts, won a posthumous Medal of Honor on Bataan. The USN submarine TROUT arrived at Corregidor with ammunition supplies.
1943	The USN submarine AMBERJACK sank a Japanese schooner off Buka.
1944	The USN bombarded Paramushiro in the Kuriles. Two USN PB4Y "Liberators" took off from Stirling Island in the Solomons to photograph the Japanese installations at Truk in preparation for upcoming air attacks by USN carriers. Both aircraft returned safely to their base. The commander of the IJN at Truk realized that the recon flight was probably an indication that his ships would soon be attacked. He ordered his fleet to depart for safer waters. By the time the USN forces actually attacked Truk on the 16th, most of the major IJN units had left. USN Task Group 58.4 (commanded by Ginder) attacked Eniwetok. 5th Air Force B25s and PBYs attacked Japanese shipping off New Hanover and sank the freighter NICHIAI MARU. The USN submarine TAMBOR sank the GOYO MARU (8,469 tons) and the ARIAKE MARU (5,149 tons).

1945 The US Army's 1st Cavalry Division reached the suburbs of Manila. The 44th Tank Battalion, 1st Cavalry Division, liberated 3,768 Allied civilians at the Santo Tomas Concentration Camp in Manila. They had been held captive since the Japanese invasion in 1942. USAAF B24s attacked Corregidor and Cavite in the Philippines. The US Army's 40th Division landed on Masbate Island in the Philippines. The USN submarine SPADEFISH sank the TAIRAI MARU (4,273 tons).
1948 The USN destroyer TRIPPE was scuttled after the Bikini tests.

China-Burma-India
1941 The Japanese took Tam-shin, east of Canton.
1942 China and Britain agreed on the deployment of Chinese troops in Burma. The IJN submarine I-162 damaged the British tanker SPONDILUS (7,402 tons).
1943 The Indian 123rd Brigade failed in its attack on Rathedaung, Burma.
1945 The Japanese took Namyung, China.

February 4th

Western Europe
1906 German resistance member Pastor Dietrich Bonhoeffer was born in Breslau. He was imprisoned on April 5, 1943 for subversion. After the July 20, 1944 attempt on Hitler's life evidence connecting him to the conspiracy was uncovered. He was executed on April 9, 1945.
1933 Hitler issued a decree that the government could ban political meetings.
1941 Thirty Royal Air Force "Hampdens" attacked Dusseldorf, Germany and lost one aircraft. Thirty-eight Royal Air Force "Wellingtons" attacked the ports of Brest and Le Havre in France. Thirty-one Royal Air Force "Whitleys" attacked Bordeaux and Calais in France. Thirty-seven Royal Air Force "Blenheims" attacked Dunkirk in France and Ostend in Belgium. Six Royal Air Force "Hampdens" dropped mines off St. Nazaire, France and lost one aircraft.
1942 Lord Max Beaverbrook was appointed as Britain's Minister of War Production.
1943 All non-essential businesses were closed in Germany. Thirty-nine American 8th Air Force B17s from the 91st, 303rd and 306th Bomb Groups attacked Emden, Germany. They lost five aircraft. This action marked the first time that the American formations had been attacked by twin-engine Luftwaffe fighters. This was the last mission for Lieutenant William J. Crumm and his crew of the 91st Bombardment Group B17 "Jack the Ripper". They were sent back to America to help prepare an

aircrew manual. Crumm would die as a Major General in a B52 collision over Guam on July 7, 1967. 128 Royal Air Force bombers attacked Lorient, France and lost one "Wellington".

1944   633 8th Air Force B17s and B24s dropped 1,984 tons of bombs on the marshalling yards at Frankfurt, Germany and lost eighteen B17s and two B24s. A 453rd Bombardment Group B24H "Liberator" landed in France and was captured. 637 8th Air Force P38s, P47s and P51s provided support for the bombers and claimed eight victories for the loss of one P38. The American 15th Air Force attacked transportation targets near Toulon, France. Fifteen Royal Air Force "Mosquitoes" attacked targets in Germany. Forty-nine Royal Air Force bombers dropped supplies to Resistance forces on the Continent. Seven B17s from the USAAF's 422nd Bomb Squadron dropped 319 bundles of supplies to resistance forces near Lorient, Tours, Nantes, Raismes, Lille, Cambrai, and Antwerp.

1945   Allied Headquarters announced that Belgium had been secured. The American 9th Division reached the first of the Roer River dams. 238 Royal Air Force bombers attacked Bonn, Germany and lost thirteen "Lancasters". Nineteen people were killed in the raid. 123 Royal Air Force bombers attacked Osterfeld, Germany. 120 Royal Air Force bombers attacked Gelsenkirchen, Germany. Sixty-nine Royal Air Force "Mosquitoes" attacked targets in Germany and lost two aircraft. Free French ace Edmond Meslee (16 victories) was shot down and killed by German anti-aircraft fire while flying a P47 "Thunderbolt".

1972   The 91st Bombardment Group B17 "Shoo Shoo Shoo Baby" left Rhein-Main Airport in Germany aboard a USAF C5A "Galaxy" en route to the USAF Museum at Wright-Patterson, Ohio.

1987   The wreckage of a USAAF P38R, which had crashed near Mount Farm in Britain in 1944, was discovered.

Eastern Europe

1939   Cvetkovich replaced Stoyadinovitch as Premier of Yugoslavia.

1940   Members of the Balkan Entente (Rumania, Greece, Yugoslavia and Turkey) declared their neutrality.

1943   Soviet commandoes landed near Novorossisk on the Black Sea.

1944   The Soviets took Gdov. Moscow announced that the Leningrad-Novgorod Railway was secured.

1945   The "Yalta Conference" began.

1949   The Soviets returned the Royal Navy battleship ROYAL SOVEREIGN, which had served as the ARKHANGELSK since 1944.

Mediterranean

1941 British reinforcements began to arrive at Mechili.

1942 The British forced the abdication of Egyptian King Farouk.

1943 188 Royal Air Force bombers flying from Britain attacked Turin, Italy and lost three "Lancasters". Twenty-three people were killed in the raid. Four Royal Air Force "Lancasters" attacked La Spezia, Italy. British forces moved into Tunisia.

1944 The American forces were pushed back near Cassino, Italy. The German 14th Army (commanded by Mackensen) attacked the British Army's 1st Division at Campleone, near Anzio in Italy.

Atlantic

1940 The U37 sank the Norwegian freighter HOP (1,365 tons) and the British freighter LEO DAWSON (4,330 tons). U37 survived the war. The U21 sank the Yugoslavian freighter VID (3,547 tons). U21 survived the war.

1941 The U52 sank the Norwegian freighter RINGHORN (1,298 tons). U52 survived the war. The U93 sank the British freighter DIONE II (2,660 tons). U93 survived until January 15, 1942. The U123 sank the British freighter EMPIRE ENGINEER (5,358 tons). U123 survived the war.

1942 The U751 sank the British freighter SILVERAY (4,535 tons). U751 survived until July 17th. The U103 sank the Panamanian freighter SAN GIL (3,627 tons) and the American tanker INDIA ARROW (8,327 tons-26 dead). U103 survived until April 15, 1945. The British armed merchant cruiser ALCANTARA rescued three survivors from the American tanker W.L. STEED which had been sunk on February 2nd by U103.

1943 The U187 was sunk by the Royal Navy destroyers VIMY and BEVERLEY. The USN destroyer STEVENSON was damaged in a collision with the freighter BERWINDALE off Rhode Island.

1945 The U745 was lost due to unknown causes. The U1014 was sunk by the Royal Navy frigates LOCH SCAVAIG, LOCH SHIN, PAPUA and NYASALAND.

North America

1902 Charles Augustus Lindbergh was born in Detroit.

1939 The destroyers ANDERSON and HAMMANN were launched. The ANDERSON was expended as a target at Bikini in 1946 and the HAMMANN was sunk June 6, 1942 by the IJN submarine I-168.

1943 The destroyer KIMBERLEY was launched. She was sold to Taiwan in 1967.

1989 Walter Whitlow of Tucson, Arizona was awarded a Distinguished Service Cross for actions in WWII.

2013 USF ace Kenneth Jernstedt died in Wilsonville, Oregon at the age of 95. He had been credited with 5 aerial victories while flying P40s with the "Flying Tigers" in 1942. He was the returned to the States and became a test pilot for Republic Aviation for the remainder of the war.

2015 Retired Lieutenant Commander James Langdell died at the age of 100 in a rest home in Yuba City, California. He was the last surviving officer from the battleship ARIZONA's loss on December 7, 1941.

South America

1983 Klaus Barbie, the "Butcher of Lyon", was expelled from Bolivia. He had commanded the German S.S. forces in that city during the war. He was flown in a C-130 to Cayenne, French Guiana. From there he was taken to Lyon, France in a DC-8. He would stand trial for war crimes.

Pacific

1937 General Hayashi became Japan's Prime Minister.

1942 Just after 1000, fifty-four Japanese bombers attacked an Allied naval group north of Bali in the Java Sea. It had departed Madoera the previous evening to attack a reported Japanese landing force off Balikpapan. During the action, the USN light cruiser MARBLEHEAD was severely damaged by two direct hits and suffered thirteen dead and more than seventy wounded. The USN heavy cruiser HOUSTON was hit by a single bomb and lost forty men as well as her number three eight-inch turret. The force, commanded by Dutch Admiral Doorman, retreated to Madoera. The IJN submarine I-155 sank the Dutch freighter VAN LANSBERGE (1,937 tons) south of Makassar. The IJN submarine I-156 damaged the Dutch freighter TOGIAN (979 tons) off Koepang. Brigadier General Clinton Pierce became the first US Army general to be wounded in WWII when he was hit while on the Bataan Peninsula, Luzon. The USN submarine SEADRAGON evacuated select personnel from Corregidor in the Philippines. The Japanese took Amboina in the Moluccas.

1943 The US Army's 147th Regiment was slowed in its attack in the Tassafaronga area of Guadalcanal. 4,977 Japanese troops were evacuated from Guadalcanal. The "Cactus Air Force" attacked the IJN losing two SBDs, four TBFs, three F4Fs and one P40.

1944 USN Task Group 94.6 (commanded by Baker) consisting of the light cruisers OMAHA, RALEIGH and RICHMOND and the destroyers PICKING, SPROSTON, WICKES, YOUNG, BADGER, LUCE, and KIMBERLEY bombarded Paramushiro in the Kuriles. Kwajalein Atoll was secured by American forces. 4,938 Japanese and 177 Americans were killed in the battle. A Royal Australian Air Force PBY rescued five survivors of a ditched USAAF B24 south of Nauru. Admiral Chester Nimitz was named as military governor of the Marshall Islands.

1945 Sixty-nine B29s dropped 160 tons of bombs on Kobe and lost two aircraft. American forces reached the outskirts of Manila. The US Army's 1st Corps took San Jose, Luzon. USAAF B24s attacked Corregidor.

China-Burma-India

1942 The Japanese demanded the surrender of British-held Singapore.

1943 The American 10th Air Force attacked the Myitnge River Bridge in Burma.

1945 Japanese forces launched a major offensive in Burma. Chinese forces attacked the Hukawng Valley in Burma.

February 5th

Western Europe

1894 British Lieutenant General Frederick Morgan (COSSAC-Chief of Staff Supreme Allied Command) was born.

1940 The Allied Supreme War Council in Paris decided that in addition to sending an expeditionary force to Finland, they would also occupy the Swedish iron ore fields with forces landed at Narvik, Norway.

1941 The last Luftwaffe "Stuka" dive-bomber shot down over Britain was claimed by Sergeant R. Fokes, of the Royal Air Force's No.92 Squadron. A Luftwaffe Fw200 "Condor" crashed near Bantry, Eire. Hitler sent a medal and a citation to an Irish nurse who had pulled the sole survivor clear of the wreckage. German S-boats sank a 501-ton British freighter between Ipswich and Newcastle.

1943 Dutch General Hendrik Seyffardt was assassinated by the Dutch underground for collaboration. Nineteen Royal Air Force bombers dropped mines off Denmark and lost two "Stirlings". Eight "Spitfires" from the USAAFs 4th Fighter Group flew patrols over the Channel and lost one aircraft.

1944 452 8th Air Force B17s and B24s dropped 1,313 tons of bombs on airfields in France and lost two B24s. Luftwaffe ace Egon Mayer (102 aerial victories) was killed in action by USAAF P47s. The 452nd Bombardment Group (B17) and the 453rd (B24) flew their first 8th Air Force missions. 634 8th Air Force P47s, P38s and P51s provided support for the bombers and claimed six victories for the loss of two P47s. Twenty-six Royal Air Force "Mosquitoes" attacked targets in Germany. Forty-six Royal Air Force bombers dropped supplies to Resistance forces and lost one "Stirling". Five B17s from the USAAF's 422nd Bomb Squadron dropped 300 bundles of leaflets near Ghent, Monceau-sur-Sambre, Antwerp and Brussels in Belgium.

1945   A German force near Colmar was attacked by French and American units. 589 American 15th Air Force bombers dropped 1,100 tons of bombs on Regensburg, Germany. Seventy-six Royal Air Force "Mosquitoes" attacked targets in Germany and lost one aircraft. Eight German "Seehund" two-man submarines unsuccessfully attempted to attack Allied shipping in the English Channel.

1948   Wehrmacht General Johannes Blaskowitz, commander of Army Group "G", committed suicide while he was being held in Nuremburg prison.

2010   Peter Calvocoressi died at the age of 97. He had served as the head of the Bletchley Park codebreakers who cracked Germany's Enigma code during World War II.

Eastern Europe

1932   Latvia and Russia signed a non-aggression pact.
1942   The Soviets took Izyum.
1943   Soviet forces reached the Donets River and took Izyum.
1944   The Soviets took Rovno and Lutsk. Soviet forces began an offensive that would get them within fifty miles of the "Curzon Line" where the Germans had begun their "Operation Barbarossa" in June 1941.
1945   Soviet forces were within fifty miles of Berlin. The U992 sank the Soviet minesweeper TSC-16 (the ex-USN-ARCADE). The German gun carrier POLARIS and the patrol boat UJ-307 were sunk by Soviet aircraft off Pillau.

Mediterranean

1935   Italy began mobilization.
1941   British forces captured 5,000 Italians in North Africa. The steamers AGIOS GEORGIUS and RANEE were sunk in the Suez Canal by Luftwaffe-laid mines.
1943   Mussolini dismissed Ciano as his Foreign Minister. The U617 sank the Norwegian freighters HENRIK (1,350 tons) and CORONA (3,264 tons).
1945   Greek Communists (E.L.A.S.) and the Greek government agreed to amnesty terms.
1946   The American freighter NATHAN HALE was a constructive loss after hitting a mine off Gorgona, Italy.

Atlantic

1940   The U41 sank the British freighter BEAVERBURN (9,874 tons) and damaged the Norwegian tanker CERONIA (8,096 tons). U41 was then sunk by the Royal Navy destroyer ANTELOPE.
1942   The U109 sank the Canadian tanker MONTROLITE (11,309 tons). U109 was sunk on May 4, 1943. The U103 sank the American tankers INDIA ARROW (8,327 tons) and CHINA ARROW (8,403 tons). U103 survived

until April 15, 1945. At 2135, the Royal Navy corvette ARBUTUS was sunk south of Iceland by the U136. U136 was sunk on July 11th. The USN destroyer BERNADOU rescued ten survivors from the Belgian freighter GANDIA which had been sunk on January 22nd by U135.
1943 The U413 sank the American freighter WEST PORTAL (5,376 tons) with all hands. U413 was sunk on August 20, 1944.
1944 The Royal Navy escort carrier SLINGER was damaged by a mine and was out of action for 8.5 months.
1945 The U245 sank the American freighter HENRY B. PLANT (7,240 tons-916 dead). U245 survived the war.

North America
1919 8th Air Force ace George Preddy (26 aerial victories) was born in Greensboro, North Carolina.
1940 The Boeing Aircraft Company's President Philip Johnson received the specifications for what would become the company's Model 341 (the B29 "Superfortress").
1942 The Alaskan Air Force became the American 11th Air Force.
1944 The destroyer CASSIN was recommissioned having been rebuilt to repair severe damage suffered in the Japanese attack on Pearl Harbor on December 7, 1941.
1945 The Panamanian freighter CLIO and the American tanker SPRING HILL collided in New York Harbor. Eighteen crewmen died.

South America
1944 Argentina broke relations with Vichy France, Bulgaria, Hungary, and Rumania.

Pacific
1942 Japanese aircraft destroyed five P40s at Den Passar, Bali. The USN submarine SEADRAGON evacuated code experts from Corregidor in the Philippines. The Hawaiian Air Force became the American 7th Air Force. The Far East Air Force became the American 5th Air Force.
1943 The Japanese Imperial Headquarters ordered that the islands of Kiska and Attu in the Aleutians be held at all costs. 5th Air Force B24s sank the Japanese freighters HOSHIKAWA MARU and SHUNKO MARU in the Solomons.
1944 The IJN battleship ISE was damaged off Indo-China by a mine. The American freighter JOHN EVANS was hit by a kamikaze off Luzon. The US Army's 2nd Cavalry Brigade captured the Balera water plant near Manila. Technical/Sergeant Donald Rudolph, of the 6th Division, won a Medal of Honor on Luzon. 2nd Lieutenant Robert Viale, of the 37th

1945   Division, won a posthumous Medal of Honor in Manila. Australian forces landed on New Britain. USAAF B25s sank the FATSUMI MARU off Wewak, New Guinea.
1945   USAAF B24s attacked Corregidor. The "Lil' Audrey" became the first 7th Air Force B24 to complete 100 missions when she returned from a raid on Iwo Jima.

China-Burma-India
1932   The Japanese occupied Hardin, China.
1942   The RMS EMPRESS OF ASIA was sunk in Singapore by the Japanese Naval Air Force. Japanese artillery began bombarding Singapoe Island.
1943   The American 10th Air Force attacked the Myitnge River Bridge in Burma.
1944   14th Air Force B24s and B25s sank the IJN gunboat ROZAN MARU and the freighters LUSHAN MARU and SEIKYO MARU off Swatow, China.
1945   The American freighter PETER SILVESTER was sunk in the Indian Ocean by the U862.

February 6th

Western Europe
1934   Six people were killed during right-wing riots in Paris.
1937   The German heavy cruiser ADMIRAL HIPPER was launched. She was scrapped in 1946.
1940   The German freighter KONSUL HORN arrived in Norwegian waters having evaded British forces off Aruba on January 7th. The German armed merchant cruiser PINGUIN was commissioned. General Erwin Rommel assumed command of the German 7th Panzer Division.
1941   Forty-nine Royal Air Force bombers attacked the ports of Boulogne and Dunkirk in France and lost one "Wellington". Hitler issued a directive for an economic war against Britain. Hitler met with Erwin Rommel, who was to assume command of the Deutches Afrika Korps. At its peak, the DAK would consist of three German divisions, the 5th, 15th Panzer and 90th, as well as the Italian Ariete, Trieste, Pavia, Bologna, Brescia, and Savona divisions. Forty-six Royal Air Force bombers dropped mines in the Baltic and lost one "Hampden". Sixty Royal Air Force bombers attacked the port of Brest, France and lost one "Wellington".
1943   USAAF General William Andrews was appointed as commander of the American Forces in Europe. He would die in an aircraft accident en route to his new assignment. Seventy-two Royal Air Force bombers dropped mines on the Atlantic coast and lost three "Wellingtons". Six "Spitfires" from the USAAF's 4th Fighter Group flew patrols over the Channel.

1944   206 American 8th Air Force B17s and B24s dropped 604 tons of bombs on French airfields and lost four B17s. 638 8th Air Force fighters provided support for the bombers and claimed eleven victories for the loss of three P38s and one P47. The German minesweeper M-156 was sunk at Abervrach, France by Royal Air Force "Typhoons".

1945   The American 3rd Army took Habscheid, Germany. Sixty 8th Air Force B17s dropped 167 tons of bombs on Giessen, Germany. 1,242 8th Air Force bombers dropped 2,508 tons of bombs on oil targets in Germany and lost three B17s and two B24s. 829 8th Air Force fighters provided escort for the bombers and claimed four victories for the loss of four P51s. Twelve Royal Air Force "Spitfires" attacked V-2 rocket launching sites at Hellendoorn, Holland. American forces cleared the last German forces from the Monschau Forest.

1948   German General Otto von Stuelpnagel, Military Governor of Occupied France, committed suicide while awaiting trial at the Cherche-Midi Prison in Paris.

1975   Royal Air Force Air Chief Marshal Keith Parker died.

Eastern Europe

1943   The Soviets took Yeysk on the Sea of Azov.

1944   The Soviets took Apostolovo and Manganets. Five German divisions were surrounded near Nikopol.

1945   Soviet forces crossed the Oder River southeast of Breslau.

Mediterranean

1941   Australian troops entered Benghazi, Libya.

1943   At 1925, the Royal Canadian Navy corvette LOUISBURG was sunk off Oran by the Luftwaffe. Fifty members of her crew survived. She was the first Royal Canadian Navy warship to be lost to air-attack in the Mediterranean. The North African Theater of Operations, commanded by Lieutenant General Dwight Eisenhower, was established.

1944   The Allies retreated along the Cassino Front.

1945   The German MTBs S-36 and S-61 were constructive losses after they collided off Pola.

1968   The USN destroyer BACHE was wrecked off Rhodes. She was later salvaged and scuttled.

Atlantic

1940   A mine laid by the U13 sank the Estonian freighter ANU (1,421 tons). U13 survived until May 31st.

1941   The U107 sank the Canadian freighter MAPLECOURT (3,388 tons). U107 survived until August 18, 1944.

1942   The U109 sank the Panamanian freighter HALCYON (3,531 tons). U109 survived until May 4, 1943. The U106 sank the British freighter OPAWA (10,354 tons). U106 survived until August 2, 1943. The U82 was sunk by the Royal Navy sloop ROCHESTER and corvette TAMARISK off the Azores. The US Coast Guard cutter NIKE rescued 38 survivors from the tanker CHINA ARROW. The British freighter HARTLEPOOL rescued two survivors from the American tanker W.L. STEED which had been sunk on February 2nd by U103. The U107 sank the American freighter MAJOR WHEELER (3,431 tons) with all hands. U107 survived until August 18, 1944.

1943   The U266 sank the Greek freighter POLYKTOR (4,077 tons). U266 survived until May 14th. The U262 sank the Polish freighter ZAGLOBA (2,864 tons). U262 survived the war.

1944   The U177 was sunk by USN VB-107.

1945   The American freighter JAMES OTIS was a constructive loss after running aground off Devon, Britain. The U1017 sank the British freighter EVERLEIGH (5,222 tons). U1017 survived until April 29th.

North America

1940   The first flight of the AT-6 "Texan" training aircraft took place.

1942   The first meeting of the Combined Chiefs of Staff took place.

1943   The destroyer DASHIELL was launched. She was stricken in December 1974.

1944   The anti/aircraft light cruiser ATLANTA (awarded two battle stars during the war) was christened by Margaret Mitchell, the author of "Gone with the Wind". She had christened the first ATLANTA three years earlier. The second ATLANTA was destroyed in explosives experiments off Florida in 1966. The destroyer LOWRY was launched. She was sold to Brazil in 1973.

1969   The USN submarine REDFISH was expended as a target. She had appeared in the 1954 movie "20,000 Leagues under the Sea" as well as "Run Silent Run Deep".

Pacific

1942   The Japanese landed reinforcements on Luzon. Japanese forces took Samarinda, Borneo. American-held Fort Drum, in Manila Bay, received its baptism of Japanese fire when the "Kondo Detachment" hit it with 105mm shells. The USN submarine SEAWOLF arrived at Surabaya, Java with twenty-five Corregidor evacuees (twelve US Army officers, eleven USN pilots, a USN yeoman and a British Army Major) aboard.

1943   The US Army's 161st Regiment reached the Umasani River on Guadalcanal. Japanese aircraft attacked the Allied airfield at Wau, New Guinea. Flight/

	Lieutenant R. Foster scored the first "Spitfire" victory in the Pacific Theater of Operations when he shot down a Japanese Ki46 "Dinah" recon aircraft off Cape Van Diemen, Australia. A 5th Air Force B24 sank the Japanese freighter GISHO MARU off New Britain. The IJN tanker NAGISAN MARU was damaged by the USN submarine FLYING FISH.
1944	USAAF A20s and P40s sank the Japanese ships KAIYO MARU and TAKEGIKU off Wewak, New Guinea.
1945	4,000 Allied prisoners of war were released from Manila prisons. USAAF B24s attacked Corregidor in Manila Bay. The USN submarine SPADEFISH sank the SHOHEI MARU (1,092 tons). The USN submarine POMPANITO sank the ENGEN MARU (6,890 tons).
1961	The Royal Canadian Navy light cruiser UGANDA arrived in Osaka, Japan to be scrapped.

China-Burma-India

1942	The American Volunteer Group and the Royal Air Force shot down ten Japanese aircraft over Rangoon, Burma. Japanese forces began advancing in Burma. Japanese aircraft began heavy attacks against refugee ships fleeing from Singapore.
1944	The British began retreating along the Arakan Front.
1945	The U862 sank the American freighter PETER SYLVESTER (7,176 tons-32 dead).

February 7th

Western Europe

1885	Luftwaffe Field Marshal Hugo Sperrle was born in Ludwigsburg. He would command Air Fleet 3 during the war.
1912	Eva Braun was born in Munich. She would marry Hitler on April 29, 1945 and commit suicide with him some 36 hours later.
1939	Ribbentrop declared that Germany would "...never come to an understanding with Bolshevist Russia".
1940	The freighter MUNSTER (4,305 tons) was sunk in Liverpool Bay by a mine laid by the U30.
1941	Sixty-four Royal Air Force bombers attacked the French ports of Boulogne and Dunkirk.
1942	The German Minister of Munitions, Fritz Todt, was killed in a plane crash. He would be replaced by Albert Speer. Thirty-two Royal Air Force "Hampdens" dropped mines in the Baltic and lost three aircraft.
1943	323 Royal Air Force bombers attacked the port of Lorient, France and lost seven aircraft.

1944 Thirty-five Royal Air Force "Mosquitoes" attacked targets in Germany. Six B17s from the USAAF's 422nd Bomb Squadron dropped 363 bundles of supplies to resistance forces near Brussels, Antwerp, Ghent, Liege, Monceau-sur-Sambre.
1945 The Germans blew up the Schwammenaul Dam flood gates. The Belgian government resigned in protest of the return of the Belgian King. Due to Bad weather only one of 295 8th Air Force bombers dispatched to Essen, Germany, only one aircraft managed to drop its bombs on the target. Seventy-five Royal Air Force "Lancasters" attacked Wanne-Eickel and lost one aircraft. The American 15th Air Force attacked refineries near Vienna, Austria. 464 Royal Air Force bombers attacked Goch and lost two "Halifaxes". 305 Royal Air Force bombers attacked Kleve and lost one "Lancaster". 188 Royal Air Force bombers attacked the Dortmund-Ems Canal and lost three "Lancasters". Ninety-five Royal Air Force "Mosquitoes" attacked targets in Germany and lost four aircraft.
1952 Britain's King George VI died of cancer.
1981 Hermann Esser, co-founder of the Nazi Party, died at age 80.

Eastern Europe
1943 Soviet forces took Azov.
1945 The Soviets took the southern rail station in Budapest, Hungary.
1977 Soviet aircraft designer Sergei Ilyushin, age 83, died.

Mediterranean
1941 British forces captured 25,000 Italians (including Generals Cona and Babini). Six Royal Air Force "Hurricanes" were sent to Greece. Several "Gladiators" had already been sent.
1943 The American 12th Air Force attacked Sardinian airfields. The U596 sank the Royal Navy LCI-162. The U77 sank the British freighters EMPIRE WEBSTER (7,043 tons) and EMPIRE BANNER (6,699 tons). The Italian submarine ACCIAIO sank the Royal Navy trawler TERVANI (409 tons).
1944 At 0900, the German 14th Army (commanded by Mackensen) attacked the British forces at Aprilia, near Anzio. Two days later, the Germans succeeded in taking the town.
1945 The American 15th Air Force attacked Vienna, Austria.

Atlantic
1942 The Royal Navy catapult-armed merchantman EMPIRE SUN (6,953 tons) was sunk by the U751. U751 survived until July 17th.
1943 The U402 sank the British freighters TOWARD (1,571 tons) and AFRIKA (8,597 tons), the American tanker ROBERT E. HOPKINS (6,625 tons-15 dead) and transport HENRY S. MALLORY (6,063 tons-86 dead) and the

Greek freighter KALLIOPI (4,965 tons) off Greenland. U402 survived until October 13th. The US Coast Guard cutter BIBBS rescued 202 survivors from MALLORY and thirty-three from the KALLIOPI. The US Coast Guard cutter INGHAM rescued thirty-three survivors from the HENRY S. MALLORY, ROBERT E. HOPKINS and WEST PORTAL. The US Coast Guard cutter ICARUS rescued twenty-two survivors from five different ships. The U614 sank the British freighter HARMALA (5,730 tons). U614 survived until July 29th. The U609 was sunk by the French corvette LOBELLIA. The U624 was sunk by the Royal Air Force's No.220 Squadron. The British freighters BALTONIA (2,013 tons), MARY SLESSOR (5,027 tons) and EMPIRE MORDRED (7,024 tons) were sunk by mines.

1944 Schnorkel-equipped German U-boats began operating in the Atlantic. The schnorkel was a device developed before the war by the Dutch that permitted submarines to operate their diesel engines while submerged rather than depending on their less effective electric auxiliaries.

North America

1886 USAAF Lieutenant General George Brett, commander of the Far East Air Force in 1942 and the Caribbean Defense Command in 1944, was born in Cleveland, Ohio. He also briefly commanded the Allied Air Forces in the Southwest Pacific until he was sent home by General Douglas MacArthur, the Theater Commander. He died in 1963.

1941 US Army Chief of Staff General George Marshall sent a letter to General Walter Short, the Army Commander, in Hawaii stating that "the risk of sabotage and the risk involved in a surprise air and submarine attack constitute the real perils of the situation". The 1941 class at Annapolis was graduated four months early due to the national emergency.

1942 FDR approved $500 million in aid for China.

1943 Shoes were rationed in America.

1944 The carrier TICONDEROGA was launched. She was still on active duty in 1972. The light cruiser BIRMINGHAM was damaged in a collision with the steamer MANUKAI off San Francisco.

1945 A Japanese balloon-bomb was found near Provost, Alberta.

1946 The destroyer-minelayer TRACY was sold for scrap.

1948 General Dwight Eisenhower retired as US Army Chief of Staff and was replaced by General Omar Bradley.

Pacific

1932 During a training exercise, the USN carriers SARATOGA and LEXINGTON successfully attacked Pearl Harbor. The action took place on a Sunday morning.

1942 Allied forces counter-attacked on Bataan Peninsula in the Philippines. The IJN submarine I-155 sank the Dutch freighter VAN CLOON (4,519 tons) off Java. The USN yacht ISABEL rescued all 187 survivors from the VAN CLOON. A seaplane from the Japanese submarine I-25 flew over Sydney, Australia. The Japanese submarines Ro-61 and Ro-62 were damaged in a collision of Kwajalein.

1943 2,639 Japanese troops were evacuated from Guadalcanal. The fact that the main Japanese force was no longer on the island was not discovered until the Americans arrived at Cape Esperance on the 9th at the conclusion of their last offensive. USN Commander Howard Gilmore, commander of the submarine GROWLER, won a posthumous Medal of Honor on her fourth war patrol. A USAAF B17 damaged the USN submarine SWORDFISH north of New Ireland.

1944 The last of the smaller Japanese-held islands in the Kwajalein Atoll surrendered. The USN submarine NARWHAL landed supplies on Negros in the Philippines and evacuated 28 people. The USN escort carrier WHITE PLAINS and the destroyer CALDWELL were damaged in a collision in the Marshalls.

1945 The IJN submarine Ro-55 was sunk by the USN destroyer escort THOMASON. The USN submarine GUAVINA sank the TAIGYO MARU (6,892 tons). The IJN escort CD-53 was sunk by the USN submarine BERGALL. The USN submarine PARCHE sank the OKINOYAMA MARU (984 tons). The USN submarine POMPANITO sank the EIFUKU MARU (3,520 tons). The USN PTs-373 and 356 entered Manila Bay on a night patrol. They were the first USN vessels to enter the Bay since 1942. Master/Sergeant Charles McGaha won a Medal of Honor on Luzon. USAAF A20 bombers attacked Corregidor in the Philippines. The US Army's 40th Division landed on Masbate in the Philippines. Royal Australian Air Force PBYs mined Surabaya, Java.

China-Burma-India

1942 Japanese forces made a landing on the eastern side of Singapore. British General Percival declared that Singapore would never surrender. Robert Sandell, one of the first American Volunteer Group aces, was killed in a crash.

1944 The American 10th Air Force destroyed the Ye Bridge in Thailand.

1945 The Japanese took the American 14th Air Force base at Kanchow, China.

February 8th

Western Europe

1937   Spanish Nationalists took Malaga, Spain.

1941   Eleven Royal Air Force bombers attacked targets in Germany and Holland. Fifteen Royal Air Force "Hampdens" attacked Mannheim, Germany.

1942   Albert Speer was named as Germany's Minister of Munitions. He replaced Fritz Todt who had been killed in a plane crash the previous day.

1943   German Admiral Karl Doenitz had his first conference with Hitler since assuming command of the Navy from Admiral Erich Raeder on January 30th. Six Royal Air Force "Lancasters" dropped mines in the Baltic.

1944   110 American 8th Air Force B24s dropped 363 tons of bombs on V-1 rocket installations at Watten and Siracourt in France. 89 8th Air Force P47s provided support for the bombers. 195 8th Air Force B17s dropped 485 tons of bombs on the marshalling yards at Frankfurt, Germany and lost thirteen bombers. 253 8th Air Force fighters provided support for the bombers and claimed sixteen victories for the loss of two P38s, three P47s and four P51s. The American 9th Air Force dispatched two raids on the same day for the first time since moving to Britain from the Mediterranean. Twelve Royal Air Force "Lancasters" of No.617 Squadron attacked the Gnome and Rhone aircraft engine factory. The target was severely damaged and no aircraft were lost. Six B17s from the USAAF's 422nd Bomb Squadron dropped 360 bundles of leaflets near Caen, Rouen, Paris, Rennes, and Amiens in France.

1945   The US Army's V Corps took Schmidt, Germany. 414 8th Air Force bombers were recalled after take-off due to bad weather. 109 8th Air Force fighters attacked rail traffic in Germany and claimed one aerial victory. The American 15th Air Force attacked rail targets in Austria. Fifteen Royal Air Force "Lancasters" attacked U-boat installations at Ijmuiden, Holland. 452 Royal Air Force bombers attacked Politz and lost twelve "Lancasters". 228 Royal Air Force bombers attacked Wanne-Eickel and lost two "Halifaxes". 151 Royal Air Force bombers attacked Krefeld and lost two "Lancasters". Forty-seven Royal Air Force "Mosquitoes" attacked Berlin. British civilian casualties up to this time in the war totalled 57,468 dead and 79,178 wounded.

Eastern Europe

1932   Bulgaria announced that it would make no more WWI reparation payments.

1941   Germany and Bulgaria agreed on arrangements for moving German troops into Bulgaria.

1942   90,000 German troops were surrounded near Demyansk.
1943   The Soviets took Kursk.
1944   The Soviets took Nikopol.
1945   The Soviets began an offensive near the Oder River.

Mediterranean
1941   The first German troops to be sent to North Africa, the 5th Panzer Regiment, left Naples for North Africa. The Royal Navy stopped the Japanese merchantship YAMFUJI MARU in the Persian Gulf and confiscated the mail that she was carrying.
1942   The American 12th Air Force lost six B25s and one P38 over Gabes, Tunisia.
1943   Major General James Doolittle, commander of the American 12th Air Force, flew a B26 on a raid to Sicily. The Italian submarine AVORIO was sunk by the Royal Canadian Navy REGINA.
1944   Major H. Sidney, of the Grenadier Guards, won a Victoria Cross in Italy. Corporal Paul Huff, of the 509th Parachute Battalion, won a Medal of Honor near Carano, Italy. 2nd Lieutenant Paul Riordan, of the 34th Division, won a posthumous Medal of Honor near Cassino, Italy. The American 15th Air Force attacked rail targets in Italy.
1945   The Italian "Fruili" Combat Group replaced the Polish "Kresowa" Division in action with the British 8th Army.

Atlantic
1941   The German battlecruisers SCHARNHORST and GNEISENAU approached convoy HX-106, but turned away when they sighted the Royal Navy battleship RAMILLIES acting as escort.
1942   At 2330, the French corvette ALYSSE was torpedoed by the U654. She foundered on the 10th. U654 survived until August 22nd. The U108 sank the British freighter OCEAN VENTURE (7174 tons). U108 survived until July 17, 1944.
1943   The U160 sank the American freighter ROGER B. TANEY (7,191 tons-3 dead). U160 survived until July 14th. The U608 sank the British tanker DAGHILD (9,272 tons) and LCT-2335, which was being carried as deck cargo. U608 survived until August 19, 1944. The U521 sank the Royal Navy trawler BREDON (750 tons). U521 survived until June 2nd. The U402 sank the British freighter NEWTON ASH (4,625 tons). U402 survived until October 13th. The Swiss freighter CARITASI rescued 14 survivors from the American freighter CHARLES E. PINCKNEY which had been sunk on January 28th by U514.
1944   The U985 sank the British freighter MARGIT (1,735 tons). U985 survived until November 15th. The U762 was sunk by the Royal Navy sloops WILD

GOOSE and WOODPECKER. The USN light cruiser MARBLEHEAD rescued survivors from the U177 which had been sunk on February 6th by a USN PB4Y.

North America

1941   The American House of Representatives passed the Lend-Lease bill by a vote of 260 to 165. This act would permit America to "loan" military supplies and equipment to countries actively fighting the Axis.

1944   The PT-boat tender CYRENE was launched. Comedian Don Rickles would serve aboard her in the Philippines.

1945   Japanese balloon-bombs were found near Camp Beale, California and Newcastle, Wyoming.

1959   William "Wild Bill" Donovan (founder of the O.S.S.-Office of Strategic Services) died in Washington D.C.

South America

1945   Paraguay declared war on the Axis.

Pacific

1942   The IJN submarine I-69 shelled American installations on Midway. The IJN destroyer NATSUSHIO was sunk off Macassar by the USN submarine S-37. Japanese General Masaharu Homma discontinued his attacks on the Allied forces located on the Bataan Peninsula. The steamer MORINDA arrived at Tulagi. She was to be the last chance of escape for the residents of the area before the Japanese forces arrived. Eight USAAF B17s attempted to attack the Japanese airfield at Kendari, Celebes, losing two aircraft.

1943   The USN submarine TUNNY sank the KUSUYAMA MARU (5,306 tons). The USN submarine TARPON sank the TATSUTA MARU (16,975 tons). The IJN submarine I-21 sank the British freighter IRON KNIGHT (4,812 tons).

1944   The USN submarine SNOOK sank the LIMA MARU (6,989 tons) and damaged the SHIRANESAN MARU (4,793 tons).

1945   The US Army's 1st Cavalry and 37th Infantry Divisions began attacks on the city of Manila.

China-Burma-India

1942   Three Japanese divisions commanded by Tomotuki Yamashita landed on Singapore Island.

1943   Orde Wingate's Chindits made their first raid in Burma.

February 9th

Western Europe
- **1933** The Oxford Union, a student group at Oxford University, passed a resolution stating that it would not fight "...for King or Country".
- **1938** Hitler invited Austrian Chancellor Kurt Schuschnigg to Berchtesgaden.
- **1940** German General Erich von Manstein was named as commander the 38th Corps. The freighter CHARGRES (5,406 tons) was sunk in Liverpool Bay by a mine that had been laid by the U30.
- **1941** Twenty-three Royal Air Force "Hampdens" attacked Wilhelmshaven, Germany.
- **1943** Twenty-one Royal Air Force bombers dropped mines along Frances Atlantic coast.
- **1944** Thirty-six American 9th Air Force B26s attacked railyards at Tergnier, France. Sixteen Royal Air Force "Mosquitoes" attacked targets in Germany and lost one aircraft.
- **1945** Allied forces eliminated the last of the German forces "Colmar Pocket" in France. The US Army's 78th Division reached the Schwammenaul Dam. Twenty-five 8th Air Force B17s dropped sixty tons of bombs on Giessen's railyards. 1,175 8th Air Force bombers dropped 2,905 tons of bombs on oil targets in Germany and lost three B24s and five B17s. 809 8th Air Force fighters provided escort for the bombers and claimed fifty-one victories for the loss of five P51s. Luftwaffe ace Rudi Linz (70 victories) was killed in action over Kristiansund, Norway by Royal Air Force Flight/Lieutenant James Butler, of No.65 Squadron (P51). The American 15th Air Force attacked oil refineries around Vienna. The KG200-flown B17F "Down and Go" (See July 29, 1943) exploded on take-off with ten Vichy officials and agents aboard, two of the nineteen aboard survived.
- **1996** Luftwaffe ace Adolf Galland died at the age of 83. He had scored 104 aerial victories and had served as General of Fighters during the war.

Eastern Europe
- **1943** The Soviets took Byelgorod, north of Kharkov.

Mediterranean
- **1941** British forces took El Agheila, Libya. The Royal Navy battleship MALAYA, the battlecruiser RENOWN and the heavy cruiser SHEFFIELD shelled the port of Genoa, sinking five ships. Royal Navy carrier ARK ROYAL aircraft mined La Spezia Harbor and attacked Pisa and Leghorn.
- **1942** Italian aircraft attacked Alexandria, Egypt. The Royal Navy destroyer FARNDALE was damaged west of Mersa Matruh by a "Stuka" dive-bomber.

1943   The U81 sank the Egyptian sailing ship EL KASSBANA (110 tons). The Italian submarine MALACHITE was sunk by the Dutch submarine DOLFIN. The Royal Navy corvette ERICA was sunk off Benghazi, Libya by a Royal Navy mine. All seventy-one members of her crew survived. Major General James H. Doolittle, commander of the American 12th Air Force, flew a 301st Bombardment Group B17 on a combat mission.

Atlantic
1941   The U37 sank the British freighters COURLAND (1,325 tons) and ESTRELLANO (1,983 tons). U37 survived the war.
1942   The U108 sank the Norwegian freighter TOLOSA (1,974 tons) off the American coast. U108 survived until July 17, 1944. The U85 sank the British freighter EMPIRE FUSILIER (5,408 tons). U85 survived until April 14th. The USN destroyer ROE rescued fourteen survivors from the British freighter OCEAN VENTURE which had been sunk the day before by U108.
1943   The USN destroyer BOYLE rescued 54 survivors from the PAN ROYAL which had been rammed and sunk by the freighters EVITA and GEORGE DAVIS while in convoy UGS-5. Eight of her crew died in the accident.
1944   The U238 was sunk by the Royal Navy sloops KITE, MAGPIE and STARLING southwest of Ireland. The U734 was sunk southwest of Ireland by the Royal Navy sloops STARLING and WILD GOOSE.
1945   The U864 was sunk west of Bergen by the Royal Navy submarine VENTURER. The Norwegian Navy discovered the wreck in March of 2003. Two years later divers recovered a cylinder of mercury. Further research revealed that U864's cargo included 1,857 cylinders containing nearly 65 tons of the chemical and that some of them were leaking. As of 2007 it had still not been resolved how to handle the situation.

North America
1940   FDR sent Under Secretary of State Sumner Welles to Europe to investigate the prospects of peace.
1941   The USN's "Helldiver" dive-bomber proto-type crashed.
1942   The French liner NORMANDIE caught fire during conversion into a transport at New York City and eventually capsized.
1943   The destroyer HAGGARD was launched. She was scrapped in 1946.
1944   The destroyer COOPER was launched. She was lost December 3, 1944.
1945   A Japanese balloon-bomb was found near Lodge Grass, Montana.
1960   The destroyer HALL was sold to Greece.
1966   The US Coast Guard cutter NEMISIS was sold.

Pacific

1932   Former Japanese Finance Minister Junnosuki Inouye was assassinated in Tokyo.

1942   The USN submarine TROUT, with ten tons of Philippine gold and silver aboard, sank the CHUWA MARU (2,719 tons) and the KURAMA MARU (6,788 tons) off Formosa. TROUT was carrying the precious metals to Pearl Harbor to prevent their capture by the invading Japanese forces. The IJN submarine I-165 sank the Dutch freighter MEROENDOENG (2,464 tons). Japanese forces took Makassar on Celebes. The IJN carrier KAGA ran aground off Palau. Japanese aircraft attacked targets in Java.

1943   Organized Japanese resistance on Guadalcanal ended at 1625 when the US Army's 161st and 132nd Regiments met at Tenaro. 2,000 Japanese soldiers were evacuated from Guadalcanal. The USN submarine GUDGEON rescued twenty-eight people from Timor.

1944   The USN submarine POGY sank the IJN destroyer MINEKAZE and the MALTA MARU (5,499 tons). The USN submarine SPEARFISH sank the TATSUWA MARU (6,345 tons).

1945   Private First Class Joseph Cicchetti (posthumous), Private First-Class John Reese (posthumous) and Private Cleto Rodriguez, of the 37th Division, won Medals of Honor in Manila. The IJN submarine I-41 was sunk by the USN submarine BATFISH.

China-Burma-India

1942   The Japanese 55th Division crossed the Salween River in Burma and cut off the town of Martaban. Chiang Kai-shek began a visit to India. The Japanese took Tengan Airfield on Singapore Island. The Royal Navy survey ship HERALD was scuttled at Singapore. She was later salvaged by the Japanese and recommissioned as the HEIYO (See November 14, 1944).

1944   The U188 sank the Norwegian freighter VIVA (3,798 tons).

1945   British secured Ramree Island off Burma. The IJN escort No.61 was a constructive loss after hitting a mine off Saigon. The American freighter CAPE EDMONT rescued survivors from the American freighter PETER SILVESTER which had been sunk on February 6th by U862.

February 10th

Western Europe

1894   Future British Prime Minister Harold MacMillan was born.

1936   Heinrich Himmler was given absolute authority over Germany's internal security and his Gestapo was placed above the law.

1941   Six Royal Air Force "Blenheims" attacked Dunkirk, France. Britain broke relations with Rumania. 222 Royal Air Force bombers attacked Hannover, Germany and lost seven aircraft. Forty-three Royal Air Force bombers attacked Rotterdam, Holland. The Rotterdam attack force included three "Stirlings" on the type's first operations. Since October 13th, the Royal Air Force's Bomber Command had flown 6,597 sorties on which it had dropped 4,350 tons of bombs and lost 126 aircraft.
1942   Fifty-five Royal Air Force bombers attacked Bremen, Germany.
1943   Twelve Royal Air Force "Venturas" attacked Caen, France. Two "Spitfires" from the USAAF's 4th Fighter Group flew patrols over the Channel.
1944   The Hungarian Ambassador in Lisbon informed the Western Allies that the Budapest government would surrender to them, but not to the Soviets. American 9th Air Force ace Lieutenant Glenn Eagleston (18.5 victories) was attacked and nearly shot down by a USAAF P47. 143 8th Air Force B17s dropped 355 tons of bombs on Brunswick, Germany and lost twenty-nine bombers. 466 8th Air Force fighters provided support for the bombers and claimed fifty-six victories for the loss of five P38s and four P47s. Twenty-seven 8th Air Force B24s dropped seventy-one tons of bombs on the Gilze-Rijen Airfield. Ninety-one 8th Air Force fighters provided support for the bombers. The American 9th Air Force attacked V-1 rocket launching sites. Twenty-five Royal Air Force "Mosquitoes" attacked targets in Germany. Five B17s from the USAAF's 422nd Bomb Squadron dropped 260 bundles of leaflets near Rennes, Antwerp, Caen, Rouen and Amiens.
1945   The Germans flooded the Roer Valley. 164 8th Air Force B17s dropped 457 tons of bombs on the oil storage depot at Dulmen, Germany. 227 8th Air Force fighters provided support for the bombers and lost two P51s. Ninety-three Royal Air Force "Mosquitoes" attacked targets in Germany. Ten German "Seehund" two-man submarines unsuccessfully attempted to attack Allied shipping in the English Channel.
1947   A group of treaties that would officially end World War II in Europe were signed in Paris. The provisions of those treaties were as follows: Italy-lost the Adriatic port of Trieste to Yugoslavia, the Dodecanese islands to Greece, was stripped of her African colonies and paid reparations of $125 million to Yugoslavia, $105 million to Greece, $100 million to Russia, $25 million to Ethiopia and $5 million to Albania: Hungary-lost territory to Rumania and Czechoslovakia and paid reparations of $300 million to Russia, $50 million to Yugoslavia and $50 million to Czechoslovakia: Rumania-lost territory to Russia and Bulgaria and paid reparations of $300 million to Russia: Bulgaria-reparations of $45 million to Greece and $25 million to Yugoslavia: Finland-lost territory to Russia and paid reparations of $300 million to Russia. As a result of the "Cold War", an

actual peace treaty with Germany was never signed. The closest thing to a treaty was eventually signed in July of 1990. The document guaranteed the borders of Poland with the soon to be reunited Germany. German reunification took place at midnight of October 1st 1990.

1993   During the construction of a car park near Munich, the buried proto-type of the Luftwaffe's Me109B was discovered.

1995   The remains of USAAF Flying Officer Frank Gallion were recovered from the cockpit of his P47 "Thunderbolt" in the sea off Holland. He had been shot down by Luftwaffe fighters on November 23, 1943, while escorting B17s on a raid against Wilhelmshaven. The wreck had been located during an October 1993 survey of the area.

Eastern Europe

1939   Poland declared that it would not allow German rail or road traffic across the Danzig Corridor.

1940   Germany and Russia signed a trade agreement.

1943   The Soviets took Chuguev and Volchansk.

1944   The Soviets took Shepetovka.

1945   The German liner VON STEUBEN was sunk in the Baltic by the Soviet submarine S-13, 2,700 died. The Soviets took Preussisch-Eylau and Elbing in East Prussia.

Mediterranean

1936   The Italians attacked Amba-Aradam, Ethiopia.

1941   The British Army, under the command of General Sir Alan Cunningham, began advancing into Ethiopia and Italian Somaliland.

1943   The U81 damaged the Dutch tanker SAROENA (6,671 tons). Major General James Doolittle, commander of the American 12th Air Force, flew a 310th Bombardment Group B25 on a shipping strike.

1944   The American 15th Air Force attacked troop concentrations near Anzio.

Atlantic

1940   The U48 sank the Dutch freighter BURGERDIJK (6,853 tons). U48 survived the war. The U37 sank the Norwegian freighter SILJA (1,259 tons). U37 survived the war.

1941   The U37 sank the British freighter BRANDENBURG (1,473 tons). U37 survived the war. The U52 sank the British freighter CANFORD CHINE (3,364 tons). U52 survived the war.

1942   The Royal Canadian Navy corvette SPIKENARD was sunk by the U136. U136 survived until July 11th.

1943   The German armed merchant cruiser CORONEL was damaged while attempting to break out into the Atlantic and was forced to put into Boulogne. The U519 was sunk by the USAAF's 2nd Squadron northwest of the Azores.

1944   The U666 was sunk by the Royal Navy escort carrier FENCER. The last victory to be scored by a Luftwaffe Fw200 was the British tanker EL GRILLO (7,264 tons) which was sunk off Iceland.

North America

1939   The first flight of the NA-40 (the B25 proto-type) took place.

1942   Ford Motor Company completed the last civilian car to be built for the duration of the war. The American 10th Air Force was activated at Patterson Field, Ohio. The French liner NORMANDIE (82,423 tons) caught fire and capsized in New York harbor.

1993   USAF Lieutenant General Elwood Ricardo Quesada, age 88, died in Florida. He had commanded 12th Fighter Command in North Africa and 9th Tactical Air Force in England.

2013   USN ace Edward Wendorf died in Le Mesa, Califonia. He had been credited with 6 aerial victories while flying F6Fs off the LEXINGTON in 1943-44.

Pacific

1920   The IJN light cruiser TAMA was launched. She was sunk on October 25, 1944.

1939   Japanese forces occupied Hainan Island in the South China Sea.

1942   The Japanese took Banjarmasin, Borneo. The IJN submarine I-69 shelled American installations on Midway, but was damaged by USMC F2A "Buffaloes". USAAF LB-30s damaged the Japanese seaplane carrier CHITOSE in the Makassar Strait.

1943   The IJN submarine I-21 sank the American freighter STARR KING (7,176 tons). The USN submarine PICKEREL sank the AMARI MARU (2,184 tons). The American 11th Air Force attacked Kiska in the Aleutians. It was the B17's last mission in the theater. Thereafter, the B24 "Liberator" would serve as the USAAF's primary heavy bomber in the Pacific until the advent of the B29.

1944   American and Australian troops took the Huon Peninsula in New Guinea. USN Task Group 58.4 (commanded by Ginder) attacked Eniwetok in the Marshalls. They repeat their attacks on the 11th and 12th. USN LST-170 was damaged by Japanese aircraft off New Guinea. The "Main Body" of the IJN Fleet left Truk after a recon flight by American aircraft on the 4th. The IJN destroyer MINEKAZE was sunk northeast of Formosa by the USN submarine POGY.

1945　USN Task Force 58 (commanded by Mitscher) left Ulithi en route to attacking Tokyo on the 16th. Tokyo was hit by an earthquake. The USN submarine BATFISH was attacked by USN aircraft. The IJN submarine Ro-50 sank the USN LST-577. Thirty-three B29s attacked the Nakajima Plant at Oba and lost two aircraft.

1948　The USN battleship PENNSYLVANIA was expended after the Bikini tests.

China-Burma-India
1942　British Field Marshal Archibald Wavell visited Singapore and ordered it held at all costs. The Royal Air Force withdrew its last fighters from Singapore. Japanese forces took Martaban, Burma.

1943　Eight American 10th Air Force B25s attacked the Maymo Railyards in Burma. The U509 sank the British freighter QUEEN ANNE (4,937 tons). U509 survived until July 15th.

1945　British forces took Myitson, Burma. The East African 18th Brigade took Seikpyu, Burma.

1952　USAF Major George A. Davis (7 aerial victories during WWII) was killed after shooting down a North Korean MiG-15 (See November 30th and December 5th and 13th of the previous year). When he died, he was the leading USAF ace in Korea and was the only F-86 "Sabre" pilot to be awarded a Medal of Honor during the war.

February 11th

Western Europe
1940　189 Royal Air Force bombers attacked Hannover, Germany.

1941　French Admiral Jean Darlan was nominated as Petain's deputy and successor. Seventy-nine Royal Air Force bombers attacked Bremen, Germany. No aircraft were lost on the raid, but twenty-two crashed while trying to land at their fog-bound bases back in Britain. Eighteen Royal Air Force bombers attacked Hannover, Germany.

1942　Forty-nine Royal Air Force bombers attacked Mannheim, Germany. Thirty-one Royal Air Force bombers attacked Le Havre, France and lost one "Wellington". Eighteen Royal Air Force "Wellingtons" attacked Brest, France and lost one aircraft.

1943　Nineteen Royal Air Force "Bostons" attacked rail targets and lost one aircraft. 177 Royal Air Force bombers attacked Wilhelmshaven, Germany and lost three "Lancasters". 120 acres of the city was destroyed in the raid.

1944　Ninety-four 8th Air Force B24s dropped 274 tons of bombs on V-1 launching sites near Siracourt, France and lost one aircraft. 126 8th and

9th Air Force fighters provided support for the bombers. 212 8th Air Force B17s dropped 535 tons of bombs on Frankfurt, Ludwigshafen and Saarbrucken in Germany and lost five aircraft. 606 8th and 9th Air Force fighters provided support for the bombers and claimed thirty victories for the loss of eight P38s, four P47s and two P51s. Lieutenant James Morris, of the 55th Fighter Group, became the first 8th Air Force P38 ace when he shot down a Me109 near Bonn, Germany. The 357th Fighter Group (P51) flew its first 8th Air Force mission. USAAF Lieutenant Colonel Kenneth R. Martin, commander of the 354th Fighter Group (P51), collided with a Me109 over Frankfurt and was captured. American 9th Air Force B26s attacked Amiens, France. Soviet aircraft attacked the German battleship TIRPITZ in Altafjord, Norway. Twenty-seven Royal Air Force "Mosquitoes" attacked targets in Germany. Five B17s from the USAAF's 422nd Bomb Squadron dropped 250 bundles of supplies for resistance forces near Ghent, Brussels and Antwerp in Belgium.

1945 Sergeant Edward Dahlgren, of the 36th Division, won a Medal of Honor at Oberhoffen, Germany. 124 8th Air Force bombers dropped 335 tons of bombs on the oil storage depot at Dulmen, Germany. 296 8th Air Force fighters provided support for the bombers and lost one P51.

1946 The French battleship JEAN BART entered Brest, France to be completed.

Eastern Europe

1940 The Soviets broke through the "Mannerheim Line" in Finland.
1943 German forces abandoned the major rail junction at Lozovaya.
1944 The Soviets took Shepetovka.
1945 The Soviets took Luben, Leignitz, Neumarkt and Kanth in East Prussia.

Mediterranean

1941 German General Erwin Rommel arrived in Rome, en route to North Africa, to assume command of the Deutsches Afrika Korps. The German 5th Light Division landed in Tripoli, Libya.
1943 The U81 sank the Lebanese sailing ship HUSNI (107 tons) and the Palestinian sailing ship DOLPHIN (135 tons).
1944 Allied counter-attacks at Anzio were repulsed.

Atlantic

1940 The German blockade runner ROSTOCK (2,592 tons) was captured by the French sloop ELAN. The U50 sank the Swedish freighter ORANIA (1,854 tons). U50 survived until April 29th. The U37 sank the British trawler TOGIMO (290 tons). U37 survived the war. The U53 sank the Norwegian freighter SNESTAD (4,114 tons). U53 survived until February 21st. The U9

	sank the Estonian freighter LINDA (1,213 tons). U9 survived until August 20, 1944.
1941	The Luftwaffe sank five British freighters off the Azores.
1942	American troops occupied Curacao and Aruba in the Dutch West Indies. At 0035, the Royal Canadian Navy corvette SPIKENARD was sunk south of Iceland by the U136. The U591 sank the Norwegian freighter HEINA (4,028 tons). U591 survived until July 30, 1943. The U564 sank the Canadian tanker VICTOLITE (11,410 tons). U564 survived until June 14, 1943. Nine survivors from the British tanker SAN ARCADIO, which had been sunk on January 31st by U107, were rescued by a USN PBM "Mariner".
1943	The Panamanian freighter PORTLAND (2,648 tons) was lost off Cape Hatteras.
1944	The U1017 sank the Belgian freighter PERSIER (5,382 tons). U1017 survived until April 29, 1945. The U283 was sunk by Royal Canadian Air Force No.407 Squadron. The U424 was sunk southwest of Ireland by the Royal Navy sloops WOODPECKER and WILD GOOSE.

North America

1887	Admiral Henry Kent Hewitt was born in Hackensack, New Jersey. He graduated 30th in his 1906 Annapolis class of 209. During WWI, he won a Navy Cross while serving on destroyers in the Atlantic. In 1939 he was promoted to rear admiral. From April 1942 he commanded the Amphibious Force, Atlantic Fleet. He commanded the naval element of the Western Task Force during "Operation Torch" on November 8, 1942. On November 20th, he was promoted to vice-admiral. He would serve as commander of the US naval forces in the Mediterranean until the end of the war. He was promoted to full admiral in September 1945. On August 1, 1945 he was named as commander of the US naval forces in Europe. He retired on March 1, 1949 at the age of 62. He died on September 15, 1972 and was buried at Annapolis.
1942	Anti-conscription riots occurred in Montreal, Canada injuring twelve.
1944	The escort carrier OMMANEY BAY was commissioned. She was sunk in 1945.
1954	USN Admiral Charles "Soc" McMorris, commander of the heavy cruiser SAN FRANCISCO and Task Force 8 in the North Pacific, died.
1972	The destroyer HOPEWELL was expended as a target.

Pacific

1942	Allied counter-attacks forced the Japanese to retreat on Bataan. The USN submarine SHARK was sunk in Molucca Strait by the IJN destroyer YAMAKAZE. The Japanese Naval Air Force attacked Samarai Island, 380 miles north of Australia.

1943 The F4U "Corsair" flew its first combat operations (with VMF-124 from Espiritu Santo). The USN submarine GRAYLING damaged the Japanese freighter HOEIZAN MARU off Corregidor.
1944 The IJN submarine I-11 was sunk by the USN destroyer NICHOLAS. The USN LST-577 was sunk off Mindanao by the IJN submarine Ro-50. Thirty American 13th Air Force B25s attacked Rabaul, New Britain. The Royal Australian Air Force attacked Yoga Yoga, New Guinea. USN PT-279 was lost in a collision with PT-282 off Buka in the Solomons.
1945 The IJN submarine Ro-112 was sunk by the USN submarine BATFISH.

China-Burma-India

1942 The final British counter-attack on Singapore Island, took place. The Japanese issued a surrender demand to the British in Singapore.
1943 The U516 sank the British freighter HELMSPREY (4,764 tons). U516 survived the war.
1944 The IJN submarine Ro-110 damaged the British freighter ASPHALION (6,274 tons) in the Bay of Biscay. The Ro-110 was then sunk by Royal Navy escorts.
1945 USAAF B29s attacked Rangoon, Burma. The last victory scored by a P38 in the theater, was a Japanese Naval Air Force "Jill" downed by the 459th Fighter Squadron. Royal Air Force B24s attacked Rangoon, Burma. The British destroyer PATHFINDER was a constructive loss after a Japanese air-attack off Akyab. She had participated in the sinking of two U-boats in the Atlantic.

February 12th

Western Europe

1885 Julius Streicher was born in Fleinhausen, Bavaria. He would be sentenced to death at the Nuremburg War Crimes Trials.
1938 Hitler met with Austrian Chancellor Kurt Schuschnigg at Berchtesgaden.
1941 The Germans sealed off the Jewish quarter in Amsterdam, Holland.
1942 Just after midnight, the German battlecruisers SCHARNHORST and GNEISENAU and heavy cruiser PRINZ EUGEN began "Operation Cerebus". It was an attempt escape from Brest, France and return to Germany by passing through the English Channel. They were escorted by six destroyers and fourteen torpedo boats. At 0028, they passed Ushant. At 0114, they entered the Channel. At 0530, they passed Alderney. At 0850, they were joined by their fighter escort. At 1042, they were sighted by an Royal Air Force "Spitfire". At 1219, the British artillery at Dover opened fire on them. Eight British motor torpedo boats then

unsuccessfully attacked and suffered damage to three of their number. At 1245, "Swordfish" torpedo bombers attacked. Royal Navy Lieutenant Commander Eugene Esmonde won a posthumous Victoria Cross for leading six No.825 Squadron "Swordfish" against the German ships. During several attacks by British aircraft the patrol boat V-1302 was sunk and the torpedo boats T-13 and JAGUAR were damaged. At 1431, the SCHARNHORST hit a mine. At 1505, the SCHARNHORST got under way again. At 1547, the British destroyers CAMPBELL, VIVACIOUS, WORCESTER, WHITSHED and WALPOLE unsuccessfully tried to penetrate the defensive screen around the German force. At 1830, the Royal Air Force made their last attack. At 1955, the GNEISENAU hit a mine. At 2134, the SCHARNHORST hit a mine. Twenty-one Royal Air Force bombers dropped mines in the Baltic. No aircraft were lost on the mission, but one crashed upon returning to Britain.

1943 Sixteen Royal Air Force "Mosquitoes" attacked targets in Belgium and Germany. Thirty-eight Royal Air Force bombers dropped mines in the Baltic. Eighteen "Spitfires" from the USAAF's 4th Fighter Group flew patrols over the Channel.

1944 Ninety-seven 8th Air Force B24s dropped 279 tons of bombs on V-1 rocket sites near Siracourt, France. 125 8th and 9th Air Force fighters provided support for the bombers. Ten Royal Air Force "Lancasters" of No.617 Squadron attacked the Antheor viaduct between France and Italy. The target was missed. Twenty-five Royal Air Force bombers dropped mines off the French coast and lost one "Halifax".

1945 Five German "Seehund" two-man submarines attacked Allied shipping in the English Channel. They sank the tanker LISETA (2,628 tons). The German minesweeper M-381 was sunk off Norway by the Royal Navy submarine VENTURER. Ninety-nine Royal Air Force "Mosquitoes" attacked targets in Germany.

Eastern Europe

1900 Soviet General Vasily Chukov was born. He died in 1982.

1940 The Finns counter-attacked in an attempt to expel the Soviets from the "Mannerheim Line". The Finnish government began moves to end the war.

1941 Zhukov was named Chief of the Soviet General Staff.

1943 The Soviets took Krasnodar. The city was a rail junction in the northern Caucasus.

1944 The Soviets took Batetskaya.

1945 The "Yalta Conference" ended. The Soviets began an offensive in the Ukraine. The Royal Navy anti-aircraft cruiser DELPHI was a constructive loss after a "Linsen" explosive attack in Split, Yugoslavia.

Mediterranean

1940   The first Anzac (Australian-New Zealand Army Corps) troops arrived in Egypt.

1941   Italian General Italo Gariboldi was named as Commander-in-Chief Libya, replacing Rodolfo Graziani. General Erwin Rommel arrived in Tripoli, Libya, to assume command of the DAK. The Luftwaffe's first raid in North Africa took place, the target was Benghazi. Richpal Ram, of the 6th Raj Putna Rifles, won a posthumous Victoria Cross in Eritrea. Italian troops retook the Forked Rock, near Keren in Eritrea. Mussolini and Franco met in Bordighera.

1942   The Royal Navy destroyer MAORI exploded after an attack by the Luftwaffe on Malta. The Royal Navy destroyer DECOY was damaged while lying alongside. A 3-ship British convoy was sunk while en route from Alexandria, Egypt to Malta.

1944   General Bernard Freyberg, commander of the New Zealand Corps, announced that the Abbey on Monte Cassino would have to be bombed before he would attack it. The American 15th Air Force attacked German troop concentrations near Anzio.

1948   The Italian sloop ERITREA was transferred to the French Navy as war reparations. She was scrapped in 1966.

Atlantic

1940   The German blockade runner MOREA (4,709 tons) was captured off the Spanish coast by the Royal Navy destroyer HASTY. The German trawler HERRLICHKEIT was captured off Tromso, Norway by the Royal Navy cruiser GLASGOW. The German steamer WAKAMA was scuttled off Brazil to prevent her capture by the British cruiser DORSETSHIRE. The U26 sank the Norwegian freighter NIDARHOLM (3,482 tons). U26 survived until July 3rd. The U53 sank the Swedish freighter DALARO (3,927 tons). U53 survived until February 21st. The U33 was sunk while laying mines in the Clyde Estuary by the Royal Navy minesweeper GLEANER. Seventeen survivors and the rotors from her "Enigma" encoding machine were captured by the GLEANER.

1941   The German heavy cruiser HIPPER sank seven of nineteen freighters in convoy SLS-64.

1942   The U108 sank the Norwegian freighter BLINK (2,701 tons-24 of her crew died). U108 survived until July 17, 1944. The U442 was sunk northwest of Cape St. Vincent by the Royal Air Force's No.48 Squadron. The American freighter DIXIE SWORD foundered.

1942   The USN tanker SALAMONIE was damaged in a collision off Bermuda with the freighter URUGUAY.

North America

1880 US labor leader John L. Lewis was born near Lucas, Iowa. His formal education ended with the seventh grade when he went to work in the coal mines. He became leader of the United Mine Workers Union. He retired in 1960 and died on June 11, 1969.

1893 General Omar Nelson Bradley was born near Clark, Missouri. He graduated 44th in his 1915 West Point class of 164. In 1929 he was assigned as an instructor at the Infantry School at Fort Benning which was commanded by future Army Chief of Staff Lieutenant Colonel George C. Marshall. Marshall put his name in his famous "Black Book" in which he kept track of what he considered exceptional officers. A decade later, Marshall would pick him to command the school. After war was declared, he was given command of the 82nd Infantry Division. On June 26, 1942 he turned over that unit to Matthew Ridgeway and assumed command of the 28th Infantry Division. On February 12, 1943, he was informed by Marshall that he was to command a corps. On the same day, he learned that his West Point classmate Dwight Eisenhower had chosen him to perform a special mission for him in North Africa. He was to be Eisenhower's "eyes and ears" and find out the reasons for the sub-standard performance of American forces in the area. On March 7, 1943, he recommended that General Fredendall be replaced as 2nd Corps commander. General Patton arrived the next day to assume command of the unit. Bradley relieved Patton as commander of the 2nd Corps on April 15th. On October 16, 1943 he was named as commander of the 12th Army Group in the upcoming invasion of France. On March 12, 1945 he was promoted to four-star general. He succeeded Eisenhower as Army Chief of Staff on February 7, 1948. On August 16, 1949 he became the first permanent Chairman of the Joint Chiefs of Staff. He was promoted to five-star rank on September 22, 1950. He retired on August 13, 1953 and was named as the Chairman of the Board at Bulova Watch in 1958. He died of a blood clot on April 8, 1981 in New York City.

1941 The destroyer WOOLSEY was launched. She was stricken in July 1971.

1942 The American 10th Air Force was activated under the command of Colonel Harry A. Halvorson (later the commander of "HalPro" in the Mediterranean). The light cruiser MONTPELIER (awarded thirteen battle stars and a Navy Unit Commendation during the war) and the destroyers COGHLAN, BUTLER and GHERARDI were launched. The MONTPELIER was scrapped in 1960 and BUTLER in 1948. The COGHLAN was stricken in July 1971 and the GHERARDI in June of the same year.

1943 A waterfront fire in Jacksonville, Florida caused $100,000 in damages.

1944 Wendell Wilkie announced his candidacy for president. The destroyer LYMAN K. SWENSON was launched.
1945 Japanese balloon-bombs were found near Hardin, Riverdale, and Cascade in Montana, Burwell in Nebraska, Nowlin in South Dakota, Cohasset in California, and Spokane in Washington.
1946 The Royal Navy escort carriers STRIKER, PURSER and BATTLER were returned to USN. The USN destroyer LAVALETTE was placed in reserve. She was sold to Peru in 1974.
1947 The destroyer DUPONT (AG-80) was sold for scrap.
1961 Admiral Richmond Kelly Turner died in Monterey, California. He would be buried in Golden Gate Cemetery south of San Francisco next to Admirals Chester Nimitz, Charles Lockwood and Raymond Spruance.

Pacific
1942 The ANZAC Squadron was formed at Fiji and was commanded by Australian Admiral Crace. It consisted of the Australian cruiser AUSTRALIA, the American cruiser CHICAGO, the New Zealand cruisers LEANDER and ACHILLES and the American destroyers LAMSON and PERKINS. The USN battleship NEVADA was raised from the bottom of Pearl Harbor. The USN destroyer WHIPPLE and the Dutch light cruiser DE RUYTER were damaged in a collision off Java. USAAF B17s damaged the Japanese freighters KOZUI MARU and KINRYU MARU off Surumi.
1944 The USMC landed on Arno Island in the Marshalls. USMC forces landed on Umboi Island, off New Britain. The USMC took Gorisso, New Britain. The USN submarine TAMBOR sank the RONSAN MARU (2,735 tons). The Royal Navy submarine STONEHENGE sank the CHOKO MARU (889 tons). Japanese aircraft destroyed a USMC bomb dump on Roi, killing 26 and wounding 130. The USN auxiliary submarine rescue ship MACAW was lost when she slid off the reef near Midway where she had run aground on January 16th.
1945 USAAF B29s attacked Iwo Jima.
1946 Paul Mullen, a former member of Boyington's "Black Sheep" VMF-214 died in a mid-air collision over Japan.

China-Burma-India
1942 Royal Air Force ace Squadron/Leader Frank Carey (28 aerial victories) shot down three "Oscars" over Rangoon, Burma.
1943 The American 10th Air Force attacked the Myitgne River Bridge in Burma.
1944 The Royal Air Force attacked Lammadaw, Burma. The IJN submarine I-27 sank the transport KHEDIVE ISMAIL (7,513 tons-1,200 died) and then was sunk herself by the Royal Navy destroyers PETARD and PALADIN. The Royal Navy RELENTLESS sank the U-boat supply ship CHARLOTTE SCHLIERMAN in the Indian Ocean.

February 13th

Western Europe

1941   Spanish Premier Francisco Franco and French Premier Phillip Petain met in Montpellier, France.

1942   "Operation Sealion", the German invasion of Britain, was formally cancelled. Eighty-five Royal Air Force bombers attacked Cologne and Aachen in Germany and Le Havre in France.

1943   Fifty-six Royal Air Force bombers attacked Ijmuiden, Holland and various targets in France. 466 Royal Air Force bombers attacked the port of Lorient, France and lost seven aircraft. Twenty-four "Spitfires" from the USAAF's 4th Fighter Group flew patrols over the Channel and lost one aircraft.

1944   416 8th Air Force B17s and B24s dropped 1,171 tons of bombs on V-1 rocket launching sites in the Pas de Calais in France and lost four B17s. 232 8th Air Force fighters provided support for the bombers and claimed six victories for the loss of one P51. The American 9th Air Force attacked V-1 launching sites in France.

1945   837 American 15th Air Force bombers attacked Vienna, Austria. British forces took Hasselt. The German minesweeper M-421 was sunk off Kolberg in the Baltic by a German mine. 804 Royal Air Force bombers attacked Dresden, Germany and lost nine "Lancasters". Due to the firestorm that occurred after the raid the number of casualties could never be established, but it was estimated that more than 50,000 people died. 386 Royal Air Force bombers attacked Bohlen and lost one "Halifax". 109 Royal Air Force "Mosquitoes" attacked targets in Germany.

1964   Werner Heyde, Head of the Euthanasia Program, committed suicide in a Butzbach prison.

Eastern Europe

1942   During this day and the next, the Soviet Navy would bring 2,109 reinforcing troops into the besieged fortress city of Sevastopol. Hitler met with Rumanian Premier Antonescu and demanded more troops for the Eastern Front.

1944   Soviet forces took Luga and began concentrating for the capture of Pskov.

1945   Budapest, Hungary, surrendered after a 45-day siege and 138,000 Germans were taken prisoner. The Soviets took Beuthen in Silesia. The U992 sank the Royal Navy corvette DENBIGH CASTLE.

Mediterranean

1917   Corporal Benito Mussolini was wounded in action. He would later become dictator of Italy.

1941　Royal Navy carrier FORMIDABLE aircraft attacked Massawa, Ethiopia.
1942　The Royal Navy submarine TEMPEST was sunk by an Italian torpedo boat.
1943　Major General James Doolittle, commander of the American 12th Air Force, flew a 17th Bombardment Group B26 on a mission against DAK supply points.
1945　An American O.S.S. team blew up an important bridge over the Piave River at San Felice.

Atlantic

1940　The German freighter WAKAMA (3,771 tons) was scuttled to prevent her capture by the Royal Navy cruiser DORSETSHIRE. The U25 sank the Danish tanker MAERSK (5,177 tons). U25 survived until August 3rd. The U53 sank the Swedish freighter NORNA (1,022 tons). U53 survived until February 21st. The U50 damaged the Norwegian tanker ALBERT L. ELLSWORTH.
1941　The U96 sank the British tanker CLEA (8,074 tons). U96 survived until March 30, 1945. The U103 and U96 sank the British tanker CORWIN (10,516 tons). U103 survived until April 15, 1945.
1942　The USN destroyer ERICSSON accidentally rammed and sank the Icelandic steamer GREEDIR off Iceland.
1944　The Royal Navy trawler STRATHELLA was rescued by the US Coast Guard cutter MODOC after being adrift in the North Atlantic for more than a month.

North America

1929　Congress authorized $19 million for the Navy's construction of its first purpose-built carrier, the RANGER.
1942　The IJN submarine I-17 shelled an oil tank farm at Goleta, California.
1947　USAAF ace Duane W. Beeson (19 air and 7 strafing victories) died and was buried at Arlington on the 19th.
1956　Medal of Honor winner Private Lloyd McCarter, of the 503rd Regimental Combat Team, committed suicide.
1970　The destroyer SOLEY was sold for scrap.
1994　Robert Lee Sherrod, age 86, died in Washington D.C. He had been a correspondent for Time-Life and had specialized in covering the USMC.

Pacific

1942　The IJN submarine I-25 sank the British freighter DERRYMORE (4,799 tons). Japanese aircraft sank the tankers MANVANTARA (8,237 tons) and MERULA (8,277 tons) and the steamer SUBADAR (5,424 tons). Many other smaller vessels were also sunk and damaged in the actions, which took place off the Dutch East Indies. The IJN submarine I-55 sank the transport DERRYMORE (4,799 tons) in the Sunda Strait. The Royal Navy gunboat SCORPION was sunk off Sumatra by IJN destroyers, twenty of her crew survived. An Allied force commanded by Dutch Admiral Doorman departed from Batavia to attack a Japanese naval force that had entered Banka Strait. It consisted of the Dutch cruisers DE RUYTER, JAVA and TROMP, the British cruiser EXETER, the Australian cruiser HOBART, the Dutch destroyers BANCKERT, KORTENAER, PIET HEIN and VAN GHENT and the American destroyers BARKER, BULMER, JOHN D. EDWARDS, PARROTT, PILLSBURY and STEWART as well as several smaller vessels. The American transport PRESIDENT TAYLOR ran aground and was lost off Canton Island. Philippine troops wiped out a Japanese force that had landed on Canas Point, Bataan.

1943   The American 13th Air Force was activated in the South Pacific. USAAF and USMC aircraft attacked Japanese shipping off New Georgia, losing three bombers and six escorting fighters. USAAF B26s attacked Munda, New Georgia and Kolombangara. A Japanese floatplane was shot down off Amchitka in the Aleutians.

1944   5th Air Force A20s sank the Japanese freighter YOSHINO MARU off Aitape. The USN battleship INDIANA arrived at Pearl Harbor for collision damage repairs (See February 1st).

1945   The US Army's 11th Airborne Division took Cavite Naval Base and Nichols Airfield on Luzon in the Philippines. Private First-Class Manuel Perez, of the 11th Airborne Division, won a posthumous Medal of Honor on Luzon. USN minesweepers began clearing mines from Manila Bay. The USN bombarded the island of Corregidor. The IJN submarine Ro-113 was sunk by the USN submarine BATFISH. The USN submarine HADDOCK sank the KOTOSHIRO MARU No.8 (109 tons). The USN submarine LOGARTO sank the SHOWA MARU No.3 (76 tons). USAAF ace Colonel Charles MacDonald shot down a Japanese "Topsy" off the Philippines.

China-Burma-India

1944   Eight American 10th Air Force B24s destroyed the Kanchanaburi Rail Bridge in Burma. The Royal Australian Air Force attacked Tarikngan, Gwarawan and Yoga Yoga in New Guinea. 14th Air Force B25s sank the Japanese freighter off Hainan Island.

1945   The USN frigate CORPUS CHRISTI rescued 102 survivors from the American freighter PETER SILVESTER which had been sunk on February 6th by U862.

February 14th

Western Europe

1939   The German battleship BISMARCK (41,700 tons) was launched. She would be sunk in May of 1941 by the Royal Navy.

1940   The German tanker ALTMARK entered Norwegian waters. Aboard were 303 British seamen who had served on merchant ships that had fallen victim to the German pocket battleship GRAF SPEE in the south Atlantic. British merchant ships in the North Sea were armed.

1941   Four Royal Air Force "Blenheims" attacked Calais, France. Hitler met with the Yugoslavian Prime Minister at Obersalzburg. A Luftwaffe He111 landed in error at Royal Air Force Debden, but recovered in time to escape. The Danish torpedo boat DRAGEN was sunk in the Baltic by a mine. Forty-four Royal Air Force "Wellingtons" attacked Gelsenkirchen, Germany. Forty-four Royal Air Force bombers attacked Homberg, Germany. Eleven Royal Air Force "Hampdens" dropped mines off the Gironde Estuary in France and lost one aircraft.

1942   The Royal Air Force's Bomber Command received the "Area Bombing Directive" from the Air Ministry. It stated that from that point on the main target of its attacks would be the morale of the German people and not specific industrial sites. Considering that they had missed most of their targets by a matter of miles, the change in policy would not tend to be noticed by the German population. Ninety-eight Royal Air Force bombers attacked Mannheim, Germany and lost two aircraft. One person was injured in the raid.

1943   Ten Royal Air Force "Mosquitoes" attacked Tours, France. 243 Royal Air Force bombers attacked Cologne, Germany and lost nine aircraft. Seventy-six people were killed in the raid, including 25 French workers. Seventy-four B17s from the USAAF's 91st, 303rd, 305th and 306th Bomb Groups attempted to attack the marshalling yards at Hamm, Germany but had to abort due to bad weather.

1944   Forty-eight P47s from the 8th Air Force 353rd Fighter Group attacked the Gilze-Rijen airfield in Holland. The USAAFs 4th Fighter Group received its first three P51Bs.

1945   The American 15th Air Force attacked oil refineries around Vienna. 1,293 8th Air Force bombers dropped 3,202 tons of bombs on Dresden, Chemnitz and Magdeburg in Germany and Prague and Brux in Czechoslovakia and lost six B17s and one B24. 881 8th Air Force fighters provided support for the bombers and lost seven P51s. 717 Royal Air Force bombers attacked Chemnitz and lost thirteen aircraft. 232 Royal Air Force bombers attacked Rositz and lost four "Lancasters". 100 Royal Air Force "Mosquitoes" attacked targets in Germany. Fifty-four Royal Air Force bombers dropped mines in the Baltic and lost six aircraft.

Eastern Europe

1941 Heavy fighting took place near Scindeli, between Italian and Greek troops.

1943 The Soviets took Rostov. The Soviet tanker EMBA was sunk in the Black Sea by a mine. The Soviet freighter KRASNYJ PROFINTERN (4,648 tons) was sunk by the U19 in the Black Sea.

1945 Luftwaffe ace Otto Kittel (267 aerial victories) was killed by Soviet flak. The U711 sank the American freighter HORACE GRAY (7,200 tons).

Mediterranean

1941 The first "Stuka" dive-bomber lost in North Africa was shot down over El Agheila, Libya.

1943 The Axis began an offensive against the Allied forces that had landed in North Africa in November 1942. 142 Royal Air Force bombers attacked Milan and lost two "Lancasters".

1944 The American 15th Air Force attacked rail targets in Italy. Allied aircraft began dropping leaflets on Monte Cassino warning the civilian population of the impending bombing attack on the abbey.

Atlantic

1940 The U57 sank the British tanker GRETAFIELD (10,191 tons). U57 survived the war. The U53 sank the Danish freighter GOLDSCHMIDT (2,095 tons). U53 survived until February 21st. The U26 sank the British freighter LANGLEEFORD (4,422 tons). U26 survived until July 3rd. The U48 sank the British freighter SULTAN STAR (12,306 tons). U48 survived the war.

1941 The Italian submarine BIANCHI sank the British freighter BELCREST (4,517 tons). The U101 sank the British freighter HOLYSTONE (5,462 tons). U101 survived the war.

1942 The U576 sank the British freighter EMPIRE SPRING (6,946 tons). U576 survived until July 15th.

1943 The German armed merchant cruiser CORONEL left Boulogne, France. The U620 was sunk in the Bay of Biscay by the Royal Air Force's No.202 Squadron.

1944 The Italian submarine TAZZOLI was sunk in the Bay of Biscay by a torpedo from an unknown source. The U738 was lost in an accident.

1945 The U989 was sunk off the Faroes by the Royal Navy frigates BAYNTUN, BRATHEWAITE, LOCH ECK and LOCH DUNVEGAN. The American freighter HORACE GRAY was a constructive loss after a torpedo attack by the U711. U711 survived until May 4, 1945.

North America

1938 The destroyer MAURY was launched. She was scrapped in 1946.
1941 Admiral Kichisaburo Nomura, Japan's new ambassador to America, presented his credentials to FDR.
1942 The submarine WAHOO was launched at Mare Island. She was lost on October 12, 1943.
1944 The first flight of the P51F ("Mustang" light-weight) took place. The destroyer JARVIS was launched. She was transferred to Spain in 1960.
1945 Two F4U "Corsairs" and five TBM "Avengers", from the USN escort carrier BLOCK ISLAND II, crashed off Santa Barbara during training, eight died and nine were injured.
1951 USAAF ace Ray S. Wetmore, 22 air and 3 strafing victories, died in a plane crash at Otis Air Force Base, Massachusetts.
1970 The destroyer RENSHAW was stricken.

South America

1942 Chile declared war on Japan.

Pacific

1941 The IJN light cruiser KASHII was launched. She was sunk on January 12, 1945.
1942 Dutch Admiral Conrad Helfrich replaced USN Admiral Thomas Hart as the Naval Commander of ABDA (the combined American-British-Dutch-Australian forces). National Guard troops of the American 148th Idaho Field Artillery Battalion boarded the transports TULAGI and PORT MAR and Australian troops boarded the MAUNA LOA and the MEIGS for movement to Timor. They left that evening escorted by the USN heavy cruiser HOUSTON and the destroyer PEARY. The IJN submarine I-23 was wrecked. 360 Japanese paratroops landed on Sumatra at Palembang. Fifty-eight Allied aircraft attacked a Japanese invasion force off Muntok and sank the transport INABASAN MARU (989 tons). The USN submarine SARGO delivered ammunition to Corregidor in the Philippines and evacuated USAAF ground personnel. The Royal Navy gunboats DRAGONFLY and GRASSHOPPER were sunk off Sumatra by Japanese aircraft. They were part of an Allied force that had left Batavia the previous evening. Also damaged during this action were the USN destroyers BULMER and BARKER. The USN Task Force 8, commanded by Admiral Halsey, departed from Pearl Harbor en route to attacking Japanese installations on Marcus and Wake Islands. It consisted of the carrier ENTERPRISE, the cruisers NORTHAMPTON and SALT LAKE CITY, the destroyers BALCH, MAURY, CRAVEN, DUNLAP, BLUE and RALPH TALBOT and the tanker SABINE.

1943 The USAAF and USMC lost two bombers and six fighters while attacking Japanese shipping off New Georgia. The USN submarine TROUT sank the HIROTAMA MARU (1,911 tons). The USN submarine THRESHER sank the IJN submarine I-62.
1944 The USN submarine SNOOK sank the NITTOKU MARU (3,591 tons). The USN submarine FLASHER sank the HOKUAN MARU (3,712 tons) and the MINRYO MARU (2,240 tons). VMTB-223 lost 6 of 16 TBFs on a mine-laying mission to Rabaul, New Britain. UIT23 was sunk in Malacca Strait by the Royal Navy submarine TALLYHO.
1945 USN Watertender 1st Class Elmer Bigelow, of the destroyer FLETCHER, won a posthumous Medal of Honor off Corregidor. The USN destroyer LAVALETTE hit a mine in Manila Bay, seven of her crew died. The USN YMS-48 was sunk in Manila Bay by shore-fire. The IJN escort CD-9 was sunk by the USN submarine GATO.

China-Burma-India
1942 Royal Navy Lieutenant T. Wilkinson, of the Royal Navy gunboat LI WO, won a posthumous Victoria Cross. The IJN submarine I-166 sank the freighter KAMUNING (2,076 tons). RAF "Blenheims" sank the Japanese transport INABASAN MARU off Palembang, Malaya.
1944 The U168 sank the Royal Navy repair ship SALVIKING (1,440 tons). U168 survived until October 5th. A USAAF B25 sank the SATSUMA MARU off Wenchow, China.

February 15th

Western Europe
1890 Robert Ley, German Minister of Labor, was born.
1901 British politician Brendan Bracken was born in Templemore, Ireland. He would serve as British Minister of Information during the war. He died of throat cancer in London on August 8, 1958.
1939 The French government ordered 100 A20 bombers from America.
1940 Germany announced that any armed merchant ship would be treated as a combatant. Julius Bursche, Bishop of the Evangelical Church of Augsburg in Poland, was sent to the Sachsenhausen Concentration Camp. He died in February 1942.
1941 Five Royal Air Force bombers attacked Calais, France and lost one "Blenheim. Seventy-three Royal Air Force bombers attacked Sterkrade, Germany and lost one "Wellington" and one "Whitley". Seventy Royal Air Force bombers attacked Homberg, Germany. Forty-three Royal Air Force bombers attacked Boulogne, France.

1942 Twenty-six Royal Air Force bombers attacked St. Nazaire, France. Three of the attacking aircraft crashed upon returning to Britain.
1943 Thirty-five Royal Air Force bombers attacked Tours and Dunkirk in France. The American 8th Air Force 44th and 93rd Bomb Groups lost two of twenty-one B24s over Dunkirk, France. Six Royal Air Force "Mosquitoes" attacked targets in Germany. Luftwaffe night-fighter ace Paul Gildner (44 aerial victories) died in a plane crash in Holland.
1944 Fifty-two American 8th Air Force B24s dropped 149 tons of bombs on V-1 sites near Siracourt, France. American 9th Air Force B26s attacked V-1 launching sites in France. 891 Royal Air Force bombers attacked Berlin and lost forty-three aircraft. 320 people were killed in the Berlin and another fifty-nine were killed outside the city. Six B17s from the USAAF's 422nd Bomb Squadron dropped 300 bundles of supplies for resistance forces near Orleans, Chartres, Cambrai, Le Mans, and Reims.
1945 The U1053 was lost in an accident in the Baltic. 1,075 8th Air Force bombers dropped 2,652 tons of bombs on rail and oil targets in Germany and lost one B17 and one B24. 460 8th Air Force fighters provided escort for the bombers and claimed two victories for the loss of one P51. Fifty-five Royal Air Force bombers dropped mines in the Baltic. The American 15th Air Force attacked Vienna, Austria.
1970 Royal Air Force Air Chief Marshal Hugh Dowding, age 87, died. He had commanded the Royal Air Force's Fighter Command during the "Battle of Britain".

Eastern Europe
1940 Finnish forces retreated from their "Mannerheim Line" under pressure from Soviet forces.
1942 Soviet paratroops that had landed in the "Demyansk Pocket" and were wiped out. The Soviet submarine S-101 sank the Norwegian steamer MIMONA (1,147 tons).
1945 Soviet forces besieged Breslau.

Mediterranean
1940 British General Archibald Wavell became Commander-in-Chief Mid-East.
1942 The Allies stopped all shipping due to heavy losses.
1943 An attack near Sidi Bou Zid, Tunisia, by the US Army's 1st Armored Division was repulsed. Major General James Doolittle, commander of the American 12th Air Force, flew a 97th Bombardment Group B17 on a mission to Palermo, Sicily.
1944 147 USAAF B17s and 82 B25s dropped 400 tons of bombs on Monte Cassino in Italy. The American freighter ELIHU YALE (7,176 tons-5 dead)

was sunk off Anzio by a Luftwaffe glide-bomb, as was LCT-35 which was alongside. The U410 sank the British freighter FORT ST. NICOLAS (7,154 tons). American 15th Air Force B24s attacked rail targets in Italy.

1945   The Italian battleship CAVOUR was sunk at Trieste by the USAAF.

Atlantic

1940   The U50 sank the Danish freighter MARYLAND (4,895 tons). U50 was sunk on April 29, 1940. The U37 sank the Danish freighter AASE (1,206 tons). U37 survived the war. The U26 sank the Norwegian freighter STEINSTAD (2,476 tons). U26 was sunk on July 3, 1940. The U48 sank the Dutch tanker DEN HAAG (8,971 tons). U48 survived the war. The U14 sank the Danish freighter SLEIPNER (1,066 tons). U14 survived the war.

1941   The U123 sank the British freighter ALNMOOR (6,573 tons). U123 survived the war.

1942   The U98 sank the British freighter BIELA (5,298 tons). U98 was sunk on November 19, 1942. The U566 sank the Greek freighter MEROPI (4,181 tons). U566 was sunk on October 24, 1943. The U432 sank the Brazilian freighter BUARQUE. The US Coast Guard cutter CALYPSO rescued 42 of her crew. U432 was sunk on March 11, 1943.

1943   The U529 was sunk southwest of Cape Farewell by the Royal Air Force's No.120 Squadron. the American tanker ATLANTIC SUN (11,355 tons-65 dead). U607 survived until July 13, 1943.

1944   The American freighters HAYM SOLOMON and SAMFORTH were damaged in a collision while en route to
Casablanca.

1945   The U245 damaged the Dutch tanker LISETA (2,628 tons). U245 survived the war.

1954   The last British "Seafire" unit, No.1833 Squadron, was re-equipped with "Sea Furies".

North America

1892   James Vincent Forrestal was born in Mattewan, New York. He became Secretary of the Navy on April 23, 1944, after the death of Frank Knox. He would later serve as the first Secretary of Defense, but would resign on March 28, 1949. He committed suicide on May 22, 1949.

1930   James H. Doolittle began working for Shell Oil Company and was placed in the USAAC Reserve as a Major.

1941   The destroyer INGRAHAM was launched. She was lost in a collision with the freighter CHEMUNG off Nova Scotia on August 22, 1942.

1942   The destroyer MEADE was launched. She was stricken in 1971.

1945   A Japanese balloon-bomb was found near Prosser, Washington.

1946 The battleship MISSISSIPPI was reclassified as AG128 (gunnery development ship).
1971 The heavy cruiser BALTIMORE was stricken.
1973 Colonel Joseph Manske retired. He had flown on the "Doolittle Raid".
1994 Admiral Richard O'Kane died. He had commanded the submarine TANG and had won a Medal of Honor.
2006 James Burt died. He had won a Medal of Honor on October 13, 1944 for actions near Wurselen, Germany.

Pacific
1922 The IJN light cruiser YURA was launched. She was sunk on October 25, 1942.
1941 USN Admiral Husband Kimmel, commander of the Pacific Fleet, received a letter from Chief of Naval Operations Harold Stark stating that anti-torpedo nets were not necessary in Pearl Harbor due to the shallow depth of that facility. Naval Station, Kaneohe, Oahu was established.
1942 The ABDA attempt to stop the invasion of Sumatra was turned back by the Japanese Naval Air Force. The Dutch destroyer VAN GHENT was wrecked in Banka Strait off Java. The Dutch minelayer PROPAYRIA was scuttled in the Musi River. 100 Japanese paratroops were dropped to reinforce a group sent to Palembang, Sumatra the previous day. Meanwhile, Japanese amphibious forces began landing nearby. The Japanese First Air Fleet departed Palau for the Dutch East Indies. The USN submarine THRESHER was attacked by a USN PBY "Catalina" off Oahu.
1943 The USN submarine PICKEREL sank the TATEYAMA MARU (1,990 tons). The USN submarine GATO sank the SURUGA MARU (991 tons). A Japanese floatplane bombed Amchitka in the Aleutians. A 5th Air Force B24 sank the Japanese freighter KOKOKU MARU off New Britain.
1944 The IJN submarine I-43 was sunk by the USN submarine ASPRO. The IJN submarine Ro-40 was sunk by the USN destroyer PHELPS. The USN submarine SNOOK sank the HOSHI MARU II and the KAMOME MARU (875 tons). The USN submarine GATO sank the TAIYO MARU No.3 (36 tons) off Rabaul. The USN submarine TINOSA sank the ODATSUKI MARU (1,988 tons). American aircraft flying from Abemama Island in the Gilberts attacked Wake Island. USN Lieutenant Nathan Gordon won a Medal of Honor while flying a PBY on a rescue mission over the Bismarck Sea, when he rescued three bomber crews off Kavieng, New Ireland. He was later elected as Lieutenant Governor of Arkansas. New Zealand troops invaded Green Island, 115 miles east of Rabaul. The American Eniwetok invasion force left Kwajalein.

1945   USN Lieutenant Commander Eugene Fluckey, commander of the submarine BARB, won a Medal of Honor for her 11th war patrol. The US Army's 38th Division landed on the southern tip of Bataan. The USN LSM-169 was sunk by a mine in Manila Bay. IJN suicide boats attacked USN landing craft off Luzon. The USAAF attacked Corregidor. Ninety-one B29s attacked targets in Japan.

China-Burma-India
1942   Allied forces in Singapore surrendered. Allied losses for the Malayan campaign were 67,340 Indian troops, 38,496 British, 18,490 Australian and 14,382 local volunteers (total-138,708). Of that number 130,000 were prisoners. Japanese losses were 9,824. The British commander, General Arthur Percival, died in 1966. The Japanese took Thaton, Burma. The IJN submarine I-165 sank the British freighter JOHANNE JUSTESEN (4,681 tons).
1944   The U168 sank the Greek freighter EPAMINONDAS C. EMBIRICOS (4,385 tons). 14th Air Force B25s sank the Vichy French patrol boat PING SANG off Hongay, Indochina. The Japanese freighter RYOKA MARU was sunk by a mine near the mouth of the Yangtze River. The Japanese freighter HOSHI MARU was sunk off the Korean coast by a mine.
2001   Fifty-nine years to the day after the Japanese took Singapore from the British in 1942, a memorial was dedicated in that city to those involved in the battle.

February 16th

Western Europe
1926   The Royal Navy heavy cruiser SUFFOLK was launched. She was scrapped in 1948.
1936   The Leftist Popular Front won a majority in the Spanish general election.
1940   A Royal Air Force "Hudson" sighted the German tanker ALTMARK in Norwegian territorial waters and notified the Royal Navy light cruiser ARETHUSA and the destroyers COSSACK, SIKH, NUBIAN, IVANHOE and INTREPID. That evening, the COSSACK attacked the ALTMARK in Josing Fjord, killing 8 Germans and rescuing 303 British sailors that were being held aboard. The British sailors had been captured when the German pocket battleship GRAF SPEE sank their ships in the South Atlantic.
1941   Nine Royal Air Force "Blenheims" attacked targets in Holland and France.
1942   Eight Royal Air Force A20 "Bostons" attacked shipping off the Dutch coast. Martin Bormann was named to succeed Rudolf Hess in his various

posts in the Nazi hierarchy. Forty-nine Royal Air Force bombers dropped mines in the Baltic and lost two aircraft.

1943 Sixty-five B17s and B24s of the USAAF's 91st, 303rd, 305th, 306th and 44th Bomb Groups attacked St. Nazaire, France and lost six B17s and two B24s. 337 Royal Air Force bombers attacked Lorient, France and lost one "Lancaster". Thirty-two Royal Air Force bombers dropped mines off the Biscay ports. A mandatory two-year labor obligation to the German occupying forces was imposed on all French men and women born between January 1, 1920 and December 31, 1922.

1945 The U309 was sunk in the Moray Firth by the Royal Canadian Navy frigate ST. JOHN. Four German "Seehund" two-man submarines and fifteen "Linsen" explosive boats unsuccessfully attempted to attack Allied shipping in the Scheldt. 263 15th Air Force bombers dropped 559 tons of bombs on Regensburg. 987 8th Air Force bombers dropped 2,734 tons of bombs on rail and oil targets in Germany and lost seven B17s and one B24. 189 8th Air Force fighters provided escort for the bombers. 100 Royal Air Force bombers attacked Wesel, Germany. The Germans launched 160 V-1s at Antwerp.

Eastern Europe

1943 Theodor Eicke, Inspector General of Concentration Camps, was killed while on a recon flight over the Front. Soviet forces took Kharkov.

Mediterranean

1942 Petty Officer T. Gould and Lieutenant P. Robert, of the Royal Navy submarine THRASHER, won Victoria Crosses off Crete.

1943 Axis forces advanced towards Feriana and Sbeitla in Tunisia. The British 8th Army reached Medenine, Tunisia. The Royal Canadian Navy corvette LOUISBURG was sunk off Oran by Italian aircraft.

1944 The Germans began a major counter-attack at Anzio, Italy. The U230 sank the Royal Navy LST-418 off Anzio. The American 15th Air Force attacked rail targets in Italy.

Atlantic

1940 The U14 sank the Danish freighter RHONE (1,064 tons) and the Swedish freighters OSMED (1,526 tons) and LIANA (1,664 tons). U14 survived the war.

1942 The U156 shelled the oil refineries at Aruba off Venezuela, sinking the British tanker ORANJESTED (2,396 tons) and damaging the British tanker PEDERNALES (4,317 tons) and the American tanker ARKANSAS (6,452 tons). U156 survived until March 8, 1943. The US Coast Guard

cutter WOODBURY rescued 40 survivors from the tanker E.H. BLUM after she wandered into a minefield off Cape Henry, Virginia. The cutter CALYPSO rescued survivors from the Brazilian steamer BUARQUE which had been sunk the day before by U432. The U502 sank the British tankers TIJUANA (2,395 tons) and SAN NICHOLAS (2,391 tons) and the Venezuelan tanker MONAGAS (2,650 tons). U502 survived until July 5th. The U108 sank the Panamanian freighter RAMAPO (2,968 tons). U108 survived the war.
1943 The French tug GEIR (323 tons) was sunk by a mine off Fedhala.

North America
1887 Admiral Jesse Oldendorf was born in California. He graduated 141st in his 1909 Annapolis class of 174. In January 1944, he assumed command of Cruiser Division 4 of Halsey's Third Fleet in the Pacific. Later in the year, he was transferred to Kinkaid's Seventh Fleet. He retired on September 1, 1949 as a full admiral. He died on April 22, 1974 at Portsmouth, Virginia.
1942 The battleship ALABAMA was launched. She would appear in the 1988 mini-series "War and Remembrance" and would be preserved as a memorial.
1943 The French battleship RICHELIEU arrived in New York to repair damages sustained in the Royal Navy attack of September 24, 1940 on Dakar.
1944 The submarine BERGALL was launched. She was transferred to the Turkish Navy in 1958.
1945 The USN destroyer EDISON was damaged when she was rammed by the British tanker BENEDICK in New York Harbor.
1946 Staff Sergeant George Hall died from the effects of his war wounds. He had won a Medal of Honor in Italy.
1959 The destroyer PLUNKETT was sold to Taiwan.
1972 The destroyer STORMES was sold to Iran.
1974 John Garand died in Springfield, Massachusetts. He had designed the M-1 Rifle.
1995 A WWII-era floating mine was destroyed by the USN off Monterey, California. It had been discovered by a fishing boat when it was caught in a net.

Pacific
1922 The IJN light cruiser NATORI was launched. She was sunk on August 18, 1944.
1942 Forty-six Japanese aircraft attacked the HOUSTON convoy (SEE February 14th). Although they scored no hits, the convoy turned back to Darwin. Japanese forces secured Palembang, Sumatra.

1943 The Japanese Naval Air Force attacked Amchitka in the Aleutians. The USN submarine AMBERJACK was sunk off New Britain by the IJN torpedo boat HIYODORI. The USN submarine FLYING FISH sank the HYUGA MARU (994 tons). The US Army's 43rd Division was transferred to Guadalcanal in preparation for the invasion of the Russell Islands. The American 6th Army (commanded by Krueger) was activated. It consisted of the 1st Corps (commanded by Eichelberger), the 2nd Special Engineers Brigade and the 503rd Parachute Regiment.

1944 In a dawn assault, a USN force consisting of the carriers ENTERPRISE, YORKTOWN, ESSEX, INTREPID and BUNKER HILL and the light carriers BELLEAU WOOD, CABOT, COWPENS, and MONTGOMERY attacked Japanese shipping located at Truk. They were escorted by the battleships NEW JERSEY, ALABAMA, IOWA, MASSACHUSETTS, NORTH CAROLINA and SOUTH DAKOTA, the heavy cruisers BALTIMORE, SAN DIEGO, SAN FRANCISCO, WICHITA, MINNEAPOLIS and NEW ORLEANS, the light cruisers BILOXI, MOBILE, OAKLAND and SANTA FE and the destroyers C.K. BRONSON, CAPERTON, COGSWELL, COTTEN, DORTCH, GATLING, HEALY, INGERSOLL, KNAPP, HICKOX, HUNT, LEWIS HANCOCK, OWEN, STACK, STEMBEL, STEPHEN POTTER, THE SULLIVANS, BELL, BRADFORD, BROWN, BURNS, CHARRETTE, CONNOR, IZARD, LANG, LOWELL, STERETT and WILSON. Only 80 of the 365 available Japanese aircraft in the area rose to meet the attackers. By 1400 hrs, not a single airborne Japanese aircraft could be seen over the anchorage. The aerial assault would continue into the next day. At 0950, the battleships IOWA and NEW JERSEY, the cruisers NEW ORLEANS and MINNEAPOLIS and the destroyers BRADFORD, IZARD, CHARRETTE, and BURNS began a counter-clockwise sweep around Truk to prevent any IJN ships from escaping the air-attacks. They were to be designated Task Group 50.9 commanded by Spruance. The first vessel this group encountered was the sub chaser SHONAN MARU No.15. At 1310, they began firing and soon sank her. Not long after this action, they took the light cruiser KATORI under fire. During this action, the KATORI fired several torpedoes which nearly hit the IOWA. The KATORI sank at 1337 after a gallant fight. Her survivors, who numbered approximately 150, were then strafed by USN aircraft. The IJN destroyer MAIKAZE was then taken under fire. She fired torpedoes at IOWA during the action, two of which nearly hit her. There were no survivors from the destroyer when she finally sank. While the USN ships were concentrating their fire on the KATORI and MAIKAZE, the destroyer NOWAKE made good her escape from the area. The next target encountered by this force was the sub-chaser Ch-24 which was assigned as a target to the destroyer BURNS. While destroying this target, the BURNS expended 265 rounds of 5" and 500 rounds 40mm ammunition. At 1350, the USN submarine SKATE sank the IJN light cruiser AGANO 160 miles off Truk. At 1423, the Japanese freighter TATSUHA MARU (5,764 tons) was sunk by USN aircraft 75 miles west of Truk. The ZUKAI MARU (2,700 tons) was sunk in the same action. The USN submarine TINOSA sank the CHOJO MARU (2,610 tons). USN Task Group 58.4 (commanded by Ginder) attacked Eniwetok.

1945 USN Task Force 58 (commanded by Mitscher) began a two day-attack on Tokyo and Yokohama. The first strikes were hampered by bad weather. USN Task Force 54 (commanded by Rodgers), consisting of the battleships ARKANSAS, NEVADA, TEXAS, NEW YORK, TENNESSEE and IDAHO, bombarded Iwo Jima. The TENNESSEE was hit by Japanese counter-fire. The American Iwo Jima invasion force left Saipan en route to their objective. Japanese suicide boats sank the USN LCSs 7, 26 and 49 and damaged LCS-27 off Luzon. The USN bombarded Kuraba Zaki in the Kuriles. The USN submarine BOWFIN sank the IJN escort CD-56. The IJN minelayer NARYU (720 tons) was sunk by the USN submarine SENNET.

China-Burma-India
1941 The Royal Navy began mining the waters off Singapore.
1944 Major C. Hoey, of the Royal Lincolnshire Regiment, won a posthumous Victoria Cross at Arakan, Burma.
1945 Allied troops landed at Ruywa on the coast of Burma.

February 17th

Western Europe
1940 The British government announced that 400,000 more children would be evacuated from Britain's larger cities.
1941 Royal Navy Admiral Sir Percy Noble replaced Admiral Sir M. Dunbar-Nasmith as Commander of the Western Approaches.
1942 Thirteen Royal Air Force bombers attacked targets in Germany.
1943 Six Royal Air Force "Wellingtons" attacked Emden, Germany. Twelve Royal Air Force "Stirlings" dropped mines in the Bay of Biscay. Two Royal Air Force "Mosquitoes" attacked targets in Germany. Thirty-eight "Spitfires" from the USAAF's 4th Fighter Group flew patrols over the Channel.
1945 Forty-five American 8th Air Force B17s dropped 109 tons of bombs on the Giessen railyards. 286 8th Air Force bombers dropped 702 tons of bombs on Frankfurt, Hanau and Aschaffenburg in Germany and lost three B17s

and two B24s. 167 8th Air Force fighters provided escort for the bombers and lost one P51. 298 Royal Air Force bombers attacked Wesel, Germany and lost three "Halifaxes". Luftwaffe ace Jurgen Harder (64 victories) was killed in action near Swinemunde. The American 15th Air Force attacked Linz, Austria. The USN PT-605 was lost when she ran aground off Ostend, Belgium.

Eastern Europe

1943 The Soviets took Slavyansk north of Kramatorsk. Hitler, Jodl and Zeitzler visited Army Group "South" (commanded by Manstein) Headquarters at Zaporozhe.

1944 The Soviet submarine ShCh-219 was sunk by German surface craft. Surrounded German forces at Korsun were relieved. A German force of 10 divisions trapped near Kanyew in the Ukraine was destroyed. 55,000 Germans were killed and 18,500 were captured.

1945 The American freighter THOMAS SCOTT (7,176 tons) was sunk in Kola Gulf by the U968. The U425 was sunk off Murmansk by the Royal Navy sloop LARK and frigate ALNWICK CASTLE. The Royal Navy sloop LARK was torpedoed by the U968. She was salvaged by the Soviets, and was scuttled in 1960 as the NEPTUN. The Royal Navy corvette BLUEBELL was sunk off Kola Inlet by the U711, 12 men survived.

Mediterranean

1942 British General Claude Auchinleck was ordered to send 2 divisions to the Far East.

1943 The Italian submarine ASTERIA was sunk by the Royal Navy destroyers WHEATLAND and EASTON. The U205 was sunk by the Royal Navy destroyer PALADIN. The American 12th Air Force attacked Sardinian airfields. The Axis took Feriana, Tunisia.

1944 The Germans evacuated the last Monks from Monte Cassino and sent them to Rome. The American 15th Air Force attacked German troop concentrations near Anzio.

1945 The American 15th Air Force attacked Trieste and Fiume. The German torpedo boats TA-44 and TA-41 (both ex-Italian craft) were sunk at Trieste.

Atlantic

1940 The U10 sank the Norwegian freighter KVERNAAS (1,819 tons). U10 survived the war. The U37 sank the British freighter PYRRHUS (7,418 tons). U37 survived the war. The U48 sank the Finnish freighter WIJA (3,396 tons). U48 survived the war.

1941   The U101 sank the British freighter GAIRSOPPA (5,237 tons). U101 survived the war. The U103 sank the British tanker BROWN (10,455 tons). U103 survived until April 15, 1945. The U69 sank the British freighter SIAMESE PRINCE (8,564 tons).

1942   The U136 sank the British freighter EMPIRE COMET (6,914 tons). U136 survived until July 11th. The USN minesweeper DETECTOR was lost in a collision with the American tanker OSWEGO off Boston. The USN destroyer JACOB JONES and the American steamer EAGLE rescued 32 survivors from the Brazilian steamer BUARQUE which had been sunk on February 15th by U432.

1943   The U69 was sunk by the Royal Navy destroyer VISCOUNT. The Royal Navy destroyer FAME sank the U201 off Newfoundland.

1945   The U300 damaged the American freighter MICHAEL J. STONE (7,176 tons) and the British tanker REGENT LION (9,551 tons). U300 survived until February 22, 1945. The U1278 was sunk northwest of Bergen by the Royal Navy frigates BAYNTUN and LOCH ECK. The U1273 was sunk by a mine in Oslofjord, Norway.

1964   USN Admiral John D. Bulkeley, Commander of the USN Naval Station Guantanamo Bay, Cuba ordered the bases waterline to the mainland cut, thus making it self-sufficient. Bulkeley would die in 1996 and had won a Medal of Honor in 1942.

North America

1942   The submarine ALBACORE was launched. She was lost on November 7, 1944.

1943   The destroyer ABBOT was launched. She was stricken in December 1974. The carrier LEXINGTON was commissioned. She would appear in the 1976 film "Midway" and the 1988 TV mini-series "War and Remembrance" and would eventually become a memorial in Corpus Christi, Texas.

1946   The light cruiser MARBLEHEAD was sold for scrap having been decommissioned November 1, 1945.

1960   The destroyer DYSON was sold to West Germany.

2013   USAAF ace Clinton Burdick died in Santa Monica, California. He had been credited with 5.5 aerial victories while flying P51s with the 356th Fighter Group in Britain. His father, Howard, had been an ace during WWI with 8 victories, making them the only father/son combination to do so in American history.

Pacific

1942   The USN submarine TRITON sank the SHINYO MARU No.5 (1,498 tons). The Dutch destroyer VAN NESS was sunk in Banka Strait off Java by the

Japanese Naval Air Force. A battalion of "Sea-Bees" landed on Bora-Bora to build an airfield. The Allies evacuated Sumatra. A Japanese aircraft flying from the submarine I-25 flew a recon mission over Sydney, Australia.

1943 The USN submarine SAWFISH accidentally sank the Soviet freighters KOLA and ILMEN off Kyushu.

1944 American forces landed on Eniwetok. The attack on Japanese shipping and installations at Truk initiated the previous day by USN forces continued throughout the day. During the operation, USN aircraft succeeded in sinking the IJN light cruiser NAKA, the destroyers OITE, FUMITSUKI and TACHIKAZE, the sub chaser Ch-29, the MTB GYORAITEI No.10, the armed merchant cruiser AKAGI MARU (7,398 tons), the submarine tender HEIAN MARU (11,614 tons), the tankers FUJISAN MARU (9,524 tons), HOYO MARU (8,691 tons), SHINOKOKU MARU (10,020 tons) and TONAN MARU (19,209 tons), the freighters AMAGISAN MARU (7,620 tons), GOSEI MARU (1,931 tons), HAKUSHUN MARU (7,112 tons), HANAKAWA MARU (4,739 tons), HOKI MARU (7,120 tons-the former New Zealand ship HAURAKI), HOKUYO MARU (4,217 tons), KENSHO MARU (4,862 tons), MATSUTAN MARU (1,999 tons), MOMOKAWA MARU (3,829 tons), NAGANO MARU (3,824 tons), NIPPO MARU (3,764 tons), REIYO MARU (5,446 tons), MINSEI MARU (378 tons), SAN FRANCISCO MARU (5,831 tons), SANKISAN MARU (4,752 tons), SEIKO MARU (5,385 tons), TAIHO MARU (2,827 tons), TAIKICHI MARU (1,891 tons), TATSUHA MARU (5,784 tons), RIO DE JANEIRO MARU (9,626 tons), UNKAI MARU No.6 (3,220 tons), YAMAGIRI MARU (6,438 tons), YUBAE MARU (3,217 tons), ZUKAI MARU (2,700 tons) and AIKOKU MARU (10,437 tons), the transport KIYOSUMI MARU (8,614 tons) and the aircraft transport FUJIKAWA MARU (6,938 tons). Another 27 ships were damaged during the action. Also lost during the action were more than 250 Japanese aircraft. American losses were: 12 fighters, 7 torpedo bombers and 6 dive-bombers and personnel losses totaled 29 aircrew. After this operation senior American commanders decided to cancel the planned invasion of Truk and invade the Marianas instead. The IJN destroyer FUMITSUKI was sunk off Truk by USN carriers. The USN carrier INTREPID was hit by an aircraft torpedo, 11 died and 17 were wounded. USN destroyers bombarded Rabaul, New Britain and Kavieng, New Ireland. The USN submarine TANG sank the GYOTEN MARU (6,854 tons) and the KUNIEI MARU (5,184 tons). The USN submarine SARGO sank the NICHIRO MARU (6,534 tons). The USN submarine CERO sank the JOZAN MARU (1,086 tons).

1945 For the 2nd consecutive day, USN carrier aircraft attacked Tokyo and Yokohama. They flew 2,761 sorties over the two days and lost sixty aircraft in combat and twenty-eight due to accidents. The US Army's 503rd Regimental Combat Team parachuted onto Corregidor. The 3/34th Infantry landed by boat. The USN LCS-26 was sunk off Luzon by a suicide boat. USN Lieutenant Rufus Herring, commander of LCI-449, won a Medal of Honor off Iwo Jima. The USN cruiser PENSACOLA was hit by counter-fire off Iwo Jima and suffered 17 dead and 119 wounded. USN Boatswain's Mate 2nd Class Owen Hammerberg won a posthumous Medal of Honor while serving as a diver in the salvage of a sunken LST in the West Loch of Pearl Harbor. The IJN escort No.56 was sunk by the USN submarine BOWFIN. 7th Air Force B24s attacked Japanese shipping off Chichi Jima and sank the tanker NANSHIN MARU No.28 and the freighter DAIBI MARU.

China-Burma-India
1943   The 55th Indian Brigade failed in its attack on Donbaik, Burma. The U516 sank the American freighter DEER LODGE (6,187 tons-2 dead). U516 survived the war. The U182 sank the British freighter LLANASHE (4,836 tons). U182 was on sunken May 16, 1943.
1944   The American 10th Air Force destroyed the Moulmein Rail Bridge in Burma.
1945   Parkash Singh, of the 13th Frontier Force Rifles, won a posthumous Victoria Cross in Burma.

February 18th

Western Europe
1913   Hitler Youth Leader Artur Axmann was born in Hagen.
1924   The Royal Navy carrier HERMES was commissioned. She was sunk in 1942 by Japanese carrier aircraft.
1937   Ben Leider, a volunteer with Republic forces in Spain, became the first American pilot killed in the Spanish Civil War.
1942   Twenty-five Royal Air Force "Hampdens" dropped mines in the Baltic and lost one aircraft.
1943   Twenty-six Royal Air Force "Mosquitoes" attacked Tours, France and lost one aircraft. 195 Royal Air Force bombers attacked Wilhelmshaven, Germany and lost four "Lancasters". Five people were killed in the raid. Eighty-nine Royal Air Force bombers dropped mines along the Atlantic coast and lost two "Halifaxes". Twenty-six "Spitfires" from the USAAF 4th Fighter Group flew patrols over the Channel.
1944   Royal Canadian Air Force and Royal Australian Air Force "Mosquitos" breached the wall of the Amiens Prison, freeing seventy Resistance

leaders. Group/Captain P. Pickard, the mission leader, was killed on the raid. SHAEF officially announced that the American 9th Air Force was operating from Britain. 187 Luftwaffe aircraft attacked Britain, losing 11 aircraft.

1945 American 15th Air Force bombers dropped 417 tons of bombs on Linz, Austria. 160 Royal Air Force bombers attacked Wesel, Germany. A German prisoner of war was recaptured while in the cockpit of a P51C at Royal Air Force Rednal. He had escaped from the Owestry Prisoner of War Camp the previous day. Audie Murphy won a Legion of Merit in Germany. Murphy would end the war as Americas most decorated soldier. Forty-four Royal Air Force "Mosquitoes" attacked targets in Germany. Twenty-five Royal Air Force bombers dropped mines in the Baltic and lost two "Lancasters". U2344 was lost in a collision with the U2336 in the Baltic.

1958 The Royal Navy battleship DUKE OF YORK was scrapped.

1994 Thirteen Royal Air Force veterans of a 1944 raid on a Gestapo prison in Amiens met at the site (See 1944). Seventy prisoners and twenty Germans had been killed in the attack.

Eastern Europe

1895 Soviet Marshal Semen Timoshenko was born. He died on March 31, 1970.

1940 Finnish forces retreated to new defensive positions.

1944 The Soviets took Staraya-Russa, south of Novgorod.

1945 General Ivan Chernyakovsky, commander of the 3rd Byelorussian Front, was killed in East Prussia near Konigsberg.

1994 The war crimes trial of Boleslav Maikovski, a 90-year-old Latvian, was discontinued because of the ill health of the defendant.

Mediterranean

1941 The Luftwaffe dropped mines in the Suez Canal. German forces in North Africa were officially designated the "Deutsches Afrika Korps".

1943 The Axis entered Sbeitla, Tunisia. British forces took Tatahouine, Tunisia.

1944 At 0730, the Royal Navy light cruiser PENELOPE was sunk off Naples by the U410. 250 members of her crew were rescued.

Atlantic

1940 The Royal Navy destroyer DARING was sunk by the U23 (commanded by Kretschmer). There were fifteen survivors from her crew. The U61 sank the Panamanian freighter EL SONADOR (1,406 tons) and the Norwegian freighter SANGSTAD (4,297 tons). U61 survived the war. The U37 sank the Greek freighter ELLIN (4,917 tons) and French freighter P.L.M.-15

(3,754 tons). U37 survived the war. The U10 sank the Dutch freighter AMELAND (4,537 tons). U10 survived the war. The U53 sank the Spanish freighter BANDERAS (2,140 tons). U53 survived until February 21st.

1941 The U96 sank the British freighter BLACK OSPREY (5,589 tons). U96 survived until March 30, 1945. The U103 sank the British freighter SEAFORTH (5,459 tons). U103 survived until April 15, 1945.

1942 The French submarine SURCOUF was rammed and sunk in the Gulf of Mexico by the American freighter THOMPSON LYKES. 159 members of her crew died. The U432 sank the Brazilian freighter OLINDA (4,053 tons). U432 survived until March 11, 1943. The U108 sank the British freighter SOMME (5,265 tons). U108 survived the war.

1943 The Brazilian freighter BRASILOIDE (6,075 tons) was sunk by the U518. U518 survived until April 22, 1945.

1944 The U406 was sunk by the Royal Navy frigate SPEY.

North America

1892 Presidential candidate Wendell Willkie was born in Elwood, Indiana. He would die on October 8, 1944.

1942 At 0410, the destroyer TRUXTEN and at 0417 the freighter POLLUX ran aground in Placentia Bay, Newfoundland. 203 men died aboard the two ships. The USN destroyer WILKES also ran aground, but was saved.

1943 The second XB29 "Superfortress" test aircraft caught fire and crashed into Frye Packing Plant on Airport Way near the Seattle Airport. The crash killed the entire crew of the aircraft as well as twenty people on the ground. The tragedy and the continuing problems with the engines were investigated by Senator Harry Truman's committee. The committee concluded that the USAAF had placed quantity before quality when it ordered 40,000 engines before they were properly developed.

1944 The escort carrier PETROF BAY was commissioned. She was scrapped in 1959.

1959 The light cruiser COLUMBIA was sold for scrap.

1960 The light cruiser CLEVELAND was sold for scrap.

1981 Aircraft designer Jack Northrup died.

Pacific

1941 USN Admiral Husband Kimmel, commander of the Pacific Fleet, requested that Chief of Naval Operations Harold Stark ensure that he receive all information pertaining to the Pacific area.

1942 The Dutch submarine KXII and the coastal defense ship SOERABAJA were sunk at Surabaya, Java by the Japanese Naval Air Force. The Japanese landed on Bali. The HOUSTON convoy (See February 16th) returned to

Darwin, Australia. The USN heavy cruiser HOUSTON and the destroyer PEARY refueled and left Darwin, Australia to join the ABDA forces near Java. PEARY expended most of her fuel hunting for a submarine and was forced to return to Darwin. The Japanese First Air Fleet arrived in the Banda Sea, northwest of Australia.

1943 USN Task Group 8.6 (commanded by McMorris), consisting of the heavy cruiser INDIANAPOLIS, the light cruiser RICHMOND and 4 destroyers bombarded Attu in the Aleutians. An 11th Air Force B24 attempted to bomb the American ships, but its bomb-release mechanism failed. A Japanese floatplane was shot down near Amchitka in the Aleutians. American reinforcements arrived on Guadalcanal in preparation for the invasion of the Russell Islands. A Royal Australian Air Force PBY attacked Kahili, Bougainville.

1944 "Avengers" torpedo bombers from the USN carrier ENTERPRISE flew the first night raid in USN history when they attacked Japanese shipping at Truk. Allied destroyers bombarded Rabaul, New Britain and Kavieng, New Ireland. The Royal Navy submarine TRESPASSER damaged the EIFUKU MARU (3,520 tons).

1945 The USN forces (commanded by Radford) attacked Iwo Jima and Chichi Jima. The USN destroyer-minelayer GAMBLE was a constructive loss after an air-attack off Iwo Jima. USN cruisers and destroyers bombarded Japanese positions in the Kuriles.

1954 Royal Australian Navy Captain R.C. Garcia died. He had commanded convoys to Suez, Singapore, Bombay and New Guinea during the war.

February 19th

Western Europe

1916 The Royal Navy battleships VALIANT and MALAYA were commissioned. They were both scrapped in 1948.

1941 German S-boats sank the British freighter ALGARVE (1,355 tons) off the Thames Estuary.

1942 Lord Beaverbrook resigned his post of British Minister of Production. He died in 1964. Eight Royal Air Force "Wellingtons" attacked targets in Germany.

1943 Twelve Royal Air Force "Venturas" attacked targets in Holland. 338 Royal Air Force bombers attacked Wilhelmshaven, Germany and lost twelve aircraft. Three people were injured in the raid. Twenty-four "Spitfires" from the USAAF's 4th Fighter Group flew a sweep in the St. Omer area of France.

1944 The Luftwaffe attacked the USAAF's 4th Fighter Groups base at Debden in Britain. 823 Royal Air Force bombers attacked Leipzig, Germany and lost seventy-four aircraft. Forty-nine Royal Air Force bombers dropped mines in Kiel Bay. Fifteen Royal Air Force "Mosquitoes" attacked Berlin and lost one aircraft.

1945   1,073 American 8th Air Force bombers dropped 3,084 tons of bombs on rail, industrial and oil targets in Germany and lost one B24. 521 8th Air Force fighters provided support for the bombers and claimed three victories for the loss of seven P51s. 168 Royal Air Force bombers attacked Wesel, Germany and lost one "Lancaster". The American 15th Air Force attacked railyards at Graz and Klagenfurt, Austria. American forces took Hammerdingen, Nusbaum, Niedergegen and Stockem in Germany. 260 Royal Air Force bombers attacked Bohlen, Germany and lost one "Mosquitoes". 106 Royal Air Force "Mosquitoes" attacked targets in Germany.

1952   Norwegian novelist Knut Hamsun, who had been fined $65,000 by a German de-nazification court for "Profiting from the Nazi Regime", died at age 93.

Eastern Europe

1940   Soviet forces penetrated the Finnish intermediate defense line.

1945   The U676 was sunk in Gulf of Finland by a mine.

Mediterranean

1937   An attempt was made on the life of the Italian Viceroy of Ethiopia (Graziani).

1942   The Luftwaffe attacked Malta. The French battleship DUNKERQUE sailed from Mers-el-Kebir for Toulon to repair damage suffered in the Royal Navy attacks of July 1940.

1943   The Axis forces commanded by German Field Marshal Erwin Rommel attacked American positions near the Kasserine Pass in Tunisia and were repulsed. During the night, Rommel would bring up reinforcements and resume his attack the next day. The U562 was sunk north of Benghazi by the Royal Navy destroyers IRIS and HURSLEY.

1944   The Allies gained more than a mile on the Anzio Front. Private First-Class William Johnston, of the 45th Division, won a Medal of Honor near Padiglione, Italy. The American freighter EDWARD BATES ((7,176 tons-dead) was sunk off Algeria by a Luftwaffe Ju88.

Atlantic

1941   The U69 sank the British freighter EMPIRE BLANDA (5,693 tons). U69 survived until February 17, 1943. The U103 sank the Norwegian freighter BENJAMIN FRANKLIN (7,034 tons). U103 survived until April 15, 1945.

1942 The U432 sank the British freighter MIRAFLORES (2,158 tons). U432 survived until March 11, 1943. The American tanker PAN MASSACHUSETTS (8,202 tons-20 dead) was sunk by the U128. The US Coast Guard cutter FORWARD rescued eighteen of her crew. U128 survived until May 17, 1943. The USN destroyer DALLAS rescued forty-six survivors from the Brazilian tanker OLINDA which had been sunk the day before by U432. The U96 sank the tanker EMPIRE SEAL (7,965 tons). U96 survived until March 30, 1945.

1943 The American submarine BLACKFISH sank the German patrol boat V-408 in the Bay of Biscay. The U403 sank the Greek freighter ZEUS (5,961 tons). U403 survived until August 17th. The U268 was sunk off La Pallice by the Royal Air Force's No.172 Squadron. U268 survived until February 19th.

1944 The U264 was sunk by the Royal Navy sloops WOODPECKER and STARLING. The U386 was sunk by the Royal Navy frigate SPEY.

North America

1936 USAAC General William "Billy" Mitchell died in New York City.

1941 Rear Admiral William Blandy relieved Rear Admiral William Furlong as Chief of the Bureau of Ordnance.

1942 FDR signed executive order No.9066 authorizing the removal of "Any and All" persons from sensitive areas (i.e. Nisei to relocation camps). Canada's Parliament voted to begin conscription. The destroyer NICHOLAS was launched. She was stricken in January 1970.

1945 A Japanese balloon-bomb was found near Takla Landing, British Columbia.

1947 The destroyer BULMER was sold for scrap.

1982 The plaster cast of the Iwo Jima Memorial was dedicated at the Marine Military Academy in Harlingen, Texas. The original statue had been unveiled at Arlington Cemetery in 1954.

Pacific

1942 188 aircraft from the IJN carriers AKAGI, KAGA, HIRYU and SORYU (the First Air Feet), while en route to Darwin, Australia, sank the freighters DON ISIDORO (3,261 tons-14 dead) and FLORENCE D. (2,638 tons-4 dead). They were blockade runners en route to the Philippines. They also shot down a USN PBY piloted by Lieutenant Thomas H. Moorer. He would be named as Chairman of the Joint Chiefs of Staff on April 14, 1970. They then attacked Darwin sinking the USN destroyer PEARY (80 of her crew died) and the freighters NEPTUNA, ZEALANDIA and BRITISH MOTORIST, and causing the American transports MEIGS (1 dead) and MAUNA LOA (1 dead) and the freighters BAROSSA, TULAGI and

PORTMAR (2 dead) to be beached. They also damaged the USN aircraft tender PRESTON and the freighter ADMIRAL HALSTEAD and the Royal Australian Navy vessels PLATYPUS, SWAN, GUNBAR, KARA-KARA, KOOKABURRA, KANGAROO, COONGOOLA and the hospital ship MANUNDA. Total Allied casualties 240 dead and 150 wounded. The Dutch destroyer PIET HEIN was sunk in Badoeng Strait, off Bali, by the IJN destroyers MICHISHIO, OSHIO and ASASHIO. The USN destroyer STEWART was damaged by the IJN. Japanese forces landed on Timor and Bali. The USN submarine SWORDFISH evacuated Philippine President Quezon from Corregidor. The Japanese Naval Air Force destroyed two B17s at Bandoeng, Java. British General Archibald Wavell asked the Combined Chiefs to dissolve the ABDA (American-British-Dutch-Australian) Command.

1943 Royal Australian Air Force PBYs and 5th Air Force B17s attacked Kahili, Bougainville and Ballale Island off southern Bougainville. The USN submarine BLACKFISH sank the IJN patrol boat VP-408 (445 tons). USN Task Group 8.6 (commanded by McMorris) sank the Japanese freighter ARAGANE MARU off Attu in the Aleutians.

1944 USN Task Group 51.11 (commanded by Hill) landed a USMC force on Eniwetok in the Marshalls. American aircraft attacked Rabaul, New Britain. After repeated attacks the Japanese abandon any attempt of defending the air over Rabaul. 5th Air Force aircraft attack Japanese shipping off Kavieng, New Ireland and sink the sub-chaser CHA-34, CH-22, CH-40 and the freighters SHINTO MARU NO.1 and SHINKIKU MARU. USAAF B25s and B24s sank the Japanese freighter EBON MARU in the Carolines. The USN submarine GRAYBACK sank the TAIKEI MARU (4,739 tons) and the TOSHIN MARU (1,917 tons). The USN submarine JACK sank the NANEI MARU (5,019 tons), the KOKUEI MARU (5,154 tons), the NICHIRIN MARU (5,162 tons), the ICHIYO MARU (5,106 tons) and the ASANAGI MARU (5,141 tons).

1945 30,000 men of the 4th and 5th USMC Divisions landed on Iwo Jima. USMC Sergeant Darrell Cole, of the 4th Division, and USMC Corporal Tony Stein, of the 5th Division, won posthumous Medals of Honor on Iwo Jima. USMC Gunnery Sergeant John Basilone was killed in action on Iwo Jima. He won a Navy Cross for his actions that day and had been awarded a Medal of Honor during the 1942 battle on Guadalcanal. Brigadier General Paul Wurtsmith assumed command of the American 13th Air Force. 119 USAAF B29s attacked Tokyo. The US Army's Americal Division landed on Samar in the Philippines. Private Lloyd McCarter, of the US Army's 503rd Regimental Combat Team, won a Medal of Honor on Corregidor. 101 B29s attacked Tokyo and lost five aircraft.

China-Burma-India
1941 The Australian 8th Division arrived in Singapore.
1944 14th Air Force B24s sank the Japanese freighter TAIRYU MARU off Formosa.

February 20th

Western Europe
1938 Anthony Eden resigned as British Foreign Minister and was replaced by Lord Halifax.
1940 Two of twenty Royal Air Force "Wellingtons" were lost on an abortive shipping strike.
1942 At 0300, the first element of the American 8th Air Force including its commanding officer General Ira Eaker and six other officers arrived at Whitechurch Airfield outside of Bristol, Britain after a flight from Lisbon, Portugal aboard a DC-3. The German minesweeper JASON was sunk off Calais by a mine.
1943 Twenty Royal Air Force "Wellingtons" dropped mines off Denmark and lost one aircraft. Two "Spitfires" from the USAAF's 4th Fighter Group flew patrols over the Channel.
1944 "Operation Argument" began. It was an intense air offensive against the German aircraft industry. 296 8th Air Force B17s dropped 708 tons of bombs on Tutow and Rostock in Germany and lost six aircraft. One of the missing B17s landed in Sweden. 584 8th Air Force B17s and B24s dropped 1,510 tons of bombs on Leipzig, Oschersleben, Brunswick, Gotha and Bernberg in Germany and lost seven B17s and eight B24s. 1st Lieutenant William Lawley, of the 305th Bomb Group (B17), won a Medal of Honor on the mission. 2nd Lieutenant Walter Truemper and Sergeant Archibald Mathies, of the 351st Bomb Group (B17), won posthumous Medals of Honor over Europe. They were the navigator and engineer aboard a damaged B17 that had a badly wounded pilot and a dead co-pilot. They flew it back to Britain and allowed the rest of the crew to bail out. On their 4th attempt to land at their base at Polebrook and save the pilot as well as the aircraft they crashed and both were killed. 835 8th and 9th Air Force fighters provided support for the bombers and claimed 61 victories for the loss of 1 P38, 2 P47s and 1 P51. American 9th Air Force B26s attacked Dutch airfields. The Luftwaffe established Kampfgeschwader 200 which was to be responsible for a variety of special missions including flying captured Allied aircraft and special agent operations. The Norwegian ferry HYDRO, while loaded with Germany's supply of heavy water, was sunk by saboteurs. 528 Royal Air Force bombers attacked Dortmund,

Germany and lost fourteen "Lancasters". 173 Royal Air Force bombers attacked Dusseldorf, Germany and lost five aircraft. 128 Royal Air Force bombers attacked Monheim and lost two "Halifaxes". 165 Royal Air Force bombers attacked the Mittelland Canal. Thirty-four Royal Air Force bombers dropped mines off the French coast and lost one "Wellington". Eighty-two Royal Air Force "Mosquitoes" attacked targets in Germany. Four B17s from the USAAF's 422nd Bomb Squadron dropped 200 bundles of supplies for resistance forces near Tours, Nantes, Brest and Lorient.

1945 The American 15th Air Force attacked Nuremburg, Germany. 860 8th Air Force bombers dropped 2,176 tons of bombs on the Nuremburg railyards and lost five B17s. 670 8th Air Force fighters provided support for the bombers and claimed forty-nine victories for the loss of six P51s and seven P47s.

1996 Jeffery Quill died at the age of 83. He had been the second man to fly the "Spitfire" prototype.

Eastern Europe

1907 Soviet General Sergei Shtemenko was born. He died on April 23, 1976 at the age of sixty-nine.

1940 Russia offered new peace terms to Finland.

1942 The Germans took Novo-Moskovsk. German casualties for the war in the East to this point were 199,448 dead, 708,351 wounded, 112,627 cases of frostbite and 44,342 missing.

1943 The Soviets took Pavlograd and Krasnograd.

Mediterranean

1941 British and Germans patrols made contact for the first time in North Africa, near El Agheila, Libya. A Luftwaffe anti/aircraft unit (the 33rd Squadron, 1st Group) joined the DAK at Tripoli.

1942 Axis aircraft attacked Malta. At 2300, the French battle cruiser DUNKERQUE arrived in Toulon from Mers el Kabir in North Africa. She would never sail again. On November 27, 1942 she was scuttled along with most of the French fleet. Her hulk was sold in 1958 for $723,000.

1943 Axis forces attacked American-held positions in the Kasserine Pass in Tunisia and forced the Americans to withdraw with the loss of almost 1,000 dead and hundreds more captured. The USAAF's 98th Bomb Group B24 "Blonde Bomber II" landed in error at Pachino, Sicily and was captured.

1944 The American 15th Air Force attacked troop concentrations near Anzio. The USN LST-348 was sunk off Anzio by the U410. The U230 sank the USN LST-305 off Anzio.

1945 The American 15th Air Force attacked Trieste, Pola and Fiume in Italy.

Atlantic

1940 The U19 damaged the British tanker DAGHESTAN. A German U-boat entered Fort du France Harbor in Martinique and requested medical aid for its executive officer. It was rendered and he was interned by the French.

1941 Luftwaffe Fw-200s damaged four ships in an Allied convoy.

1942 The Italian submarine TORELLI sank the British freighter SCOTTISH STAR (7,224 tons). The U129 sank the Norwegian freighter NORDVANGEN (2,400 tons). U129 was scuttled in 1944. The U96 sank the American freighter LAKE OSWEYA (2,398 tons) with all hands. U96 was sunk on March 30, 1945. The U156 sank the American freighter DELPLATA (5,127 tons). The USN seaplane tender LAPWING rescued her fifty-two survivors. U156 survived until March 8, 1943. The U432 sank the American freighter AZALEA CITY (5,529 tons-with all hands). U432 survived until March 11, 1943.

1943 The U525 sank the British freighter RADHURST (3,454 tons). U525 survived until August 11, 1943.

1944 At 0001, the Royal Navy sloop WOODPECKER was torpedoed by the U764 and foundered on the 27th while under tow. She had participated in the sinking of 5 U-boats before her loss. U764 survived the war. At 1145, the Royal Navy destroyer WARWICK (launched in 1918) was sunk off Cornwall by the U413. Ninety-three of her crew survived. U413 survived until August 20, 1944.

1945 The Royal Navy corvette VERVAIN was sunk south of Ireland by the U1208. U1208 survived until February 20th.

North America

1936 The destroyer SMITH was launched at Mare Island, California. She was scrapped in 1947.

1939 20,000 members of the German-American Bund staged a rally at Madison Square Garden.

1942 America granted a $1-billion loan to Russia. The destroyers DUNCAN, HUTCHINS, LANSDOWNE, and GUEST were launched. DUNCAN was sunk by the IJN on October 11, 1942, HUTCHINS was scrapped in 1948, LANSDOWNE was transferred to Turkey in 1949 and GUEST was transferred to Brazil in 1959.

1943 The escort carrier BARNES was commissioned. She was scrapped in 1960. The USN minesweeper YMS-133 foundered off Coos Bay, Oregon.

1944 The light cruiser OKLAHOMA CITY (awarded 2 battle stars during WWII and 13 more during the Viet Nam War) was launched. She was stricken in 1979.

1968 The destroyer SAUFLEY was expended as a target.

Pacific

1942 Japanese forces took Bali and Timor. USN forces commanded by Admiral Wilson Brown, including the carrier LEXINGTON, attempted to raid Rabaul, but were driven off by Japanese aircraft. Lieutenant Edward O'Hare, of the carrier LEXINGTON, won a Medal of Honor while flying an F4F "Wildcat" off the LEXINGTON. The USN destroyer STEWART was damaged in action with the IJN destroyers ASASHIO and OSHIO off Bali. The USN submarine SWORDFISH departed Mariveles with Philippine President Quezon, his family, and members of his cabinet aboard. As a result of the Japanese air-raid, the Allies abandoned Darwin, Australia as a naval base.

1943 The IJN destroyer OSHIO was sunk off Manus Island by the USN submarine ALBACORE. The USN submarine HALIBUT sank the SHINKOKU MARU (3,991 tons) off Saipan.

1944 USN Task Group 58.1 (commanded by Reeves) attacked Jaluit in the Marshalls. USMC Captain John Glenn, American astronaut, and senator, began flying F4U "Corsairs" in the Marshalls; he would fly fifty-nine missions and win two Distinguished Flying Crosses. The New Zealand 3rd Division secured Green Island off New Ireland. The Japanese withdrew their last fifty-seven aircraft from Rabaul and sent them to Truk. The Royal Australian Air Force attacked Aiyau, New Guinea. The USN submarine POGY sank the NANYO MARU (3,614 tons) and the TAIJAN MARU (5,154 tons).

1945 USMC Private First-Class Jacklyn Lucas, of the 5th Division, won a Medal of Honor on Iwo Jima. The IJN destroyer NOKAZE was sunk by the USN submarine PARGO. The USN submarine HAWKBILL sank the DAIZEN MARU (5,396 tons). The USN submarine GUAVINA sank the EIYO MARU (8,673 tons).

China-Burma-India

1932 The Japanese occupied Tunhua, China.

1941 The German pocket battleship SCHEER took the freighters BRITISH ADVOCATE, GREGORIOS and CANADIAN CRUISER, northeast of Madagascar.

1942 The IJN submarine I-165 sank the British freighter BHIMA (5,280 tons).

1943 The hospital ship ATLANTIS rescued the last 10 survivors from the American freighter DEER LODGE which had been sunk off South Africa on February 16th by U607.

February 21st

Western Europe
1917   Luftwaffe ace Otto Kittel (267 aerial victories) was born in Kronsdorf. He died on the Eastern Front.
1934   Hitler told Anthony Eden that he was prepared to reduce the S.A. by two-thirds and eliminate their military training.
1939   The Royal Navy battleship KING GEORGE V was launched. She was scrapped in 1958.
1940   Hitler designated General Nikolaus von Falkenhorst as commander of the Norwegian invasion. Falkenhorst was chosen because of his experience in amphibious operations during the First World War.
1941   Thirty-four Royal Air Force bombers attacked Wilhelmshaven, Germany and lost one "Wellington". Forty-two Royal Air Force "Hampdens" dropped mines off Brest, France.
1942   The German pocket battleship SCHEER and heavy cruiser PRINZ EUGEN left Germany for Norway. Forty-two Royal Air Force bombers attacked targets in Germany and lost three aircraft. Fifteen Royal Air Force bombers attacked Norwegian airfields and lost one "Manchester".
1943   German General Heinz Guderian was appointed Inspector General of Armored Troops. He had been retired by Hitler as a result of his action in Russia the previous year. 143 Royal Air Force bombers attacked Bremen, Germany.
1944   762 American 8th Air Force B17s and B24s dropped 1,978 tons of bombs on airfields in Germany and lost thirteen B17s and three B24s. Two of the lost B17s went down over Britain after colliding soon after take-off. In 1964, the wreckage was excavated. Among the items recovered was a parachute which was donated to the Air Force Museum at Wright-Patterson in Ohio. 679 8th Air Force fighters provided support for the bombers and claimed thirty-three victories for the loss of two P47s and three P51s. The 457th Bomb Group (B17) flew its first 8th Air Force mission. American 9th Air Force B26s attacked French and Dutch airfields. The Allied High Command considered crossing the Irish border and closing the Axis embassies. Forty-one Royal Air Force bombers dropped mines off the French coast and lost one "Stirling". Five B17s from the USAAF's 422nd Bomb Squadron dropped 250 bundles of supplies for resistance forces near Rouen, Caen, Paris, and Amiens in France.
1945   The British Army's XXX Corps took Goch, Germany. 1,219 American 8th Air Force bombers dropped 2,891 tons of bombs on Nuremburg, Germany. 743 8th Air Force fighters provided support for the bombers and claimed four victories for the loss of seven P51s. The American 15th Air Force attacked Vienna, Austria. The first flight of the Hawker "Sea

Fury" took place. Royal Air Force "Typhoons" attacked V-2 launching sites at Heek and Zeist in Holland. 373 Royal Air Force bombers attacked Duisburg, Germany and lost ten aircraft. 349 Royal Air Force bombers attacked Worms, Germany and lost eleven aircraft. 239 people were killed in the raid. 177 Royal Air Force bombers attacked the Mittelland Canal and lost thirteen aircraft. Eighty-two Royal Air Force "Mosquitoes" attacked targets in Germany. Luftwaffe night-fighter ace Heinz-Wolfgang Schnaufer shot down 7 Royal Air Force "Lancasters" over Germany.
2010 RAF Wing Commander Bob Doe died at the age of 89. He had scored 14 aerial victories during the Battle of Britain.

Eastern Europe
1940 The construction of the Auschwitz Concentration Camp began.
1942 German forces took Pavlograd.
1943 Luftwaffe ace Hans Hahn (108 aerial victories) was forced down by engine trouble and captured.
1944 The Soviets took Kholm and Soltsy, south of Leningrad.
1945 Hungary declared war on the Axis.

Mediterranean
1941 The Royal Navy carrier INDOMITABLE attacked Massawa, Ethiopia. The Royal Navy submarine REGENT damaged a 5,609-ton German steamer.
1942 Axis aircraft attacked Malta.

Atlantic
1940 The German blockade runner WAHEHE (4,709 tons) was captured by the Royal Navy's cruiser MANCHESTER and destroyer KIMBERLEY. The U50 sank the Dutch freighter TARA (4,760 tons). U50 survived until April 29th. The U57 and U23 sank the British freighter LOCH MADDY (4,996 tons). U57 survived the war and U23 survived until September 10, 1944. The U53 was sunk off the Orkneys by the Royal Navy destroyer GURKHA.
1941 The Royal Navy destroyer CLARE (the ex-USN UPSHUR) was damaged in a collision with the freighter PETERTOWN. A Luftwaffe Fw-200 damaged a 6,999-ton tanker.
1942 The U432 sank the American freighter AZALEA CITY (5,529 tons). U432 survived until March 11, 1943. The U161 sank the British tanker CIRCE SHELL (8,207 tons). U161 survived until April 27, 1943. The U67 sank the American tanker J.N. PEW (9,033 tons-33 dead). U67 survived until July 16, 1943.
1943 The U332 and U603 sank the Norwegian tanker STIGSTAD (5,964 tons). U332 survived until May 2nd and U603 survived until March 1, 1944.

The U225 was sunk by the US Coast Guard cutter SPENCER. The U623 was sunk by the Royal Air Force's No.120 Squadron. The U664 sank the American freighter ROSARIO (4,659 tons-thirty-three dead) and the Panamanian tanker H.H. ROGERS (8,807 tons). U664 survived until August 9th. The U92 sank the British freighter EMPIRE TRADER (9,990 tons). U92 was scrapped after the war. The British freighter PENRITH CASTLE rescued 28 survivors from the American freighter ROGER B. TANEY which had been sunk on February 8th by U160.

1945 The U1064 sank the Icelandic freighter DETTIFOSS (1,564 tons). U1064 survived the war.

North America

1943 The destroyer BROWN was launched. She was transferred to Greece in 1962. The submarine BLUEFISH was launched. She was discarded in 1959. The USN YMS-133 foundered in Coos Bay, Oregon.

1945 A Japanese balloon-bomb was found near Sumas, Washington.

1946 USN Admiral Theodore Wilkinson, commander of the 3rd Amphibious Force in the Pacific, died in a car wreck in Norfolk, Virginia.

1947 George C. Marshall was appointed as US Secretary of State.

Pacific

1941 The USN carrier ENTERPRISE arrived off Oahu and launched thirty USAAC P-36s which would be based at Wheeler Field.

1942 The USN submarine TRITON sank the SHOKYU MARU (4,486 tons). The USN destroyer STEWART was moved into a floating drydock in Surabaya, Java to repair damage suffered the previous day in action with IJN forces off Bali. While being positioned within the confines of the drydock she capsized and was seriously damaged.

1943 The Dutch submarine 0-24 sank the BANDAI MARU (165 tons). The US Army's 43rd Division occupied Banika and Pavuvu in the Russells.

1944 The Royal Navy submarine TALLY HO sank the DAIGEN MARU No.6 (510 tons). A 5" shell exploded aboard the USN battleship ALABAMA off the Marianas and five of her crew died. Japanese resistance ended on Eniwetok. Royal Australian Air Force attacked Saidor, New Guinea. General Hidecki Tojo was named as military ruler of Japan. American SBDs and TBFs attacked Rabaul, New Britain. 5th Air Force B25s attacked a Japanese convoy off New Hanover and sank the sub chasers CHA-38 and CHA-48, the transport KOKAI MARU and the gunboat KOWA MARU.

1945 American forces secured Bataan Peninsula on Luzon. The USN carrier SARATOGA (123 of her crew died), the escort carrier LUNGA POINT, the freighter KEOKUK and the LSTs 477 and 809 were hit by kamikazes off Iwo Jima. The USN escort carrier BISMARCK SEA was sunk by a kamikaze off Iwo Jima. 218 of her crew died. The USN attack-transport NAPA was rammed by the attack-transport LOGAN off Iwo Jima. USMC Captain Robert Dunlap and Private First Class Donald Ruhl (posthumous), of the 5th Division, won Medals of Honor on Iwo Jima. USMC Captain Joseph McCarthy and Sergeant Ross Gray (posthumous), of the 4th Division, won Medals of Honor on Iwo Jima. The USN submarine GATO sank the TAIRIKU MARU (2,325 tons). The IJN submarine Ro-43 damaged the USN destroyer RENSHAW.

China-Burma-India
1941   The German pocket battleship SCHEER took the Dutch freighter RANTAU PANTJANG.
1942   The USN light cruiser MARBLEHEAD arrived in Ceylon, en route to America from action in the Southwest Pacific.
1944   The U168 damaged the Norwegian tanker FENRIS (9,804 tons).

February 22nd

Western Europe
1941   425 Jews were arrested in Amsterdam, Holland. Twenty-nine Royal Air Force "Wellingtons" attacked Brest, France. No aircraft were lost on the raid, but four aircraft crashed upon returning to their bases in Britain.
1942   Air Chief Marshal Sir Arthur Harris assumed command of the Royal Air Force's Bomber Command. The Commands strength at this time consisted of 469-night bombers and 78-day bombers. Fifty Royal Air Force bombers attacked Wilhelmshaven, Germany. Since November 11th, the Bomber Command had flown 5,544 sorties on which it had dropped 5,322 tons of bombs and lost 165 aircraft. The headquarters for the USAAF's 8th Bomber Command was activated at High Wycombe.
1943   Hans and Sophie Scholl (of "The White Rose Movement") were hung in Munich. "The White Rose Movement" was an anti-Nazi program organized by students in Munich.
1944   255 8th Air Force B17s and B24s dropped 667 tons of bombs on targets in Holland and Germany and lost thirty-eight B17s and three B24s. B24s dropped their bombs on Nijmegen, Holland killing 200 Dutch civilians. Luftwaffe ace Horst Sternberg (23 aerial victories), was killed by USAAF B17 gunners over Magdeburg. 659 8th and 9th Air Force fighters provided support for the bombers and claimed fifty-nine victories for the loss of eight P47s and three P51s. Luftwaffe ace Edward Tratt (38 aerial victories) was killed by USAAF 354th Fighter Group P51s. USAAF 353rd Fighter Group (P47) ace Walter Beckham (16 victories) was shot down

by ground-fire over France and captured. The American 15th Air Force attacked the Messerschmitt factory at Obertraubling near Regensburg and lost nineteen bombers and two escorting fighters. A USAAF 92nd Bomb Group B17 accidentally dropped a bomb on the 445th Bomb Group (B24) base at Tibenham killing two airmen and a civilian woman. American 9th Air Force B26s attacked Dutch airfields. Twenty-one Royal Air Force "Mosquitoes" attacked targets in Germany. In a speech before the House of Commons, Churchill pledged support for Marshal Tito in Yugoslavia.

1945   1,372 8th Air Force bombers dropped 3,895 tons of bombs on transportation targets in Germany and lost three B17s and four B24s. 817 8th Air Force fighters provided support for the bombers and claimed twenty-eight victories for the loss of thirteen P51s. The Swiss town of Schaffhausen was accidentally bombed by the 8th Air Force. USAAF's 4th Fighter Group P51s shot down a USAAF 479th Fighter Group P51. 167 Royal Air Force bombers attacked oil installations in Germany and lost one "Lancaster". The US Army's 6th Armored Division took Irrhausen and Olmscheid. The Canadians took Moyland. The Royal Canadian Navy corvette TRENTONIAN was sunk by the U1004, six of her crew died. Eighty-three Royal Air Force "Mosquitoes" attacked targets in Germany and lost one aircraft.

1946   Luftwaffe ace Gerhard Michalski (73 aerial victories) died.

1961   French Admiral Philippe Auboyneau died in Paris. He had served as Commander-in-Chief of the Free French Naval Forces.

Eastern Europe

1897   Soviet Marshal Leonid Govorov was born. He died on March 19, 1955.

1940   Russia gained control of Finland's Baltic islands.

1942   The Soviet cruiser KRASNY KRIM and the destroyer BOIKI delivered supplies to the besieged city of Sevastopol.

1943   German General Erich von Manstein's counter-offensive began. The Free French fighter group "Regiment Normandie" began operations on the Russian Front.

1944   The American 15th Air Force attacked Zagreb and Sibenek in Yugoslavia.

Mediterranean

1941   The Royal Navy monitor TERROR was damaged at Benghazi, Libya by "Stukas". She sank the next day with no loss in personnel. The Luftwaffe dropped mines in the Suez Canal. General Henry Maitland Wilson assumed command of the British Greek Expedition.

1942   Axis aircraft attacked Malta.

1944   1st Lieutenant Jack Montgomery, of the 45th Division, won a Medal of Honor near Padiglione, Italy. The American freighters GEORGE

CLEEVE (7,176 tons-1 dead) and PETER SKEEN OGDEN (7,176 tons) were constructive losses after an attack by the U969. U969 survived until August 6, 1944.

Atlantic

1940   The German destroyers SCHULTZ (308 of her crew died) and MAASS (282 of her crew died) were sunk in a Royal Navy minefield off Borkum, after being attacked in error by the Luftwaffe. The U50 sank the British tanker BRITISH ENDEAVOR (4,580 tons). U50 survived until April 29, 1940.

1941   The U96 sank the British tanker SCOTTISH STANDARD (6,999 tons). U96 survived until March 30, 1945. The U108 sank the Dutch freighter TEXELSTROOM (1,617 tons). U108 survived the war. The German battlecruisers SCHARNHORST and GNEISENAU sank five Allied freighters (totaling 25,748 tons) in a convoy 500 miles east of Newfoundland. The Italian submarine MARCELLO was sunk by Allied escorts.

1942   The U504 sank the American tanker REPUBLIC (5,287 tons-five dead). U504 survived until July 30, 1943. The U502 sank Norwegian tanker 9,467 tons). U502 survived until July 5, 1942. The U96 sank the Norwegian freighter TORUNGEN (1,948 tons) and the British tanker KARS (8,888 tons). U96 survived until March 30, 1945. The U155 sank the British tanker ADELLEN (7,984 tons) and the Norwegian freighter SAMA (1,799 tons). U155 survived the war. The U128 sank the American tanker CITIES SERVICE EMPIRE (8,103 tons-14 dead). U128 survived until May 17, 1943. The US Coast Guard cutter VIGILANT rescued two survivors from the American tanker PAN MASSACHUSETTS. The tanker had been sunk on the 19th by the U128. U129 sank the American freighter WEST ZEDA (5,658 tons) and the Canadian freighter GEORGE TORAIN (1,754 tons). U129 was scuttled in 1944.

1943   The U753 sank the Norwegian whaler NIELSEN ALONSO (9,348 tons). U753 was lost due to unknown causes on May 15, 1943. At 1056, the Royal Canadian Navy corvette WEYBURN was sunk by a mine. The explosions of her depth charges damaged the Royal Navy WIVERN. The U107 sank the British freighter ROXBOROUGH CASTLE (7,801 tons). U107 survived until July 18, 1944. The U606 sank the American freighter CHATTANOOGA CITY (5,687 tons) and the British freighter EMPIRE REDSHANK (6,615 tons). U606 was sunk later in the day by the US Coast Guard cutter CAMPBELL and the Polish destroyer BURZA. There were twelve survivors.

1945   The U1004 sank the British freighter ALEXANDER KENNEDY (1,313 tons). U1004 survived the war. The U300 was sunk by the Royal Navy minesweepers RECRUIT and PINCER and armed yacht EVADINE.

North America

1941 The USAAF accepted delivery of its first four B26 "Marauders".

1942 FDR ordered General Douglas MacArthur, the Allied Commander in the Philippines, to leave the Philippines and relocate in Australia.

1943 The battleship IOWA was commissioned at New York City. The submarine CREVALLE was launched. She was scrapped in 1971.

1944 The heavy cruiser PITTSBURGH (awarded two battle stars during the war) was launched. She was scrapped in 1973.

1945 Japanese balloon-bombs were found near Manyberries in Alberta, North Bend in Oregon, Kirby, Powell and Glendo in Wyoming and Trementon in Utah.

1972 The destroyer FLETCHER was sold for scrap. It had been planned to preserve her as a memorial, but the plan failed.

1992 USN Admiral Harry D. Felt died. He had served as Commander Air Group aboard the (CV-3) SARATOGA during the Guadalcanal campaign.

Pacific

1942 The USN submarine GUDGEON was attacked near Marcus Island by an SBD from the USN carrier ENTERPRISE. The Japanese 48th Division arrived at Balikpapan from the Philippines. The IJN submarine I-158 sank the Dutch freighter PIJNACKER HORDIJK (2,982 tons), south of Java. Equipment from the damaged USN destroyer STEWART (See February 21st) in the harbor of Surabaya, Java was salvaged by other ships of the ABDA forces and her crew was reassigned to other duties. USN forces ashore in the area were ordered to destroy the hulk if it became necessary. The USN submarine SWORDFISH disembarked Philippine President Quezon and his cabinet at San Jose, Panay.

1943 The USN submarine THRESHER sank the KUWAYAMA MARU (5,724 tons). The USN YP-72 ran aground off Kodiak, Alaska and was lost.

1944 The USMC's 22nd Regiment landed on Parry Island in the Eniwetok Atoll against heavy opposition. The TEIKU MARU (the ex-French D'ARTAGNAN) and IJN minelayer NATSUSHIMA were sunk off Kavieng, New Ireland by the USN destroyers AUSBURNE, DYSON and STANLEY. The FUKUYAMA MARU (3,581 tons), CHIYODA MARU No.15 (408 tons), TAKATORI MARU No.2 (521 tons) and KYOSEI MARU (556 tons) were sunk by the USN submarine TANG. The USN submarine PUFFER sank the TEIKO MARU (15,105 tons). The USN submarine BALAO sank the NIKKI MARU (5,857 tons). An 11th Air Force B24 crashed on take-off, destroying two C47s and killing six on Amchitka in the Aleutians.

1945   USMC Colonel Justice Chambers, of the 4th Division, won a Medal of Honor on Iwo Jima. The USN submarine BECUNA sank the NICHIYOKU MARU (1,945 tons).
1946   An Allied force was ambushed seventy miles southwest of Manila by thirty Japanese troops and lost six Americans and two Filipinos. The American freighter SEA SATYR was damaged off Makassar, Celebes. Four of her crew were wounded.
1980   Japanese Naval Air Force ace Sadaaki Akamatsu (30 victories) died of pneumonia in Kochi, Japan.

China-Burma-India
1932   The first American-built aircraft shot down over China was a Boeing-218 flown by American Robert Short. It was downed by aircraft from the IJN carrier KAGA.
1942   American 10th Air Force B24s dropped forty mines into the Rangoon River.
1944   The U510 sank the British tanker SAN ALVARO (7,385 tons) and the American freighter E.G. SEUBERT (9,181 tons) and damaged the Norwegian tanker ERLING BROVIG (9,970 tons). The IJN submarine I-37 sank the British tanker BRITISH CHIVALRY (7,118 tons).
1945   The British landed 6,000 men Kangaw, Burma.

February 23rd

Western Europe
1915   Luftwaffe ace Frank Liesendahl (50 aerial victories) was born in Wupper-tal-Barman. He was killed on July 17, 1942.
1920   Hitler staged the first major meeting of the German Worker's Party, at the Hofbrauhaus in Munich.
1939   Hugh Dowding was informed that he would remain in command of the Royal Air Forces Fighter Command until 1940.
1941   Three Royal Air Force "Blenheims" attacked Boulogne, France. Twenty-six Royal Air Force bombers attacked Boulogne, France and lost one "Wellington".
1942   Twenty-three Royal Air Force "Hampdens" dropped mines in the Baltic and lost one aircraft.
1944   102 American 15th Air Force bombers dropped 214 tons of bombs on the ball-bearing factory at Steyr, Austria, losing seventeen aircraft. Forty 8th Air Force P38s flew a sweep over Holland, Belgium and France. Seventeen Royal Air Force "Mosquitoes" attacked Dusseldorf, Germany. Five B17s from the USAAF's 422nd Bomb Squadron dropped 250 bundles of supplies

for resistance forces near Rennes, Le Mans, Chartres, Lille and Orleans in France.

1945   The American 1st and 3rd Armies attacked between Köln and Koblenz, while the American 9th Army attacked out of bridge-heads over the Roer River. 1,211 8th Air Force bombers dropped 3,316 tons of bombs on road and rail targets in Germany and lost one B24. 667 8th Air Force fighters provided support for the bombers and claimed fifteen victories for the loss of six P51s. 342 Royal Air Force bombers attacked Essen, Germany and lost one "Halifax". 155 people were killed in the raid. 133 Royal Air Force bombers attacked Gelsenkirchen, Germany. 455 American 15th Air Force bombers attacked transportation targets in Germany. The French destroyer LA COMBATTANTE (the ex-Royal Navy HALDON) was sunk off the South Falls Bank by a "Seehund" midget submarine. 380 Royal Air Force bombers attacked Pforzheim and lost twelve aircraft. 17,600 people were killed in the raid. South African Air Force Captain Edwin Swales, No.582 Squadron, won a posthumous Victoria Cross while serving as Master Bomber on the mission. Eighty-three Royal Air Force bombers attacked Horton, Germany and lost one aircraft. Eighty-eight Royal Air Force "Mosquitoes" attacked targets in Germany and lost one aircraft.

1948   The Royal Navy battleship RAMILLIES was sold for scrap.

1974   Hans Gisevius, German vice-consul in Zurich and liaison between the Abwehr and the OSS, died in West Germany.

Eastern Europe

1940   Finnish forces destroyed the Soviet 18th Rifle Division.

1942   The Soviet submarine SHCH-213 sank the Turkish steamer CANKAYA (454 tons). The Soviets took Dorogobuzh on the Dnieper.

1943   The Soviets took Sumy in the Ukraine.

1944   The Soviets took Strugi Krasnye.

1945   The Soviet First Byelorussian Front took the city of Poznan in western Poland.

Mediterranean

1941   As of this date the Allies had suffered 604 dead and 2,326 wounded in action in North Africa. Free French forces landed in Eritrea. The Royal Navy monitor TERROR sank while under tow between Benghazi and Alexandria. The Greek government accepted a British offer of 100,000 men, 272 guns and 142 tanks.

1942   The Royal Navy submarine P-38 was sunk by an Italian torpedo boat. Axis aircraft attacked Malta.

1943   The Axis forces under the command of German Field Marshal Erwin Rommel were forced back through the Kasserine Pass in Tunisia (See

February 20th). The U371 sank the British freighter FINTRA (2,089 tons). The U443 was sunk off Algiers by the Royal Navy destroyers LAMERSTON, BICESTER and WHEATLAND. Major General James Doolittle, commander of the American 12th Air Force, flew as a guest of the Royal Air Force on a mission to Bizerte.

1944 US Army General Truscott relieved General Lucas as commander of the Allied forces at Anzio. The U510 sank the American tanker E.G. SEUBERT (9,181 tons- 6 dead) in the Gulf of Aden. U510 was scrapped in 1958.

Atlantic

1941 The U107 sank the British freighter MANISTREE (5,360 tons). U107 survived until August 18, 1944. The U96 sank the British freighter HUNTINGTON (10,946 tons). U96 survived until March 30, 1945. The U69 sank the British freighter TEMPLE MOAT (4,427 tons). U69 survived until February 17, 1943.

1942 The German heavy cruiser PRINZ EUGEN was torpedoed off Trondheim by Royal Navy submarine TRIDENT and was out of action for eight months. The U504 sank the American tanker W.D. ANDERSON (10,227 tons-35 dead). U504 survived until July 30, 1943. The U161 sank the American freighter LIHUE (7,001 tons). U161 survived until October 27, 1943. The U502 sank Panamanian tanker THALIA (8,329 tons). U502 survived until July 5, 1942. The U129 sank the Canadian freighter LENNOX (1,904 tons). U129 was scuttled in 1944.

1943 The U604 sank the British freighter STOCKPORT (1,683 tons). U604 survived until August 3, 1943. The U303 sank the American freighter EXPOSITOR (4,959 tons-nine dead). U303 survived until May 21, 1943. The U522 sank the British tanker ATHELPRINCESS (8,882 tons). U522 survived until February 23, 1943. The U603 sank the Norwegian tanker GLITTRE (6,409 tons). U603 survived until March 1, 1944. The U223 sank the Panamanian tanker WINKLER (6,907 tons). U223 survived until March 30, 1944. The U456 sank the British freighter KYLECLARE (700 tons). U456 survived until May 13, 1943. The U558 sank the British tanker EMPIRE NORSEMAN (9,811 tons). U558 survived until July 20, 1943. The U522 was sunk southwest of Madeira by the Royal Navy cutter TOTLAND. The U606 was sunk by the US Coast Guard cutter CAMPBELL. The U202 sank the American tanker ESSO BATON ROUGE (7,989 tons-three dead). U202 survived until June 2, 1943. The U186 sank the American freighter HASTINGS (5,401 tons-nine dead) and the British tanker EULIMA (6,207 tons). U186 survived until May 12, 1943. The Royal Canadian Navy corvette WEYBURN was sunk by a mine.

1945 The American freighter HENRY BACON (7,177 tons-twenty-two dead), sailing with Convoy RA-64 in the Barents Sea, was the last Luftwaffe (Ju88) victory at sea.

North America

1889 American Ambassador to Britain John Winant was born in New York City. He replaced Joe Kennedy as ambassador on February 6, 1941. He committed suicide in 1947.

1933 The heavy cruiser PORTLAND was commissioned. She was scrapped in 1959.

1942 At 1830, the IJN submarine I-17 entered the Santa Barbara channel off the California coast. At 1840, she surfaced off her target the Ellwood Oil Field in Santa Barbara. She fired several rounds from her deck gun and caused $500 in damage before withdrawing at 2020.

1943 The light cruiser BILOXI was launched. She was scrapped in Portland, Oregon in 1962. The USN YP-336 was sunk when she ran aground in the Delaware River.

1944 The destroyer SAMUEL N. MOORE was launched. She was sold to Taiwan in June 1969.

1945 A Japanese balloon-bomb was shot down near Elmira, California by a P38. Others were found near Rigby in Idaho, Bigelow in Kansas, Grand Rapids in Michigan, Boyd in Montana and Burns and Deer Islands in Oregon.

1990 US Army General James Gavin, age 82, died in Baltimore. He had commanded the 82nd Airborne Division in Europe.

Pacific

1942 Six USAAF B17s flew from Australia and attacked Rabaul, New Britain. The ABDA Command held its last conference before it was disolved. The IJN submarine I-19 sent its aircraft on a recon mission over Pearl Harbor. FDR ordered MacArthur to assume command of the Allied forces in Australia.

1943 The IJN destroyer OOSHIO was sunk by the USN submarine ALBACORE off Manus Island. American 5th Air Force B17s attacked Rabaul.

1944 Eniwetok Atoll was secured. The battle had cost 300 American and 2,534 Japanese dead. USN Task Group 58.2 (commanded by Montgomery) and Task Group 58.3 (commanded by Sherman) attacked Rota, Tinian and Saipan sinking 20,000 tons of Japanese shipping. The KIMISHIMA MARU (5,193 tons) was sunk by the USN submarine PLUNGER. The PLUNGER's commander was Richard Bass. He had won a Gold Medal for rope-climbing in the 1932 Olympics. The USN submarine TANG sank the YAMASHIMO MARU (6,777 tons). The USN submarine SNOOK sank the KOYO MARU (5,471 tons). The HOREI MARU (5,588 tons) was sunk by the USN submarine POGY. The USN submarine SUNFISH sank the SHINIUBARI MARU (5,354 tons) and the MIKKI MARU. The USN submarine COD sank the OGURA MARU No.3 (7,358 tons). The Royal Australian Air Force attacked Saidor, New Guinea. The Japanese garrison at Rabaul was ordered to withdraw.

1945 The American 1st Corps took Pantabangan, Luzon. The US Army's 11th Airborne Division rescued 2,147 civilians from a Japanese prison camp at Los Banos, Luzon. Private First Class William Grabiarz, of the 1st Cavalry Division, won a posthumous Medal of Honor in Manila. USMC forces reached the summit of Mount Suribachi on Iwo Jima. USMC Corporal Hershel Williams, of the 3rd Division, won a Medal of Honor on Iwo Jima. The USN submarines FLOUNDER and HOE collided while submerged off Indo-China, both survived. The IJN escort YAKU (940 tons) was sunk by the USN submarine HAMMERHEAD.

China-Burma-India
1942 The 17th Indian Division was destroyed near the Sittang River in Burma.
1944 The Chinese 22nd Division took Yawngbang, Burma.
1945 The U510 sank the Canadian freighter POINT PLEASANT PARK (7,136 tons).

February 24th

Western Europe
1880 British Samuel Hoare was born in London. He would serve as foreign minister in 1935 and was responsible for the notorious Hoare-Laval proposal. He died on May 7, 1959.
1940 Germany completed plans for its invasion of the West. Germany and Italy signed a trade agreement. The Royal Navy battleship ANSON was launched. She was scrapped in 1957. The first flight of the Royal Air Forces Hawker "Typhoon" took place.
1941 French Admiral Jean Darlan was named as head of the Vichy government. Fifty-seven Royal Air Force bombers attacked Brest, France. It was the first operation for the "Manchester" bomber.
1942 Fifty-one Royal Air Force bombers dropped mines in the Baltic and lost two "Hampdens".
1943 The Royal Navy submarine VANDAL was lost in the Firth of Clyde. 115 Royal Air Force bombers attacked Wilhelmshaven, Germany. Four Royal Air Force "Mosquitoes" attacked targets in Germany. Fourteen "Spitfires" from the USAAF's 4th Fighter Group flew patrols over the Channel.

1944   295 8th Air Force B17s dropped 685 tons of bombs on Rostock, Germany and lost five aircraft. 451 American 8th Air Force B17s and B24s dropped 1,061 tons of bombs on Schweinfurt, Rostock, Gotha and Eisenbach in Germany and lost eleven B17s and thirty-three B24s. The 458th Bomb Group (B24) flew its first 8th Air Force mission. 767 8th and 9th Air Force fighters provided support for the bombers and claimed thirty-eight victories for the loss of four P38s, four P47s and two P51s. The American 15th Air Force attacked Steyr, Austria, losing sixteen bombers and three escorting fighters. American 9th Air Force B26s attacked Dutch and Belgian airfields and V-1 launching sites. Luftwaffe ace Rudolf Leuschel (8 aerial victories) was killed in action over Belgium by American 9th Air Force B26s. 734 Royal Air Force bombers attacked Schweinfurt, Germany and lost thirty-three aircraft. 110 Royal Air Force bombers dropped mines in the Baltic and lost two "Stirlings". Five B17s from the USAAF's 422nd Bomb Squadron dropped 250 bundles of supplies for resistance forces near Lorient, Tours, Nantes, Brest, and Reims.

1945   1,055 American 8th Air Force bombers dropped 2,775 tons of bombs on rail and oil targets in Germany and lost one B17 and one B24. 557 8th Air Force fighters provided support for the bombers and claimed one victory for the loss of eleven P51s. 340 Royal Air Force bombers attacked Kamen, Germany and lost one "Halifax". American forces took Doveren, Julich, Stetternich, Hambach and Niederzier in Germany.

1950   German General Erich von Manstein was sentenced to eighteen years by a British court for war crimes.

1953   German Field Marshal Gerd von Rundstedt died in Hannover.

Eastern Europe

1940   The Soviets took Koivisto, Finland.

1942   The Bulgarian steamer STRUMA was sunk in the Black Sea by a torpedo. Of the 769 Jewish refugees aboard only one survived. The German II Corps was surrounded on the Northern Front.

1943   The U649 was lost in a collision with the U232 in the Bay of Danzig.

1944   The Soviets took Dno and Rogachev.

Mediterranean

1941   The Royal Navy destroyer DAINTY (launched in 1932 and suffering thirty-three casualties) was sunk by Luftwaffe Ju-88s off Tobruk, Libya. British forces crossed the Juba River in Italian Somaliland.

1942   The Italian blockade runner ORSEOLO arrived at Bordeaux, France from Kobe, Japan.

1943   The American freighter NATHANAEL GREENE (7,176 tons) was a constructive loss after an attack by the U565 off Oran. The Royal Navy submarine UREDD was sunk by a mine. Ribbentrop met with Mussolini in Rome.

1944　The U761 was sunk off Tangiers by the Royal Navy destroyers WISHART and ANTHONY. The American 15th Air Force attacked Fiume, Italy and lost one B17.

1945　The American 15th Air Force attacked the Brenner Pass Railway. Egyptian Prime Minister Ahmed Maher Pasha was assassinated after declaring war on the Axis.

Atlantic

1940　The British freighter ROYAL ARCHER (2,266 tons) was sunk by a mine laid by the U21. The U63 sank the Swedish freighter SANTOS (3,840 tons). U63 survived until February 25th.

1941　The U95 sank the British freighters CAPE NELSON (3,807 tons), MARSLEW (4,542 tons) and ANGELO PERUVIAN (5,457 tons). U95 survived until November 28th. The U123 sank the Dutch freighter GROOTEKERK (8,685 tons). U123 survived the war. The U96 sank the Norwegian freighter SVEIN JARL (1,908 tons) and the British freighter SIRIKISHNA (5,458 tons). U96 survived until March 30, 1945. The U97 sank the British freighters MANSEPOOL (4,894 tons) and JONATHAN HOLT (4,973 tons) and the tanker BRITISH GUNNER (6,894 tons). U97 survived until June 16, 1943. The Italian submarine BIANCHI sank the British freighter LINARAIA (3,385 tons). The U73 sank the British freighter WAYNEGATE (4,260 tons). U73 survived until December 16, 1943. The U48 sank the British freighter NAILSEA LASS (4,289 tons). U48 survived the war.

1942　The U94 sank the British freighter EMPIRE HAIL (7,005 tons). U94 survived August 28th. The U558 sank the British tankers INVERARDER (5,578 tons), ANADARA (8,009 tons), FINNANGER (9,551 tons), EIDANGER (9,432 tons) and the freighter WHITE CREST (4,365 tons). U558 survived until July 20, 1943. The U162 sank the British tanker EMPIRE CELT (8,032 tons). U162 survived until September 3rd. The U432 sank the American freighter NORLAVORE (2,713 tons) with all hands. U432 survived until March 1, 1943.

1943　The U649 was lost in a collision with U232. The U707 sank the American freighter JONATHAN STURGES (7,176 tons). U707 survived until November 9th. The U600 and U628 sank the Norwegian freighter INGRIA (4,391 tons). U600 survived until November 25th and U628 survived until July 3rd. The Italian submarine BARBARIGO sank the Spanish freighter MONTE IGUELDO (3,453 tons).

1944　The U257 was sunk by the Royal Canadian Navy frigate WASKESIU. The U713 was sunk northwest of Narvik by the Royal Navy destroyer KEPPEL.

1945　The U480 sank the British freighter ORISKANY (1,644 tons). U480 was then sunk in the English Channel by the Royal Navy frigates DUCKWORTH and ROWLEY. The U1203 sank the Royal Navy trawler ELLESMERE (580 tons). U1203 survived the war. The U972 was sunk in the English Channel by the Royal Air Force's No.179 Squadron.

North America
1885　Admiral Chester William Nimitz was born in Fredricksburg, Texas. He graduated 7th in his 1905 Annapolis class of 144. By the time he was 20-years old he was in command of the destroyer DECATUR. In 1909 he was assigned to the submarine service. He was later to command the heavy cruiser AUGUSTA. He was promoted to rear admiral in 1938. He then commanded Cruiser Division 2 and later a Battleship Division. He then became Chief of the Bureau of Navigation. On December 16, 1941 he was notified that he was to immediately take over as Commander-in-Chief of the Pacific Fleet. He would remain in that position until November 24, 1945 when he turned it over to Admiral Raymond Spruance. On December 15th, he replaced King as Commander-in-Chief of the US Fleet. Two years later he retired. He died on February 20, 1966 in San Francisco.
1937　The heavy cruiser VINCENNES was commissioned. She was sunk in August 1942 during the "Battle of Savo Island".
1942　"The Battle of Los Angeles" (a false alarm air-raid) took place.
1945　A Japanese balloon-bomb was shot down over Attu in the Aleutians.
1964　The US Coast Guard cutter DIONE was sold.
1971　The light cruiser TUCSON was sold for scrap.

Pacific
1938　A Japanese firm paid $90,000 for the rights to build the Douglas DC-3 under license.
1942　The USN carrier ENTERPRISE attacked Wake Island, losing two SBDs. The island was also bombarded by the cruisers NORTHAMPTON and SALT LAKE CITY and the destroyers BALCH and MAURY. Lewis Brereton, Commander of the Far East Air Force, left Bandoeng, Java for Ceylon aboard an LB-30 "Liberator". A seaplane from the IJN submarine I-9 flew over Pearl Harbor. The Panamanian freighter SNARK was destroyed by a mine while attempting to enter Noumea, New Caledonia. Japanese forces completed the conquest of Timor.
1943　General Douglas MacArthur's Headquarters began planning for the invasion of the Philippines.
1944　American forces reached Biliau, New Guinea. The USN submarine GRAYBACK sank the NANHO MARU (10,033 tons). The USN submarine

TANG sank the ECHIZEN MARU (2,424 tons). The USN destroyers BUCHANAN and FARENHOLT were damaged by shore-fire off New Ireland. American aircraft sank the Japanese transport SHUNZAN MARU in the Carolines. The Royal Australian Air Force attacked Hansa Bay, New Guinea.

1945   The USN submarine LOGARTO sank the IJN submarine Ro-49 and the TATSUMOME MARU (880 tons). The USN submarine TREPANG sank the UZUKI MARU (875 tons). The USMC secured part of Iwo Jima's second airfield. Staff Sergeant Raymond Cooley, of the 25th Division, won a Medal of Honor on Luzon. The American 6th Division took the towns of Montalban and San Isidoro on Luzon.

China-Burma-India

1943   The American 10th Air Force attacked the Gokteik Viaduct in Burma.

1945   105 USAAF B29s, of the 20th Bomber Command, attacked Singapore. They destroyed 40% of the warehouses in the city. The 17th Indian Division took Taungtha, Burma.

February 25th

Western Europe

1932   Adolf Hitler became a German citizen. He had been born in Austria.

1933   Japan withdrew from the League of Nations in response to a vote by that body condemning Japan's invasion of Manchuria.

1941   The Royal Navy destroyer escort EXMOOR was sunk by the German S-30 off Lowestoft. She had participated in the sinking of two U-boats. German torpedo boats laid a minefield off Eastbourne. Eighty Royal Air Force bombers attacked Dusseldorf, Germany and lost one "Wellington".

1942   Sixty-one Royal Air Force bombers attacked Kiel, Germany and lost three "Wellingtons". 146 people were killed in the raid. Twenty-one Royal Air Force "Whitleys" attacked aluminum factories in Norway.

1943   337 Royal Air Force bombers attacked Nuremburg, Germany and lost nine aircraft. Fourteen people were killed in Nuremburg and another twenty-six died in the nearby town of Furth.

1944   685 American 8th Air Force bombers dropped 1,702 tons of bombs on Furth, Regensburg, Augsburg, and Stuttgart in Germany and lost twenty-five B17s and six B24s. 899 8th and 9th Air Force fighters provided support for the bombers and claimed twenty-six victories for the loss of one P47 and two P51s. It was the last operation of "Big Week", in which the 8th Air Force flew 3,800 sorties, dropped 10,000 tons of bombs, and lost 226 bombers and twenty-eight fighters. 594 Royal Air Force bombers attacked

Augsburg, Germany and lost twenty-one aircraft. 762 people were killed in the raid. The Royal Air Force had flown 2,351 sorties during "Big Week", dropped 9,198 tons of bombs and lost 157 bombers. The American 15th Air Force attacked Regensburg, losing thirty-three bombers. During "Big Week", the 15th had lost eighty-nine bombers. American 9th Air Force B26s attacked Dutch and Belgian airfields. 131 Royal Air Force bombers dropped mines in Kiel Bay and lost four aircraft. Five B17s from the USAAF's 422nd Bomb Squadron dropped 250 bundles of supplies for resistance forces near Grenoble, Toulouse, Chartres, Caen and Raismes.

1945 1,157 8th Air Force bombers dropped 3,180 tons of bombs on tank factories, jet airfields, rail targets and oil depots in Germany and lost five B17s. Three of the lost B17s landed in Switzerland. 704 8th Air Force fighters provided support for the bombers and claimed thirty-four victories for the loss of eight P51s. The USAAF's 387th Bomb Group (B26) attacked the railway bridge at Ahrweiler, Germany. 153 Royal Air Force bombers attacked Kamen and lost one "Lancaster". Sergeant A. Cosens, of the Queen's Own Rifles of Canada, won a posthumous Victoria Cross in Holland. The US Army's VII Corps took Duren, Germany. The American 15th Air Force attacked Linz, Austria. Seventy-three Royal Air Force "Mosquitos" attacked V-2 launching sites at Holten, Xanten and Marienburg in Germany. American O.S.S agents in Bern, Switzerland were advised that S.S. General Karl Wolff wanted to negotiate the surrender of the German forces in Italy. Eighty-nine Royal Air Force "Mosquitoes" attacked targets in Germany.

1948 Communists overthrew the Edvard Benes government in Czechoslovakia.

1964 Heinrich Lohse, Reich Commissioner for Baltic States and White Russia, died in Schleswig-Holstein.

Eastern Europe

1944 Luftwaffe ace Siegfried Schnell (93 aerial victories) was killed in action.

Mediterranean

1941 British forces commanded by Lieutenant General Sir Alan Cunningham took Mogadishu, the capital of Italian Somaliland. At 0245, the Italian light cruiser ARMANDO DIAZ was sunk east of Sfax, Tunisia by the Royal Navy submarine UPRIGHT. The Royal Navy destroyers DECOY and HEREWARD landed 200 British commandoes on the island of Castelorizo in the Aegean Sea. They would be driven off by Italian forces within two days.

1943 The US Army's II Corps re-occupied Kasserine Pass.

1944   The Royal Navy destroyer INGLEFIELD was sunk off Anzio by a Luftwaffe Hs293 glide-bomb. 157 of her crew survived. She had participated in the sinking of two U-boats before her loss. The American 15th Air Force attacked rail targets in Italy losing six bombers.

Atlantic
1940   The U63 was sunk south of the Shetlands by the Royal Navy destroyers INGLEFIELD and IMOGEN.
1942   The U156 sank the British tanker LA CARRIERE (5,685 tons) and the Brazilian freighter CABEDELO (3,557 tons). U156 survived until March 8, 1943. The Italian submarine TORELLI sank the Panamanian tanker ESSO COPENHAGEN (9,245 tons).
1943   The U628 sank the British freighter MANCHESTER MERCHANT (7,264 tons). U628 survived until July 3rd.
1944   The U91 was sunk by the Royal Navy frigates AFFLECK, GORE and GOULD. The U601 was sunk northwest of Narvik by the Royal Air Force's No.210 Squadron. The US Coast Guard cutter HURST rescued survivors from the steamer EL COSTEN. The US Coast Guard cutter MARCHLAND rescued fifty more from the steamer EL COSTEN. The US Coast Guard cutter RICKETTS rescued thirty-three survivors from the steamers EL COSTEN and MURFREESBORO. At 2210, the Royal Navy destroyer MAHRATTA was sunk by the U990, sixteen of her crew survived. U990 survived until May 25th.
1945   The U2322 sank the British freighter EGHOLM (1,317 tons). U2322 survived the war.

North America
1933   The carrier RANGER was launched. She was scrapped in 1947.
1937   The destroyer CRAVEN was launched. She was scrapped in 1947.
1942   The Coast Guard assumed responsibility for port security in the continental U.S.
1943   The light carrier PRINCETON was commissioned. She was sunk on October 24, 1944.
1944   The escort carrier RUDYERD BAY was commissioned. She was scrapped in 1960.
1945   A Japanese balloon-bomb was found near Boise, Idaho.
1946   The destroyers BABBITT, KANE and GILMER were stricken.
1947   The destroyer HELMS was sold for scrap at Oakland, Calif. The destroyers SMITH and PATTERSON were stricken.
1984   Junior Spurrier died. He had won a Medal of Honor in Europe in 1944.
1988   "Doolittle Raider" Technical/Sergeant Waldo Blither died.

South America
2004 A salvage team recovered the 27-ton command tower of the German pocket battleship GRAF SPEE from the waters off Montevideo, Uruguay where she had been scuttled on December 17, 1939.

Pacific
1925 The IJN heavy cruiser FURUTAKE was launched. She was sunk on October 11, 1942.

1942 American-British-Dutch-Australian Command was disbanded and its commander, British General Archibald Wavell, left Java to assume his new post of Commander-in-Chief India and Burma. The USN submarine PERCH was damaged by gunfire off Celebes. The IJN submarine I-158 sank the Dutch freighter BOERO (7,135 tons) south of Java.

1944 USN destroyers shelled Rabaul, New Britain and Kavieng, New Ireland. The USN submarine HOE sank the tanker NISSHIO MARU, the KYOKUTO MARU (10,051 tons) and the NISSHO MARU (10,526 tons). The USN submarine TANG sank the CHOKO MARU (1,790 tons). The USN submarine RASHER sank the TANGO MARU (6,200 tons) and the RYUSEI MARU (4,805 tons). The USMC's 5th Regiment landed at the Iboki Plantation on New Britain.

1945 USN Task Force 58 attacked Tokyo. Ninety-four B29s attacked Tokyo and lost four aircraft. Twenty American "Sherman" tanks were destroyed by the Japanese near Airfield No.2 on Iwo Jima. The US Army's 24th Division landed on San Augustin in the Philippines. The IJN escort SHONAN (940 tons) was sunk by the USN submarine HOE. The USN submarine PIPER sank the HOSEN MARU No.3 (111 tons). The USN submarine FLASHER sank the KOHO MARU (850 tons).

China-Burma-India
1944 The West African 81st Division took Kyauktaw, Burma.

1945 The Indian 17th Division took Mahlaing, Burma.

February 26th

Western Europe
1894 German General Wilhelm Bittrich was born. He commanded the 2nd S.S. Panzer Corps in Normandy and assisted in the wiping out of the British airhead at Arnhem in 1944. After the war, he was held by the French until 1954. He died on April 19, 1979.

1924 Adolf Hitler's treason trial began in Munich; it would last twenty-four days.

1941	The German S-28 sank the British freighter MINORCA (1,123 tons) off Cromer. Twelve Royal Air Force "Blenheims" attacked Calais, France. 126 Royal Air Force bombers attacked Cologne, Germany.
1942	Four Royal Air Force "Bostons" attacked shipping off Holland. Forty-nine Royal Air Force bombers attacked Kiel, Germany and lost three aircraft. They scored a direct hit on the battle cruiser GNEISENAU and put her out of the war as well as killing 116 of her crew. Sixteen people were killed in Kiel during the raid. Three people were killed and six were injured in the town of Vejle, Denmark which was 100 miles from the target in Kiel. Also attacked was the Danish town of Odense which lost one dead. This was an extreme example, but it still gives an indication of the Royal Air Force's navigation capabilities at this point in the war.
1943	Sixty-five B17s and B24s of the USAAF's 91st, 303rd, 305th, 306th, 44th and 93rd Bomb Groups attacked Wilhelmshaven, Germany and lost five B17s and two B24s. This was the first mission that American news correspondents were allowed to go on. Of the six that actually went, one was lost when the B24 he was aboard was shot down. His name was Robert Post of the New York Times. Seventy-six sorties by USAAF's 4th Fighter Group "Spitfires" escorted sixty Royal Air Force "Ventura" bombers against German armed merchant cruisers at Dunkirk. Twenty Royal Air Force "Mosquitoes" attacked Rennes, France and lost two aircraft. 427 Royal Air Force bombers attacked Köln, Germany and lost ten aircraft. 109 people were killed in the raid.
1944	Sixteen Allied airmen escaped from France aboard a Royal Navy MTB.
1945	1,135 8th Air Force bombers dropped 2,886 tons of bombs on Berlin and lost three B17s. 687 8th Air Force fighters provided escort for the bombers and claimed six victories for the loss of three P51s. 149 Royal Air Force bombers attacked Dortmund, Germany. The US Army's 102nd Division took Erkelenz, Germany. Seventy-six Royal Air Force "Mosquitoes" attacked targets in Germany.
1946	The American freighter CYRUS ADLER was damaged by a mine off Belgium. The American 8th Air Force returned its last base in Britain, Honington, to the Royal Air Force.
1952	Joseph Thorak, one of Hitler's favorite sculptors, died in Hartmannsberg, Bavaria.
1969	Karl Jaspers, anti-Nazi professor at Heidelberg, died in Basel, Switzerland. British aircraft designer George Carter died. He had designed the Royal Air Force's "Meteor" jet.
1985	A memorial service was held in Westminster Abbey for Brian Horrocks. He had commanded the British Army's XXX Corps during the war.

Eastern Europe

1940 Finnish forces retreated to their final defensive positions.

1943 Admiral Karl Doenitz flew to Hitler's headquarters at Vinnitsa in the Ukraine. The main purpose for his visit was to acquire more air support for his U-boats.

1944 The Soviets took Porkhov, east of Dno.

Mediterranean

1941 The British occupied Harar, East Africa. British Major General John Campbell, commander of the 7th Armored Division, was killed when his staff car skidded off the road near Halfaya Pass.

1943 The Germans launched an offensive in Tunisia.

1944 The USN LST-349 was lost when she ran aground off Gaeta, Italy.

1945 General Wladyslaw Anders was named as Acting Commander-in-Chief of all Polish Armed Forces. He died in London in 1970.

Atlantic

1941 The U47 sank the Belgian freighter KASONGA (5,254 tons), the Swedish freighter RYDBOHOLM (3,197 tons) and the Norwegian freighter BORGLAND (3,636 tons). U47 survived until March 7th. The U70 sank the Swedish freighter GOTEBORG (820 tons). U70 survived until March 8th.

1942 The U504 sank the Dutch tanker MAMURA (8,245 tons). The American tanker JOHN D. GILL rescued 25 survivors. Another fifteen landed on the North Carolina shore. U504 survived until July 30, 1943. The American tanker CASSMIR was lost in a collision with the freighter LARA off North Carolina.

1944 The U66 sank the British freighter SILVERMAPLE (5,313 tons). U66 survived until May 6th. The American freighter WILLIAM H. WELCH (forty-two dead) ran aground in Loch Ewe, Scotland and was lost.

North America

1882 USN Admiral Husband Edward Kimmel was born in Henderson, Kentucky. He would be in command of the Pacific Fleet at Pearl Harbor on December 7, 1941.

1894 General Ernest Harmon was born in Lowell, Massachusetts. He graduated 76th in his 1917 West Point class of 139. From July 1942 until January 1945, he commanded the 2nd Armored Division. On January 29th, he assumed command of the 22nd Corps. He retired on February 29, 1948 and died on November 13, 1979 at White River Junction, Vermont.

1896 USMC Colonel Evans Fordyce Carlson was born in Sidney, New York. He would command the USMC Raiders on Guadalcanal.

1936   The destroyer TUCKER was launched at Portsmouth, Virginia. She was sunk off Espiritu Santo, on August 4, 1942 by a mine.
1940   The US Air Defense Command was formed. Captain Raymond A. Spruance relieved Commander Reuben L. Walker as the Commandant of the Tenth Naval District.
1944   The US Army transport MOUNT BAKER was lost when she caught fire off British Columbia.
1945   A Japanese balloon-bomb was found near Eugene, Oregon.
1954   The destroyers BENSON and HILARY P. JONES were sold to Taiwan.

Pacific

1936   Japanese Finance Minister Korekiyo Takahashi and former Prime Minister Makoto Saito were assassinated.
1942   The seaplane tender LANGLEY, with thirty-two fighters aboard, was sunk off Java by the Japanese Naval Air Force having suffered five direct hits. The USN destroyers WHIPPLE and EDSALL rescued all but sixteen of the crew and passengers. A Japanese aircraft flying from the submarine I-25 flew a recon mission over Melbourne, Australia. The USN submarine S-38 bombarded a Japanese radio station that had been set up the previous day on Bawean Island 85 miles north of Java.
1944   The USN submarine GRAYBACK was lost. The USN submarine GATO sank the DAIGEN MARU No.3 (5,255 tons). The USN PT251 was sunk off Bougainville by artillery fire. The American transport PRESIDENT GRANT was lost by grounding off New Guinea.
1945   American forces declared the island of Corregidor in Manila Bay secured. American losses were 1,000, while the Japanese lost 5,000. The IJN submarines I-368 and Ro-43 were sunk by the USN escort carrier ANZIO's escort group. The USN destroyer escort FINNEGAN sank the IJN submarine I-370. The USN submarine BLENNY sank the AMATO MARU (10,238 tons). USMC Private First-Class Douglas Jacobson, of the 4th Division, won a Medal of Honor on Iwo Jima. The American 8th Army surrounded the last Japanese forces on Leyte.

China-Burma-India

1903   Orde Wingate was born in India. He would command the "Chindits" in the CBI during WWII.
1943   The IJN minesweeper No.3 KYO MARU was sunk by a mine off Rangoon, Burma.
1944   The IJN submarine I-37 sank the British freighter SUTLEJ (5,189 tons). 14th Air Force B-25s attacked shipping off Tourane, Indochina and sank the Vichy French vessels GILMOT and ASTROLABE.
1945   The Indian 17th Division took Thabutkon Airfield near Meiktila, Burma.

February 27th

Western Europe

- **1933** The "Reichstag Fire" took place.
- **1939** Britain and France formally recognized Franco's government in Spain.
- **1940** Norway and Sweden refused Finland's request for transit rights in her fight against Russia.
- **1942** Sixty-eight Royal Air Force bombers attacked Kiel, Germany but failed to drop a single bomb within the city limits. Thirty-three Royal Air Force bombers attacked Wilhelmshaven, Germany and lost three "Whitleys". Three bombs landed within the target area.
- **1943** Twenty-four USAAF 4th Fighter Group "Spitfires" escorted twenty-four Royal Air Force "Venturas" in a raid against German armed merchant cruisers at Dunkirk. Ninety-one Royal Air Force bombers dropped mines in the Baltic and lost one "Halifax". Sixty B17s and B24s of the USAAF's 91st, 303rd, 306th, 44th and 93rd Bomb Groups attacked Brest, France.
- **1944** A VB-10 PB4Y crashed into Skellig Rock off Ireland, killing all ten aboard.
- **1945** 1,062 American 8th Air Force bombers dropped 2,728 tons of bombs on communication targets at Bitterfeld, Halle and Leipzig in Germany and lost two B24s. 690 8th Air Force fighters provided escort for the bombers and claimed eighty-nine victories for the loss of two P51s. 430 American 15th Air Force bombers attacked Augsburg, Germany. 458 Royal Air Force bombers attacked Mainz, Germany and lost two aircraft. 1,112 people were killed in the raid. 149 Royal Air Force bombers attacked Gelsenkirchen, Germany and lost one "Lancaster". The first US Army T-26 "Pershing" tank action took place at Elsdorf, Germany. Private First-Class Herman Wallace, of the 76th Division, won a posthumous Medal of Honor near Prumzurley, Germany.
- **1948** Dieter Wisliceny, German S.S. Major, and Adolf Eichmann's deputy, was executed in Czechoslovakia.

Eastern Europe

- **1943** Luftwaffe "Stukas" attacked shipping in Murmansk Harbor. German forces took Lozovaya.

Mediterranean

- **1941** The Italian armed merchant cruiser RAMB I was sunk by the Royal New Zealand Navy light cruiser LEANDER.
- **1943** The U565 damaged the British tanker SEMINOLE (10,389 tons).
- **1944** The U407 sank the Egyptian sailing ship ROD EL FARAG (55 tons).
- **1945** Lebanon and Syria declared war on the Axis.

Atlantic

1941 The Italian submarine BIANCHI sank the British freighter BALTISTAN (6,803 tons).

1942 The U578 sank the American tanker R.P. RESOR (7,451 tons-39 died). U578 survived until August 10th. The U432 sank the American freighter MARORE (8,215 tons). U432 survived until March 11, 1943. The U156 sank the British freighter MACGREGOR (2,498 tons). U156 survived until March 8, 1943.

1943 The U66 sank the British freighter ST. MARGARET (4,312 tons). U66 survived until May 6, 1944.

1945 The U1018 sank the Norwegian freighter CORVUS (1,317 tons). U1018 was then sunk in the English Channel by the Royal Navy frigate LOCH FADA. The U327 was sunk in the English Channel by the Royal Navy sloop WILDGOOSE and frigates LABAUN and LOCH FADA. The British freighter SAMPA was sunk nine miles northwest of Ostend by a mine.

North America

1896 Admiral Arthur Radford was born in Chicago. He graduated 59th in his 1916 class of 177. He qualified as a naval aviator in 1920. He was commander of the Naval Air Station at Seattle 1937-40, executive officer of the carrier 1940-41 and commander of the Naval Air Station at Trinidad in 1941. He was promoted to captain in January 1942 and named as Director of Aviation Training. In April 1943, he joined the staff of Carrier Division 2 in the Pacific. Three months later he was promoted to rear admiral and given command of Carrier Division 11. In January 1944, he began a series of staff assignments that ended in November 1944 when he assumed command of Carrier Division 6. After the war, he became Deputy Chief of Naval Operations for Air. In February 1947, he took over the 2nd Fleet in the Atlantic. The next year, he was named as Vice Chief of Naval Operations. On April 7, 1949 he assumed command of the Pacific Fleet. He served as Chairman of the Joint Chiefs of Staff 1953-57. He retired on August 1, 1957 and he died on August 17, 1973.

1940 The RMS QUEEN ELIZABETH arrived in New York for conversion to a troop transport.

1944 The destroyer ENGLISH was launched. She was sold to Taiwan in August 1970. The submarine BESUGO was launched. She was sold to Italy in 1966.

1945 Japanese balloon-bombs were found near Goldendale, Washington and Bethel, Alaska.

1946 The light cruiser CINCINNATI was sold for scrap.

Pacific

1942 At 1612, an ABDA (American-British-Dutch-Australian) force commanded by Dutch Admiral Karl Doorman, made contact with the IJN in the Java Sea. The ABDA group included the USN heavy cruiser HOUSTON, the Royal Navy heavy cruiser EXETER, the Dutch light cruisers DE RUYTER and JAVA, the Royal Australian Navy light cruiser PERTH, the USN destroyers ALDEN, JOHN D. EDWARDS, JOHN D. FORD and PAUL JONES, the Royal Navy destroyers ELECTRA, ENCOUNTER and JUPITER and the Dutch destroyers KORTENAER and WITTE DE WITTE. The IJN force included the heavy cruisers NACHI and HAGURO, the light cruisers JINTSU and NAKA and fourteen destroyers. At 1708, the EXETER was severely damaged and had her speed cut in half. At 1712, the KORTENAER was sunk by the HAGURO. At 1740, the ELECTRA was sunk by the IJN destroyer ASAGUMO in the Java Sea. The USN submarine S-38 rescued fifty-four survivors. At 1820, contact was broken off. At 2125, the JUPITER was sunk off Surabaya by a Dutch mine. At 2300, contact was regained. At 2320, the JAVA was sunk by the NACHI and the DE RUYTER was sunk by the HAGURO. USN Captain Albert Rooks, commander of the HOUSTON, won a Medal of Honor for his actions during the battle. The IJN submarine I-153 sank the Dutch freighter MOESIE (913 tons). The American freighter SEA WITCH delivered twenty-seven crated USAAF P-40s to Tjilajap, Java. They were later destroyed on the docks to prevent their capture by Japanese forces.

1944 The USN carrier INTREPID was hit by an aircraft torpedo. The USN submarine COD sank the TAISOKU MARU (2,473 tons). American aircraft attacked Momote and Lorengau in the Admiralties and Wewak on New Guinea. The Royal Australian Air Force attacked Madang and Alexishafen in New Guinea.

1945 The US Army's 63rd Infantry Regiment took Mount Pacawagan near Manila on Luzon. The USN light carrier SAN JACINTO was damaged in a storm off Iwo Jima. USMC Gunnery Sergeant William Walsh, of the 5th Division, won a posthumous Medal of Honor on Iwo Jima. USMC Private Wilson Watson, of the 3rd Division, won a Medal of Honor on Iwo Jima. Organized Japanese resistance on Corregidor ended. The USN submarine SCABBARDFISH sank the KIKAKU MARU No.6 (137 tons).

China-Burma-India

1943 The U516 sank the Dutch submarine tender COLUMBIA (10,972 tons). 10th Air Force B24s sank the Japanese freighter ASAKASAN MARU off Rangoon, Burma.

1945 American 14th Air Force B25s destroyed four bridges in Indo-China.

February 28th

Western Europe

1900 British General Francis De Guingand was born. He graduated from Sandhurst in 1919 and two years later would serve under Captain Bernard Montgomery. In 1942, after assuming command of the 8th Army in North Africa, General Montgomery would name De Guingand as his Chief of Staff. He would hold this position until the end of the war. He would spend much of his time reconciling differences between Montgomery and the American commanders. By 1946, even he had become tired of Montgomery's petty slights and he retired as a major general. He died on June 29, 1979 in Cannes, France.

1933 The German Reichstag passed an ordinance empowering police to arrest political opponents of the government.

1940 The Royal Navy battleship DUKE OF YORK was launched. She was scrapped in 1957. The German blockade runner WANGONI arrived at Kiel, Germany after evading the Allied blockading fleet.

1941 116 Royal Air Force bombers attacked Wilhelmshaven, Germany and lost one "Blenheim".

1942 British commandoes raided the German radar station at Bruneval, France. British civilian casualties in Luftwaffe raids during the month were twenty-two dead and twenty-one wounded. Six Royal Air Force "Blenheims" attacked the port of Ostend.

1943 Ten Royal Air Force "Mosquitoes" attacked targets in Holland. The Norwegian Resistance destroyed the heavy water plant at Vemork. Having all but destroyed the town of Lorient, France and its U-boat facilities, the Royal Air Force began concentrating its efforts against similar targets in St. Nazaire, France. 437 Royal Air Force bombers attacked the town and lost five aircraft. Twenty-nine people were killed and up to 60% of the town was destroyed. Twelve USAAF 4th Fighter Group "Spitfires" flew patrols over the Channel.

1944 Forty-nine American 8th Air Force B24s dropped 131 tons of bombs on V-1 launching sites near Ecalles-sur-Buchy, France. Sixty-one 8th Air Force P47s provided support for the bombers. 132 8th Air Force B17s dropped 379 tons of bombs on Pas de Calais, France losing seven bombers. 197 8th Air Force fighters provided support for the bombers and claimed one victory. The USAAF's 4th Fighter Group (P47) transitioned into P51s while en route to their targets in Europe. Lieutenant Colonel Frederick C. Grambo, commander of the 364th Fighter Group (P38), was killed in action over Zwolle, Holland while gaining combat experience by accompanying 20th Fighter Group (P38s) on its missions. American 9th Air Force B26s attacked V-1 launching sites. Five B17s from the USAAF's 422nd Bomb Squadron dropped 250 bundles of leaflets near Amiens, Rouen, Paris, Rouen, and Le Mans in France. Eight Royal Air Force "Wellingtons" dropped leaflets over France.

1945   1,072 American 8th Air Force bombers dropped 2,881 tons of bombs on rail targets in Germany and lost one B17. 707 8th Air Force fighters provided support for the bombers and claimed 18 victories for the loss of five P51s. 156 Royal Air Force bombers attacked Gelsenkirchen, Germany. The American Ninth Army was within sixteen miles of Köln, Germany. During the first flight of the Luftwaffe's experimental rocket fighter "Natter", the canopy blew off killing the pilot. Eighty-six Royal Air Force "Mosquitoes" attacked targets in Germany and lost one aircraft. The British government awarded ten Victoria Crosses in the month of February during the war. British civilian casualties for the month were 483 dead and 1,152 wounded.

1953   A German de-Nazification court posthumously exonerated General Alfred Jodl of the crimes for which he had been executed in 1946.

Eastern Europe

1941   The Germans crossed the Danube in Bulgaria as per the agreement of February 8th.

1943   Luftwaffe "Stuka" dive-bombers attacked shipping in Murmansk Harbor. German forces took Kramatorsk.

1945   The Soviets took Neustettin and Prechlau in East Prussia.

1946   Bela Imredy, Hungarian Premier and Finance Minister during the war, was executed for collaboration.

Mediterranean

1941   The Royal Air Force attacked Asmara, Eritrea. Sixteen Royal Air Force "Hurricanes" and twelve "Gladiators" fought fifty Italian fighters near the Albanian border. The Italians lost twenty-seven aircraft and the Royal Air Force lost none. The Luftwaffe dropped mines off Tobruk.

1943   The U371 damaged the American freighter DANIEL CARROL (7,176 tons). The German S-boat S-35 was sunk by a mine northwest of Bizerte by a mine. The German S-boat S-56 was damaged by the Royal Air Force at Palermo, Sicily. The Italian submarine FR-111 (the ex-French PHOQUE) was sunk ten miles south of Augusta by the Royal Air Force. The American 12th Air Force attacked Cagliari, Sicily.

1944   A major German attack took place at Anzio, Italy.

1945   755 American 15th Air Force aircraft attacked the Brenner Pass Railway.

Atlantic

1940 The Axis sank 226,920 tons of neutral and Allied shipping in February and lost five U-boats. The U20 sank the Italian freighter MARIA ROSA (4,211 tons) in error. U20 survived until September 10, 1944.

1941 The Axis sank 403,393 tons of neutral and Allied shipping in February and lost no U-boats. The U47 sank the British freighter HOLMELEA (4,223 tons). U47 survived until March 7th. The U108 sank the British freighter EFFNA (6,461 tons). U108 survived the war.

1942 At 0600, the USN destroyer JACOB JONES was torpedoed off the Delaware Capes by the U578 and sank an hour later. Eleven members of her crew survived. The U129 sank the Panamanian freighter BAYOU (2,605 tons). U129 was scuttled in August 1944. The Italian submarine DA VINCI sank the Latvian freighter EVERASMA (3,644 tons). The U653 sank the Norwegian freighter LEIF (1,582 tons). U653 survived until March 15, 1944. The U156 sank the American tanker OREGON (7,017 tons). U156 survived until March 8, 1943. The USN destroyer EDISON accidentally attacked the British submarine SEVERN off Nova Scotia. A USN PBY accidentally attacked and damaged the USN submarine GREENLING off New London, Connecticut. The Axis sank 679,632 tons of neutral and Allied shipping in February and lost three U-boats.

1943 The U405 sank the American freighter WADE HAMPTON (7,176 tons-nine dead). Her deck cargo included the ex-USN PTs-85 and 86, which were being sent as Lend-Lease to Russia. U405 survived until November 1st. The Axis sank 403,062 tons of neutral and shipping in February and lost twenty U-boats.

1944 The Axis sank 116,855 tons of neutral and Allied shipping in February and lost twenty-two U-boats.

1945 The Axis sank 95,316 tons of neutral and Allied shipping and lost twenty-two U-boats. The U1022 sank the Panamanian freighter ALCEDO (1,392 tons). U1022 survived the war. The U1302 sank the Panamanian freighter SORELDOC (1,926 tons-fifteen dead) and the British freighter NORFOLK COAST (646 tons). U1302 survived until March 7th.

North America

1942 It was announced that the Navy and Army commanders (Kimmel and Short) in Hawaii at the time of the December 7th attack on Pearl Harbor would be court-martialed.

1943 The light carrier MONTEREY and the destroyers THORN, TURNER, BULLARD, and KIDD were launched. The THORN was expended as a target in August 1974, the TURNER was lost January 3, 1944, the BULLARD was stricken in December 1972 and the KIDD was stricken in December 1974. The attack-transport DU PAGE was commissioned.

She would serve off Kwajalein, New Britain, Guam, Peleliu, Leyte, Luzon and Okinawa and would be scrapped in 1973. She would also be the last American ship damaged during the war when she was hit by a kamikaze off Okinawa in 1945. The submarine RAY was launched. She was discarded in 1960. The new light cruiser SANTA FE left Philadelphia en route to Pearl Harbor and operations in the Pacific. Aboard her and serving as members of her crew were 350 survivors from the heavy cruisers ASTORIA, QUINCY and VINCENNES which had been sunk off Savo Island on August 8, 1942.

1944 The minelayer OGLALA was recommissioned as ARG-1 (repair ship for diesel-propelled craft). She had been sunk during the December 7, 1941 attack on Pearl Harbor by the IJN and was later salvaged.

1945 Japanese balloon-bombs were found near Lake Bay, Washington and Holstein, Iowa. The American government awarded fifty-two Medals of Honor in the month of February during the war.

1954 Nuclear physicist Enrico Fermi died of cancer.

1961 USN Admiral Aaron "Tip" Merrill, commander of the battleship INDIANA and Cruiser Division 12-Pacific, died.

1967 The destroyer VAN VALKENBURGH was sold to Turkey.

1989 USAF Colonel Vincent W. "Squeek" Burnett died in Lynchburg, Virginia of emphysema. He had been instrumental in the development of the B26 "Marauder".

South America

1949 Major Lucian Youngblood died in a plane crash in Mexico. He had flown on the "Doolittle Raid".

Pacific

1942 The Allies sank 33,248 tons of Japanese shipping (nine ships) in January. The IJN submarine I-153 sank the British freighter CITY OF MANCHESTER (8,917 tons) and the Dutch freighter PARIGI (1,172 tons). The IJN submarine I-158 damaged the British tanker BRITISH JUDGE (6,735 tons). The IJN submarine I-4 sank the Dutch freighter BAN HO GUAN (1,693 tons). Japanese forces began landing on Java. The hulk of the USN destroyer STEWART (See February 22nd) was dynamited by retreating Allied forces.

1943 The Allies sank 93,175 tons of Japanese shipping (nineteen ships) in February. The IJN tanker IRO was damaged by the USN submarine PLUNGER. USN aircraft attacked Kahili Airfield on Bougainville. The Japanese freighter KASHII MARU was lost in a collision off Honshu with the KASAGISAN MARU.

1944   The Allies sank 519,559 tons of Japanese shipping (115 ships) in February. The USN submarine SAND LANCE sank the KAIKO MARU (3,538 tons). The USN submarine BALAO sank the AKIURA MARU (6,803 tons) and the SHOHO MARU (2,723 tons). The Royal Australian Air Force attacked Madang and Alexishafen in New Guinea. The USN destroyer ABNER READ was damaged when she ran aground off New Guinea.

1945   The Allies sank 87,464 tons of Japanese shipping (twenty-nine ships) in February. USN Pharmacist's Mate First Class John Willis, of the 5th USMC Division won a posthumous Medal of Honor on Iwo Jima. Motoyama Village on Iwo Jima was taken by American forces. The US Army's 186th Regimental Combat Team landed on Palawan in the Philippines.

February 29th

Western Europe

1944   218 American 8th Air Force B17s dropped 457 tons of bombs on Brunswick, Germany and lost one bomber. 554 8th and 9th Air Force fighters provided support for the bombers and claimed one victory for the loss of two P38s, one P47 and one P51. Thirty-eight 8th Air Force B24s dropped 112 tons of bombs on the Lottingham, France V-1 launching site. Seventy-nine 8th Air Force P47s provided support for the bombers and lost one aircraft. The USAAF's 387th Bomb Group (B26) attacked the V-1 site near Behen, France. Luftwaffe ace Johannes Kiel (21 heavy bomber victories), was killed in action by defensive fire from American 8th Air Force B17s. The Royal Air Force Fighter Command was re-named the Air Defense Command of Britain. Fifteen Royal Air Force "Mosquitoes" attacked Dusseldorf, Germany. A Royal Air Force "Mosquito" attacked the V-1 site at Sottevast, France. Five B17s from the USAAF's 422nd Bomb Squadron dropped 250 bundles of leaflets near Orleans, Lille, Reims, Cambrai, and Chateauroux in France.

Eastern Europe

1944   The Soviet government confirmed that the Finns wanted to discuss peace terms. Soviet Marshal Vatutin, commander of the First Ukrainian Front, was ambushed and mortally wounded by Ukrainian Nationalists.

Mediterranean

1944   German forces attacked the Allied-held beach-head at Anzio. The U407 damaged the British tanker ENSIS (6,207 tons). The German corvette Uj-201 (the ex-Italian EGERIA) was a constructive loss after an air-raid on Monfalcone.

North America
1944 There were thirty-one ship collisions on this day in New York Harbor due to heavy fog.
1960 The light cruiser DENVER was sold for scrap.
1966 Admiral Chester A. Nimitz died at his home on Yerba Buena Island in San Francisco Bay. He had commanded the USN Pacific Fleet during the war.

Pacific
1944 The USN submarine TROUT sank the SAKITO MARU (7,126 tons) and was then sunk by the IJN destroyers KISHINAMI, OKINAMI and ASASHIMO. The American Fifth Air Force attacked Alexishafen, New Guinea. USN PB4Y-1s operating out of Abamama in the Gilberts attacked Wake Island. USAAF B-24s sank the Japanese freighter NARITA MARU off Hollandia, New Guinea. 1,500 men of the US Army's 5th Cavalry Regiment landed at Hyane Harbor on Los Negros in the Admiralties. The USN submarine SARGO sank the UCHIDE MARU (5,275 tons). USN destroyers bombarded Rabaul, New Britain.

China-Burma-India
1944 The IJN submarine I-37 sank the British freighter ASCOT (7,005 tons). The U183 sank the British freighter PALMA (5,419 tons).

CHAPTER 3

THE MONTH OF MARCH

March 1st

Western Europe
1887 German General Georg Reinhardt was born. He died on November 22, 1963.
1899 German General Erich von Bach-Zelewski was born in Lauenburg, Pomerania. He commanded the forces that put down the Warsaw uprising that began on August 1, 1944. Polish resistance had ended on October 2, 1944 after sixty-three days of house-to-house fighting. After the war, he avoided war criminal charges until 1962 when he was sentenced to life in prison for murdering six communists in 1933. He died on March 8, 1972 in the prison hospital at Munich-Harlaching.
1938 Hermann Goering was named as Chief of Staff of the German Luftwaffe.
1940 Adolf Hitler issued the final directive for the invasion of Norway and the occupation of Denmark. The American Under Secretary of State, Sumner Welles, arrived in Berlin and met with German Foreign Minister Joachim Ribbentrop.
1941 John G. Winant arrived in Britain to replace Joseph Kennedy as American Ambassador to that country. No.485 Squadron became the first Royal New Zealand Air Force fighter squadron when it was formed at Driffield in Yorkshire, Britain. 131 Royal Air Force bombers attacked Cologne, Germany and lost twenty-two aircraft. Twenty-one people were killed in the raid.
1943 302 Royal Air Force bombers attacked Berlin and lost seventeen aircraft. 875 buildings were destroyed and 191 people were killed in the raid. Forty-nine Royal Air Force bombers dropped mines off the French and German coasts and lost two "Wellingtons". Twenty-four "Spitfires" from the American 4th Fighter Group flew patrols over the English Channel.
1944 The USAAF's 7th Photo Group sent two "Spitfires" on missions over Germany and lost one of them. 557 Royal Air Force bombers attacked Stuttgart, Germany and lost four aircraft. 125 people were killed in the raid. Five B17s from the USAAF's 422nd Bomb Squadron dropped 250 bundles of leaflets near Brest, Tours, Lorient, Nantes and Reims in France.

1945　American forces took Venlo in Holland and Sefferweich, Malbergweich, and Munchen-Gladbach in Germany. The German High Command issued orders that no staff officer could cross to the east bank of the Rhine from the west. This was to prevent unauthorized retreats in the face of the Allied advance. 1,209 American 8th Air Force bombers dropped 3,354 tons of bombs on rail targets in Germany. 460 8th Air Force fighters provided escort for the bombers and claimed twelve victories for the loss of seven P51s. 478 Royal Air Force bombers attacked Mannheim, Germany and lost three "Lancasters". 151 Royal Air Force bombers attacked Kamen, Germany and killed nine people. Forty-five Royal Air Force "Spitfires" attacked V-2 rocket launching sites in Holland. Private J. Stokes, of the Shropeshire Light Infantry, won a posthumous Victoria Cross in Germany. Ninety-five Royal Air Force "Mosquitoes" attacked targets in Germany.

1958　The Royal Navy battleship DUKE OF YORK was scrapped.

2011　Royal Navy Lieutenant Commander Barklie Lakin died at the age of 96. He had been awarded a DSO and two DSCs while in command of the submarine URSULA in the Mediterranean during the war.

Eastern Europe

1942　The Soviets began an offensive in the Crimea.

1943　Moscow informed the Polish government-in-exile that it would reclaim eastern Poland as Soviet territory. Soviet forces took Demyansk, Lychkovo and Zaluchie. The Germans evacuated their salient at Rzhev, thereby shortening their front by 200 miles and releasing twenty divisions for other duties.

1944　The Soviets took Russaki.

Mediterranean

1941　Free French forces took Kufra.

1943　At 1330, the Italian destroyer GENIERE was severely damaged at Palermo, Sicily by the USAAF. She was later towed to Taranto, France and repaired. At 1800, the Italian destroyer MONSONE was sunk at Naples by the USAAF.

1944　A German offensive against the Allies in Anzio was stopped. 100,000 Italian workers went on strike in Turin.

1945　Turkey and Saudi Arabia declared war on the Axis. Iran declared war on Japan.

Atlantic

1940　The German freighter TROJA (2,390 tons) was scuttled to prevent her capture by the Royal Navy cruiser DESPATCH. The U20 sank the Italian freighter MIRELLA (5,340 tons). U20 survived until September 10, 1944.

1941   The U552 sank the British tanker CADILLAC (12,062 tons). U552 survived the war.
1942   The U588 sank the British freighter CARPERBY (4,890 tons). U588 survived until July 31st. The U656 was sunk south of Newfoundland by a USN "Hudson" bomber of VP-82. It was the first U-boat victory for the USN.
1943   The American freighter FITZ-JOHN PORTER (7,176 tons-one dead) was sunk by the German U518, which had previously torpedoed her on February 28th. U518 survived until April 22, 1945.
1944   The U66 sank the French freighter SAINT LOUIS (5,202 tons). U66 survived until May 6, 1944. At 1920, the Royal Navy frigate GOULD (the ex-USN LOVERING) was sunk north of the Azores by the U358, which was then sunk by the Royal Navy frigates GORE, AFFLECK and GORLIES. The U603 was sunk by the USN destroyer escort BRONSTEIN. The U709 was sunk by the USN destroyer escorts BRONSTEIN and BOSTWICK.
1945   The American freighter ROBERT VANN was sunk off Ostend, Belgium by a mine.

North America

1940   The RMS QUEEN MARY completed her conversion to a troopship in New York.
1942   The 92nd Heavy Bomb Group (B17) was activated. It would be among the first units assigned to the new 8th Bomber Command in Britain. The carrier HORNET left Norfolk, Virginia en route to the Pacific and the "Doolittle Raid".
1943   It was announced that General Walter Short and Admiral Husband Kimmel would be court-martialed for dereliction of duty while serving as commanders of American forces at Pearl Harbor on December 7th. Processed food and fire-wood were rationed in America. By this date, the Soviet ferry pilots in Alaska had accepted 106 A20s, 34 B25s, 151 P39s, 48 P40s and 30 C47s for movement to Russia under the Lend-Lease program.
1944   The French battleship RICHELIEU left America en route to joining the Royal Navy's Eastern Fleet at Trincomalee, Ceylon. She had been undergoing repairs and modernization since her capture the previous year.
1959   The light cruiser SANTA FE was sold for scrap. She had been awarded fourteen battle stars and a Navy Unit Commendation during the war. The light cruisers SAN DIEGO, HOUSTON and BIRMINGHAM were stricken.
1962   USN Admiral Richard Conolly, commander of Destroyer Squadron 6, Task Force 86-Sicily and Task Force 53-Kwajalein, Saipan and Guam, died.
1964   The escort carrier THETIS BAY was decommissioned.

1968 The destroyers NELSON and WELLES were sold for scrap.
1969 The destroyer KALK was expended as a target this month.
1975 The destroyers PORTERFIELD and PICKING were stricken.

South America
1974 Luftwaffe "Stuka" pilot Hans Rudel and German aircraft designer Kurt Tank met with Argentine President Juan Peron.

Pacific
1942 At 0035, the USN heavy cruiser HOUSTON was sunk in Sunda Strait by the IJN heavy cruisers MOGAMI and MIKUMA and destroyers. HOUSTON's commanding officer Captain Albert H. Rooks was awarded a posthumous Medal of Honor. There were over 300 survivors. At 0108, the Royal Australian Navy light cruiser PERTH (6,980 tons and launched in 1936) was sunk in Sunda Strait by the same group. There were 307 survivors. At 1100, the Royal Navy heavy cruiser EXETER was scuttled after being damaged by the IJN heavy cruisers NACHI and HAGURO and the destroyer IKAZUCHI. Her 300 survivors were captured by the Japanese. At 1135, the Royal Navy destroyer ENCOUNTER was sunk by the IJN heavy cruisers MYOKO and ASHIGARA. At 1230, the USN destroyer POPE was damaged by the IJN heavy cruisers MYOKO and ASHIGARA. She was later scuttled. She had been awarded three battle stars and a Presidential Unit Citation before her loss. The Dutch destroyer EVERTSEN was damaged by the IJN destroyers SHIRAKUMO and MURAKUMO and was beached in Sunda Strait. The USN destroyer PILLSBURY was sunk in Bali Strait by the IJN heavy cruiser ASHIGARA. There were no survivors. The USN destroyer EDSALL was sunk in Sunda Strait by the IJN battleships HIEI and KIRISHIMA. Only five of her crew survived the action and they died as prisoners of war. It wasn't until seven years after the end of the war that her final story and that of her crew would be known. The Dutch submarine K-10 was sunk by the IJN. The IJN submarine I-154 sank the Dutch freighter MODJOKERTO (8,806 tons). The USN tanker PECOS, with the LANGLEY'S survivors aboard, was sunk off Java by the Japanese Naval Air Force. The USN destroyer WHIPPLE rescued 232 survivors and took them to Fremantle, Australia. The IJN minesweeper W-2 was sunk off Java by a mine. Japanese casualties on Luzon in the Philippines to this date were 2,700 dead and 7,000 wounded. A seaplane from the Japanese submarine I-25 flew over Hobart, Tasmania.
1943 A 5th Air Force B24 attacked a Japanese convoy that was en route from Rabaul, New Britain to New Guinea and sank the freighter KOKOKU

MARU. The American tanker GULFWAVE (7,141 tons) was damaged by the IJN submarine I-10.
1945 The USMC had secured two airfields on Iwo Jima and had a foothold on the remaining third. The USN destroyer COLHOUN was hit by Japanese shore-fire off Iwo Jima and suffered one dead and sixteen wounded. USN Task Force 58 attacked Okinawa, sinking the IJN ammunition ship KINESAKI, the escort TSUBAME and the torpedo boat MANAZURU. Japanese resistance in Manila, Luzon was confined to the Finance Ministry Building. The USN submarine STERLET sank the TATEYAMA MARU (1,148 tons).
1946 This was the designated date for "Operation Coronet", the American invasion of Honshu.

China-Burma-India
1942 The IJN submarine I-159 sank the Dutch freighter ROOSEBOOM (1,035 tons).
1943 The Burma Road was completed. It would be used to supply China from Burma.
1944 The "Chindits" crossed the Chindwin River in Burma. They were a British commando unit commanded by Orde Wingate.
1945 The French battleship RICHELIEU and the Royal Navy battleship QUEEN ELIZABETH arrived at the Royal Navy's base at Columbo, Ceylon.

March 2nd

Western Europe
1911 Luftwaffe ace Wolfgang Schellman (26 aerial victories) was born in Kassel. He was killed on June 24, 1941 by the Soviet NKVD two days after he had been shot down.
1935 France and the Soviet Union signed a mutual aid treaty.
1940 The American Under Secretary of State, Sumner Welles, met with Hitler in Berlin. In the first attack by the Luftwaffe on shipping in the southern portion of the English Channel, the transport DOMALA (8,441 tons) was damaged off the Isle of Wight.
1941 Fifty-four Royal Air Force bombers attacked German U-boat installations at Brest, France and lost one "Wellington".
1942 Four Royal Air Force "Bostons" attacked German shipping off Holland.
1943 Sixty Royal Air Force bombers dropped mines along the Atlantic coast and lost three aircraft. The German armed merchant cruiser CORONEL arrived in Kiel, Germany. Six Royal Air Force "Mosquitoes" attacked targets in the Ruhr area of Germany. Twelve "Spitfires" from the American 4th Fighter Group flew patrols over the Channel.

1944   375 American 8th Air Force bombers dropped 889 tons of bombs on Limburg, Ludwigshafen, Frankfurt, and Fischbach in Germany and lost eight B17s and one B24. 589 8th and 9th Air Force fighters provided support for the bombers and claimed seventeen victories for the loss of three P47s and one P51. Eighty-four 8th Air Force B17s dropped 158 tons of bombs on Chartres, France and lost one bomber. 281 8th and 9th Air Force fighters provided support for the bombers and claimed two victories. Luftwaffe ace Egon Mayer (102 victories) was killed in action by USAAF P47 fighters near Montmedy, France. An 8th Air Force B24 "Carpetbagger" was shot down over France. American 9th Air Force B26s attacked German V-1 rocket launching sites. 123 Royal Air Force bombers attacked Meulan-les-Meureaux, France. Five B17s from the USAAF's 422nd Bomb Squadron dropped 250 bundles of leaflets near Caen, Amiens, Rouen, Chartres, and Rennes in France.

1945   The American Third Army took Trier, Germany. The American Ninth Army took Roermond, Germany. Fifteen-year-old males were called up for service in the German Wehrmacht. 1,167 American 8th Air Force bombers dropped 2,589 tons of bombs on synthetic oil plants and tank factories in Germany and lost eleven B17s and three B24s. 713 8th Air Force fighters provided escort for the bombers and claimed 102 victories for the loss of thirteen P51s. 858 Royal Air Force bombers attacked Cologne, Germany and lost nine aircraft. Sixty-nine Royal Air Force "Spitfires" attacked German V-2 launching sites in Holland. The U3519 was sunk in the Baltic by a mine. The German minesweeper M-575 capsized in the Baltic. The Canadian Army's 53rd Division took Weeze, Germany. Seventy Royal Air Force "Mosquitoes" attacked targets in Germany.

Eastern Europe

1940   Soviet forces began an offensive against the Finns last defensive positions.
1941   German troops began crossing the Danube into Bulgaria in preparation for invading Greece.
1942   The German 4th Army evacuated Yukhnov.
1943   German forces (commanded by von Kluge) evacuated Rzhev. The German 1st Panzer Army took Slavyansk and Bogorodichno.
1945   The U995 sank the Soviet patrol craft BO-223 (the ex-USN PC-1507).

Mediterranean

1876   Pope Pius XII was born in Rome. He died in 1958.
1939   Italian Foreign Minister Count Ciano, while returning from Poland, received report of Cardinal Pacellis' election as Pope Pius XII.
1941   The Italian dictator, Benito Mussolini, arrived in Albania to inspect his troops.

1942   Royal Air Force bombers attacked Palermo, Sicily.
1944   426 Italians died of carbon-monoxide poisoning when their train stalled in a tunnel near Salerno, Italy. American Lend-Lease to Turkey was stopped due to that countries lack of any contribution to the war effort. The American 15th Air Force attacked German troop concentrations near Anzio, Italy. General Howard Kippenberger (died in 1957), commander of the New Zealand Division, had both feet blown off by a land-mine near Monte Cassino in Italy. Audie Murphy won a Bronze Star in Italy. He would end the war as America's most-decorated soldier.
1945   500 British troops, supported by the destroyer LIDDESDALE, captured the island of Piskopi northwest of Rhodes.
1949   The Italian light cruiser AOSTA was transferred to the Soviet Navy as war reparations. She was scrapped in 1957.

Atlantic

1940   The German freighter HEIDELBERG (6,530 tons) was scuttled to prevent her capture by the Royal Navy cruiser DUNEDIN. The U32 sank the Swedish freighter LAGAHOLM (2,818 tons). U32 survived until October 30th. The U17 sank the Dutch freighter RIJNSTROOM (695 tons). U17 survived the war.
1941   The U95 sank the British freighter PACIFIC (6,034 tons). U95 survived until November 28th. The U147 sank the Norwegian freighter AUGVALD (4,811 tons). U147 survived until June 2nd.
1942   The U126 sank the Norwegian freighter GUNNY (2,362 tons). U126 survived until July 3, 1943.
1943   The American freighter MERIWETHER LEWIS (7,176 tons) was sunk with all hands by the U634. U634 survived until August 30th. The Brazilian freighter ALFONSO PENA (3,540 tons) was sunk by the Italian submarine BARBARIGO. The BARBARIGO was lost on June 19th. The USN SC-1024 was lost in a collision off North Carolina. The American salvage tug WELLFLEET, which was en route to being turned over to the British, was rammed and sunk off Cape Hatteras, North Carolina by the American tanker EDWARD L. DOHENEY. The tugs 17-man crew survived. The USN sub chaser SC-1024 was lost in a collision off North Carolina.
1944   The U744 sank the Royal Navy LST-362. U744 survived until March 6th.
1945   The U1302 sank the British freighter KING EDGAR (4,536 tons) and the Norwegian freighter NOVASLI (3,204 tons). U1302 survived until March 7th.

North America

1942   The destroyer AULICK was launched. She was transferred to Greece in 1959.

1944   The escort carrier SAGINAW BAY was commissioned. She was scrapped in 1960. The USN destroyer escort ALEXANDER J. LUKE was damaged when she ran aground off Boston, Massachusetts.
1966   The destroyer KENDRICK was expended as a target.

Pacific

1942   Japanese forces took Batavia, Java and landed on Mindanao in the Philippines. USAAF P40s based on Bataan, sank the IJN sub chaser No.11 KYO MARU in Subic Bay. The Dutch Navy scuttled eleven minesweepers at Tandjok-Priok, Java. The Dutch minelayer RAM and the patrol craft FORMALHOUT and MEREL were scuttled at Tjilatjap, Java. The Dutch submarine K-X and the destroyers BANCKERT and WITTE DE WITH were scuttled at Surabaya, Java. The Japanese Naval Air Force sank the Dutch minesweeper ENDEH in Java Sea. The IJN aircraft ferry KAMAGAWA MARU (6,440 tons) was sunk by the USN submarine SAILFISH. The SAILFISH was scrapped in 1948. The USN destroyer STEWART was scuttled at Surabaya, Java. She would later be salvaged by the Japanese. The USN submarine PERCH was badly damaged by IJN destroyers. She would later be scuttled and her crew captured. Australia declared war on Thailand.

1943   The "Battle of the Bismarck Sea" began when 5th Air Force B17s and B24s attacked a Japanese convoy that had been sighted the previous day. It consisted of eight merchant ships and eight destroyers and was headed for Lae, New Guinea. The freighter KYOKUSAI MARU was the first ship sunk. The freighter KEMBU MARU and the transport TEIYO MARU were also damaged in the first attacks. A Royal Australian Air Force "Catalina" tracked the convoy during the night and into the next morning. The USN submarine THRESHER sank the TOEN MARU (5,232 tons) in the Makassar Straits. THRESHER was scrapped in 1948.

1944   The USN submarine PICUDA sank the SHINKYO MARU (5,139 tons). USN submarine NARWHAL landed supplies on Mindanao and evacuated 28 personnel. 1,000 men of the US Army's 5th Cavalry Regiment landed on Los Negros in the Admiralties. USN PBJs (the USN version of the B25) attacked Japanese installations at Rabaul, New Britain.

1945   USN forces (commanded by Whiting) bombarded Okino Daito Jima. General Douglas MacArthur returned to Corregidor aboard the USN PT-373. He had been evacuated in 1942 from the same island aboard another PT-boat. The USMC 3rd Division took Airfield No.3 on Iwo Jima. The USN submarine BOWFIN sank the CHOKAI MARU (135 tons).

China-Burma-India

1944   The West African 81st Division took Apaukwa, Burma, but was then driven out by Japanese troops.

1945   Fazal Din, of the Baluch Regiment, won a posthumous Victoria Cross in Burma. Gian Singh, of the 4/15th Punjab Regiment, won a Victoria Cross in Burma. USAAF B29s attacked Singapore. Royal Air Force B24s attacked Bangkok, Thailand.

1946   The American freighter OSHKOSH VICTORY was damaged by a mine in the Yangtze River.

March 3rd

Western Europe

1912   Luftwaffe ace Hannes Trautloft (57 victories) was born in Grossobringen. He survived the war.

1919   Luftwaffe ace Karl Schoerner (46 victories) was born in Nuremburg. He survived the war.

1941   A Luftwaffe He111 bomber crashed near Lackenshane, Eire and one crewman died. Seventy-one Royal Air Force bombers attacked Cologne, Germany and lost one "Hampden". No bombs fell within the city limits. At this point in the Royal Air Forces air war, this was a fairly common occurrence. Seven Royal Air Force "Stirlings" attacked the port of Brest, France and lost one aircraft. It was the first of the type to be lost in action.

1942   223 Royal Air Force bombers dropped 462 tons of bombs on the Renault Works in Billancourt, France and lost one "Wellington" and killed 623 civilians. It was estimated that the French company was making 18,000 trucks a year for the Germans. Four Royal Air Force "Wellingtons" attacked Emden, Germany and lost one aircraft. A Luftwaffe Ju-88 bomber crashed into Mount Gabriel in Eire. Four of the crew died.

1943   Ten Royal Air Force "Mosquitoes" attacked targets in Norway and lost one aircraft. 173 people died of suffocation when they panicked in an air-raid shelter in London. 417 Royal Air Force bombers attacked Hamburg and lost ten aircraft. Twenty-seven people were killed in the raid. Fourteen Royal Air Force bombers dropped mines off Denmark and lost one "Stirling". Twenty-eight "Spitfires" from the American 4th Fighter Group flew patrols over the Channel.

1944   Seventy-nine American 8th Air Force bombers attacked the port facilities at Wilhelmshaven, Germany and lost nine B17s and two B24s. 55th Fighter Group P38 "Lightnings" became the first USAAF aircraft to fly over Berlin. The 364th Fighter Group (P38 then converted to the P51) flew its first 8th Air Force mission. A damaged 100th Bomb Group B17 landed near

Schleswig, Germany and was captured. 730 8th and 9th Air Force fighters provided support for the bombers and claimed eight victories for the loss of one P38 and six P51s. Two 8th Air Force "Carpetbagger" B24s were shot down over France. Curtis Lemay was promoted to Major General in the USAAF. He would later command the 20th Air Force in the Pacific. American 9th Air Force B26s attacked French airfields. Twenty-seven Royal Air Force "Mosquitoes" attacked targets in Germany.

1945   American forces took Rath, Sinsteden, Stommeln, Giessen, Krefeld, and Dansweiler in Germany. Royal Canadian Air Force ace Flight/Lieutenant Richard Audet (10 victories) was killed in action. Wolf Harnack, a German Social Democrat, was executed by Gestapo for his part in the July 20th conspiracy. German forces began retreating from the west bank of the Rhine. In Germany, 15-year-olds conscripts were sent to the front. 1,069 8th Air Force bombers dropped 2,895 tons of bombs on rail and oil targets in Germany and lost five B17s and four B24s. 684 8th Air Force fighters provided support for the bombers and claimed twenty-two victories for the loss of eight P51s. The Royal Air Force sent 106 "Spitfires", 44 B25s and 17 A20s against German V-2 launching sites in Holland. A Luftwaffe KG200-flown B17 was shot down by a Royal Air Force "Mosquito" near Luvigny, France. 234 Royal Air Force bombers attacked Kamen, Germany and killed seventeen people. 222 Royal Air Force bombers attacked the Dortmund-Ems Canal in Germany and lost seven "Lancasters". Ninety-six Royal Air Force "Mosquitoes" attacked targets in Germany. The Luftwaffe sent more than 200 intruder aircraft over Britain. They shot down thirteen "Halifaxes", nine "Lancasters", one "Fortress" and one "Mosquito". British ace Richard Audet (10.5 aerial victories) was killed by anti-aircraft fire.

1946   The American freighter MINOR C. KEITH was damaged by a mine in Bremerhaven, Germany.

Eastern Europe
1941   Moscow criticized Germany's occupation of Bulgaria.
1943   The Soviets took Rzhev and Lgov. The Germans took Slavyansk and Lisichansk.
1945   Finland declared war on Germany.

Mediterranean
1913   The Italian battleship ANDREA DORIA was launched. She was scrapped in 1961.
1941   Greek forces were within 25 miles of Tirania, the capital of Albania. The first British convoy destined for Greece left Alexandria, Egypt. General

Maitland Wilson arrived in Athens. He had been appointed on February 28th to command the British troops in Greece.

1942 Sixteen Royal Air Force "Wellingtons" flying from Malta attacked Palermo, Sicily. They sank the ammunition ship CUMA (8,260 tons) and damaged thirteen other vessels.

1944 The Italian corvette MARANGONE was sunk by Allied aircraft while serving with the Germans. The last German attack on the Allies Anzio beach-head took place. The American 15th Air Force attacked rail and aircraft targets in Italy.

Atlantic

1940 The German freighter WOLFSBURG (6,201 tons) was scuttled in the Denmark Strait to prevent her capture by the Royal Navy heavy cruiser BERWICK. The British freighter CATO (710 tons) was sunk by a mine.

1942 The U129 sank the American freighter MARY (5,104 tons). U129 was scuttled in August 1944. The U68 sank the British freighter HELENUS (7,366 tons). U68 survived until April 10, 1944.

1943 The American freighter STAG HOUND (8,591 tons) was sunk off Brazil by the Italian submarine BARBARIGO. BARBARIGO was lost on June 19th. The U43 sank the German blockade runner DOGGERBANK (5,154 tons) in error. The British destroyer BEVERLEY rescued the last survivor from the American freighter WADE HAMPTON which had been sunk by U405 on February 28th.

1944 The Royal Navy destroyer LAFOREY was sunk by the U223, which was then sunk by the Royal Navy destroyers TUMULT, BLENCATHRA and HAMBLETON.

1945 The U1022 sank the British trawler SOUTHERN FLOWER (328 tons). U1022 survived the war. The Royal Navy submarine SEALION was scuttled for use as an Asdic target.

North America

1895 General Matthew Bunker Ridgeway was born in Fort Monroe, Virginia. He graduated 56th in his 1917 West Point class of 139. In June 1942 he succeeded Omar Bradley as commander of the 82nd Airborne Division. In September 1944 he assumed command of the 18th Airborne Corps. On June 4, 1945 he was promoted to lieutenant general. In 1950 he would take over the 8th Army in Korea. After MacArthur's recall in April 1951, he was promoted to four-star rank and given MacArthur's post of C-in-C Far East Command. On May 30, 1952 he replaced Eisenhower as Supreme Allied Commander Europe. After an unsatisfactory performance there, he was sent back to the States where he served a shortened tour as Army Chief of Staff. He retired in 1955 and died in August 1993 in Pittsburgh.

1900 Uzal Ent, future commander of the 2nd Air Force and leader of the Ploesti low-level raid, was born in Northumberland, Pa.
1942 17th Bomb Group B25s arrived at Eglin Field, Florida, from their base at Pendleton, Oregon, to begin training for the "Doolittle Raid" on the Japanese Home Islands. The escort carrier CHARGER was commissioned. She was stricken in 1949 and converted into the freighter FAIRSEA.
1944 The escort carrier CAPE ESPERANCE was launched. In 1961 she was scrapped in Japan. FDR announced that the remains of the Italian Fleet would be distributed among the Soviet Union, Great Britain, and the U.S.
1945 A Japanese balloon-bomb was found near Nanaimo, British Columbia.
1978 Robert W. Prescott died in Palm Springs of cancer at age 64. He had flown with the American Volunteer Group and had founded the Flying Tigers Airline.
2009 USN ace Earling Zaeske, age 87, died in Spring Valley, Illinois. He had scored 5 victories in the Pacific while flying the F6F.

Pacific

1942 The USN submarine PERCH was scuttled after being damaged the previous day. Nine of her crew would die in captivity. The USN gunboat ASHEVILLE was sunk with all hands by the IJN destroyers ARASHI and NOWAKI. Her only survivor would die in a POW camp in 1945. At 2315, the Royal Navy destroyer STRONGHOLD (launched in 1919) was sunk south of Sunda Strait by the IJN heavy cruiser MAYA and the destroyers ARASHI and NOWAKI. The Royal Australian Navy sloop YARRA and the minesweeper MMS-51, the tanker FRANCOL and the freighter ANKING were sunk south of Java by the IJN. IJN carrier aircraft sank two Allied freighters at Tjilatjap, Java. The IJN submarine I-1 sank the Dutch freighter SIANTAR (8,667 tons). The Japanese Naval Air Force attacked Broome, Australia, destroying twenty-four aircraft. The USN submarine TROUT arrived at Pearl Harbor with twenty tons of Philippine government gold and silver, which was then transferred to the light cruiser DETROIT. Two Japanese Naval Air Force "Emily" flying boats attacked Oahu, Hawaii, bombing Mount Tantalus.
1943 The 5th Air Force continued attacking a Japanese convoy off New Guinea. The action had begun the previous day. The destroyers ASASHIO, TOKITSUKAZE and SHIRAYUKI were sunk and the destroyer ARASHIO was badly damaged. The collier NOSHIMA, the freighters AIYO MARU, SHINAI MARU, TAIMEI MARU and KEMBU MARU and the transport TEIYO MARU were also sunk during the action. The freighter OIGAWA MARU was damaged and abandoned. She would be sunk later that night by USN PTs-143 and 150. USAAF ace Hoyt Eason,

the 5th Air Force's first P38 ace, was killed during the convoy's attacks. 5th Air Force ace Captain Thomas Lynch shot down a Japanese "Oscar" off Lae, New Guinea. Japanese aircraft attacked Allied shipping off Tulagi and damaged the USN freighter CARINA. A USN PB4Y sank the IJN gunboat CHOEI MARU off Vella Lavella in the Solomons.

1944   The Japanese attacked the American beach-head on Los Negros in the Admiralties. The USN submarine SAND LANCE sank the AKASHISAN MARU (4,541 tons) and the Soviet freighter BELORUSSIA (5,900 tons). The SAND LANCE was sold to Brazil in 1963. The USN submarine NARWHAL damaged the IJN patrol gunboat KARATSU (the ex-USN LUZON) which was towed to Manila and scuttled on February 3, 1945. The NARWHAL was scrapped in 1945. The USN submarine RASHER sank the NITTAI MARU (6,484 tons). The IJN minelayer SHIRAKAMI was sunk in a collision with the transport NICHIRAN MARU off the Kuriles.

1945   General Millard Harmon, commander of the USAAF in the Pacific, was listed as missing while on a C-47 flight out of Hawaii. The IJN auxiliary tanker HARIO was sunk by a Royal Australian Air Force-laid mine. The USN submarine TREPANG sank the NISSHO MARU No.2 (1,386 tons). USMC Corporal Charles Berry, Private First-Class William Caddy (posthumous), Pharmacist Mate Third Class Jack Williams (posthumous), Sergeant William Harrell and Pharmacist Mate Second Class George Wahlen, all of the 5th USMC Division, won Medals of Honor on Iwo Jima. Japanese resistance ended in Manila in the Philippines. The US Army's Americal Division landed on Romblin and Burias in the Philippines. Royal Australian Air Force PBYs mined Yulinkan Bay off Hainan Island.

China-Burma-India

1942   Japanese forces crossed the Sittang River in Burma and surrounded the town of Pegu.

1943   The Chindits cut the Mandalay-Myitkyina railway. The American freighter HARVEY W. SCOTT (7,176 tons) and the British freighter NIRPURA (5,961 tons) were sunk and the Dutch tanker TIBIA (10,356 tons) was damaged by the U160.

1944   The Chinese 22nd Division took Ngam Ga, Burma. The IJN submarine I-162 sank the British freighter FORT MCLEOD (7,127 tons).

1945   The British Army's IV Corps took Meiktila, Burma. Lt. W. Weston, of the Green Howards, won a posthumous Victoria Cross in Burma. 14th Air Force B24s sank the Japanese freighter YAEI MARU No.1 and the tanker IYASAKI MARU No.1. RAAF aircraft dropped mines off Hainan Island.

March 4th

Western Europe

1916 The Royal Navy battlecruiser RENOWN was launched. She was scrapped in 1948.

1941 Adolf Hitler met with Yugoslavia's Prince Paul at Obersalzburg. A Royal Navy force of two light cruisers, five destroyers and two transports attacked Lofoton, Norway with 500 British Commandoes, 52 Royal Engineers and 52 Norwegian volunteers. They destroyed fishery processing plants and sank the steamers HAMBURG (5,470 tons), FELIX NEUMANN (2,468 tons), PASAJES (1,996 tons), EILENAU (1,404 tons), BERNHARD SCHULTE (1,058 tons), GUMBINNEN (1,381 tons) and MIRA (1,152 tons). They capture 213 Germans and 12 Norwegians. The Swedish press reported that at least twenty errant British barrage-balloons had caused damage in western Sweden with their trailing cables.

1943 Twelve Royal Air Force "Mosquitoes" attacked targets in France. Forty-four B17s of the American 8th Air Forces 91st, 303rd and 305th Bomb Groups attacked Hamm, Germany and lost five aircraft. The 91st was awarded a Distinguished Unit Citation for the mission. Twenty-seven Royal Air Force bombers dropped mines and lost one "Lancaster".

1944 249 American 8th Air Force B17s dropped 570 tons of bombs on Bonn, Dusseldorf, Frankfurt, Berlin, Cologne and Machnow in Germany and lost fifteen aircraft. 770 8th and 9th Air Force fighters provided support for the bombers and claimed eight victories for the loss of four P38s, four P47s and sixteen P51s. The Luftwaffe attacked the 8th Air Force base at Metfield (485th Bomb Group-B24), killing one man. Twenty-two Royal Air Force "Mosquitoes" attacked targets in Germany. Seventy-six Royal Air Force bombers dropped supplies to Resistance forces.

1945 671 8th Air Force bombers dropped 1,712 tons of bombs on airfields and industrial targets in Germany and lost one B24. Nine USAAF 466th Bomb Group B24s accidentally attacked Basel, Switzerland and six 392nd Bomb Group B24s attacked Zurich. Swiss casualties were five killed and nineteen wounded. 482 8th Air Force fighters provided escort for the bombers and lost one P51. 128 Royal Air Force bombers attacked Wanne-Eickel, Germany. USAAF Lieutenant Colonel Earle Aber, commander of the 406th Squadron (a night-leaflet unit), died when his B17 was shot down by British anti/aircraft fire near Woodbridge in Suffolk. Forty-five "Spitfires" attacked German V-2 launching sites in Holland. The British XXX Corps took Geldern, Holland. American forces took Repeln, Kaldenhausen, Derikum and Hausweiler in Germany. The American VII Corps reached the Rhine north of Cologne. Sixty-three Royal Air Force "Mosquitoes" attacked targets in Germany.

Eastern Europe
1943 Soviet forces took Sevsk west of Kursk.
1944 Soviet forces under Zhukov began an offensive west of Berdichev. The U703 sank the British freighter EMPIRE TOURIST (7,062 tons).
1945 The Soviet First Byelorussian Front reached the Baltic near the Pomeranian city of Kolberg. Kolberg held out until March 18th. It was the last German-held territory between the Polish Corridor and Stettin Bay.

Mediterranean
1943 The U83 was sunk by the Royal Air Force's No.500 Squadron.
1965 Nazi author Johann Leers died in Cairo.

Atlantic
1940 The U29 sank the British freighters THURSTON (3,072 tons) and PACIFIC RELIANCE (6,717 tons). U29 was scuttled on May 5, 1945.
1943 The U172 sank the British freighter CITY OF PRETORIA (8,049 tons). U172 survived until December 13th. The U515 sank the British freighter CALIFORNIA STAR (8,300 tons). U515 survived until April 9, 1944. The U87 was sunk by the Royal Canadian Navy destroyer ST. CROIX and frigate SHEDIAC. The Argentine steamer RIO COLORADO rescued 84 survivors from the American freighter STAGHOUND which had been sunk the previous day by the Italian submarine BARBARIGO.
1944 The U472 was sunk by aircraft from the Royal Navy escort carrier CHASER and the destroyer ONSLAUGHT.

North America
1937 The US Army was ranked as the seventeenth strongest in the world at this time. The police department of New York City was numerically larger than the Army.
1943 The submarine SKATE was launched at Mare Island, California. She was expended on October 16, 1948 after having served as a target ship for the Bikini A-bomb tests. Rocky Marciano, the boxer, was drafted.
1945 A Japanese balloon-bomb was found near Big Creek, British Columbia.
1949 A Japanese balloon-bomb was found near Montesano, Washington.
1982 USAAF Major General Pierpont Hamilton died. He had won a Medal of Honor in North Africa during the first days of "Operation Torch".

Pacific
1942 Aircraft from the USN carrier ENTERPRISE attacked Japanese installations on Marcus Island. The USN submarine GUDGEON was attacked in error by USN carrier ENTERPRISE aircraft. The Dutch minesweeper JAN VAN AMSTEL was sunk in Madura Strait by the IJN. The Dutch

minesweeper PIETER DE BITTER was scuttled at Surabaya, Java. The Dutch minesweeper ELAND DUBOIS was scuttled in Gili Genteng Roads, Java. The USN submarine S-39 sank the IJN tanker ERIMO in Sunda Strait. The S-39 was lost August 14th. The USN submarine NARWHAL sank the TAKI MARU (1,235 tons). The NARWHAL was scrapped in 1945. The USN submarine GRAMPUS sank the tanker KAIJO MARU (8,632 tons) south of Truk. The GRAMPUS was lost on March 5, 1943. The IJN submarine I-7 sank the Dutch freighter LE MAIRE (3,271 tons). IJN "Emily" seaplanes refueled at French Frigate Shoals on their return trip from attacking Hawaii. The USN submarine SARGO was attacked and damaged off Fremantle by an Australian "Hudson".

1943 The Royal Navy carrier VICTORIOUS arrived at Pearl Harbor. The USN battleship MASSACHUSETTS arrived at Noumea, New Caledonia for duty in the Pacific. The "Battle of the Bismarck Sea" continued as 5th Air Force bombers destroyed the abandoned hulk of the IJN destroyer ARASHIO. From this point on, action mainly consisted of strafing rafts and boats. Twelve USAAF A20 bombers attacked Lae Airfield on New Guinea. USAAF Lieutenant Harry Brown, who had scored his first aerial victory over Pearl Harbor on December 7, 1941, scored his second, a Japanese "Oscar" over the Bismarck Sea. The USN submarine PERMIT sank the HOKUTO MARU (2,267 tons). The USN submarine TRITON sank the KIRIHA MARU (3.057 tons).

1944 USN Task Force 74 (commanded by Crutchley) bombarded Hauwei and Norilo in the Admiralties. Sergeant Troy McGill, of the US Army's 1st Cavalry Division, won a posthumous Medal of Honor on Los Negros in the Admiralties. The American airfield on Green Island became operational. American aircraft attacked Choiseul Island in the Solomons. USN PBJs (the USN version of the B25) attacked Rabaul, New Britain. The USN submarine PETO sank the KAYO MARU (4,368 tons). The USN submarine BLUEFISH sank the OMINESAN MARU (10,356 tons).

1945 Ninety-four B29s made the types last precision raid of the war and lost one aircraft. The target was the Musashino aircraft plant outside Tokyo. Thereafter they would use "carpet-bombing". Eight B29s made a night-raid on Nagato. The "Dinah Might" became the first B29 to land on the newly captured airfield on Iwo Jima. USMC ace Major Robert Stout (six victories) was killed in action near Peleliu. The USN submarine BAYA sank the PALEMBANG MARU (5,236 tons). The Royal Navy submarines TRENCHANT and TERRAPIN sank the IJN patrol craft Cha-8 (309 tons). The Royal Navy submarine CLYDE sank the KIKU MARU (233 tons). The USN destroyers YARNALL and RINGGOLD were damaged in a collision.

China-Burma-India

1943 The U160 sank the British freighters EMPIRE MAHSEER (5,087 tons) and MARIETTA (7,628 tons) and damaged the freighter SHEAF CROWN (4,868 tons).

1945 Indian troops took Meiktila, Burma. 14th Air Force dropped mines in the Yangtze River.

March 5th

Western Europe

1920 The Royal Navy battlecruiser HOOD was commissioned. She was sunk by the German battleship BISMARCK on May 24, 1941.

1936 The first flight of the Royal Air Force's Supermarine "Spitfire" fighter took place.

1941 German torpedo boats laid a minefield off Eastbourne. Five Royal Air Force "Blenheims" attacked Boulogne, France. Britain broke relations with Bulgaria.

1942 General Alan Brooke replaced Admiral Dudley Pound as Chairman of the British Chiefs of Staff Committee.

1943 442 Royal Air Force bombers attacked Essen, Germany and lost fourteen aircraft. 482 people were killed in the raid. Since the 20th of December, the Royal Air Force's Bomber Command had flown 9,980 sorties on which it had dropped 17,834 tons of bombs and had lost 276 aircraft. The first flight of the Royal Air Force's Gloster "Meteor" jet took place. Four "Spitfires" from the American 4th Fighter Group flew patrols over the Channel.

1944 Colonel Henry Spicer, commander of the 357th Fighter Group (P51), was shot down and would spend two days drifting in the English Channel before being captured by the Germans. 164 American 8th Air Force B24s dropped 392 tons of bombs on French airfields and lost four bombers. 307 8th and 9th Air Force fighters provided support for the bombers and claimed fourteen victories for the loss of two P38s and three P51s. American 9th Air Force B26s attacked V-1 rocket launching sites. Ten Royal Air Force "Mosquitoes" attacked targets in Germany. Five B17s from the USAAF's 422nd Bomb Squadron dropped 250 bundles of leaflets over Le Mans, Paris, Orleans and Reims.

1945 The American First Army reached Cologne, Germany. The American 4th Division reached the Rhine at Orsoy. The American 104th Division took Junkersdorf. The Germans began blowing the Rhine bridges. 396 8th Air Force bombers dropped 992 tons of bombs on Chemnitz, Hamburg, Fulda and Plauen in Germany and lost one B17. 624 8th Air Force fighters provided support for the bombers. 170 Royal Air Force bombers attacked

Gelsenkirchen, Germany and lost one "Lancaster". Fifty-one "Spitfires" attacked V-2 launching sites in Holland. 760 Royal Air Force bombers attacked Chemnitz and lost twenty-two aircraft. A further nine had been lost soon after take-off due to icy conditions, including one that crashed in the city of York and killed several civilians. 258 Royal Air Force bombers attacked Bohlen, Germany and lost four "Lancasters". 126 Royal Air Force "Mosquitoes" attacked targets in Germany and lost three aircraft.

Eastern Europe

1940 Finland agreed to discuss Soviet peace terms.
1942 Soviet forces took Yucknov.
1943 German Army Group "South" (commanded by Manstein) advanced towards Kharkov. The U255 sank the American freighter EXECUTIVE (4,978 tons).
1944 Soviet forces under Koniev began an offensive near Uman.
1945 The Soviets took Stargard and Naugard near Stettin.

Mediterranean

1942 Royal Air Force bombers attacked Benghazi, Libya. Royal Navy Commander A. Miers, commander of the Royal Navy submarine TORBAY, won a Victoria Cross.

Atlantic

1940 The U17 sank the Dutch freighter GRUTTO (920 tons). U17 survived the war.
1941 The U95 sank the Swedish freighter MURJEK (5,070 tons). U95 survived until November 28th.
1942 The U404 sank the American freighter COLLAMER (5,112 tons-seven dead). U404 survived until July 28, 1943. The U126 sank the American freighter MARIANA (3,110 tons) with all hands. U126 survived until July 3, 1943. The U128 sank the Norwegian tanker KNUDSEN (11,007 tons). U128 survived until May 17, 1943. The U505 sank the British freighter BENMOHR (5,920 tons). U505 was captured on June 4, 1944 and is now a memorial in Chicago, Illinois.
1943 The American freighter HARTWELSON ran aground and was lost off Maine. The United States Coast Guard cutter HEX rescued thirty-five of her crew. The U130 sank the British freighters FIDRA (1,574 tons), EMPIRE TOWER (4,378 tons), TREFUSIS (5,299 tons) and GER-Y-BRYN (5,108 tons). U130 survived until March 12th. The German trawler V-1252 was lost in a collision with the trawler FJ-27 north of Borkum.
1944 The U66 sank the British freighter JOHN HOLT (4,964 tons). U66 survived until May 6th. The U366 was sunk by aircraft from the Royal Navy escort carrier CHASER and the destroyer BEAGLE.

The Month of March

North America
1937 US Secretary of State Cordell Hull expressed official US government regrets to the German government over remarks made by New York City Mayor Fiorello H. La Guardia. La Guardia had referred to Adolf Hitler as a "brown-shirted fanatic".
1944 The destroyer COLLETT was launched. She was sold to Argentina in 1974.
1945 The USN LCS-127 was wrecked in San Pedro Bay, California.
2013 USN ace Charles Mallory died in Charleston, West Virginia at the age of 92. He had been credited with 10 aerial victories while flying F6Fs off the INTREPID.

South America
1941 American officials seized the Italian liner CONTE BIANCAMAO at Colon, Panama.

Pacific
1923 The IJN light cruiser YUBARI was launched. She was sunk on April 27, 1944.
1932 The Japanese industrialist Takuma Dan was assassinated by military extremists in Tokyo.
1942 The Japanese took Batavia, Java. The Japanese New Guinea invasion force left Rabaul, New Britain. The Japanese transport TAKAO MARU, which had run aground off Vigan, Luzon, was destroyed by Philippine saboteurs. USMC Colonel Lemuel Sheperd assumed command of the 9th Regiment, 1st Division. In January 1952 he would become USMC Commandant.
1943 The "Battle of the Bismarck Sea" concluded with attacks by RAAF "Beaufighters" and USN PT-boats on Japanese landing barges, rafts and boats which had survived the action of the previous days. The USN submarine GRAMPUS was sunk in Blackett Strait by IJN destroyers. The USN submarine TAMBOR landed agents, 2 tons of ammunition and $10,000 in currency on Mindanao.
1944 All the first-class restaurants in Japan were closed with the female employees being sent to work in factories. The US Army's 32nd Division landed at the Yalau Plantation on New Guinea, 30 miles west of Saidor. 1,400 men of the US Army's 7th Cavalry Regiment landed on northern Los Negros. USAAF Colonel Neel Kearby (22 aerial victories and a Medal of Honor) was killed in action. USN PBJs (B25s) attacked Rabaul, New Britain. The USN submarine NARWHAL delivered supplies to Tawi Tawi in the Phillippines and evacuated 8 personnel.
1945 The USN submarine SEA ROBIN sank the MANYO MARU (2,904 tons), the SHOYU MARU (855 tons) and the NAGARA MARU (855 tons). The

USN submarine BASHAW sank the SEISHIN MARU (5,239 tons). The IJN minesweeper W-15 was sunk by the USN submarine TILEFISH.

China-Burma-India

1879 British economist William Beveridge was born in Rangpur, Bengal.
1942 Aircraft from the IJN light carrier RYUJO attacked targets on the east coast of India. Japanese forces took Pegu, Burma. British General Harold Alexander (died in 1969) arrived in Rangoon relieve General Thomas Hutton, (died in 1981), as commander of the British forces in Burma. USAAF General Lewis Brereton assumed command of the 10th Air Force in India. He had previously commanded the Far East Air Force in the Philippines.
1944 The Chinese 22nd Division took Maingkwan, Burma.
1945 Japanese forces counter-attacked the British IV Corps at Meiktila, Burma. Bhanbhagta Gurung, of the 3/2nd Gurkha Rifles, won a Victoria Cross in Burma. The 25th Indian Division took Tamandu, Burma. American 14th Air Force B25s destroyed five bridges in Indo-China.

March 6th

Western Europe
1934 The Royal Navy light cruiser ARETHUSA was launched. She was scrapped in 1950.
1940 The French battleship JEAN BART was launched at St. Nazaire. France and Italy signed a trade agreement.
1941 German S-boats attacked two British convoys off Cromer and Southwold and sank seven freighters. Five Royal Air Force "Blenheims" attacked targets in Holland and Belgium. The Gestapo executed eighteen members of the Dutch Resistance.
1943 Eighty B17s and B24s of the American 8th Air Force attacked Lorient and Brest in France and lost three B17s. The German minelayer SKAGERRAK laid a minefield off Bergen, Norway.
1944 672 8th Air Force bombers attacked targets in and around Berlin and lost fifty-three B17s and sixteen B24s. One B24 and three B17s landed in Sweden. Brigadier General Russell Wilson, commander of the 4th Combat Wing, died when his 385th Bomb Group B17 was shot down over Berlin. Piloting the aircraft was Medal of Honor winner 1st Lieutenant John C. Morgan, who survived. 810 8th and 9th Air Force fighters provided support for the bombers and claimed eighty-one victories for the loss of one P38, five P47s and five P51s. American 9th Air Force B26s attacked French airfields and railyards. 267 Royal Air Force bombers attacked

the railyards at Trappes, France to check the feasibility of such attacks in support of "Operation Overlord", the Allied invasion of Northern France. Five B17s from the USAAF's 422nd Bomb Squadron dropped 250 bundles of leaflets on Nantes, Cambrai, Lille, Chateauroux and Lorient in France.

1945 Canadian forces took Sonsbeck. 119 Royal Air Force bombers attacked the oil refinery at Salzbergen and lost one "Lancaster". Forty-eight Royal Air Force "Mosquitoes" attacked Wesel, Germany and lost one aircraft. The German destroyer Z-28 was sunk by the Royal Air Force. 198 Royal Air Force bombers attacked Sassnitz, Germany and lost one "Lancaster". 138 Royal Air Force bombers attacked Wesel, Germany.

1946 French Admiral Georges Robert, the former commander of the French garrison in Martinique, was sentenced by a French court to a dishonorable discharge and 10-years hard labor.

Eastern Europe

1929 Bulgarian/Turkish treaty was signed.

1940 Finnish peace negotiators left for Moscow.

1942 The Soviet destroyer SMYSHLENY was sunk off Kerch by a mine.

1943 The German 4th Panzer Army began an offensive west of Kharkov. The Soviets took Gzhatsk on the Moscow/Smolensk Railway.

1944 Soviet forces under Malinovsky began an offensive against German Army Group "A".

1945 The Germans began their last offensive in Hungary in an attempt to secure their last source of oil at Nagykanisza. Soviet forces took Grudziadz, Poland.

1953 Soviet dictator Josef Stalin died of a heart attack.

Mediterranean

1941 The Italian submarine ANFITRITE was sunk by the Royal Navy destroyer GREYHOUND. The Luftwaffe dropped acoustic mines in the Suez Canal.

1943 The DAK lost fifty-five tanks in action along the Mareth Line.

1944 The American freighters DANIEL CHESTER FRENCH (thirty-three dead) and VIRGINIA DARE were sunk in an Allied minefield off Bizerte.

Atlantic

1940 The German blockade runner ARUCAS (3,359 tons) was scuttled east of Iceland to prevent her capture by the Royal Navy cruiser YORK. The German freighter URUGUAY (5,846 tons) was scuttled in the Denmark Strait to prevent her capture by the Royal Navy cruiser BERWICK.

1942 The U587 sank the Greenland freighter HANS EGEDE (900 tons). U587 survived until the 27th. The Italian submarine TAZZOLI sank the Dutch freighter ASTREA (1,406 tons) and the Norwegian freighter TONSBERGFJORD (3,156 tons). The Italian submarine FINZI sank the British tanker MELPOMENE (7,011 tons). The U505 sank the Norwegian tanker SYDHAV (7,587 tons). U505 survived the war and is now a memorial in Chicago, Illinois. The U129 sank the American freighter STEEL AGE (6,188 tons-33 dead). U129 was scuttled in August 1944. The U701 sank the Faroes trawler NYGGJABERG (272 tons). U701 survived until July 7th.

1943 The U410 sank the British freighter FORT BATTLE RIVER (7,133 tons). U402 survived until October 13th. The U172 sank the Norwegian freighter THORSTRAND (3,041 tons). U172 survived until December 13th.

1944 The U744 was sunk by the Royal Navy destroyer ICARUS, frigate KENILWORTH CASTLE and the Royal Canadian Navy destroyers CHAUDIERE and GATINEAU and corvettes FENNEL and CHILLIWACK. The U973 was sunk by the Royal Navy escort carrier CHASER northwest of Narvik, Norway.

1945 The U775 damaged the British freighter EMPIRE GERAINT (6,991 tons). U775 survived the war. The German destroyer Z-28 was sunk by the Royal Air Force.

North America

1942 The submarine AMBERJACK was launched. She was lost on February 16, 1943.

1943 The light cruiser ASTORIA (awarded five battle stars during the war) and the destroyer LUCE were launched. ASTORIA was scrapped in 1971 and LUCE was lost on May 3, 1945.

1944 The submarine ATULE was launched.

1962 The destroyer MONSSEN was wrecked while under tow. She was later salvaged and sold for scrap on October 21, 1963.

1972 The destroyer KNAPP was stricken.

1986 USN Admiral Winfield Scott Cunningham, commander of Wake Island in 1942, died.

Pacific

1943 The IJN destroyers MURASAME and MINEGUMO were sunk in the Kula Gulf by the USN light cruisers DENVER, MONTPELIER and CLEVELAND and the destroyer WALLER. Only forty-nine men survived from the two ships. The IJN patrol boat No.34 collided with the target ship YAKAZE south of Kavieng, New Britain. She would be sunk at Truk on July 3, 1944 by USN aircraft. The Japanese Naval Air Force attacked the American forces in the Russell Islands.

1944   The USN submarine NAUTILUS sank the AMERICA MARU (6,069 tons). American forces landed on the Willaumax Peninsula on New Britain and took Salami and Porlaka on Los Negros. USN PBJs (B25s) attacked Rabaul, New Britain.
1945   Twenty-eight P51s and twelve P61s of the USAAF's 15th Fighter Group arrived at Airfield No.2 on Iwo Jima. The USN transport YANCEY was damaged in a collision off Iwo Jima.

China-Burma-India
1942   A convoy carrying reinforcements for the Allied forces defending Rangoon turns back when the senior commanders decided that the Japanese were too close to the city to justify sending in more troops.

March 7th

Western Europe
1881   British politician Ernest Bevin was born. He served as Minister of Labor and died on April 14, 1951 in London.
1904   Reinhard Heydrich was born in Halle. He would later serve as Himmler's deputy and leader of the Seicher-Dienst (security police).
1936   Germany re-occupied the Rhineland. The Allies failure to react to this action greatly enhanced Hitler's position with the German military and as well as the public.
1942   Seventeen Royal Air Force bombers attacked German U-boat installations at St. Nazaire, France. Seventeen Royal Air Force "Hampdens" dropped mines off Lorient, France and lost one aircraft.
1943   Twenty Royal Air Force bombers dropped mines off Denmark and lost two aircraft. Two "Spitfires" from the USAAF's 4th Fighter Group flew a patrol over the Channel.
1944   Irish Prime Minister Eamon de Valera (died in 1975) sent FDR a telegram concerning Eire's "friendly neutrality" towards America. American 9th Air Force B26 "Marauders" attacked German shore-batteries on the French coast. Eighteen 9th Air Force A20 "Havocs" attacked the Conches Airfield in France. 304 Royal Air Force bombers attacked Le Mans, France. The German minesweeper M-4405 was sunk west of La Pallice, France in an air-attack.
1945   The US Army's 3rd Armored and 104th Infantry Divisions took Cologne, Germany. The German forces killed eighty hostages in Holland. The US Army's 9th Division took the town of Remagen on the Rhine. Sergeant Alex Drabik led his squad from A Company, 27th Armored Infantry Battalion, 9th Division across the Ludendorff rail bridge in Remagen. The

first American tank to cross was a "Sherman" commanded by Lieutenant Windsor Miller. American forces took Boxberg, Dockweiler and Kelberg in Germany. Royal Air Force bombers attacked shipping in the Kattegat. 859 American 8th Air Force bombers dropped 2,610 tons of bombs on communication and oil targets in Germany. 311 8th Air Force fighters provided support for the bombers and lost one P51. The Allies declared Germany's Foreign Minister Joachim von Ribbentrop and Propaganda Minister Joseph Goebbels war criminals. 531 Royal Air Force bombers attacked Dessau, Germany and lost eighteen "Lancasters". 281 Royal Air Force bombers attacked Hemmingstedt, Germany and lost five aircraft. 241 Royal Air Force bombers attacked Harburg, Germany and lost fourteen "Lancasters". 422 people were killed in the raid. 112 Royal Air Force "Mosquitoes" attacked targets in Germany and lost one aircraft. The German patrol boats V-1610 and V-1612 were sunk by Allied aircraft at Lysekiel, Norway.

Eastern Europe
1940   Finnish Marshal Carl Mannerheim advised his government to seek terms with the Soviets.
1942   The Soviet freighter IZHORA was sunk by German destroyers.
1945   Luftwaffe ace Erich Leie (118 aerial victories) died when his Fw190 collided with a Soviet Yak-9.

Mediterranean
1941   The first British troops disembarked in Greece. They had been withdrawn from the British 8th Army in North Africa to support the Greeks in their war against the Italians.
1942   The Royal Navy carriers EAGLE and ARGUS launched fifteen "Spitfires" for Malta in "Operation Spotter".
1943   At 1310, the Italian torpedo boat CICLONE was mined off Bizerte and sank the next day.
1945   The Jewish Brigade entered action along the Montone River in Italy.

Atlantic
1940   The German freighter HANNOVER was captured by the Royal Navy cruiser DUNEDIN. The U14 sank the Dutch freighter VECHT (1,965 tons). U14 was scuttled on May 5, 1945. The British freighter COUNSELLOR (5,064 tons) was sunk by a mine.
1941   The U99 sank the British whaler TERJE VIKEN (20,638 tons) and the tanker ATHELBEACH (6,568 tons). U99 survived until March 17th. The U37 sank the Greek freighter MENTOR (3,050 tons). U37 was scuttled on May 5, 1945. The U47 (commanded by Prien) was sunk by the Royal Navy destroyer WOLVERINE.

1942   The Italian submarine FINZI sank the Swedish freighter SKANE (4,528 tons). The U94 sank the Royal Navy trawler NORTHERN PRINCESS (655 tons). U94 survived until August 28th. The American freighters BARBARA (4,637 tons-nineteen dead) and freighter CARDONIA (5,104 tons-one dead) were sunk off Cuba by the U126. U126 survived until July 3, 1943. The U161 sank the Canadian tanker UNIWALECO (9,755 tons). U161 survived until September 27, 1943. The Brazilian freighter ARABUTAN (7,874 tons) was sunk off Virginia by the U155. The US Coast Guard cutter CALYPSO rescued fifty-four of her crew. U155 survived the war.

1943   The U230 sank the British freighter EGYPTIAN (2,868 tons). U230 was scuttled on August 21, 1944. The U591 sank the British freighter EMPIRE IMPALA (6,116 tons). U591 survived until July 30th. The U221 sank the Norwegian freighter JAMAICA (3,015 tons). U221 survived until September 27th. The U633 was sunk south of Iceland by the Royal Air Force's No.200 Squadron. The American freighter ALCOA GUARD rammed and sank the Norwegian freighter TAMESIS off Bermuda.

1944   The U518 sank the Panamanian freighter VALERA (3,401 tons). U518 survived until April 22, 1945.

North America

1907   Future US Army Chief of Staff George C. Marshall was promoted to First Lieutenant. USAAF General Lauris Norstad was born in Red Wing, Minnesota. He graduated 139th in his 1903 West Point class of 299. At the start of the war, he was serving in USAAF headquarters in Washington D.C. He was later transferred to the Mediterranean Theater and the 12th Air Force. He was promoted to brigadier general and named as that unit's operation officer. In August 1944, he returned to Washington D.C. as Deputy Chief of Staff of the USAAF. He was then assigned as Chief of Staff of the 20th Air Force in the Pacific. On June 4, 1945 and at the age of thirty-eight he was promoted to major general. He was promoted to four-star rank in 1952. He retired in 1963. He died in Tucson, Arizona on September 12, 1988.

1942   The first class of Black USAAF fighter pilots graduated their segregated school at Tuskegee, Alabama. The entire class was retained as instructors. The USN blimp K-5 dropped the first sonobouy in a test with the submarine S-20 off New London, Connecticut.

1943   The destroyers MILLER and BRAINE were launched. The submarine BONEFISH was launched. She was lost on June 18, 1945.

1944   The destroyer escort ULVERT M. MOORE was launched. She would be commanded by Franklin Roosevelt Jr., son of the President and would be expended as a target in July 1966.

2010 USN Lieutenant Commander James Billo died at the age of 90 in Gold Beach, Oregon. He had scored five aerial victories while flying an F4F "Wildcat" during the Battle of Santa Cruz Island in 1942.

Pacific

1942 Japanese forces took Tjilatjap and Lembang on Java. The Dutch minelayer LEEUW was scuttled at Surabaya, Java. The Japanese began landing at Salamaua and Lae on New Guinea.

1942 The USN submarine TAUTOG laid mines off the coast of Borneo.

1944 USN PT-337 was sunk in Hansa Bay, New Guinea by Japanese shore batteries. American forces took Papitalai on Los Negros. USN PBJs (B25s) attacked Rabaul, New Britain.

1945 USMC Second Lieutenant John Leims, of the 3rd Division, won a Medal of Honor on Iwo Jima. The US Army's 127th Infantry Regiment took Aringay, Luzon.

1950 Admiral Arthur Radford, Commander-in-Chief of the Pacific Fleet, ordered that from this day forward the national flag would fly over the wreck of the battleship ARIZONA in Pearl Harbor. This would lead to the mistaken assumption by many that the ship was still in commission.

China-Burma-India

1942 3,500 Allied troops were evacuated from Rangoon, Burma. The operation was supported by the USN destroyer ALLEN and the Indian sloop HINDUSTAN. The Japanese Southern Army, commanded by General Iida, received a directive from Tokyo ordering it to destroy the Allied forces in Burma and to chase the remnants into China.

1943 The U506 sank the British freighter SABOR (5,212 tons).

1944 The U510 sank the Norwegian freighter TARIFA (7,229 tons).

1945 The Chinese 38th Division took Lashio, Burma. The Japanese counter-attacked at Meiktila, Burma.

March 8th

Western Europe

1884 German General Georg Lindemann was born. He died on September 25, 1963.

1921 Luftwaffe ace Georg-Peter Eder (seventy-eight aerial victories) was born in Oberdachstetten. He survived the war.

1937 A week-long battle began near Guadalajara, Spain in which the rebel force of two divisions was routed.

1941   Eight Royal Air Force "Blenheims" attacked targets in Holland and Germany. The Luftwaffe attacked London.

1942   Twenty-four Royal Air Force "Bostons" attacked targets in France and lost one aircraft. 211 Royal Air Force bombers attacked Essen, Germany and lost eight aircraft. Ten people were killed in the raid. It was the first operation for the Royal Air Forces "Gee" navigational aid.

1943   Sixteen Royal Air Force "Mosquitoes" attacked targets in France and lost one aircraft. Sixty-seven American 8th Air Force B17s and B24s attacked the marshalling yards at Rennes and Rouen in France and lost two B17s and two B24s. 335 Royal Air Force bombers attacked Nuremburg, Germany and lost eight aircraft. 343 people were killed in the raid.

1944   539 8th Air Force bombers dropped 1,059 tons of bombs on targets in and around Berlin and lost twenty-eight B17s and nine B24s. 891 8th and 9th Air Force fighters provided support for the bombers and claimed seventy-nine victories for the loss of three P38s, ten P47s and five P51s. Luftwaffe ace Rudolf Ehrenberger (forty-nine aerial victories) was killed in action by USAAF fighters. The USAAF 390th Bomb Group B17 "Phyllis Marie" landed near Werben, Germany and was captured. American 9th Air Force B26s attacked Dutch airfields.

1945   The US Army's 1st Division entered Bonn, Germany. The German minesweepers M-412, M-432, M-442 and M-452 along with three gun carriers and six smaller vessels carried troops from the Channel Islands and staged a raid on American-held Granville on the Contentin Peninsula. They destroyed the American patrol boat PC-564 and four freighters of 3,612 tons. They also captured the collier ESKWOOD (791 tons), released sixty-seven German prisoners of war and blew up harbor installations. The M-412 was lost when she ran aground during the attack. Sixty-nine 8th Air Force B17s dropped 240 tons of bombs on the marshalling yards at Giessen, Germany. 245 8th Air Force bombers dropped 3,530 tons of bombs on rail, communication, and oil targets in Germany. 314 8th Air Force fighters provided escort for the bombers. 312 Royal Air Force bombers attacked Hamburg, Germany and lost one aircraft. 118 people were killed in the raid. 276 Royal Air Force bombers attacked Kassel, Germany and lost one "Mosquito". Eighty-nine Royal Air Force "Mosquitoes" attacked targets in Germany. Fifteen USAAF 492nd Bomb Group B24s dropped thirty-seven tons of bombs on the Dortmund, Germany marshalling yards in a night raid.

1972   S.S. General Erich Bach-Zelewski died in a prison hospital in Munich-Harlaching. He had commanded the German forces that put down the Warsaw Uprising in 1944.

Eastern Europe
1940   The Finns sued for peace in their war with Russia.
1943   The Soviets took Sychevka north of Vyazma.
1944   The Soviets returned the USN light cruiser MILWAUKEE which had served with them as the MURMANSK. She was scrapped later in the year at Wilmington, Delaware.

Mediterranean
1944   At 1900, the German torpedo boat TA-15 (the ex-Italian FRANCESCO CRISPI) was sunk off Crete by the Royal Air Force. She was later salvaged (See October 12, 1944). The British destroyers TENACIOUS and TROUBRIDGE bombarded Korcula Island in the Adriatic.
1945   Talks concerning the ending of the Italian war began between German S.S. General Wolff and American diplomat Allen Dulles. American forces took Carviano, Italy.

Atlantic
1941   The U105 sank the British freighter HARMODIUS (5,229 tons). U105 survived until June 2, 1943. The U124 sank the British freighters NARDANA (7,974 tons), HINDPOOL (4,897 tons), TIELBANK (5,084 tons) and LAHORE (5,304 tons). U124 survived until April 2, 1943. The U70 was sunk south of Iceland by the Royal Navy destroyer WOLVERINE. U70 survived until March 8, 1941.
1942   The U701 sank the Royal Navy trawler NOTTS COUNTRY (541 tons). U701 survived until July 7, 1942. The U68 sank the British freighter BALUCHISTAN (6,992 tons). U68 survived until April 10, 1944. The U569 sank the British freighter HENGIST (984 tons). U569 survived until May 22, 1943. The USN net tender MULBERRY rescued fourteen survivors from the American freighter CARDONIA which had been sunk the day before by U126. The USCG cutter CALYPSO rescued fifty-four survivors from the Brazilian ARABUTAN.
1943   The U156 was sunk by the USN's VP-53. The American freighter J.L.M. CURRY was scuttled by Allied warships after being damaged by heavy seas northeast of Iceland. The U432 sank the British freighter GUIDO (3,921 tons). U432 survived until March 11, 1943. The U527 sank the British freighter FORT LAMY (5,242 tons) and the LCT-2480 which was being carried as deck cargo. U527 survived until July 23, 1943. The U591 sank the Yugoslavian freighter VIJVODA PUTNIK (5,879 tons). U591 survived until July 30, 1943. The U190 sank the British freighter EMPIRE LAKELAND (7,015 tons). U190 survived the war. The U642 sank the British freighter LEADGATE (2,125 tons). U642 survived until July 5,

1944. The US Coast Guard cutter SPENCER rescued thirty-five survivors from the freighter GUIDO.
1945 The U275 sank the British freighter LORNASTON (4,934 tons). U275 survived until March 10th.

North America
1941 The US Senate passed the Lend-Lease bill by a vote of sixty to thirty-one. This act eliminated the need for cash payments by the Allies for American-made goods.
1942 Colonel W.O. Butler became commander of the American 11th Air Force in Alaska. The destroyer CARMICK was launched. She was stricken in 1971.
1943 The escort carrier BLOCK ISLAND and the training-carrier SABLE were commissioned. The SABLE would serve on the Great Lakes and the BLOCK ISLAND would be sunk on May 29, 1944.
1944 500 P82 "Twin-Mustangs" were ordered. USAAF Chief of Staff General Henry H. Arnold inspected B29 units training in Kansas.
1945 A Japanese balloon-bomb was found near Platinum, Alaska.
1949 The trial of Mildred Gillars, alias "Axis Sally", ended with a conviction for treason. She was sentenced to ten to thirty years in prison and fined $10,000.
1962 The destroyer HOWORTH was expended as a target.
1963 The US Coast Guard cutter MARION was sold.
2010 USAF Colonel Jack Walker died at the age of 89 in Riverside, California. He had scored 5 aerial victories while flying the P38 "Lightning" in the Mediterranean.

Pacific
1942 The Japanese took Surabaya, Java. Within the harbor, they discovered the scuttled hulk of the USN destroyer STEWART (See February 28th). She would be repaired and commissioned into the Japanese Navy. The Dutch minelayer KRAKATAU was scuttled off Madura, Java. The Dutch minesweeper AMSTEL was sunk in Madura Strait by the IJN. The Dutch minesweeper DUBOIS was scuttled at Gili Genteng, Java. Dutch Lieutenant General Heinter Poorten surrendered his forces on Java. A seaplane from the Japanese submarine I-25 flew over Wellington, New Zealand.
1943 The USN submarine PERMIT sank the HISASHIMA MARU (2,747 tons).
1944 Japanese forces attacked the US Army's 37th Division at Torokina, Bougainville. Three F4U "Corsairs" and one B24 "Liberator" were destroyed by artillery fire during the action. The 1st USMC Division attacked Japanese forces on New Britain. American forces secured Los

Negros in the Admiralties. The Royal Navy submarine SEA ROVER sank the SHOBU MARU (2,005 tons).

1945 USMC Private First-Class James LaBelle and First Lieutenant Jack Lummus, of the 5th Division, won posthumous Medals of Honor on Iwo Jima. The US Army's 1st Corps took Mount Magabang on Luzon in the Philippines. American forces secured Palawan Island in the Philippines. The US Army's 503rd Regimental Combat Team left Corregidor Island in Manila Bay having landed on February 17th. The US Army's 24th Division landed on Mindanao in the Philippines. The IJN escort No.69 was damaged by the USAAF off Hainan. She would sink while under tow on the 16th.

1948 The USN destroyers RALPH TALBOT and WILSON were expended after the Bikini A-bomb tests.

1962 The USN destroyer HOWORTH was expended off San Diego, California.

1969 Rear Admiral Richard Antrim died. He had won a Medal of Honor as a prisoner of war after his ship, the destroyer POPE, was sunk early in the Pacific war.

China-Burma-India

1942 The Japanese took Rangoon and Payagyi in Burma. Rangoon had been evacuated by the Allies the previous day.

1944 The Royal Air Force attacked Sakhan, Burma.

March 9th

Western Europe

1907 Baldur von Schirach was born in Berlin. He would serve as leader of the Hitler Youth and as Governor of Vienna. He served a twenty-year sentence for war crimes after the war. He died on August 8, 1974 at the age of sixty-seven.

1935 Germany announced that the formation of the Luftwaffe had occurred on March 1st.

1937 The Luftwaffe's He111 bomber flew its first operational sortie when KG88 attacked Republican airfields at Alcala and Barajas in Spain.

1941 Fifteen Royal Air Force "Mosquitoes" attacked targets in France and lost one aircraft. The Luftwaffe attacked Portsmouth, Britain. The British Air Ministry ordered the Bomber Command to begin operations against German U-boats and the long-range aircraft threat. 264 Royal Air Force bombers attacked Munich, Germany and lost eight aircraft. 291 buildings were destroyed and 208 people were killed in the raid. Sixty-two Royal Air Force bombers dropped mines in the Baltic and lost three "Wellingtons".

1942   187 Royal Air Force bombers attacked Essen, Germany and lost three aircraft. Ten people were killed in Essen and another seventy-four were killed in nearby towns. Admiral Harold Stark, the former Chief of Naval Operations, assumed command of the USN Forces in the European Theater of Operations.

1943   Forty "Spitfires" from the USAAF's 4th Fighter Group flew missions over the Channel.

1944   490 American 8th Air Force bombers dropped 1,207 tons of bombs on Berlin, Hannover, Brunswick and Nienburg in Germany and lost six B17s and two B24s. One of the lost B17s landed in Sweden. 808 8th and 9th Air Force fighters provided support for the bombers and lost one P38. Forty-four Royal Air Force "Lancasters" attacked Marignane, France.

1945   The American 1st Division took Bonn, Germany. The American First Army took Godesberg, Germany. 1,021 8th Air Force bombers dropped 2,427 tons of bombs on rail and industrial targets in Germany and lost six B17s and one B24. 421 8th Air Force fighters provided support for the bombers. The American 9th Air Force attacked rail and communication targets on the east bank of the Rhine. 159 Royal Air Force bombers attacked Datteln, Germany and lost one "Lancaster". Canadian forces took Veen, Holland. Ninety-four "Spitfires" attacked V-2 targets in Holland. The German minesweeper M-412 was scuttled by her crew at Granville in Normandy. Ninety-two Royal Air Force "Mosquitoes" attacked Berlin.

1946   The American freighter LORD DELAWARE was damaged by a mine off Fehmarn Island, Germany.

Eastern Europe

1890   Soviet politician Vyacheslav Molotov was born. He died in 1986.
1935   Nikita Khrushchev became Chief of the Communist Party.
1936   Poland proposed to France that they jointly attack Germany.
1943   Russian public was first told of Allied aid. The U586 sank the American freighter PUERTO RICAN (6,076 tons).
1944   The Soviets took Staronstantinov. German Army Group South attacked Soviet positions at Tarnopol in the Ukraine.

Mediterranean

1940   The Royal Navy submarine UTMOST sank the Italian transport CAPO VITA.
1941   The Italians began offensive against the Greeks near Bubesh, Albania.
1943   Hans-Jurgen von Arnim replaced Erwin Rommel as commander of the DAK. The U596 damaged the British freighters FORT NORMAN (7,133 tons) and EMPIRE STANDARD (7,047 tons).

1944   The American transport WOODS was sunk off Palermo, fifty-one died. The American freighter CLARK MILLS was a constructive loss after an air-raid off Bizerte.

Atlantic
1940   The U14 sank the British freighters BORTHWICK (1,079 tons), ABBOTSFORD (1,585 tons) and AKELD (643 tons). U14 was scuttled on May 5, 1945. The U38 sank the British trawler LEUKOS (216 tons). U38 was scuttled in May 1945. The U28 sank the Greek freighter MARGARONIS (4,979 tons). U28 survived until March 1944.
1942   The U587 sank the Greek freighter LILY (5,719 tons). U587 survived until the 27th. The Italian submarine TAZZOLI sank the Uruguayan freighter MONTEVIDEO (5,785 tons). The U94 sank the Brazilian freighter CAYRU (5,152 tons). U94 survived until August 28th. The U126 sank the Panamanian tanker HANSEAT (8,241 tons). U126 survived until July 3, 1943. The U96 sank the Norwegian freighter TYR (4,265 tons). U96 survived until March 30, 1945. The US Coast Guard cutter BEDLOE rescued sixteen survivors from the tanker GULFTRADE. The American freighter ALCOA SCOUT rescued survivors from the American freighter MARY which had been sunk on March 3rd by U129.
1943   On this day, German submarines attacked five different convoys, two transatlantic convoys, one bound for northern Russia, one moving from Brazil to Trinidad and one en route from Britain to Gibraltar. The U510 sank the American freighters THOMAS RUFFIN (7,191 tons-six dead) and JAMES K. POLK (7,177 tons) and the British freighter KELVINBANK (3,872 tons) 175 miles north of French Guiana. U510 survived the war. The U530 sank the Swedish freighter MILOS (3,058 tons). U530 survived the war. The U409 sank the American freighter MALANTIC (3,837 tons-twenty-five dead), the Norwegian BONNEVILLE (4,665 tons) and the LCT-2341, which was being carried as deck cargo and the British tanker ROOSEWOOD (5,989 tons). U409 survived until July 12th. The US Coast Guard cutter BIBB rescued three survivors from the freighter COULMORE and one each from the freighters BONNEVILLE and MELROSE.
1944   At 0130, the Royal Navy corvette ASPHODEL was sunk northwest of Spain by the U575. Her five survivors were rescued by the Royal Navy corvette CLOVER. U575 survived until March 13th. At 2100, the US Coast Guard-manned destroyer escort LEOPOLD (171 dead) was torpedoed south of Iceland by the U255. The US Coast Guard-manned destroyer escort JOYCE rescued twenty-eight of her crew. U255 survived the war.

North America

1886 General Robert Eichelberger was born in Urbana, Ohio. He graduated 68th in his 1909 West Point class of 103. He won a Distinguished Service Cross and a Distinguished Service Medal while fighting the Bolsheviks in Siberia in 1919. He was promoted to brigadier general in 1940. He got his second star the next year. He was superintendent of West Point from November 18, 1940 until January 11, 1942. In March of 1942 he assumed command of the 77th Division. On June 22, 1942 he was named as commander of the 1st Corps. In August, he and his staff reached Australia. He was promoted to lieutenant general on October 15, 1942. On December 1st, he flew to New Guinea with orders from General MacArthur to "Take Buna or don't come back alive." He took Buna, as well as the rest of New Guinea. After leading forces in the battles for New Britain, the Admiralties and Morotai, on September 4, 1944, he was named as commander of the 8th Army. He led it during the conquest of the Philippines and the occupation of Japan. He retired on September 3, 1948 and died on September 26, 1961.

1892 Major General John Cannon, future commander of the 12th Air Force in the Mediterranean, was born in Salt Lake City, Utah.

1933 The heavy cruiser SAN FRANCISCO (awarded 17 battle stars during the war-only the carrier ENTERPRISE would earn more) was launched. She was scrapped at Panama City, Florida in 1961.

1940 The destroyers KEARNY and PLUNKETT were launched. The KEARNY was stricken in 1971 and the PLUNKETT was transferred to China in 1959.

1942 Ernest King became Chief of Naval Operations. Construction of the Alaska-Canada Highway began.

1943 The destroyer HAILEY was launched. She was transferred to Brazil in 1961.

1944 The escort carrier SARGENT BAY was commissioned. She was scrapped in 1959. The light cruiser SPRINGFIELD (awarded two battle stars during the war) was launched. She was scrapped in 1978.

1945 Comedian Red Skelton was drafted into the Army.

1948 Congress approved the Medal of Honor for WWII's Unknown Soldier.

1953 Escaped German prisoner of war Reinhold Pabel was recaptured in Chicago (See September 9th).

1989 Kermit Beahan died at age 70. He had been the bombardier on the Nagasaki A-bomb mission.

2012 Medal of Honor recipient Van Thomas Barfoot died at the age of 92. He had received the Medal for his actions at Carrano, Italy on May 23, 1944.

Pacific

1943 USN aircraft attacked Munda in the Solomons. The Japanese Naval Air Force attacked Wau, New Guinea. The American 11th Air Force attacked Kiska and Attu islands in the Aleutians.

1944 The USN submarine LAPON sank the TOYOKUNI MARU (5,792 tons) and the NICHIREI MARU (5,396 tons). USAAF ace Tommy Lynch (20 aerial victories) was killed in the Southwest Pacific by ground fire near Wewak, New Guinea. The last major Japanese attack on the Bougainville beach-head. It was made by 15,000 troops led by General Hyakutake.

1945 The American 13th Air Force and USN units attacked the Zamboanga Peninsula on Mindanao in the Philippines in preparation for an invasion by the US Army's 41st Division. A major Japanese suicide attack took place on Iwo Jima. 282 USAAF B29s fire-bombed Tokyo and lost fourteen aircraft, while killing 83,000 and burning 15.8 square miles of the city. The USN submarine TREPANG sank the KAIKO MARU (139 tons) and the TSUKIYURA MARU (115 tons).

China-Burma-India

1943 The German merchant ships DRACHENFELS (6,342 tons), EHRENFELS (7,752 tons) and BRAUNFELS (7,847 tons) scuttled themselves in Mormugao. The U506 sank the Norwegian freighter TABOR (4,768 tons).

1944 The Royal Air Force attacked Le-U, Burma. The U183 sank the British tanker BRITISH LOYALTY (6,993 tons).

1945 The Indian 19th Division surrounded Mandalay, the former capital of Burma.

March 10th

Western Europe

1918 Luftwaffe ace Gunther Rall (275 aerial victories) was born in Gaggenau. He survived the war.

1933 Jewish Scientist Albert Einstein vowed that he would never return to Germany. He would be instrumental in the development of the American atomic bomb.

1936 The first flight of the Royal Air Forces Fairey "Battle" light bomber took place. The Royal Navy light cruiser SOUTHAMPTON was launched. She was sunk on January 11, 1941.

1941 The Luftwaffe attacked Portsmouth, Britain. Nineteen Royal Air Force "Hampdens" attacked Cologne, Germany and killed twenty-four people. Fourteen Royal Air Force bombers attacked Le Havre, France. It was the first operation for the "Halifax" bomber, one of which was shot down in error over Surrey by a Royal Air Force fighter. Fourteen Royal Air Force bombers attacked U-boat installations at St. Nazaire, France.

1942 126 Royal Air Force bombers attacked Essen, Germany and lost four aircraft. Five people were killed in the raid.

1943 The USAAF's 4th Fighter Group flew its first P47 mission when fourteen P47s and twelve "Spitfires" flew a fighter sweep over Ostend. Thirty-five Royal Air Force bombers dropped mines and lost two "Lancasters".

1944 The government of Eire refused to expel Axis diplomats. 102 Royal Air Force bombers attacked targets in France and lost one "Lancaster". Five B17s from the USAAF's 422nd Bomb Squadron dropped 250 bundles of leaflets on Brussels, Antwerp, Ghent and Monceau-sur-Sambre.

1945 1,347 American 8th Air Force bombers dropped 2,958 tons of bombs on rail targets in Germany. 644 8th Air Force fighters provided support for the bombers and claimed two victories for the loss of two P51s. 155 Royal Air Force bombers attacked Schloven/Buer, Germany. Hitler named Field Marshal Albert Kesselring to replace Gerd von Rundstedt as German Commander in the West. Sixty-four "Spitfires" attacked German V-2 rocket targets in Holland. Seventy-two Royal Air Force "Mosquitoes" attacked targets in Germany. Thirteen USAAF 492nd Bomb Group B24s dropped thirty-one tons of bombs on marshalling yards in Munster, Germany in a night raid. The German patrol boat Uj-302 was lost during a storm in the Baltic.

1954 Royal Navy Admiral Sir Ralph Leatham died. He had held commands in the East Indies, Malta and Plymouth, Britain during the war.

1957 The Royal Air Force's No.603 Squadron "City of Glasgow", which had been the first to fly the "Spitfire" in action (See October 16, 1939) and the first to shoot down a Luftwaffe aircraft over British soil (an He111 near Humber, Scotland) was disbanded.

1988 Hugh Wolfe Frank, age 75, was found dead in his fume-filled car outside London. He had been suffering from Parkinson's Disease. He had served as Chief Interpreter at the Nuremburg War Crimes Trials after the war.

Eastern Europe

1943 The Germans took Kharkov. The U255 sank the American freighter RICHARD BLAND (7,191 tons).

1944 The Soviets took Uman.

1945 The heavy cruiser PRINZ EUGEN began supporting the retreating German Army in the Danzig area.

Mediterranean

1940 The Royal Navy submarine UNIQUE sank the Italian transport FENICIA.

1943   The Royal Navy submarine TIGRIS was sunk by a mine. Allied aircraft attacked Palermo, Sicily.

1944   The U343 was sunk south of Sardinia by the Royal Navy trawler MULL. The U450 was sunk off Anzio by the Royal Navy destroyers BLANKNEY, EXMOOR, BRECON and BLENCATHRA. The American freighter WILLIAM B. WOODS (7,176 tons-fifty-two dead) was damaged off Palermo, Sicily by the U952 and would sink five days later.

Atlantic

1941   The U552 sank the Icelandic trawler REYKJABORG (687 tons). U552 survived the war.

1942   The Italian submarine FINZI sank the Norwegian tanker CHARLES RACINE (9,957 tons). The U588 sank the American tanker GULFTRADE (6,676 tons-eighteen dead). U588 survived until July 31st.

1943   The U229 sank the British freighter NAILSEA COURT (4,969 tons). U229 survived until September 29th. The U185 sank the American tanker VIRGINIA SINCLAIR (6,151 tons-seven dead) and American freighter JAMES SPRUNT (7,177 tons) with all hands. U185 survived until August 24th. The U221 sank the American freighter ANDREA F. LUCKENBACH (6,565 tons-twenty-two dead) and the British freighter TUCURINCA (5,412 tons). U221 survived until September 27th. The German blockade-runner KARIN (7,322 tons) was scuttled when approached by the American cruiser SAVANNAH and destroyer EBERLE.

1944   The U625 was sunk west of Iceland by the Royal Navy destroyer FORESTER, the Royal Canadian Navy destroyer ST. LAURENT and the frigates SWANSEA and OWEN SOUND.

1945   The U714 sank the Norwegian minesweeper NORDHAV II (425 tons). U714 survived until March 14, 1945. The U532 sank the British freighter BARON JEDBURGH (3,656 tons). U532 survived the war.

North America

1943   The submarine APOGON was launched. She was expended as a target during the Bikini A-bomb tests in 1946.

1945   Japanese balloon-bombs were found near Bernice in Montana, Nelson House in Manitoba, Wolf Creek in Oregon, Nicola in British Columbia, and Moxee City, Status Pass and Toppenish in Washington. Another was shot down over Galiano Island, British Columbia.

South America

1944   General Edelmero Farrell assumed the Presidency of Argentina. He had been Acting President since the military had staged a coup on February 25th to prevent a declaration of war against the Axis.

Pacific

1942 The USN carriers LEXINGTON and YORKTOWN, commanded by Admiral Wilson Brown, attacked Japanese installations near Lae and Salamaua on New Guinea. The IJN armed merchant cruiser KONGO MARU was sunk in the attack on Salamaua. Also sunk were the minelayer TENYO MARU and the transport YOKOHAMA MARU. The Japanese took Finschafen, New Guinea. Allied forces in the Dutch East Indies surrendered. An IJN Kawanishi patrol plane was shot down near American-held Midway by USMC "Buffalos". It had flown from Wotje in the Marshalls. The Japanese collier KOSEI MARU was sunk by a mine in Lingayen Gulf.

1943 The Japanese Naval Air Force attacked the Russell Islands. The American 11th Air Force attacked Kiska in the Aleutians. USN PT-114 captured 18 Japanese who had drifted ashore on Kiriwina in the Trobriand Islands after the Battle of the Bismarck Sea. A 5th Air Force B24 destroyed the IJN tanker KAEJO MARO off Celebes.

1944 Japanese forces retained Hill 260 despite repeated attacks by American forces and attacked the American perimeter on Bougainville. American forces took Talasea, New Britain. The USN SC-700 caught fire and was lost off Vella Lavella.

1945 Private First Class Thomas Atkins, of the 32nd Division, won a Medal of Honor on Luzon. USAAF B29s attacked Tokyo destroying 16.8 square miles of the city and killing 83,793 and lost fourteen aircraft. The US Army's 41st Division landed on Basilan Island in the Philippines. The USN submarine KETE sank the KEIZAN MARU (2,116 tons), the SANKA MARU (2,495 tons) and the DOKAN MARU (2,270 tons).

1947 Japanese General Haruyoshi Hyakutake died.

1959 The USN destroyers HEYWOOD L. EDWARDS and RICHARD P. LEARY were sold to Japan (See 1974).

1974 The Japanese destroyers ARIAKE (the ex-USN HEYWOOD L. EDWARDS) and YUGURE (the ex-USN RICHARD P. LEARY) were sold to the Republic of Korea as spare parts ships.

China-Burma-India

1942 The IJN submarine I-162 sank the British sailing ship LAKSHIMI GOVINDA (235 tons).

1943 The U182 sank the American freighter RICHARD D. SPAIGHT (7,177 tons).

1945 French and Japanese forces fought in Hanoi, Indo-China. The British took Mongmit, Burma. The French sloops AMIRAL CHARNER and MARNE were scuttled at My Tho in Indo-China to prevent their capture by Japanese forces. The USN submarine ROCK rescued the last 15 survivors from the American freighter PETER SILVESTER which had been sunk on February 6th by U862.

March 11th

Western Europe

1913 Luftwaffe ace Wolf-Dietrich Wilke (162 aerial victories) was born in Schrimm/Proving. He died on March 23, 1944.
1926 The Royal Navy heavy cruiser CORNWALL was launched. She was sunk on April 5, 1942.
1940 The French battleship BRETAGNE and cruiser ALGERIE left Toulon, France with 2,379 bars of gold aboard. They were en route to Halifax, Nova Scotia on April 10th.
1941 Four Royal Air Force "Blenheims" attacked targets in Holland. Twenty-seven Royal Air Force "Wellingtons" attacked Kiel, Germany and killed six people.
1942 The German S-70 sank a 951-ton freighter in the English Channel.
1943 314 Royal Air Force bombers attacked Stuttgart, Germany and lost eleven aircraft. 118 buildings were destroyed and 112 people were killed in the raid. Eighteen "Spitfires" from the USAAF's 4th Fighter Group flew patrols over the Channel.
1944 124 American 8th Air Force B17s dropped 242 tons of bombs on Munster, Germany and lost one aircraft. 140 8th Air Force fighters provided support for the bombers and lost two P51s. Thirty-four 8th Air Force B24s dropped 127 tons of bombs on German V-1 rocket sites near Wizernes, France. 253 8th Air fighters provided support for the bombers and lost two P47s. The American 15th Air Force attacked Toulon, France. American 9th Air Force B26s attacked V-1 launching sites in France. Forty-seven Royal Air Force "Mosquitoes" attacked targets in Germany. Forty-three Royal Air Force bombers dropped mines off the Biscay ports of France and lost one "Stirling".
1945 1,079 Royal Air Force bombers attacked Essen, Germany and lost three aircraft. 1,226 American 8th Air Force bombers dropped 3,021 tons of bombs on U-boat and oil targets in Germany and lost one B17. The U2515 and U2530 and the dredge CARL (the ex-Soviet AMGA-947 tons) were sunk at Hamburg by the 8th Air Force. The German minesweepers M-266, M-804 and M-805 were sunk at Kiel by the 8th Air Force. 766 8th Air Force fighters provided escort for the bombers and lost four P51s. The American 9th Air Force attacked airfields from which the Luftwaffe had

been attacking the American-held Remagen bridge-head over the Rhine. Major League baseball pitcher Warren Spahn was wounded while serving with the American Army in the Remagen area. 108 Royal Air Force "Mosquitoes" attacked targets in Germany. The German minesweeper M-2 was sunk in Fedjefjord, Norway by Allied aircraft.

1946 Rudolf Hoss, German commandant of the Auschwitz concentration camp, was arrested near Flensburg.

1949 French General Henri Giraud died in Dijon.

Eastern Europe

1943 The Germans counter-attacked near Kharkov.

1944 The Soviets took Berislav east of Kherson.

Mediterranean

1942 At 2000, the Royal Navy anti/aircraft light cruiser NAIAD was sunk 50 miles north of Solum by the U565.

1944 The American VI Corps began an offensive along the Albano Road near Anzio. The American 15th Air Force attacked rail targets in Italy. Vichy's former Minister of the Interior, Pierre Pucheau, was tried in Algiers for collaboration and found guilty. He was sentenced to death.

Atlantic

1940 The U28 sank the Dutch freighter EULOTA (6,236 tons). U28 survived until March 1944.

1941 The U106 sank the British freighter MEMNON (7,506 tons). U106 survived until August 2, 1943.

1942 The U701 sank the Royal Navy trawler STELLA CAPELLA (440 tons). U701 survived until July 7th. The U94 sank the Norwegian freighter HVOSLEFF (1,630 tons). U94 survived until August 28th. The U158 sank the American freighter CARIBSEA (2,609 tons-twenty-one dead). U158 survived until June 30th. The Italian submarine TAZZOLI sank the Panamanian freighter CYGNET (3,628 tons). The USN minesweeper AMc-202 rescued seven survivors from the Brazilian steamer CAYRU which had been sunk on March 9th by U94.

1943 The U757 sank the Norwegian ammunition ship BRANT COUNTY (5,001 tons-no survivors) and the American freighter WILLIAM C. GORGAS (7,197 tons). U757 survived until January 8, 1944. The U183 sank the Honduran freighter OLANCHO (2,493 tons). U183 survived until April 23, 1945. The U621 sank the British freighter BARON KINNAIRD (3,355 tons). U621 survived until August 18, 1944. The U444 was sunk by the Royal Navy destroyer HARVESTER and the French corvette ACONIT.

The Royal Navy destroyer HARVESTER sank after ramming the U432, which was then sunk by the French corvette ACONIT. The HARVESTER had participated in the sinking of three U-boats. The British light cruiser NIGERIA rescued 30 survivors from the American freighter JAMES B. STEPHENS which had been sunk on March 8th by U160. The British trawler NORWICH CITY rescued 19 more.

1944 The UIT-22 was sunk off the Cape of Good Hope by South African Air Force PBYs while she was en route to the Pacific with a cargo for Japan. The French submarine CAIMAN was lost.

1945 The U681 was sunk by the USN's VPB-103 after being wrecked in the Scillies.

North America

1890 Vannevar Bush was born in Everett, Massachusetts. Until the transfer of the program to the US Army Corps of Engineers in 1943, he had overseen the project to develop the American atomic bomb. He died in 1974.

1916 The battleship NEVADA was commissioned. She was expended on July 31, 1948 after participating in the Bikini A-bomb tests.

1937 The submarine POMPANO was launched at Mare Island. She was lost in August 1943.

1941 The American Lend-Lease Bill was signed into law. The US Army Air Corps Ferry Command was organized (See March 20th).

1942 The American transport MOUNT MCKINLEY ran aground off Alaska and was lost.

1944 The battleship WASHINGTON arrived at Bremerton to repair collision damage (See February 1st). American 5th Air Force ace Ken Starks (11 victories) died when his P38 crashed in California.

1945 Japanese balloon-bombs were found near Hammond in Montana, Meridian in California, Cold Creek in Washington, Kunghit Island, British Columbia, and Edson in Alberta. The USN battlecruiser HAWAII was launched. She would be scrapped in 1960, never having been commissioned.

1946 The destroyer-minelayer MONTGOMERY was sold for scrap.

1989 John McLoy, age 93, died in Stamford, Conn. He had been Assistant Secretary of War during WWII.

South America

1942 The USN carrier HORNET passed through the Panama Canal en route to San Francisco and the "Doolittle Raid".

Pacific

1942 US Army General Douglas MacArthur left Corregidor Island in Manila Bay aboard the USN PT-41 en route to Australia. The USN submarine POLLACK sank the FUKUSHI MARU (1,454 tons) and the BAIKAL MARU (5,266 tons). The IJN submarine I-2 sank the British freighter CHILKA (4,360 tons).

1943 American 5th Air Force ace Lieutenant Richard Bong shot down two Japanese "Oscars" over the Bismarck Sea.

1944 The USN submarine BOWFIN sank the TSUKIKAWA MARU (4,673 tons). Japanese ground forces attacked the American perimeter on Bougainville.

1945 Eleven Japanese Naval Air Force "Francis" bombers staged a kamikaze attack on Ulithi damaging the USN carrier RANDOLPH. The USN submarine SEGUNDO sank the SHORI MARU (3,087 tons). Iwo Jima-based USAAF P51 "Mustangs" began giving ground support to USMC fighting on the northern part of the island. The US Army's 41st Division occupied Azmboang, Mindanao. 286 USAAF B29s dropped 1,800 tons of incendiaries on Nagoya, destroying two square miles of the city and lost one aircraft. The US Army's 24th Division landed on Siniara in the Philippines.

China-Burma-India

1942 The Japanese landed on the Irrawaddy Delta in Burma.
1943 The U160 sank the British freighter AELYBRYN (4,986 tons).
1944 The Indian 7th Division took Buthidaung, Burma. The Royal Air Force attacked Nanbon, Tanga, Gwengu and Nyaungintha in Burma.
1945 Royal Air Force B24s attacked Rangoon.

March 12th

Western Europe

1933 The first German concentration camp at Oranianburg near Berlin.
1935 The first flight of the Luftwaffe's He111 bomber took place.
1938 The Austrian "Anschluss" took place. It was the annexation of Austria by Germany.
1940 The Royal Navy re-occupied Scapa Flow as its main anchorage. It had been abandoned until its defenses could be improved after the sinking of the battleship ROYAL OAK by a German submarine.
1941 Six Royal Air Force "Blenheims" attacked targets in Holland. Eighty-eight Royal Air Force bombers attacked Hamburg, Germany and killed eight people. Eighty-six Royal Air Force bombers attacked Bremen, Germany

and lost two "Wellingtons" and one "Blenheim". Seventy-two Royal Air Force bombers attacked Berlin and lost three aircraft. Eleven people were killed in the raid on Berlin. Since February 10th the Royal Air Forces Bomber Command had flown 1,729 sorties on which it had dropped 1,517 tons of bombs and had lost twenty-eight aircraft. A further seventy more aircraft had crashed in England after completing their missions. The Luftwaffe attacked Merseyside in Britain. Royal Air Force ace Sergeant J. Glendenning (five aerial victories) was killed in action by Luftwaffe ace Werner Moelders.

1942 Sixty-eight Royal Air Force "Wellingtons" attacked the U-boat yards at Kiel, Germany and lost five aircraft. Twelve people were killed in the raid. Forty Royal Air Force bombers attacked Emden, Germany and lost three aircraft. The nearest bomb landed five miles from the target area.

1943 Twelve Royal Air Force "Mosquitoes" attacked Liege, Belgium and lost one aircraft. Sixty-three American 8th Air Force B17s attacked the Rouen/Sotteville marshalling yards in France. 457 Royal Air Force bombers attacked Essen, Germany and lost twenty-three aircraft. Nearly 500 buildings were destroyed and 198 people were killed in the raid.

1944 Fifty-two American 8th Air Force B24s dropped 202 tons of bombs on Siracourt, France. The British government halted all travel between Britain and Ireland because the Irish would not expel Axis diplomats. Fourteen Royal Air Force "Mosquitoes" attacked targets in Germany.

1945 1,108 Royal Air Force bombers attacked Dortmund, Germany and lost two "Lancasters". The Germans began firing V-2 rockets at the American-held Ludendorff Rail Bridge in Remagen, Germany. One of them missed the bridge by less than 300 yards. The Soviets took Kustrin, a German strongpoint near Berlin. 1,315 American 8th Air Force bombers dropped 3,003 tons of bombs on rail targets in Germany and lost one B17. The lost B17 landed in Sweden. 734 8th Air Force fighters provided support for the bombers and claimed four victories for the loss of four P51s. Thirty-three Royal Air Force "Spitfires" attacked V-2 rocket targets in Holland. Ninety-three Royal Air Force "Mosquitoes" attacked targets in Germany. Nineteen Royal Air Force bombers dropped mines in the Kattegat and lost three aircraft. The German patrol boats Uj-303 and Uj-305 were lost in a storm in the Baltic. The German depot ship PARIS was sunk off Haugesund, Norway by British motor torpedo boats.

1966 Sydney Camm, age 72, died. He had designed the Royal Air Force's Hawker "Hurricane" fighter.

1995 Odette Hallowes, age 82, died. She had been tortured by the Gestapo in 1943 while serving as a British secret agent. She was the first woman to be awarded the George Cross, Britain's second highest decoration.

Eastern Europe

1940 The Russo-Finnish Treaty was signed ending the war between the two countries. Russian losses in the war were 68,000 men, 1,600 tanks and 700 aircraft. Finland lost 24,923 men during the conflict.

1945 The German transport GERRIT FRITZEN (1,761 tons) was sunk by Soviet aircraft off Danzig.

Mediterranean

1943 At 2220, the Royal Navy destroyer LIGHTNING was sunk off Bizerta, Algeria by a German S-boat. Her 170 survivors were rescued by the Royal Navy destroyer LEGION. 100,000 Italian workers went on a general strike in Turin, Italy.

Atlantic

1941 The U37 sank the Icelandic trawler PETRUSY (91 tons). U37 was scuttled on May 3, 1945.

1942 The U126 sank the American freighters TEXAN (7,005 tons-ten dead) and OLGA (2,496 tons-one dead). The U126 survived until July 3, 1943. The Italian submarine MOROSINI sank the British freighter STANGARTH (5,966 tons). The U578 sank the Norwegian freighter INGERTO (3,089 tons). U578 survived until August 10th.

1943 The U653 sank the American freighter THOMAS HOOKER (7,176 tons). U653 survived until March 15, 1944. The U468 sank the British tanker EMPIRE LIGHT (6,537 tons). U468 survived until August 1st. The U130 was sunk west of the Azores by the USN destroyer CHAMPLAIN. The USN destroyer BELKNAP rescued 7 survivors from the American freighter JONATHAN STURGES and 3 from the Dutch freighter MADOERA both of which had been sunk on February 23rd by U707. The sole survivor of the American freighter PUERTO RICAN, which had been sunk on March 19th by U586, was rescued by the British trawler ST. ELSTAN.

1945 The U260 was sunk south of Ireland by a mine. The U683 was sunk in the English Channel by the Royal Navy sloop WILD GOOSE and frigate LOCH RUTHVEN.

North America

1938 The light cruiser PHOENIX was launched. She was transferred to Argentina in 1951.

1941 FDR requested a $7 billion appropriation for financing his "Lend-Lease" program.

1942 Admiral Harold "Betty" Stark was relieved as Chief of Naval Operations. FDR combined the duties of Chief of

Naval Operations with those of Commander-in-Chief.
1945 The USN submarine BASS was scuttled as a sonar target 8 miles off Block Island. In 1963 the hulk was sold for $1,278.
1947 Raymond Cooley died in a car wreck. He had won a Medal of Honor in the Philippines in 1945. The destroyer DUPONT was sold for scrap.

Pacific
1942 17,500 US Army troops, under the command of General Alexander Patch, landed at Noumea, New Caledonia to build a base and garrison it. The Japanese landed on northern Sumatra.
1943 The USN submarine PLUNGER sank the TAIHOSAN MARU (1,804 tons).
1944 American forces landed on Hauwri in the Admiralties, and Wotje in the Marshalls. Japanese forces attacked the American perimeter on Bougainville. The USN submarine GATO sank the OKINOYAMA MARU No.3 (871 tons). The USN submarine FLYING FISH sank the TAIJUN MARU (1,924 tons).

China-Burma-India
1942 US Army General Joseph Stilwell and the Chinese Army arrived in Burma.
1944 Nand Singh, of the 1/11th Sikhs, won a Victoria Cross at Arakan.
1945 USAAF B29s attacked oil installations in Singapore. The 20th Indian Division took Myotha, Burma.

March 13th

Western Europe
1941 The Luftwaffe attacked Clydeside and Merseyside in Britain. They also attacked Liverpool and sank one ship of 5,644 tons and damaged seven others of 45,114 tons. 139 Royal Air Force bombers attacked Hamburg, Germany and lost seven aircraft. Fifty-one people were killed in the raid.
1942 Eleven Royal Air Force "Bostons" attacked Hazebrouck, Belgium. 135 Royal Air Force bombers attacked Köln, Germany and lost one "Manchester". Sixty-two people were killed in the raid. Nineteen Royal Air Force bombers attacked Dunkirk, France and lost two "Wellingtons". Twenty Royal Air Force bombers attacked Boulogne, France and lost one "Wellington".
1943 British Lieutenant General Frederick E. Morgan was appointed as COSSAC, Chief of Staff Supreme Allied Commander. He and his staff would be responsible for the preliminary planning for the Allied invasion of northern France which would take place on June 6, 1944. Seventy-five American 8th

Air Force B17s attacked the Amiens/Longeau marshalling yards and the airfield at Abbeville/Drucat in France. Sixty-eight Royal Air Force bombers dropped mines along the Atlantic coast and lost three aircraft.

1944   271 American 8th Air Force bombers attempted to attack German V-1 rocket sites in Pas de Calais, but were unable to locate their targets because of bad weather. They lost two B17s and one B24. 213 8th Air Force P47 fighters flew support for the bombers. At this time, all P51 "Mustang" fighters in the Theater were grounded for modifications. 222 Royal Air Force bombers attacked Le Mans, France and lost one "Halifax". Thirty-five Royal Air Force bombers dropped mines off the French coast. Seven B17s from the USAAF's 422nd Bomb Squadron dropped 350 bundles of leaflets on Reims, Orleans, Paris, Amiens, Rouen, and Chartres.

1945   Technical/Sergeant Morris Crain, of the 36th Division, won a posthumous Medal of Honor at Haguenau, France. 354 Royal Air Force bombers attacked Wuppertal, Germany and killed 562 people. The American 9th Air Force attacked airfields from which the Luftwaffe had been attacking the American-held Remagen bridgehead over the Rhine. 146 Royal Air Force "Spitfires" attacked German V-2 rocket targets in Holland. American forces took Hargarten, Germany. 227 Royal Air Force bombers attacked oil targets in Germany and lost one "Lancaster". The German patrol boat Uj-1414 was sunk at Lorient, France by gunfire.

1948   The Swiss government bought thirteen P51D fighters from the USAAF in Germany.

Eastern Europe

1940   A treaty was signed by Finland and the Soviet Union.

1942   The Soviet submarine ShCh-210 was sunk by the Luftwaffe. The Soviet freighter CHEKOV was sunk by a mine.

1943   Hitler arrived at Smolensk to inspect Army Group "Center". In an attempt to assassinate Hitler Henning von Treschow planted a bomb on Hitler's aircraft, but the bombs fuse froze. The Soviets evacuated Kharkov.

1944   The Soviets took Kjerson and crossed the Dnieper River.

1945   The Soviets attacked Konigsberg in East Prussia.

Mediterranean

1946   The American freighter EXANTHIA was damaged by a mine off Leghorn, Italy. Three of her crew died.

Atlantic

1940   The German freighter LA CORUNA was scuttled to prevent her capture by the Royal Navy armed merchant cruiser MALOJA.

1942   The U158 sank the American tanker JOHN GILL (11,641 tons-23 died). U158 survived until June 30, 1942. The U404 sank the Chilean freighter TOLTEN (1,858 tons). U404 survived until July 28, 1943. The U332 sank the American schooner ALBERT PAUL (735 tons-with all hands) and the Yugoslavian freighter TREPCA (5,042 tons). U332 survived until May 2, 1943. The Italian submarine TAZZOLI sank the British freighter DAYTONIAN (6,434 tons).

1943   The U107 sank the British freighters CLAN ALPINE (5,442 tons), MARCELLA (4,592 tons), OPORTO (2,352) and the Dutch freighter SEMBILANGEN (4,990 tons). U107 survived until August 18, 1944. The U68 sank the Dutch freighter CERES (2,680 tons) and the American tanker CITIES SERVICES MISSOURI (7,506 tons-two dead). U68 survived until April 10, 1944. The U172 sank the American freighter KEYSTONE (5,565 tons-two dead). U172 survived until December 13, 1943.

1944   The U852 sank the Greek freighter PELEUS (4,695 tons). U852 survived until May 3, 1944. The U575 was sunk north of the Azores by the USN escort carrier BOGUE and destroyer escort HAVERFIELD, destroyer HOBSON and the Royal Canadian Navy frigate PRINCE RUPERT.

1945   The American transport MCANDREWS was lost in a collision with the French carrier BEARN off the Azores, sixty-eight died.

North America

1887   USMC General Alexander Archer Vandegrift was born in Charlotteville, Virginia. He would command the USMC forces on Guadalcanal in 1942, serve as Marine Corps Commandant and become the Corps first four-star general. He died on May 8, 1973 after eighteen months as a patient at Bethesda Naval Hospital.

1914   Edward Henry "Butch" O'Hare, future USN ace and Medal of Honor winner, was born in St. Louis, Missouri.

1938   The light cruiser PHOENIX (awarded nine battle stars during the war) was launched. She was sunk by an Royal Navy submarine during the Falklands War in 1982, while serving as the Argentine GENERAL BELGRANO.

1944   The Main Headquarters Group of the 3rd Army left Camp Shank, New York aboard the liner ILE DE FRANCE en route to Europe. The destroyers CHARLES S. SPERRY and PORTER were launched.

1945   Japanese balloon-bombs were found near Baril Lake in Alberta, Montana Divide, Legg, Harlowton and Broadus in Montana, Farmington and Everett in Washington, Echo and Malheur Lake in Oregon, Delta in Colorado, American Falls in Idaho and Port Hardy in British Columbia.

Pacific

1942   The USN PT-32 was scuttled off Tagauayan Island in the Philippines. The USN submarine GAR sank the CHICHIBU MARU (1,462 tons). A seaplane from the Japanese submarine I-25 flew over Auckland, New Zealand.

1943   The USN submarine GRAYBACK sank the NOSHIRO MARU (7,184 tons). The USN submarine SUNFISH sank the KOSEI MARU (3,262 tons). The Dutch submarine 0-21 sank the KASUGA MARU No.3. 5th Air Force B17s attacked Japanese shipping off Wewak, New Guinea and sank the freighter MOMOYAMA MARU. The first USN F6F "Hellcat" fighters were assigned to the carrier ESSEX. The American 11th Air Force attacked Kiska in the Aleutians.

1944   The IJN light cruiser TATSUTA and the KOKUYO MARU (4,667 tons) were sunk southwest of Yokosuka by the USN submarine SANDLANCE. The USN submarine TAUTOG sank the RYUA MARU (1,915 tons) and the SHOJIN MARU (1,942 tons). The American freighter RUSSELL CHITTENDEN was wrecked off Vassel Island near New Guinea. American forces counter-attacked on Bougainville.

1945   275 USAAF B29s destroyed 8.1 square miles of Osaka. The IJN escort No.66 was sunk off Amoy, Formosa by the USAAF.

China-Burma-India

1942   The IJN submarine I-164 sank the Norwegian freighter MABELLA (1,513 tons). USAAF personnel arriving at Karachi, were the first American detachment to arrive in the CBI Theater.

1944   Second Lieutenant G. Cairns, of the Somerset Light Infantry, won a posthumous Victoria Cross, while on a Chindit operation in Burma. The IJN submarine I-26 sank the American tanker H.D. COLLIER (8,298 tons-forty-five died).

March 14th

Western Europe

1879   Scientist Albert Einstein was born in Ulm, Germany.

1939   Slovakia declared itself independent of Prague and a protectorate of Germany.

1941   The Luftwaffe attacked Clydeside, Britain. 101 Royal Air Force bombers attacked Gelsenkirchen, Germany and lost one "Wellington. Nine people were killed in the raid. Twenty-four Royal Air Force "Blenheims" attacked Dusseldorf, Germany. Twelve Royal Air Force bombers attacked Rotterdam, Holland.

1942   Pierre Laval was renamed premier of France.
1942   Thirteen Royal Air Force bombers dropped mines off Denmark.
1943   Thirty-seven "Spitfires" from the USAAF's 4th Fighter Group flew patrols over the Channel.
1944   British Prime Minister Winston Churchill announced a policy of isolating Eire from the rest of the world. At 2145, the German minesweeper M-10 was sunk off Dunkirk by the Royal Navy MTB-353. Thirty Royal Air Force "Mosquitoes" attacked Dusseldorf, Germany.
1945   The German torpedo boats T-3 and T-5 were sunk in the Baltic by mines. The U745 was lost in the Gulf of Finland. American forces took Heddert, Weiskirchen and Niederfelle in Germany. Second Lieutenant Harry Michael, of the 80th Division, won a posthumous Medal of Honor near Niederzerf. 372 Luftwaffe aircraft attacked the Rhine bridges and lost 80 aircraft. 169 Royal Air Force bombers attacked oil targets in Germany and lost one aircraft. 1,439 American 8th Air Force bombers dropped 3,498 tons of bombs on industrial, oil and rail targets in Germany and lost three B17s. 766 8th Air Force fighters provided support for the bombers and claimed seventeen victories for the loss of one P47 and one P51. Eighty-seven "Spitfires" attacked German V-2 rocket targets in Holland. Sweden purchased fifty USAAF P51s. 255 Royal Air Force bombers attacked Lutzkendorf, Germany and lost eighteen "Lancasters". 230 Royal Air Force bombers attacked Zweibrucken, Germany. 161 Royal Air Force bombers attacked Homberg, Germany and lost two "Halifaxes". Luftwaffe night-fighter ace Martin Becker shot down nine Royal Air Force bombers over Germany. Eighty-seven Royal Air Force "Mosquitoes" attacked targets in Germany. Seven USAAF 492nd Bomb Group B24s dropped 13.5 tons of bombs on the marshalling yards at Wiesbaden, Germany in a night raid.
1946   German Field Marshal Werner von Blomberg died while waiting to testify at the Nuremburg Trials.

Eastern Europe
1940   The Finns began evacuating areas ceded to Russia after the Russo-Finnish War.
1943   The last Soviet resistance ended in Kharkov.
1944   The German Army lost 10,000 killed and 4,000 taken prisoner after they were surrounded near Nikolayev.
1945   The German torpedo boats T-3 and T-5 were sunk off Danzig by the Soviet submarine L-21.

Mediterranean
1942   Axis aircraft attacked Malta. Royal Air Force bombers attacked Benghazi. The U133 was sunk in the Aegean Sea by a mine. The Italian submarine

MOCENIGO sank the French sailing ship STE.MARCELLE (1,518 tons). The Royal Navy submarine ULTIMATUM sank the Italian submarine MILLO.
1943 The Royal Navy submarine THUNDERBOLT was sunk by an Italian corvette. The Royal Navy submarine TURBULENT was sunk by a mine.

Atlantic
1941 The Italian submarine EMO sank the British freighter WESTERN CHIEF (5,759 tons).
1942 The U67 sank the Panamanian tanker PENELOPE (8,436 tons). U67 survived until July 16, 1943. The U161 sank the Canadian freighter SARNIADOC (1,940 tons). U161 survived until September 27, 1943. The U404 sank the American freighter LEMUEL BURROWS (7,610 tons-20 dead). U404 survived until July 28, 1943. The U124 sank the British tanker BRITISH RESOURCE (7,209 tons). U124 survived until April 2, 1943.
1943 The Italian submarine DA VINCI sank the British transport EMPRESS OF CANADA (21,517 tons).
1945 The U714 sank the Swedish freighter MAGNE (1,226 tons). U714 was then sunk in the Firth of Forth by the Royal Navy frigate NATAL.

North America
1942 The American government established a nation-wide 40 mph speed limit to help conserve tires. The destroyer O'BANNON was launched. She was stricken in 1970. The submarine WHALE was launched. She was discarded in 1960.
1944 Presidential candidates Willkie and Roosevelt won their party primaries in New Hampshire.
1945 Japanese balloon-bombs were found near Yamhill in Oregon, Hay Lake in Alberta, and Grimes in California.
2013 USAAF ace Robert Rankin died in Jensen Beach, Florida at the age of 94. He had been credited with 10 aerial victories while flying P47s with the 56th Fighter Group based in Britain.

Pacific
1934 The IJN heavy cruiser MOGAMI was launched. She was sunk on October 25, 1944.
1940 Australian Prime Minister Menzies formed a new coalition government to direct his country's war effort.
1942 US Army General Douglas MacArthur arrived at Mindanao aboard a PT-boat, en route to Australia. The first American troops arrived in Australia.

1944   B24s of the 30th Bomb Group, American 7th Air Force flying from Kwajalein attacked the IJN base at Truk in a night raid. They damaged several buildings and destroyed seven aircraft on the ground.
1945   US Army Major General Edwin D. Patrick, commander of the 6th Division, was wounded by a Japanese machine-gunner and died three days later in a Manila hospital. USMC Private George Phillips (posthumous) and Private Franklin Sigler, of the 5th Division, won Medals of Honor on Iwo Jima. The USN submarine BREAM sank the KEIHEIN MARU (76 tons). The American tanker ESSO WASHINGTON was lost by grounding off Eniwetok.

China-Burma-India
1940   The Japanese Air Force shot down twenty-seven Chinese aircraft over Chengtu.
1942   Japanese forces stopped to reorganize in front of the British Prome-Toungou defensive postions in Burma.

March 15th

Western Europe
1930   German President Paul von Hindenburg accepted the American "Young Plan" for WWI reparations to be paid by Germany.
1933   German Chancellor Adolf Hitler announced the creation of the "Third Reich".
1939   Czech President Hacha signed an agreement with Hitler at Berchtesgaden. German troops marched into Czechoslovakia the same day.
1940   The German armed merchant cruiser THOR was commissioned.
1941   The Luftwaffe attacked London. Thirty-seven Royal Air Force bombers attacked Lorient, France. Twenty-one Royal Air Force bombers attacked Dusseldorf, Germany.
1942   The German S-53 was sunk by a mine in the English Channel. The Royal Navy destroyer VORTIGEN was sunk off Cromer by the German S-104. The German S-111 sank after an engagement with British torpedo boats in the English Channel. Three Royal Air Force "Blenheims" attacked Dutch airfields.
1943   Eleven Royal Air Force "Venturas" attacked La Pleine airfield in France and lost one aircraft. Twenty-four "Spitfires" from the USAAF's 4th Fighter Group flew patrols over the Channel.
1944   Erwin Rommel and Hans Speidel, his Chief of Staff, met to discuss the "Schwarz Kapelle" ("Black Orchestra"- a group of German conspirators opposed to Adolf Hitler). 330 American 8th Air Force B17s and B24s dropped

745 tons of bombs on Brunswick, Germany and lost one B17 and two B24s. 588 8th Air Force fighters provided support for the bombers and claimed thirty-eight victories for the loss of four P38s and one P47. American 9th Air Force B26s attacked airfields and railways in France and the Low Countries. 863 Royal Air Force bombers attacked Stuttgart, Germany and lost thirty-seven aircraft. Eighty-eight people were killed in the raid. 140 Royal Air Force bombers attacked Amiens, France and lost three aircraft. Twenty-two Royal Air Force bombers attacked Woippy, France. Seven B17s from the USAAF's 422nd Bomb Squadron dropped 350 bundles of leaflets on Rennes, Lille, Reims, Le Mans, Paris and Chartres in France.

1945 American forces took Lorscheid and Notscheid in Germany. Private Silvestre Herrara, of the 36th Division, won a Medal of Honor near Mertzwiller, France. 1,310 American 8th Air Force bombers dropped 3,348 tons of bombs on Zossen, Oranianburg and Wittenberg in Germany and lost one B24 and eight B17s. 764 8th Air Force fighters provided support for the bombers and claimed one victory for the loss of four P51s. 188 Royal Air Force bombers attacked oil targets in Germany and lost one "Halifax". The American 15th Air Force attacked various oil targets in Austria. 367 Royal Air Force bombers attacked Hagen, Germany and lost ten aircraft. 505 people were killed in the raid. 265 Royal Air Force bombers attacked Misburg, Germany and lost four "Lancasters". A force of 107 Royal Air Force "Mosquitoes" attacked targets in Germany. Fourteen USAAF 492nd Bomb Group B24s dropped 35.7 tons of bombs on the marshalling yards at Munster, Germany in a night raid.

1946 Sweden purchased ninety P51 "Mustangs" from the USAAF.

1948 The Royal Navy carrier FURIOUS was scrapped.

1949 The Royal Navy battleship NELSON was scrapped.

1995 Lord Simon Lovat, age 83, died in his sleep. He had been awarded the British Distinguished Service Order, the Military Cross, and the French Croix de Guerre for his actions while leading troops on D-Day in Normandy.

Eastern Europe

1938 Stalin ordered the execution of eighteen top Soviet officials.

1942 Hitler announced that the Soviet army would be destroyed in the summer of 1942.

1943 The Soviets evacuated Kharkov.

1944 The Soviets took Vapnyarka and Kalinkova.

1945 The German battleship SCHLEISEN began supporting the retreating Wehrmacht in the Danzig area. She continued to do so until the 21st when she had to withdraw due to a lack of ammunition.

Mediterranean

1942 The British cruisers DIDO and EURYALUS and six destroyers bombarded the island of Rhodes. During the next four nights, German torpedo boats laid 165 mines off Malta.

1943 The U380 sank the British freighter OCEAN SEAMAN (7,178 tons).

1944 New Zealand ground troops attacked Cassino, Italy. The American 15th Air Force attacked Cassino.

Atlantic

1941 The German battlecruisers GNEISENAU and SCHARNHORST sank sixteen merchant ships in the North Atlantic.

1942 The U503 was sunk south of Newfoundland by the USN's VP-82. The USN light cruiser MARBLEHEAD arrived at Durban, South Africa en route to America from the southwest Pacific. The U158 sank the American tanker ARIO (6,952 tons-eight dead). U158 survived until June 30th. The US Coast Guard light house tender ACACIA was sunk off Haiti by the U161. U161 survived until September 27, 1943. The Italian submarine TAZZOLI sank the British tanker ATHELQUEEN (8,780 tons).

1943 The U524 sank the French freighter WYOMING (8,062 tons). U524 survived until the 22nd. The U653 was sunk by the Royal Navy escort carrier VINDEX and the sloops WILD GOOSE and STARLING.

North America

1874 Secretary of the Interior Harold Ickes was born in Pennsylvania.

1930 The submarine NAUTILUS was launched at Mare Island in California. She was scrapped in 1946.

1934 The destroyer FARRAGUT was launched. She was scrapped in 1947.

1938 The submarine STURGEON was launched at Mare Island. She was scrapped in 1948.

1942 The 761st Tank Battalion (Light) was activated at Camp Claiborne, Louisiana. It was to be the first Black combat unit in the US Army.

1944 Actor Art Carney was drafted into the US Army. He would be wounded at "Omaha" beach in Normandy and lose one inch off his right leg. The escort carrier SHAMROCK BAY was commissioned. She was scrapped in 1959.

1943 The Navy established that American fleets in the Pacific would have odd numbers and those in the Atlantic would have even.

1945 Japanese balloon-bombs were found near Chase Baker Creek in British Columbia and Coquille in Oregon.

1947 The minelayer OGLALA was scrapped. She had been sunk at Pearl Harbor and had also helped lay the huge minefield in the North Sea during WW I.

1956   The ex-battleship OREGON (IX-22) was sold for scrap having served at Guam as a floating munitions depot since July 1944.
1958   President Eisenhower signed a bill authorizing the USN to build a memorial over the wreck of the battleship ARIZONA at Pearl Harbor.
1982   The USN submarine POMPANITO was opened as a public memorial at Pier 45 in San Francisco Bay.

Pacific
1942   The Japanese began shelling the fortified islands in Manila Bay. The USAAF's 67th Pursuit Squadron (P400 "Airacobra") was disembarked at Noumea, New Caledonia. On August 22nd, they would become the first USAAF unit to operate from Henderson Field on Guadalcanal. Up to this time, only USMC and USN units had been stationed at Henderson. The US 27th Division arrived in Hawaii.
1943   The USN submarine TRITON was sunk north of New Guinea by IJN destroyers. The USN 7th Fleet (commanded by Carpender) was formed to control the seas around New Guinea. The USN submarine TRIGGER sank the MOMOHA MARU (3,103 tons). Seven Japanese Naval Air Force aircraft and Royal Australian Air Force "Spitfires" were shot down in a battle over Darwin, Australia. The American 11th Air Force attacked Kiska and lost one P38.
1944   The Japanese counter-attacked on Bougainville. The US Army's 8th Cavalry Regiment landed on Manus Island in the Admiralties and took the airfield at Lorengau. Twenty-two B24s made the American 7th Air Force's first raid on Truk. USAAF Major General Hubert Harmon became Commander-Air-Solomons.
1945   USN forces (commanded by McCrea) bombarded Matsuwa in the Kuriles.

March 16th

Western Europe
1911   Josef Mengele, Auschwitz' "Angel of Death", was born in Gunzburg, Bavaria.
1926   The Royal Navy heavy cruisers CUMBERLAND and KENT were launched. CUMBERLAND was scrapped in 1959 and KENT was scrapped in 1948.
1933   Belgium began building fortifications along the Meuse River.
1935   Hitler denounced the disarmament clauses of the Versailles Treaty and decreed universal military for all Germans.
1940   A Luftwaffe raid on Scapa Flow caused the first British civilian casualties of the war.

1941 The Luftwaffe attacked Bristol, Britain.
1943 Sixteen Royal Air Force "Mosquitoes" attacked Paderborn, Germany and lost one aircraft. Twelve Royal Air Force "Wellingtons" dropped mines off Denmark. Fourteen "Spitfires" from the USAAF's 4th Fighter Group flew patrols over the Channel.
1944 675 American 8th Air Force bombers dropped 1,579 tons of bombs on Friedrichshaven, Ulm and Augsburg in Germany and lost eighteen B17s and five B24s. Four B17s and three B24s landed in Switzerland. 868 8th Air Force fighters provided support for the bombers and claimed seventy-seven victories for the loss of one P38, three P47s and six P51s. French Maquis forces assassinated the Police Adjutant in Axat, France who was a known collaborator. 130 Royal Air Force bombers attacked Amiens, France. Twenty-one Royal Air Force "Lancasters" attacked Clermont-Ferrand, France.
1945 The US Army's 78th Division cut the autobahn that ran between Köln and Frankfurt in Germany. The American 7th Army took Bitche, France. German swimmers tried to blow up the US-held bridge at Remagen on the Rhine. The American 15th Air Force attacked oil targets in Austria. 293 Royal Air Force bombers attacked Nuremburg, Germany and lost twenty-four "Lancasters". 529 people died in the raid. 236 Royal Air Force bombers attacked Wurzburg, Germany and lost five "Lancasters". Ninety-two Royal Air Force "Mosquitoes" attacked targets in Germany. The German patrol boat Uj-1105 was sunk in the Skagerrak by Allied aircraft.
1994 The trial of Paul Touvier, age 78, began in Versailles, France. He had been the Vichy Intelligence Chief in the Lyons area. He was charged with killing seven Jews in June 1944 (See April 20, 1994).

Eastern Europe
1943 The Germans took Kharkov. The Soviets evacuated Byelgorod.
1947 Luftwaffe General Alexander Lohr was hung in Yugoslavia for war crimes.

Mediterranean
1941 The Italians stopped their offensive in Albania.
1943 The U77 sank the British freighter HADLEIGH (5,222 tons) and damaged the British freighter MERCHANT PRINCE (5,229 tons).
1944 New Zealand attacks near Cassino were repulsed by German paratroops. The U392 was sunk in the Straits of Gibraltar by the Royal Navy destroyer VANOC and the frigate AFFLECK. The American 15th Air Force attacked troop concentrations near San Georgio, Italy. The German trawler UJ-2209 was sunk at Leghorn in an air-raid.
1945 An Allied air attack on Monfalcone destroyed the German minesweeper R-14 and the incomplete submarines UIT-6, UIT-7, UIT-8 and UIT-9.

Atlantic

1941 The German battlecruiser GNEISENAU sank the freighter CHILEAN REEFER. The U106 sank the Dutch freighter ALMKERK (6,810 tons). U106 survived until August 2, 1943. The U99 sank the Norwegian tankers FERM (6,593 tons) and BEDUIN (8,136 tons), the British tanker VENETIA (5,728 tons), and the Canadian freighter J.B. WHITE (7,375 tons). U99 survived until the 17th.

1942 The Italian submarine MOROSINO sank the Dutch tanker OSCILLA (6,341 tons). The U504 sank the British freighter MANAQUI (2,802 tons). U504 survived until July 30, 1943. The U332 sank the American tanker AUSTRALIA (11,628 tons-four dead). U332 survived until May 2, 1943. The U68 sank the British freighter BARON NEWLANDS (3,386 tons). U68 survived until April 10, 1944.

1943 The American freighter BENJAMIN HARRISON (7,191 tons-three dead) was torpedoed off the Azores by the U172 and later scuttled. U172 survived until December 13th. The U603 sank the Norwegian freighter ELIN K. (5,214 tons). U603 survived until March 1, 1944.

1944 The U801 was sunk off the Cape Verde Islands by the USN escort carrier BLOCK ISLAND, destroyer CORRY and destroyer escort BRONSTEIN.

1945 The U772 sank the British freighter INGER TOFT (2,190 tons).

North America

1914 The battleship ARIZONA's keel was laid at New York Navy Yard. She would be sunk during the December 7, 1941 attack on Pearl Harbor.

1915 The battleship PENNSYLVANIA was launched. She was expended on February 10, 1948 after participating in the Bikini A-bomb tests.

1942 The destroyer CHARLES AUSBURNE was launched. She was transferred to Germany in 1960.

1945 A Japanese balloon-bomb was found near Coram in Montana.

1946 The submarine FLASHER was placed in "mothballs". She had sunk 100,231 tons of Japanese shipping during the war and had been awarded a Presidential Unit Citation and six battle stars. She was scrapped in 1959.

1982 Claus von Bulow was convicted of trying to kill his heiress wife in order to collect $14 million. He had served as a page in Hermann Goering's wedding.

Pacific

1926 The IJN light cruiser ABUKUMA was launched. She was sunk on October 26, 1944.

1942 The IJN submarine I-162 sank the Dutch freighter MERKUS (865 tons). The USN submarine PERMIT delivered ammunition to Corregidor and evacuated communications specialists.

1943 Royal Australian Air Force Flight/Lieutenant W.E. Newton, of No.22 Squadron, won a posthumous Victoria Cross over New Guinea. The USN destroyers STRONG, CHEVALIER TAYLOR and O'BANNON (McIrnerney) bombarded the Villa-Stanmore Plantation on Kolombangara Island. The American 11th Air Force attacked Kiska and lost one B25 "Mitchell" bomber.

1944 The USN submarine TAUTOG sank the IJN destroyer SHIRAKUMO and the transport NICHIREN MARU (5,460 tons) off Hokkaido, Japan. The USN submarine FLYING FISH sank the ANZAN MARU (5,493 tons). The USN submarine SILVERSIDES sank the KOFUKU MARU (1,919 tons).

1945 The US Army's 41st Division landed on Basilian in the Philippines. 307 USAAF B29s destroyed three square miles of Kobe and lost three aircraft. The USN carriers INTREPID (two dead) and YORKTOWN (five dead) were bombed south of Shikoku, Japan. The USN submarine SPOT sank the IKOMASAN MARU (3,173 tons).

China-Burma-India

1944 The IJN submarine Ro-111 sank the Indian freighter EL MADINA (3,962 tons).

March 17th

Western Europe

1917 Luftwaffe ace Hans Philipp (206 aerial victories) was born in Meissen. He died on October 10, 1943.

1927 The Royal Navy heavy cruiser AUSTRALIA was launched. She was scrapped in 1955.

1938 The Royal Navy heavy cruiser BELFAST was launched. She was preserved as a memorial in 1971.

1941 Fifty-seven Royal Air Force bombers attacked Bremen and Wilhelmshaven in Germany and lost one "Wellington". Hitler decided that when he invaded Russia Army Group "South" would move towards Kiev, the 11th Army would guard the Rumanian oil fields and the 6th Army and the 1st Panzer Group would surround Soviet forces near the Black Sea.

1942 FDR recalled Admiral Leahy from his post as Ambassador to Vichy.

1943 Seventy-eight American 8th Air Force B17s attempted to attack the Rouen/Sotteville marshalling yards in France but had to abort due to bad weather.

1944 The U1013 was lost in a collision with U236 in the Baltic. 135 American 8th Air Force P47 "Thunderbolts" attacked French airfields and lost two aircraft. The American 15th Air Force attacked Vienna, Austria. American

9th Air Force B26s attacked railyards. Thirty Royal Air Force bombers attacked targets in Germany.

1945   The US Army's 87th Division entered Koblenz, Germany. The American-held Ludendorff Bridge at Remagen collapsed. A second bridge had been opened the same day by US Army engineers. A Luftwaffe intruder shot down an Royal Air Force "Lancaster" over Britain. 1,281 American 8th Air Force bombers dropped 3,464 tons of bombs on rail, oil and industrial targets in Germany and lost five B17s. 756 8th Air Force fighters provided support for the bombers and lost two P51s. 167 Royal Air Force bombers attacked oil targets in Germany. 148 "Spitfires" attacked rail targets near The Hague and lost one aircraft. American forces took Birkenfeld and Boppard in Germany. Eighty-one Royal Air Force "Mosquitoes" attacked targets in Germany.

1973   Franz Rademacher, the acknowledged "Jewish Expert" of the German Foreign Office, died in Bonn.

1991   A Luftwaffe Me109 captured in Libya in November 1942 flew again at Benson, Britain.

Eastern Europe

1899   Soviet official Lavrentiy Beria was born. He headed the NKVD (Soviet secret police) during the war. He was arrested after the death of Stalin in 1953 and was executed on December 23rd of that year.

1944   The Soviets took Dubno in the Ukraine. The Finns rejected Russia's terms for an armistice.

1945   The Soviet submarine K-53 sank the German freighter MARGARETHE CORDS (1,912 tons) in the Baltic.

Mediterranean

1934   Treaties between Italy, Hungary and Austria were signed.

1942   The U83 damaged the British freighter CRISTA (2,590 tons). The Italian submarine GUGIELMOTTI was sunk by the Royal Navy submarine UNBEATEN.

1944   New Zealand troops reached the rail station in Cassino, Italy. The U371 sank the American freighter MAIDEN CREEK II (5,031 tons-eleven dead) and the Dutch freighter DEMPO (17,024 tons).

Atlantic

1940   The U38 sank the Danish freighter ARGENTINA (5,375 tons). U38 survived the war.

1941   The U99 sank the Swedish freighter KORSHAMN (6,673 tons). The U99 and U100 were sunk south of Iceland by the Royal Navy destroyers WALKER and VANOC. The U106 sank the British freighter ANDALUSIAN (3,082 tons) and the Dutch freighter TAPANOELI (7,031 tons). U106 survived until August 2, 1943.

1942   The U124 sank the Honduran freighter CEIBA (1,698 tons-44 died). U124 survived until April 2, 1943. The U404 sank the British tanker SAN DEMETRIO (8,073 tons). U404 survived until July 28, 1943. The U68 sank the British freighters ILE DE BATZ (5,755 tons), ALLENDE (5,081 tons) and SCOTTISH PRINCE (4,917 tons). U68 survived until April 10, 1944. The U373 sank the Greek freighter MOUNT LYCABETTUS (4,292 tons). U373 survived until June 8, 1944. The U71 sank the Norwegian tanker RANJA (6,355 tons). U71 survived the war.

1943   The U756 sank the Dutch freighter ZAANLAND (6,813 tons). The U338 sank the British freighters KINGSBURY (4,898 tons), KING GRUFFYDD (5,072 tons) and ALDERAMIN (7,886 tons) and the Panamanian freighter GRANVILLE (4,071 tons). U338 survived until September 20th. The U91 sank the American freighters HARRY LUCKENBACH (6,366 tons-lost with all hands), JAMES OGELTHORPE (7,176 tons-44 dead) and WILLIAM EUSTIS (7,196 tons), IRENE DU PONT (6,125 tons-13 dead) and the British freighter NARIVA (8,714 tons). U91 survived until February 25, 1944. The U600 sank the British whaler SOUTHERN PRINCESS (12,156 tons). U600 survived until November 25th. The U665 sank the British freighter FORT CEDAR LAKE (7,134 tons). U665 survived until the 22nd. The U384 sank the British freighter CORACERO (7,252 tons). U384 survived until the 20th. The U631 sank the Dutch freighter TERKOELEI (5,158 tons). U631 survived until October 17th. The U305 sank the British freighter ZOUAVE (4,256 tons). U305 survived until January 17, 1944.

1945   The Royal Canadian Navy minesweeper GUYSBOROUGH was sunk by the U878, fifty-four of her crew died. U878 survived until April 10th.

North America

1942   The destroyers DOYLE and FRAZIER were launched. DOYLE was stricken in 1970 and FRAZIER was stricken in 1971.

1945   A Japanese balloon-bomb was found near Babine in British Columbia. The American freighter ALVARADO was lost by grounding off Coos Bay, Oregon.

Pacific

1942   US Army General Douglas MacArthur arrived in Australia, aboard a B17, from the Philippines. He landed at Batchelor Field, near Darwin. The USN submarine GRAYBACK sank the ISHIKARI MARU (3,291

	tons) off Chichi Jima. The USN carrier WASP collided with the USN destroyer STACK. The USAAF began operating out of Darwin, Australia. The America assumed strategic responsibility for the Pacific. The USN submarine PERMIT was damaged by depth charges off Tayabas Bay in the Philippines. Aboard were evacuees from Corregidor.
1943	The USN PTs 67 and 119 were destroyed by fire at Tufi, New Guinea.
1944	America forces took Lorengau airfield on Manus. The USN PT-283 was sunk off Bougainville by artillery fire.
1945	Admiral Chester Nimitz announced that Iwo Jima had been secured. Fighting would continue for two more weeks. Japanese resistance on Iwo Jima was confined to an area of 300 yards by 625 yards. The USN submarine SPOT sank the NANKING MARU (3,005 tons). The USN submarine SEALION sank the Siamese tanker SAMUI (1,458 tons).
1984	Sergeant Major Jacob Vouza was buried on Guadalcanal. He had been knighted in 1979 by Queen Elizabeth for his actions there in 1942.

China-Burma-India

1945	British forces took Ava Fort south of Mandalay. The Chinese 6th Army took Hsiphaw on the Burma Road. IJN Admiral Seigo Yamagata committed suicide after his damaged "Emily" seaplane was attacked by Chinese guerillas near Lin-Hai, China. It had been damaged by a USN VB-104 PB4Y1 and forced to land.

March 18th

Western Europe

1913	Luftwaffe ace Werner Moelders (115 aerial victories) was born in Gelsenkirchen. He died in an accident after he had been appointed as Inspector of Fighters.
1929	The Royal Navy heavy cruiser DEVONSHIRE was launched. She was scrapped in 1954.
1935	Britain protested German reinstitution of military conscription.
1937	Spanish Loyalist forces defeated a rebel force at Brihuega.
1939	Spain and Portugal signed a non-aggression pact.
1940	Hitler and Mussolini met at Brenner Pass.
1941	German S-boats sank the French freighter DAPHNE (1,970 tons) off the Humber. Ninety-nine Royal Air Force bombers attacked Kiel, Germany and killed five people. Forty-four Royal Air Force "Blenheims" attacked Wilhelmshaven, Germany. Nineteen Royal Air Force bombers attacked Rotterdam, Holland.
1942	Lord Mountbatten was named to command British Combined Operations.

1943   Ninety-seven American 8th Air Force B17s and B24s dropped 268 tons of bombs on Vegesack, Germany and lost one B17 and one B24. This was the first time that the 93rd Bomb Group (B24) penetrated German airspace. 1st Lieutenant Jack Mathis, of the 303rd Bomb Group (B17), won a posthumous Medal of Honor on the mission. It was the first use of the automatic flight control linked to the bombsight. Twelve Royal Air Force "Venturas" attacked targets in Holland.

1944   678 American 8th Air Force bombers dropped 1,546 tons of bombs on Munich, Friedrichshaven, Landsberg and Lechpeld in Germany and lost fifteen B17s and twenty-eight B24s. Twelve of the lost B24s landed in Switzerland and one landed near Eger, Germany and was captured. 925 8th Air Force fighters provided support for the bombers and claimed thirty-six victories for the loss of five P38s, two P47s and six P51s. USAAF 20th Fighter Group (P38) ace Lindol Graham (five victories) was killed in action near Ulm, Germany. Colonel Joseph A. Miller, commander of the USAAF's 453rd Bomb Group (B24), was shot down and captured near Friedrichshaven. Lieutenant Colonel Mark E. Hubbard, commander of the USAAF's 20th Fighter Group (P38), was shot down over France and captured. 846 Royal Air Force bombers attacked Frankfurt, Germany and lost twenty-two aircraft. 421 people were killed in the raid. Seventeen Royal Air Force "Mosquitoes" attacked airfields in France, Belgium, and Holland. Ninety-eight Royal Air Force bombers dropped mines off Heligoland. Six B17s from the USAAF's 422nd Bomb Squadron dropped 300 bundles of leaflets on Cambrai, Lille, Paris, Amiens, Rouen, and Caen in France.

1945   1,184 American 8th Air Force bombers dropped 3,373 tons of bombs on rail and tank targets in Berlin and lost twelve B17s and one B24. 426 8th Air Force fighters provided escort for the bombers and claimed fourteen victories and lost six P51s. 100 Royal Air Force bombers attacked oil targets in Germany. 111 Royal Air Force "Spitfires" attacked rail targets around The Hague. Thirty-three Royal Air Force "Spitfires" attacked V-2 launching sights in Holland. The American 3rd Army took Bad Kreuznach and Bingen in Germany. Private William McGee, of the 76th Division, won a posthumous Medal of Honor near Mulheim, Germany. Private First-Class Frederick Murphy, of the 65th Division, won a Medal of Honor at Saarlautern, Germany. Captain Jack Treadwell and Corporal Edward Wilkin, of the 45th Division, won Medals of Honor near Niederwurzbach. 324 Royal Air Force bombers attacked Witten, Germany and lost eight aircraft. 285 Royal Air Force bombers attacked Hanau, Germany and lost one "Lancaster". More than 2,000 people were killed in the raid. Seventy-two Royal Air Force "Mosquitoes" attacked targets in Germany.

German torpedo boats attacked a British convoy off Lowestoft and sank the freighters CRICHTOUN (1,097 tons) and ROGATE (2,871 tons).
1958   The Royal Navy battleship DUKE OF YORK was scrapped at Faslane, Scotland.

Eastern Europe

1943   The Germans took Byelgorod.
1944   The Soviets took Zhmerinka. Admiral Miklos Horthy, Regent of Hungary, was arrested at Rastenburg after he refused Hitler's offer of troops in his country. Hitler ordered the invasion of Hungary. The Soviets reached the Rumanian border.
1945   The Soviets took Kolberg in Pomerania. The German minesweeper M-3137 and the patrol boat Uj-303 were sunk by Soviet aircraft off Danzig.

Mediterranean

1941   At 0001, the Italian torpedo boat ALDEBARAN was sunk off Albania by Royal Navy aircraft.
1942   The Italian submarine TRICHECO was sunk by the Royal Navy submarine UPHOLDER.
1943   The Allies took Gafsa and El Guittar in Tunisia. The U593 sank the British freighters DAFILA (1,940 tons) and KAYING (2,626 tons).
1944   An Australian attack on Cassino, Italy was repulsed. The American 15th Air Force attacked aircraft targets in Italy. At 2025, the German torpedo boat TA-36 (the ex-Italian STELLA POLARE) was sunk southwest of Fiume by a mine.
1945   The German torpedo boats TA-29 (the ex-Italian ERIDANO) and TA-24 (the ex-Italian ARTURO) were sunk off Corsica by the Royal Navy destroyers METEOR and LOOKOUT. It was the last action between destroyers in the European war.

Atlantic

1941   The U105 sank the British freighter MEDJERDA (4,380 tons). U105 survived until June 2, 1943.
1942   The American freighter LIBERATOR fired three 4" shells at the USN destroyer DICKINSON, hitting her with one and killing four of her crew, including her captain. The U124 sank the American tanker E.M. CLARK (9,647 tons-one dead) and the Greek freighter KASSANDRA LOULOUDI (5,106 tons). U124 survived until April 2, 1943. Eight survivors from the British tanker SAN DEMITRIO, which had been sunk on March 16th by U404, were rescued by the USCG cutter CUYAHOGA and the USN yacht TOURMALINE.

1943   The U521 sank the American freighter MOLLY PITCHER (7,200 tons- four dead). U521 survived until June 2nd. The U305 sank the British freighter PORT AUCKLAND (8,789 tons). U305 survived until January 17, 1944. The U663 sank the British freighter CLARISSA RADCLIFFE (5,754 tons). U663 survived until May 7th. The U221 sank the American freighter WALTER Q. GRESHAM (7,191 tons-27 dead) and the British freighter CANADIAN STAR (8,293 tons). U221 survived until September 27th. The US Coast Guard cutter ICARUS rescued the crew of American freighter MATTHEW LUCKENBACK (5,848 tons) after she was damaged by the U527. U527 survived until July 23rd.

1944   The U263 was sunk in Bay of Biscay by a mine.

1945   The U866 was sunk northeast of Boston by the USN destroyer escorts LOWE, MENGES, PRIDE and MOSLEY.

North America

1942   The Alaskan-Canadian highway was completed.

1943   The destroyer COWELL was launched. She was sold to Argentina in 1971.

1945   Japanese balloon-bombs were found near Garrison and Laure in Utah and at Kinak Bay, Alaska.

1946   Official hearings began before the Military Affairs Committee of the US House of Representatives. The hearings concerned the crossing of the Rapido River in Italy by the US Army's 36th Division during the war. The unit had suffered extremely heavy casualties during the crossing which was considered by many to be ill-advised and poorly planned. The operation was generally white-washed, and the target of the investigation, General Mark Clark, was vindicated.

1964   Joseph O'Callahan died. He had won a Medal of Honor while serving as Chaplain aboard the carrier FRANKLIN in 1945.

1981   FDR's yacht sank at its moorings at Treasure Island Naval Base, California. She had been confiscated by the Drug Enforcement Agency after being involved in illegal drug operations. On the 30th she was raised from the bottom. On April 28th the Port of Oakland would pay $15,000 for her in the hope of turning her into a museum.

1995   James Howard, age 82, died in Bay Pine, Florida. He had won the Medal of Honor on January 1, 1944. While flying a P51 "Mustang" he personally saved a formation of B17s on a mission over Germany. He was the only USAAF fighter pilot to win the Medal in the European Theater of Operations. He had previously served with the "Flying Tigers" in the Far East and had scored six victories there.

South America
1943 French Guiana declared itself for the Free French.

Pacific
1941 Rear Admiral William Furlong became Commander Minecraft Battle Force at Pearl Harbor.
1942 American forces arrived on Efate in the New Hebrides to build an airfield.
1943 The American 11th Air Force attacked Kiska in the Aleutians.
1944 USN Task Group 50.10 (commanded by Lee) attacked Mili Atoll. It consisted of the carrier LEXINGTON, the battleships IOWA and NEW JERSEY and the destroyers DEWEY, HULL, MACDONOUGH, PHELPS, BANCRIFT, MEADE and EDWARDS. The USN battleship IOWA was hit by two 152mm shells during the attack. Five USN 7th Fleet destroyers bombarded Wewak, New Guinea. The USN submarine LAPON sank the HOKURIKU MARU (8,359 tons).
1945 USN Task Force 58 began a 3-day attack on Japan. The USN carrier INTREPID was hit by a kamikaze (two dead) and carriers ENTERPRISE and YORKTOWN (five dead) were hit by bombs off Japan. American 20th Air Force B29s destroyed three square miles of Nagoya. 14,000 men of the US Armys 40th Division (commanded by Brush) landed on Panay in the Philippines. Also invaded the same day, by the 8th Army, were Bohol, Negros, and Caballo in the Visayan Islands in the Philippines. The USN submarine SPRINGER sank the IJN destroyer-transport T-18 (1,500 tons) and the minelayer W-17. The USN submarine BALAO sank the DAITO MARU No.2 (188 tons). The USN submarine TRIGGER sank the TSUKUSHI MARU No.3 (1,012 tons). The IJN destroyer-transport T-18 was sunk by a mine.
1946 Four Japanese officers were tried for the execution of three "Doolittle Raiders".

China-Burma-India
1942 Japanese forces took Taikkyi, Burma.
1943 The Chindits crossed the Irrawaddy River in Burma.
1944 The IJN submarine I-165 sank the British freighter NANCY MOLLER (3,916 tons).
1945 The British 2nd Division took Ava, Burma. Lieutenant Karanjeet Singh Judge, of the 15th Punjab Regiment, won a posthumous Victoria Cross in Burma.

March 19th

Western Europe

1905   Albert Speer was born in Mannheim. He would serve as German Minister of Production during the war.

1906   Adolf Eichmann was born in Solingen, Germany. When he was four years old his family moved to Austria. On April 1, 1932 he joined the Austrian Nazi Party. In September 1934 he joined the S.S. In August 1938, he was named as head of the S.S. Department for Jewish Immigration. After the Wannsee Conference of January 20, 1942, he was named as the director of the "final solution" to the Jewish problem. After the war, his actions would remain in obscurity until uncovered by the Nazi hunter Simon Wiesenthal in 1948. In 1953, Wiesenthal discovered that Eichmann was living in Argentina and living as a worker for a water company. On May 23, 1960 the Israeli government announced that Eichmann was their prisoner after being kidnapped by Jewish agents. His trial lasted from April 11th until August 14th of 1961. He was hanged on May 31, 1962 at Ramle. His body was cremated and his ashes were scattered in the Mediterranean outside of Israeli territorial waters.

1911   Luftwaffe ace General Adolf Galland (103 aerial victories) was born in Westerholt, Germany. In October 1934, he was commissioned into what was to become the Luftwaffe. He commanded a squadron of ground support aircraft in Spain from May 1937 until July 1938. During the attack against Poland, he won an Iron Cross 2nd Class and was promoted to captain. He was transferred to fighters in October 1939. He scored his first three victories on May 12, 1940 over Liege, Belgium. He was the highest scoring German ace during the "Battle of Britain". He served as General of Fighters from November 1941 until the end of 1944. On November 19, 1942, he became the Wehrmacht's youngest general. He was be relieved of his post and would end the war commanded in squadron of Me262 jet fighters. After two years as a prisoner of war, he served as a technical advisor in Argentina until January 1955. He returned to Germany where he worked as an aerospace consultant, airline president and business executive. He would die in 1995 at the age of 83.

1929   The Royal Navy heavy cruiser SUSSEX was launched. She was scrapped in 1950.

1940   Paul Reynaud formed a new French cabinet, with Edouard Daladier as Minister of Defense. Fifty Royal Air Force bombers attacked a German seaplane base at Hornum. One "Whitley" was lost.

1941   370 Luftwaffe aircraft attacked London. It was the heaviest raid since December 29th. Thirty-six Royal Air Force "Wellingtons" attacked Cologne, Germany.

1943 The U5 was lost in a collision in the Baltic. The German minesweeper M-3408 ran aground off the Hook of Holland and was lost. Six "Spitfires" from the USAAF's 4th Fighter Group flew patrols over the Channel.

1944 173 American 8th Air Force B17s dropped 505 tons of bombs on V-1 rocket launching sites at Wizernes, Watten, and Mimoyecques in France and lost one aircraft. Eighty-two 8th Air Force fighters provided support for the bombers. Thirty-five 8th Air Force P47s attacked the Gilze-Rijen airfield and were escorted by thirty-nine P51s. The American 15th Air Force attacked refineries in Austria. Twenty-one Royal Air Force "Mosquitoes" attacked targets in Germany. Six B17s from the USAAF's 422nd Bomb Squadron dropped 300 bundles of leaflets on The Hague, Rotterdam, Leeuwarden, Utrecht, and Amsterdam in Holland.

1945 Hitler ordered a "scorched earth" policy on all fronts. This was a policy originally utilized by the Soviets earlier in the war and demanded the destruction of anything that could be used by an advancing enemy. 1,224 American 8th Air Force bombers dropped 3,143 tons of bombs on airfields and rail targets in Germany and lost five B17s and one B24. 623 8th Air Force fighters provided support for the bombers and claimed forty victories for the loss of ten P51s. Seventy-nine Royal Air Force bombers attacked Gelsenkirchen, Germany. An American 8th Air Force A26 "Carpetbagger" was shot down near Bramsche, Germany. The American 15th Air Force attacked refineries around Vienna, Austria. Forty "Spitfires" attacked rail and V-2 targets in Holland. The American 7th Army took Saarlouis. A third bridge was opened over the Rhine at Remagen. The US Army's 3rd Division took Zweibrucken, Germany. Staff Sergeant Herbert Burr, of the 11th Armored Division, won a Medal of Honor near Dorrmoschel, Germany. German General Friedrich Fromm, commander of the Reserve Army, was executed for his part in the July 20th conspiracy. The British freighter SAMSELBU was sunk in the Scheldt by a mine. The first operational cruise for a German Type XXI U-boat began when U2511 left Kiel. She returned eight days later with mechanical problems. A USAAF 353rd Fighter Group P51 was shot down over Berlin by Soviet aircraft. American forces took Webenheim and Wissembourg in Germany. Thirty-four Royal Air Force "Mosquitoes" attacked Berlin. The British submarine VENTURER sank the German freighter SIRIUS (998 tons) off Namsos, Norway.

1948 The Royal Navy battleships QUEEN ELIZABETH and VALIANT were sold for scrap.

Eastern Europe

1943 The Germans took Byelgorod.

1944   The Soviets took Soroki and Krzeimienic. German paratroops attacked Hungarian airfields. The American 15th Air Force attacked rail targets in Yugoslavia.

Mediterranean
1943   The Royal Navy destroyer escort DERWENT was a constructive loss after an air-attack in Tripoli. The Italian destroyer ALPINO was sunk at La Spezia in a Royal Air Force air-raid.
1945   German S.S. General Karl Wolff met with two American O.S.S agents near Locarno to discuss the surrender of German forces in Italy.

Atlantic
1940   The U19 sank the Danish freighters MINSK (1,229 tons) and CHARKOW (1,026 tons). U19 was scuttled on September 10, 1944.
1941   The U105 sank the Dutch freighter MANDALIKA (7,750 tons). U105 survived until June 2, 1943.
1942   The U124 sank the American tankers PAPOOSE (5,939 tons-two dead) and W.E. HUTTON (7,076 tons-thirteen dead). U124 survived until April 2, 1943. The U332 sank the American freighter LIBERATOR (7,720 tons-five dead), which had damaged the USN destroyer DICKERSON the previous day. U332 survived until May 2, 1943.
1943   The U523 sank the American freighter MATTHEW LUCKENBACH (5,848 tons). U532 survived the war. The Italian submarine DA VINCI sank the British freighter LULWORTH HILL (7,628 tons). The U333 sank the Greek freighter CARRAS (5,234 tons). The British freighter SVEND FOYNE was sunk by an iceberg 100 miles south of Greenland.
1944   The U1059 was sunk by the USN escort carrier BLOCK ISLAND southwest of the Cape Verde Islands. The U311 sank the American tanker SEAKEY (10,342 tons). U311 survived until April 24th.

North America
1883   General Joseph Warren Stilwell was born in Palatka, Fla. He graduated 32nd in his 1904 West Point class of 124. He would command the American forces in the CBI and would serve as Chiang Kai-shek's Chief of Staff. He died on October 12, 1946.
1892   General James Van Fleet was born in New Jersey. He graduated 92nd in his 1915 West Point class of 164. He won a Purple Heart and a Silver Star during WWI. Long after his classmates Eisenhower and Bradley had been promoted to general, he was still a colonel. After the invasion of Normandy, Eisenhower informed Army Chief of Staff Marshall that he had a colonel by the name of Van Fleet who should be promoted. Marshall refused saying that he had been scratching that name from promotion lists

	for years because he was known as a drunk. After further discussion, it was discovered that the offending officer's name was Van Vliet. Marshall then proceeded to make up for lost time and by the end of the war, Van Fleet was a major general in command of the 3rd Corps. On February 19, 1948 he was promoted to lieutenant general. He retired on March 31, 1953 as a full general. He died on September 23, 1992 in Polk City, Florida.
1943	The destroyers HALLIGAN and HARADEN were launched. HALLIGAN was lost March 26, 1945 and HARADEN was expended in 1972.
1944	The light cruiser DAYTON and the destroyer MADDOX were launched. DAYTON was scrapped in 1962 and MADDOX was sold to Taiwan in 1972
1945	Japanese balloon-bombs were found near Cedarville in British Columbia and Sonoyta in Mexico.
1971	The destroyer ZELLARS was sold to Iran.

Pacific

1938	The IJN heavy cruiser CHIKUMA was launched. She was sunk on October 25, 1945.
1941	The USN destroyers AYLWIN and FARRAGUT collided off Hawaii. One man aboard the AYLWIN was killed.
1942	The Allied commander in the Philippines, Jonathan Wainwright, was promoted to Lieutenant General. Philippine President Quezon arrived at Oroquito, Mindanao after a 240-mile voyage aboard USN PT-41 from Dumaguete, Negros. A seaplane from the Japanese submarine I-25 flew over Suva, Fiji. The US 41st Infantry Division left San Francisco for Australia.
1943	The USN submarine WAHOO sank the ZOGEN MARU (1,428 tons) and the KOWA MARU (3,217 tons). The USN submarine KINGFISH sank the TAKACHIHO MARU (8,154 tons). Five 5th Air Force B25s attacked Lae, New Guinea and damaged the IJN I-176 which was unloading supplies.
1945	290 USAAF B29s destroyed three square miles of the city of Nagoya and lost one aircraft. The USN carriers WASP (101 dead) and FRANKLIN (832 dead) were bombed off Japan. FRANKLIN's crew was awarded two Medals of Honor-Lieutenant (junior grade) Donald Gary and Chaplain Joseph O'Callahan (See March 18, 1964), nineteen Navy Crosses and twenty-two Silver Stars. Her Captain, Leslie Gehres, had been the first enlisted man to work his way through the ranks to the command of a carrier. The IJN submarine I-205 was sunk at Kure by carrier aircraft. The USN submarine BALAO sank the HAKOZAKI MARU (10,413 tons), the DAITO MARU No.1 (156 tons) and the TATSUHARA MARU (6,345 tons). The US Army's 33rd Division took Bauang, Luzon.

China-Burma-India
1942   British General William Slim assumed command of the British troops in Burma. The Japanese 56th Division left Singapore for Rangoon.
1943   Eight American 10th Air Force B25s attacked the Myitgne River in Burma.
1944   The U510 sank the American freighter JOHN A. POOR (7,176 tons).
1945   The British 36th Division took Mogok, Burma. The American 10th Air Force attacked rail targets in Burma and lost two B24s. The IJN escort SUMA was sunk on the Yangtze by a mine.

March 20th

Western Europe
1892   German General Ludwig Cruewell was born. He commanded the 11th Panzer Division until October 1941 when he assumed command of the Afrika Korps. His airplane was shot down on May 29, 1942 and he was captured. He died in 1958 at the age of 66.
1919   Luftwaffe ace Erich Barkhorn (301 victories) was born in Konigsberg. He survived the war.
1920   The Royal Navy light cruiser FROBISHER was launched. She was scrapped in 1949.
1940   Edouard Daladier resigned as the French Premier. The British freighter BARN HILL (5,439 tons) was sunk off the Isle of Wight by the Luftwaffe. The RMS MAURETANIA was requisitioned as a troopship.
1941   The Luftwaffe attacked Plymouth, Britain. Sixty-six Royal Air Force bombers attacked German U-boat bases at Lorient, Brest, and St. Nazaire in France.
1942   Nineteen Royal Air Force bombers dropped mines in the Baltic. The armed merchant cruiser MICHEL left Germany for the Atlantic.
1943   An attempt on Hitler's life was made by Colonel Rudolf von Gertsdorff. Sixteen Royal Air Force bombers dropped mines off the Biscay ports. Two "Spitfires" from the USAAF's 4th Fighter Group flew a patrol over the Channel.
1944   American 9th Air Force B26s attacked the Criel railyards. 147 American 8th Air Force bombers dropped 268 tons of bombs on Frankfurt, Bingen and Mannheim in Germany and lost five B17s and two B24s. 594 8th Air Force fighters provided support for the bombers and claimed four victories for the loss of six P47s and two P51s. American 9th Air Force B26s attacked V-1 launching sites in Holland and lost two aircraft. Thirty-five Royal Air Force "Mosquitoes" attacked targets in Germany. Royal Air Force Pilot Officer C.J. Barton, of No.578 Squadron, won a posthumous Victoria Cross over Nuremburg, Germany. The British submarine GRAPH (the ex-German U570) was wrecked on the west coast of Islay.

1945   Adolf Hitler made his last public appearance when he awarded medals to members of the Hitler Youth outside his bunker in Berlin. A 4th bridge was opened by the American forces at Remagen on the Rhine River. The bridgehead now measured thirty miles wide by nineteen miles deep. The American 7th Army took Saarbrucken and Kaiserslautern in Germany. Royal Air Force "Mosquitos" shot down a Luftwaffe intruder ten miles northeast of Cromer, but other intruders shot down a Royal Air Force "Halifax" and a "Stirling". The last Luftwaffe bombs to land on the British Isles were dropped on Royal Air Force Swanton Morley. 418 American 8th Air Force dropped 1,175 tons of bombs on Hamburg, Hemmingstedt and Kiel in Germany and lost three B17s and one B24. The German minesweepers M-15, M-16, M-18, M-19 and M-522 were sunk at Kiel in the raid. 338 8th Air Force fighters provided support for the bombers and claimed eight victories for the loss of two P51s. 153 Royal Air Force bombers attacked Recklinghausen, Germany. 113 Royal Air Force bombers attacked rail targets in Germany. The American 3d and 7th Armies linked up at Neunkirchen, Germany. 125 "Spitfires" attacked The Hague area railways. Thirty-four "Spitfires" attacked V-2 targets in Holland. 235 Royal Air Force bombers attacked Bohlen, Germany and lost nine "Lancasters". 166 Royal Air Force bombers attacked the oil refinery at Hemmingsatdt and lost one aircraft. Eighty-one Royal Air Force "Mosquitoes" attacked targets in Germany. The USAAF's 492nd Bomb Group dispatched two A26 "Invaders" on "Carpetbagger" missions and lost one aircraft.

1948   The Royal Navy battleship RAMILLIES was sold for scrap.

Eastern Europe

1943   The Germans recaptured Byelgorod.
1944   Soviet forces advanced into Rumania. The Soviets took Vinnitsa in the Ukraine. German forces completed their occupation of Hungary.
1945   The Soviets took Braunsburg. The American freighter HORACE BUSHNELL (7,176 tons-five dead) was a constructive loss after an attack by U995. The U968 sank the Royal Navy sloop LAPWING and the American freighter THOMAS DONALDSON (7,210 tons-four dead).

Mediterranean

1941   The British took Jarabub.
1942   At 1100, the Royal Navy destroyer escort HEYTHORP was torpedoed east of Tobruk by the U625. She sank five hours later while under tow by the Royal Navy destroyer ERIDGE.
1943   Eighteen USAAF B25s attacked Mareth, Tunisia. The U81 sank the Syrian sailing ship MAWAHAB ALLAR (77 tons) and the Egyptian sailing ship BOURGHIEH (244 tons).

Atlantic

1940 The U20 sank the Danish freighters VIKING (1,153 tons) and BOTHAL (2,109 tons) southwest of Narvik. U20 was then sunk by the Royal Navy destroyer FORTUNE. The U44 was sunk north of the Shetlands by the Royal Navy destroyer FORTUNE.

1941 The Royal Navy battleship MALAYA was torpedoed by the U106 northwest of Cape Verde.

1942 The U71 sank the American freighter OAKMAR (5,766 tons-6 dead). U71 survived the war.

1943 The U518 sank the Dutch freighter MARISO (7,659 tons). U518 survived until April 22, 1945. The U384 was sunk southwest of Ireland by the Royal Air Force's No.201 Squadron. The Brazilian freighter BAJE rescued 27 survivors from the American freighter ROGER B. TANEY which had been sunk on February 8th by U160. USN YP-438 was lost after she ran aground off Florida.

1945 The U905 was sunk south of the Faeroes by the Royal Air Force's No.86 Squadron.

North America

1920 The battleship MARYLAND was launched. She would be scrapped in 1959.

1941 The US Army Air Corp's Ferry Command was renamed the Air Transport Command.

1942 The carrier HORNET arrived at San Francisco to load Doolittle's B25s for the attack on Tokyo. The battleship SOUTH DAKOTA was commissioned. She would be scrapped in 1962. The Eastern Theater of Operations became the Eastern Defense Command. The light cruiser BIRMINGHAM (she was awarded nine battle stars and a Navy Unit Commendation during the war) and the destroyers LARDNER and MCCALLA were launched. BIRMINGHAM was scrapped in Long Beach in December 1959 and LARDNER was transferred to Turkey in 1950 as was MCCALLA in 1949.

1945 The carrier MIDWAY was launched. George Gay, sole survivor of Torpedo 8 at the "Battle of Midway", was present at the ceremony. Japanese balloon-bombs were found near Timnath in Colorado, Chadron in Nebraska, Fort Chipewyan, Formost and Delburne in Alberta, Denman Island and Williams Lake in British Columbia.

1970 The destroyer CONY was expended as a target.

1975 The light cruiser TOPEKA was sold for scrap.

1992 USN Admiral George W. Anderson died. He had commanded CV-2, the LEXINGTON and CV-5, the YORKTOWN.

Pacific

1942   Lieutenant General Jonathan Wainwright was appointed commander all US forces in the Philippines. The USN submarine RUNNER laid 32 mines in the approaches to Singapore Harbor.

1943   The IJN armed merchant cruiser BANGKOK MARU was sunk off Jaluit Atoll by the USN submarine POLLACK. The USN submarine SAWFISH sank the SHINSEI MARU (148 tons).

1944   The USN battleships NEW MEXICO, IDAHO, MISSISSIPPI, and TENNESSEE bombarded Kavieng, New Ireland, while the USMC invaded Emirau Island, 90 miles to the north. The USN submarine POLLACK sank the HAKUYO MARU (1,327 tons). The USN submarine PICUDA sank the HOKO MARU (1,504 tons).

1945   Staff Sergeant Ysmael Villegas, of the 32nd Division, won a posthumous Medal of Honor on Luzon. The USN submarine BAYA sank the KAINAN MARU (525 tons). The USN submarine BLENNY sank the NANSHIN MARU No.21 (834 tons), the HOSEN MARU (1,039 tons) and the YAMAKUNI MARU (500 tons). USN Admiral James Fife left Fremantle aboard the USN submarine HARDHEAD becoming the second and last USN admiral to make a combat patrol. The first was Ralph Christie who had gone out on the BOWFIN and the HARDER. The USN destroyer HALSEY POWELL was hit by a kamikaze, twelve of her crew died.

China-Burma-India

1942   The Japanese took Tharrawaddy, Burma.

1943   The IJN submarine I-27 sank the British freighter FORT MUMFORD (7,132 tons). The U516 sank the Panamanian freighter NORTUN (3,663 tons).

1944   The British submarine was lost in the Malacca Strait.

1945   The British 19th Division, commanded by Thomas Rees, took Mandalay, Burma. General Rees died in 1959.

March 21st

Western Europe

1889   New Zealand General Bernard Freyberg was born in Richmond, Britain. His family moved to New Zealand when he was a child. He was commissioned into the territorials in 1912. He returned to London in August 1914 and was commissioned into the Royal Navy Reserve. During WWI, he was promoted to lieutenant colonel and won three Distinguished Service Orders and a Victoria Cross. He retired as a major general in 1937. He was recalled to active duty in 1939. On November 23rd, he was offered command of New Zealand's Expeditionary Force. After the war, he served as Governor General of New Zealand 1946-52. He died on July 4, 1963 while serving as Lieutenant Governor and Deputy Constable of Windsor Castle.

1933 The opening of the Dachau Concentration Camp was announced in the German press.

1940 Paul Reynaud became Premier of France. The Luftwaffe scored its first sinking in the Channel when they bombed the freighter BARN HILL which had been sailing alone. The Royal Navy heavy cruiser TRINIDAD was launched. She was sunk on May 15, 1942.

1941 The Luftwaffe attacked Plymouth, Britain. Sixty-six Royal Air Force bombers attacked the German U-boat base at Lorient, France and lost one "Blenheim" and one "Hampden.

1942 Hitler named Fritz Sauckel as Labor Minister and ordered him to import 300,000 forced laborers from the occupied countries each month.

1943 The Royal Air Force air-crews that would fly the "Dambuster's Raid" on May 16th were assembled for the first time. They would not be told of their target until the day before the attack. The first "Liberty" ship to arrive in Britain was the JOAQUIN MILLER.

1944 The headquarters group of the American 3rd Army arrived at the Firth of Clyde in Scotland. Fifty-six American 8th Air Force B24s dropped 213 tons of bombs on German V-1 rocket sites near Watten, France. Forty-eight 8th Air Force P47s provided escorts for the bombers. Forty-one 8th Air Force P51s flew sweeps near Bordeaux, France and claimed twenty-one victories for the loss of seven aircraft. Twenty-seven Royal Air Force "Mosquitoes" attacked targets in Germany. Six B17s from the USAAF's 422nd Bomb Squadron dropped 300 bundles of leaflets on The Hague, Amsterdam, Leeuwarden, Rotterdam, and Utrecht in Holland.

1945 Eighteen "Mosquitoes" attacked the Gestapo headquarters in Copenhagen, killing thirty-five, but they also hit a Catholic School that was located next to it and killed 103 students. A fifth bridge was opened by the American forces at Remagen on the Rhine. 178 Royal Air Force bombers attacked Rheine, Germany and lost one aircraft. 160 Royal Air Force bombers attacked Munster, Germany and lost three aircraft. 139 Royal Air Force bombers attacked Bremen, Germany. The German destroyer Z-51 was sunk in the Bremen air-raid. A V-2 rocket hit near the USAAF's 4th Fighter Group's base at Debden, Britain. 1,353 American 8th Air Force bombers dropped 3,114 tons of bombs on jet airfields and lost seven B17s. 751 8th Air Force fighters provided support for the bombers and claimed fifty-five victories for the loss of nine P51s. 366 American 15th Air Force B24s dropped 800 tons of bombs on Neuburg, Austria. 116 Royal Air Force "Spitfires" attacked The Hague area railways. General Heinz

Guderian (died in 1953) was dismissed as Chief of the German General Staff. American forces took Neustadt, Darmstadt, Annweiler, Demsieders, Queichhambach and Worms in Germany. 159 Royal Air Force bombers attacked Hamburg, Germany and lost four "Lancasters". 153 Royal Air Force bombers attacked Bochum, Germany and lost one "Lancaster". 145 Royal Air Force "Mosquitoes" attacked targets in Germany. The German MTB S-203 was sunk off Texel by Allied aircraft.

Eastern Europe

1942   Elements of the German 16th Army surrounded at Demyansk began attempts to break out.

1945   The Soviets took Tatabanya, Hungary. The German battleship SCHLESWIG-HOLSTEIN was scuttled at Gydnia, Poland.

Mediterranean

1941   Gariboldi replaced Graziani as Italian Governor of Libya and commander of Italian forces in North Africa.

1942   The Royal Navy carrier EAGLE launched nine "Spitfires" for Malta in "Operation Picket I".

1943   Second Lieutenant M. Ngarimu, of the 28th New Zealand Battalion, and Lieutenant D. Seagrim, of the Green Howards, won posthumous Victoria Cross' on the "Mareth Line" in Tunisia.

1944   The US Army's 34th Division arrived to reinforce the Anzio beachhead.

1945   The German torpedo boat TA-42 (the ex-Italian ALABARDA) was sunk at Venice by the USAAF.

Atlantic

1940   The U38 sank the Danish freighters ALGIER (1,654 tons) and CHRISTIANSBORG (3,270 tons). U38 survived the war. The U57 sank the Norwegian freighter SVINTA (1,267 tons). U57 survived the war.

1941   The U105 sank the British freighters CLAN OGILVY (5,802 tons), BENWYVIS (5,920 tons) and JHELUM (4,038 tons). U105 survived until June 2, 1943.

1943   German surface craft sank the Soviet submarine K-3 off Batsfjord, Norway. The U163 was sunk in the Bay of Biscay by the USN submarine HERRING. The US Coast Guard cutters ALGONQUIN rescued twenty-two survivors, the FREDRICK LEE rescued twenty and the MODOC rescued twenty-eight from the freighter SVEND FOYNE which had sunk after hitting an iceberg.

1944   The U66 sank the British tanker MATADIAN (4,275 tons). U66 survived until May 6, 1944.

1945   The American freighter JOHN R. PARK (7,184 tons) was sunk in the English Channel by the U399. The U1195 damaged the America freighter JAMES EAGAN LAYNE (7,176 tons).

North America
1903   USAAF General La Verne George "Blondie" Saunders was born in Stratford, South Dakota. He graduated 214th in his 1928 West Point class of 261. His 11th Bomb Group's sixteen B17s were the first USAAF formation to be involved in the Guadalcanal campaign of August 1942. He was promoted to brigadier general on December 25, 1942. Later in the war, he would command the 58th Bomb Wing of LeMay's 20th Air Force in the Pacific. He retired in 1947 as a brigadier general and died in Aberdeen, South Dakota on November 16, 1988.
1941   Actor James Maitland Stewart reported for duty at Moffet Field, California. He would fly twenty combat missions with the 8th Air Force B24-equipped 445th and 453rd Bomb Groups and return as to the States a Colonel.
1943   The destroyers OWEN and ERBEN were launched. The OWEN was stricken in 1972 and ERBEN was transferred to Korea in 1963. The submarine COD was launched. She was preserved as a memorial in 1975.
1944   The escort carrier SHIPLEY BAY was commissioned. She was scrapped in 1961.
1945   Japanese balloon-bombs were found near Dillingham in Alaska, Camsell-Portage in Saskatchewan, and Glen in Montana.
1946   USAAF Chief of Staff Carl Spaatz announced the formation of Strategic Air Command with General George C. Kenney in command.

Pacific
1942   General Jonathan Wainwright moved his headquarters to Corregidor.
1943   The USN submarine WAHOO sank the HOZAN MARU (2,260 tons) and the NITTSU MARU (2,183 tons). The American 11th Air Force attacked Japanese-held Kiska in the Aleutians.
1944   American 5th Air Force B24s attacked Wewak, New Guinea.
1945   The American Kerama Retto invasion force left Ulithi.

China-Burma-India
1942   The IJN submarine I-162 damaged the British tanker SAN CIRILO (8,012 tons).
1944   The IJN submarine I-26 sank the Norwegian tanker GRENA (8,117 tons).
1945   Lieutenant C. Eaymond, of the Royal Engineers, won a posthumous Victoria Cross in Burma.

March 22nd

Western Europe

1938 The British government abandoned its rearmament policy of "no interference with the normal course of trade". Under this policy, rearmament would only occur after the consequences on the civilian economy and trade were considered.

1941 The German battlecruisers GNEISENAU and SCHARNHORST arrived at Brest, France. During their foray into the Atlantic, they had destroyed 115,000 tons of Allied shipping. Thr 5th Division left Britain for Madagascar.

1943 Eighty-four American 8th Air Force B17s and B24s dropped 224 tons of bombs on the U-boat construction yards in Wilhelmshaven, Germany and lost one B17 and two B24s. 357 Royal Air Force bombers attacked St. Nazaire, France and lost one "Lancaster".

1944 657 American 8th Air Force bombers dropped 1,471 tons of bombs on Berlin and lost seven B17s and five B24s. One of the lost B24s landed on Switzerland. The 466th Bomb Group (B24) flew its first 8th Air Force mission. The 482nd Bomb Group (B17 then B24) flew the last of its 8th Air Force missions, having lost seven aircraft. It was then transferred to the 8th Composite Command where its role would be that of training and experimentation. 817 8th Air Force fighters provided support for the bombers and claimed one victory for the loss of three P38s, five P47s and four P51s. 816 Royal Air Force bombers attacked Frankfurt, Germany and lost thirty-three aircraft. 948 people were killed in the raid. 146 Royal Air Force bombers dropped mines in the Baltic and lost one "Halifax". Six B17s from the USAAF's 422nd Bomb Squadron dropped 263 bundles of leaflets on Paris, The Hague, Amsterdam and Leeuwarden.

1945 1,301 American 8th Air Force bombers dropped 3,069 tons of bombs on barracks and airfields in Germany and lost one B17. 632 8th Air Force fighters provided support for the bombers and claimed twenty-seven victories for the loss of three P51s. 235 Royal Air Force bombers attacked Hildesheim, Germany and lost four "Lancasters". 1,645 people were killed in the raid. 130 Royal Air Force bombers attacked Dulmen, Germany. 124 Royal Air Force bombers attacked Dorsten, Germany. 100 Royal Air Force bombers attacked Bocholt, Germany. 102 Royal Air Force "Lancasters" attacked bridges in Germany. The US Army's 5th Division crossed the Rhine at Oppenheim. American forces took Mainz, Landau, and Steinfeld in Germany. 136 American 15th Air Force B17s attacked Ruhland, Austria. 120 "Spitfires" attacked V-2 targets in Holland. 70 Royal Air Force "Mosquitoes" attacked targets in Germany and lost two aircraft.

1946 Cardinal Clemens von Galen, arch-bishop of Munster, who had been sent to Sachsenhausen Concentration Camp in 1944, died in Munich.

1947   S.S. Brigadefuhrer Juergen Stroop, who had overseen stopping the Warsaw Rebellion, was sentenced to death by an American court at Dachau for shooting hostages in Greece.

Eastern Europe
1944   Berlin announced the formation of a new government in Hungary. The Soviets took Pervomaysk north of Odessa.
1945   G.S. Heinrici replaced Heinrich Himmler as commander of Army Group "Vistula". The German 9th Army attacked the Soviet bridgehead on the Oder west of Kustrin. The German transport FRANKFURT (1,186 tons) was sunk by Soviet aircraft in the Baltic. The Soviet submarine L-21 sank the German patrol boat V-2022 in the Baltic.

Mediterranean
1943   USAAF 301st Bomb Group B17s attacked Palermo, Sicily. The British gunboat APHIS bombarded Gabes in support of the 8th Army.
1944   Two officers and thirteen men of the US Army's 267th Special Recon Battalion landed behind German lines in Italy, via landing craft, to destroy a railroad tunnel between La Spezia and Genoa. The American 15th Air Force attacked rail targets in Italy. Mount Vesuvius erupted, damaging sixty B25 bombers stationed at nearby Pompeii Airfield.

Atlantic
1941   The German armed merchant cruiser KORMORAN took the British tanker AGNITA (3,561 tons). Two American grain ships were permitted through the British blockade to Vichy France.
1942   The U123 sank the American tanker MUSKOGEE (7,034 tons-with all hands). U123 survived the war. The U373 sank the British freighter THURSOBANK (5,575 tons). U373 survived until June 8, 1944.
1943   The U524 was sunk south of Madeira by USAAF's 1st Squadron. The U665 was sunk in the Bay of Biscay by the Royal Air Force's No.172 Squadron.
1944   The U802 sank the Canadian freighter WATUKA (1,621 tons). U802 survived the war.
1945   The U315 sank the British freighter EMPIRE KINGSLEY (6,996 tons). U315 survived the war. The U296 was sunk in the North Sea by the Royal Air Force's No.120 Squadron.

North America
1907   General James Maurice Gavin was born in Brooklyn, New York. He would graduate 185th in his 1929 West Point class of 299. In 1942, he assumed command of the 505th Regiment of the 82nd Airborne Division. In

September 1943, he became deputy division commander. In August 1944, he succeeded Matthew Ridgeway as division commander, thus becoming the youngest US Army division commander since the Civil War. He was promoted to major general on October 20, 1944, becoming the youngest in the US Army. He retired as a lieutenant general in 1958 after refusing to support military programs with which he did not agree. He died on February 23, 1990 in Baltimore, Maryland.

1921 The battleship COLORADO was launched. She was scrapped in 1959.
1945 A Japanese balloon-bomb was shot down near Reno, Nevada by a USAAF P63 "Kingcobra", others were found near Rogerson in Idaho, Volcano in California, Rome in Oregon and Ree Heights in South Dakota.
1948 The shore batteries of HDSF (Harbor Defense-San Francisco) fired their last target practice.
1962 The light cruiser RENO was sold for scrap.
1966 "Bazooka Charlie" Carpenter, who had won a Silver Star for destroying six German tanks, while flying an L-4 recon plane with the 4th Armored Division, 3rd Army, died of Hodgkin's Disease in Urbana, Illinois.
2007 Jay Zeamer died in a Boothsbay Harbor, Maine nursing home at the age off 88. He had won a Medal of Honor on June 16, 1943 while flying a B17 on a photo mission over Buka in the Solomons.

Pacific

1943 The USN submarine GUDGEON sank the MEIGEN MARU (5,434 tons). The American 11th Air Force attacked Kiska in the Aleutians.
1944 The IJN tanker IRO was damaged by the USN submarine TUNNY.
1945 The Japanese Air Force made its last raid on Morotai Island in the Moluccas. Corporal R. Rattey, of the Australian 25th Infantry Battalion, won a Victoria Cross in the Solomons. USN carriers attacked Okinawa.
1948 The USN destroyers MUGFORD and RHIND were expended off Kwajalein after the Bikini tests.

China-Burma-India

1945 Japanese forces took Pyu, Burma.
1945 The 7th Indian Division took Myingan, Burma.

March 23rd

Western Europe

1912 German rocket scientist Werner von Braun was born in Wirsitz, Prussia. He would be moved to America after the war where he became a major player in the American space program.

1933 The German Reichstag passed the Enabling Act which gave Hitler dictatorial powers.

1939 Germany declared that the populations of occupied territories would not have to serve in the armed forces, but would have to be available for service in forced labor battalions.

1941 Sixty-three Royal Air Force bombers attacked Berlin. Thirty-one Royal Air Force bombers attacked Kiel, Germany and killed ten people. Twenty-six Royal Air Force bombers attacked Hannover, Germany and lost one "Blenheim".

1942 Seventeen Royal Air Force bombers dropped mines off Lorient, France. Hitler ordered the construction of the "Atlantic Wall".

1943 Fifteen Royal Air Force "Mosquitoes" attacked Nantes, France. Forty-five Royal Air Force bombers dropped mines in the Baltic and lost two "Wellingtons". Eight "Spitfires" from the USAAF's 4th Fighter Group flew patrols over the Channel.

1944 707 American 8th Air Force bombers dropped 1,755 tons of bombs on Brunswick, Munster, Osnabruck, Handorf and Achmer in Germany and lost twenty-two B17s and six B24s. 841 8th Air Force fighters provided support for the bombers and claimed twenty-two victories for the loss of four P51s. Luftwaffe ace Wolf-Dietrich Wilke (162 victories) was killed in action over Brunswick, Germany by USAAF 4th Fighter Group P51s. American 9th Air Force B26s attacked Dutch railyards. 143 Royal Air Force bombers attacked Laon, France. Five B17s from the USAAF's 422nd Bomb Squadron dropped 262 bundles of leaflets on Grenoble, Vichy, Lyon, Toulouse and Limoges in France.

1945 The British 2nd and Canadian 1st Armies crossed the Rhine in "Operation Plunder". The American 3rd Army took Ludwigshafen, Germany. 1,244 American 8th Air Force bombers dropped 3,140 tons of bombs on rail targets in Germany and lost three B24s and four B17s. 469 8th Air Force fighters provided support for the bombers and claimed one victory. 128 Royal Air Force bombers attacked rail bridges in Germany and lost two "Lancasters". Eighty Royal Air Force bombers attacked Wesel, Germany. 157 American 15th Air Force bombers dropped 437 tons of bombs on the Valentin tank factory in Ruhland, Austria. Seventeen Royal Air Force "Typhoons" and 126 "Spitfires" attacked German V-2 rocket sites in Holland. In a second raid, 218 Royal Air Force bombers attacked Wesel. By the end of the war, 97% of the buildings in the city had been destroyed in air-raids. Eighty-eight Royal Air Force "Mosquitoes" attacked targets in Germany. The USAAF's 492nd Bomb Group dispatched nineteen B24s on "Carpetbagger" missions over Denmark.

1946 The American freighter JEAN LYKES was damaged by a mine off Copenhagen, Denmark.

Eastern Europe

1939 Germany seized Memel, Lithuania.

1942 The Soviet minelayer OSTROVSKY was sunk by the Luftwaffe. The Soviet freighter CHAPAYEV was sunk by a mine.

1944 Soviet forces took German defensive positions east of Tarnopol. The German patrol boat V-6109 was sunk by Soviet aircraft off northern Norway.

1945 The Soviets took Szekefehervar, Hungary. The German cruiser LUTZOW began supporting the retreating Wehrmacht near Danzig.

Mediterranean

1919 Future Italian dictator Benito Mussolini founded the Fasci Di Combattimento in Milan. It was the beginning of Italian Fascist Party.

1941 The Greek submarine TRITON sank an Italian ship of 5,451 tons off Valona.

1942 At 0545, the Italian destroyer SCIRROCO foundered during a storm in the Ionian Sea. At 1007, the Italian destroyer LANCIERE foundered during the same storm.

1943 The Italian submarine DELFINO was lost in a collision off Sicily. USAAF B17s attacked Bizerte, Tunisia. Luftwaffe ace Joachim Muncheberg (135 victories) died when his Me109 collided with a USAAF "Spitfire" over Tunisia.

1944 A bomb detonated by the Italian Resistance exploded in Rome. It killed thirty-two German soldiers. Hitler's first reaction was to demand that all able-bodied males in the city be sent to concentration camps. General Albert Kesselring convinced him that would be impractical. Instead, 335 Romans were taken to nearby Grotto via Ardeantina and executed.

1945 Heinrich von Vietinghoff succeeded Albert Kesselring as German Commander-in-Chief in Italy.

1981 British Field Marshal Claude Auchinleck died in Marrakech. He had commanded the British forces in North Africa.

Atlantic

1941 The U97 sank the British tanker CHAMA (8,077 tons). U97 survived until June 16, 1943. The U551 was sunk
south of Iceland by the Royal Navy trawler VISENDA.

1942 The German armed merchant cruiser THOR took the Greek freighter PAGASITIKOS (3,942 tons). The U754 sank the British tanker BRITISH PRUDENCE (8,620 tons). U754 survived until July 31st. The U124 sank the American tanker NAECO (5,373 tons). U124 survived until April 2, 1943. The Italian submarine MOROSINI sank the British tanker PEDER BOGEN (9,741 tons).

1944   The U218 laid two mines off St. Lucia in the West Indies.
1945   The American freighter CHARLES D. MCIVER was sunk off Ostend, Belgium by a mine. The American freighter ELEFTHERIA was sunk by a mine.

North America
1914   The battleship OKLAHOMA was launched. She would be sunk during the Pearl Harbor attack of December 7, 1941.
1920   The destroyer POPE was launched in Philadelphia. She was sunk on March 1, 1942.
1941   FDR received a request from Churchill that the Royal Navy's battleship MALAYA be allowed to enter an American shipyard to repair torpedo damage. FDR was able to comply with the request because of the fact that the Lend-Lease Bill had been passed by Congress earlier in the month.
1942   Lieutenant Colonel James Doolittle led twenty-two B25s from Eglin Field in Florida to McClellan Field in California on the first leg of their trip to Tokyo and the famous "Doolittle Raid". The USN submarine GATO was attacked off San Francisco by the USN blimp TC-13.
1943   The USN yard craft No.869 was wrecked at Imperial Beach, California.
1944   The submarine TREPANG was launched at Mare Island.
1945   Japanese balloon-bombs were found near Desdemona in Texas and Parkersburg in Oregon.
1972   The destroyer GANSEVOORT was expended as a target.
2006   Desmond Doss died. He had won a Medal of Honor on Okinawa for actions that took place between April 29 and May 21 in 1945. He had been serving as a medic because he was a conscientious objector.

Pacific
1943   The USN submarine WHALE sank the KENYO MARU (6,484 tons).
1944   Japanese forces attacked the American perimeter on Bougainville. The IJN submarine Ro-41 was sunk by the USN destroyer HAGGARD. The USN submarine TUNNY sank the IJN submarine I-42. USN carrier aircraft attacked Okinawa. The Royal Navy carriers INDEFATIGABLE, ILLUSTRIOUS, INDOMITABLE and VICTORIOUS left Manus as Task Force 57.
1945   San Fernando on Luzon was taken by the American I Corps. USN Task Force 58 began a 3-day attack on Okinawa. The USN submarine SPADEFISH sank the DORYO MARU (2,274 tons).

China-Burma-India
1942   The Japanese took the Andaman Islands in the Bay of Bengal.
1945   The Allies took Wundwin and Myingan in Burma.

March 24th

Western Europe

1888   British Admiral William Wake-Walker was born. He died on September 24, 1945.

1917   The Royal Navy light cruiser CERES was launched. She was scrapped in 1946.

1933   Adolf Hitler was given supreme power by the German Reichstag.

1937   The Royal Navy heavy cruiser LIVERPOOL was launched. She was scrapped in 1958.

1941   Nine Royal Air Force "Blenheims" attacked shipping off the Dutch coast and lost one aircraft.

1942   Eighteen Royal Air Force "Bostons" attacked targets in France. Thirty-five Royal Air Force bombers dropped mines off Lorient, France and lost two aircraft. One of them was the first "Lancaster" to be lost in action. The German minesweeper M-3625 was sunk by a mine off Vissingen.

1943   Three Royal Air Force "Mosquitoes" attacked targets in the Ruhr. Twenty-six "Spitfires" from the USAAF's 4th Fighter Group flew patrols over the Channel.

1944   403 American 8th Air Force B17s and B24s dropped 1,081 tons of bombs on Schweinfurt and Frankfurt in Germany and St. Dizier and Nancy in France and lost three B17s. 540 8th Air Force fighters provided support for the bombers and claimed three victories for the loss of two P38s and three P51s. 811 Royal Air Force bombers attacked Berlin and lost seventy-two aircraft. 150 people were killed in Berlin and another thirty were killed in 126 various other smaller towns and villages that were hit. This was the last major raid that the Royal Air Force made on the city. Five B17s from the USAAF's 422nd Bomb Squadron dropped 250 bundles of leaflets on Tour, Lorient, Brussels, Charleroi, and Antwerp.

1945   1,714 American 8th Air Force bombers dropped 4,774 tons of bombs on airfields in Germany and lost five B17s and fourteen B24s. All fourteen B24s that were lost were shot down by small arms fire while dropping supplies to Allied ground troops that were crossing the Rhine under British Field Marshal Bernard Montgomery. 1,297 8th Air Force fighters provided support for the bombers and claimed fifty-three victories for the loss of nine P51s. The American 15th Air Force made its only attack on Berlin when 150 B17s dropped 357 tons of bombs and lost two aircraft. Lieutenant Roscoe C. Brown, of the Negro-manned 332nd Fighter Group-P51, shot down a Luftwaffe Me262 jet during the raid. American 15th Air Force B24s attacked jet targets in southern Germany and Czechoslovakia. 177 Royal Air Force bombers attacked Sterkrade,

Germany. 175 Royal Air Force bombers attacked Gladbeck, Germany and lost one "Halifax". 185 Royal Air Force bombers attacked oil targets in Germany and lost three "Lancasters". 110 Royal Air Force "Spitfires" attacked The Hague area railways. 14,000 paratroops of the American 17th Airborne and British 6th Airborne Divisions landed northeast of Wesel, Germany. Private George Peters and Private First-Class Stewart Stryker, of the 17th Airborne Division, won posthumous Medals of Honor near Wesel, Germany. Corporal F. Topham, of the 1st Canadian Parachute Regiment, won a Victoria Cross near Wesel. Seventy-seven Royal Air Force "Mosquitoes" attacked targets in Germany.

1946 The German destroyer Z-34 was scuttled in the Skagerrak with a cargo of poison gas aboard.

1976 British Field Marshal Bernard Montgomery died at Isington Mill. He had commanded the British 8th Army in North Africa and the 21st Army Group in Northern Europe.

Eastern Europe

1944 The Soviets took Cherkov.

1945 The Soviets took Mor Veszprem and Kisber in Hungary and Soran in Czechoslovakia.

Mediterranean

1940 The French destroyer LA RAILLEUSE was sunk in an accidental mine explosion at Casablanca, twenty died.

1941 Deutsches Afrika Korps commander Erwin Rommel began his first offensive in North Africa, with the taking of El Agheila, Libya. The DAK suffered its first casualties when a tank ran over a mine near El Agheila.

1942 At 1117, the Royal Navy destroyer escort SOUTHARD hit a mine off Malta. She sank at 1800.

1943 The USAAF attacked Messina and Ferryville in Tunisia. The German minesweeper R-10, the ex-French destroyer L'AUDACIEUX and the Italian freighter CITTA DI SAVONA were sunk during the raid on Ferryville. At 0730, the Italian destroyer LANZERETTO MALOCELLO hit a mine north of Cap Bon and sank at 0845. At 1300, the Italian destroyer ASCARI was sunk off Cap Bon by three mines. 947 died aboard the two ships including 550 German troops who were aboard as passengers.

1944 A 15-man US Army commando unit was captured by the Germans in Italy (See March 22nd). The Germans executed 335 civilians near Rome in reprisal for a partisan attack which had killed 32 Germans. In 1995, one of the officers in charge would be extradited from Argentina and charged with the crime. The American 15th Air Force attacked rail targets in Italy.

1945 General Ira C. Eaker left his position as commander of the Middle East Air Force to become Deputy Commander of the USAAF.

Atlantic
1941 The Italian submarine VENIERO sank the British freighter AGNETE MAERSK (2,104 tons). The U97 sank the Norwegian freighter HORDA (4,301 tons). U97 survived until June 16, 1943.
1942 The U123 sank the British tanker EMPIRE STEEL (8,138 tons). U123 survived the war. The U655 was sunk by the Royal Navy sloop SHARPSHOOTER.
1944 The British submarine TERRAPIN torpedoed the German catapult ship SCHWABENLAND off Norway.

North America
1902 US politician Thomas Dewey was born in Owosso, Michigan. He became governor of New York in 1943. In 1944, he lost the presidential election to FDR. He tried again four years later against Truman and suffered the same result.
1919 The battleship IDAHO was commissioned. She was scrapped in 1947.
1921 The light cruiser MILWAUKEE was launched. She was scrapped in Wilmington, Delaware in 1949.
1936 The destroyer BALCH was launched. She was scrapped in 1946.
1942 Typewriters were rationed in America.
1943 The American Chiefs of Staff approved the plan to invade the island of Attu in the Aleutians.
1944 The destroyer HARRY E. HUBBARD was launched. She was scrapped in 1970.
1945 Japanese balloon-bombs were found near Woodson in Texas and Osceolo in Nebraska.
1958 USAF Lieutenant Colonel Jacob E. Manch died in a plane crash in Las Vegas, Nevada. He had flown as a co-pilot on the "Doolittle Raid".

Pacific
1892 Japanese Admiral Koso Abe was born. He commanded the garrisons in the Marshall Islands and was hanged in 1946 for war crimes.
1925 The IJN light cruiser NAKA was launched. She was sunk on February 17, 1944.
1928 The IJN heavy cruiser HAGURO was launched. She was sunk on May 16, 1945.
1942 Japanese aircraft began daily bombing of American positions on Corregidor. Port Moresby, New Guinea was bombed by Japanese aircraft.

The USN battleship CALIFORNIA was raised from the bottom of Pearl Harbor where she had rested since the December 7th attack.

1943 The USN submarine WAHOO sank the TEISHO MARU (9,849 tons). The American 11th Air Force attacked the island of Kiska in the Aleutians.

1944 The IJN submarine I-32 was sunk by the USN destroyer escort MANLOVE and PC-1135. The USN submarine BOWFIN sank the SHINKYO MARU (2,672 tons) and the BENGAL MARU (5,399 tons). Japanese forces attacked the American perimeter on Bougainville. The last major battle on the island of Los Negros in the Admiralties was fought when troops of the 5th and 12th Cavalry Regiments took several key hills from the Japanese.

1945 250 B29s attacked the Mitsubishi plant in Nagoya, Japan. Five battleships and eleven destroyers (commanded by Lee) bombarded Okinawa. The USN began minesweeping off the Kerama Group off Okinawa. The IJN torpedo boat TOMOZURU, two freighters and two minesweepers were sunk off Okinawa by Task Force 58.

China-Burma-India

1942 The American Volunteer Group attacked Chiang-Mai Airfield and lost two aircraft. One of those lost was flown by ace Jack Newkirk-10 victories.

1943 The American 10th Air Force attacked the Myitgne River Bridge in Burma.

1944 Orde Wingate, commander of the Chindits, was killed in a USAAF plane crash in Burma. All the victims were buried in a common grave in Arlington Cemetery in Washington D.C.

March 25th

Western Europe

1879 US production director William Knudsen was born in Copenhagen. At the age of twenty he moved to America. During WWI he was production manager at Ford. In 1919 he moved to General Motors and by 1937 he was president of the company. In 1940 he became head of the seven-member National Defense Commission. On January 7, 1941 he became director of the Office for Production Management. During the war he settled labor disputes and sped up production, mainly in the aircraft industry. He died in 1948.

1913 Luftwaffe ace Oberstleutnant Heinz Baer (220 victories) was born in Sommerfeld. He would fly more than 1,000 missions during the war and was shot down eighteen times. 124 of his 220 aerial victories were against western pilots. Of those, sixteen were scored while flying the Me262 jet fighter. He survived the war, but died in the crash of a private plane near Brunswick on April 28, 1957.

1939	The Royal Navy light cruiser PHOEBE was launched. She was scrapped in 1956.
1941	Five Royal Air Force "Blenheims" attacked shipping off Holland.
1942	Nine Royal Air Force "Bostons" attacked Le Trait, France. 254 Royal Air Force bombers attacked Essen, Germany and lost nine aircraft. Five people were killed in the raid. Thirty-eight Royal Air Force bombers dropped mines off Lorient, France and lost one "Hampden". Twenty-seven Royal Air Force bombers attacked St. Nazaire, France and lost one "Wellington".
1943	Twelve "Spitfires" from the USAAF's 4th Fighter Group flew patrols over the Channel.
1944	"The Great Escape" took place at Stalag Luft III. The last of seventy-six Allied officers to escape, slipped into the woods at 0455. Fifty of them would later be shot while "attempting to escape". American 9th Air Force B26s attacked Dutch railyards. 192 Royal Air Force bombers attacked Aulnoye, France. Six B17s from the USAAF's 422nd Bomb Squadron dropped 300 bundles of leaflets on Brussels, Antwerp, Charleroi, and Amsterdam.
1945	The US Army's III Corps began its break-out from the Remagen bridgehead. The American 3rd Army took Darmstadt, Germany. 243 American 8th Air Force B24s dropped 484 tons of bombs on oil plants and a tank factory in Germany and lost four aircraft. 275 Royal Air Force bombers attacked Hannover, Germany and lost one "Lancaster". 175 Royal Air Force bombers attacked Munster, Germany and lost three "Halifaxes". 156 Royal Air Force bombers attacked Osnabruck, Germany. The US Army's 87th and 89th Divisions crossed the Rhine north of Koblenz, Germany. The American 15th Air Force attacked targets around Prague, Czechoslovakia. 102 Royal Air Force "Spitfires" attacked railways in The Hague. The British took Wesel, Germany.

Eastern Europe

1941	Yugoslavia signed the Tripartite Pact with Germany.
1944	The Soviets took Proskurov, northwest of Vinnitsa.
1945	The Soviets took Heiligenbeil, East Prussia and Oliva in Poland. German General Lothar Rendulic (died in 1971) assumed command of Army Group "South". The German cruiser LEIPZIG began supporting the retreating Wehrmacht near Danzig.

Mediterranean

1937	An Italian-Yugoslavian treaty was signed.
1941	The Royal Navy submarine RORQUAL laid a minefield off Sicily which would sink two ships.

1947 The American freighter ST. LAWRENCE VICTORY was damaged off Dubrovnik, Yugoslavia by a mine. One of her crew died.

Atlantic
1940 The U47 sank the Danish freighter BRITTA (1,146 tons). U47 survived until March 7, 1941. The U57 sank the British tanker DAGHESTAN (5,742 tons). U57 was lost in a collision with the German freighter RONA on September 3rd.
1941 The German armed merchant cruiser KORMORAN took the Canadian freighter CANDOLITE (11,309 tons). The German armed merchant cruiser THOR took the British freighter BRITANIA and the Swedish coal ship TROLLENHOLM.
1942 The U552 sank the Dutch tanker OCANA (6,256 tons). U552 survived the war. U105 sank the British tanker NARRAGANSETT (10,389 tons). U105 survived until June 2, 1943.
1943 U518 sank the Swedish freighter INDUSTRIA (1,688 tons). U518 survived until April 22, 1945. U469 was sunk south of Iceland by Royal Air Force's No.206 Squadron.
1944 U976 was sunk in Bay of Biscay by Royal Air Force's No.248 Squadron.

North America
1940 Contracted American aircraft manufacturers were authorized to sell aircraft to countries fighting the Axis. The submarine TRITON was launched. She was lost on March 15, 1943.
1941 FDR authorized the repair of damaged British warships in American shipyards.
1942 Task Force 39 (the carrier WASP, one battleship, two heavy cruisers and eight destroyers left for Scapa Flow. The USN destroyer STEWART, which was missing in action in the Pacific, was stricken from the Navy's list of active ships. Her name was assigned to a new destroyer escort of the EDSALL class.
1943 The destroyer JOHNSTON was launched. She was lost on October 24, 1944.
1945 USMC Major General William Rupertus died. He had commanded the 1st Division at Cape Gloucester, New Britain and the island of Peleliu in the Palaus. A Japanese balloon-bomb was found near Farmington in Michigan.
1956 The IX-Prairie State (the ex-battleship ILLINOIS) was stricken.
1965 Admiral Calvin Durgan, commander of the carrier RANGER, Task Group 88.2 off Southern France and Carrier Division 29-Pacific, died.
1989 Russell Fisher received a Distinguished Flying Cross for actions while serving as a B17 crewman over Germany on March 25, 1945.

Pacific

1943 The USN submarine WAHOO sank the TAKAOSAN MARU (2,076 tons) and the SATSUKI MARU (830 tons). American aircraft attacked Nauru Island in the Gilberts. The American 11th Air Force attacked the island of Kiska in the Aleutians.

1944 The USN submarine POLLACK sank the IJN patrol craft Cha-54 off the island of Chichi Jima. Japanese resistance ended in the Admiralties.

1945 Lieutenant A. Chowne, of the Australian 2nd Infantry Battalion, won a posthumous Victoria Cross on New Guinea. Seventeen USN escort carriers (commanded by Durgan-See North America 1965) began attacking Kerama Retto, 15 miles west of Okinawa, and Okinawa itself. The US Army's 1st Cavalry Division took Los Banos, Luzon. 223 USAAF B29s dropped 1,508 tons of bombs on Nagoya, Japan. The USN submarine TIRANTE sank the FUJI MARU (703 tons).

1961 Royal Australian Air Force ace Sub/Lieutenant A. Goldsmith (16 victories) died. Elvis Presley gave a benefit concert for the ARIZONA Memorial. The event raised over $64,000.

China-Burma-India

1938 The battle of Taiechuang, China began. 16,000 Japanese and 15,000 Chinese would die during the action.

1942 The Japanese took Kyangin and Kyungon in Burma.

1945 The Japanese took the USAAF base at Laohokow, China. The first B29 built in Omaha, Nebraska, "Satan's Angel", was lost in a collision over the Bay of Bengal.

March 26th

Western Europe

1908 Nazi war criminal Franz Stangl was born in Altmuenster, Austria. He commanded the extermination camps at Sobibor and Treblinka. He was arrested in Brazil on February 28, 1967 and extradited back to Europe. He was sentenced to life imprisonment on October 22, 1970, but died on June 28, 1971 of a heart attack.

1922 Luftwaffe ace Hans Strelow (63 victories) was born in Berlin. He died on December 14, 1942.

1927 The German light cruiser KONIGSBERG was launched. She was sunk on January 10, 1940 in Norway and was later salvaged.

1940 Royal New Zealand Air Force "Hurricane" pilot Edgar J. Kain became the first Royal Air Force ace of WWII when he shot down multiple Luftwaffe

Me109Es over France. The Royal Navy carrier INDOMITABLE was launched. She was scrapped in 1955.

1941 Eighteen Royal Air Force "Blenheims" attacked shipping off Holland.

1942 Twenty-four Royal Air Force "Bostons" attacked Le Havre, France and lost one aircraft. At 1500, a Royal Navy force carrying British Commandoes for an attack on St. Nazaire, France left Falmouth Bay in Cornwall. 104 Royal Air Force bombers attacked Essen, Germany and lost eleven aircraft. Six people were killed in the raid. Two "Blenheims" and two "Hampdens" were lost on other operations.

1943 455 Royal Air Force bombers attacked Duisburg, Germany and lost six aircraft. Eleven people were killed in the raid. Eight "Spitfires" from the USAAF's 4th Fighter Group flew patrols over the Channel.

1944 A group of 465 French Maquis was attacked on the Glieres Plateau in the French Alps by a force of 12,000 Vichy and German troops. The Maquis group lost more than half its strength in what was the first major battle between the Maquis and German troops. Axis losses were not known, but were believed to be more than 850. 500 American 8th Air Force bombers dropped 1,271 tons of bombs on V-1 launching sites near Cherbourg and Pas de Calais in France and lost four B17s and one B24. 338 American 9th Air Force B26s attacked Ijmuiden, Holland and lost one aircraft. 266 8th Air Force P47s provided support for the bombers and claimed one victory for the loss of one aircraft. 240 American 9th Air Force fighters attacked railyards and "Crossbow" (V-1 rocket) targets in France. 705 Royal Air Force bombers attacked Essen, Germany and lost nine aircraft. 599 people were killed in the raid. 109 Royal Air Force bombers attacked Courtrai, France. 252 French civilians died in the raid. Six B17s from the USAAF's 422nd Bomb Squadron dropped 300 bundles of leaflets on Caen, Rennes, Amiens, Paris and Rouen in France.

1945 The Rhein-Main Airport near Frankfurt was taken by American forces. The American 7th Army crossed the Rhine between Worms and Mannheim in Germany. The American 1st Army captured a bridge over the Lahn River at Limburg in Germany, but got only four tanks across before the Germans blew it up. "Task Force Baum" left Aschaffenburg in its attempt to rescue American prisoners of war at a camp near Hammelburg. It would be ambushed by the Germans and all but destroyed. 330 American 8th Air Force bombers dropped 892 tons of bombs on airfields and oil targets. 450 8th Air Force fighters provided support for the bombers. British statesman and former Prime Minister David Lloyd-George died. The Royal Navy corvette PUFFIN was a constructive loss after ramming a German midget submarine in the Scheldt. Eighty-six Royal Air Force "Mosquitoes" attacked Berlin.

1948   The Royal Navy battleship RODNEY was scrapped.
1994   RAF Sergeant Norman Jackson died at the age of 74. He had been awarded the Victoria Cross while serving as a crewman aboard a "Lancaster" bomber on a mission over Schweinfurt, Germany on April 26, 1944. He was one of 10 "Lancaster" crewmen to be awarded the medal during the war.
2011   Royal Navy Rear-Admiral Godfrey Place died at the age of 73. He had been awarded the Victoria Cross while serving as the commander of a midget submarine during an attack on the German battleship Tirpitz in a Norwegian fjord on September 21, 1943.

Eastern Europe
1926   The Rumanian-Polish alliance was signed.
1942   The Soviets counter-attacked in the Crimea.
1944   The Soviets reached the Prut River in the Ukraine.
1945   The Soviets took Devecser and Papa in Hungary. The German transports BILLE (665 tons) and WESER (999 tons) were sunk by Soviet aircraft in the Baltic.

Mediterranean
1941   The British occupied Hara in East Africa. The Royal Navy heavy cruiser YORK and the Norwegian tanker PERICLES (8,324 tons) were crippled by six Italian MTBs and was beached in Suda Bay, Crete. The YORK was scrapped in 1952.
1942   The Royal Navy destroyer LEGION and the submarine P-39 were sunk at Malta by aircraft. At 0445, the U652 sank the Royal Navy destroyer JAGUAR, 53 of her crew survived, and the British tanker SLAVOL (2,623 tons).
1943   The U431 sank the British freighter CITY OF PERTH (6,415 tons). The U755 sank the French freighter SERGEANT GOUARNE (1,147 tons).
1944   A 15-man US Army commando unit was executed by order of General Anton Dostler, commander of the LXXV Corps, (See March 22 and 24, 1944 and October 12, 1945). The American 15th Air Force attacked rail, aircraft and shipping targets in Italy.
1995   A 53-gallon drum of Nazi aviation fuel was found floating off the coast of Israel. It was stamped Wehrmacht-1942. Israeli officials theorized that it had originated in Italy.

Atlantic
1940   The U38 sank the Norwegian freighter COMETA (3,794 tons). U38 survived the war.

1942   The American tanker DIXIE ARROW (8,046 tons-11 dead) was sunk by the U71. U71 survived the war.

1943   The American freighter LILLIAN LUCKENBACH was rammed and sunk by the American freighter CAPE HENLOPEN.

1945   The U399 sank the Dutch freighter PACIFIC (362 tons). U399 was then sunk in the English Channel by the Royal Navy frigate DUCKWORTH.

North America

1940   The destroyer MAYO was launched. She was stricken in 1970.

1942   The "Doolittles Raiders" B25s arrived at McClellan Field near Sacramento, California.

1943   The first woman to win an Air Medal was 2nd Lieutenant Elsie Ott for a med-evac flight from India to Washington D.C.

1944   The destroyers AULT, WALDRON and PUTNAM were launched. AULT was stricken in 1973, WALDRON was sold to COLOMBIA the same year and PUTNAM was stricken in 1973.

1993   US Army Colonel Jerry Sage, age 75, died in Dothan, Alabama of cancer. He had been the prisoner of war that Steve McQueen had portrayed in the movie "The Great Escape". The USN destroyer tender PRAIRIE was decommissioned. She had been commissioned December 9, 1939.

Pacific

1942   The Japanese 1st Carrier Fleet (commanded by Nagumo) departed from Staring Bay in Southern Celebes. They were en route to attacking British installations on Ceylon. It consisted of five carriers, four battleships, three cruisers and nine destroyers. The USN carrier LEXINGTON arrived at Pearl Harbor from a cruise that lasted fifty-four days in the South Pacific. While there, she had her 8"gun turrets removed.

1943   The "Battle of the Komandorski Islands" took place in the Aleutians. The USN ships involved were the heavy cruiser SALT LAKE CITY, the light cruiser RICHMOND, and the destroyers BAILEY, COGHLAN, MONAGHAN and DALE. The IJN ships involved were the heavy cruisers NACHI and MAYA, the light cruisers TAMA and ABUKUMA and the destroyers INAZUMI, IKAZUCHI, USUGUMO, WAKABA and HATSUSHIMO. At 0840, NACHI was hit by a shell from RICHMOND. By 0900, NACHI had been hit several more times. At 0930, the IJN squadron began concentrating its fire on the SALT LAKE CITY. At 1010, the SALT LAKE CITY was seriously damaged. The USN destroyers drove the Japanese off when they attempted to finish her, thus effectively ending the battle. USN PBYs and 13th Air Force B24s attacked Nauru Island in the South Pacific.

1944   The USN submarine TULLIBEE was sunk by circular run of one of its own torpedoes. There was only one survivor, a gunner's mate who had been on the bridge.

1945   The USN submarine BALAO sank the SHINTO MARU No.1 (884 tons). 14,000 men of the US Army's Americal Division (commanded by Arnold) landed south of Cebu City in the Philippines. 280 Japanese troops mounted the last "Banzai" charge on Iwo Jima killing 75 and wounding 119 American troops. All but eighteen of the Japanese were killed. USMC 1st Lieutenant Harry Martin won a posthumous Medal of Honor on Iwo Jima. It was the last of twenty-seven that were awarded during the invasion of the island. The US Army's 77th Division landed on Kerama Retto. USN Task Force 54 (commanded by Deyo) began the primary bombardment of Okinawa. The USN destroyer HALLIGAN was sunk off Okinawa by a mine, 162 of her crew died. Her hulk would rest on a reef in the area until 1958 when she was donated to the government of the Ryukyu Islands as scrap. The USN battleship NEVADA and the destroyer KIMBERLEY (four of her crew died) were hit by kamikazes off Okinawa. Sixty Royal Navy F4Us and F6Fs and twenty-four TBMs attacked airfields on Miyako Island. The Royal Navy's Task Force 57 (commanded by Rawlings) attacked Sakashima Gunto.

China-Burma-India
1942   The Japanese attacked Toungoo, Burma.
1944   The IJN submarine I-8 sank the Dutch freighter TJISALAK (5,787 tons). Ninety-eight members of the crew were murdered after the attack.

March 27th

Western Europe
1940   The Royal Navy light cruiser CLEOPATRA was launched. She was scrapped in 1958.
1941   Ten Royal Air Force "Blenheims" attacked shipping off Holland. Thirty-nine Royal Air Force bombers attacked Koln, Germany and lost one "Wellington". Thirty-nine Royal Air Force bombers attacked Dusseldorf, Germany and lost one "Manchester" and one "Whitley".
1942   Twelve Royal Air Force "Bostons" attacked Ostend, Belgium. Sixty-two Royal Air Force bombers attacked St. Nazaire, France in support of the Commando raid that was scheduled to begin the next morning and lost one "Whitley". Four Royal Air Force bombers were lost on other operations. The German minesweeper SPERRBRECHER-147 was sunk by a mine off the Hook of Holland.
1943   At 1645, the Royal Navy escort carrier DASHER was sunk on the River Clyde by an accidental fire and explosion. There were 149 survivors. Royal Navy Admiral Sir Henry Harwood, the victor at the "Battle of the River

Plate", retired for health reasons. 396 Royal Air Force bombers attacked Berlin and lost nine aircraft. Most of the bombs fell up to seventeen miles from the target area. 102 people were killed in the raid.

1944 701 American 8th Air Force bombers dropped 1,852 tons of bombs on French airfields and lost three B24s and three B17s. 960 8th Air Force fighters provided support for the bombers and claimed thirty-eight victories for the loss of two P38s, five P47s and three P51s. USAAF 56th (P47) Fighter Group ace Gerald Johnson (18 victories) was shot down over France but survived. 56th Fighter Group ace Walter Mahurin (20 victories in European Theater of Operations as well as a Japanese "Dinah" in the Pacific Theater of Operation and 3.5 North Korean "Migs" during the Korean War) was shot down by a Luftwaffe Do217 gunner. He avoided capture and returned to Britain on May 7th and was then sent to the Pacific Theater Operations. US Army nurse Reba Tobiason was captured when the American 9th Air Force B26 she was riding in was shot down near Aachen, Germany. Seventeen Royal Air Force "Mosquitoes" attacked targets in Germany.

1945 Eighty-three Royal Air Force "Spitfires" attacked Hague area railways. 276 Royal Air Force bombers attacked Paderborn, Germany. They were escorted by thirty-seven P47s and seventy-eight P51s from the American 8th Air Force. 150 Royal Air Force bombers attacked Hamm, Germany. 115 Royal Air Force bombers attacked Farge, Germany. The American 3rd Army took Hanau, Germany. A German V-2 rocket hit Stepney in east London killing 130. The 1,115th and last V-2 to hit Britain impacted at Kynaston Road in Ordington, Kent. V-2s had killed 2,700 people and wounded 6,500. An additional 2,050 V-2s had been fired at Antwerp, Brussels and Liege in Belgium. Ninety-nine Royal Air Force "Mosquitoes" attacked targets in Germany and lost four aircraft.

Eastern Europe

1941 A coup in Yugoslavia, led by General Simovic, instigated a German invasion on April 6th.

1942 The German minesweepers M-5607 and M-5608 were sunk by mines.

1943 The Germans shot 140 Poles in retaliation for "Operation Mexico", in which Polish Resistance rescued one of its members from the Gestapo in Warsaw.

1944 German troops began moving into Rumania after a request from the Rumanian government. The Soviets took Kaments-Podolsky.

1945 Sixteen Anti-Soviet Polish leaders arrived in Moscow and were arrested. The Soviets entered Danzig. The hulk of the German battlecruiser GNEISENAU was scuttled as a block ship at Gotenhafen.

Mediterranean

1941 At 1300, a Royal Air Force "Sunderland" patrol bomber sighted the Italian heavy cruisers TRIESTE, TRENTO and BOLGANO. With this indication that the Italian fleet was at sea, the British began to sortie their own fleet. At 1900, Royal Navy Admiral Sir Andrew Cunningham left Alexandria with the carrier FORMIDABLE, the battleships VALIANT, BARHAM and WARSPITE and nine destroyers. Royal Navy Admiral Henry Pridham-Whippell with the cruisers ORION, AJAX, PERTH and GLOUCESTER and the destroyers ILEX, HASTY, HEREWARD and VENDETTA, prepared to sail from Piraeus. These actions will lead to the "Battle of Cape Matapan" the next day.

1943 The U593 sank the British freighter CITY OF GUILDFORD (5,157 tons).

1944 Royal Navy MTBs and USN PTs sank six vessels in a German convoy off Vado, Italy. The German corvette Uj-205 (the ex-Italian COLUBRINA) was sunk at Venice by the USAAF.

Atlantic

1941 The U98 sank the British freighter KORANTON (6,695 tons). U98 survived until November 19, 1942. The German armed merchant cruiser KORMORAN rendezvoused with the U105 and U106 and the supply ship NORDMARK.

1942 The USN Q-ship ATIK was sunk by the U123. Her entire crew of 141 died. U123 survived the war. The freighter BATEAU was sunk off North Cape by the German destroyer Z-28, which was then sunk by the Royal Navy light cruiser TRINIDAD. The U160 sank the Panamanian freighter EQUIPOISE (6,210 tons). U160 survived until July 14, 1943. The U105 sank the Norwegian tanker SVENOR (7,616 tons). U105 survived until June 2, 1943. The U587 was sunk by the Royal Navy destroyers GROVE, LEAMINGTON, ALDENHAM and VOLUNTEER. USN Admiral John W. Wilcox, commander of Task Force 59, fell off the battleship WASHINGTON and was lost while en route to Scapa Flow.

1945 The U722 was sunk by the Royal Navy frigates FITZROY, REDMILL, and BYRON. The U965 was sunk by the Royal Navy frigate CONN north of Scotland.

North America

1940 The submarine TAUTOG was launched. She was scrapped in 1960.

1970 The destroyer EATON was expended as a target.

South America

1945 Argentina declared war on the Axis.

Pacific

1933   Japan quit the League of Nations.

1941   IJN Ensign Takeo Yoshikawa arrived in Honolulu to assume his duties as a naval clerk and spy with the Japanese embassy there.

1942   The USN submarine GUDGEON sank the NISSHO MARU (6,526 tons). Royal Navy Admiral Sir James Somerville assumed command of the Royal Navy's Far East Fleet, which consisted of three carriers, five battleships, seven cruisers, and fourteen destroyers. He would die in 1949.

1944   The USN submarine RASHER sank the NICHINAN MARU (2,732 tons). The USN submarine HAKE sank the YAMAMIZU MARU (5,154 tons). USN PTs 121 and 353 were sunk in error by the Royal Australian Air Force in Bangula Bay, New Britain. The Japanese began retreating on Bougainville.

1945   105 aircraft of the USAAF's 313th Bomb Wing flew the first B29 mining mission, when they dropped 1,000 1-ton mines in the Shimonoseki Strait on the Inland Sea. They would eventually plant 12,000 that would sink 500,000 tons of shipping. The USN battleships NEVADA and TENNESSEE, the light cruiser BILOXI, the destroyers PORTERFIELD (one of her crew was wounded), O'BRIEN (fifty of her crew died), MURRAY (one died) the destroyer escort FOREMAN (one of her crew was wounded), the minesweepers DORSEY and SOUTHARD, the minelayers SKIRMISH and SMITH, the destroyer-transport GILMER and the transport KNUDSON were hit by Japanese kamikazes. The USN battlecruiser ALASKA bombarded Minami Daito Jima. American forces landed on Fort Hughes in Manila Bay. American forces took Cebu City on Cebu. The IJN minesweeper Ma-1 was sunk by a mine.

China-Burma-India

1944   The U510 sank the Norwegian whaler MAALOY (249 tons). The U532 sank the British freighter TULAGI (2,281 tons). Major General W. Lentaigne succeeded Wingate as commander of the "Chindits" (See March 25th). The Japanese Air Force attacked the American 10th Air Force bases near Ledo.

1945   Royal Air Force B24s attacked Bangkok.

March 28th

Western Europe

1933   The Nazi Party organized a boycott against Jewish businesses in Germany.

1939   The Spanish Civil War ended. The Loyalist government fled the country. The war had caused 745,000 fatalities among the Spanish population.

THE MONTH OF MARCH

1940   A "No separate peace" agreement was signed by France and Britain. The Allies decided to mine Norwegian territorial waters. They neglected to inform the Norwegian government of their decision. The German tanker ALTMARK arrived in Kiel, Germany (See February 16th).

1941   The heavy cruiser HIPPER returned to Germany from a raid in the Atlantic.

1942   The British Commando raid on St. Nazaire, France ("Operation Chariot") took place. The objective of the raid was to disable the "Normandie" drydock which was the only one of its type that could handle German capital ships. At 0030, the ships carrying the Commandoes entered the Loire estuary. At 0134, the destroyer CAMPBELLTOWN rammed the drydock. At 1130, the CAMPBELLTOWN exploded destroying the drydock and killing 380 Germans who were on or near the ship. Of the 611 British commandoes and sailors involved, 397 were lost. The following personnel won Victoria Crosses, Royal Navy Lieutenant Commander S. Beattie, Royal Navy Able Seaman W. Savage (posthumous), Royal Navy Commander R. Ryder, Lieutenant Colonel A. Newman-2nd Commando and Sergeant T. Durrant-1st Commando. The first train-load of Paris Jews was sent to the German extermination camp at Auschwitz. The Vatican established diplomatic relations with Japan. 234 Royal Air Force bombers attacked Lubeck, Germany and lost twelve aircraft. It was the first major success for the Royal Air Force's Bomber Command. 190 acres of the city were destroyed and 320 people were killed.

1943   Twenty-four Royal Air Force "Venturas" attacked Rotterdam, Holland. Six Royal Air Force "Mosquitoes" attacked Liege, Belgium and lost two aircraft. Seventy American 8th Air Force B17s dropped 209 tons of bombs on the marshalling yards at Rouen/Sotteville in France and lost one aircraft. Royal Australian Air Force ace Sub/Lieutenant K. Truscott (17 victories) was killed in an aircraft accident. 323 Royal Air Force bombers attacked St.Nazaire, France and lost two aircraft.

1944   364 American 8th Air Force B17s dropped 936 tons of bombs on airfields in France and lost two aircraft. 453 8th Air Force fighters provided support for the bombers and claimed thirty victories for the loss of three P51s.

1945   General Heinz Guderian was replaced by General Hans Kreb as Chief of the German General Staff. Technical/Sergeant Clinton Hedrick, of the 17th Airborne Division, won a posthumous Medal of Honor near Lembeck, Germany. US Army Lieutenant David Waybur was killed in action in Germany. He had won a Medal of Honor on Sicily. The US Army's III Corps took Marburg, Germany. The American 3rd Army took Wiesbaden, Germany. 891 American 8th Air Force bombers dropped 2,520 tons of bombs on German tank and armament factories and lost two B17s. 345

8th Air Force fighters provided support for the bombers. The last German V-2 rocket that was fired during the war landed in Belgium.

Eastern Europe

1944 The Soviets took Nikolaev east of Odessa. The German 1st Panzer Army was surrounded.

1945 The Soviets took Gydnia, Poland.

Mediterranean

1940 The Royal Navy submarine UTMOST sank the German freighter HERAKLIA and damaged the freighter RUHR.

1941 The "Battle of Cape Matapan" began. The Italian fleet met a Royal Navy force under Admiral Pridham-Whippell off Gaudo, an island south of Crete. The major portion of the Royal Navy fleet would soon join the action. At 1505, the Italian battleship VITTORIO VENETO was hit by an aerial torpedo. At 1630, the battleship again got under way. The action then shifted to Cape Matapan on the southern tip of the Peloponnesus. At 1930, the Italian cruiser POLA was damaged by an aircraft torpedo. She was scuttled the next day by the Royal Navy destroyers JERVIS and NUBIAN. The Italian heavy cruisers ZARA, FIUME and the destroyers VITTORIO ALFIERI, GIOBERTI, GIOSU CARDUCCI and ORIANI were sent to escort her. At 1033, the Royal Navy battleships VALIANT, BARHAM and WARSPITE began shelling the group. At 2230, the ZARA was damaged by the Royal Navy battleships. She was scuttled at 0200 the next morning. At 2230, the FIUME was sunk by the Royal Navy battleships. The destroyers ALFIERI and CARDUCCI were sunk by the Royal Navy destroyers STUART, GREYHOUND, GRIFFEN and HAVOC. 2,400 Italian sailors died during the battle. The Italian torpedo boat GENERALE ANTONIO CHINOTTO was sunk off Palermo by a mine laid by Royal Navy submarine RORQUAL. The Royal Navy submarine UTMOST sank one ship of 1,927 tons and damaged another of 5,954 tons.

1942 "Bread Riots" took place in Venice, Italy. The riots were incited by Italian women protesting food shortages.

1943 The British transport BRECONSHIRE was sunk during an air-raid on Malta. The U81 sank the Egyptian freighter ROUSHDY (133 tons). The U77 was sunk off Cartagena by the Royal Air Force's Nos.40 and 233 Squadrons.

1944 The American 15th Air Force flew its first 1,000-ton raid in Italy. The Allies conceded a "temporary failure" at Anzio. The Royal Navy submarine SURTIS was sunk by a mine. The American 15th Air Force attacked rail targets in Italy.

The Month of March

Atlantic

1940 The German freighter MIMI HORN was scuttled in the Denmark Strait to prevent her capture by the Royal Navy armed merchant cruiser TRANSYLVANIA.

1942 Luftwaffe Ju88s, based in Norway, sank the freighters RACELAND and EMPIRE RANGER.

1943 The U167 sank the Belgian freighter MOANDA (4,621 tons). U167 survived until April 5th. The U159 sank the British freighter LAGOSIAN (5,449 tons). U159 survived until July 15, 1943. The Italian submarine FINZI sank the Greek freighter GRANICOS (3,689 tons).

1945 The U532 sank the American tanker OKLAHOMA (9,298 tons-50 dead). U532 survived the war.

North America

1890 Major General Davenport Johnson, commander of the 11th Air Force, was born in Tyler, Texas. He died on October 21, 1963 in Denver.

1935 The first flight of the Consolidated PBY "Catalina" patrol plane took place.

1940 MacKenzie King's Liberal government was returned to power in Canada. The American Under Secretary of State Sumner Welles returned from his fact-finding trip to Europe.

1943 The destroyers BLACK and CHAUNCEY were launched. BLACK was stricken in 1969 and CHAUNCEY was stricken in 1972.

1944 The destroyer PAUL HAMILTON accidentally fired 6 5" shells during training exercises in Chesapeake Bay which impacted near civilian areas. The escort carrier SITKOH BAY was commissioned. She was scrapped in 1961. The submarines SEA DOG and SEA FOX were launched. SEA DOG was stricken in 1968 and SEA FOX was sold to Turkey in 1970.

1945 Japanese balloon-bombs were found near Strathmore, Alberta and Whitewater, British Columbia; another was shot down south of the Imperial Valley in California.

1946 The destroyer NEWCOMB was stricken.

1969 Dwight Eisenhower died in Washington D.C. He had commanded the Allied forces in the Mediterranean and in Europe. He was later elected as President of the United States.

1972 Admiral Louis Denfield, commander of BatDiv-9 in the Pacific, died in Westboro, Massachusetts.

1989 Joseph Eckert, age 65, was deported to Austria for concealing his past as a guard at the extermination camp at Auschwitz.

Pacific

1914 The IJN battleship FUSO was launched. She was sunk on October 25, 1944.

1943   The Japanese Air Force attacked Oro Bay, New Guinea. The US Army freighter MASAYA (2 dead) was sunk by the Japanese Air Force.
1944   The USN submarine SILVERSIDES sank the IJN LST No.3 (948 tons). The USN submarine BARB sank the FUKUSEI MARU (2,219 tons). The Royal Navy submarine TRUCULENT sank the YASUSHIMA MARU (1,910 tons). B24s of the 30th Bomb Group, American 7th Air Force flying from their base on Kwajalein attacked the IJN anchorage at Truk.
1945   The USN minesweeper SKYLARK was sunk off Okinawa by a mine. The IJN escort No.33 was sunk by USN carriers. The IJN minesweeper W-11 was sunk off Macassar, Celebes by the USAAF. The USN submarine TIRANTE sank the NASE MARU (1,218 tons). The USN submarine THREADFIN sank the IJN escort MIKURA (940 tons).

March 29th

Western Europe
1932   Eamon de Valera was elected as Ireland's Prime Minister. He would serve in that capacity throughout the war.
1939   Serious talks between the French and British military staffs began. They concerned future co-operation against expected hostile action by Germany's military forces. The British government authorized the increase of the Regular Army to thirty-two divisions and to double the size of the Territorial Army.
1940   Royal Air Force "Hurricanes" of No.1 Squadron attacked nine Luftwaffe Me110s near the Franco-German border and shot down one of them. It was the first time that one of Goering's "Destroyers" had been lost in combat with the Royal Air Force.
1941   Twenty-five Royal Air Force bombers dropped mines off Brest, France and lost one "Hampden".
1942   As a result of the previous night's raid on the historic city of Lubeck by the Royal Air Force, Hitler ordered reprisal raids on historic cities in Britain. These would be called the "Baedeker Raids" after the famous tour books. Twenty-six Royal Air Force bombers dropped mines off Denmark and lost two "Manchesters".
1943   Sixty-one Royal Air Force "Ventura" bombers attacked targets in Holland and France. 329 Royal Air Force bombers attacked Berlin and lost twenty-one aircraft. 148 buildings were destroyed and 148 people were killed in the raid. 157 Royal Air Force bombers attacked Bochum, Germany and lost twelve "Wellingtons". Eighteen "Spitfires" from the USAAF's 4th Fighter Group flew patrols over the Channel.

THE MONTH OF MARCH

1944   233 American 8th Air Force B17s dropped 475 tons of bombs on Stedorf, Unterluss and Brunswick in Germany and lost nine aircraft. 428 8th Air Force fighters provided support for the bombers and claimed fifty-seven victories for the loss of two P38s, one P47 and nine P51s. Luftwaffe ace Detler Rohwer (38 victories) was killed in action by USAAF P38s. USAAF 56th Fighter Group ace Stan Morrill (10 victories) was killed in an explosion at his base at Halesworth. Thirty American 8th Air Force B24s dropped 115 tons of bombs on V-1 rocket sites near Watten, France. Two American 8th Air Force B24s collided during assembly over Henham and killed eighteen of the twenty crewmen. A further nineteen were killed on the ground by munitions explosions during rescue attempts. Thirty-seven 8th Air Force P47s provided support for the bombers. Eighteen of the Allied officers, who had escaped from Stalag Luft III at Sagan on March 24th, were shot at various sites around Germany. Eighty-four Royal Air Force bombers attacked Vaires, France and lost one "Halifax". Nineteen Royal Air Force "Lancasters" attacked Lyons, France. Fifty-two Royal Air Force "Mosquitoes" attacked targets in Germany.

1945   Frankfurt, Germany was secured by the US Army's 5th Division. The American 1st and 3rd Armies linked up at Wiesbaden, Germany. Soviet forces entered Austria. The American 3rd Army took Bad Nauheim, Germany. Staff Sergeant Robert Dietz, of the 7th Armored Division, won a posthumous Medal of Honor at Kerchain, Germany. 130 Royal Air Force bombers attacked Salzgitter. The last German V-1 rocket to hit Britain impacted in Datchworth, Kent. The Royal Canadian Navy frigate TEME was a constructive loss after an attack by the U246 off Lands End, four of her crew died. The American actor James Stewart was promoted to the rank of Colonel in the USAAF. Sixty-one Royal Air Force "Mosquitoes" attacked targets in Germany.

Eastern Europe
1940   Russia declared its neutrality in the European war.
1944   The Royal Air Force attacked the German 2nd Panzer Corps, which was en route from the Eastern Front to the Western. Soviet forces took Kolomya, Rumania.

Mediterranean
1941   The British took Diredawa in East Africa.
1942   The Royal Navy carrier EAGLE launched seven "Spitfires" for Malta in "Operation Picket II". The Luftwaffe attacked Tobruk. "Bread Riots" took place in Matera, Italy.
1943   The British took Gabes and El Hamma in Tunisia.

1944 The American 15th Air Force attacked Bolzano, Italy. The USAAF's 449th Bomb Group B24H "Sunshine" landed in error at Venegono Airfield in Italy and was captured.

Atlantic

1941 The U48 sank the British freighters GERMANIC (5,352 tons), HYLTON (5,197 tons) and EASTLEA (4,267 tons), the Belgian freighter LINBOURG (2,483 tons). U48 survived the war. The U46 sank the Swedish freighter LIGURIA (1,751 tons). U46 survived the war.

1942 The U585 was sunk by the Royal Navy destroyer FURY. At 0920, the German destroyer Z-26 was sunk by the Royal Navy light cruiser TRINIDAD and the destroyers FURY and ECLIPSE. The TRINIDAD was damaged by one of her own torpedoes during the action, but survived. The Italian submarine CALVI sank the British freighter TREDINNICK (4,589 tons). The U571 sank the British freighter HERTFORD (10,923 tons). U571 survived until January 28, 1944. The U160 sank the American transport CITY OF NEW YORK (8,272 tons-26 dead). U160 survived until July 14, 1943.

1943 The U172 sank the British freighter SILVERBEACH (5,319 tons). U172 survived until December 13th. The U404 sank the British freighter NAGARA (8,791 tons). U404 survived until July 28th. The U662 sank the British freighters EMPIRE WHALE (6,159 tons) and UMARIA (6,852 tons). U662 survived until July 21st. The American freighter WILLIAM PIERCE FRYE (7,176 tons-57 dead) was sunk by the U610. U610 survived until October 8th.

1944 The U961 was sunk off Iceland by the Royal Navy sloop STARLING. "Seafires" from the Royal Navy escort carrier STRIKER, shot down a USAAF C-54, killing six.

1945 The U246 was sunk in the English Channel by the Royal Navy frigate DUCKWORTH. The U1106 was sunk north of the Faeroes by the Royal Air Force's No.224 Squadron.

North America

1943 The American tanker ESSO MANHATTAN broke in half after hitting a mine in the approaches to New York Harbor. The harbor was closed for 24 hours while the entrance was swept. The ship was later welded back together.

1945 Japanese balloon-bombs were found near Nyssa in Oregon and Pyramid Lake in Nevada.

1946 The destroyer CLARK was sold for scrap.

1957 USAF Colonel Charles Ross Greening died at Bethesda, Maryland. He had been a pilot on the "Doolittle Raid".

1975   The destroyer LAFFEY was stricken.
1994   Ex-Nazi Peter Mueller, age 70, left America for Germany. He had been facing charges that he had concealed his past as a concentration guard.
2015   USAF Lieutenant Colonel Rbert Hite died at the age of 95 in Nashville, Tennessee. He had been a pilot on the "Doolittle Raid" of April 1942. He was captured and spent 40 months in captivity, most of it in solitary confinement.

Pacific
1938   The IJN battleship MUSASHI's keel was laid at Nagasaki.
1942   The Japanese landed on Christmas Island, south of Java.
1943   The USN submarine GUDGEON sank the TOHO MARU (9,987 tons). The USN submarine WAHOO sank the YAMABATO MARU (2,556 tons). The USN submarine GATO landed twelve Australian commandos on Bougainville to assist the Coastwatchers Jack Read and Paul Mason who had been on the island since before the war began. When GATO left the area, she had aboard fifty-one refugees. American 5th Air Force ace Lieutenant Richard Bong shot down a Japanese "Doris" over the Bismarck Sea. The USAAF 11th Air Force attacked the Japanese-held island of Kiska in the Aleutians.
1944   In the first day-light raid of its type twenty-four American 13th Air Force B24s flying from Bougainville attacked Japanese-held Truk and lost two bombers. The American 7th Air Force attacked Truk in a night-raid. The IJN battleship YAMATO was damaged by the USN submarine TUNNY.
1945   The US Army's 40th Division landed on the island of Negros in the Philippines. The USN submarine BLUEGILL sank the HONAN MARU (5,542 tons).

China-Burma-India
1942   The commander of the British Far Eastern Fleet (Somerville) received information that Japanese forces were going to attack Ceylon. He split his forces into two groups. A "Fast Group" consisting of the carriers INDOMITABLE and FORMIDABLE, the battleship WARSPITE, the cruisers CORNWALL, DORSETSHIRE, EMERALD and ENTERPRISE and six destroyers and a "Slow Group" made up of the carrier HERMES, the battleships RESOLUTION, RAMILLIES, ROYAL SOVEREIGN and REVENGE, the cruisers CALEDON, DRAGON, and JACOB VAN HEEMSKERCK (Dutch) and eight destroyers. Both units were to cruise south of Ceylon. The Japanese fleet was not located until the 4th of April by which time these arrangements had been discarded. Japanese forces took Lashio, Burma. Britain announced dominion status for India, effective

after the war. General Clair Chennault was informed by General Joseph Stilwell and Clayton Bissel that the American Volunteer Group (the "Flying Tigers") would be inducted into the USAAF.
1944 Japanese forces cut the road between Imphal and Kohima isolating the British units in Imphal. The American freighter RICHARD HOVEY (7,176 tons-4 dead) was sunk in the Indian Ocean by the IJN submarine I-26.
1945 American 20th Air Force B29s flew their last mission from India before moving to the Marianas. Royal Air Force B24s attacked Rangoon.

March 30th

Western Europe
1892 Future Luftwaffe Field Marshal Erhard Milch was born.
1926 The Royal Navy heavy cruiser BERWICK was launched. She was scrapped in 1948.
1939 A Luftwaffe He100 raised the world speed record to 463.92 mph.
1941 The German pocket battleship SCHEER arrived in Bergen, Norway after a cruise of 5-months during which she scored 21 victories. Royal Air Force bombers attacked the German battlecruisers SCHARNHORST and GNEISENAU in Brest, France. British civilian casualties in German air raids totaled 28,859 dead and 40,166 wounded so far in the war. 109 Royal Air Force bombers attacked Brest, France. Hitler ordered that during the invasion of Russia all Commissars and Communist officials were to be executed.
1942 Thirty-four Royal Air Force "Halifaxes" attacked the German battleship TIRPITZ near Trondheim, Norway and lost one aircraft.
1943 Ten Royal Air Force "Mosquitoes" attacked Eindhoven, Holland. Twenty-eight USAAF 4th Fighter Group "Spitfires" flew patrols over the Channel.
1944 Seventy-four American 8th Air Force P47s attacked the Soesterburg and Eindhoven airfields in Holland. Twenty-two American 8th Air Force P47s strafed the Venlo, Twente/Enschede and Deleen airfields in Holland and lost one aircraft. USAAF Colonel James Stewart was transferred from the 445th Bombardment Group to the 453rd Bombardment Group, where he became Operations Officer. Three Allied officers, who had escaped from Stalag Luft III at Sagan on the 24th, were shot. 795 Royal Air Force bombers attacked Nuremburg, Germany and lost ninety-five aircraft. It was highest casualty rate for the entire war for the Royal Air Force. Sixty-nine people were killed in the raid. Royal Air Force Pilot Officer C.J. Barton, of No.578 Squadron, won a posthumous Victoria Cross over Nuremburg, Germany. Forty-nine Royal Air Force bombers dropped

mines off Heligoland. Six B17s from the USAAF's 422nd Bomb Squadron dropped 300 bundles of leaflets on Rouen, Rennes, Reims, Paris, and Amiens in France.

1945   1,320 American 8th Air Force bombers dropped 3,720 tons of bombs on the U-boat building yards at Hamburg, Bremen, Wilhelmshaven, and Farge in Germany and lost four B17s and one B24. The German light cruiser KÖLN, the sloop KONIGIN LUISE, the minesweeper M-329 and the U96 and U429 were sunk at Wilhelmshaven. The U72, U430 and U870 were sunk at Bremen. The U358, U350 and U1167 were sunk at Hamburg. The U239 was damaged at Kiel and was later scrapped. 852 8th Air Force fighters provided support for the bombers and claimed eight victories for the loss of four P51s. German radio announced the destruction of the Hammelburg rescue force (Task Force Baum). It had been dispatched by the American 3rd Army to capture a prisoner of war camp located near the town of Hammelburg in Germany. The American 3rd Army took Heidelberg, Germany. Staff Sergeant George Peterson and First Lieutenant Walter Will, of the 1st Division, won posthumous Medals of Honor near Eisern, Germany. US Army Major General Maurice Rose, commander of the 3rd Armored Division, was killed by machine gun fire near Paderborn, Germany. Canadian forces took Emmerich. 128 Royal Air Force "Spitfires" attacked The Hague area railways. Ninety-six Royal Air Force "Mosquitoes" attacked targets in Germany. The USAAF's 492nd Bomb Group dispatched nineteen B24s on "Carpetbagger" missions and lost two aircraft.

1957   Max Amann, Hitler's personal banker, died in Munich.

Eastern Europe

1940   A Royal Air Force Lockheed 12A flew a reconnaissance mission over the Soviet refineries at Baku in the Caucasus in preparation for an air-raid.

1942   The U376 sank the British freighter INDUNA (5,086 tons). The U435 sank the American freighter EFFINGHAM (6,421 tons).

1943   Stalin was told that the Murmansk convoys would be suspended due to heavy losses.

1944   Manstein was relieved by Model of command of German Army Group "North" and Kleist (died in 1954) was relieved of command of Army Group "South" by Schorner. The Soviets occupied Cernauti, Rumania. The American 15th Air Force attacked Sofia, Bulgaria.

1945   The Soviets took the city of Danzig in Poland.

Mediterranean

1941   The Deutsches Afrika Korps began an offensive against Agedabia, Libya. The Royal Navy submarine RORQUAL damaged a ship of 3,645 tons.

1943 The British took Sejenane, Tunisia. The U596 sank the Norwegian tanker HALLANGER (9,551 tons) and the British freighter FORTA LA CORHE (7,133 tons).

1944 At 0110, the Royal Navy destroyer LAFOREY (69 survivors) was sunk northeast of Palermo by the U223, which was then sunk by the Royal Navy destroyers TUMULT, BLENCATHRA and HAMBLETON. She was the last Royal Navy vessel to be sunk in the Mediterranean by a U-boat.

Atlantic

1941 The U69 sank the British freighter COULTARN (3,759 tons). U69 survived until February 17, 1943. The U124 sank the British freighter UMONA (3,767 tons). U124 survived until April 2, 1943.

1942 The German armed merchant cruiser THOR took the freighter WELLPACK (4,649 tons). The U68 sank the British freighter MUNCASTER CASTLE (5,853 tons). U68 survived until April 10, 1944.

1943 The Italian submarine FINZI sank the British freighter CELTIC STAR (5,575 tons). The U404 sank the British freighter EMPIRE BOWMAN (7,031 tons). U404 survived until July 28th.

1945 The U1021 was sunk by the Royal Navy frigates CONN and PRINCE RUPERT.

North America

1880 General Walter Campbell Short was born in Fillmore, Illinois. He would command the US Army forces in Hawaii at the time of the Pearl Harbor attack. He died on September 3, 1949 in Dallas, Texas at the age of sixty-nine.

1941 America and Mexico decided to take all Axis ships in their ports into protective custody.

1942 Lieutenant Colonel James Doolittle and Admiral William Halsey, commander of Task Force 16, met for the first time in a San Francisco restaurant to discuss the upcoming Tokyo raid. Ground was broken for a new Bell Aircraft B29 plant near Marietta, Georgia.

1945 Japanese balloon-bombs were found near Duchesne in Utah, Grafton in North Dakota, Bozeman in Montana, Red Elm in South Dakota, and Consul in Saskatchewan. Martin Aircraft completed the last of 5,157 B26 "Marauders" to be built.

1970 Heinrich Brunning, Germany's Chancellor from 1930 until 1932, died in Norwich, Vermont.

South America

1941 Costa Rica and Venezuela decided to take all Axis ships in their ports into protective custody.

Pacific

1942 The USN submarine STURGEON sank the CHOKO MARU (842 tons). The USN destroyer PHELPS was damaged at Pearl Harbor when a crane fell into her drydock. The Pacific Ocean was divided into the Central and Southwest operational areas by the American Joint Chiefs of Staff.

1943 An American 11th Air Force B24 was shot down over the island of Kiska in the Aleutians. Six 11th Air Force B25s attacked Kiska. All six pilots were awarded the Distinguished Flying Cross for the low-level mission. The USN submarine TUNA sank the KUROHIME MARU (4,697 tons).

1944 USN Task Force 58 attacked Palau in the Carolines (See January 15, 1988). The IJN destroyer WAKATAKE and the patrol boat No.31 were sunk by USN carrier aircraft off Palau. The USN submarine DARTER sank the FUJIKAWA MARU (2,829 tons). The USN submarine STINGRAY sank the IKUSHIMA MARU (3,940 tons). The USN submarine PICUDA sank the ATLANTIC MARU (5,782 tons). The USN submarine GUITARRO attempted to rescue an Australian commando team from Borneo. Eleven American 5th Air Force B24s attacked Truk and lost three aircraft. Sixty-five 5th Air Force B24s attacked Hollandia, New Guinea destroying seventy-three Japanese aircraft. The American 13th Air Force attacked Truk and lost three B24s.

1945 The USN submarine TIRANTE sank the EIKICHI MARU (19 tons). USAAF B29s attacked the Mitsubishi plant in Nagoya. The USN transports ROPER and ARTHUR MIDDLETON were damaged in a collision.

China-Burma-India

1940 A Chinese puppet government was formed in Manchukio.

1942 The 200th Indian Division took Kyaukse, Burma. The Chinese evacuated Toungoo, Burma.

1944 USAAF B29s flew their last mission from India. The IJN submarine I-8 sank the British freighter CITY OF ADELAIDE (6,589 tons).

March 31st

Western Europe

1886 German General Otto Knobelsdorff was born. He died in 1966.

1938 The Royal Navy heavy cruiser EDINBURGH was launched. She was sunk on May 2, 1942.

1939 Britain guaranteed Poland's integrity.

1940 The armed merchant cruiser ATLANTIS left Germany for the Atlantic.

1941 Twenty Royal Air Force bombers attacked German shipping and lost two "Blenheims". The Royal Navy battleship PRINCE OF WALES was commissioned. She would be sunk in December 1941 by Japanese aircraft off Malaya. British civilian air-raid casualties for the month totaled 4,259 dead and 5,557 wounded. Twenty-eight Royal Air Force "Wellingtons" attacked Bremen, Germany and lost one aircraft. It was the first operation for the Royal Air Forces 4,000-pound bomb.

1942 Seventeen Royal Air Force bombers attacked targets in Germany.

1943 Thirty-three B17s from the USAAFs 303rd and 305th Bomb Groups dropped ninety-nine tons of bombs on the dock-yards of Rotterdam, Holland and lost four aircraft. They missed their German S-boat pen target and caused 300 Dutch casualties. British civilian casualties for the first three months of the year were 973 dead and 1,191 wounded.

1944 British civilian air-raid casualties for the month were 279 dead and 633 wounded. Eighteen Allied officers who had escaped from Stalag Luft III at Sagan on the 24th were shot by the Germans. The American 8th Air Force dropped over 20,000 tons of bombs in a month for the first time in the war. Nazi Minister of Labor Fritz Sauckel admitted that only 200,000 of the 5,000,000 foreign workers in Germany were volunteers. Twenty-eight Royal Air Force bombers dropped supplies to French Resistance forces. Since November 18th, the Royal Air Force's Bomber Command had flown 29,459 sorties on which it had dropped 78,477 tons of bombs and had lost 1,117 aircraft.

1945 1,302 American 8th Air Force bombers dropped 2,460 tons of bombs on synthetic oil plants and armament factories and lost three B17s and two B24s. 847 8th Air Force fighters provided escort for the bombers and claimed six victories for the loss of four P51s. 469 Royal Air Force bombers attacked Hamburg, Germany and lost eleven aircraft. Seventy-five people were killed in the raid. American 9th Air Force B26s attacked Heilbronn, Germany. French Air Force B26 "Marauders" attacked Boblingen, Germany. Ninety-three Royal Air Force "Spitfires" attacked The Hague area railways. The Germans began withdrawing from the Netherlands. The last V-1 German rocket fired during the war impacted in Belgium. The British government awarded twenty-one Victoria Crosses in the month of March during the war.

1946 British Lord John Gort died in London. He had served as Chief of the Imperial General Staff and had also commanded the British Expeditionary Force in France during 1940.

1967 The French carrier BEARN was sold for scrap.

Eastern Europe

1943 The Soviet tanker SOVETSKAJA NYEFT (8,228 tons) was sunk by the U24 in the Black Sea.

Mediterranean

1941 At 0307, the Royal Navy light cruiser BONAVENTURE was sunk south of Crete by the Italian submarine AMBRA. 310 members of her crew were rescued. The Italian submarine CAPPONI was sunk by the Royal Navy submarine RORQUAL. The German 15th Panzer Division arrived in Tripoli, Libya. The Axis attacked Mersa Brega, northeast of El Agheila in Libya.

1942 Liberia granted the American rights to establish bases there.

1943 The American 12th Air Force attacked Cagliari, Sardinia. The British took Cap Serrat, Tunisia.

Atlantic

1940 The Axis sank 107,009 tons of Allied and neutral shipping in March and lost one German U-boat.

1941 The Axis sank 537,493 tons of Allied and neutral shipping in March and lost five German U-boats. The U46 sank the Swedish tanker CASTOR (8,714 tons). U46 survived the war.

1942 The Axis sank 834,164 tons of Allied and neutral shipping in March and lost six German U-boats. The U754 sank the US Coast Guard tug MENOMENEE (441 tons-16 dead), the barges ALLEGHENY (914 tons) and BARNEGAT (914 tons) and damaged the barge ONTARIO (490 tons). U754 survived until July 31st. The U71 sank the British tanker SAN GERADO (12,915 tons). U71 survived the war. The Italian submarine PIETRO CALVI sank the American tanker T.C. MCCOBB (7,452 tons-4 dead).

1943 The Axis sank 693,389 tons of Allied and neutral shipping in March and lost fifteen German U-boats.

1944 The Axis sank 157,960 tons of Allied and neutral shipping in March and lost eighteen German U-boats.

1945 The Axis sank 111,204 tons of Allied and neutral shipping in March and lost twenty-three German U-boats. An American 8th Air Force B24 "Carpetbagger" crashed off the Orkney Islands while on a mission for the OSS.

North America

1941 The US Senate passed the Lend-Lease Bill by a vote of sixty to thirty-two. FDR ordered the Coast Guard to seize thirty Axis and thirty-five Danish ships that were moored in American harbors. Fifteen B18 bombers arrived at Elmendorf Airfield to form the nucleus of the American 11th Air Force in Alaska.

1942 The USN carrier HORNET arrived at Alameda Naval Air Station and began loading the "Doolittle Raiders" B25s.

1945 Japanese balloon-bombs were found near Marcus in South Dakota and Barrier Lake in British Columbia. The American government awarded thirty-one Medals of Honor in the month of March during the war.

1956 General Lawton Collins retired from active duty. He had commanded the US Army's VII Corps in Europe.

Pacific

1942 The Allies sank 78,159 tons of Japanese shipping (15 ships) in March. A member of Sorge's spy ring, Yoshio Kawamura, was arrested by Japanese police.

1943 The Allies sank 150,573 tons of Japanese shipping (38 ships) in March. The Japanese Naval Air Force attacked the Russell Islands. The Japanese freighter NANSHIN MARU was lost in a collision off Honshu with the freighter ONA MARU.

1944 The Allies sank 225,766 tons of Japanese shipping (61 ships) in March. Admiral Mineichi Koga, Commander-in-Chief of the IJN, was lost in a plane crash off the Philippines. Sixty-eight American 5th Air Force B24s attacked Hollandia, New Guinea. Twenty-two American 13th Air Force B24s flying from Bougainville attacked Truk and lost four aircraft.

1945 The Allies sank 186,118 tons of Japanese shipping (73 ships) in March. The USN heavy cruiser INDIANAPOLIS, the minelayer ADAMS and the LST-724 were hit by Japanese kamikazes. The IJN submarine I-8 was sunk by the USN destroyers MORRISON and STOCKTON. The USN submarine SPOT was attacked by the USN destroyer CASE. The American freighter JOHN FREMONT was a constructive loss, after hitting a mine in Manila Bay. The USN seaplane tender COOS BAY was damaged in a collision with the freighter MATAGORDA off Eniwetok. USAAF B29s attacked airfields on Kyushu. Private First-Class William Shockley, of the 32nd Division, won a posthumous Medal of Honor on Luzon. American forces emplaced twenty-four 155mm cannon on Keise Islet, eight miles west of Naha, Okinawa, to supply fire-support for American troops on Okinawa.

CHAPTER 4

THE MONTH OF APRIL

April 1st

Western Europe
- **1885** Clementine Churchill, Winston's wife, was born in London. She married Winston on September 12, 1908 and she died on December 12, 1977.
- **1920** Adolf Hitler's German Worker's Party became the National Socialist German Workers Party.
- **1933** The German pocket battleship ADMIRAL SCHEER was launched. The ADMIRAL SCHEER was the first of her class to be commissioned. She weighed in at 10,000 tons, was armed with six 11" guns and could cruise 21,500 miles. She was sunk on April 9, 1945. The boycotting of Jewish businesses began in Germany.
- **1934** Heinrich Himmler was appointed as commander of the Bavarian Political Police. The first unit of the new Luftwaffe, JG-132, was activated.
- **1935** Austria re-instituted military conscription.
- **1936** General Werner von Blomberg, Reich Defense Minister, decreed that German soldiers couldn't marry Jews.
- **1937** Rebel forces took Bilbao, Spain.
- **1939** The German battleship TIRPITZ was launched. She was sunk on November 12, 1944.
- **1940** In a final review of his planned invasion of Norway and Denmark Hitler told his commanders that the main purpose of the operation was to forestall British action in Scandanavia, secure Swedish ore supplies and to establish air and naval installations for future operations against the Allies.
- **1941** Luftwaffe attacked a convoy off Bristol and sank the tankers SAN CONRADO (7,982 tons) and HIDLEFJORD (7,693 tons). They also damaged three more tankers totaling 26,002 tons. Twelve Royal Air Force bombers attacked shipping off Belgium. The pocket battleship ADMIRAL SCHEER returned to Germany after a cruise which had netted her twenty-one victories. Her captain, Theodor Kranke, received the Knight's Cross and the rest of the crew received Iron Crosses. A Luftwaffe He111 crash-landed in Eire.

1942 Twelve Royal Air Force "Bostons" attacked Boulogne, France. Fifty-six Royal Air Force bombers attacked Le Havre, France and lost one "Wellington". Forty-nine Royal Air Force bombers attacked Hanau, Germany and lost thirteen aircraft. Forty-one Royal Air Force bombers attacked Paris/Poissy and lost one "Wellington".

1943 Twelve Royal Air Force "Mosquitoes" attacked Trier, Germany. Fourteen "Spitfires" from the USAAF's 4th Fighter Group flew patrols over the Channel. This was the last "Spitfire" operation for the American 8th Fighter Command. Thereafter they would fly American-built aircraft.

1944 165 American 8th Air Force B17s and B24s dropped 485 tons of bombs on Strasbourg, Ludwigshafen, Grafenhausen and Pforzheim and lost twelve B24s. One of the lost B24s was interned in Switzerland. Colonel James Thompson, commander of the USAAF's 448th Bomb Group (B24), was shot down on the mission. 475 8th Air Force fighters provided support for the bombers and claimed eighteen victories for the loss of two P47s and two P51s. Schaffhausen, Switzerland was accidentally bombed by thirty-eight B24s of the USAAF's 44th and 392nd Bomb Groups. The American government paid $1 million in damages to the Swiss government. Thirty-five Royal Air Force "Mosquitoes" attacked Hannover, Germany. Thirty-four Royal Air Force "Halifaxes" dropped mines off the Dutch coast.

1945 The US Army's 3rd Division took Paderborn, Germany. With the capture of Paderborn, the American 9th and 3rd Armies completed their encirclement of Germany's industrial Ruhr and captured more than 100,000 German troops. Four Royal Air Force "Mosquitoes" attacked airfields in Southern Germany and lost one aircraft.

1947 Franz Seldte, Reich Minister of Labor, died in Furth.

1948 The Soviets announced restrictions on road and rail traffic into Berlin.

1950 The French battleship JEAN BART was commissioned this month. She had been launched in 1940, but had not been completed until after the war.

1993 British Lord Solly Zuckerman died of a heart attack. He had been scientific advisor to Winston Churchill during the war.

Eastern Europe

1942 The U436 sank the Norwegian trawler SULA (250 tons). The German trawler UJ-1201 was sunk by a mine off Finland.

1944 40,000 German troops were trapped at Skala in the Ukraine.

1945 The Soviets took Sopron, Hungary.

Mediterranean

1941 The British took the capital of Eritrea, Asmara. At 0700, the Italian destroyer LEONE was lost by grounding in the Red Sea.

1942   The Royal Navy submarines P-36 and PANDORA were sunk in a Malta air-raid. At 0900, the Italian light cruiser GIOVANNI DELLE BANDE NERE was sunk off Stromboli, in the Tyrrhenian Sea, by the Royal Navy submarine URGE.

1943   Allied aircraft attacked the El Maou Airfield near Sfax, Tunisia. At 0400, the Italian destroyer LUBLIANA ran aground and was lost in the Gulf of Tunis.

1945   The British crossed the Reno River in Italy.

Atlantic

1941   Between this date and the end of June the Germans would sink 1,600,000 tons of shipping and would lose seven submarines. During the same period, the Allies would build 500,000 tons of new shipping.

1942   A partial convoy system was finally introduced along the east coast of the America. The German armed merchant cruiser THOR took the freighter WILLESDEN (4,563 tons). The U71 sank the British freighter EASTMOOR (5,812 tons). U71 survived the war. The U160 sank the British freighter RIO BLANCO (4,086 tons). U160 survived until July 14, 1943. The U754 sank the American tanker TIGER (5,992 tons-1 dead). U754 survived until July 31st. The U202 sank the British freighter LOCH DON (5,249 tons). U202 survived until June 1, 1943. Between this date and the end of June the Germans would sink 1,350,000 tons of shipping and would lose ten submarines. During the same period, the Allies would build 850,000 tons.

1943   The German trawler V-1241 was sunk off Terschelling by British MTBs. Between this date and the end of June the Germans would sink 900,000 tons of shipping and would lose seventy-three submarines. During the same period, the Allies would build 3,000,000 tons. The USN YP-235 exploded in the Gulf of Mexico.

1944   The U355 was sunk by the Royal Navy destroyer BEAGLE. The U218 laid fifteen mines off San Juan, Puerto Rico. U218 survived the war. Between this date and the end of June the Germans would sink 310,000 tons of shipping and would lose sixty-eight submarines. During the same period, the Allies would build 3,500,000 tons.

North America

1888   US Army General Terry Allen, commander of the 1st and 104th Divisions, was born in Fort Douglas, Utah.

1932   The battleship UTAH was re-commissioned as a target ship. She would be sunk at Pearl Harbor on December 7, 1941.

1939   The submarine SWORDFISH was launched at Mare Island. She was lost in January 1945.

1942	The USN carrier HORNET, with the "Doolittles Raiders" aboard, was moved from Alameda Naval Air Station across the Bay to San Francisco. The forced evacuation of Japanese-Americans from the Pacific coast was begun. The destroyer CLAXTON was launched. She was transferred to Germany in 1959. This month, FDR issued an Executive Order seizing temporary control of Brewster Aeronautical Corporation. The company had suffered problems with production. It was eventually issued a contract to build the F4U "Corsair". When it failed in that endeavor the company was closed on July 4, 1944.
1943	The Soviet freighter UZBEKISTAN was stranded on Vancouver Island, British Columbia. Twelve ships were involved in collisions in a fog-bound New York Harbor.
1945	Japanese balloon-bombs were found near Dillon in Montana, Tampico and Colville in Washington and on the Hoopa Indian Reservation in northern California.
1964	Herschel Green retired as a USAAF colonel. He had scored 18 victories while with the 325th Fighter Group in the Mediterranean.
1965	The destroyers SMALLEY and MCDERMUT were stricken.
1966	The light cruiser VINCENNES was sunk as a target.
1970	Medal of Honor winner Lawson Patterson Ramage retired as a Vice Admiral.
1974	The destroyer PERRY was stricken.
1982	The US Coast Guard cutter CAMPBELL was decommissioned.
1987	A federal appeals court approved the deportation of Karl Linnas, age 67, who had been in charge of a concentration camp in which 12,000 people had died.
1992	"Doolittle Raider" Lieutenant Robert Emmens died of cancer.

Pacific

1939	The first flight of the Japanese A6M "Zero" took place.
1942	The Royal Navy submarine TRUANT sank the YAE MARU (6,780 tons) and the SHUNSEI MARU (4,939 tons). US Army General Douglas MacArthur was awarded a Medal of Honor for his actions in the Philippines. Rations for the troops on Bataan were halved.
1943	The American 11th Air Force attacked Kiska in the Aleutians.
1944	USN Task Force 58 attacked Woleai in the Carolines. American forces occupied Ndrilo and Koniniat in the Admiraties. Twenty-two American 13th Air Force B24s made a night-raid on Truk. The USN submarine FLYING FISH sank the MINAMI MARU (2,398 tons). The IJN submarines I-46 and RO-46 were damaged in a collision in the Inland Sea.
1945	American forces invaded the island of Okinawa. The USN battleship WEST VIRGINIA (four of her crew died), the destroyer CALLAGHAN,

the freighters ARCHENAR, ALPINE, and TYRREL, the transport HINSDALE and the Royal Navy carriers INDEFATIGABLE (fourteen of her crew died), INDOMITABLE and ILLUSTRIOUS and battleship KING GEORGE V were hit by Japanese kamikazes. The Royal Navy destroyer ULSTER was hit by a bomb. The USN submarine QUEENFISH sank the Japanese hospital ship AWA MARU (11,249 tons). The AWA MARU had been guaranteed safe passage by the American government. Her cargo consisted of more than $5 billion in plunder instead of the wounded soldiers as agreed to in the guarantee. This was not known until after the war. The Captain of the QUEENFISH was court-martialed and found guilty of negligence in the misidentification and the sinking of what was in reality a treasure ship. The US Army's 158th Infantry Regiment landed at Legaspi on Luzon. The B29 "Joltin' Josie" crashed on Saipan (See October 12, 1944). Six USAAF 313th Bomb Wing B29s dropped mines in Kure Harbor. B29s dropped 1,000 tons of bombs on the Nakajima Plant near Tokyo. Only four tons fell within the target area.
1946 This month forty-one Japanese hold-outs from the war on Lubang in the Philippines and thirty-three on Peleliu in the Palaus surrendered.
2001 The wreck of the USN tanker MISSISSINEWA (25,425 tons) was located on the bottom of Ulithi Lagoon. She had been sunk by a Japanese Kaiten suicide torpedo on November 20, 1944.

China-Burma-India
1944 The U852 sank the British freighter DAHOMIAN (5,277 tons).

April 2nd

Western Europe
1941 Nineteen Royal Air Force bombers attacked shipping off the North Sea coast and lost one "Blenheim". The Royal Air Force dropped 75,000 tea bags over Holland to disprove German claims of a tea shortage in Britain. The first flight of the Luftwaffe's experimental He280 V-1 jet took place.
1942 Fifty Royal Air Force bombers attacked Paris/Poissy and lost one "Wellington". Forty-nine Royal Air Force bombers attacked Le Havre, France. Thirty Royal Air Force bombers dropped mines in the Bay of Biscay and lost two aircraft.
1943 Ninety-two Royal Air Force bombers attacked St. Nazaire and Lorient in France and lost one aircraft. Thirty-three Royal Air Force bombers dropped mines off the Biscay coast and lost one "Lancaster".
1944 A USAAF B29 was sent to Britain in an attempt to convince the Germans that the type would be used in the European Theater of Operations. The

American 15th Air Force attacked Steyr, Austria and lost twenty bombers. Royal Air Force Flight Officer Pawel Tobolski was shot by the Germans. He had been one of seventy-six Allied officers who had escaped from Stalag Luft III at Sagan on March 24th.
1945 The British 2nd Army took Munster, Germany. The US Army's 80th Division reached the outskirts of Kassel, Germany. Corporal E. Chapman, of the Monmouthshire Regiment, won a Victoria Cross in Germany. 708 American 8th Air Force bombers attempted to attack Luftwaffe airfields in Denmark, but were recalled due to bad weather conditions over their target. Fifty-two "Spitfires" attacked The Hague area railways. 114 Royal Air Force "Mosquitoes" attacked targets in Germany and lost one aircraft. The German minesweeper R-256 was sunk by Allied aircraft in the Baltic.
1948 The Swiss bought fourteen P51 "Mustangs" from the USAAF in Germany.
1952 Royal Navy Admiral Sir Henry Pridham-Wippel died. He had served as second-in-command in the Mediterranean in 1940 and had commanded Dover from 1942 until 1945.
1972 Wehrmacht General Franz Halder died in Aschau, Bavaria.

Eastern Europe
1944 The Soviets entered Rumania and took the town of Gertza. The American 15th Air Force attacked rail targets in Yugoslavia. German General Hans Hube, commander of the 1st Panzer Army, received an ultimatum from Soviet Marshall Zhukov demanding that he surrender or one-third of his troops who were captured would be shot.
1945 The Soviets and the Bulgarians took Nagykanizsa, Hungary.

Mediterranean
1941 The British evacuated Agedabia, Libya.
1943 The U755 sank the French freighter SIMON DUHAMEL II (928 tons).
1945 Corporal T. Hunter, of the 43rd Royal Marine Commando, won a posthumous Victoria Cross in Italy.

Atlantic
1941 The Royal Navy submarine TIGRIS sank the German tanker THORN off St. Nazaire, France. The U46 sank the British tanker BRITISH RELIANCE (7,000 tons). U46 survived the war.
1942 The U552 sank the American freighter DAVID H. ATWATER (23 dead). U552 survived the war.
1943 The U155 sank the Norwegian freighter LYSEFJORD (1,091 tons). U155 survived the war. The U129 sank the British freighter MELBOURNE STAR (12,806 tons). U129 was scuttled in August 1944. The U124 sank the British freighters KATHA (4,357 tons) and GOGRA (5,190 tons). U124

was then sunk west of Oporto by the Royal Navy sloop BLACK SWAN and the corvette STONECROP.
1944 The U360 was sunk in the Arctic Ocean by the Royal Navy destroyer KEPPEL.
1945 The U321 was sunk southwest of Ireland by the Royal Air Force's No.304 (Polish) Squadron.

North America
1940 The USN Pacific Fleet sailed from San Diego for maneuvers near Hawaii. After the maneuvers were over FDR decided to station the fleet in Hawaii as a possible deterrent to the Japanese.
1941 FDR informed Churchill that he had allotted funds for the construction of additional ship-building facilities in America as well as 200 ships. Actor Efrem Zimbalist Jr. enlisted.
1942 The USN carrier HORNET left San Francisco with the B25 "Mitchells" of the "Doolittle Raiders" aboard. She was escorted by the heavy cruiser VINCENNES, the light cruiser NASHVILLE and the destroyers GWIN, MEREDITH, GRAYSON and MONSSEN and accompanied by the tanker CIMMARON. The destroyer KENDRICK was launched. She was stricken in 1966 and used as a target. The submarine BARB was launched. She was transferred to the Italian Navy in 1955.
1943 The Soviet freighter LAMUT was stranded near Lapush, Washington and was lost.
1945 The USN blimp K-87 sighted a floating mine off Grays Harbor, Washington and was assisted by the USN blimp K-119 in exploding it.
1954 General Hoyt Vandenberg, commander of the 9th Air Force from August 1944, died in Washington D.C.

Pacific
1931 The IJN light carrier RYUJO was launched. She was sunk on August 24, 1942.
1941 The German steamers MUNCHEN (5,619 tons) and HERMONTHIS (4,833 tons) were scuttled off Peru to avoid capture by the Canadian armed merchant cruiser PRINCE HENRY.
1942 The IJN light cruiser OYODO was launched. She was sunk on July 28, 1945.
1943 The USN submarine TUNNY sank the TOYO MARU No.2 (4,162 tons). The American 11th Air Force attacked Japanese positions on Attu and Kiska in the Aleutians.
1944 The American 13th Air Force attacked Truk and lost four B24s. The IJN submarine I-196 was lost in an accident at Truk. She had submerged to

avoid the air-raid. A defective valve caused the loss of the submarine and her entire crew.

1945 The USN destroyer-transport DICKERSON (54 of her crew died), the transports HENRICO, CHILTON, GOODHUE and TELFAIR, the LST-599, the LCI-568 and the destroyer-transport HERBERT were damaged off Okinawa by Japanese aircraft. The USN destroyer SHAW was a constructive loss after being wrecked in the Leyte Gulf. The USN destroyer FRANKS was severely damaged after colliding with the USN battleship NEW JERSEY. The IJN escort No.186 and the transport T-17 were sunk by USN carrier aircraft. The USN submarine SEA DEVIL sank the TAIJO MARU (6,866 tons), the EDOGAWA MARU (1,972 tons), the NISSHIN MARU (1,179 tons) and the TAMA MARU (396 tons). The US Army's 185th Regimental Combat Team took Talisay on Negros. The US Army's 163rd Regimental Combat Team landed on Tawi-Tawi, in the Sulu Archipelago, off North Borneo.

China-Burma-India

1942 The American 10th Air Force flew its first mission; the target was the Andaman Islands in the Bay of Bengal. The Japanese took Prome, Burma. The IJN submarine I-6 sank the British freighter CLAN ROSS (5,897 tons).

1943 The British freighter CITY OF BARODA (7,129 tons) was a constructive loss after an attack by the U509.

1944 The first USAAF B29 "Superfortress" to arrive in the CBI landed at Chakulia, India. It was flown by Colonel Jake Harmon. The British freighter SAMCALIA rescued 25 survivors from the American freighter RICHARD HOVEY which had been sunk on March 29th by the IJN submarine I-26.

April 3rd

Western Europe

1938 Francisco Franco's Nationalist forces took Lerida, Spain.

1940 Seven German freighters left Hamburg for the upcoming invasion of Norway. Aboard were the first of the Wehrmacht troops that would land in Norway at Narvik, Trondheim and Stavanger. Royal Air Force fighters flying from Britain suffered their first loss of the war when an aircraft of No.41 Squadron was shot down by a Luftwaffe He111 over the Channel. Winston Churchill was appointed Chairman of the British Ministerial Defense Committee. Edgar Ludlow-Hewitt was replaced as Commander of the Royal Air Force's Bomber Command by Charles Portal.

1941	The Luftwaffe attacked Bristol, Britain. Ninety Royal Air Force bombers attacked Brest, France and lost three aircraft.
1943	Eight Royal Air Force "Mosquitoes" attacked targets in Belgium and lost one aircraft. 348 Royal Air Force bombers attacked Essen, Germany and lost twenty-one aircraft. 635 buildings were destroyed and 118 people were killed in the raid.
1944	122 aircraft from the Royal Navy carriers FURIOUS and VICTORIOUS attacked the German battleship TIRPITZ in Norway and lost three aircraft. The TIRPITZ suffered fifteen hits in the raid.
1945	The Soviets took Wiener Neustadt, Austria. The French 1st Army took Karlsruhe, Germany. 255 Royal Air Force bombers attacked Nordhausen, Germany and lost two "Lancasters". 719 American 8th Air Force bombers dropped 2,229 tons of bombs on U-boat yards at Kiel, Germany and lost two B17s. One of the lost B17s landed in Sweden. The U1221 and U2542 and the minesweeper M-802 were sunk at Kiel. Twenty-four Royal Air Force "Spitfires" attacked The Hague area railways. Captain I. Liddell, of the Coldstream Guards, won a Victoria Cross in Germany. Private First-Class Walter Wetzer, of the 8th Division, won a posthumous Medal of Honor at Birken, Germany. The American 9th Army took Munster, Germany. The British XXX Corps reached the Dortmund-Ems Canal in Germany. 108 Royal Air Force "Mosquitoes" attacked targets in Germany and lost one aircraft.
1995	A Luftwaffe 1,100-pound bomb that had been dropped in July 1941 was defused near Portland, Britain. It had been discovered two weeks earlier under a soccer field.

Eastern Europe

1941	Stalin was told by the British that Germany intended to attack Russia. Hungarian premier Pal Teleki committed suicide in protest of his country's collaboration with Germany.
1942	The Luftwaffe attacked Murmansk and sank the British freighters EMPIRE STARLIGHT (6,850 tons) and NEW WESTMINISTER (4,747 tons).
1943	Major fighting took place near Leningrad.
1944	The American 15th Air Force sent 375 bombers against Budapest, Hungary. Eighty-seven Royal Air Force bombers attacked Budapest, Hungary and lost five aircraft. The American 15th Air Force attacked rail targets in Yugoslavia.
1945	The Soviets took Wiener Neustadt, Austria.

Mediterranean

1941 The British evacuated Benghazi, Libya. A pro-Axis group took over the government in Iraq. At 0615, the Italian destroyer NAZARIO SAURO was sunk in the Red Sea by Royal Navy aircraft. At 0745, The Italian destroyer DANIELE MANIN was sunk by Royal Navy aircraft. At 1400, the Italian destroyer CESARE BATTISTI was damaged by Royal Navy aircraft and was scuttled later in the day. The Italian destroyers PANTERA and TIGRE were scuttled off Saudi Arabia. The Italian torpedo boat GIOVANNI ACERBI was sunk at Massawa by the Royal Air Force. The Royal Navy carrier ARK ROYAL launched twelve "Hurricane" fighters to reinforce Malta in "Operation Winch". The Luftwaffe attacked British convoys off Greece and sank three ships totaling 21,155 tons.

1943 Axis forces began retreating in Tunisia.

Atlantic

1941 The U46 sank the British freighter ALDERPOOL (4,313 tons). U46 survived the war. The U73 sank the British freighters ATHENIC (5,351 tons), BRITISH VISCOUNT (6,895 tons) and WESTPOOL (5,724 tons). U73 survived until December 16, 1943. The U74 sank the Belgian freighter INDIER (5,409 tons) and the Greek freighter CAMBANIS (4,274 tons). U74 survived until May 2, 1942. The U69 sank the Finnish freighter DAPHNE (1,939 tons). U69 survived until February 17, 1943.

1942 The German armed merchant cruiser THOR took the Norwegian steamer AUST (5,630 tons). The U552 sank the American freighter DAVID ATWATER (2,438 tons). U552 survived the war. The U754 sank the American freighter OTHO (4,839 tons-31 dead). U754 survived until July 31st. The U505 sank the American freighter WEST IRMO (5,775 tons-10 dead). U505 was captured by the USN escort carrier GUADALCANAL on June 4, 1944 and is still on display in Chicago.

1943 The American tanker GULFSTATE (6,882 tons-36 dead) was sunk by the U155. U155 survived the war. The British destroyer SHIKARI rescued 7 survivors from the American freighter PIERCE FRYE which had been sunk on March 29th by U160.

1944 The U288 was sunk by the Royal Navy escort carriers TRACKER and ACTIVITY.

1945 The U1276 was sunk northwest of Bergen by Royal Air Force's No.224 Squadron.

North America

1888 Admiral Thomas Cassin Kinkaid was born in Hanover, New Hampshire. He graduated 136th in his 1908 Annapolis class of 201. He was promoted to rear admiral in 1941. He would command the 7th Fleet in the Pacific. He retired on May 30, 1950 and died on November 17, 1972 at his home in Washington D.C.

1892   Major General Hubert Harmon, commander of the 13th Air Force, was born in Chester, Pennsylvania.

1941   The Soviet freighter VOROVSKY was stranded off the Oregon Coast. FDR ordered the transfer of ten US Coast Guard cutters to the Royal Navy.

1942   Charles Lindbergh began working as a consultant at Ford's Willow Run B24 "Liberator" plant in Michigan.

1945   Japanese balloon-bombs were found near Harper in Oregon and Walla Walla in Washington.

2009   USAAF Colonel Harold Comstock, age 88, died in California. He had scored 5 victories while flying P47s in the European Theater.

2010   USN Commander Thomas Harris died at the age of 88 in New Haven, Missouri. He had scored 9 aerial victories while flying the F6F "Hellcat" in the Pacific.

2013   USAAF ace Urban Drew died in Vista, California at the age of 89. He had been credited with 6 aerial victories while flying P51s with the 361st Fighter Group. Two of his victories were Me262 jets which he shot down on the same mission. 38 years after that action, he was awarded the Air Force Cross in a somewhat belated ceremony.

Pacific

1942   Japanese forces began their final assault on Allied positions on Bataan, Luzon. The USN blimp L-8 delivered navigator's windows for Doolittle's B25s when the carrier HORNET was one day out of San Francisco.

1943   The USN submarine PICKEREL sank the IJN patrol boat Ch-13. The USN submarine HADDOCK sank the ARIMA MARU (7,389 tons) and the TOYO MARU No.1 (1,916 tons). The 5th Air Force attacked Japanese shipping off Kavieng, New Ireland sinking the transport FLORIDA MARU and damaging the heavy cruiser AOBA and the destroyer FUMIZUKI. The IJN destroyer KAZAGUMO was damaged by a mine off Kahili Bay, Bougainville.

1944   The USN submarine POLLACK sank the TOSEI MARU (2,814 tons). The IJN submarine I-74 was wrecked. 236 American 5th Air Force bombers dropped 500 tons of bombs on Hollandia, New Guinea. 5th Air Force ace Captain Richard Bong shot down an "Oscar" over Hollandia. 13th Air Force B25s attacked Rabaul, New Britain.

1945   The USN escort carrier WAKE ISLAND, the destroyer PRICHETT, the destroyer escort FOREMAN and the destroyer-minesweeper HAMBLETON were hit by kamikazes off Okinawa. The FOREMAN sustained major damage but suffered no casualties. The US Army's 40th Division landed on Masbate in the Philippines. The USN YMS-71 was sunk off Brunei by a mine. The American Joint Chiefs of Staff appointed General Douglas MacArthur as Commander of all-American Land Forces in the Pacific and Admiral Chester Nimitz Commander of all Naval Forces. The Japanese government announced the establishment of a "National Volunteer Force" (civilian army).

1946   Japanese General Masaharu Homma was executed in Los Banos, Luzon for war crimes.

China-Burma-India

1942   The IJN submarine I-7 sank the British freighter GLENSHIEL (9,415 tons). Six American 10th Air Force B17s attacked Rangoon, Burma and lost one aircraft. 2,000 people were killed in a Japanese Air Force raid on Mandalay, Burma.

1945   American 10th Air Force B24s attacked "The Bridge on the River Kwai" near Kanchanaburi, Burma. The IJN escort MANJU was sunk at Hong Kong by the USAAF.

April 4th

Western Europe

1889   German Hans-Jurgen von Arnim was born in Ernsdorf, Silesia. He would command the DAK in North Africa after Rommel was recalled to Germany. He was captured on May 12, 1943. He died on September 1, 1962 at a nursing home in Bad Wildungen at the age of 73.

1941   Fourteen Royal Air Force "Blenheims" attacked shipping and lost one aircraft. The French sloop LA CONQUERANTE SUIPPE was sunk in an air-raid on Falmouth, Britain. Adolf Hitler and Japanese Foreign Minister Matsuoka met in Berlin to discuss a Japanese attack on Singapore and the possibility of war with America. Fifty-four Royal Air Force bombers attacked Brest, France and lost one "Hampden".

1942   Sixteen Royal Air Force bombers attacked St. Omer, France. USN Task Force 39 arrived at Scapa Flow.

1943   Sixty Royal Air Force "Venturas" attacked targets in Holland and France and lost two aircraft. Eighty-five American 8th Air Force B17s dropped 251 tons of bombs on the Renault works in Billancourt near Paris and lost four aircraft. The 305th Bomb Group won a Distinguished Unit Citation for the mission. 577 Royal Air Force bombers attacked Kiel, Germany and lost twelve aircraft. Eleven buildings were destroyed and twenty-six people were killed in the raid.

1944	Six Royal Air Force "Mosquitoes" attacked Gestapo headquarters in The Hague. An American 8th Air Force B24 "Carpetbagger" was shot down over France. French General Charles De Gaulle named two communists to his Committee of National Liberation. He pronounced himself head of the Free French armed forces at the same time. Luftwaffe ace Rudolf Ehrenberger (49 aerial victories) was killed in his parachute by a USAAF fighter. Seventy-one Royal Air Force "Mosquitoes" attacked targets in Germany.
1945	The US Army's 80th Division took Kassel, Germany. French forces took Karlsruhe, Germany. The USAAF's 4th Fighter Group shot down three Luftwaffe Me262 jets. Luftwaffe ace Heinrich Ehrler (209 aerial victories) was killed in action when his Me262 jet was shot down. 244 Royal Air Force bombers attacked Nordhausen, Germany and lost one aircraft. 950 American 8th Air Force bombers dropped 2,686 tons of bombs on Luftwaffe airfields throughout Germany and shipping yards at Hamburg and Kiel and lost six B24s and four B17s. One of the lost B17s landed in Sweden. The U237, U749 and U3003 were sunk at Kiel. 812 8th Air Force fighters provided escort for the bombers and claimed twenty-four victories for the loss of four P51s and one P47. The American 9th Army was officially transferred from the British 21st Army Group to the American 12th Army Group. The American 3rd Army liberated the first of the slave labor camps at Ohrdruf, Germany. After being forced to view the camp the Mayor of Ohrdruf and his wife hung themselves. The British entered Osnabruck, Germany. General Gothard Heinrici (died in 1971) assumed command of German Army Group "Vistula". 341 Royal Air Force bombers attacked Leuna, Germany and lost two "Lancasters". 327 Royal Air Force bombers attacked Hamburg, Germany and lost three aircraft. 272 Royal Air Force bombers attacked Lutzkendorf, Germany and lost six "Lancasters". Sixty-six Royal Air Force "Mosquitoes" attacked targets in Germany and lost two aircraft. Thirty Royal Air Force bombers dropped mines in the Kattegat and lost three "Lancasters".
1960	Alfred Naujocks died in Hamburg, Germany. He had led the phony Polish raid on the German radio station at Gleiwitz that had preceded the German attack on Poland.
1971	A Luftwaffe He111 shot down off East Wittering; Britain on August 26, 1940 was recovered.

Eastern Europe

1934	Russian extended its non-aggression pacts with Latvia, Lithuania and Estonia thru 1945.
1942	The Luftwaffe attacked Soviet Naval vessels in Leningrad.

1944 The Germans counter-attacked near Kovel. The American 15th Air Force attacked Bucharest, Rumania and lost seven B24s.
1945 The Soviets took Bratislava. The German battleship SCHLEISEN was sunk by a mine.

Mediterranean
1941 The Axis took Benghazi, Libya. Axis forces began an offensive in Cyrenaica. The British 2nd Armored Division was left without supplies when the British garrison at Msus, Egypt panicked and destroyed a supply dump. The Italians evacuated Addis Ababa, Ethiopia. The Italian liner COLOMBO was sunk off Massawa, Ethiopia. The Greek torpedo boat PROUSSA was sunk by Italian aircraft.
1942 The Royal Air Force attacked Benghazi and Derna.
1943 The USAAF B24 "Lady Be Good" went down in North Africa on her maiden combat flight. She would be located 10 years after the war by an oil company team. Ninety-one USAAF B17s attacked Naples. Allied aircraft attacked Palermo and Syracuse on Sicily and Carloforte on Sardinia.

Atlantic
1941 The German armed merchant cruiser THOR sank the Royal Navy armed merchant cruiser VOLTAIRE (13,245 tons) and rescued 197 survivors. The German armed merchant cruiser KORMORAN took the Greek freighter NICHOLAS D.L. (5,486 tons). The U98 sank the Norwegian freighter HELLE (2,467 tons) and the British freighter WELLCOMBE (5,122 tons). U98 survived until November 19, 1942. The U94 sank the British freighter HARBLEDOWN (5,414 tons). U94 survived until August 28, 1942. The U97 sank the British tanker CONUS (8,132 tons). U97 survived until June 16, 1943. The U124 sank the British freighter MARLENE (6,507 tons). U124 survived until April 2, 1943.
1942 The U154 sank the American tanker COMOL RICO (5,034 tons-3 dead). U154 survived until July 3, 1944. The U702 was lost in the North Sea. The U505 sank the Dutch freighter AAPHACCA (5,759 tons). On June 4, 1944 U505 was captured by the USN escort carrier GUADALCANAL.
1943 The U635 sank the British freighter SHILLING (5,529 tons). U635 survived until April 6th.

North America
1936 The carrier YORKTOWN was launched. She was sunk on June 7, 1942.
1939 The carrier WASP was launched. She was sunk on September 15, 1942.
1941 FDR agreed to let damaged Royal Navy ships be repaired in American ports.

The Month of April

1942   The escort carrier NASSAU and the light cruiser DENVER (awarded eleven battle stars and a Navy Unit Citation during the war) were launched. The NASSAU was scrapped in 1961 and the DENVER was scrapped in November 1960.

1943   The light carrier CABOT and the destroyers THE SULLIVANS, HALE and CHARLES F. BADGER were launched. The CABOT was sold to Spain in 1967, THE SULLIVANS was dedicated as a memorial, the HALE was transferred to Columbia in 1960 and CHARLES F. BADGER was stricken in 1970. The submarines REDFIN and CERO were launched. The REDFIN was scrapped in 1971 and the CERO was scrapped in 1970.

1944   The 20th Air Force was activated. It would be commanded by USAAF Chief of Staff General Henry Arnold and would make use of the B29 "Superfortress". Arnold would thus have control of the new aircraft and would be answerable only to the President. As his duties required him to stay in Washington D.C. his deputy, General Haywood Hansen, would actually run the organization. The escort carrier STEAMER BAY was commissioned. She was scrapped in 1959.

1946   Escaped German prisoner of war Erich Gellert was arrested in Cedarburg, Wisconsin.

1961   The destroyer BALDWIN broke its tow and was wrecked on Montauk Point. She was salvaged on June 4th and scuttled.

Pacific

1942   The Allies began retreating on Bataan, Luzon.

1943   The USN submarine PORPOISE sank the KOA MARU (2,023 tons). The IJN submarine Ro-34 was sunk by the USN destroyer O'BANNON. USN Admiral Marc Mitscher became Commander Air Solomons.

1944   The American 20th Air Force was activated.

1945   American forces began meeting stiff resistance on Okinawa. The Royal Navy carriers FORMIDABLE and INDOMITABLE were hit by Japanese kamikazes off Okinawa. The USN destroyer-transports DICKERSON and HERBERT were scuttled after being damaged by Japanese kamikazes off Okinawa on April 2nd. The USN LCI-82 was sunk by an IJN suicide boat. The IJN escort MOKUTU was sunk by a mine. The USN LSM-12 foundered off Okinawa.

1948   The USN destroyer MAYRANT was scuttled after the Bikini Tests.

China-Burma-India

1942   A PBY "Catalina", flown by Royal Canadian Air Force Squadron Leader Leonard Birchall, sighted an IJN carrier force 250 miles southeast of Ceylon. The sighting report enabled the Allied forces at Colombo, Ceylon to prepare for the upcoming attack. The PBY was shot down immediately after transmitting the report and its surviving crewmembers were captured. All operational ships in Colombo, Ceylon were immediately ordered to sea.

April 5th

Western Europe

1939 The Royal Navy carrier ILLUSTRIOUS was launched. She was scrapped in 1956.

1940 Britain and France informed Norway that they reserved the right to deprive Germany of Norway's resources and they began mining Norwegian territorial waters.

1941 Hitler pledged that Germany would "promptly take part" in any conflict between Japan and America.

1942 263 Royal Air Force bombers attacked Köln, Germany and lost five aircraft. Twenty-three people were killed in the raid. Twenty Royal Air Force "Whitleys" attacked Paris/Gennevilliers.

1943 Eighty-two American 8th Air Force B17s and B24s dropped 502 tons of bombs on Antwerp, Belgium and lost four B17s. The 306th Bomb Groups Technical/Sergeant Roscovitch became the first member of the American 8th Bomber Command to complete his 25-mission tour. The Belgian Ambassador to America made a formal complaint concerning the inaccurate bombing by USAAF forces over his country. Twelve Royal Air Force "Venturas" attacked Brest, France and lost three aircraft.

1944 Twenty-one American 8th Air Force B24s dropped fifty-seven tons of bombs on V-1 rocket sites at Siracourt, France. Fifty 8th Air Force P47s provided support for the bombers. 456 8th Air Force fighters attacked Luftwaffe airfields in Germany and claimed ninety-eight victories for the loss of one P38, one P47 and seven P51s. USAAF 352nd Fighter Group (P51) ace Captain Virgil Meroney (9 victories) was shot down over Germany. Ernst Kaltenbrunner issued orders for Allied air-crew to be shot if they resisted or were dressed in civilian clothes. USAAF 4th Fighter Group ace Duane Beeson (24 victories) was shot down and captured near Brandenburg. 145 Royal Air Force bombers attacked Toulouse, France and lost one "Lancaster". The USAAF's 801st Bomb Group dispatched seventeen B24s on "Carpetbagger" missions and lost one aircraft.

1945 1,039 American 8th Air Force bombers dropped 2,815 tons of bombs on rail and aircraft targets in Germany and lost five B17s and five B24s. 606 8th Air Force fighters provided escort for the bombers and claimed eight victories for the loss of one P51. The American 3rd Army took

Mulhouse, Gotha, and Eisenbach in Germany. The American 7th Army took Wurzburg, Germany. Corporal Thomas Kelly, of the 7th Armored Division, won a Medal of Honor at Almert, Germany. The Norwegian submarine UTSIRA sank the German freighter TORRIDAL (1,501 tons) off Follafjord, Norway

1949   The Royal Navy battleship ROYAL SOVEREIGN was sold for scrap.

2012   The last known survivor of the "Great Escape" which took place on March 24, 1944 at Stalg Luft III near Sagan, Germany, died. Royal Air Force serviceman Richard Bittle died of a heart attack at the age of 92.

Eastern Europe

1940   A Royal Air Force Lockheed 12A flew a recon mission over the Soviet refineries at Batum in the Caucasus in preparation for a raid by the French Air Force. The first flight of the Soviet Mig-3 fighter took place. German Abwehr agents stopped an Allied attempt to block the Danube by sinking cement-filled barges at the "Iron Gate", a gorge between Yugoslavia and Rumania.

1942   Hitler ordered a summer offensive in the southern sector of the Eastern Front.

1943   Luftwaffe ace Friedrich Geisshardt (102 victories) was wounded. He died the next day.

1944   The Soviets took Tarnopol. The American 15th Air Force sent 146 B24s and 90 B17s to Ploesti, Rumania. They dropped 588 tons of bombs and lost thirteen aircraft on the first high-level raid against the oil refineries located there. It was the first mission flown from the Foggia airfields in Italy. The 15th Air Force also attacked rail targets in Yugoslavia.

1945   The USSR informed Japan that their 1941 non-aggression pact would not be renewed.

Mediterranean

1941   The Italians evacuated Addis Ababa, Ethiopia. The DAK took Tengeder and Barce in Libya.

1942   The Royal Navy battleship QUEEN ELIZABETH moved into the Alexandria dry-docks after being sunk in shallow waters by Italian "Pigs" (midget submarines) on December 18, 1941. The Royal Navy destroyer LANCE and the minesweeper ABINGTON were constructive losses after a Luftwaffe raid on Malta. The Royal Navy destroyer HAVOCK ran aground near Kelibia and was later destroyed by a torpedo from the Italian submarine ARADAM.

1943   USAAF fighters shot down fourteen Luftwaffe Ju52 transports over Tunisia. Ten more were destroyed on the ground in Sicily. USAAF 82nd

Fighter Group ace William Sloan (12 victories) was captured when his P38 was shot down near Cap Bon, Tunisia. Captain Denver Truelove was killed over Italy. He had been a bombardier on the "Doolittle Raid".

1945 Private First Class Sadao Munemori, of the 442nd Combat Team (Nisei), won a posthumous Medal of Honor near Serravezza, Italy.

Atlantic

1941 The U105 sank the British freighter LARRINAGA (5,200 tons). U105 survived until June 2, 1943. The U76 was sunk by the Royal Navy destroyer WOLVERINE and sloop SCARBOROUGH south of Iceland.

1942 The U552 sank the American tanker BYRON D. BENSON (7,953 tons-10 dead). U552 survived the war. The U154 sank the American tanker CATAHOULA (5,030 tons-10 dead). U154 survived until July 3, 1944.

1943 The U530 sank the American tanker SUNOIL (9,005 tons-with all hands). U530 survived the war. The U630 sank the British freighter WAROONGA (9,365 tons). U630 survived until May 4th. The U229 sank the Swedish freighter VAALAREN (3,406 tons). U229 survived until September 22nd. The U706 sank the British tanker BRITISH ARDOUR (7,124 tons). U706 survived until August 2nd.

1945 The U857 damaged the American tanker ATLANTIC STATES (8,537 tons). The U1169 was sunk by a mine in St. George's Channel.

North America

1937 Douglas Aircraft took over Northrop Aviation.
1942 The destroyer ENDICOTT was launched. She was stricken in 1969.
1943 The escort carrier CASABLANCA was launched. She was scrapped in 1947.
1945 A Japanese balloon-bomb was found near Massacre Lake in Nevada.
1964 General Douglas MacArthur died in Washington D.C.

Pacific

1931 The IJN heavy cruiser CHOKAI was launched. She was sunk on October 25, 1944.

1942 The USAAF's 22nd Bomb Group flew the first operational mission with the B26 "Marauder"; the target was Rabaul, New Britain.

1943 The American 11th Air Force attacked Kiska in the Aleutians.

1944 The IJN sub chaser No.46 was sunk off Wake by a USN PB4Y. The 5th Air Force attacked Hollandia and sank the Japanese freighters CHOUN MARU and IWAKUNI MARU.

1945 The IJN submarine Ro-49 was sunk by the USN destroyer HUDSON. The USN battleship NEVADA was hit five times by shore-fire off Okinawa (2

of her crew died). The IJN tanker ARAOSAN MARU was sunk by the USN submarine HARDHEAD. IJN Admiral Kantori Suzuki replaced General Kuniaki Koiso as Japan's Prime Minister.
1948   Stan Bailey, a former member of the Boyington's "Black Sheep Squadron", was killed on a night-mission out of Hawaii.

China-Burma-India
1942   Fifty-three level bombers, thirty-eight dive-bombers and thirty-six fighters from the IJN carriers AKAGI, SHOKAKU, ZUIKAKU, SORYU and HIRYU attacked Royal Navy forces at Colombo on the west coast of Ceylon. They would shoot down nineteen "Hurricanes" and "Fulmars" and six "Swordfish" over the harbor. At 0800, the Royal Navy armed merchant cruiser HECTOR (11,198 tons) and the destroyer TENEDOS (launched in 1919 and had 33 of her crew killed) were sunk in Colombo Harbor in Ceylon. The HECTOR was later salvaged. Near mid-day, a Japanese reconnaissance aircraft from the cruiser TONE sighted British naval units south of Ceylon. Fifty-three dive-bombers were immediately launched from the Japanese carriers and by 1355 the Royal Navy heavy cruisers CORNWALL (launched in 1928 and had 190 of her crew killed) and DORSETSHIRE (launched in 1930 and had 234 of her crew killed) were sunk. The 1,122 survivors were not rescued until thirty hours later by the cruiser ENTERPRISE and two destroyers. Having failed to locate the main British fleet, the Japanese began withdrawing from the area.
1943   The U182 sank the British freighter ALOE (5,047 tons).
1945   The USAAF sank the IJN tanker KAMOI in Hong Kong Harbor.

April 6th

Western Europe
1938   Leading Jewish figures in Vienna were sent to Dachau Concentration Camp by the Germans.
1940   The Royal Air Force stopped its leaflet raids having dropped 6.5 million of them since September 4, 1939.
1941   The first successful Royal Air Force torpedo attack took place when 71 bombers attacked German warships at Brest, France. The target was the German battlecruiser GNEISENAU in Brest, France. Royal Air Force Flying Officer K. Campbell won a posthumous Victoria Cross during the attack. Fourteen Royal Air Force bombers attacked shipping off the Belgian and Dutch coasts. Gloster Aircraft made its first taxi tests with the E28/39 jet interceptor proto-type.

1942 157 Royal Air Force bombers attacked Essen, Germany and lost five aircraft. There were no casualties in the city.
1943 Eight Royal Air Force "Mosquitoes" attacked Namur, France. Forty-seven Royal Air Force bombers dropped mines off the Biscay ports and lost two aircraft.
1944 Twelve American 8th Air Force B24s dropped forty-four tons of bombs on V-1 rocket sites near Watten, France. Twenty-seven 8th Air Force P47s flew as escorts for the bombers. Eleven Allied officers who had escaped from Stalag Luft III at Sagan on March 24th were shot. Thirty-five Royal Air Force "Mosquitoes" attacked Hamburg and lost one aircraft. Thirty-nine people were killed in the raid.
1945 646 American 8th Air Force bombers dropped 1,628 tons of bombs on rail targets in Halle, Eisleben and Leipzig and lost four B17s. 630 8th Air Force fighters provided escort for the bombers and lost one P51. The Soviets attacked Vienna, Austria. The American 1st Army crossed the Weser River. First Lieutenant Raymond Beaudoin and First Lieutenant James Robinson, of the 63rd Division, won posthumous Medals of Honor near Hamelin, Germany. A Luftwaffe KG200 B17 was shot down by German anti/aircraft fire, while another crashed into a mountain during a flight between Wackersleben and Furstenfeldbruck. Canadian forces took Zutphen and Almelo in Holland. The USAAF's 492nd Bomb Group dispatched three B24s on "Carpetbagger" missions and lost one aircraft.
1947 Nazi Food Minister Herbert Backe hung himself in Nuremburg Prison.
1955 Winston Churchill resigned as Britain's Prime Minister.

Eastern Europe
1941 At 0515, German forces invaded Yugoslavia. The Luftwaffe attacked Belgrade, Yugoslavia and killed thousands. The Royal Air Force attacked Sofia, Bulgaria. The Yugoslavian Air Force shot down ten Luftwaffe aircraft and lost fifteen of their own.
1944 The American 15th Air Force attacked Zagreb, Yugoslavia.
1945 The Soviets entered Konigsberg.

Mediterranean
1941 German forces invaded Greece. Besides the ill-equipped Greek Army, they also faced 31,000 troops from the British Commonwealth. Italy declared war on Yugoslavia. The South African Division took Addis Ababa, Ethiopia. The Axis took Mechiland Msus in Cyrenaica. A German patrol captured three British generals (O'Connor, Neame and de Wiart) near Derna in Libya.

The Month of April

1942   Axis aircraft attacked Alexandria, Egypt. The Royal Navy destroyer HAVOC ran aground off Tunisia with the loss of one man. The crew and 100 passengers bound for Malta were interned by Vichy French.

1943   Private E. Anderson, of the East Yorkshire Regiment, won a posthumous Victoria Cross at Wadi Akarit, Lieutenant Colonel L. Campbell, of the Argyll and Sutherland Highlanders, and Lalbahadur Thapa, of the 2nd Gurkha Rifles, also won Victoria Crosses during the battle. French Major General Edouard Welvert, commander of the "Constantin Division", was killed by a mine while entering Kairouan, Tunisia. The USAAF sank the German freighter SAN DIEGO (6,013 tons) and damaged the Italian ROVERETO (8,564 tons) off Bizerte. The German trawler UJ-2202 was sunk off Trapani by Allied aircraft.

1944   The German minesweeper R-192 was sunk in the Tyrrhenian Sea by British MTBs. The U455 was lost off Spezia.

1945   Ali Haidar, of the 6/13th Frontier Force Rifles, won a Victoria Cross in Italy.

Atlantic

1940   The U59 sank the Norwegian freighter NAVARRA (2,118 tons). U59 survived the war.

1941   The U94 sank the Norwegian tanker LINCOLN ELLSWORTH (5,580 tons). U94 survived until August 28, 1942. The Royal Navy armed merchant cruiser CORMORIN was scuttled by Royal Navy destroyer BROKE after an on-board fire. Only 20 of her 425-man crew were lost.

1942   The U571 sank the Norwegian tanker KOLL (10,044 tons). U571 survived until January 28, 1944. The U754 sank the Norwegian tanker KOLLSKEGG (9,858 tons). U754 survived until July 31st.

1943   The U632 sank the Dutch freighter BLITAR (7,065 tons). U632 was then sunk by the Royal Air Force's No.86 Squadron southwest of Iceland. The U635 was sunk by the Royal Navy frigate TAY off Iceland. The American freighter JOHN SEVIER (7,176 tons) was sunk north of Cuba by the U185. U185 survived until August 24th. The U336 rescued the last 6 survivors from the American freighter JONATHAN STURGES which had been sunk on February 23rd by U707.

1944   The U302 sank the Norwegian tanker SOUTH AMERICA (6,246 tons) and the freighter RUTH I (3,531 tons). U302 was then sunk by the Royal Navy frigate SWALE northwest of the Azores.

1945   The U1195 sank the British transport CUBA (11,420 tons) was sunk in the English Channel. U1195 was then sunk by the Royal Navy destroyer WATCHMAN.

North America

1920 The destroyer PEARY was launched in Philadelphia. She was sunk on February 19, 1942.

1938 The first flight of the USAAF's P39 "Airacobra" took place.

1941 The Royal Navy battleship MALAYA arrived in New York to repair damages inflicted by the U106.

1946 The B17D "Swoose" was transferred to the city of Los Angeles from Kingman, Arizona. She eventually ended up in storage at the Smithsonian in Washington D.C. As of 2009, she was undergoing restoration at the Air Force Museum at Wright-Patterson Field in Ohio.

1967 "Doolittle Raider" Lieutenant George Barr died.

1996 USN Vice Admiral John D. Bulkeley died. He had won a Medal of Honor while serving as the commander of the PT-boat squadron that rescued General Douglas MacArthur from the Philippines in 1942.

2009 Medal of Honor recipient Russell E. Dunham, age 89, died. He had won the Medal of Honor near Kayserberg, France on January 8, 1945 while serving with the 3rd Infantry Division. USAAF Colonel Edward Roddy, age 89, died in Fresno, California. He had scored 8 victories in the Pacific while flying the P47.

Pacific

1942 The Japanese landed in the Admiralty Islands. The USN submarine SEADRAGON arrived at Corregidor to evacuate personnel. The American freighter BIENVILLE was sunk by the Japanese Air Force.

1944 Thirty-one American 13th Air Force bombers attacked Truk and lost one B24. Royal Australian Air Force "Beaufighters" sank the Japanese tanker MYOSHO MARU at Koepang, Timor. The Japanese freighter ARABIA MARU was damaged by a mine off Formosa.

1945 355 Japanese kamikazes attacked the USN fleet off Okinawa. The USN destroyers BUSH (87 died), COLHOUN (34 died) the destroyer-minesweeper EMMONS (64 died), the American freighters LOGAN VICTORY (15 died) and HOBBS VICTORY (12 died) were sunk off Okinawa by kamikazes. The Royal Navy carrier ILLUSTRIOUS and the USN destroyers WITTER (6 died), HYMAN (11 died), HOWORTH (9 died), HAYNESWORTH (12 died), HARRISON (no casualties), HUTCHINS (1 died) and MULLANY (30 died) and the destroyer escort FIEBERLING (no casualties) were damaged by kamikazes off Okinawa. The USN destroyers MORRIS (12 died), LEUTZE (8 died), and NEWCOMB (40 died) were constructive losses after air attacks off Okinawa. The USN battleship NORTH CAROLINA was hit by an American 5" shell off Okinawa and suffered 3 dead and 44 wounded. The IJN battleship YAMATO was sighted by the B29 "Yokohama Yo-Yo" leaving the Inland Sea. She was en route to Okinawa on what was basically a kamikaze mission. She was to run aground off Okinawa and fore on American positions until she had been destroyed or ran out of ammunition. She did not have enough fuel for a return trip. USMC Corporal Richard Bush, of the 6th Division, won a Medal of Honor on Okinawa. The USN submarine HARDHEAD sank the ARAOSAN MARU (6,886 tons). The IJN destroyer AMATSUKAZE and the escort No.134 were sunk by the USAAF. The IJN minesweeper W-12 was sunk by the USN submarine BESUGO.

China-Burma-India
1942   The Japanese Air Force attacked targets in India for the first time. The primary targets were the towns of Coconada and Vizagupatam. The Royal Indian Navy's sloop INDUS was sunk near Akyab by the Japanese Air Force. The IJN cruisers KUMANO and SUZUYA and the destroyer SHIRAKUMO (commanded by Kurita) sank nine ships including the American freighter EXMOOR. Another group made up of the cruisers CHOKAI, YURA and ASAGIRI and the destroyer YUGIRI sank (Ozawa) sank four ships. Another unit comprised of the cruisers MIKUMA and MOGAMI and the destroyer AMAGIRI sank three more ships. Aircraft flying from the carrier RYUJO sank three ships including the American freighter SELMA CITY. The IJN would sink more than 92,000 tons of Allied shipping during its foray into the Indian Ocean. The IJN submarine I-15 submarine sank the American freighter WASHINGTONIAN (6,617 tons). Japanese forces took Kama, Burma.
1944   The second USAAF B29 to arrive in the CBI, landed at Chakulia, India. Abdul Hafiz, of the Jat Regiment, won a posthumous Victoria Cross in Burma.

April 7th

Western Europe
1882   German General Kurt von Schleicher was born. He would be the last Chancellor of the Weimar Republic and was assassinated by the Nazis during the "Night of the Long Knives" on June 30, 1934.
1925   Adolf Hitler renounced his Austrian citizenship.
1939   Spain joined the Anti-Comintern Pact along with Germany and Italy.
1940   The German task force that was to invade Norway weighed anchor. The German general in charge of the invasion of Denmark, Kurt Himer, arrived in Copenhagen, Denmark wearing civilian clothes. He was there to reconnoiter the city. Royal Navy mine-layers left port en route to the

coast of Norway where they were to attempt to block the movement of iron ore from northern Sweden to Germany.

1941 Twenty-five Royal Air Force "Blenheims" attacked shipping off the Dutch and Danish coasts and lost one aircraft. 229 Royal Air Force bombers attacked Kiel and lost two "Wellingtons" and two "Whitleys". Eighty-eight people were killed in the raid. Twenty-four Royal Air Force "Blenheims" attacked Bremerhaven, Germany.

1943 Adolf Hitler met Benito Mussolini at Klessheim Castle outside Salzburg to discuss the situations in Russia and Africa.

1944 British General Bernard Montgomery presented his final plan for "Overlord" at a staff meeting at St. Paul's School in London. Joseph Goebbels was named as Administrator of Berlin. Twelve Royal Air Force "Halifaxes" dropped mines off the Dutch coast.

1945 1,261 American 8th Air Force bombers dropped 3,451 tons of bombs on aircraft and rail targets in Germany and lost fourteen B17s and three B24s. 830 8th Air Force fighters provided escort for the bombers and claimed sixty-four victories for the loss of three P51s and two P47s. Seventeen Royal Air Force bombers attacked shipping at Ijmuiden, Holland. The American 3rd Army discovered the Reichsbank monetary and gold reserves in the Kaiseroda Mine in Merkers, Germany. Private First-Class Mike Colalillo, of the 100th Division, won a Medal of Honor near Untergriesheim, Germany. The US Army's 14th Division took Neustadt on the Saar River. The American 3rd Army took its 400,000th prisoner. An American 1st Army military commission convicted German Captain Curt Bruns of having caused the murders of two American prisoners of war during the "Battle of the Bulge". 186 Royal Air Force bombers attacked Molbis.

1953 Luftwaffe Field Marshal Hugo Sperrle was buried in Munich.

1959 A Luftwaffe 1,000kg bomb was uncovered in London.

Eastern Europe

1941 The Royal Air Force attacked Sofia, Bulgaria. German forces took Skopje, Yugoslavia. The Yugoslavian Air Force lost twelve aircraft in action against the Germans.

1942 The Soviets opened a railway to Leningrad.

1944 Two Slovakian Jews, Alfred Weczlar and Rudolf Vrba, escaped from Auschwitz and brought the first information of such camps to the outside world. Luftwaffe ace Kurt Ebener (fifty-seven aerial victories) was captured.

1945 The Soviets entered Vienna, Austria.

1947 After a trial, Rudolf Hoess, German commander of Auschwitz, was executed at the camp.

Mediterranean

1939 The Italians landed in Albania.

1941 The DAK took Derna, Libya. Eleven Luftwaffe He111s attacked Piraeus, Greece and hit the British explosives-carrier CLAN FRASER (7,529 tons). The ensuing explosion destroyed 13 ships of 41,942 tons of shipping, 25 motor sailing ships and 60 lighters.

1942 Malta had its 2,000th air-raid alert of the war. The U453 damaged the British freighter SOMERSETSHIRE (9,716 tons).

1943 Units of the British 8th Army and the US Army's 2nd Corps met near Graiba, Tunisia. Axis forces continued their retreat towards Enfidaville, Tunisia. German Lieutenant Colonel Claus von Stauffenberg (See July 20, 1944) was wounded by strafing Allied fighters, while with the 10th Panzer Division in Tunisia. He lost his right hand, left eye and two fingers on his left hand.

1944 The American 15th Air Force attacked rail targets in Italy.

Atlantic

1941 The US naval base on Bermuda was activated. The U124 sank the British freighter PORTADOC (1,746 tons). U124 survived until April 2, 1943.

1942 The German U552 sank the British tanker BRITISH SPLENDOR (7,138 tons) and the Norwegian whaler LANCING (7,866 tons). U552 survived the war.

1945 The U1024 damaged the American freighter JAMES W. NESMITH (7,176 tons).

North America

1925 The carrier SARATOGA was launched. She was expended during the Bikini A-bomb tests in 1946.

1943 The destroyers PAUL HAMILTON and TWIGGS and the submarine ASPRO were launched. PAUL HAMILTON was stricken in 1968, TWIGGS was lost on June 16, 1945 and ASPRO was discarded in 1962.

2009 USN Captain John Strane, age 88, died in San Diego, California. He had scored 13 victories in the Pacific while flying the F6F.

South America

1977 Karl Ritter, Nazi film director, died in Buenos Aires.

Pacific

1941 The carrier YORKTOWN and the destroyers MAYRANT, TRIPPE, RHIND, MUSTIN and RUSSELL were transferred to the Atlantic.

1942 The first USAAF P38 "Lightnings" to arrive in the Southwest Pacific Area landed in Australia. They were four F-4 recon aircraft belonging to the 8th

Photo Squadron. Admiral William Halsey's Task Force 16.1, consisting of the USN carrier ENTERPRISE, the heavy cruisers NORTHAMPTON and SAN FRANCISCO, the destroyers BALCH, BENHAM, ELLET and FANNING and the tanker SABINE, left Pearl Harbor to rendezvous with the carrier HORNET and "Doolittles Raiders". The last Allied positions on Bataan were attacked. The Alaska Defense Command ordered the internment of the 263 Japanese-Americans living in Alaska.

1943 The Japanese Naval Air Force sent 71 bombers and 117 fighters to attack the American forces in the Guadalcanal area. The USN destroyer AARON WARD (27 died), the HMNZ corvette MOA and the USN tanker KANAWHA were sunk off Tulagi in the raid. USMC 1st Lieutenant James Swett, of VMF 221, won a Medal of Honor for actions over the Solomons. The USN submarine TUNNY sank the KOSEI MARU (8,237 tons). The USN submarine PICKEREL sank the FUKUEI MARU (1,113 tons). The USN submarine TROUT laid 23 mines off Sarawak, Borneo. The IJN carrier TAIHO was launched. She was sunk on June 19, 1944.

1944 The IJN submarine I-2 was sunk by the USN destroyer SAUFLEY.

1945 The IJN battleship YAMATO, the light cruiser YAHAGI, and the destroyers ISOKAZE, HAMAKAZE, ASASHIMO and KASUMI were sunk by Task Force 58 aircraft. The USN carrier HANCOCK (72 of her crew died), the battleship MARYLAND (10 of her crew died), the destroyer BENNETT (3 of her crew died) and the destroyer escort WESSON (8 of her crew died) were hit by kamikazes off Okinawa. The USN PGM-18 was sunk off Okinawa by a mine. The IJN light cruiser ISUZU was sunk by the USN submarines GABILAN and CHARR in the Java Sea. The USN submarine TIRANTE sank the TAMA MARU (396 tons). USAAF B29s attacked the Mitsubishi plant in Nagoya and the Musashino plant outside Tokyo. The first USAAF P51 escort mission was flown from Iwo Jima.

China-Burma-India

1942 The IJN submarine I-3 damaged the British freighter ELMDALE (4,872 tons). The IJN submarine I-6 sank the British freighter BAHADUR (5,224 tons).

1944 The Japanese surrounded the British 161st Brigade at Jotsoma in Burma.

April 8th

Western Europe

1940 At 0700, the French and British governments informed the Norwegian government that they had laid three minefields off the Norwegian coast. Despite reports of the impending invasion of Norway by the Germans the Norwegian government failed to take decisive action. Although coastal defensive units were alerted, they were forbidden to lay defensive minefields. Airfields were not fortified and military reservists were notified by ordinary mail. Since the war began, the Royal Air Force's Bomber Command had flown 1,527 sorties on which it had dropped seventy-one tons of bombs and lost sixty-two aircraft.

1941   Seventeen Royal Air Force "Blenheims" attacked shipping targets. 160 Royal Air Force bombers attacked Kiel and lost four aircraft over the target and a further nine that crashed on returning to Britain. 125 people were killed in the raid. Twenty-two Royal Air Force bombers attacked Bremerhaven, Germany. One Royal Air Force "Hampden" was lost on a mine-laying mission.

1942   272 Royal Air Force bombers attacked Hamburg, Germany and lost 5 aircraft. Seventeen people were killed in the raid.

1943   Twenty-three P47s from the USAAF's 4th, 56th and 78th Fighter Groups flew a sweep near Dunkirk, France. 392 Royal Air Force bombers attacked Duisburg, Germany and lost 19 aircraft. Forty buildings were destroyed and thirty-six people were killed in the raid.

1944   611 American 8th Air Force bombers dropped 1,388 tons of bombs on Brunswick, Germany and various Luftwaffe airfields and lost 30 B24s and 4 B17s. 780 8th and 9th Air Force fighters provided support for the bombers and claimed 137 victories for the loss of 5 P38s, 4 P47s and 14 P51s. 163 American 9th Air Force B26s dropped 263 tons of bombs on Hasselt, Belgium. The U2 was lost in collision with the fishing boat HEINRICH FREESE in the Baltic. The American 15th Air Force attacked aircraft targets in Austria. Forty Royal Air Force "Mosquitoes" attacked Essen, Germany. Five B17s from the USAAF's 422nd Bomb Squadron dropped 1,000,000 leaflets on Liege, Brussels, Ghent, Antwerp, and Mont-sur-Sombre in Belgium.

1945   1,103 American 8th Air Force bombers dropped 3,179 tons of bombs on airfields and rail targets in Germany and lost nine B17s. 763 8th Air Force fighters provided escort for the bombers and lost 1 P47. The US Army's 5th Armored Division crossed the Leine River, south of Hannover. Staff Sergeant John Crews, of the 63rd Division, won a Medal of Honor near Lobenbacherhof. The American 3rd Army received ninety of the new T26E3 "Pershing" tanks. The French 1st Division took Pforzheim. The American 7th Army took Schweinfurt. The Soviets occupied the suburbs of Vienna. Ferdinand Schorner, Commander of German Forces in Czechoslovakia, was promoted to Field Marshal. Hans von Dohnanyi, a member of the Abwehr, was executed at Sachsenhausen for his part in the July 20th conspiracy. 4,000 American prisoners of war where force-marched 400 kilometers from Krems, Austria to Branau, where they were liberated on May 2nd. 440 Royal Air Force bombers attacked Hamburg, Germany and lost six aircraft. The U677, U747, U982, U2509, U2514, U2516 and U2537 were sunk in the raid. 242 Royal Air Force bombers attacked Lutzkendorf, Germany and lost six "Lancasters". 107 Royal Air Force "Mosquitoes" attacked targets in Germany.

1949 Wehrmacht General Wilhelm Adam died in Garmisch. He had commanded Germany's western front until relieved by Hitler in 1938.

Eastern Europe

1941 German forces, under von Kleist, took Nis, Yugoslavia.

1944 Soviets attack in the Crimea. Stalin was informed of the date for "Overlord". Royal Air Force "Wellingtons" and American 15th Air Force B24s mined the Danube near Belgrade.

1945 The German tanker FRANKEN (11,115 tons) and the patrol boat Uj-301 were sunk by Soviet aircraft off Hela in the Baltic.

Mediterranean

1941 General Maitland Wilson, Commander of the Commonwealth forces in Greece, ordered the 1st Armored Brigade to block the German forces moving in from the north. The Italian minelayer OSTIA and the torpedo boats GIORDANO and ORSINI were scuttled at Massawa. The Allies took Massawa, Ethiopia.

1942 Malta suffered its heaviest attacks of the war.

1943 Axis forces continued their retreat towards Enfidaville in Tunisia.

1945 Major A. Lassen, a Dane serving with the Royal Army Commandos, won a posthumous Victoria Cross in Italy.

Atlantic

1940 The Royal Navy began mining Norwegian waters. At 0905, the Royal Navy destroyer GLOWWORM, which was escorting the minelayers, was sunk after ramming the German heavy cruiser HIPPER west of Trondheim, Norway. Only thirty-eight of her crew survived. Her commander, Lieutenant Commander Gerard Roope, won a posthumous Victoria Cross. The HIPPER suffered a 120-foot gash in her side. The German transport RIO DE JANEIRO was sunk en route to Norway by the Polish submarine ORZEL.

1941 The USN Task Group 7.3 arrived at the newly activated USN base on Bermuda. The Task Group consisted of the carrier RANGER, the cruisers TUSCALOOSA and WICHITA and the destroyers KEARNY and LIVERMOORE. In May, they would be reinforced by the cruisers

QUINCY and VINCENNES, the destroyers SAMPSON, EBERLE, GWIN, GRAYSON, MEREDITH, MONSSEN and ERICSSON and the carrier WASP. The U124 sank the British freighter TWEED (2,697 tons). U124 survived until April 2, 1943. The U107 sank the British freighters ESKDENE (3,829 tons) and HELENA MARGARETA (3,316 tons). U107 survived until August 18, 1944. The Royal Navy armed merchant cruiser RAJPUTANA was sunk by the U108, forty of her crew died. The Royal Navy destroyer LEGION rescued 277 survivors. U108 survived until April 11, 1944.

1942 The U84 sank the Yugoslavian freighter NEMANJA (7,966 tons). U84 survived until August 24, 1943. The Italian submarine CALVI sank the American tanker EUGENE THAYER (7,138 tons-eleven dead).

1943 The Italian submarine ARCHIMEDE sank the Spanish freighter CASTILLO MONTEALLEGRE (3,972 tons).

1944 The U843 sank the British freighter NEBRASKA (8,261 tons). U843 survived until April 9, 1945. The U962 was sunk by the Royal Navy sloops CRANE and CYGNET northwest of Cape Finisterre.

1945 The U774 was sunk by the Royal Navy frigates CALDER and BENTINCK southwest of Ireland. The U1001 was sunk southwest of Land's End by the Royal Navy frigates FITZROY and BYRON.

North America

1939 The destroyer SIMS was launched at Bath, Maine. She was sunk on May 7, 1942.

1944 The destroyer HYMAN was launched. She was scrapped in 1970.

1945 A Japanese balloon-bomb was found near Merrit, British Columbia.

1981 US Army General Omar Bradley died in New York City at age 88. He had commanded the 12th Army Group in Europe.

Pacific

1942 Almost 2,000 of the 78,000 men defending Bataan escaped to Corregidor before the final defenses on the peninsula collapsed. The USN minesweeper BITTERN was scuttled in Manila Bay. She had been an engine-less hulk since being damaged in an air-raid on December 10th.

1944 The USN submarine SEAHORSE sank the ARATAMA MARU (6,783 tons).

1945 American forces took the Motobu Peninsula on Okinawa. The USN destroyer GREGORY (2 wounded) was hit by a Japanese kamikaze off Okinawa. The USN submarine BULLHEAD was attacked by a USAAF B24. The USN YMS-103 was sunk off Okinawa by a mine. The USN submarine SPADEFISH sank the RITSU GO (she was the ex-Chinese LEE TUNG-1,834 tons). USAAF B29s attacked Kagoshima on Kyushu.

1989 The previously undiscovered wreck of the CHUYO MARU was located in Palau Lagoon.

China-Burma-India
1942 The USAAF began to airlift supplies over the "Hump". The operation involved flying over the Himalayas from Assam, India to Kunming, China and would continue until the end of the war. By the time it ended, 460 aircraft and almost 800 American air-crew would be lost, but more than 650,000 tons of supplies would be delivered. The American Volunteer Group shot down 11 Japanese aircraft over Loiwing. A British "Catalina" patrol plane located the Japanese fleet, which was approaching Ceylon. The British commander (Somerville) ordered the operational ships in Trincomalee out to sea. The IJN submarine I-3 sank the British freighter FULTALA (5,051 tons).
1943 Kawabe replaced Iida as Japanese Commander-in-Chief in Burma.

April 9th

Western Europe
1872 French statesman Leon Blum was born. He was Premier for two different periods in the mid-thirties and was arrested by Vichy authorities. He survived the war and died on March 30, 1950.
1879 Erich Ludendorff was born. Ludendorff would be Quartermaster-General of the German Army during WWI and would participate in the Nazis Putsch attempt in Munich in 1923.
1899 Luftwaffe General Hans Jeschonneck was born in Allenstein. He would be the Luftwaffe Chief of Staff until his suicide on August 19, 1943.
1935 Future Luftwaffe commander Hermann Goering married actress Emmy Sonnemann.
1940 At 0235, the German heavy cruiser BLUCHER was sunk by Norwegian defenses at Bolaerne near Oslo in southern Norway. 125 German sailors and 195 soldiers died when she went down. The German torpedo boat ALBATROS was damaged in the same action. At 0415, ten German destroyers attacked Narvik in northern Norway. At 0425, the Norwegian coastal battleship EIDSVOLD was sunk by the German destroyer WILHELM HEIDKAMP off Narvik. At 0530, the Norwegian coastal battleship NORGE was sunk in Narvik harbor by the German destroyer BERND VON ARNIM. The Norwegian torpedo boat TOR was scuttled at Frederikstad. She was later raised by the Germans and renamed the TIGER. German ground forces landed at Bergen, Oslo, Kristiansand, Trondheim and Narvik. German airborne units attacked Sola Airport and

the city of Stavanger in southern Norway. Twenty-four Royal Air Force bombers attempted to locate German naval units off Bergen, Norway. The Germans captured the Norwegian coastal defense ships HARALD HAARFAGRE and TORDENSKJOLD and at Horton and renamed them THETIS and NYMPHE. The Germans captured the torpedo boats BALDER, ODIN, GYLLER and the minelayer OLAV TRYGGVASON at Horton and renamed them LEOPARD, PANTHER, LOWE and BRUMMER respectively. At 1900, the German light cruiser KARLSRUHE was torpedoed and sunk in the Skagerrak off Kristiansand in southern Norway by the Royal Navy submarine TRUANT. At 2130, five Royal Navy destroyers approached Narvik. They would attack the German ships located there, the next morning. The Norwegian torpedo boat AEGER was sunk at Stavanger by the Luftwaffe. The German light cruiser KONIGSBERG was damaged at Bergen by Norwegian shore batteries. The Royal Navy heavy cruisers SOUTHAMPTON and GLASGOW were damaged and the destroyer GURKHA was sunk by the Luftwaffe west of Bergen. The Royal Navy battleship HOWE was launched. She was scrapped in 1957.

1941 Twenty Royal Air Force "Blenheims" attacked German shipping. The Luftwaffe attacked Birmingham, Britain. Eighty Royal Air Force bombers attacked Berlin and lost 5 aircraft. Three more "Wellingtons" were lost in other operations.

1942 Seven Royal Air Force "Wellingtons" attacked Essen, Germany.

1943 Four Royal Air Force "Mosquitoes" attacked targets in Germany. 109 Royal Air Force bombers attacked Duisburg, Germany and lost 8 "Lancasters". Fifty buildings were destroyed and twenty-seven people were killed in the raid.

1944 402 American 8th Air Force bombers dropped 957 tons of bombs on industrial targets in Germany and lost 18 B17s and 14 B24s. One of the lost B17s landed in Sweden. 719 8th and 9th Air Force fighters provided support for the bombers and claimed 39 victories for the loss of 2 P38s, four P47s and 4 P51s. A 452nd Bomb Group B17 landed near Vaerlose, Denmark and was captured. 239 Royal Air Force bombers attacked Lille, France and lost 1 "Lancaster". 456 French civilians were killed in the raid. 225 Royal Air Force bombers attacked Villeneuve-St-Georges, France. Ninety-three French civilians were killed in the raid. Five B17s from the USAAF's 422nd Bomb Squadron dropped 2,752,000 leaflets on Rouen, Paris, Amiens and Caen in France. The USAAF's 801st Bomb Group sent twenty-three B24s on "Carpetbagger" missions.

1945 The American 9th Army reached the Krupp factories in the Ruhr. Royal Air Force bombers attacked Lutzendorf, Germany. 729 American 9th Air

Force bombers attacked Bad Berka, Kummersruck, Naumburg and Jena in Germany. Fifty-seven Royal Air Force bombers attacked Hamburg, Germany and lost 2 "Lancasters". 1,215 American 8th Air Force bombers dropped 3,108 tons of bombs on airfields and oil targets in Germany and lost 6 B17s and 1 B24. 812 8th Air Force fighters provided support for the bombers and claimed 85 victories for the loss of 5 P51s. Commander of the Abwehr, Wilhelm Canaris, his chief of staff, Hans Oster and Protestant Theologian Dietrich Bonhoeffer were executed at Flossenburg Concentration Camp by the Germans. Johann Elser (See November 8, 1939) was executed at Dachau. The Royal Navy escort carrier BITER was sold to France. She had participated in the sinking of 2 U-boats during the war. 599 Royal Air Force bombers attacked Kiel and lost 3 aircraft. In the raid, the German pocket battleship ADMIRAL SCHEER was sunk, as well as the torpedo boat T-1, the minesweeper M-504 and the submarines U804, U843, U1065, U1131 and U1227. The heavy cruiser ADMIRAL HIPPER and the light cruiser EMDEN were also badly damaged in the attack. 105 Royal Air Force "Mosquitoes" attacked targets in Germany.

Eastern Europe
1942   The Soviets began offensive in the Crimea. General Mikhail Yefremov committed suicide rather than surrender his 33rd Army to the Germans.
1944   The 1st Panzer Army rejoined German forces after a 150-mile forced march through Soviet territory.
1945   The Soviets took Konigsburg, East Prussia.

Mediterranean
1941   The Italian liner OCEANIA was sunk by the Royal Navy submarine UPHOLDER. The British Commonwealth forces in Greece under General Maitland Wilson retreated to defensive positions near Mount Olympus. The Greek Army was forced to halt its offensive against the Italians and move troops to stop the Germans that were moving in from Yugoslavia. The Greek "Metaxas Line" was broken. The German 2nd Panzer Division captured Salonika, Greece. The 70,000 men of the 2nd Greece Army surrendered in Thrace.
1942   The Royal Navy destroyer LANCE was sunk off Malta by German "Stukas".
1943   The British 8th Army continued its advance towards Sfax, Tunisia. Private Robert Booker, of the 34th Division, won a posthumous Medal of Honor near Fondouk, Tunisia.
1945   The British 8th Army (commanded by McCreery) began an offensive in Italy. Richard McCreery would die in 1967. Namdeo Jadhao, of the

1/5th Mahratta, won a Victoria Cross in Italy. 825 American 15th Air Force bombers attacked tactical targets in Italy. The American freighter CHARLES HENDERSON exploded while unloading 2,000 tons of explosives at Bari, Italy, all hands were lost.

Atlantic
1940   In a brief battle off the coast of Norway between the Royal Navy battlecruiser RENOWN and the German battlecruisers SCHARNHORST and GNEISENAU, the GNEISENAU suffered one 15"shell hit.
1941   The U107 sank the British freighter HARPATHIAN (4,671 tons) and the tanker DUFFIELD (8,516 tons). U107 survived until August 18, 1944. The U98 sank the Dutch freighter PRINS WILLEM II (1,304 tons). U98 survived until November 19, 1942. The German armed merchant cruiser KORMORAN took the British freighter CRAFTSMAN (8,022 tons).
1942   The U160 sank the American freighter MALCHACE (3,516 tons-1 dead). U160 survived until July 14, 1943. The U552 sank the American tanker ATLAS (7,137 tons-2 dead). U552 survived the war. The U123 sank the American freighter ESPARTA (3,365 tons-1 dead). U123 survived the war.
1943   The U515 sank the French freighter BAMAKO (2,357 tons). U515 survived until April 9, 1944.
1944   The U515 was sunk north of Madeira by the USN escort carrier GUADALCANAL, the destroyer POPE and the destroyer escorts CHATELAIN, FLAHERTY, and PILLSBURY.
1945   The British freighter SAMIDA was sunk by a German midget submarine.

North America
1941   The battleship NORTH CAROLINA was commissioned at the New York Navy Yard. She was the first USN battleship to be completed since December 1923 when the WEST VIRGINIA was commissioned. NORTH CAROLINA was dedicated as a memorial in 1961. The American government took action to declare Greenland a protectorate until Denmark was freed from German occupation.
1943   The escort carrier PRINCE WILLIAM was commissioned. She was scrapped in 1961.
1944   The escort carrier CAPE ESPERANCE was commissioned. She was scrapped in 1961. The submarines KETE and BLENNY were launched. KETE was lost in March 1945 and BLENNY was stricken in 1973 and expended as a target. The battleship WASHINGTON completed collision repairs at Bremerton, Washington (See February 1st).
1963   Former British Prime Minister Winston Churchill became an Honorary American citizen.

1977 Donald Gary died. He had won a Medal of Honor aboard the USN carrier FRANKLIN in 1945.
1987 Don Whitaker, of Rolla Missouri, received a Distinguished Service Cross for his actions while serving as a Staff Sergeant with the 6th Division on Luzon in 1944.

Pacific

1942 General Edward King surrendered the American forces on Bataan. The USN submarine SNAPPER delivered forty-six tons of supplies to Corregidor. The USN PT-34 was scuttled off Cebu. The USN tug NAPA was scuttled off Corregidor.
1943 The USN submarine TAUTOG sank the IJN destroyer ISONAMI and the freighter PENANG MARU (5,214 tons) off Celebes. The USN submarine GRAYLING sank the SHANGHAI MARU (4,103 tons). The USN submarine DRUM sank the OYAMA MARU (3,809 tons).
1944 American forces landed on Pak Island in the Admiralties. The last Japanese forces on Manus Island surrendered. The IJN light cruiser SAKAWA was launched. She was expended in 1946 after the Bikini A-bomb tests. The USN submarine WHALE sank the HONAN MARU (5,401 tons). The USN submarine SEAHORSE sank the BISAKU MARU (4,467 tons) and the MIMASAKI MARU (4,667 tons). The USN SC-984 ran aground off the New Hebrides and was lost.
1945 The US Army's 163rd Regimental Combat Team landed on Jolo in the Philippines. The US Army's 186th Regimental Combat Team landed on Busuanga in the Philippines. Private First-Class Edward Moskala, of the 96th Division, won a posthumous Medal of Honor on Okinawa. USAAF B29s attacked airfields on Kyushu. The IJN submarine Ro-46 was sunk by the USN destroyers MONSSEN and MERTZ. The USN submarine TIRANTE sank the NIKKO MARU (5,057 tons) and the IJN escort CD-102 (940 tons). The IJN minesweeper W-3 (702 tons) was sunk by the USN submarine PARCHE. The USN LCT-876 was sunk by a Japanese kamikaze. The USN destroyer CHARLES J. BADGER (no casualties) was damaged by a kamikaze.

China-Burma-India

1942 At 1120, 91 bombers and 38 fighters from the IJN carriers AKAGI, SORYU, HIRYU, SHOKAKU and ZUIKAKU attacking Royal Navy facilities at Trincomalee on the east coast of Ceylon. They shot down 9 of the 23 British fighters that rose to defend the harbor. Five of nine British "Blenheim" bombers that attacked the Japanese fleet were shot down. After locating British naval units, the Japanese carriers launched 80 bombers to attack them. They sank the carrier HERMES (10,850 tons, launched in 1924 and had 307 of her crew killed). At 1130, the Royal Australian Navy destroyer VAMPIRE (8 of her crew died) went down and at 1200; the corvette HOLLYHOCK (53 died) sank. The transport SAGAING went down in the same action east of Ceylon. After this action the Japanese decided to return to the Pacific. They had destroyed 23 merchant ships totaling 112,312 tons. This was in addition to the warships that had been destroyed. By the 12th of April, all Japanese surface ships had vacated the Indian Ocean. The Japanese submarines that had accompanied them had sunk 9 ships and would remain in the area. Japanese Naval Air Force ace Kenji Okabe (15 victories) would score his first, two Hawker "Hurricanes" over Trincomalee, Ceylon. He would survive the war.

1944 Lance Corporal J. Harman, of the Royal West Kent Regiment, won a Victoria Cross at Kohima. 14th Air Force B25s sank the Japanese freighter HOKUREI MARU off Hainan Island.

April 10th

Western Europe

1918 The Royal Navy light cruiser DAUNTLESS was launched. She was scrapped in 1946.
1932 Paul von Hindenburg defeated Adolf Hitler in Germany's general elections.
1937 The Luftwaffe's Ju88V1 (the Ju88 prototype) was lost in an accident.
1940 The Royal Navy destroyers HOTSPUR, HARDY, HAVOCK, HUNTER and HOSTILE, under Captain Warburton-Lee, attacked German naval forces at Narvik, Norway. At 0415, the German destroyers WILHELM HEIDKAMP (81 dead-including the German commander, Commodore Friedrich Bronte) and ANTON SCHMIDT were sunk by the Royal Navy destroyers. The Royal Navy destroyer HUNTER sank after colliding with the Royal Navy destroyer HOTSPUR. At 0615, the Royal Navy destroyer HARDY was beached after being damaged. Captain Warburton-Lee won a posthumous Victoria Cross aboard the destroyer HARDY. At 0700, the German light cruiser KONIGSBERG was sunk at Bergen by fifteen "Skuas" from the Royal Navy carrier FURIOUS. She was later raised, but would capsize on September 22, 1944. Six Royal Air Force bombers attacked Stavanger airfield and lost one "Hampden". Royal Air Force bombers attacked shipping in the Baltic and lost one "Whitley".
1941 Twenty-one Royal Air Force "Blenheims" attacked shipping targets and lost one aircraft. Fifty-three Royal Air Force bombers attacked Brest, France and lost one "Wellington". The raid scored four bomb hits on the

German battlecruiser GNEISENAU that killed fifty of her crew. Fifty-three Royal Air Force bombers attacked Dusseldorf, Germany and lost five "Hampdens".

1942   Royal Air Force ace Wing Commander M. Lister-Robinson (19 victories) was killed in action. 254 Royal Air Force bombers attacked Essen, Germany and lost 14 aircraft. Seven people were killed in the raid. Forty Royal Air Force bombers attacked Le Havre, France and lost one "Manchester". One of three Royal Air Force "Hampdens" that dropped mines off Heligoland was lost.

1943   502 Royal Air Force bombers attacked Frankfurt, Germany and lost 21 aircraft. Eighteen people on the ground were killed in the raid. A Royal Canadian Air Force "Wellington" crashed near Birmington in Warwickshire, Britain. The wreckage was recovered in 1989.

1944   The USAAF's 4th Fighter Group scored its 405th victory. Fifty-six American 9th Air Force P51s attacked rail targets at Hasselt, Belgium. 148 9th Air Force B26s dropped 184 tons of bombs on Namur. Forty 9th Air Force B26s attacked Charleroi, Belgium. 655 American 8th Air Force bombers dropped 1,690 tons of bombs on airfields in Belgium and France and lost two B17s and one B24. 496 8th and 9th Air Force fighters provided support for the bombers and claimed fifty-two victories for the loss of one P47 and one P51. 171 American 8th Air Force P38s and P47s attacked airfields in France and claimed two victories for the loss of three P38s. 180 Royal Air Force "Lancasters" attacked Tours, France and lost one aircraft. 157 Royal Air Force "Halifaxes" attacked Tergnier, France and lost ten aircraft. 163 Royal Air Force bombers attacked Laon, France and lost one "Lancaster". 147 Royal Air Force bombers attacked Aulnoye, France and lost seven "Lancasters". Fourteen French civilians were killed in the raid. 132 Royal Air Force bombers attacked Ghent, Belgium. 428 civilians were killed in the raid. Five B17s from the USAAF's 422nd Bomb Squadron dropped 2,000,000 leaflets on Lille, Le Mans, Reims, Chartres, and Orleans in France. The USAAF's 801st Bomb Group dispatched twenty-three B24s on "Carpetbagger" missions.

1945   An Arado Ar234 recon plane flew from Stavanger, Norway to Scotland on the Luftwaffe's last mission over the British Isles. 315 Royal Air Force bombers dropped 1,139 tons of bombs on Plauen, Germany. 1,232 American 8th Air Force bombers dropped 3,402 tons of bombs on rail and aircraft targets in Germany and lost eighteen B17s and one B24. 868 8th Air Force fighters provided support for the bombers and claimed 311 victories for the loss of eight P51s. Luftwaffe ace Franz Schall (106 victories) died when his Me262 jet crashed at Parchim. Luftwaffe jets shot down ten 8th Air Force bombers near Berlin. 230 Royal Air Force bombers attacked

Leipzig, Germany and lost one "Lancaster". The German torpedo boat T-13 was sunk in the Skagerrak by the Royal Air Force. The American 9th Air Force attacked Schweinfurt, Germany. The American 9th Army entered Hannover and Essen in Germany. Canadian forces took Groningen and Leeuwarden in Holland. Ninety-five Royal Air Force bombers attacked Leipzig and lost seven "Lancasters". 105 Royal Air Force "Mosquitoes" attacked targets in Germany.

1961 Royal Navy Lieutenant Donald Cameron died. He had commanded one of the "X-craft" submarines that had attacked the German battleship TIRPITZ in Altenfjord, Norway on September 22, 1943.

Eastern Europe

1941 Axis forces took Zagrib, Yugoslavia. The Yugoslavian minesweeper KOBAC was captured at Sebenico and recommissioned as the Italian UNIE.

1944 Soviet forces occupied Odessa. The Germans had evacuated 24,000 men and 55,000 tons of supplies by sea. The German minesweeper M-459 was sunk and the M-413 was damaged by the Soviet Air Force in the Gulf of Finland.

Mediterranean

1941 The Australian 9th Division withdrew into Tobruk. British forces were ordered to withdraw from Greece.

1942 Luftwaffe ace Herman Neuhoff (40 victories) was shot down over Malta and captured.

1943 Twenty-four American 9th Air Force B24s attacked La Madallena, Sardinia and sank the Italian light cruiser TRIESTE and the torpedo boats MAS-501 and MAS-503. The heavy cruiser GORIZIA was also damaged during the attack. Allied fighters shot down five German Ju52s over Tunisia. 15th Air Force B24s attacked Naples, Italy. The British 8th Army took Sfax, Tunisia.

1945 The US Army's 92nd Division entered Massa, Italy.

Atlantic

1940 The U37 sank the Swedish tanker SVEABORG (9,076 tons) and the Norwegian freighter TOSCA (5,128 tons). U37 survived the war. The U4 sank the British freighter THISTLE (1,090 tons). U4 survived the war.

1941 America took over the protection of Greenland. The U52 sank the Dutch freighter SALEIER (6,563 tons). The USN destroyer NIBLACK dropped three depth charges on a suspected U-boat contact off Iceland while rescuing her survivors. U52 survived the war.

1942 The German armed merchant cruiser THOR took the British freighter KIRKPOOL (4,842 tons). The U654 sank the British freighter EMPIRE PRAIRIE (7,010 tons). U654 survived until August 22nd. The U203 sank the British tanker SAN DELFINO (8,072 tons). U203 survived until April 25, 1943. The U552 sank the American tanker TAMAULIPAUS (6,943 tons-2 dead). U552 survived the war. The U85 sank the Norwegian freighter KNUDSEN (4,904 tons).

1943 The U376 was sunk in the Bay of Biscay by the Royal Air Force's No.172 Squadron.

1944 The U68 was sunk by aircraft from the USN escort carrier GUADALCANAL.

1945 The U878 was sunk west of St. Nazaire, France by the Royal Navy destroyer VANQUISHER and frigate TINTAGEL CASTLE.

North America

1930 The heavy cruiser CHICAGO (awarded 3 battle stars during the war) was launched. She was lost on January 30, 1943.

1941 FDR extended the limits of the USN's "Neutrality Patrol". He also removed the Red Sea from the list of areas forbidden to American shipping.

1944 The destroyer COLHOUN was launched. She was lost on April 6, 1945.

1945 A Japanese balloon-bomb was found near Bald Mountain in Oregon.

1994 Konrad Kalejs, age 80, was deported to Australia for concealing his past as an Einstazcommando in occupied Latvia.

2010 RCAF Wing Commander Douggie Oxby died in Toronto at the age of 88. As a navigator/radar operator aboard night-fighters during the war, he had been involved in the destruction of 22 German aircraft.

Pacific

1925 The IJN heavy cruiser KAKO was launched. She was sunk on August 10, 1942.

1941 Nagumo assumed command of IJN's 1st Air Fleet.

1942 The "Bataan Death March" began. It would be a 60-mile trek for 76,000 Allied prisoners of war. Of those, 12,000 were American and the rest were Filipino. Approximately 5,200 Americans died during the trip, but the death toll for the Filipinos was greater than the Americans. The USN submarine SNAPPER evacuated personnel from Corregidor. Japanese forces landed on Cebu and Billiton in the Philippines. The USN submarine tender CANOPUS was scuttled off Bataan. The USN minesweeper FINCH was sunk in shallow water off Corregidor by Japanese bombs. She was later salvaged by the IJN and placed in service as patrol boat No.103 and was sunk by USN aircraft off Cap Padaran on January 12, 1945. The USN minesweeper QUAIL was damaged by Japanese artillery while sweeping a channel from American-held Corregidor to the open sea. USN Lieutenant Commander John Bulkeley, commander of MTB Squadron No.3, won a Medal of Honor for actions in the Philippines. It was his unit that had evacuated US Army General Douglas MacArthur and his family from Corregidor. The USN submarine THRESHER sank the SADO MARU (3,039 tons). An IJN radio intelligence unit at Combined Fleet Headquarters at Hagashishima picked up transmissions indicating that 2 to 3 USN carriers ("Doolittle's Raiders") were headed for Japan.

1943 The American 11th Air Force attacked Kiska in the Aleutians.

1945 The USN destroyer escort MILES was damaged by a Japanese kamikaze off Okinawa. The USN destroyer COLQUON was damaged by Japanese aircraft off Okinawa and was later sunk by gunfire from the USN destroyer CASSIN YOUNG. The Dutch submarine 0-19 sank the HOSEI MARU (676 tons). The US Army's 1st Cavalry Division took Mauban and the 11th Airborne Division took Atimonan on Luzon.

China-Burma-India

1942 The American Volunteer Group shot down 5 Japanese aircraft over Loiwing.

April 11th

Western Europe

1933 Hermann Goering was appointed Prime Minister of Prussia.

1940 Ruge relieved Laake as Commander-in-Chief of the Norwegian Army. Six Royal Air Force "Wellingtons" attacked Stavanger, Norway.

1941 The Norwegian destroyer MANSFIELD destroyed a fish factory at Lopphavet, Norway. Twenty Royal Air Force "Blenheims" attacked German shipping targets and lost 1 aircraft. The Luftwaffe attacked Bristol, Britain.

1942 185 Royal Air Force bombers dropped 225 tons of bombs on Essen, Germany. During the raid a "Halifax" bomber dropped the first 8,000-pound bomb.

1943 Eight Royal Air Force "Mosquitoes" attacked targets in France and Holland and lost two aircraft. Six P47s from the USAAF's 4th Fighter Group attacked targets near Calais, France. The conference at Salzburg, Austria between Hitler and Mussolini ended. Fritz Sauckel and Pierre Laval signed a pact making French prisoners of war laborers for Germany. Forty-six Royal Air Force bombers dropped mines off French ports and lost two aircraft.

1944   828 American 8th Air Force bombers dropped 2,047 tons of bombs on industrial targets in Germany and lost fifty-two B17s and twelve B24s (nine of the lost B17s landed in Sweden). 819 8th and 9th Air Force fighters provided support for the bombers and claimed 116 victories for the loss of 7 P47s and 9 P51s. Supreme Allied Commander General Dwight Eisenhower made a fact-finding tour of the 91st Bomb Group (B17) based at Bassingbourn, the 4th Fighter Group (P51) at Debden and the 386th Bomb Group (B26) at Great Dunmow. While he was visiting the 91st at Bassingbourn he christened a B17 named "General Ike". First Lieutenant Edward Michael, of the 305th Bomb Group (B17), won a Medal of Honor over Germany. 193 American 9th Air Force bombers attacked Charleroi, Belgium. The last German rail convoy to leave Lyons, France took 650 French civilians to the concentration camps at Ravensbruck and Auschwitz. 341 Royal Air Force bombers attacked Aachen, Germany and lost nine "Lancasters". 1,525 people were killed in the raid. Five B17s from the USAAF's 422nd Bomb Squadron dropped 2,000,000 leaflets on Paris, Rouen, Le Mans, Rennes, Vichy, Lyon, Limoges and Toulouse in France. The USAAF's 801st Bomb Group dispatched twelve B24s on "Carpetbagger" missions.

1945   1,270 American 8th Air Force bombers dropped 3,363 tons of bombs on rail targets and airfields in Germany and lost one B17. 871 8th Air Force fighters provided support for the bombers. 129 Royal Air Force bombers attacked Nuremberg, Germany. 100 Royal Air Force bombers attacked Bayreuth, Germany. The American 9th Air Force attacked Bamberg, Germany. The American 9th Army reached the Elbe River south of the city of Magdeburg, Germany and also captured a V-2 rocket assembly plant in Nordhausen. Also taken in the same area was a huge slave labor camp that had supported the V-2 facility. The American 3rd Army took Weimar and liberated nearby the Buchenwald Concentration Camp. It would be used by the Soviets until 1951 to detain political prisoners. American forces took Coburg, Germany. The German minesweeper M-2 was sunk off Norway by the Royal Air Force. 107 Royal Air Force "Mosquitoes" attacked Berlin and lost one aircraft. The German minesweeper M-2 was sunk in Fedjefjord, Norway by British aircraft.

1947   The trial of the Buchenwald staff began at the Dachau concentration camp near Munich.

Eastern Europe

1944   The Soviets took Simferpol, Kerch and Zhankoi.

1945   The Soviets took the City Hall and Parliament Building in Vienna. The Soviet Air Force sank the German hospital ship POSEN (1,104 tons), the minesweeper M-376 and the patrol boat Uj-1102 off Hela.

Mediterranean

1933   Hermann Goering led a diplomatic mission to Rome to ease Italian fears of German aggression in Austria.

1941   German forces surrounded and launched a major attack on Tobruk.

1942   The Royal Navy destroyer KINGSTON was wrecked by German "Stukas" at Malta.

1943   The U593 sank the British freighter RUNO (1,858 tons). Allied fighters shot down 18 Luftwaffe Ju52 transports off Tunisia. The Italian minesweeper RD-20 was sunk by Allied aircraft. USAAF B24s attacked Naples. USAAF B26s attacked Oudna Airfield near Tunis in Tunisia. Faid Pass in Tunisia was captured by American forces.

1944   The USN destroyer escort HOLDER (16 dead) was constructive loss after a Luftwaffe torpedo attack northeast of Algiers. She was sold for scrap June 20, 1947.

1945   The US Army's 92nd Division took Carrara, Italy.

1985   The Turkish gunboat YILDIRIM (the ex-USN DEFIANCE) exploded off Lesbos.

Atlantic

1940   The German light cruiser KARLSRUHE was sunk off Norway by the Royal Navy submarine TRUANT. The German pocket battleship LUTZOW was torpedoed by the Royal Navy submarine SPEARFISH off Norway.

1941   The U124 sank the Greek freighter AEGEON (5,285 tons). U124 survived until April 2, 1943.

1942   The U123 sank the American tanker GULFAMERICA (8,081 tons-19 dead). U123 survived the war. The Italian submarine CALVI sank the Norwegian freighter BALKIS (2,161 tons). The U252 sank the Norwegian freighter FANEFJELD (1,355 tons). U252 survived until April 14th. The U130 sank the Norwegian freighter GRENAGER (5,393 tons). U130 survived until March 12, 1943. The U160 sank the British freighter ULYSSES (14,647 tons). U160 survived until July 14, 1943. Norwegian-based Luftwaffe Ju88s sank the freighters EMPIRE COWPER and HARPALION. The US Coast Guard patrol boat No.455 rescued 11 survivors from the freighter CITY OF NEW YORK.

1943   The U571 sank the Norwegian freighter INGERFIRE (3,835 tons). U571 survived until January 28, 1944. The U181 sank the British freighter EMPIRE WHIMBREL (5,983 tons). U181 survived the war. The American freighter EDWARD B. DUDLEY (7,177 tons-69 dead) was sunk by the U615. U615 survived until August 7th. At 0400, the Royal Navy destroyer BEVERLY (the ex-USN BRANCH) was sunk southwest of Iceland by the U188.

North America

1942 The destroyers GANSEVOORT and CHEVALIER and the freighter STEPHEN HOPKINS were launched. The GANSEVOORT was stricken in 1971 and CHEVALIER was lost October 7, 1943.

1955 Admiral Clifton Sprague, commander of "Taffy 3" in Leyte Gulf, died in San Diego.

1969 Admiral Daniel Barbey, commander of the Amphibious Forces of the 7th Fleet, died in Bremerton.

Pacific

1940 Admiral Claude C. Bloch relieved Admiral Orin G. Murfin as Commandant Fourteenth Naval District and Commandant Navy Yard Pearl Harbor.

1942 The Japanese freighter TAIJUN MARU (1,274 tons) caught fire and sank at Truk. The first attempt to right minelayer OGLALA at Pearl Harbor was made. She had capsized during the Japanese attack on December 7th.

1943 The Japanese Air Force attacked Oro Bay, New Guinea sinking 2 freighters. The IJN submarine I-26 sank the Yugoslavian freighter RECINA (4,732 tons). The American 11th Air Force attacked Kiska in the Aleutians.

1944 The USN submarine REDFIN sank the IJN destroyer AKIGUMO southeast of Zamboanga. The Japanese evacuated Cape Hoskins and Gasmata on New Britain. The USN submarine CERO was attacked by a 5th Air Force B24 off Biak.

1945 The USN battleship MISSOURI, the carrier ENTERPRISE and the destroyers HANK (3 of her crew died), KIDD (38 died), HALE (2 wounded) and BULLARD (her commander Lieutenant Commander Thomas Hart, killed in the attack, was Admiral Thomas Hart's son) and the destroyer escort MANLOVE (1 died) and the LCS-36 were hit by Japanese kamikazes off Okinawa. In 1987 the KIDD was dedicated as a memorial in Baton Rouge, Louisiana. The USN carrier ESSEX was hit by a bomb off Okinawa. The USN submarine PARCHE sank the TOGO MARU (302 tons). The USN submarine SPADEFISH sank the HINODE MARU No.17 (235 tons). The US Army's Americal Division landed on Bohol in the Philippines.

China-Burma-India

1945 The British Eastern Fleet (commanded by Walker) attacked Sabang.

April 12th

Western Europe

1885 German General Hermann Hoth was born.

1917	The Royal Navy light cruiser CARDIFF was launched. She was scrapped in 1946.
1935	The first flight of the Royal Air Force's "Blenheim" bomber took place.
1940	German forces took the town of Halden in southern Norway near the Swedish border. Eighty-three Royal Air Force bombers attacked German shipping at Stavanger, Norway and lost six "Hampdens" and three "Wellingtons". The Luftwaffe lost five fighters during the action.
1941	Twenty Royal Air Force "Blenheims" attacked targets in Germany and Holland and lost one aircraft. Sixty-six Royal Air Force bombers attacked Brest and Lorient in France. Twenty-four Royal Air Force bombers attacked the airfield at Bordeaux, France and lost one "Wellington".
1942	Nine Royal Air Force "Bostons" attacked Hazebrouck, Belgium and lost one aircraft. 251 Royal Air Force bombers attacked Essen, Germany and lost ten aircraft. Twenty-seven people were killed in the raid.
1943	German radio announced the discovery of the graves of more than 4,000 Polish Army officers who had been executed by Soviet forces in the Katyn forest near Smolensk.
1944	455 American 8th Air Force bombers attempted to attack industrial targets in Germany, but had to abort due to bad weather and lost six B17s. 766 8th and 9th Air Force fighters provided support for the bombers and claimed nineteen victories for the loss of three P38s and two P51s. The American 15th Air Force attacked aircraft targets in Austria and lost seven bombers. Three Allied officers who had escaped from Stalag Luft III at Sagan on March 24th were shot by the Germans. Thirty-nine Royal Air Force "Mosquitoes" attacked Osnabruck, Germany. Twenty-one Royal Air Force bombers dropped supplies to Resistance forces in France and lost two "Stirlings".
1945	The American 3rd Army took Erfurt, Germany. The American 9th Army took Braunschweig and Brunswick in Germany and also established a bridge-head over the Elbe River. French forces took Baden-Baden and Heilbronn in Germany. Private First Class Joe Hastings, of the 97th Division, won a posthumous Medal of Honor at Drabenderhohe, Germany. The American 7th Army took Schweinfurt, Germany. The American 9th Air Force attacked an ordinance depot at Klempten, Germany. The USAAF's 453rd Bomb Group (B24) flew the last of its 259 8th Air Force missions, having lost 58 aircraft in combat. Luftwaffe Do217s flew their last mission of the war; the targets were Soviet-held bridges over the Oder. The USN LST-493 ran aground at Plymouth, Britain and was lost. 107 Royal Air Force "Mosquitoes" attacked targets in Germany.
1948	The Royal Navy battleship MALAYA was sold for scrap.
1962	Nazi author Erwin Kolbenheyer died in Munich.

1987 The wreckage of a Royal Air Force No.172 Squadron "Wellington" that crashed during the war near Clovelly, Scotland was recovered.

Eastern Europe
1941 The Germans entered Belgrade, Yugoslavia.
1943 The Germans found the bodies of 4,143 Polish officers in the Katyn Forest near Smolensk.
1944 The American 15th Air Force attacked Zagreb and Split in Yugoslavia and lost one B24.
1945 The Germans evacuated Zenica, Yugoslavia.

Mediterranean
1941 The Greek 1st Army began a general retreat in Albania. In the only tank battle of the war in Greece, units of the German 9th Panzer Division defeated the British 1st Armored Brigade near Kozani. Axis forces took Sollum, Egypt and Fort Capuzzo in Libya. The Royal Navy submarine TETRARCH sank a 2,474-ton Italian tanker off Tripoli.
1943 The Axis forces around Enfidaville were attacked by the British 8th Army. Allied forces took Sousse, Tunisia.
1945 The British cruiser ORION bombarded San Remo.

Atlantic
1939 Germany claimed 230,000 square miles of Antarctica.
1940 The U37 sank the British freighter STANCLIFFE (4,511 tons). U37 survived the war. The U54 was sunk in the North Sea by the Royal Navy submarine SALMON. The Dutch torpedo boat FRISCO was sunk by the Luftwaffe.
1941 American troops occupied Greenland. U124 sank the British freighter ST. HELENA (4,313 tons). U124 survived until April 2, 1943.
1942 The Italian submarine CALVI sank the Panamanian tanker BEN BRUSH (7,691 tons). The U154 sank the American freighter DELVALLE (5,032 tons-2 dead). U154 survived the war. The U130 sank the American tanker ESSO BOSTON (7,699 tons). U130 survived until March 12, 1943.
1943 The American freighter JAMES W. DENVER (7,200 tons-2 dead) was sunk west of the Canaries by the U195. U195 survived the war. The U404 sank the British freighter LANCASTRIAN PRINCE (1,914 tons). U404 survived until July 28th. The U563 sank the British freighter PACIFIC GROVE (7,117 tons) and the Dutch freighter ULYSSES (2,666 tons). U563 survived until May 31st. The U706 sank the British freighter FRESNO CITY (7,261 tons). U706 survived until August 2nd.
1945 The U1024 damaged the American freighter WILL ROGERS (7,200 tons). The U486 was sunk by the Royal Navy submarine TAPIR off Bergen.

North America

1933 The heavy cruiser NEW ORLEANS (awarded 16 battle stars during the war) was launched. She was scrapped in Baltimore in 1959.

1939 The destroyer WILSON was launched. She was scuttled in 1948 after serving as a target ship in Bikini.

1943 The escort carrier BRETON was commissioned. She was still on active duty in 1969.

1945 FDR died of a stroke at Warm Springs, Georgia. A Japanese balloon-bomb was found near Rome, Oregon and another was shot down off Attu in the Aleutians.

Pacific

1942 The USN PT-35 was scuttled at the Cebu Shipyard to prevent her capture by the Japanese. RAAF "Hudsons" attacked Koepang, Timor.

1943 The USN submarine FLYING FISH sank the SAPPORO MARU (2,865 tons). 174 Japanese aircraft attacked Port Moresby, New Guinea and lost 26. It was to be their last attack on the port. 5th Air Force B17s and B24s attacked Japanese shipping in Hansa Bay and sank the freighter SYDNEY MARU. The American 11th Air Force attacked Kiska and lost one P40.

1944 The USN submarine HALIBUT sank the TAICHU MARU (3,213 tons). USN PT-135 was scuttled near Crater Point, New Britain. The USN PT-135 was scuttled after she ran aground off New Britain. 5th Air Force attacked Hollandia and sank the Japanese freighter NARITA MARU.

1945 Seventy-one USAAF B29s attacked Koriyama, Japan. Staff Sergeant Henry Erwin, of the 29th Bomb Group, won a Medal of Honor on the mission. The IJN submarine Ro-64 was sunk in Hiroshima Bay by a mine. The USN submarine SILVERSIDES sank the SHIRATORI MARU (269 tons). The Royal Navy submarine STYGIAN sank the IJN minesweeper Wa-104 off the coast of Bali. The USN destroyer MANNERT L. ABELE (82 of her crew died) and the LCS-33 were sunk off Okinawa by Japanese kamikazes. The USN battleships NEW MEXICO, TENNESSEE and IDAHO, the destroyers ZELLAR, YOUNG, CASSIN YOUNG (1 died), BENNION (1 died), STANLY (3 wounded) and PURDY (13 died), the destroyer escorts RIDDLE (1 died), RALL (21 died), WANN and WHITEHURST (37 died), the Destroyer-Minesweeper JEFFERS, the minesweeper GLADIATOR, the minelayer LINDSEY, the LSM-89 and the LCS-57 were hit by kamikazes off Okinawa. Royal Navy aircraft attacked Formosa airfields.

China-Burma-India

1942 The Japanese took Migyaungye, Burma.

1945 The 7th Indian Division took Kyaukpadaung, Burma.

April 13th

Western Europe

1892   British Air Marshal Arthur Harris was born. During WWI, he flew with No.45 Squadron in France and No.44 Squadron in Britain. He was promoted to group captain in 1933. In 1937 he assumed command of No.4 Bomb Group. He was promoted to air vice marshal in 1938. On February 22, 1942 he took over Bomber Command. During the war, his Bomber Command would lose 57,143 men, of which 41,548 have no known grave. He retired in 1946 as a Marshal of the Royal Air Force and died in South Africa in 1984.

1937   The Royal Navy carrier ARK ROYAL was launched. She was sunk on November 14, 1941.

1940   The Royal Navy battleship WARSPITE and the destroyers BEDOUIN, COSSACK, ESKIMO, PUNJABI, HERO, ICARUS, KIMBERLEY, FORESTER and FOXHOUND attacked the German naval forces at Narvik, Norway. The U64 was sunk at Narvik by WARSPITE's aircraft. At 1015, the WARSPITE and the BEDOUIN and ESKIMO sank the German destroyer KOELLNER (thirty-one dead). At 1230, the German destroyer ERICH GIESE (eighty-three dead) was sunk by the COSSACK and FOXHOUND. The German destroyer HANS LUDEMANN was sunk by the HERO. At 1230, the German destroyer DIETHER VON ROEDER was scuttled (sixteen dead). At 1330, the German destroyers BERND VON ARNIM (broken up in 1960) and HERMANN KUNNE were scuttled due to lack of fuel or ammunition. At 1500, the German destroyer GEORG THIELE (27 dead-broken up in 1963) was beached and later sank. The German destroyer WOLFGANG ZENKER was scuttled (broken up in 1960). Nine Royal Air Force "Blenheims" attacked German patrol boats in the North Sea. In the Royal Air Force's first mine-laying operation of the war, fifteen "Hampdens" dropped mines in the Baltic and lost one aircraft.

1941   Sixteen Royal Air Force bombers attacked targets in Holland and lost one "Blenheim".

1942   Louis Mountbatten was appointed Chief of Combined Operations. The German "Mirus Battery" on Guernsey Island was test-fired. It was made up of cannon salvaged from the Russian battleship IMPERATOR ALEKSANDER III, obtained by Germany after WW I. Forty-seven Royal Air Force bombers dropped mines in the Baltic and lost one "Stirling".

1943   Twenty-four Royal Air Force "Venturas" attacked targets in France. The USAAF's 4th, 56th and 78th Fighter Groups sent seventy-six P47s on missions over France and lost one aircraft to engine failure. This was the first of 450 missions that would be flown by the 78th during which it would lose 167 aircraft. It was also the first for the 56th. Ten Royal Air Force "Lancasters" dropped mines off the German coast and lost one aircraft. Six Royal Air Force "Mosquitoes" attacked targets in Germany.

1944 USAAF 4th Fighter Group (P51) ace Don Gentile (23 victories) crashed his fighter, "Shangri-la", while buzzing his base at Debden on the completion of his tour. He survived, but was reprimanded and would not fly in combat again. 566 American 8th Air Force bombers dropped 1,354 tons of bombs on industrial targets in Germany and lost thirty-two B17s and six B24s (ten B17s and three B24s landed in Switzerland). 871 8th and 9th Air Force fighters provided support for the bombers and claimed seventy-seven victories for the loss of three P38s, two P47s and four P51s. The American 9th Air Force and the British 2nd Tactical Air Force began a campaign against shore-batteries on the Channel coast. Twenty-nine Royal Air Force "Mosquitoes" attacked Berlin. Four B17s from the USAAF's 422nd Bomb Squadron dropped 800,000 leaflets on Amsterdam, The Hague, and Eindhoven in Holland.

1945 212 American 8th Air Force B17s dropped 577 tons of bombs on the marshalling yards at Neumunster, Germany and lost two aircraft. The USAAF's 56th Fighter Group (P47) scored its 1,002nd victory. The German 15th Army in the Ruhr surrendered to American forces. The American 3rd Army took Jena, Germany. The American 7th Army took Bamburg, Germany. British forces liberated the Belsen Concentration Camp. The American 9th Army took Duisburg and Dortmund in Germany. A Luftwaffe KG200-flown B24 (See June 20, 1944) was destroyed by its crew after its nose-gear failed on take-off from Quedlinburg, Germany. The German torpedo boat T-16 was sunk at Friedrichshaven, Germany by the Royal Air Force. 482 Royal Air Force bombers attacked Kiel, Germany and lost two "Lancasters". Fifty people were killed in the raid. 109 Royal Air Force "Mosquitoes" attacked targets in Germany and lost one aircraft.

Eastern Europe
1940 Russia and Japan signed a neutrality treaty.
1941 Royal Air Force bombers attacked Sofia, Bulgaria.
1942 The Soviet freighter KIEV (5,823 tons) and the Panamanian freighter EL OCCIDENTE (6,008 tons) was sunk by the U435.
1944 The American 15th Air Force attacked Budapest, Hungary and lost eighteen bombers and three escorting fighters. The Soviets took Simferpol in the Crimea and 20,000 prisoners.
1945 The Soviets took Vienna, Austria.

Mediterranean

1941 General Maitland Wilson, Commander of the British Commonwealth forces in Greece, decided to retreat 100 miles to the area around Thermopylae. The Greek destroyer PSARA was sunk by the Luftwaffe. Corporal J. Edmondson, of the Australian 17th Infantry Battalion, won a posthumous Victoria Cross at Tobruk, Libya. The Luftwaffe attacked Malta. The Persian sloops BABR and PALANG were sunk by Royal Australian Navy and Royal Navy surface forces.

1943 211 Royal Air Force bombers flying from Britain attacked La Spezia, Italy and lost four aircraft.

1945 The German torpedo boat TA-45 (the ex-Italian SPICA) was sunk by the Royal Navy MTBs 697 and 670.

Atlantic

1940 The Danish Faeroes Islands to the north of Britain were seized by British forces.

1941 The U108 sank the Royal Navy armed merchant cruiser RAJPUTANA (16,444 tons). Forty of her crew died. U108 survived until April 11, 1944. The U124 sank the British freighter CORINTHIC (4,823 tons). U124 survived until April 2, 1943.

1942 The U123 sank the American freighter LESLIE (2,609 tons-4 dead) and the Swedish freighter KORSHOLM (2,647 tons). U123 survived the war. The U154 sank the British tanker EMPIRE AMETHYST (8,032 tons). U154 survived until July 3, 1944. The U402 sank the British freighter EMPIRE PROGRESS (5,249 tons). U402 survived until October 13, 1943.

1943 The German blockade-runner PORTLAND (7,132 tons) was scuttled when approached by the Free French cruiser GEORGES LEYGUES.

North America

1896 USAAF General Ira Clarence Eaker was born in Field Creek, Texas. On August 15, 1917, he was commissioned as a reserve officer in the infantry. On November 15, 1917, he received his Regular Army commission and won his wings in October 1918. In 1921, he and Major Carl Spaatz set an aerial endurance record of almost 151 hours. In 1936, he became the first to navigate solely on instruments across the American continent. He was promoted to brigadier general in January 1942 and was named to command 8th Bomber Command. On December 1, 1942 he was promoted to major general and assumed command of the entire 8th Air Force from General Carl Spaatz. On September 13, 1943, he was promoted to lieutenant general. He was designated as Commander USAAF in the United Kingdom on October of that year. On December 22nd, Spaatz assumed command of the USAAF in Europe and Eaker went to the Mediterranean to replace Tedder as commander of the Mediterranean Allied Air Forces. He reached his new command in mid-January 1944. He stayed there until the end of the war. In 1947, he was named as the USAF's Chief of Staff. On August 31st of that year, he retired. He died on August 6, 1987.

1904   USAAF General Elwood Richard Quesada was born in Washington D.C. He was promoted to brigadier general on December 11, 1942 and given command of a wing. Within a few weeks, he assumed command of the 12th Fighter Command in the Mediterranean. In October 1943 he took over the 9th Fighter Command in Britain. He was promoted to major general on April 28, 1944. He became Air Force Chief of Intelligence in April 1945. He retired in 1947 as a lieutenant general. He died in 1973.

1943   The USAAF ordered 2,500 of the D-model of the P51 "Mustang".

1945   The last B17G "Flying Fortress" was delivered to the USAAF. Ten Japanese balloon-bombs were shot down over the Aleutians.

1950   The US Coast Guard cutter SOUTHWIND was returned after being lend-leased to Russia during the war.

1959   Flying Officer Robert J. Stephens died. He had been a bombardier on the "Doolittle Raid".

1998   An expedition left San Diego, California en route to Midway Atoll northwest of Hawaii. Its objective was to locate the wreck of the USN aircraft carrier YORKTOWN. The YORKTOWN had been sunk by Japanese forces in June of 1942 during the "Battle of Midway". The leader of the expedition was Robert Ballard. Previous to this, Ballard had located the wrecks of the German battleship BISMARCK and the passenger liner TITANIC in the Atlantic and various Allied and Japanese warships off Guadalcanal in the Southwest Pacific.

South America

1967   A B17G crashed at Santa Ana, Bolivia.

Pacific

1942   The USN submarine GRAYLING sank the RYUJIN MARU (6,243 tons), off Bungo Strait.

1943   American radio monitoring stations intercepted a message that Yamamoto would be inspecting bases in the Solomons. The American 11th Air Force attacked Kiska in the Aleutians and lost one P38.

1944   The Australians took Bogadjim, New Guinea. The USN submarine HARDER sank the IJN destroyer IKAZUCHI.

1945   American forces burned out the Japanese occupied Fort Drum, the "Concrete Battleship", located in Manila Bay. 327 USAAF B29s fire-bombed Tokyo, they dropped 2,139 tons of bombs and destroyed 11.4 square miles of the city. The USN submarine PARCHE sank the MISAGO MARU No.1 (265 tons) and the KOSHO MARU No.2 (302 tons). The USN submarine TIRANTE sank the JUZAN MARU (3,943 tons) and the IJN frigates CD-31 and NOMI. The USN submarine GABILAN sank the KAKO GO (762 tons). Technical/Sergeant Beaufort Anderson, of the 96th Division, won a Medal of Honor on Okinawa. Private First Class Dexter Kerstetter, of the 33rd Division, won a Medal of Honor on Luzon. Royal Navy aircraft attacked Formosa airfields.

April 14th

Western Europe
1914   Luftwaffe ace Hans Hahn (108 victories) was born in Gotha. He survived the war as a prisoner of the Soviets.
1931   King Alphonso XIII of Spain abdicated and fled to France. Alcala Zamora set up a provisional government and was elected as president on December 10th.
1940   The German gunnery training ship BRUMMER was sunk by the Royal Navy submarine STERLET in the Kattegat. The Norwegian torpedo boat TEIST was scuttled at Drange. Twenty-eight Royal Air Force bombers dropped mines off Denmark and lost two "Hampdens".
1941   Twenty Royal Air Force "Blenheims" attacked targets in Holland and lost one aircraft. The first of twenty B17Cs, on loan to the Royal Air Force from America, arrived in Britain. They would form the Royal Air Force's 90th Squadron. Ninety-four Royal Air Force bombers attacked Brest, France.
1942   Twelve Royal Air Force "Bostons" attacked Mondeville, France. The British accepted "Bolero", a plan submitted by US Army General George Marshall for preparing for the invasion of France. 208 Royal Air Force bombers attacked Dortmund, Germany and lost nine aircraft. Four people were killed in the raid. Twenty-three Royal Air Force bombers attacked Le Havre, France and lost one "Wellington".
1943   Luftwaffe Fw190 fighter-bombers destroyed a ball-bearing plant at Chelmsford in Essex. At 0300, the Norwegian destroyer escort ESKDALE was sunk in the Channel by the German torpedo boats S-65, S-90 and S-112. 462 Royal Air Force bombers attacked Stuttgart, Germany and lost twenty-three aircraft. 393 buildings were destroyed and more than 200 people were killed in the raid. Also killed were 257 French prisoners of war and 143 Russian prisoners of war.

1944   USAAF 354th Fighter Group (P51) ace Captain Walter Koraleski (8 victories) was shot down over Germany and captured. Sub/Lieutenant Klaus Donitz, elder son of the Grand-Admiral, was killed aboard the S-141. It had been part of a group that attacked Allied landing craft off the Isle of Wight. 1,500 Jews were shipped from Drancy, France to Auschwitz, where 105 survived the war.

1945   1,133 American 8th Air Force bombers dropped 3,318 tons of bombs on German forces still resisting on the Atlantic coast and lost two B24s. The Reichsbank currency reserves were loaded onto two trains in Berlin for shipment to Bavaria, while the gold reserves were sent by truck convoy. The American 9th Army took Magdeburg, Germany. Royal Canadian Air Force ace Sub/Lieutenant D. Laubman (15 victories) was shot down over Germany and captured. The American 1st Army reached the Mulde River. The American 3rd Army took Jena and Erfurt in Germany. The U235 was sunk in the Kattegat by the German torpedo boat T-17. 512 Royal Air Force bombers attacked Potsdam, Germany and lost one "Lancaster". This was the last major raid on a German city by the Royal Air Force's Bomber Command. Seventy-two Royal Air Force "Mosquitoes" attacked targets in Germany.

Eastern Europe

1943   Stalin's son died in Sachsenhausen Concentration Camp. He had been captured in action. The Germans had tried to arrange a trade, but Stalin had ignored them.

Mediterranean

1941   Axis aircraft attacked Malta. Axis forces attacked the Australian 6th Division at Tobruk, Libya. Forty Luftwaffe "Stukas" attacked Tobruk. Rommel stopped his advance at Salum just inside the Egyptian border.

1942   The Royal Navy submarine UPHOLDER was sunk off Tripoli, Libya by the Italian torpedo boat PEGASO. She was on her 23rd patrol and had sunk two submarines, two destroyers, 94,900 tons of merchant shipping and had won a Victoria Cross for her commander, Malcolm Wanklyn. Luftwaffe ace Karl-Heinz Krahl (24 victories) was killed in action over Malta by anti/aircraft fire.

1944   The first Jews from Greece were sent to Auschwitz.

1945   The American 5th Army took Vergato. Private First-Class John Magrath, of the 10th Mountain Division, won a posthumous Medal of Honor near Castel D'Aiano, Italy. Lieutenant Robert Dole, of the 10th Mountain Division, was wounded in Italy. The future US Senator and presidential candidate suffered a shattered shoulder, a punctured lung and a damaged kidney. He would spend 3 years in various hospitals recovering and would never regain full use of his right hand.

Atlantic

1940 The Royal Navy submarine TARPON was sunk by German trawlers.

1941 The U52 sank the Belgian freighter VILLE DE LIEGE (7,430 tons). U52 survived the war.

1942 The USN destroyer ROPER scored the USN's first U-boat victory when she sank the U85. The U203 sank the British freighter EMPIRE THRUSH (6,160 tons). U203 survived until April 25, 1943. The U66 sank the Greek freighter KORTHIAN (2,116 tons). U66 survived until May 6, 1944. The U571 sank the American freighter MARGARET (3,352 tons) with all hands. U571 survived until January 28, 1944. The U252 was sunk by the Royal Navy sloop STORK and corvette VETCH southwest of Ireland. Prior to being sunk, the U252 had landed agents on Iceland. The USN carrier WASP left the Clyde with a load of "Spitfires" for Malta.

1943 The U526 was sunk by a mine in the Bay of Biscay.

1944 The U448 was sunk by the Royal Navy sloop PELICAN and the Royal Canadian Navy frigate SWANSEA north of the Azores. The Royal Navy LSI (L) EL HIND caught fire and sank.

1945 The U879 sank the Belgian freighter BELGIAN AIRMAN (6,959 tons). The U1206 was lost in an accident in the North Sea. The U235 was sunk in error by the German torpedo boat T-17 in the North Sea.

North America

1942 Actor Ronald Reagan enlisted.

1971 The destroyer ALBERT W. GRANT was stricken.

1981 General Omar Bradley was buried in Arlington Cemetery. He had commanded the 12th Army Group in Northern Europe.

Pacific

1942 USN Task Force 17 (formed around the carrier YORKTOWN), under Admiral Frank Fletcher, went to Tongatapu to replenish in preparation for the upcoming battle in the Coral Sea.

1943 5th Air Force B17s and B24s attacked Japanese shipping in Hansa Bay and sank the freighter INDIA MARU. 5th Air Force ace Lieutenant Richard Bong shot down a "Betty" over Milne Bay, New Guinea. The American 11th Air Force attacked Kiska in the Aleutians and lost one B24.

1944 The IJN destroyer IKAZICHI was sunk southeast of Guam by the USN submarine HARDER. USN Commander David MacDonald became Air Officer aboard the carrier ESSEX. In August 1963 he would become Chief of Naval Operations.

1945   The USN destroyer LINDSEY (57 of her crew died) was crashed by 2 Japanese "Vals". The USN destroyer SIGSBEE (3 died) was hit by a Japanese kamikaze. The US Army's I Corps took Calauag on Luzon. USN Commander George Street, commander of the submarine TIRANTE, won a Medal of Honor on her first war patrol. The IJN escorts NOMI and No.31 were sunk by the USN submarine TIRANTE.

China-Burma-India
1942   The British began destroying the oil fields at Yenangyaung, Burma. Japanese forces took Myohla and Migyaungwe in Burma.
1944   The British 161st Brigade, which had been surrounded at Jotsoma in Burma, was relieved. The ammunition ship FORT STIKENE (7,142 tons) exploded in Bombay. Other ships lost in the incident were the Dutch freighters GENERAAL VAN DER HEYDEN (1,215 tons), GENERAAL VAN SWIETEN (1,300 tons) and TINOMBO (872 tons). Three Indian warships and fourteen merchant ships totaling 50,500 tons were damaged. 336 people were killed and more than 1,000 were injured. The British freighter SAMUTA rescued 38 survivors from the American freighter RICHARD HOVEY which had been sunk on March 29th by the I-26.

April 15th

Western Europe
1892   Luftwaffe ace Theodore Osterkamp (32 victories in WWI and 6 in WWII) was born. He survived the war.
1940   Vidkun Quisling resigned as head of the Norwegian government and was replaced by Christensen. The British 24th Guard's Brigade as well as French and Polish troops landed on Hinnoy Island, sixty miles from Narvik in northern Norway. Eleven Royal Air Force bombers attacked Stavanger airfield in southern Norway. One of two Royal Air Force "Blenheims" attacking German patrol boats off Wilhelmshaven in the Baltic was lost.
1941   Twenty-nine Royal Air Force "Blenheims" attacked German shipping and lost one aircraft. Ninety-six Royal Air Force bombers attacked Kiel, Germany and lost one "Wellington". Five people were killed in the raid. Twenty-three Royal Air Force bombers attacked Boulogne, France and lost one "Whitley".
1942   Nine Royal Air Force "Bostons" attacked Cherbourg, France. The French resistance forces attacked the German headquarters at Arras, France. 152 Royal Air Force bombers attacked Dortmund, Germany and lost four aircraft. Two people were killed in the raid.
1943   Thirteen Royal Air Force "Venturas" attacked Cherbourg, France. Twenty-three Royal Air Force bombers dropped mines off the Biscay

ports. Fifty-nine P47s from the USAAF's 4th, 56th and 78th Fighter Groups flew sweeps near St. Omer, France. They claimed three victories and lost three of their own. The German minesweeper M-5613 ran aground near Odderoy, Norway and was lost.

1944 Rommel and his Chief of Staff Speidel met to discuss the "Schwarz Kapelle". That was the code name for the conspiracy against Hitler. 616 American 8th and 9th Air Force fighters flew sweeps over Germany and claimed fifty-eight victories for the loss of 11 P38s, 7 P47s and 15 P51s. The American 9th Air Force attacked Pointe Du Hoc on the Normandy coast of France. The USAAF 56th Fighter Group (P47) ace Leroy Schreiber (14 victories) was killed in action over Flensburg, Germany.

1945 The Canadians took Arnhem. The last of the Reichsbank reserves that had been discovered at Merker were transferred to a bank in Frankfurt. The German 12th Army destroyed an American 9th Army bridgehead over the Elbe near Magdeburg. The American 3rd Army took Bayreuth. The concentration camp at Bergen/Belsen was liberated. American 12th Army Group commander General Omar Bradley informed General Simpson that his 9th Army was to stop at the Elbe River. 1,287 American 8th Air Force bombers dropped 2,855 tons of bombs on German units that were still resisting along the French coast. The German Panzer Lehr Division surrendered to American forces. The German minesweeper M-368 was sunk off Norway by a mine. 118 Royal Air Force "Mosquitoes" attacked targets in Germany and lost one aircraft. The German minesweeper M-368 was sunk by a mine off Kindesnes, Norway. The German harbor defense boats NO-37 and NO-31 deserted their posts and defected to Sweden. Both sank while being towed into Goteborg.

1948 Twenty-eight B29s landed in Munich to reinforce the USAAF in Europe.

1956 Nazi artist Emil Nolde died in Seebull.

1996 85-year-old Szymon Serafimowicz, a native of Russia, was ordered to face charges in Dorking, England, that he had murdered three Jews during WWII.

Eastern Europe

1944 Soviet forces took Tarnopol. The American 15th Air Force attacked Nis, Yugoslavia and Bucharest and Ploesti in Rumania.

1945 The Soviets took Radkesburg in Austria.

Mediterranean

1941 The British Admiralty ordered Admiral Andrew Cunningham to scuttle the battleship BARHAM to block the entrance to Tripoli Harbor, he refused. Cunningham would die in 1963.

1942	The population of the island of Malta was awarded the George Cross by the British government.
1943	General Omar Bradley relieved General George Patton as commander of the US Army's II Corps in North Africa. American 9th Air Force B24s attacked Catania, Sicily.
1944	The American 15th Air Force lost 3 of 137 bombers over Ploesti, Rumania.
1945	1,235 American 15th Air Force aircraft attacked tactical targets around Bologna.

Atlantic

1940	The U49 was sunk off Narvik, Norway by the Royal Navy destroyer FEARLESS.
1941	The Italian submarine TAZZOLI sank the British freighter AURILLAC (4,733 tons).
1942	The U575 sank the American freighter ROBIN HOOD (14 dead). U575 survived until March 13, 1944.
1943	The Italian submarine ARCHIMEDE was sunk off Brazil by USN VP-83 "Liberators". The USN YP-453 was lost after she ran aground off the Bahamas.

North America

1914	The battleship NEW YORK was commissioned. She was scuttled in 1948 after participating in the Bikini A-bomb tests.
1935	The first flight of the Douglas TBD "Devastator" torpedo bomber took place. It was the first USN aircraft to have hydraulically-operated folding wings. It would remain in frontline service until after the "Battle of Midway" in June 1942.
1938	The light cruiser ST. LOUIS (awarded 11 battle stars and a Navy Unit Citation during the war) was launched. She was transferred to Brazil in 1951 and was stricken in 1975.
1941	William Pawley organized the Central Aircraft Manufacturing Company. Its main purpose would be to organize the American Volunteer Group in China. FDR signed a secret executive order allowing American military personnel to volunteer for duty with the American Volunteer Group.
1942	The destroyer DYSON was launched. She was transferred to Germany in 1960. The submarine SHAD was launched. She was discarded in 1960.
1943	The A-bomb laboratory at Los Alamos was activated. The carrier YORKTOWN II was commissioned, she would participate in the 1944 movie "A Wing and a Prayer", 1968's "Tora Tora" and 1984's "The Philadelphia Experiment". She was eventually preserved as a memorial outside of Charleston, South Carolina. The 99th Fighter Squadron (Negro) left New York en route to the Mediterranean.

1944	The carrier HANCOCK (stricken in 1976), the escort carrier TAKANIS BAY (scrapped in 1960) and the destroyer HAYNESWORTH (sold to Taiwan in 1970) were commissioned.
1945	A Japanese balloon-bomb was found near Midas Creek, Alaska. The first flight of the P82 "Twin Mustang" took place.
1971	The destroyer BENNION was stricken.
1973	The destroyers OWEN, HART and LAWS were stricken.
1981	USN Lieutenant Commander John Smith Thach (he had devised the defensive maneuver known as the "Thach Weave") died in San Diego, having retired as an admiral in 1967.
1990	Vice Admiral Lawson P. "Red" Ramage died of cancer in Bethesda, Maryland at the age of 81. He had won a Medal of Honor while in command of the submarine PARCHE.

Pacific

1887	Australian General Henry Bennett was born in Melbourne. He commanded the Australian forces in Singapore in 1942. On he escaped capture by the Japanese when he and other Australian officers commandeered a Chinese junk and sailed to Batavia. This was after he had advised British General Percival to surrender Singapore. He was promoted to Lieutenant General and given command of the Third Corps after returning to Australia. Due to criticism of his escape from Singapore he was never given another combat command. He died in 1962.
1942	The USN PT-41 was scuttled off Mindanao. She was part of the group that was transporting US Army General Douglas MacArthur and his party from the Philippines to Australia and was the last of her kind in the Philippines. The USN carrier LEXINGTON left Pearl Harbor for the Coral Sea.
1943	The USN submarine SEAWOLF sank the KAIHEI MARU (4,575 tons). 5th Air Force B17s attacked Wewak, New Guinea and damaged the IJN destroyer TACHIKAZE. American forces completed their first airfield on Banika Island in the Russells. The American 11th Air Force attacked Kiska in the Aleutians.
1944	The IJN picket boat KOTOHIRA MARU (30 tons) was sunk at Truk by USAAF B24s. Royal Australian Air Force PBYs mined the waters off Woleai in the Carolines. The Alaskan Sea Frontier (commanded by Vice Admiral Frank Jack Fletcher) was established on Adak in the Aleutians. USAAF B25s attacked Ponape in the Carolines. The Japanese freighter SUMIDA MARU was sunk off Hokkaido by a mine.
1945	USMC Private First Class Harold Gonsalves, of the 6th Division, won a posthumous Medal of Honor on Okinawa. 303 USAAF B29s dropped

1,930 tons of incendiaries and burned out 6 square miles of Tokyo, 3.6 square miles of Kawasaki and 1.5 square miles of Yokohama. The Japanese Naval Air Force ace Shoichi Sugita (120 victories) was killed in action by USN F6F fighters over Kanoya Airfield in Japan. American forces took San Francisco, Luzon.

China-Burma-India
1943 The five surviving members of the "Doolittle Raid" in Japanese captivity were transferred to Nanking Prison.
1944 The IJN minesweeper W-7 was sunk southeast of Andaman Island by the Royal Navy submarine STORM. By this date, there were thirty-two USAAF B29s in India.

April 16th

Western Europe
1881 Lord Edward Halifax was born. When Eden resigned as Foreign Minister on February 20, 1938, Prime Minister Chamberlain appointed Halifax as his replacement. He held that position until December 1940 when Eden returned. He then went to the US as British ambassador. He remained there until May 1946. He died in 1959.
1940 The British 146th Brigade landed at Namsos in central Norway. British troops occupied Denmark's Faeroe Islands. Twelve Royal Air Force bombers attacked Stavanger airfield in Norway.
1941 The Luftwaffe attacked London. 107 Royal Air Force bombers attacked Bremen, Germany and lost one "Wellington" and one "Whitley".
1942 Twelve Royal Air Force "Bostons" attacked Le Havre, France. Twenty-one Royal Air Force bombers dropped mines off French ports and lost two aircraft.
1943 Twenty-five Royal Air Force "Venturas" attacked targets in Holland. Eighty-five Dutch civilians died in the raids. Seventy-eight American 8th Air Force B17s and B24s dropped 199 tons of bombs on Lorient and Brest in France and lost one B17 and three B24s. 327 Royal Air Force bombers attacked Pilsen, Czechoslovakia and lost thirty-six aircraft. The important Skoda factory target was not hit. 271 Royal Air Force bombers attacked Mannheim, Germany and lost eighteen aircraft. 130 buildings were destroyed and 130 people were killed in the raid.
1945 General Carl Spaatz, commander of the USAAF Strategic Air Force in Europe, declared that the strategic air war in Europe was over. The 8th Air Force's 4th Fighter Group (P51) destroyed 105 German aircraft on the ground near Prague, Czechoslovakia and lost eight aircraft. The

American 9th Air Force's 387th Bomb Group (B26) attacked rail yards at Gunzehausen, Germany. 1,208 American 8th Air Force bombers dropped 3,448 tons of bombs on German strong points and railways near Bordeaux, France marshalling yards around Regensburg, Germany and lost one B24. 860 8th Air Force fighters provided support for the bombers scoring 724 strafing victories and three more in the air. Thirty P51s and one P47 were lost. Eighteen Royal Air Force "Lancasters" attacked the German pocket battleship LUTZOW at Swinemunde and sank her with the loss of one aircraft. The American 7th Army reached the outskirts of Nurnburg, Germany. The special prisoner of war camp at Colditz was liberated by the US Army's 9th Armored Division. The U78 was sunk by a Soviet shore battery near Pillau. Stalin ordered the final assault on Berlin with 2.5 million men (150 divisions), 8,354 aircraft, 42,973 cannon and 6,287 tanks. The Canadians took Groningen. 233 Royal Air Force bombers attacked Pilsen, Czechoslovakia and lost one "Lancaster". 175 Royal Air Force bombers attacked Schwandorf and lost one "Lancaster". Eighty-seven Royal Air Force "Mosquitoes" attacked targets in Germany. The German harbor defense boat NO-21 (ex-Norwegian torpedo boat ORN) deserted from Oslo, Norway to Sweden.

Eastern Europe

1922 The Treaty of Rapallo was signed. It provided German aviators with training facilities in Russia.

1941 German forces occupied Sarajevo, Yugoslavia.

1942 The U403 sank the British freighter EMPIRE HOWARD (6,985 tons).

1944 The Soviets took Yalta in the Crimea. The American 15th Air Force attacked Belgrade, Yugoslavia and rail targets in Rumania.

1945 The German transport GOYA was sunk during the evacuation of Danzig, 6,500 died. The U78 was sunk at Pillau by Soviet artillery. She had been serving as a transformer station. Hungarian ace Dezso Szentgyorgyi shot down a Soviet Yak-9 fighter for his 34th aerial victory.

Mediterranean

1941 The Greek Commander-in-Chief Alexander Papagos asked that the British forces leave Greece to prevent further destruction of the country. British Prime Minister Churchill approved the evacuation, but stipulated that the island of Crete be held at all costs. The Royal Navy destroyers MOHAWK, JANIS, JERVIS and NUBIAN attacked an Axis convoy consisting of three Italian destroyers and five freighters off Tunisia. At 0220, the Italian destroyer LUCA TARIGO was damaged and sank at 0300. At 0225, the Italian destroyer BALENO was damaged and sank the next day. At 0225 the MOHAWK (launched in 1938) was torpedoed by the TARIGO and was scuttled by the JANUS. The Italian freighter SABAUDIA and four German freighters were sunk were also sunk in the action.

1942 British Royal Marines landed on Crete to destroy a wireless station. They had been transported by the British destroyers KELVIN and KIPLING. The U81 sank the French trawler VIKING (1,150 tons), the Egyptian sailing ships FATOUH EL KHER (97 tons) and BAB EL FARAG (105 tons) and the British tanker CASPIA (6,018 tons).

1943 At 0330, the Italian torpedo boat CIGNO (2 dead) was sunk and the torpedo boat CASSIOPEA was damaged by the Royal Navy destroyers PAKENHAM and PALADIN. The PAKENHAM was damaged by the CIGNO and was scuttled at 0800 by the PALADIN. The USAAF attacked Palermo and Catania on Sicily, sinking the Italian torpedo boat MEDICI at Catania.

1944 The American freighter THOMAS MASARYK (7,176 tons) was a constructive loss and the American freighter MEYER LONDON (7,210 tons) was sunk off Derna, Libya after an attack by the U407.

1945 Brigadier General William O. Darby, Assistant Division Commander of the 10th Mountain Division, was killed in the Po Valley by 88mm fire. He had commanded the US Army Rangers until they were all but wiped out near Anzio on January 29, 1944. After that he had commanded a regiment of the 45th Division. The German minesweeper R-15 was sunk in the northern Adriatic by a British MTB.

Atlantic

1940 The U-1 was sunk in the North Sea by the Royal Navy submarine PORPOISE. The Royal Navy submarine STERLET was sunk by German surface craft.

1941 The British freighter SIR ERNEST CASSEL (7,739 tons) was taken by the German armed merchant cruiser THOR.

1942 The U575 sank the American freighter ROBIN HOOD (6,887 tons). U575 survived until March 13, 1944. The U66 sank the Dutch tanker AMSTERDAM (7,329 tons). U66 survived until May 6, 1944. The U572 sank the Panamanian freighter DESERT LIGHT (2,368 tons). U572 survived until August 3, 1943.

1944 The U550 sank the American tanker PAN PENNSYLVANIA (11,017 tons-25 dead). U550 was then sunk off New York by the USN destroyer escorts GANDY, JOYCE, and PETERSON. The USN destroyer escort ENRIGHT was damaged in a collision with the Portuguese freighter THOME.

1945 The U2324 sank the British freighter MONARCH (1,150 tons). The U1274 sank British tanker ATHELDUKE (8,966 tons). The Royal Canadian Navy minesweeper ESQUIMALT was sunk by the U190. Forty-four of her crew died. The U880 was sunk by the USN destroyer escorts STANTON and FROST. The Royal Navy destroyer escort EKINS was a constructive loss after hitting a mine in the North Sea.

North America
1923 The light cruiser TRENTON was launched. She was scrapped in Baltimore in 1946.
1938 The destroyer BENHAM was launched. She was lost November 15, 1942.
1940 Captain Albert C. Read relieved Captain Aubrey C. Fitch as Commandant Naval Air Station, Pensacola, Florida.
1942 The destroyers FULLAM and BENNETT were launched. FULLAM was sunk as a target in 1962 and BENNETT was transferred to Brazil in 1959.
1944 The battleship WISCONSIN was commissioned. She was preserved as a memorial.
1947 The American freighter GRANDCAMP (the ex-BENJAMIN R. CURTIS) caught fire and exploded at Texas City, destroying the freighters HIGHFLYER and WILSON KEENE, more than 500 died.
1961 The destroyer BALDWIN ran aground and was scuttled on the 5th of June.
2010 Genearl John Vogt died at the age of 90 in Melbourne, Florida. He had scored 8 aerial victories while flying the P47 "Thunderbolt" in the European Theater.

Pacific
1927 The IJN heavy cruiser MYOKO was launched. She survived the war and was scuttled by the British in Malacca Strait on July 8, 1946.
1942 The USN submarine TAMBOR sank the KITAMI MARU (394 tons) southeast of Kavieng, New Ireland. USN Task Force 11 (formed around the carrier LEXINGTON) left Pearl Harbor en route to the Coral Sea. 4,000 Japanese landed on Panay in the Philippines.
1943 The American 11th Air Force attacked Kiska in the Aleutians. The USN battleship IDAHO arrived at Adak for the invasions of Attu and Kiska.
1944 The USN submarine PADDLE sank the MITO MARU (7,061 tons) and the HINO MARU (2,671 tons). The USN submarine REDFIN sank the YAMAGATA MARU (3,807 tons). The USN battleship COLORADO ran aground off Kahoolawe, Hawaii but suffered no damage.
1945 The USN destroyer HARDING was a constructive loss after an air attack off Okinawa and was sold for scrap April 16, 1947 (22 of her crew died). The USN destroyer PRINGLE was sunk by a Japanese kamikaze off Okinawa (62 of her crew died), the carrier INTREPID (9 died) was also hit. The USN destroyer MCDERMUT (2 died), BRYANT (34 died) and

the destroyer escort BOWERS (48 died) were hit by kamikazes. The USN destroyer LAFFEY (32 died) was hit by four bombs and five kamikazes, but would survive to become a memorial after serving on active duty well into the 1970's. The USN submarine SUNFISH sank the IJN frigate CD-73 and the MANRYU MARU (1,630 tons). The USN submarine SEA DOG sank the TOKO MARU (530 tons). The USN submarine SEA OWL sank the IJN submarine Ro-56. The USN destroyer MCDERMUT was hit by a 5" shell fired from the battleship MISSOURI off Okinawa, two died. American author William Manchester was seriously wounded while serving with 29th USMC Regiment on Okinawa. The US Army landed on Fort Frank in Manila Bay and found it abandoned. The US Army's 186th Regimental Combat Team landed on Balabac in the Philippines.

China-Burma-India
1942   Six American 10th Air Force bombers attacked Rangoon. Japanese forces took Yenang-Yaung.
1945   The 5th Indian Division took Shwemyo, Burma.

April 17th

Western Europe
1889   General Alfred Godwin-Austen, commander of the British XXX Corps in Libya 1941-42, was born.
1940   The Royal Navy heavy cruiser SUFFOLK bombarded Stavanger Airfield in Norway and was damaged before retiring. Thirty-two Royal Air Force bombers attacked Stavanger airfield in Norway and lost two "Blenheims" and one "Wellington". The Norwegian torpedo boats RAVIN, GRIB and JO were scuttled south of Lyngor.
1941   German S-boats sank two freighters of 2,744 tons and damaged another of 5,673 tons off Great Yarmouth. Thirty-five Royal Air Force "Blenheims" attacked German shipping and lost one aircraft. 118 Royal Air Force bombers attacked Berlin and lost eight aircraft. Three "Wellingtons" were lost on other operations.
1942   Royal Air Force Squadron/Leader. J. Nettleton, of the No.44 Rhodesian Squadron, won a Victoria Cross for leading twelve "Lancasters" on a daylight raid against the U-boat engine factory at Augsburg, Germany, seven of which were lost. The first operational use of "Moonshine" took place, it gave an exaggerated numbers of radar echoes, was on an American 8th Air Force mission to Rouen, France.
1943   Thirty-seven Royal Air Force "Venturas" attacked targets in France and Holland. 107 B17s of the American 8th Air Force dropped 265.5 tons of

bombs on Bremen, Germany and lost sixteen aircraft. A Luftwaffe Fw190 landed in error at Royal Air Force West Malling. Twenty-four Royal Air Force bombers dropped mines off the Biscay coast.

1944 Fourteen American 8th Air Force B24s dropped fifty-one tons of bombs on V-1 rocket launching sites at Wizernes, France. Thirty-three 8th Air Force P47s flew as escorts for the bombers. American 9th Air Force B26s dropped ninety-two tons of bombs on the Creil rail yards. Twenty-six Royal Air Force "Mosquitoes" attacked Cologne, Germany. Five B17s from the USAAF's 422nd Bomb Squadron dropped 1,480,000 leaflets on Rennes, Brest, Nantes, Lorient, and St. Nazaire in France.

1945 981 American 8th Air Force bombers dropped 2,724 tons of bombs on rail targets in Germany and Czechoslovakia and lost eight B17s. 756 8th Air Force fighters provided escort for the bombers and claimed 299 victories, of which 286 were on the ground, and lost seventeen P51s. USAAF ace Lieutenant Colonel Elwyn G. Righetti (27 ground and 7 air victories) was killed by civilians after he crash-landed his P51 near Dresden, Germany. First Lieutenant Frank Burke, of the 3rd Division, won a Medal of Honor in Nuremburg. The Soviet forces took Zisterdorf, Wihelmsdorf and Polten in Austria. The French forces took Freudenstadt. 101 Royal Air Force bombers attacked Cham, Germany.

Eastern Europe

1894 Soviet politician Nikita Khrushchev was born. During the war he served as political commissar on various fronts. He died on September 1, 1971.

1939 Diplomatic talks began between Russia and Germany.

1941 Yugoslavia surrendered to the Germans. The Germans had lost only 151 killed in the entire operation. Yugoslavian King Peter escaped in a British "Sunderland" at Kotor. The Yugoslavian the destroyer ZAGREB was scuttled at Kotor to avoid capture. The following Yugoslavian ships were captured at Kotor: the destroyer DUBROVNIK (the future Italian PREMUDA), the destroyer BEOGRAD (the future Italian SEBENICO), the LJUBLJANA (the future Italian LUBIANA-See April 1, 1943), the cruiser DALMACIJA (the future Italian CATTARO-See December 22, 1943), the aircraft tender ZMAJ (the future Italian DRACHE-See December 22, 1943), the minesweepers GALEB (the future Italian SELVE-See November 6, 1942), JASTREB (the future Italian ZIRONA-See November 25, 1941), LABUD (the future Italian ORIOLE-See July 10, 1943), ORAO (the future Italian VERGADA) and SOKOL (the future Italian ESO-See January 19, 1943). The Italians forces took Dubrovnik, Yugoslavia.

1942 The Soviet freighter SVANETIA was sunk by the Luftwaffe at Sevastopol.

1944 The American 15th Air Force attacked aircraft and rail targets in Yugoslavia and Sofia, Bulgaria.

Mediterranean

1941 The Royal Navy bombarded Fort Capuzzo, Libya. The Royal Navy submarine TRUANT sank two ships of 2,753 tons off Cyrenaica.

1943 American 12th Air Force B17s attacked Palermo, Catania, and Syracuse on Sicily.

1944 The American freighter JAMES GUTHERIE was a constructive loss after hitting a mine south of Capri.

1945 The British took Argentia. The French destroyer TROMBE was torpedoed by German S-boats off San Remo. S.S. General Karl Wolff was ordered to report to Hitler's headquarters in Germany to explain his unauthorized surrender negotiations with the Allies (See Western Europe- February 25th and Mediterranean-March 19th.

Atlantic

1940 The U13 sank the British freighter SWAINBY (4,935 tons). U13 survived until May 31st.

1941 The German armed merchant cruiser ATLANTIS took the Egyptian freighter ZAMZAM (8,299 tons). She rescued the entire complement of the ship including 138 American passengers. The U123 sank the Swedish freighter VENEZUELA (6,991 tons). U123 survived the war.

1942 The U123 sank the American freighter ALCOA GUIDE (4,834 tons-6 dead). U123 survived the war. The U66 sank the Panamanian tanker RIEDEMANN (11,020 tons). U66 survived until May 6, 1944.

1943 The U175 was sunk by the US Coast Guard cutter SPENCER, which rescued one of the submarine's crew, while the US Coast Guard cutter DUANE rescued twenty-two more. The U628 sank the British freighter FORT RAMPART (7,134 tons). U628 survived until July 3rd.

1944 The U986 was sunk by the USN minesweeper SWIFT and PC-619 southwest of Ireland. The U342 was sunk by a Royal Canadian Air Force No.162 Squadron PBY "Catalina". In 1985, that actual aircraft still in use in Ontario, Canada working as a water-bomber.

1945 The German patrol boat Uj-1207 was sunk off Heligoland by Allied aircraft.

North America

1915 USMC ace Joseph Jacob Foss was born in Sioux Falls, South Dakota.

1924 The light cruiser MEMPHIS was launched. She was scrapped in Baltimore in 1946.

1945 Japanese balloon-bombs were found near Boundary Bay and Morice Lake in British Columbia.

1949 Filming of the movie "12 O'clock High" began at Eglin Field in Florida. Some of the twelve B17s used had seen service as drones during the Bikini atomic bomb tests and could be used for only short periods of time due to radioactivity.
2013 USAAF ace John Bolyard died in Pensacola, Flrida at the age of 91. He had been credited with five aerial victories while flying P51s with the 23rd Fighter Group in China.

Pacific

1942 USN Vice-Admiral Robert Ghormley was named as Commander South Pacific Area. The American 5th Air Force sank the KOMAKI MARU at Rabaul, New Britain. The USN submarine SEARAVEN began evacuating Australian military personnel from Timor.
1943 The USN submarine FLYING FISH sank the AMAHO MARU (2,772 tons). Four USAAF B24 "Liberators" landed at Henderson Field, Guadalcanal with long-range fuel tanks for the P38s which were going to ambush IJN Admiral Yamamoto. The Japanese transport SHINNAN MARU was sunk by a mine off Buin, Bougainville. The American 11th Air Force attacked Kiska in the Aleutians.
1944 The USN submarine HARDER sank the MATSUE MARU (7,061 tons). The USN submarine SEARAVEN sank the NOSHIRO MARU No.2 (216 tons). The USN submarines BARB and STEELHEAD shelled the Japanese phosphate works on Rasa, Island. Royal Australian Air Force PBYs mined Woleai in the Carolines.
1945 USN destroyer BENHAM was hit by a Japanese kamikaze off Okinawa. Philippine guerillas liberated Malabang, Mindanao.

China-Burma-India

1943 Ten American 10th Air Force B25s attacked the Myitgne River Bridge in Burma. The Italian submarine DA VINCI sank the Dutch freighter SEMBILAN (6,566 tons).
1944 The Japanese began their last offensive in China.

April 18th

Western Europe

1907 British commando leader Robert Laycock was born in London. He died on March 10, 1968 of a heart attack.
1939 The French liner PARIS caught fire at Le Havre and sank the next day.

The Month of April

1940 The British 148th Brigade landed at Andalsnes in southern Norway and French troops landed at Namsos to the north. Nine Royal Air Force bombers attacked shipping off Norway and lost one "Whitley".

1941 Twenty-six Royal Air Force bombers attacked German shipping and lost one "Blenheim" and one "Hampden".

1942 173 Royal Air Force bombers attacked Hamburg, Germany and lost eight aircraft. Twenty-three people were killed in the raid. Two Royal Air Force bombers were lost in other operations.

1943 Twelve Royal Air Force "Venturas" attacked Dieppe, France. Sixteen P47s from the USAAF's 4th Fighter Group flew a sweep near Dunkirk, France.

1944 A rehearsal for the D-Day glider operations took place over Britain. 733 American 8th Air Force bombers dropped 1,645 tons of bombs on industrial targets in Germany and lost seventeen B17s and two B24s (one B17 landed in Switzerland). 634 8th and 9th Air Force fighters provided support for the bombers and claimed twenty victories for the loss of one P38, one P47 and three P51s. Twelve 8th Air Force B24s dropped forty-four tons of bombs on V-1 rocket sites near Watten, France. They were escorted by thirty-six 8th Air Force P47s. 289 Royal Air Force bombers attacked Rouen, France. 202 Royal Air Force bombers attacked Juvisy, France and lost one "Lancaster". 181 Royal Air Force bombers attacked the marshalling yards at Noisy-le-Sec, France and lost four "Halifaxes". The target was damaged so badly, that it would be six years before it was completely repaired. 464 French civilians were killed in the raid. 171 Royal Air Force bombers attacked Tergnier, France and lost six "Halifaxes". 168 Royal Air Force bombers dropped mines in the Baltic and lost three aircraft. Five B17s from the USAAF's 422nd Bomb Squadron dropped 2,560,000 leaflets on Stavanger, Oslo, Bergen and Trondheim in Norway.

1945 317,000 German troops surrendered in the "Ruhr Pocket". The American Army ordered the inhabitants of Weimer to visit the Buchenwald Concentration Camp. Private Joseph Merrell, of the 3rd Division, won a posthumous Medal of Honor near Lohe. A patrol from the US Army's 90th Infantry Division crossed the border into Czechoslovakia. The American 3rd Army began an unauthorized offensive into Czechoslovakia to rescue the Lipizzaner Stallions that had been moved from the Spanish Riding School in Vienna. The American 9th Army took Magdeburg, Germany. The US 1st Army took Dusseldorf, Germany. American 9th Air Force B26s attacked storage areas at Neuberg. 760 American 8th Air Force bombers dropped 2,088 tons of bombs on rail targets in Germany and lost two B17s. 778 8th Air Force fighters provided support for the bombers and claimed sixteen victories for the loss of two P51s. Luftwaffe ace Johannes "Macky" Steinhoff (176 victories) was severely burned in the crash of his Me262 jet. He would retire as a General in the new German Air Force in 1972 and would die in 1995. 969 Royal Air Force bombers attacked military installations on Heligoland Island and lost three "Halifaxes". British forces took Soltau and Ulzen. 123 Royal Air Force bombers attacked Komotau, Czechoslovakia. Ninety-three Royal Air Force "Mosquitoes" attacked targets in Germany. The German KFK-298 deserted from Pillau to Karlskrona, Sweden.

1970 Royal Air Force Air Marshal Richard Atcherley died at Aldershot. He had served as a Group Commander during the war.

1986 French aircraft designer Marcel Bloch, age 94, died. He had also designed under the professional name of Marcel Dassault.

Eastern Europe

1942 Field Marshal Wilhelm von Leeb was removed as commander of German Army Group "North". All action on the Eastern Front ended as the spring thaw set in.

1943 Adolf Hitler released the Italian 2nd Corps from duty with Army Group "Center", thus ending Italian participation on the Eastern Front. German aircraft attacked shipping at Murmansk and damaged the American freighter THOMAS HARTLEY.

1944 The Soviets took Balaklava in the Crimea. The Soviet submarine KARBONARI was sunk German surface craft.

Mediterranean

1941 The Greek Prime Minister Alexandros Korizis committed suicide.

1943 The Royal Navy submarine REGENT was sunk by a mine. In what became known as the "Palm Sunday Massacre", 58 USAAF P40 "Warhawks" and 12 Royal Air Force "Spitfires" shot down 51 Luftwaffe Ju52 transports and 16 fighters off Cape Bon, Tunisia and lost 1 "Spitfire" and seven P40s. Thirty-one American 12th Air Force B17s attacked Palermo, Sicily. 173 Royal Air Force bombers attacked La Spezia, Italy and lost one "Lancaster".

Atlantic

1941 The Royal Navy submarine URGE sank the Italian tanker FRANCO MARTELLI (10,535 tons) which was en route from Brazil.

1943 The Royal Navy submarine P-615 (the ex-Turkish ULUC ALI REIS) and the British freighter EMPIRE BRUCE (7,459 tons) were sunk by the U123. U123 survived the war. The Spanish freighter CABO HUERTAS rescued 11 survivors from the American freighter JAMES W. DENVER which had been sunk on April 11th by U195.

1945 The U1107 sank the American freighter CYRUS MCCORMICK (7,181 tons-6 dead) and the British tanker EMPIRE GOLD (8,028 tons) off Brest, France. The American tanker SWIFTSCOUT (8,300 tons-91 dead) was sunk by the U548. The U245 sank the Norwegian freighter KARMT (4,991 tons) and the British freighter FILLEIGH (4,856 tons).

North America

1892 Major General Westside Larson, commander of the 3rd Air Force, was born in Vernalis, California.
1936 The destroyer SELFRIDGE was launched. She was scrapped in 1947.
1942 The destroyer SHUBRICK was launched. She was scrapped in 1947. The submarine BLACKFISH was launched. She was discarded in 1959. Eastern seaboard lights were finally turned out despite protests by local merchants. German U-boats had been using them to silhouette their merchant ship targets. The "Stars and Stripes" newspaper began publication.
1943 The destroyer CLARENCE K. BRONSON (sold to Turkey in 1967) and the submarines ESCOLAR and DRAGONET were launched. ESCOLAR was lost in October 1944 and DRAGONET was expended as a target in 1961.
1955 Scientist Albert Einstein died in Princeton.
1980 Lieutenant Colonel Harry McCool retired from Civil Service. He had flown on the "Doolittle Raid".
1994 The "Liberty" ship JEREMIAH O'BRIEN left San Francisco. She was en route to 50th anniversary ceremonies in Normandy.
2011 The last five surviving "Doolittle Raiders" met for a reunion at the Strategic Air Museum near Omaha, Nebraska. They were Dick Cole-co-pilot on Plane No.1, Tom Griffin-navigator on Plane No.9, Bob Hite-co-pilot on Plane No.16, David Thatcher-engineer-gunner on Plane No.7 and Ed Saylor-engineer on Plane No.15.
2013 USAAF ace Joseph Forster died in Tempe, Arizona at the age of 93. He had beed credited with 9 aerial victories while flying P38s with the 475th Fighter Group in the Southwest Pacific.

Pacific

1941 A Japanese G3M2 Mitsubishi made a photo-recon flight over Legaspi, Luzon.
1942 At 0738, USN Task Force 16 (including the carriers HORNET and ENTERPRISE) was sighted by Japanese patrol boat No.23 NITTO MARU. At 0803, while still 650 miles from Japan, the carrier HORNET prepared to launch Lieutenant Colonel James Doolittle's B25s. At 0825, Doolittle's personal aircraft took off. At 0920, the last of 16 B25s took off from the

HORNET. The "Doolittle Raiders" attacked Tokyo, Yokohama, Kobe and Nagoya in Japan. Doolittle won a Medal of Honor and was promoted to the rank of Brigadier General skipping the rank of colonel, while the rest of the participants received Distinguished Flying Crosses. US 5th Air Force B26s sank the Japanese aircraft transport KOMAKI MARU at Rabaul, New Britain.

1943   IJN Admiral Isoroku Yamamoto was killed by USAAF P38s over Bougainville, eight Japanese aircraft and one P38 were lost (See November 26, 1987). The USN submarine DRUM sank the NISSHUN MARU (6,380 tons). The American 11th Air Force attacked Kiska in the Aleutians.

1944   American 13th Air Force B24s attacked Woleai Island in the Carolines. Royal Australian Air Force PBYs mined its harbor later that night. The American freighter JOHN STRAUB sank off Sanak Island in the Aleutians after hitting a mine. Fifty-five died.

1945   The USN submarines ROCK and TIGRONE destroyed a Japanese radio station on Bataan Island north of the Philippines. The IJN submarine I-56 was sunk by aircraft from the USN escort carrier BATAAN. USAAF B29s attacked airfields on Kyushu. American Correspondent Ernie Pyle was killed by a Japanese machine gunner on Ie Shima, a small island off Okinawa.

1948   The destroyer MUSTIN was expended off the Marshalls after the Bikini tests.

China-Burma-India

1942   The Chinese 55th Division was destroyed by the Japanese 56th Division.

1943   The U180 sank the British tanker CORBIS (8,132 tons). The Italian submarine DA VINCI sank the British freighter MANAAR (8,007 tons).

1944   The Japanese began an offensive against the US 14th Air Forces bases in China. The British relieved Kohima, India, which had been surrounded.

April 19th

Western Europe

1922   Luftwaffe ace Erich Hartmann (352 victories) was born in Weissach. In the fall of 1942, Lieutenant Hartmann reported to JG52 on the Eastern Front. He was promoted to captain on September 1, 1944 and was a major by the end of the war. He scored his 352nd victory on May 8, 1945, a Yak-11 over Brno, Czechoslovakia. During the war he flew 1,425 combat sorties, was shot down sixteen times, and bailed out twice. After the war he was imprisoned in Russia until 1955. He joined the new West German Air

Force after his release, but never really adapted and he retired in 1968. He died in 1995.

1939 The Royal Navy light cruiser BONAVENTURE was launched. She was sunk on March 31, 1941.

1940 German troops moving north from Trondheim took the town of Steinkjer in central Norway. German forces also took Elverum in southern Norway. Additional British troops landed at Andalsnes, Norway. One of nine Royal Air Force "Blenheims" attempting to attack Stavanger airfield in Norway was lost.

1941 Thirty-six Royal Air Force bombers attacked German shipping. 712 Luftwaffe aircraft attacked London, killing 2,300 people.

1942 Fifty-one Royal Air Force bombers dropped mines in the Baltic and lost one "Wellington".

1943 The Royal Navy submarine SERAPH left Britain with Major Martin, "The Man Who Never Was", aboard. Martin's body was to be dropped near the Spanish coast. With the body would be information leading the Germans to believe that the Allies would not attack Sicily in the Mediterranean. Six Royal Air Force "Mosquitoes" attacked Namur, Belgium.

1944 182 American 9th Air Force B26s attacked Malines, Namur, and Hasselt in Belgium. A Royal Air Force No.161 Squadron "Hudson" landed in Sweden, with its crew claiming to have lost its way over the Irish Sea. 744 American 8th Air Force B17s and B24s dropped 1,674 tons of bombs on industrial targets in Kassel, airfields at Lippstadt, Werl, Paderborn and Gutersloh and targets of opportunity in Limburg, Soest, Koblenz and Buren in Germany and lost five B17s. 697 8th and 9th Air Force fighters provided support for the bombers and claimed sixteen victories for the loss of two P51s. Twenty-seven American 8th Air Force B24s dropped seventy-seven tons of bombs on V-1 rocket sites near Watten, France and lost one aircraft. Forty-seven 8th Air Force P47s provided support for the bombers.

1945 The American First Army took Leipzig and Halle in Germany. The British cut the autobahn between Bremen and Hamburg in Germany. Berlins Reichsbank gold reserves were sent out of Munich after Martin Bormann refused to store it in his bunker. Forty-nine Royal Air Force bombers attacked Munich. Thirty-six Royal Air Force "Lancasters" attacked shore batteries on Heligoland. U251 and the minesweeper M-403 were sunk in the Kattegat by the Royal Air Force. The American 9th Air Force attacked transportation targets in Germany. 589 American 8th Air Force B17s dropped 1,523 tons of bombs on rail targets in Germany and lost five aircraft. The USAAF's 306th Bomb Group (B17) flew the last of its 342 8th Air Force missions, having lost 171 aircraft. 546 8th Air Force fighters provided support for the bombers and claimed twelve victories for the loss of two P51s. 122 Royal Air Force "Mosquitoes" attacked targets in Germany.

Eastern Europe
1943 Heavy fighting took place in the Kuban region. Heinrich Himmler ordered the massacre of the Jews in the Warsaw ghetto.

Mediterranean
1941 The Greek commander in Macedonia, General Zolakoglu, began unauthorized surrender negotiations with the Germans. The British Expeditionary Force took over the defense of Thermopylae.
1942 The U81 sank the Egyptian sailing ship HEFZ EL RAHMAN (90 tons).
1943 Chelu Ram, of the 6th Rajputana Rifles, won a posthumous Victoria Cross in Tunisia. At 0100, the Italian destroyer ALPINO was damaged at La Spezia by the Royal Air Force and sank at 0235.

Atlantic
1942 The German armed merchant cruiser MICHEL took the British freighter PATELLA (7,468 tons). The American freighter EXMINSTER was lost in a collision with the freighter ALGIC.
1943 The U974 was sunk off Stavanger by the Norwegian submarine ULA.
1945 The U879 was sunk by the USN destroyer escorts BUCKLEY and REUBEN JAMES off Boston.
1989 A turret explosion aboard the USN battleship IOWA killed 47 members of her crew.

North America
1924 The light cruiser TRENTON (awarded 1 battle star during the war) was launched. She was scrapped in 1946.
1943 The heavy cruiser CANBERRA (awarded 7 battle stars during the war) and the escort carrier LISCOME BAY were launched. CANBERRA was scrapped in 1978 and LISCOME BAY was lost November 24, 1943.
1987 General Maxwell Taylor died of "Lou Gehrig's Disease" at Walter Reed Hospital in Washington D.C. He had commanded the 101st Airborne Division.

Pacific
1940 The Japanese government informed the American government that it had no hostile intentions towards the Dutch East Indies.
1943 The Japanese recovered the remains of Yamamoto and his staff from the jungle on Bougainville. They had been killed by USAAF P38s. The USN

submarine SEAWOLF sank the BANSHU MARU No.5 (389 tons). The USN submarine SCORPION laid twenty-two mines off Inubo Saki. USN TBFs attacked Tonolei Harbor, Bougainville and damaged the Japanese freighter SHIROGARE MARU. The American 11th Air Force attacked Kiska in the Aleutians.

1944 The US Army's I Corps took Vigan, Luzon. The USN submarine SUNFISH sank the KAIHO MARU (1,093 tons) and the TAISEI MARU (1,948 tons). The USN submarine SENNET sank the HAGANE MARU (1,901 tons) and the IJN sub chaser Cha-97. The USN submarine CERO sank the ISUZU MARU No.3 (74 tons). The USN submarine SILVERSIDES sank the KAIRYU MARU (180 tons). An Allied naval force commanded by Royal Navy Admiral James Somerville attacked the Dutch East Indies.

China-Burma-India

1944 Royal Navy Admiral James Somerville's Eastern Fleet (the Royal Navy carrier ILLUSTRIOUS, the French battleship RICHELIEU and the USN carrier SARATOGA) attacked Sabang. The Allies lost one aircraft and the Japanese lost twenty-seven.

1945 The Indian 20th Division took Magwe and Myingun in Burma.

April 20th

Western Europe

1889 Adolf Hitler was born in Branau on the Inn River in Austria.

1916 The Royal Navy battle cruiser GLORIOUS was launched. She was sunk in 1940 by German battlecruisers after she had been converted into a carrier.

1940 The Luftwaffe attacked Namsos, Norway. Three Royal Air Force bombers attempted to attack the Luftwaffe airfield at Stavanger in Norway.

1941 Twenty-two Royal Air Force "Blenheims" attacked German shipping. Sixty-one Royal Air Force bombers attacked Köln, Germany and lost two "Hampdens" and one "Wellington". Twenty-four Royal Air Force bombers attacked Rotterdam, Holland.

1942 The French Resistance tried to assassinate Jaques Doriot, the Chief of the French Fascist Party.

1943 Thirty-six Royal Air Force "Venturas" attacked targets in Holland and France. 339 Royal Air Force bombers attacked Stettin, Germany and lost twenty-one aircraft. 100 acres of the city were destroyed and 586 people were killed in the raid. Eighty-six Royal Air Force "Stirlings" attacked Rostock, Germany and lost eight aircraft. Eleven Royal Air Force "Mosquitoes" attacked Berlin and lost one aircraft.

1944 570 American 8th Air Force bombers dropped 1,892 tons of bombs on V-1 rocket sites near Cherbourg and the Pas de Calais in France and lost seven B17s and two B24s. 388 8th Air Force fighters provided support for the bombers and claimed eight victories for the loss of two P51s. Sixty-six 8th Air Force P47s and P51s attacked the Cambrai/Epinoy airfield in France. American 9th Air Force B26s attacked the Creil rail yards. 379 Royal Air Force bombers attacked Köln, Germany and lost four "Lancasters". 664 people were killed in the raid. 269 Royal Air Force bombers attacked La Chapelle, France and lost six "Lancasters". 196 Royal Air Force bombers attacked Ottignies, France. 175 Royal Air Force bombers attacked Lens, France and lost one "Halifax". Five B17s from the USAAF's 422nd Bomb Squadron dropped 1,920,000 leaflets on Nantes, Orleans, Paris, and Tours in France.

1945 100 Royal Air Force "Lancasters" attacked Regensburg, Germany and lost one aircraft. 809 American 8th Air Force bombers dropped 1,953 tons of bombs on rail targets in Germany and lost one B17. 846 8th Air Force fighters provided support for the bombers and claimed seven victories. The following Heavy Bombardment Groups flew their last American 8th Air Force missions of the war: the 34th (B24 then converted to B17)-170 missions-having lost seventy-three aircraft, the 95th (B17) 320 missions-having lost 196 aircraft, the 100th (B17)-306 missions-having lost 229 aircraft, the 385th (B17)-296 missions-having lost 149 aircraft, the 390th (B17)-300 missions-having lost 176 aircraft, the 457th (B17)-237 missions-having lost eighty-three aircraft, the 490th (B24 then converted to B17)-158 missions-having lost fifty-four aircraft, the 493rd (B24 then converted to B17)-157 missions-having lost seventy-two aircraft, as did the following Fighter Groups: the 359th (P51)-346 missions-having lost 106 aircraft, the 361st Fighter Group (P51)-441 missions-having lost eighty-one aircraft. A Luftwaffe night-fighter shot down an American 8th Air Force B24 "Carpetbagger" over Norway. The American 9th Air Force attacked transportation targets in Germany. The American Seventh Army took Nuremburg and Stuttgart in Germany. Adolf Hitler celebrated his 56th birthday in the Chancellory bunker in Berlin. The American Third Army took Grafenwohr, Germany. German Luftwaffe Commander Hermann Goering and Foreign Minister Joachim Ribbentrop left Berlin. Seventy-six Royal Air Force "Mosquitoes" attacked Berlin.

1994 Paul Touvier was sentenced in France to life in prison. He had been charged with ordering the execution of seven Jews at Rillieux-la-Pape outside Lyon, while he was Militia Chief for the Vichy government.

Eastern Europe

1944 In response to Allied pressure, Turkey stopped its chrome shipments to Germany. The USN light cruiser MILWAUKEE was transferred to the Soviet Navy and renamed MURMANSK.

1945 The Soviets began bombarding central Berlin.

Mediterranean

1941 The ANZAC (Australian-New Zealand Army Corps) forces, consisting of the Australian 6th Division and the New Zealand Division, withdrew to the Pass of Thermopylae in Greece. Royal Air Force Squadron/Leader M. Pattle (28 victories) was killed in action by Luftwaffe Me110s over Greece. The Greek destroyer PSARA was sunk by the Luftwaffe. Forty of her crew died. The British attempted to reinforce Tobruk, Libya but failed.

1942 The USN carrier WASP launched forty-seven "Spitfire" fighters for Malta in "Operation Calendar", one aircraft was lost.

1943 The British Eighth Army attacked Enfidaville, Tunisia. U565 sank the French freighter SIDI-BEL-ABBES (4,392 tons) and the American freighter MICHIGAN (5,594 tons).

1944 At 2105, the USN destroyer LANSDALE was sunk off Cape Bengut by the Luftwaffe. Forty-seven of her crew died. The US Coast Guard-manned destroyer escort MENGES rescued 113 of her survivors and the US Coast Guard-manned destroyer escort NEWELL rescued another 120. The American transport PAUL HAMILTON was sunk off Algiers by the Luftwaffe, all 608 aboard died. The first German "Neger" (midget submarine) operation took place off Anzio, when twenty-three of them attacked Allied shipping. They had no success, but lost ten of their own. The Italian corvette TERSICORE was sunk while serving with the Germans. The American 15th Air Force attacked shipping and rail targets in Italy.

Atlantic

1941 The U73 sank the British freighter EMPIRE ENDURANCE (8,570 tons). U73 survived until December 16, 1943.

1942 The U572 sank the British freighter EMPIRE DRYDEN (7,164 tons). U572 survived until August 3, 1943. The U654 sank the American freighter STEELMAKER (6,176 tons) and the Swedish freighter AGRA (4,569 tons). U654 survived until August 22nd. The U109 sank the British freighter HARPAGON (5,719 tons). U109 survived until May 4, 1943. The U154 sank the British freighter VINELAND (5,587 tons). U154 survived until July 3, 1944. USN Rear Admiral Arthur Bristol, commander of Task Force 24 based at Argentia, Newfoundland, died.

1945 The British trawler ETHEL CRAWFORD (200 tons) was sunk by a mine.

North America

1882 USMC General Holland McTyeire Smith was born in Seale, Alabama. He was commissioned in the Marines on March 29, 1905. He retired in March 1946 and died on January 12, 1967.

1918 Author Edward Beach was born in New York City. He would serve aboard the USN submarines TRIGGER and TIRANTE during the war. He would write several best-selling books after the war, most of them concerning submarines.

1942 Future President Gerald Ford enlisted in the USN. He would serve as assistant navigator aboard the light carrier MONTEREY.

1943 The US War Department issued a formal communiqué on the "Doolittle Raid", stating that "Shangri-la" was in fact the carrier HORNET. At a press conference after the raid, FDR had stated that the aircraft had taken off from Shangri-la.

1945 A Japanese balloon-bomb was found near Tikchik Lake, Alaska. The submarine COCHINO was launched. She was lost on August 26, 1949.

1988 The US Senate passed a bill authorizing $1.3 billion in payments to Japanese detainees of WW II.

2009 USMC Colonel Bruce Porter, age 88, died in Fresno, California. He had scored 5 victories in the Pacific while flying the F4U and the F6F.

Pacific

1943 Twenty-four B24 "Liberators" made the first American 7th Air Force raid on Tarawa while flying from Funafuti in the Ellis Islands. 5th Air Force B17s attacked Wewak, New Guinea and sank the Japanese freighter KOSEI MARU. The USN submarine SCORPION sank the MEIJI MARU No.1 (1,934 tons). The American freighter PHOEBE HEARST was sunk off Fiji by the IJN submarine I-19. The USN submarine RUNNER laid mines off Hong Kong. The American 11th Air Force attacked Kiska in the Aleutians and sank the freighter NOJIMA MARU.

1944 The USN submarine SEAHORSE sank the IJN submarine I-174. American 13th Air Force B25s attacked Rabaul, New Britain.

1945 The US Army's III Corps secured the Motobu Peninsula on Okinawa.

China-Burma-India

1942 Five captured "Doolittle Raiders" (Farrow, Hite, Barr, Spatz and DeShazer) were sent to Japan for interrogation. The Japanese took Pyinmana, Burma.

2011 Victoria Cross recipient 88-year-old Tur Badahur Pun died in his hometown of Banduk, Burma. He had received his award for actions during the Second Chindit Expedition in 1944.

April 21st

Western Europe

1904   German S.S. commander Odilo Globocnik was born in Trieste into a Croat family. He moved to Austria in 1918. He served as a gauleiter from 1933 until 1939 when he was dismissed for speculating in foreign currencies. On November 9th, he became S.S. and Police commander in the Lublin District of Poland. He established death camps at Belzec, Majdanek, Sobibor and Treblinka. In 1941, he was placed in command of all the death camps in Poland. In 1943, he was relieved for stealing S.S. property (victim's belongings) and sent to Trieste as a police leader. He either committed suicide or was killed on May 31, 1945.

1938   Germany completed plans for the invasion of Czechoslovakia.

1940   German forces took Lillehammer in southern Norway. Thirty-six Royal Air Force bombers dropped mines off Norway and lost one "Hampden". Twelve Royal Air Force bombers attacked Norwegian airfields and lost one "Wellington". Captain Robert Losey, of the United States Army Air Corps Weather Service, became the first member of the US military to be killed in action in WWII when he died in a Luftwaffe raid on Dombas, Norway. He had been serving as an observer. The Luftwaffe dropped twenty-six mines in the Edinburgh Channel.

1941   Thirty-six Royal Air Force "Blenheims" attacked German shipping. The Luftwaffe attacked Plymouth, Britain.

1942   French General Henri Giraud escaped from occupied France.

1943   Eleven Royal Air Force "Venturas" attacked Abbeville, France and lost three aircraft. Eighty-two American 8th Air Force P47s flew sweeps over Holland and Belgium.

1944   Three USAAF 447th Bomb Group B17s were destroyed at Rattlesden in a bomb-loading accident. The German minesweeper M-553 (the ex-Dutch WILLEM VAN EWIJCK) was sunk by a mine in the Baltic. Twenty-four Royal Air Force "Mosquitoes" attacked Cologne, Germany. The USAAF's 801st Bomb Group dispatched six B24s on "Carpetbagger" missions.

1945   The Soviets reached the outskirts of Berlin. Eighteen miles north of Berlin, the Germans began evacuating the Sachsenhausen concentration camp to prevent its inmates from falling into Soviet hands. 330 American 8th Air Force bombers dropped 827 tons of bombs on rail targets and airfields in Germany and lost one B24 and one B17. 408 8th Air Force fighters provided support for the bombers and lost two P51s. The following 8th Air Force Heavy Bombardment Groups flew their last missions of the war: the 94th(B17)-324 missions-having lost 180 aircraft, the 96th (B17)-321 missions-having lost 239 aircraft, the 447th-257 missions-having lost 180 aircraft, the 452nd (B17)-250 missions-having lost 158 aircraft, the 486th (B24 then converted to B17)-188 missions, having lost 67 aircraft, the 487th (B24 then converted to B17)-185 missions-having lost 67 aircraft, as did the following Fighter Groups: the 55th (P38 then converted to P51)-having lost 181 aircraft, the 56th (P47)-447 missions-having lost 128 aircraft and the 339th (P51)-264 missions-having lost 97 aircraft. The German Gestapo and S.S. Chief Heinrich Himmler met with the deputy head of the Swedish Red Cross, Count Folke Bernadotte, to offer to surrender the German forces in the west, but to continue the fight in the east. French forces took Stuttgart, Germany. Reich Finance Minister Walther Funk issued orders that the Reichsbank gold reserves be sent to Mittenwald in Bavaria. An Fw200 carrying the baggage of the Luftwaffe Berlin headquarters, crashed after leaving Munich while en route to Barcelona, Spain. It was found near Piesenkofen, Bavaria in 1954. German Field Marshal Walther Model committed suicide outside Dusseldorf. Private E. Charlton, of the Irish Guards, won a posthumous Victoria Cross in Germany. 107 Royal Air Force "Mosquitoes" attacked Kiel, Germany and lost two aircraft. Fifty people were killed in the raid. The British destroyer escort RETALICK engaged a group of German "Linsen" explosive boats twenty-eight miles southwest of Ostend. She would sink four of them before the action was over. The German minelayer OSTMARK (the ex-French COTE D'ARGENT) was sunk in the Baltic by British aircraft.

1966 German S.S. General Sepp Dietrich died of a heart attack in Ludwigsburg, Germany.

Eastern Europe

1942 A German force surrounded at Demyansk was relieved.

1943 Finnish ace Eero Aulis Kinnunen (22.5 aerial victories) was killed by Soviet anti-aircraft fire, while flying a Brewster "Buffalo".

1944 The American 15th Air Force attacked the oil refineries Ploesti, Rumania.

Mediterranean

1941 The Germans took Ioannina, Greece. The last Royal Air Force "Blenheims" on Crete were flown back to Egypt in anticipation of the upcoming German attack. The Royal Navy battleships BARHAM, VALIANT and WARSPITE bombarded Benghazi, Libya.

1943 The Royal Navy submarine SPLENDID was sunk by German surface craft.

1944 The US Army's 34th Division landed at Anzio, Italy. General Henri Giraud resigned as Commander-in-Chief of French Forces in North Africa.

1945 The Polish II Corps took Bologna, Italy.

Atlantic

1940 The U26 sank the British freighter CEDARBANK (5,159 tons). U26 survived until July 3rd.

1941 The U107 sank the British freighter CALCHAS (10,305 tons). U107 survived until August 18, 1944.

1942 The U84 sank the Panamanian freighter CHENANGO (3,014 tons). U84 survived until August 24, 1943. The U201 sank the Norwegian freighter BRIS (2,027 tons). U201 survived until February 17, 1943. The U752 sank the American freighter WEST IMBODEN (5,751 tons). The USN destroyer BRISTOL rescued two boatloads of her survivors. U752 survived until May 23, 1943. The American freighter PIPESTONE COUNTY (5,102 tons) was sunk off Virginia by the U576. U576 survived until July 15th.

1943 The U415 sank the British freighters ASHANTIAN (4,917 tons) and WANSTEAD (5,486 tons). U415 survived until July 14, 1944. The U191 sank the Norwegian freighter SCEBELI (3,025 tons). U191 survived until April 23rd.

1945 The U636 was sunk by the Royal Navy frigates BAZELY, DRURY and BENTINCK west of Ireland.

North America

1932 The heavy cruiser PORTLAND was launched. She was scrapped in 1959.

1939 The submarine SEADRAGON was launched. She was scrapped in 1948.

1942 FDR ordered the seizure of all patents belonging to nations at war with America.

1944 The escort carrier THETIS BAY was commissioned. She was scrapped in 1960.

1945 Japanese balloon-bombs were found near Elko, Nevada and Phillipsburg, Montana.

1992 In commemoration of the "Doolittle Raid", 50 years before, 2 B25s ("In the Mood" and "Heavenly Body") were launched from the USN carrier RANGER off San Diego. After take-off, they joined with 3 other B25s and flew over retired General James Doolittle's home near Monterey.

2009 USAAF Lieutenant Colonel Richard Suehr, age 91, died in Fayetteville, North Carolina. He had scored 5 victories in the Pacific while flying P39s and P38s. USN Commander Harry Hill, age 89, died in Virginia Beach, Virginia. During the war he had flown F6F "Hellcats" off the carrier YORKTOWN and had been credited with 7 aerial victories.

2010 Whitney R. Harris died of cancer in Frontenac, Missouri at the age of 97. He had been the last surviving American prosecutor from the Nuremburg war crimes trials that took place after the war.

Pacific

1941 The battleship ARIZONA and the destroyer DAVIS collided off Hawaii during training operations.

1943 The Japanese Naval Air Force attacked the American 7th Air Force base on Funafuti, destroying two B24s. Twelve 7th Air Force B24s flying from Funafuti attacked Japanese-held Tarawa. The USN submarine GRENADIER was scuttled off Malaya and its crew was captured. Four of them died in captivity. Admiral Mineichi Koga was named as Commander-in-Chief of the IJN.

1944 USN Task Force 58 attacked Wakde Island, Sawar, Sarmi and Hollandia. American 13th Air Force B25s attacked Rabaul, New Britain.

1945 Ie Shima, a small island off Okinawa, was secured by American forces. 4,706 Japanese died during the operation. Private First-Class Martin May, of the 77th Division, won a posthumous Medal of Honor on Ie Shima. The USN destroyer AMMEN (8 wounded) was hit by a Japanese kamikaze off Okinawa.

China-Burma-India

1942 Japanese forces in China were ordered to take airfields to prevent a recurrence of the "Doolittle Raid". 250,000 Chinese were killed during the offensive.

1943 The Italian submarine DA VINCI sank the American freighter JOHN DRAYTON (7,177 tons). The USN submarine STINGRAY laid mines off Wenchow, China.

1945 The 5th Indian Division took Yedashe, Burma.

April 22nd

Western Europe

1940 Seven Royal Air Force bombers attacked Norwegian airfields and lost one "Whitley". The Luftwaffe dropped thirty-four mines off Harwich.

1941 Fourteen Royal Air Force "Blenheims" attacked German shipping off Norway. The Luftwaffe attacked Plymouth, Britain. Twenty-six Royal Air Force bombers attacked Brest, France and lost one "Wellington".

1942 Fifteen Frenchmen were executed in Paris by the Germans in retaliation for actions by the Resistance forces. Sixty-nine Royal Air Force bombers attacked Cologne, Germany and lost two "Wellingtons". Four people were killed in the raid. Two Royal Air Force bombers were lost in other operations.

1943 The Convoy ONS-5 left Liverpool, Britain for Halifax, Nova Scotia. It would lose twelve of forty ships and sink five U-boats. Thirty-two Royal

Air Force bombers dropped mines off the Biscay ports and lost two aircraft.

1944   American 9th Air Force B26s attacked V-1 rocket launching sites at Wisques, France. 779 American 8th Air Force bombers dropped 1,983 tons of bombs on Hamm, Soest, Bonn and Koblenz in Germany and lost eight B17s and seven B24s. 859 8th and 9th Air Force fighters provided support for the bombers and claimed forty victories for the loss of two P38s, five P47s and six P51s. Luftwaffe intruders shot down nine USAAF B24s over Britain. 596 Royal Air Force bombers attacked Dusseldorf, Germany and lost twenty-nine aircraft. 593 people were killed in the raid. 255 Royal Air Force bombers attacked Brunswick, Germany and lost four "Lancasters". Forty-four people were killed in the raid. 181 Royal Air Force bombers attacked Laon, France and lost nine aircraft. Five B17s from the USAAF's 422nd Bomb Squadron dropped 1,440,000 leaflets on Orleans, Tours, Paris, Nantes, Lille, Chartres, and Rouen in France.

1945   Luftwaffe Commander Hermann Goering blew up his estate at Karinhall to prevent it from falling into the hands of the advancing Soviet forces. Adolf Hitler informed his companions in the Chancellory Bunker that he had decided to remain in Berlin and die. Ernst Kaltenbrunner ordered S.S. Brigadier General Josef Spacil to remove, at gunpoint, the last $9 million in the Berlin Reichsbank and load it on aircraft for shipment to Salzburg, Austria. The Reichsbank gold reserves arrived in Mittenwald from Munich. 767 Royal Air Force bombers attacked Bremen and lost two "Lancasters". The American 7th Army crossed the Danube. US Army General Jacob Devers, commander of the 6th Army Group, ordered de Lattre, commander of the French Forces, to turn Stuttgart over to American forces, he refused. Four USAAF 492nd Bomb Group B24s flew "Carpetbagger" missions to Norway. Fifty-one Royal Air Force "Mosquitoes" attacked targets in Germany.

1948   The Swiss received nine P51Ds from the USAAF in Germany. The Soviets stopped rail traffic from West Germany into Berlin.

1982   120 Allied survivors of the "St. Nazaire Raid" of 1942, returned to that city aboard the Royal yacht BRITANNIA.

Eastern Europe

1944   Russian-Finnish peace talks were concluded.

1945   The U997 sank the Soviet freighter ONEGA (1,603 tons).

Mediterranean

1937   Italian dictator Benito Mussolini met in Venice with Austrian Chancellor Kurt Schuschnigg.

1941   The British forces began evacuating Greece. The Greek destroyer LEON was damaged in Suda Bay, Crete by the Luftwaffe and was sunk on May 15th. The Greek destroyers YDRA and THYELLA and the torpedo boat KIOS were sunk by the Luftwaffe. Emmanuel Tsouderos was named Premier of Greece.
1942   Axis aircraft attacked Malta. The U81 sank the Egyptian sailing ship EL SAADIAH (122 tons).
1943   Allied fighters shot down 16 Luftwaffe Ju52s and 18 Me323s, off Tunisia. USAAF B26s attacked Arbatax, Sardinia and Carloforte, Sicily.
1944   Yugoslavian partisans took the Adriatic Island of Korcula. It had been occupied by the Germans.
1945   American forces took Modena.

Atlantic
1942   The German armed merchant cruiser MICHEL took the American tanker CONNECTICUT (8,684 tons-36 dead). The German "Milch Cow" U459 met the U108 northeast of Bermuda, in what was the first rendezvous of its kind. The "Milch Cows" were primarily a supply base for the U-boat force that was used to enable the individual boats to remain on patrol longer. U459 survived until July 24, 1943 and U108 survived until April 11, 1944. The U201 sank the American transport SAN JACINTO (6,069 tons-14 dead) and the British freighter DERRYHEEN (7,217 tons). U201 survived until February 17, 1943. The USN destroyer BRISTOL rescued all thirty-five survivors from the American freighter WEST IMBODEN which was sunk on April 20th by U752. The USN destroyer ROWAN rescued eighteen survivors from the American STEEL MAKER which had been sunk on April 19th by U136.
1943   The U306 sank the British freighter AMERIKA (10,218 tons). U306 survived until October 31st. The German freighter DUNA (the ex-Soviet KANDAVA) was sunk off Norway by a mine.

North America
1941   The Navy's authorized enlisted strength was increased to 232,000.
1942   The first unit of the 8th Air Force to leave the America, the 689th Quartermaster Company, departed from New York en route to Britain, aboard the transport CATHAY.
1943   The destroyer LAWS was launched. She was stricken in 1973.
1945   The light cruiser GALVESTON was launched. She was stricken in 1973.
1994   Mathias Denuel, age 74, left America en route to Germany. He was expelled for concealing his past as concentration camp guard at Gusen, a sub camp of Mauthausen in Austria.

Pacific

1925 The IJN carrier AKAGI was launched. She was sunk on June 5, 1942.

1928 The IJN heavy cruiser ASHIGARA was launched. She was sunk on June 8, 1945.

1941 2,000 US Army troops arrived in the Philippines.

1942 The USN battleship NEVADA left Pearl Harbor for repairs at Bremerton. An American-New Zealand Naval Committee was established.

1943 The Dutch submarine 0-21 sank the YAMAZATO MARU (6,925 tons). The Japanese Naval Air Force attacked Funafuti in the Ellice Islands. Royal Australian Air Force PBYs mined Silver Sound off New Ireland.

1944 American forces attacked Aitape, New Guinea. New Britain was secured by American forces. The US Army's I Corps landed near Hollandia, New Guinea. American forces occupied Ungelap in the Marshalls. The Royal Navy submarine TAURUS sank the HOKUAN MARU (558 tons).

1945 The USN LCS-15 and the minesweeper SWALLOW (2 died) were sunk by Japanese kamikazes off Okinawa. The USN destroyers WADSWORTH and HUDSON (1 wounded) was hit by kamikazes. The US Army's 96th Division took Nishibaru, Okinawa. Private First-Class William Thomas, of the 38th Division, won a posthumous Medal of Honor on Luzon. The USN submarine CERO sank the AMIJI MARU (107 tons).

China-Burma-India

1945 Indian troops took Yenangyaung Burma. It contained the largest oil fields in Burma.

April 23rd

Western Europe

1940 The British 15th Brigade landed at Andalsnes, Norway. Thirty-four Royal Air Force bombers attacked airfields and shipping in the western Baltic and lost one "Whitley" and one "Blenheim".

1941 Thirty-seven Royal Air Force bombers attacked targets along the Belgian and Dutch coasts. The Luftwaffe attacked Plymouth, Britain. The German armed merchant cruiser THOR returned to Brest, France from a cruise of 322 days and twelve victories. Sixty-seven Royal Air Force bombers attacked German naval units at Brest.

1942 161 Royal Air Force bombers attacked Rostock, Germany and lost four aircraft. Most of the bombs fell two to six miles from the target area.

1943 COSSAC (Chief of Staff Supreme Allied Commander) received its first directive. It was to draft plans for diversionary operations, an assault on France if a German collapse appeared imminent and an invasion of Northwest France in 1944.

1944 382 American 8th Air Force fighters attacked targets in Germany, France and Belgium and claimed eleven victories for the loss of two P38s and five P47s. Colonel Einar A. Malstrom, commander of the USAAFs 356th Fighter Group (P47), was killed in action. Luftwaffe Me410s attacked Cambridge, Britain. The American 15th Air Force attacked aircraft targets in Austria and lost thirteen bombers and three fighters. American 9th Air Force B26s dropped 381 tons of bombs on the Creil rail yards. 114 Royal Air Force bombers dropped mines in the Baltic and lost five aircraft. Twenty-five Royal Air Force "Mosquitoes" attacked Mannheim, Germany. Twelve Royal Air Force "Stirlings" attacked Brussels, Belgium. Five B17s from the USAAF's 422nd Bomb Squadron dropped 1,780,000 leaflets Rennes, Brest, Lorient, St. Nazaire, and Nantes in France. The USAAF's 801st Bomb Group dispatched nine B24s on "Carpetbagger" missions. The German minesweeper R-208 sank while under tow by the tug FRITZ on the Danube when she struck an air-laid mine.

1945 Adolf Hitler officially took command of Berlin's defenses and announced that he would never leave the city. Luftwaffe commander Hermann Goering, from his home in Bavaria, offered to assume control of Germany. Hitler ordered his arrest for treason. German Propaganda Minister Joseph Goebbels family moved into the Chancellory bunker. The Soviets took Frankfurt-on-Oder and Cottbus. 148 Royal Air Force bombers attacked Flensburg. The British forces reached the Elbe River opposite Hamburg. The American 3rd Army found a ammunition dump near Grafenwohr, Germany containing 3,000,000 chemical warfare shells. Albrecht Haushofer, a professor at the Berlin School of Politics, and Klaus Bonhoffer, brother of Pastor Dietrich Bonhoffer, were executed at the Moabit Prison for their parts in the July 20th conspiracy. French General Eugene Deletraint was executed at Dachau. S.S. General Karl Wolff arrived in Bern, Switzerland to sign the surrender of German forces in Italy, but he was informed that Washington had prohibited contact. Sixty Royal Air Force "Mosquitoes" attacked Kiel, Germany. Fourteen USAAF 492nd Bomb Group B24s flew "Carpetbagger" missions to Denmark.

1948 The Royal Navy battleship RAMILLIES was scrapped.

Mediterranean

1941 Luftwaffe Me110s destroyed thirteen Royal Air Force "Hurricanes" on the ground near Argos, Greece. The Greek battleship LEMNOS (the ex-USN IDAHO) and battleship KILKIS (the ex-USN MISSISSIPPI) were sunk by the Luftwaffe. The Royal Air Force flew the King of Greece to Crete. The

	Greek government representatives signed a surrender document in the presence of an Italian official; it had been previously signed at German headquarters on the 21st.
1942	South Africa broke relations with Vichy France. The U565 sank the British freighter KIRKLAND (1,361 tons).
1943	The U602 was sunk by the Royal Air Force's No.560 Squadron off Oran. Maj. J. Anderson, of the Argyll and Sutherland Highlanders, won a Victoria Cross in Tunisia. Lieutenant W. Clarke, of The Loyals, won a posthumous Victoria Cross in Tunisia.
1945	The Allies reached the Po River. The German corvette Uj-2222 (the ex-Italian TUFFETTO) was sunk off Genoa by USN PTs.
1946	The remains of Benito Mussolini were stolen from the Musocco Cemetery in Milan by 3 Fascists, and were hidden at various sites until they were returned to his widow in 1957.

Atlantic

1942	The U752 sank the American freighter REINHOLT (4,799 tons). U752 survived until May 23, 1943. The U125 sank the American freighter LAMMOT DUPONT (5,102 tons-19 dead). U125 survived until May 6, 1943. The USN destroyer GREER rescued twenty-four survivors from the American freighter ROBIN HOOD which had been sunk by U575.
1943	The U189 was sunk southwest of Iceland by the Royal Air Force's No.120 Squadron. The U191 was sunk south of Greenland by the Royal Navy destroyer HESPERUS. The U306 sank the American freighter ROBERT GRAY (7,176 tons) with all hands. U306 survived until October 31st.
1945	The U2329 damaged the Norwegian freighter SVERRE HELMERSON (7,209 tons). The U1023 damaged the British freighter RIVERTON (7,345 tons). The U548 damaged the Norwegian tanker KATY (6,825 tons). The U853 sank the USN corvette EAGLE No.56 (430 tons). U853 survived until May 6th. The U396 was sunk southwest of the Shetlands by the Royal Air Force's No.86 Squadron.
1947	The Royal Navy battleship WARSPITE ran aground near Land's End on the way to the scrappers.

North America

1917	The battleship NEW MEXICO was launched. She was scrapped in 1957.
1934	The heavy cruiser SAN FRANCISCO was commissioned. She was scrapped in 1961.
1941	The "America First" committee held its first mass meeting. It was a group that America should remain isolated from conflicts in the rest of the world.

1944 The destroyers STRONG and MANNERT L. ABELE were launched. STRONG was sold to Brazil in 1973 and MANNERT L. ABELE was lost on April 12, 1945.
1945 A Japanese balloon-bomb was found near Queen Charlotte Island, British Columbia. The USN PE-56 exploded off Portland, Maine.

Pacific
1880 Carl Lucas Norden, the bomb sight inventor, was born in Semarang, Java.
1942 In the first action for the B26 "Marauder" in the Pacific Theater of Operations, Lieutenant Ralph E. Hankey won a Distinguished Flying Cross. The USN minesweeper OGLALA was righted at Pearl Harbor. She had capsized during the Japanese attack of December 7th.
1943 The Australian government ordered 100 P51s. The Japanese Naval Air Force attacked Funafuti, destroying two B24s and one F4F. The IJN patrol boat No.39 was sunk off Formosa by the USN submarine SEAWOLF.
1944 The American 13th Air Force attacked Japanese installations at Truk. American forces occupied Hollandia, New Guinea. The IJN destroyer AMAGIRI, which had sunk JFK's PT-109, was sunk by a mine off Balikpapan, Borneo. The USN submarine SEADRAGON sank the TAIJU MARU (6,886 tons).
1945 The US Army's 24th Division took Kabacan, Mindanao. The American 8th Army secured Cebu in the Philippines. The USN submarine BESUGO sank the U-183.
1954 The Royal Navy destroyer DEFENDER located the wreckage of the Royal Navy battleship PRINCE OF WALES and the battle cruiser REPULSE off Kuantan, Malaya (See December 10, 1942).

China-Burma-India
1942 The Japanese took Loilem and Loikaw in Burma.
1945 American 5th Air Force B24s attacked Saigon.

April 24th

Western Europe
1856 Philippe Petain, leader of the Vichy Government of France, was born.
1876 German Navy Commander Admiral Erich Raeder was born in Wandsbek near Hamburg.
1882 British airman Hugh Dowding was born. He received his civilian pilot's license on December 20, 1913 and his Army commission in 1900. He was promoted to air vice marshal in 1929 and to air marshal in January 1933. He assumed command of Fighter Command in 1936. He was relieved of

his command on November 25, 1940 after winning the "Battle of Britain". He retired in July 1942. He died on February 15, 1970 in Kent.

1932 In state elections in Germany, the Nazis increased their number of seats in the Prussian parliament from 6 to 162.

1939 Adolf Hitler was informed of the possibility of an atomic bomb and immediately banned the export of uranium.

1940 German forces took Rendal in southern Norway. An attempt by British ground forces to reach Trondheim, Norway failed. 18 "Gladiators", of Royal Air Force No.263 Squadron, took off from the Royal Navy carrier GLORIOUS and landed on frozen Lake Lesjaskog in Norway. All were destroyed by German forces within three days. The remains of one of them are now on display at the Royal Air Force Museum at Hendon in Britain. Josef Terboven was appointed as Reich Commissar for Norway.

1941 Twenty-four Royal Air Force bombers attacked German shipping. Sixty-nine Royal Air Force bombers attacked Kiel, Germany and lost one "Whitley". One person on the ground was killed in the raid.

1942 Twelve Royal Air Force "Bostons" attacked Flushing, Belgium. A Luftwaffe raid on Exeter marked the beginning of the "Baedeker Raids". Jews were prohibited from using public transportation in Germany. 125 Royal Air Force bombers attacked Rostock, Germany and lost one "Hampden". One Royal Air Force "Blenheim" was lost while on an intruder flight.

1943 Five Royal Air Force "Mosquitoes" attacked targets in France and Germany.

1944 716 American 8th Air Force bombers dropped 1,739 tons of bombs on airfields at Landsberg, Gablingen and Leipheim and industrial targets at Oberpfaffenhofen, Erding, Friedrichafen, Lowenthal and Neckarsulm in Germany and lost thirty-six B17s and four B24s (thirteen of the lost B17s and one of the B24s landed in Switzerland). 867 8th and 9th Air Force fighters provided support for the bombers and claimed 124 victories for the loss of five P47s and twelve P51s. Luftwaffe ace Franz Schwaiger (67 victories) was killed in action by American P51s. 637 Royal Air Force bombers attacked Karlruhe, Germany and lost nineteen aircraft. 260 Royal Air Force bombers attacked Munich and lost nine "Lancasters". Eighty-eight people were killed in the raid. Five B17s from the USAAF's 422nd Bomb Squadron dropped 1,120,000 leaflets on Amsterdam, The Hague, Rotterdam, Utrecht, Lille and Reims. The USAAF's 801st Bomb Group dispatched eight B24s on "Carpetbagger" missions.

1945 The Soviets entered Berlin. The American 1st Army took Dessau on the Elbe River. The Allies took Ulm, Germany. 110 Royal Air Force bombers attacked Bad Oldesloe. 700 people were killed in the raid. Luftwaffe ace Gunther Lutzow (108 victories) died when his Me262 jet was shot down over Donauworth. The U108 was scuttled at Stettin. Thirty-seven Royal Air Force bombers dropped leaflets and medical supplies on eight prisoner of war camps in Northern Germany. Ninety-five Royal Air Force "Mosquitoes" attacked targets in Germany. Eleven American 8th Air Force B24s dropped leaflets on France, Holland and Germany.

1953   Winston Churchill was knighted by Queen Elizabeth.

Eastern Europe

1942   The Soviet submarine ShCh-401 was sunk by German surface craft.

1944   The American 15th Air Force attacked Ploesti and Bucharest in Rumania and aircraft and rail targets in Yugoslavia. Luftwaffe ace Emil Omert (70 victories) was killed in action over Ploesti, Rumania. A USAAF C87 transport, the "Becky", was shot down near the Crimea by Soviet anti/aircraft fire.

1945   The Soviet freighter ONEGA was sunk by the U997. The Soviets liberated the prisoner of war Camp at Kief Heide in Pomerania.

Mediterranean

1913   The Italian battleship CAIO DUILIO was launched. She was scrapped in 1957.

1941   The German 5th Panzer Division broke through the ANZAC (Australian 6th and New Zealand Divisions) line at Thermopylae in Greece. German forces occupied the islands of Limnos, Thasos and Samothrace in the Aegean Sea. The British began evacuating their forces from Greece in an operation that would last until the 29th. Over 50,000 were evacuated, but of those 21,000 were sent to Crete. Bulgarian forces invaded Greek territory. The Italian torpedo boat SIMONE SCHIAFFINO was sunk off Cap Bon, Tunisia by a mine. The Greek torpedo boat KYZIKOS was sunk by the Luftwaffe.

1943   The Royal Navy submarine SAHIB was sunk by Italian corvettes. Sergeant William Nelson, of the 9th Division, won a posthumous Medal of Honor at Djebel Dardys, Tunisia.

1944   The U311 was sunk by aircraft from the Royal Navy carrier FORMIDABLE northwest of Algiers. USN PTs and Royal Navy MTBs attacked a German convoy destroying 10 vessels. The German S-54 was a constructive loss after hitting a mine off Greece. Private First-Class John Squires, of the 3rd Division, won a Medal of Honor near Padiglione, Italy.

1945   The Allies took Ferra. The US Army's 92nd Division took La Spezia. The German submarines UIT-2 and UIT-3, the torpedo boats TA-31 and TA-32, the sloops SG-15 and SG-23, the corvettes Uj-2221, Uj-2226, Uj-2227, Uj-2228, Uj-6083 and Uj-6084 were scuttled at Genoa.

Atlantic

1940 The German armed merchant cruiser ORION took the steamer HAXBY (5,207 tons).

1942 The U136 sank the British freighter EMPIRE DRUM (7,244 tons). U136 survived until July 11th.

1943 The U710 was sunk by the Royal Air Force's No.206 Squadron south of Iceland. The U129 sank the American freighter SANTA CATALINI (6,507 tons). U129 survived until August 1944. The U386 sank the British freighter ROSENBORG (1,997 tons). U386 survived until February 19, 1944. The British freighter CAMPANA rescued 15 survivors from the American freighter JAMES W. DENVER which had been sunk on April 11th by U195. The Swedish steamer VENEZIA rescued 85 survivors from the American freighter SANTA CATALINA which had been sunk the previous day by U129.

1945 The U956 sank the British freighter MONMOUTH COAST (878 tons). U956 survived the war. The USN destroyer escort FREDERICK C. DAVIS was sunk by the U546. She was the last USN ship lost to a U-boat. U546 was then sunk by the USN destroyer escorts FLAHERTY, NEUNZER, CHATELAIN, VARIAN, HUBBARD, KEITH, JANSEN, and PILLSBURY northwest of the Azores.

North America

1940 The destroyer MEREDITH was launched. She was lost October 15, 1942.

1941 FDR, Stimson (Secretary of War) and Marshall (US Army Chief of Staff) reviewed the defenses of Hawaii.

1943 The US Army's 7th Division left San Francisco en route to Attu. The destroyer SIGOURNEY was launched. The Panamanian steamer El ESTERO was scuttled after catching fire in New York Harbor.

Pacific

1943 The USN submarine FLYING FISH sank the KASUGA MARU (1,374 tons). The IJN submarine I-26 sank the Australian freighter KOWARRA (2,125 tons). Royal Australian Air Force PBYs mined Ysabel Passage off New Ireland and Balikpapan, Borneo. 7th Air Force B24s attacked Tarawa in the Gilberts. The American 11th Air Force attacked Kiska in the Aleutians.

1944 American forces occupied Aitape, New Guinea. The Australians occupied Madang, New Guinea.

1945 The U183 was sunk in the Java Sea by the USN submarine BESUGO. USAAF B29s attacked the Hitachi plant and lost four aircraft.

1948 The USN destroyer STACK was scuttled after being used as a target in the Bikini tests.

China-Burma-India
1941 Australian reinforcements arrived in Singapore.
1942 The Japanese took Hopang, Burma.
1944 The first two USAAF B29s to fly over the "Hump" arrived at Kwankhan, China.
1945 Forty American 10th Air Force B24s attacked the Burma-Thailand railway.

April 25th

Western Europe
1937 Luftwaffe aircraft attacked Guernica, Spain.
1940 The U22 was sunk by a mine in the Skagerrak. Six Royal Air Force bombers attacked shipping near Bergen, Norway and lost one "Blenheim".
1941 Twenty-seven Royal Air Force "Blenheims" attacked coastal targets and lost one aircraft. Sixty-two Royal Air Force bombers attacked Kiel, Germany and lost one "Wellington". Seven people were killed in the raid.
1942 Thirty-six Royal Air Force "Bostons" attacked targets in France and lost two aircraft. The Luftwaffe attacked Bath, Britain. 128 Royal Air Force bombers attacked Rostock, German. Six Royal Air Force "Stirlings" attacked Pilsen, Czechoslovakia and lost one aircraft.
1944 The German destroyer Z-24 was sunk at Le Verdon by the Royal Air Force. Royal Canadian Air Force ace Sub/Lieutenant G. Hill (14 victories) was shot down and captured. 294 American 8th Air Force bombers dropped 766 tons of bombs on the marshalling yards at Mannheim and Landau in Germany and airfields at Nancy, Metz and Dijon in France and lost five B24s and two B17s (three of the lost B24s landed in Switzerland). 719 8th and 9th Air Force fighters provided support for the bombers and claimed thirty-four victories for the loss of two P51s. Twenty-seven American 8th Air Force B24s dropped eighty-eight tons of bombs on the Wizernes V-1 rocket launching sites in France. They were escorted by forty 8th Air Force P47s. Twenty-five Royal Air Force "Stirlings" dropped mines off the French coast. Six B17s from the USAAF's 422nd Bomb Squadron dropped 4,200,000 leaflets on twenty different targets in France. The USAAF's 801st Bomb Group dispatched six B24s on "Carpetbagger" missions.
1945 At 1330, a 69th Division patrol led by Lieutenant Albert Kotzebue met Soviet troops at Stehla on the Elbe River. The official meeting however took place ten miles northwest of Stehla at 1640, at the town of Torgau, when a patrol led by Lieutenant William Robertson, also of the 69th Division, met the Soviets. The first meeting was disallowed because Kotzebue was unsure of his exact location. The Soviet forces surrounded Berlin. German SS troops stole 85,000 Swiss Francs from the Munich

Reichsbank. German Field Marshal Ewald von Kleist was captured. He would die in Soviet custody nine years after the war ended. 482 Royal Air Force bombers attacked Wangerooge, Germany and lost seven aircraft. 306 people died in the raid, including twenty Allied prisoners of war. 375 Royal Air Force bombers attacked Hitler's headquarters at Obersalzburg near Berchtesgaden in Bavaria. 554 American 8th Air Force bombers dropped 500 tons of bombs on Pilsen, Czechoslovakia and 885 tons on rail targets and airfields in Czechoslovakia and southeast Germany and lost six B17s. 539 8th Air Force fighters provided support for the bombers and claimed one victory for the loss of one P51. This was the last action of the war for the following 8th Air Force Heavy Bombardment and Fighter Groups that participated in this the last heavy bomber raid of the war, the type of aircraft flown, the number of missions and combat losses suffered by each during the war: the 44th (B24)-343 missions-having lost 192 aircraft, the 91st (B17)-340 missions-having lost 197 aircraft, the 92nd (B17)-308 missions-having lost 154 aircraft, the 93rd (B24)-396 missions-having lost 140 aircraft, the 303rd (B17)-364 missions-having lost 165 aircraft, the 305th (B17)-337 missions-having lost 154 aircraft, the 351st (B17)-311 missions-having lost 124 aircraft, the 379th (B17)-330 missions-having lost 141 aircraft, the 381st (B17)-296 missions-having lost 131 aircraft, the 384th (B17)-314 missions-having lost 159 aircraft, the 389th (B24)-321 missions-having lost 153 aircraft, the 392nd (B24)-285 missions-having lost 184 aircraft, the 398th (B17)-195 missions-having lost 58 aircraft, the 445th (B24)-282 missions-having lost 133 aircraft, the 446th (B24)-273 missions-having lost 86 aircraft, the 448th (B24)-262 missions-having lost 135 aircraft, the 458th (B24)-240 missions-having lost 65 aircraft, the 466th (B24)-232 missions-having lost 71 aircraft, the 467th (B24)-212 missions-having lost 48 aircraft, the 491st (B24)-187 missions-having lost 70 aircraft, the 20th (P51)-312 missions-having lost 132 aircraft, the 353rd (P51)-447 missions-having lost 137 aircraft, the 355th (P51)-having lost 175 aircraft, the 357th (P51)-313 missions-having lost 128 aircraft, the 364th (P51)-342 missions-having lost 134 aircraft and the 479th (P51)-351 missions-having lost 69 aircraft. Luftwaffe ace Joachim Brender scored the last of his 189 victories. American 9th Air Force B26s attacked Schwab-Munchen and Ebenhausen in Germany. A Luftwaffe Ju290 loaded with Nazi officials flew to Barcelona, Spain. 109 Royal Air Force bombers attacked Tonsberg, Norway and lost one "Lancaster". It was the last of more than 3,300 "Lancasters" to be lost in the war. The Royal Navy battleship ANSON left for operations in the Pacific.

Eastern Europe
1883 Soviet General Semen Budenny was born. He died on October 26, 1973 and was buried in the Kremlin Wall.
1943 Moscow broke relations with the Polish government-in-exile.
1945 The Soviets took Pillau in East Prussia.

Mediterranean
1941 Hitler issued his War Directive No.28 which called for the invasion of Crete. German forces attacked Halfaya Pass, near the Egyptian border. The Greek torpedo boat PERGAMOS was sunk by the Luftwaffe.
1944 The American 15th Air Force attacked aircraft and rail targets in Italy. At 0145, the German torpedo boat TA-23 (ex-Italian IMPAVIDO) was sunk by a mine.
1945 American forces took Verona, Mantua, and Parma. 1st Lieutenant Raymond Knight won posthumous Medal of Honor over the Po Valley while flying a P47 "Thunderbolt". Italian partisans took control of Milan, Italy. The German sloop SG-20 was scuttled at Oneglia.

Atlantic
1941 The German armed merchant cruiser PINGUIN took the British freighter EMPIRE LIGHT (6,828 tons). The U103 sank the Norwegian freighter POLYANA (2,267 tons). U103 survived until April 15, 1945. German naval units operating in the Atlantic were ordered by Berlin to avoid incidents with American shipping.
1942 The U108 sank the British freighter MODESTA (3,849 tons). U108 survived until April 11, 1944.
1943 The French freighter ROUENNAIS (3,777 tons) was sunk by a mine. The U203 was sunk by the Royal Navy escort carrier BITER and the destroyer PATHFINDER.
1944 The U990 was sunk by the Royal Air Force's No.59 Squadron.

North America
1888 Admiral John Reeves was born in Haddonfield, New Jersey. He graduated 74th in his 1911 Annapolis class of 193. He became a naval aviator in 1936 and served as executive officer of the carrier LANGLEY and Commander of the Naval Air Station Pearl Harbor. He commissioned the carrier WASP and commanded her until April 1942 when he was promoted to rear admiral commanding the Alaskan Sector, Northwest Frontier. He remained there until May 1943. He then took command of Carrier Division 4. In July 1944 he became Commander Western Carolines. He retired on May 1, 1950 as a full admiral. He died on July 15, 1967 at Pensacola, Florida.

1929   The heavy cruiser PENSACOLA (awarded 13 battle stars during the war) was launched. She was scuttled in 1948 after serving as a target at Bikini in 1946.

1940   The carrier WASP was commissioned. She was sunk on September 15, 1942. FDR proclaimed American neutrality in the war between Germany and Norway.

1941   FDR publicly labeled Charles Lindbergh "...a defeatist and an appeaser". The B17D "Swoose" was accepted by USAAC. She is still in storage at the Smithsonian and is the oldest of her type still in existence.

1943   The first all-Black USAAF unit, the 99th Fighter Squadron, was ordered to North Africa. Its commander, Lieutenant Colonel Benjamin O. Davis, would later become the USAF's first Black general. The USN YP-481 was lost after she ran aground off Charleston, South Carolina. The submarine DACE was launched. In 1954, she was transferred to the Italian Navy.

1944   An Royal Canadian Air Force bomber crashed into a Montreal street, killing nine. The light cruiser AMSTERDAM (awarded one battle star during the war) was launched. She was scrapped in 1971.

1945   US Secretary of War, Henry L. Stimson, informed President Harry Truman that within 4 months America would have a bomb that could destroy an entire city. The San Francisco Conference began. It would last two months and end with a charter for the United Nations.

1973   Admiral Frank Jack Fletcher died at Bethesda, Maryland. He had commanded carrier forces in the Pacific early in the war.

Pacific

1921   The IJN light cruiser NAGARA was launched. She was sunk on August 7, 1944.

1942   The USN carriers HORNET and ENTERPRISE returned to Pearl Harbor from the "Doolittle Raid". American troops arrived in New Caledonia.

1943   The IJN submarine I-177 sank the British freighter LIMERICK (8,724 tons).

1944   The USN submarine CREVALLE sank the KASHIWA MARU (976 tons). American 13th Air Force B24s attacked Truk. Eleven American 7th Air Force B25s attacked Wotje.

1945   The USN destroyer escort ENGLAND and the freighter YOUNG were hit by kamikazes. The USN destroyer-transport HORACE BASS was sunk by the IJN submarine Ro-109. The USN submarine COD sank the IJN minelayer W-41. Private First-Class David Gonzales, of the 32nd Division, won a posthumous Medal of Honor on Luzon.

China-Burma-India
1942 "Doolittle Raiders" Nielsen, Meder and Hallmark were sent to Japan for interrogation. The Japanese took Pyawbwe, Burma. A British convoy left Durban, South Africa. It consisted of two landing ships, six freighters, one tanker and one hospital ship. Its target was French-held Diego Suarez, Madagascar. It was escorted by the cruiser DEVONSHIRE, three destroyers and various small craft.
1943 The Italian submarine DA VINCI sank the British tanker DORYSSA (8,078 tons).
1944 American 14th Air Force P38s attacked the Japanese Air Force base at Heho.
1945 The Japanese took Wukang, China. American 5th Air Force B24s attacked Saigon. The British took Salin, Burma.

April 26th

Western Europe
1886 German General Hans von Seeckt was born. He would command the Commander-in-Chief of the German Reichswehr from 1920 until 1926. He died on December 29,1936.
1896 Luftwaffe General Ernst Udet was born in Frankfurt-am-Main. He would be Director-General of Equipment for the Luftwaffe. He committed suicide on November 17, 1941.
1925 Field Marshal Paul von Hindenburg was elected a President of Germany.
1933 The Gestapo (secret police) was established in Prussia by Hermann Goering.
1937 The Spanish town of Guernica was destroyed by the Luftwaffe.
1939 Prime Minister Neville Chamberlain announced military conscription in Britain. A Luftwaffe Me109R set a new world speed record of 469.22 mph. The record would stand until 1946, when it was broken by a American-made F8F "Bearcat".
1940 The Norwegian destroyer GARM was sunk at Bjordal by the Luftwaffe. Two Royal Navy carrier ARK ROYAL "Skuas" shot down a Luftwaffe He111 over Norway (it was salvaged in 1976). Three of twenty-eight Royal Air Force "Hampdens" were lost on an abortive mine-laying operation off Norway.
1941 Twenty-five Royal Air Force "Blenheims" attacked shipping and lost three aircraft. Fifty Royal Air Force bombers attacked Hamburg, Germany and lost one "Hampden". Six people were killed in the raid.
1942 Twelve Royal Air Force "Bostons" attacked rail targets in France. The Luftwaffe attacked Bath, Britain. 106 Royal Air Force bombers attacked

Rostock, Germany and lost three aircraft. This was the fourth consecutive night that Rostock had been attacked. The four raids had destroyed 130 acres of the city and killed 204 people.

1943 Six Royal Air Force "Mosquitoes" attacked targets in France and Belgium. 561 Royal Air Force bombers attacked Duisburg, Germany and lost seventeen aircraft. 300 buildings were destroyed and 183 people were killed in the raid.

1944 344 American 8th Air Force B17s dropped 810 tons of bombs on industrial targets in Brunswick, Hannover, and Paderborn in Germany. 554 8th and 9th Air Force fighters provided support for the bombers and lost one P38 and four P51s. Sixty-two 8th Air Force B17s attempted to attack Cologne, Germany, but had to abort due to bad weather. It was to have been the first operation for the new 2,000-pound glide-bomb. They were to have been escorted by ninety 8th Air Force P47s and P51s. Fifty-one 8th Air Force P38s attacked the Le Mans airfield in France. Twenty-eight 8th Air Force P51s attacked the Cormeilles-en-Vexin airfield in France. At 0420, the German torpedo boat T-29 was sunk off Brittany by the Royal Canadian Navy destroyer HAIDA. 493 Royal Air Force bombers attacked Essen, Germany and lost seven aircraft. 217 Royal Air Force bombers attacked Schweinfurt and lost twenty-one "Lancasters". Only two people were killed in the raid. Royal Air Force Sergeant Norman Jackson, of No.106 Squadron, won a Victoria Cross over Schweinfurt. 217 Royal Air Force bombers attacked Villeneuve-St-Georges, France and lost one "Halifax". Twenty-nine French civilians were killed in the raid. Five B17s from the USAAF's 422nd Bomb Squadron dropped 800,000 leaflets on Ghent, Antwerp, Brussels, Liege and Gosselies in Brussels.

1945 The Soviets took Brno in Czechoslovakia and the Berlin suburbs of Moabit and Neukolln. The American 3rd Army took Regensburg and Ingolstadt in Germany. The British XXX Corps took Bremen. The French 1st Army reached Lake Constance in southern Germany. Heinrich Himmler was informed by his advisors that food supplies for the German public would run out by May 10th. French Premier Petain was arrested as he tried to cross the Swiss border. The American 3rd Army crossed the Austrian border. Eighty-three Royal Air Force "Mosquitoes" attacked targets in Germany. The German patrol boat V-1114 was sunk by Allied aircraft in the Heligoland Bight.

Eastern Europe

1942 The Soviet Navy delivered reinforcements and supplies to the surrounded city of Sevastopol.

1945 The Soviets took Stettin, East Prussia.

Mediterranean

1894 Rudolph Hess was born in Alexandria, Egypt. He would serve as Hitler personal secretary.

1941 The Allies took Dessie, East Africa and 8,000 Italian prisoners. General Friedrich von Paulus arrived at Tobruk to observe the DAK's operations for the German High Command. The Greek torpedo boat KYDONIA was sunk by the Luftwaffe. To cut off the retreating British forces German airborne forces took Corinth in Greece. The German 5th Panzer Division captured 7,000 Commonwealth troops in Kalamata in the Peloponnesus. "Ultra" intercepts revealed the Luftwaffe's selection of bases for "Operation Crete" and a need for maps and photographs of the island.

1942 The U81 sank the Egyptian sailing ship AZIZA (100 tons).

1943 Sixty-two USAAF B24s attacked Bari, Italy.

1945 The British crossed the Adige River. The German patrol boat Uj-2229 was sunk off Genoa by the British submarine UNIVERSAL.

Atlantic

1941 The U110 sank the French freighter ANDRE MOYRANT (2,471 tons). U110 survived until May 9th.

1942 At 1515, the USN destroyer STURTEVANT was sunk by two USN mines off Key West, fifteen of her crew died. Three Allied merchant ships would later be lost in the same "friendly" minefield. The U66 sank the American freighter ALCOA PARTNER (5,513 tons-10 dead). U66 survived until May 6, 1944.

1944 Royal Navy carriers attempted to attack the German battleship TIRPITZ in Norway. They were diverted by bad weather and attacked a convoy west of the Faeroes instead, sinking three ships. One of those sunk was the German transport KT-3. The U859 sank the Panamanian freighter COLIN (6,255 tons). U859 survived until September 23rd. The U488 was sunk northwest of Cape Verde by the USN destroyer escorts FROST, HUSE, BARBER and SNOWDON. The German T-29 was sunk in the English Channel by the Royal Navy light cruiser BLACK PRINCE.

North America

1897 General Lucius Clay was born in Marietta, Georgia. He graduated 27th in his 1918 West Point class of 137. During the war, he mainly served in Washington D.C. On March 15, 1946, he became military governor of Germany. He retired in 1949 at the age of 51. He died on April 16, 1978 in Chatham, Massachusetts.

1933 Future Chief of Naval Operations Ernest King was promoted to Rear Admiral.

1939   The first P40 contract was awarded to Curtiss for 524 aircraft.
1943   The USN YP-47 was lost when she collided with the YMS-110 off Staten Island, New York. The carrier INTREPID was launched. After she was retired, she would be dedicated as a museum in New York City.
1944   The submarine SPIKEFISH was launched. She was discarded in 1963. The US Army seized the Montgomery Wards plant in Chicago after Wards Chairman Sewell Avery refused to comply with a War Labor Board directive. They withdrew on the 29th. Avery submitted a bill for $480,000 to the government for damages incurred during the occupation.
1947   A Japanese balloon-bomb was found near Eureka, California.

Pacific
1942   The USN destroyer OVERTON was sunk off the Marquessas by a mine. The IJN submarine Ro-30 was sunk by the USN submarine TAUTOG.
1943   The USN Task Group 8.6 (commanded by McMorris) bombarded Attu. It consisted of the cruisers DETROIT, RICHMOND, and SANTA FE and six destroyers. The American 11th Air Force attacked Kiska in the Aleutians.
1944   The IJN submarine I-180 was sunk by the USN destroyer GILMORE. The USN submarine JACK sank the YOSHIDA MARU No.1 (5,425 tons). The USN submarine SARGO sank the WAZAN MARU (4,851 tons). The USN submarine GUAVINA sank the NOSHIRO MARU (2,333 tons). The USN submarine BONEFISH sank the TOKIWA MARU (806 tons). The Australian 5th Division took Alexishafen, New Guinea.
1945   The US Army's 37th Division took Mount Mirador on Luzon.

China-Burma-India
1942   Lieutenant Colonel James Doolittle arrived at Chuchow, China after his raid on the Japanese homeland and found that he had been promoted to Brigadier General, skipping the rank of Colonel.

April 27th

Western Europe
1921   Luftwaffe ace Joachim Brendel (189 victories) was born in Ulrichshalben. He survived the war.
1939   Adolf Hitler abrogated the Anglo-German Naval Treaty.
1940   German forces took Arendal in southern Norway. The British decided to evacuate their forces in Namsos and Andalsnes in Norway.
1941   Thirty-three Royal Air Force bombers attacked targets in Germany and Holland.

1942 Eighteen Royal Air Force "Bostons" attacked Lille, France and Ostend, Belgium and lost one aircraft. The Luftwaffe attacked Norwich, Britain. At 1210, the Royal Navy minesweeper FITZROY was sunk off Great Yarmouth, Britain by a mine. Ninety-seven Royal Air Force bombers attacked Cologne, Germany and lost seven aircraft. Eleven people were killed in the raid. The Royal Air Force's "Whitley" flew its last mission for Bomber Command when two aircraft attacked Dunkirk, France. Forty-three Royal Air Force bombers attacked the battleship TIRPITZ near Trondheim, Norway and lost five aircraft. One of the aircraft lost, a "Halifax", was recovered from the bottom of Lake Hoklingen in Norway in 1973 and is now in the Royal Air Force Museum at Hendon outside of London. Five Royal Air Force bombers were lost on other operations.

1943 The British destroyers GOATHLAND and ALBRIGHTON attacked a German convoy off Ouessant and sank the trawler UJ-1402. 160 Royal Air Force bombers dropped mines off the French ports and lost one "Lancaster".

1944 The U803 was sunk in the Baltic by a mine. 476 American 8th Air Force bombers dropped 1,847 tons of bombs on V-1 rocket sites on the Pas de Calais in France and near the port of Cherbourg and lost three B17s and one B24. Colonel Robert H. Kelly, commander of the USAAF's 100th Bomb Group (B17), was killed in action on the mission. 357 8th Air Force fighters provided support for the bombers and lost one P47 and one P51. Fifty-four 8th Air Force P38s dropped fifty-two tons of bombs on the Roye-Amy airfield in France. Forty-eight 8th Air Force P38s dropped thirty-five tons of bombs on the Albert/Meaulte airfield in France. Twenty-eight 8th Air Force P51s dropped eight tons of bombs on the Cormeilles-en-Vexin airfield in France. 471 8th Air Force B17s and B24s dropped 1,303 tons of bombs on French marshalling yards and airfields and lost four B24s. 543 8th Air Force fighters provided support for the bombers and claimed seven victories for the loss of four P47s. 100 American 9th Air Force B26s attacked Cambrai, France. Seventy-one 9th Air Force A20 "Havocs" attacked Arras, France in the type's first operations with the American 9th Air Force. 322 Royal Air Force "Lancasters" attacked Friedrichshaven and lost eighteen aircraft. Ninety-nine acres of the town were destroyed and 136 people were killed in the raid. 223 Royal Air Force bombers attacked Aulnoye, France and lost one "Halifax". 144 Royal Air Force bombers attacked Montzen, France and lost fifteen aircraft. Five B17s from the USAAFs 422nd Bomb Squadron dropped 3,360,000 leaflets on Cambrai, Orleans, Rennes, Nantes, Brest, Tours, Lorient, Caen, Le Mans, Limoges, and Chateauroux in France. The USAAF's 801st Bomb group dispatched twenty-one B24s on "Carpetbagger" missions and lost one aircraft.

1945   The Soviets took Templehof airfield and controlled 75% of Berlin. American forces took the Flossenburg concentration camp near the Czech border. British troops took Bremen. Charles De Gaulle refused to hand over Stuttgart to either American or British forces. Luftwaffe Commander Hermann Goering and his family were taken to Schloss Mauterndorf by S.S. troops. Hitler had ordered the action taken after accusing Goering of treason.

Mediterranean
1941   The Royal Navy destroyer DEFENDER left the port of Kalamata, Yugoslavia with 250 evacuees and that country's crown jewels. The Greek destroyer VASILEVS GEORGIOS was sunk. She would be salvaged by the Germans and recommissioned as the ZG-1 (See March 30, 1943). The Royal Navy destroyer DIAMOND (launched in 1932) and the destroyer escort WRYNECK were sunk in the Gulf of Navplion off Greece) by the Luftwaffe. They were carrying 700 survivors from the Dutch liner SLAMAT. Only fifty survivors from the three crews were found. British forces counter-attacked to relieve Tobruk, Libya and were defeated. The Germans entered Athens, Greece. The Royal Navy carrier ARK ROYAL launched twenty-four "Hurricanes" for Malta in "Operation Dunlop", one aircraft was lost.
1943   Captain the Lord Lyell, of the Scot's Guards, won a posthumous Victoria Cross in Tunisia. The U371 sank the Dutch freighter MEROPE (1,162 tons).
1945   Genoa, having been taken by partisans, was secured by American forces. Italian Marshal Rodolfo Graziani was captured by partisans. He died in 1955.

Atlantic
1941   The Royal Navy catapult-armed merchantman PATIA was sunk off the Tyne. The U552 sank the British freighter BEACON GRANGE (10,160 tons) and the Royal Navy trawler COMMANDER HORTON. U552 survived the war. The U147 sank the Norwegian freighter RIMFASKE (1,334 tons). U147 survived until June 2nd.
1943   The U169 was sunk by the Royal Air Force's No.206 Squadron off Iceland. U174 was sunk by USN VB-125 off Newfoundland.
1944   The U193 was sunk by the Royal Air Force's No.612 Squadron in the Bay of Biscay.
1945   The Royal Navy destroyer escort REDMILL was a constructive loss after an attack by the U1105 west of Ireland. Twenty-two of her crew died.

North America

1882 Admiral Wilson Brown was born in Philadelphia. He graduated 44th in his 1902 Annapolis class of fifty-nine. On February 1, 1941, he was named as Commander, Scouting Force with the rank of Vice Admiral. After the attack on Pearl Harbor, he became commander of Task Force 11 which was built around the carrier LEXINGTON. He led that unit until April 3, 1942 when he returned to the United States to become Roosevelt's naval aide. He died on January 2, 1957.

1942 1,850 men of the 8th Air Force left New York, aboard the transport ANDES. They would be the first members of that unit to arrive in Britain.

1944 The escort carrier MAKASSAR STRAIT was commissioned. She was discarded in 1959.

1974 Admiral Jesse Oldendorf, commander of CruDiv-4, BatRon-1 and BatDiv-4 in the Pacific, died.

Pacific

1941 British, Dutch and American military officials met to prepare a defensive plan to be used in case of a Japanese attack on Singapore.

1943 The USN submarine SCORPION sank the YUZAN MARU ((6,380 tons). The IJN submarine I-178 sank the American freighter LYDIA M. CHILD (7,176 tons) off Newcastle, Australia. An Australian PBY "Catalina" crashed on Bougainville while dropping supplies to coastwatcher Jack Read. Three of the 7-man crew died in the accident and two of the survivors were later killed by the Japanese.

1944 The USN submarine TRIGGER sank the MIIKE MARU (11,738 tons). The USN submarine SEAHORSE sank the AKIGAWA MARU (5,244 tons). The USN submarine HALIBUT sank the GENBU MARU (1,872 tons) and the IJN minelayer KAMOME. The USN submarine BLUEGILL sank the IJN light cruiser YUBARI off Palau. The USN submarine SEADRAGON sank the HAWAII MARU (9,467 tons). American 13th Air Force B24s attacked Truk. Royal Australian Air Force PBYs mined Balikpapan, Borneo.

1945 American forces took Baguio, Luzon. USAAF B29s attacked airfields on Kyushu. The USN heavy cruiser WICHITA was hit by Japanese shore-fire off Okinawa. The USN destroyer HUTCHINS and the destroyer-transport RATHBURNE were constructive losses after a Japanese air attack off Okinawa. The American freighter CANADA VICTORY was sunk by a kamikaze (3 of her crew died). The USN destroyers ISHERWOOD (42 died) and RALPH TALBOT (5 of her crew died) were hit by kamikazes. The port of Nagoya, Japan was closed due to the American blockade. Three USN cruisers and six destroyers (commanded by Berkey) bombarded Tarakan, Borneo.

China-Burma-India
1941 The American-Dutch-British Conference in Singapore ended. An agreement on combined local defense had been signed.
1942 The Japanese took Thazi, Burma.

April 28th

Western Europe
1937 Rebel forces took Guernica and Durango in Spain.
1941 Fourteen Royal Air Force bombers attacked targets in Holland and Germany. Six Royal Air Force "Blenheims" attacked German shipping in the Channel. Twenty Royal Air Force bombers attacked Brest, France. Five Royal Air Force "Hampdens" dropped mines off La Rochelle, France and lost two aircraft.
1942 Six Royal Air Force "Bostons" attacked French rail targets. Eighty-eight Royal Air Force bombers attacked Kiel, Germany and lost six aircraft. Fifteen people were killed in the raid. Thirty-four Royal Air Force bombers attacked the German battleship TIRPITZ near Trondheim, Norway and lost two "Halifaxes". One Royal Air Force "Blenheim" was lost on another operation.
1943 207 Royal Air Force bombers carried out the Royal Air Force's largest mine-laying operation of the war. It was concentrated mainly in the Baltic. Twenty-two aircraft were lost in the action. Royal Air Force Wing Commander G. MacDonald died when a barge he was strafing near Hasselt, Holland exploded.
1944 116 American 8th Air Force B17s dropped 310 tons of bombs on the Avord Airfield and lost two aircraft. 205 8th Air Force fighters provided support for the bombers and claimed eight victories for the loss of two P51s. Eighteen 8th Air Force B17s dropped fifty-four tons of bombs on V-1 rocket sites near Sottevast, France. They were escorted by forty-six 8th Air Force P47s. Forty-five 8th Air Force P38s dropped seventeen tons on the Tours airfield in France. Eighty-eight 8th Air Force fighters attacked the Chateaudun airfield and claimed one victory. Forty-seven 8th Air Force B24s dropped 183 tons of bombs on rocket V-1 sites near Mimoyecques, France. They were escorted by fifty 8th Air Force P47s. Twenty-four 8th Air Force P47s dropped twenty-four tons of bombs on airfields near Paris. A Luftwaffe Me110, flown by Lieutenant Wilhelm Johnen and carrying the latest radar, codes and recognition signals, landed in Switzerland by mistake and was detained. The incident would lead to protracted negotiations between Germany and Switzerland over the return of the aircraft. Ninety-two Royal Air Force bombers attacked St. Medard-en-Jalles, France. Two

Royal Air Force "Lancasters" were shot down in Swiss airspace by the Luftwaffe. Fifty-five Royal Air Force bombers attacked Oslo, Norway. The USN LSTs-507 (13 dead) and 531 (736 dead) were sunk in Lyme Bay, off Britain's southern coast, by German S-boats. They had been participating in "Exercise Tiger", a practice landing in preparation for D-Day. The dead included 551 sailors and 198 soldiers. Five B17s from the USAAF's 422nd Bomb Squadron dropped 1,640,000 leaflets on Antwerp, Brussels, Paris, Tours, Lorient, Nantes, Orleans, and Leeuwarden. The USAAF's 801st Bomb Group dispatched twenty-one B24s on "Carpetbagger" missions.

1945 The American 7th Army took Augsburg, Germany. Stalag 11-B, a prisoner of war camp near Fallingbostel, was liberated. Franz Halder, Chief of the Army General Staff until September 24, 1942, Schuschnigg, Chancellor of Austria and Hjalmar Schacht, Reich Finance Minister were liberated at Niederdorf, South Tyrol, after being held prisoner at Dachau Concentration Camp. The Soviets were within a mile of Hitler's Chancellory in Berlin. The German 12th Army tried to relieve besieged Berlin. The U56 was sunk by the USAAF at Kiel. The U1223 was sunk by Allied aircraft at Wesermunde. The American government authorized O.S.S. agents in Bern, Switzerland to resume negotiations with S.S. General Karl Wolff for the surrender of German forces in Italy.

1957 Luftwaffe ace Heinz Baer (220 victories) died in the crash of his light plane near Brunswick in Germany. It was the 30th anniversary of his 200th victory.

1976 Walter von Seydlitz, Paulus' Chief of Staff at Stalingrad, died in Bremen.

1984 A memorial was dedicated at Slapton Sands on Lyme Bay in memory of the 749 Americans who died during "Exercise Tiger" (See 1944).

Eastern Europe

1942 The Soviet Navy delivered reinforcements and supplies to the surrounded city of Sevastopol. The Royal Navy light cruiser EDINBURGH left Murmansk with 5 tons of Soviet gold aboard.

1944 The deportation of Hungarian Jews by German forces began.

Mediterranean

1941 43,000 British and Polish troops are evacuated from Greece. The Allied force sent to aid Greece has lost 12,712 men, plus most of their equipment. The Italians had lost 13,755 dead, while the Greeks had suffered 15,700 dead. The Germans, in their invasions of Greece and Yugoslavia, had lost 1,684 dead. German forces took Sollum. Axis aircraft attacked Malta. The Royal Navy submarine USK was sunk by a mine.

1942 Royal Air Force Sergeant J. Lynch claimed Malta's 1,000th aerial victory. He was an American who later transferred to the USAAF. The Royal Navy

	submarine URGE was sunk by a mine off Malta. The Italian submarine CORALLO sank the Turkish sailing ships DAR-EL-SALAM (138 tons) and TUNIS (81 tons) off Bone.
1943	Private Nicholas Minue, of the 1st Armored Division, won a posthumous Medal of Honor near Medjez-el-Bab, Tunisia. American 9th Air Force B24s attacked Naples. At 0935, the Italian torpedo boat CLIMENE was sunk by the Royal Navy submarine UNSHAKEN. Fifty-three of her crew died.
1944	464 American 15th Air Force bombers dropped 1,348 tons of bombs on aircraft and shipping targets in Italy.
1945	Former Italian dictator Benito Mussolini was killed by Italian partisans. Fifteen others were also killed, including his mistress Clara Petacci, the Secretary of the Fascist Party Alessandro Pavolini and four former Cabinet Ministers. The bodies were taken to Milan and hung upside down near a gas station. The American 5th Army took the Italian towns of Brescia, Bergamo and Allesandria. The Allies took Venice.

Atlantic

1941	The U96 sank the British tanker OILFIELD (8,516 tons) and freighter PORT HARDY (8,897 tons) and the Norwegian tanker CALEDONIA (9,892 tons). U96 survived until March 30, 1945. The U65 was sunk by the Royal Navy corvette GLADIOLUS south of Iceland. The German armed merchant cruiser PINGUIN took the British freighter CLAN BUCHANAN (7,880 tons).
1942	The U136 sank the Dutch freighter ARUNDO (5,163 tons). U136 survived until July 11th.

North America

1941	Charles Lindbergh resigned his Colonel's commission in the USAAC Reserves. This was done in reaction to his disapproval of the American government's foreign policies.
1942	The destroyer LAUB was launched. She was stricken in 1971.
1943	The escort carrier CROATAN (scrapped in 1971) and destroyer STEPHEN POTTER (stricken in 1972) were commissioned.
1944	US Secretary of the Navy Frank Knox died.
1945	A Japanese balloon-bomb was found near Akiak, Alaska.
1980	Admiral Thomas Settle, age 84, died of cancer at Bethesda. He had commanded the heavy cruiser PORTLAND during the war.
1989	A memorial was dedicated in New Bedford, Massachusetts in memory of the 749 Americans who died in "Exercise Tiger" (See Western Europe-1944).
1992	A B26 that had crashed near Watson Lake, British Columbia while en route to Alaska during the war was flown at Chino, California after being restored.

Pacific
1943 The IJN aircraft tender KAMAKURA MARU (17,526 tons) was sunk off New Ireland by the USN submarine GUDGEON.
1944 Forty-seven American 5th Air Force B24s attacked Biak Island. American 13th Air Force B25s attacked Buka on Bougainville. The IJN submarine I-183 was sunk by the USN submarine POGY.
1945 USAAF B29s attacked airfields on Kyushu. The USN destroyers TWIGGS (9 of her crew died) and DALY (3 died) and the hospital ship COMFORT were hit by Japanese kamikazes off Okinawa. TWIGGS would survive until June 16th when she was sunk by a kamikaze. Private First-Class Alejandro Ruiz won a Medal of Honor on Okinawa. The USN submarine SENNET sank HATSUSHIMA (1,564 tons). The USN submarine TREPANG sank the IJN destroyer-transport T-146 (890 tons). The USN submarine SPRINGER sank the IJN patrol craft Cha-17.

China-Burma-India
1942 The Japanese took Kehsi-Mausam, Burma. The American Volunteer Group shot down thirteen Japanese aircraft over Lashio, Burma. A British convoy comprised of five attack transports, three troop transports, the battleship RAMILLIES, the carrier ILLUSTRIOUS, the cruiser HERMIONE and six destroyers left Durban, South Africa. It was to rendezvous with another that had left on the 25th. Together they would attack Diego Juarez on French-held Madagascar.
1945 British forces took Taungup, Burma.

April 29th

Western Europe
1915 The Royal Navy battleship ROYAL SOVEREIGN was launched. She was sold in 1949.
1919 The Royal Navy light cruiser DIOMEDE was launched. She was scrapped in 1946.
1937 Luftwaffe commander Hermann Goering stopped production of the Luftwaffe's 4-engined bomber program.
1940 German forces moving north from Oslo and south from Trondheim took Dragset in central Norway. Six Royal Air Force bombers attacked an airfield near Oslo and lost one "Whitley". The King of Norway boarded the Royal Navy cruiser GLASGOW at Molde, Norway and was taken north to Tromso, Norway. Thirty-nine Royal Air Force bombers attacked coastal targets and lost two "Blenheims". Seventy-one Royal Air Force bombers attacked Mannheim, Germany and lost one "Wellington". Four people

were killed in the raid. Thirty-one Royal Air Force bombers attacked Rotterdam, Holland.

1942   Six Royal Air Force "Bostons" attacked Dunkirk, France. The Luftwaffe attacked Norwich, Britain. German dictator Adolf Hitler and Italian dictator Benito Mussolini met in Salzburg, Austria. Eighty-eight Royal Air Force bombers attacked Paris/Gennevilliers and lost three "Wellingtons". Three Royal Air Force bombers were lost on other operations.

1943   112 P47s from the USAAF's 4th, 56th and 78th Fighter Groups flew sweeps over France and Belgium. The 56th lost two aircraft. The German trawler V-1408 was sunk off Ijmuiden by a torpedo.

1944   618 American 8th Air Force bombers dropped 1,498 tons of bombs on Berlin, Magdeburg and Brandenburg and lost thirty-eight B17s and twenty-five B24s (one B24 landed in Sweden). 814 8th and 9th Air Force fighters provided support for the bombers and claimed twenty-two victories for the loss of three P38s and ten P51s. General James Doolittle, commander of the 8th Air Force, announced that henceforth there would be no more spares or back-ups on 8th Air Force missions, all available aircraft would go on the mission. 573 American 15th Air Force bombers dropped 1,312 tons of bombs on Toulon, France. The U421 was sunk in the attack. 101 Luftwaffe aircraft attacked Plymouth, Britain. Seventy-three Royal Air Force bombers attacked St. Medard-en-Jalles, France. Fifty-nine Royal Air Force bombers attacked Clermont-Ferrand, France. Four B17s from the USAAF's 422nd Bomb Squadron dropped 1,060,000 leaflets on twenty-one different targets in Northern France and the Low Countries. The USAAF's 801st Bomb Group dispatched fourteen B24s on "Carpetbagger" missions.

1945   The Berlin city commandant, General Helmuth Weidling, informed Hitler that Soviet forces had reached the Potsdam rail station not far from the Chancellory Bunker. Adolf Hitler married his mistress Eva Braun at the Reich's Chancellory in Berlin. The Citadel Commandant of the Chancellory Bunker, Major General Mohnke, awarded the Knight's Cross to French S.S. volunteer Eugene Vaulot for destroying six Soviet tanks and Major Herzig, commander of the panzers defending the Bunker. The original guards at Dachau were replaced by 560 members of the S.S. "Wiking" Division under the command of Lieutenant Heinrich Skodzensky. The camp and its 30,000 inmates were taken later in the day by troops of the American 7th Army. Of the 30,000 surviving inmates, 2,466 would die in the following month and a half due to ill health. The British crossed the Elbe River at Lauenburg. The American 3rd Army discovered a chemical depot near Nieder-Leirdorf containing 60,000 gas-filled aircraft bombs. French troops landed on Oleron Island in the

Gironde estuary. The last German forces on the island would surrender on the 1st of May. Between this date and May 7th, the Royal Air Force would drop 6,672 tons of food for the starving Dutch civilian population. This was possible due to a truce with the German forces in that country that permitted unescorted low-level flights. The last American 8th Air Force mission sent a 482nd Bomb Group B17 and a B24 on a radarscope sortie over Kiel, Germany (the B24 aborted). American forces took Fussen, Germany. The US Army's 14th Armored Division liberated Stalag VII, a prisoner of war camp at Moosburg, Germany. The Soviets took Austerlitz, Austria.

1956 German Field Marshal Wilhelm von Leeb died in Hohen-Schwangau, Bavaria.

1959 British General Kenneth Anderson died at Gibraltar. He had commanded 1st Army in North Africa.

2009 It was revealed that wanted Nazi war criminal Herbertus Bikker had died in November of the previous year at the age of 93 in Hagen, Germany. He had been sentenced to life in prison for his crimes, but had escaped and fled to Germany in 1952.

Eastern Europe

1943 The German minesweeper R-36 was sunk in the Black Sea by one of its own mines.

1945 The U968 sank the Royal Navy destroyer escort GODDALL (the ex-USN REYBOLD).

Mediterranean

1941 The Royal Air Force attacked Benghazi, Libya. The Luftwaffe attacked Malta. The last of the Commonwealth troops in Greece were evacuated. Their losses in the campaign were more than 2,000 casualties and 10,000 captured. German losses for the entire Balkans operation were: 2,500 killed in action, 5,800 wounded in action and 3,100 missing in action.

1942 The British sailing ship TERPSITHEA (157 tons) and the tug ALLIANCE (81 tons) were sunk by mines.

1943 General H.L.N. Salmon, commander of the Canadian 1st Division, was killed in an aircraft accident.

1944 Sergeant J. Hinton, of the 20th New Zealand Battalion, won a Victoria Cross in Greece.

1945 The surrender of German forces in Italy took place at Caserta. The British 56th Division took Venice. The Italian Air Force's leading ace, Adriano Visconti (26 victories) was killed as he tried to surrender to Italian partisans.

Atlantic

1940 The U50 was sunk by the Royal Navy destroyer HERO north of the Shetlands. The Royal Navy submarine UNITY was lost in collision.

1941 The U75 sank the British freighter CITY OF NAGPUR (10,146 tons). U75 survived until December 28th.

1942 The U66 sank the Panamanian tanker HARRY SEIDEL (10,354 tons). U66 survived until May 6, 1944. The U108 sank the American tanker MOBILOIL (9,925 tons). U108 survived until April 11, 1944.

1943 The U258 sank the American freighter MCKEESPORT (6,198 tons-1 dead). U258 survived until May 20th. The U123 sank the Swedish freighter NANKING (5,931 tons). U123 survived the war. The U515 sank the British freighters CORABELLA (5,682 tons), BANDAR SHAHPUR (5,236 tons) and NAGINA (6,551 tons) and the Dutch freighter KOTA TJANDI (7,295 tons). U515 survived until April 9, 1944. The German trawler V-807 was sunk off Terschelling by Royal Air Force "Beauforts".

1944 At 0415, the Royal Canadian Navy destroyer ATHABASKAN was sunk off Brittany by German torpedo boats. At 0435, the German torpedo boat T-27 was damaged by the destroyer HAIDA during the same action and beached. She was destroyed on May 7th by the Royal Navy MTB-673.

1945 The last convoy battle of WWII took place in the Arctic when fourteen U-boats attacked Convoy RA-66, which was comprised of twenty-four merchant ships and was en route from Murmansk to Scotland. The U286 was sunk by the Royal Navy frigates LOCH INSH, ANGUILLA, and COTTON off Murmansk. The U307 was sunk by the Royal Navy frigate LOCH INSH off Murmansk. The Royal Canadian Navy frigate GOULD was sunk by U968. She had participated in the sinking of two U-boats before her loss. The U1017 was sunk by the Royal Navy frigate LOCH FADA in the English Channel.

North America

1885 Admiral Frank Jack Fletcher was born in Marshalltown, Iowa. He graduated 26th in his 1906 Annapolis class of 116. He won a Medal of Honor during the action at Vera Cruz, Mexico in 1914. On December 7, 1941, he was commanding the heavy cruiser MINNEAPOLIS. Soon promoted, he was given command of Task Force 17 which was to relieve the garrison on Wake Island. While en route, he stopped on December 22nd to refuel his ships. The delay would prove to be fatal to the expedition when temporary Pacific Fleet Commander Admiral W.S. Pye cancelled the project. On May 3, 1942, he attacked Japanese installations on Tulagi with aircraft from his flagship the carrier YORKTOWN. He would later command USN forces at the battles of the Coral Sea and Midway. His actions during the campaign for Guadalcanal would lead to the end of his combat career. He would command the USN forces in the North Pacific and would retire on June 1, 1947. He died on April 25, 1973.

1942 The destroyer MURPHY was launched. She was stricken in 1970.

1944 The carrier BON HOMME RICHARD was launched. She was placed in reserve in 1980.

Pacific

1901 Japanese Emperor Hirohito was born. He died on January 7, 1989.

1942 Two USN PBYs landed at Corregidor after flying from Australia. Japanese air and artillery attacks were launched against Corregidor.

1943 The IJN submarine I-180 sank the Australian freighter WOLLONGBAR (2,239 tons). The USN submarine GATO landed 16 commandos on Bougainville to assist the coastwatchers that had been operating there since the beginning of the war.

1944 USN Task Force 58 began a 2-day attack on Truk. The Allies reopened the airfields at Hollandia and Aitape on New Guinea. The USN submarine POGY sank the IJN submarine I-183. The USN submarine BANG sank the TAKEKAWA MARU (1,930 tons). The USN submarine FLASHER sank the SONG GIANG GO (1,065 tons). The IJN submarine I-174 was sunk by the USN light carrier MONTEREY and the destroyers POTTER and MACDONOUGH. The USN PTs 346 and 347 were sunk in error by American aircraft near Cape Pomas, New Britain. American 13th Air Force B25s attacked Buka on Bougainville.

1945 The US Army's 185th Regimental Combat Team (commanded by Brush) landed near Padan Point, Los Negros. The USN destroyers HAZELWOOD (46 of her crew died) and HAGGARD (11 died) and the minelayers SHANNON and BAUER were hit by Japanese kamikazes. The USN destroyer HAGGARD was a constructive loss after an air attack off Okinawa and was scrapped in 1946 (11 died). The USN LCS-37 was sunk by a suicide boat. The IJN submarine I-44 was sunk by the USN escort carrier TULAGI. The USN submarine BESUGO sank the OTOME MARU (199 tons). The USN submarine CERO sank the TAISHU MARU (6,925 tons). The USN submarine BREAM sank the TEISHU MARU (1,230 tons). The Royal Navy submarine TRADEWIND sank the TAKASEGO MARU (1,116 tons).

China-Burma-India

1942 The Japanese took Lashio and Hsipaw in Burma. The American 10th Air Force attacked Rangoon, Burma.

1944 The French corvette TAHURE was sunk off Indo-China by the USN submarine FLASHER.

April 30th

Western Europe

1893   Joachim Ribbentrop was born in Wesel. He would become Germany's Foreign Minister and would be executed on October 16, 1946 for war crimes.

1930   The Royal Navy heavy cruiser NORFOLK was launched. She was scrapped in 1950.

1934   The Austrian Parliament gave Chancellor Dollfuss dictatorial powers, and then voted itself out of existence.

1937   Spanish Loyalists sank the rebel battleship ESPANA.

1940   The Royal Navy sloop BITTERN was damaged off Namsos, Norway by the Luftwaffe. She was later scuttled by the Royal Navy light cruiser CARLISLE. At 1415, the French destroyer MAILE BREZE was destroyed by an explosion while loading ammunition on the Clyde, twenty-seven died. The Royal Navy minelayer DUNOON was sunk by a mine off Great Yarmouth, Britain. The German torpedo boat LEOPARD was lost in a collision with the German auxiliary PREUSSEN in the Skagerrak. Six Royal Air Force bombers attacked Stavanger airfield in Norway and lost two "Blenheims". Thirty-five Royal Air Force bombers attacked Norwegian airfields and lost seven aircraft. German forces moving north from Oslo linked-up to the east of Andalsnes in southern Norway. The British began evacuating their forces from Andalsnes. The first British civilian casualties were suffered when a Luftwaffe mine-laying bomber crashed into Clacton, Essex, killing two and injuring 160.

1941   Thirteen Royal Air Force "Blenheims" attacked German shipping and lost one aircraft. The German armed merchant cruiser THOR arrived at Hamburg, Germany after a cruise of 329 days and twelve victories. Eighty-one Royal Air Force bombers attacked Kiel, Germany.

1942   Twenty-four Royal Air Force "Bostons" attacked targets in France. British civilian air-raid casualties for the month were 938 dead and 998 wounded.

1943   Major Martin, "The Man Who Never Was", was set adrift off the Spanish coast by the Royal Navy submarine SERAPH. Attached to the body was a brief case containing papers which the British hoped would convince the Germans that Sicily would not be the Allies next objective in the Mediterranean. 305 Royal Air Force bombers attacked Essen, Germany and lost twelve aircraft. 189 buildings were destroyed and fifty-three people were killed in the raid. Twelve Royal Air Force bombers attacked targets in Holland and lost one "Stirling".

1944   284 American 8th Air Force B17s and B24s dropped 775 tons of bombs on Lyons, Aulnat and Siracourt in France and lost one B17. 644 8th and

9th Air Force fighters provided support for the bombers and claimed twenty-nine victories for the loss of one P38 and four P51s. 128 8th Air Force fighters attacked airfields in France. The USAAF's 4th Fighter Group (P51) scored its 505th victory. The USAAF's 339th Fighter Group (P51) flew its first 8th Air Force mission. Seventy-one American 9th Air Force A20s attacked Busig and 143 B26s attacked Bethune and Somain. The Allied Air Forces dropped 80,000 tons of bombs on Western Europe. 143 Royal Air Force bombers attacked Somain, France and lost one "Halifax". 128 Royal Air Force bombers attacked Acheres, France. 116 Royal Air Force bombers attacked Maintenon, France. British civilian air-raid casualties for the month were 146 dead and 226 dead. Four B17s from the USAAF's 422nd Bomb Squadron dropped 2,230,000 leaflets on Zwolle, Reims, Metz, Strasbourg, Tours, Mulhouse, and Orleans. The USAAF's 801st Bomb Group dispatched twenty B24s on "Carpetbagger" missions.

1945   Adolf Hitler and his new wife, Eva committed suicide at 1530 in the Chancellory bunker in Berlin. Supreme Allied Commander US Army General Dwight Eisenhower informed the Soviets that American troops would advance no further in Austria than the city of Linz. Soviet forces attacked the Reichstag in Berlin. Soviet troops liberated 23,000 prisoners at the women's concentration camp at Ravensbruck, north of Berlin. 115,000 more women had died in the previous two years at the camp. The American 7th Army entered Munich. The German guards left the prisoner of war camp at Stalag Luft I near Barth, leaving the prisoners in control. The German minesweeper M-455 was sunk at Cuxhaven by the Royal Air Force. The British government awarded twenty-three Victoria Crosses in the month of April during the war.

1952   American forces blew up Adolf Hitler's home, the Berghof, at Obersalzburg.

Eastern Europe

1944   Stalin admitted publicly for the first time that the Allies were supplying aid to Russia. The U711 sank the American freighter WILLIAM S. THAYER (43 dead-7,176 tons).

Mediterranean

1930   Italy began a massive naval construction program.

1941   British General Archibald Wavell flew to Crete and appointed General Bernard Freyberg as commander of the island. The DAK attacked Tobruk, Libya. The Pro-German government in Iraq sent 9,000 troops against the Royal Air Force base at Habbaniyah.

1943   At 1230, the Italian destroyer LEONE PANCALDO (124 died) was sunk off Cap Bon, Tunisia by the USAAF. The German destroyer HERMES was damaged in the action and later scuttled on May 7th. At 1700, the Italian destroyer LAMPO was damaged by the USAAF off Tunisia and sank at 1912. The German minesweeper RA-10 (ex-RN MTB-314) was sunk off Tunisia in an air-attack. Lance Corporal J. Kennealey, of the Irish Guards, won a Victoria Cross in Tunisia.

1944   The American 15th Air Force attacked aircraft and rail targets in Italy.

1945   American forces entered Turin, Italy. Yugoslavian partisans entered Trieste.

1946   The American freighter PARK was damaged by a mine off Patras, Greece.

1967   German S.S. Major Walter Reder, commander of troops who had massacred over a thousand Italian civilians on Monte Sole south of Bologna in 1944, wrote to the citizens of Monte Sole requesting a pardon from a life sentence as per Italian law.

Atlantic

1940   The Axis sank 158,218 tons of neutral and Allied shipping in April and lost five German U-boats.

1941   The Axis sank 687,901 tons of neutral and Allied shipping in April and lost two German U-boats. The U107 sank the British freighter LASSELL (7,417 tons). U107 survived until August 18, 1944.

1942   The Axis sank 674,457 tons of neutral and Allied shipping in April and lost three German U-boats. The Royal Navy light cruiser EDINBURGH was torpedoed by the U456 in the Barents Sea. U456 survived until May 13, 1943. The U162 sank the British tanker ATHELEMPRESS (8,941 tons). U162 survived until September 3rd. The U576 sank the Norwegian freighter TABORFJELL (1,339 tons). U576 survived until July 15th. The U402 sank the Soviet freighter ASCHABAD (5,284 tons). U402 survived until October 13, 1943. The U507 sank the American tanker FEDERAL (2,881 tons-5 dead). U507 survived until January 13, 1943.

1943   The Axis sank 344,680 tons of neutral and Allied shipping in April and lost fifteen German U-boats. The U227 was sunk by the Royal Air Force's No.455 Squadron off the Faroes. The American freighter MCKEESPORT was sunk south of Greenland.

1944   The Axis sank 82,327 tons of neutral and Allied shipping in April and lost eighteen German U-boats.

1945   The Axis sank 104,512 tons of neutral and Allied shipping in April and lost forty-three German U-boats. The U242 and U235 were sunk by the Royal Navy destroyers HESPERUS and HAVELOCK in the Irish Sea. The U538 was sunk by the USN destroyer escorts THOMAS, BOSTWICK and COFFMAN and the frigate NATCHEZ off Cape Hatteras, North Carolina. The U1055 was sunk by USN VPB-63 west of Brest, France. The only German Type XXI U-boat to go to sea on operations was the U2511.

North America

1919   The battleship TENNESSEE was launched. She was scrapped in 1959.

1942   The battleship INDIANA (scrapped in 1963) and destroyer MCCOOK (stricken in 1972) were commissioned. The submarine PETO was launched. She was scrapped in 1960.

1943   The Soviet freighter UZBEKISTAN was wrecked at Darling Creek, British Columbia.

1944   The submarine KRAKEN was launched. She was transferred to the Spanish Navy in 1959.

1945   The American government awarded thirty-one Medals of Honor in the month of April during the war.

1953   John C. Garand, inventor of the M-1 rifle, retired as an engineer at the Springfield Armory in Massachusetts.

1955   Admiral John H. Towers, commander of the Pacific Fleet Air Force and Nimitz' Deputy from February 1944 until the end of the war, died at St. Albans Hospital in New York City.

1962   Lieutenant Colonel Horace Crouch died. He had flown on the "Doolittle Raid".

1974   The destroyer AULT was sold for scrap.

Pacific

1942   The Allies sank 36,684 tons of Japanese shipping (seven ships) in April. The IJN carriers SHOKAKU and ZUIKAKU and light carrier SHOHO left Truk for the Coral Sea. The USN carriers HORNET and ENTERPRISE left Pearl Harbor for the Coral Sea. Two PBY "Catalinas" evacuated forty-nine people from Corregidor. Thirteen USAAF P39s saw the type's first action in the Pacific Theater of Operations, when they strafed Salamaua and Lae on New Guinea.

1943   The Allies sank 131,782 tons of Japanese shipping (twenty-seven ships) in April. The USN submarine SCORPION sank the EBISU MARU (131 tons) and laid twenty-four mines off Shanghai. The IJN submarine I-19 sank the American freighter PHOEBE A. HEARST (7,176 tons). USAAF ace Boyd "Buzz" Wagner shot down three Japanese "Zeros" over Lae, New Guinea, while flying a P39 "Airacobra". He had scored five victories over the Philippines in the first days of the war and would die in a stateside crash later in 1943. The American 11th Air Force attacked Kiska in the Aleutians. During the month of April, the 11th Air Force had flown 144 missions against Kiska and five against Attu.

1944   The Allies sank 129,846 tons of Japanese shipping (thirty-seven ships) in April. USN Task Force 58 consisting of the carriers HORNET, YORKTOWN, ENTERPRISE, BUNKER HILL, LEXINGTON and the light carriers BELLEAU WOOD, COWPENS, BATAAN, MONTEREY, CABOT, PRINCETON, and LANGLEY continued the assault on Truk which they had begun the previous day. During the operation they sank the IJN submarine chaser No.38, the HINO MARU No.2 and the MINSEI MARU. USN aircraft losses over Truk were thirty-five while the Japanese lost ninety-three. The USN submarine TANG rescued 22 USN downed aircrew off Truk. This would be the last major American action Truk. Although it would be attacked by small forces of B24 "Liberators", throughout the summer, by October it would be reduced to a practice target for the new B29 "Superfortress". The USN submarine BANG sank the NITTATSU MARU (2,859 tons). A USN force of nine cruisers and eight destroyers, commanded by Admiral Oldendorf, attacked the Sawatan Islands. Forty-two American 7th Air Force B24s dropped ninety-four tons of bombs on Wake Island.

1945 The Allies sank 101,702 tons of Japanese shipping (fifty-one ships) in April. The USN submarine TREPANG sank the MIHO MARU (4,667 tons). The YUNO MARU (2,345 tons) was sunk by a mine. The American freighter S. HALL YOUNG and the USN destroyer BENNION (no casualties) were damaged by Japanese kamikazes.

China-Burma-India
1943 Ten American 10th Air Force B25s attacked the Gokteik Viaduct in Burma.
1944 General Masaki Honda assumed command of the Japanese 33rd Army in Burma. He died in 1964 of cancer.

CHAPTER 5

THE MONTH OF MAY

May 1st

Western Europe
1887 British General Alan Cunningham was born in Scotland. He would command the 8th Army in North Africa.
1912 German U-boat ace Otto Kretschmer was born. During the war he was responsible for sinking more than 266,000 tons of Allied shipping. He was captured on March 17, 1941 when his submarine U99 was sunk. He was awarded the Swords to his Knight's Cross on December 25, 1941 while a prisoner of war at Bowmanville, Canada. After the war he became an admiral in the new German Navy.
1939 The Royal Navy battleship PRINCE OF WALES was launched. She would be sunk in December 1941 by Japanese aircraft.
1940 The Royal Navy submarine SEAL was damaged by a mine in the Kattegat and was captured by the Germans on the 5th. The British evacuated 4,400 troops from Andalsnes, Norway. German forces captured 4,000 Norwegian soldiers near Lillehammer in southern Norway. German forces that moved from Oslo in the south and Bergen to the west linked-up west of Gol in southern Norway. Nine Royal Air Force bombers attacked Stavanger airfield in Norway. Eighteen Royal Air Force bombers attacked other Norwegian airfields and suffered no losses. The Luftwaffe dropped forty-two mines in the Tyne and Humber Estuaries in Britain. The French embassy in Bern, Switzerland warned Paris that the Germans would attack in the West by the 10th of May.
1941 Twenty-two Royal Air Force "Blenheims" attacked coastal targets in Holland and lost one aircraft. The Luftwaffe attacked Liverpool and Merseyside in Britain. Between this date and the 7th of the month, the Luftwaffe would sink eighteen ships in the port of Liverpool and badly damage twenty-five more. It was during the month of May that the first "Einsatzgruppe" was formed by order of Reinhard Heydrich, Chief of the Central Security Agency (RSHA). Four such units were formed. The total force numbered about 3,000 men. Their main function was to eliminate Jews and other "undesirables" in occupied territories.

The Month of May

1942 Twelve Royal Air Force "Bostons" attacked Calais and St. Omer in France.

1943 Twenty-nine American 8th Air Force B17s attacked U-boat installations at St. Nazaire losing seven aircraft. Staff Sergeant Maynard "Snuffy" Smith, of the 306th Bomb Group, won a Medal of Honor on the mission. Thirty Royal Air Force bombers dropped mines off the French coast and lost one "Stirling".

1944 The original planned date for "Overlord", the invasion of France. 130 American 8th Air Force bombers dropped 429 tons of bombs on V-1 rocket sites at Poix-Montdidier and Pas de Calais in France. 209 8th Air Force fighters provided support for the bombers. 328 8th Air Force bombers dropped 1,092 tons of bombs on Belgian and French marshalling yards and lost three B17s. 558 8th Air Force fighters provided support for the bombers and claimed six victories for the loss of two P38s and one P51. The American 9th Air Force attacked transportation targets. 139 Royal Air Force bombers attacked Toulouse, France. 137 Royal Air Force bombers attacked St. Ghislain, France and lost two aircraft. 132 Royal Air Force bombers attacked Malaines, Belgium and lost one "Halifax". 171 Belgian civilians were killed in the raid. 120 Royal Air Force bombers attacked Chambly, France and lost five aircraft. Seventy-five Royal Air Force bombers attacked Lyon, France. Fifty Royal Air Force bombers attacked Tours, France. Five B17s from the USAAF's 422nd Bomb squadron dropped 1,550,000 leaflets on twenty-five towns in France and Holland. The USAAFs 801st Bomb Group dispatched twenty-five B24s on "Carpetbagger" missions.

1945 392 American 8th Air Force bombers dropped 776 tons of food on Rotterdam and The Hague in Holland. The formation of German Admiral Karl Doenitz' "Flensburg Government" was announced. Hitler had designated Doenitz as his replacement as leader of the German government. German Propaganda Minister Joseph Goebbels' entire family and General Hans Krebs, Chief of Staff of the Wehrmacht, committed suicide in the Chancellory Bunker in Berlin. German Field Marshal Gerd von Rundstedt was captured in Bad Tolz in Bavaria. The U3001, U3005, U3009, U3051, U3527 and U3528 were scuttled at Wesermunde on the Baltic coast. The U3006 and U3504 were scuttled at Wilhelmshaven, Germany. The French 1st Army took Bregenz, Austria. Switzerland reported that its airspace had been violated 6,501 times and that it had suffered 350 dead during eighty-nine air-raids. They had also shot down twenty-six aircraft, mostly Axis. 218 aircraft had landed or crashed in Switzerland, most of them were from the Allied air forces.

Eastern Europe

1942 The Axis had 178 infantry, 14 motorized, 20 Panzer and 4 cavalry divisions, as well as 15 infantry, 2 motorized and 3 cavalry brigades on the Eastern Front.

1945 Between this date and the 8th of May, German small craft would evacuate 150,000 Germans from the Lower Vistula to Hela on the Baltic coast. From there it was planned that they would be moved back to Germany.

Mediterranean

1941 The Commander of the Allied forces on Crete, New Zealand General Bernard Freyberg, received word from London that the Germans were going to attack the island with seaborne and airborne forces. The German DAK attacked Allied positions at Tobruk. Axis aircraft attacked Malta. The Italian Navy laid a defensive minefield off Tripoli.

1943 American forces took "Hill 609" in Tunisia. The Axis had a total of seven Italian tanks, fifty-eight Panzer MkIII, seventeen MkIV and four MkVIs (Tigers) in North Africa.

1944 In Allied air-raids, the German transport KT-2 was sunk at Genoa and the corvette UJ-209 (ex-Italian SCURE) was destroyed on a slipway at Breda. "Hells Belles", a USAAF 319th Bomb Group B26 "Marauder", became the first Allied bomber to complete 100 missions.

1945 The German forces on the island of Rhodes surrendered. The surrender of the German forces in Italy was signed at Caserta. It was to take effect the next day (See Western Europe-February 25th and April 17th, 23rd, 28th and Mediterranean-March 19th. The German torpedo boats TA-41 and TA-43 were scuttled at Trieste.

Atlantic

1941 The U552 sank the British freighter NERISSA (5,583 tons). U552 survived the war. The U103 sank the British freighter SAMSO (1,494 tons). U103 survived until April 15, 1945.

1942 At 1345, the Royal Navy battleship KING GEORGE V rammed and sank the Royal Navy destroyer PUNJABI while with convoy PQ15 in the Arctic Sea. Only four members of the 212-man crew of the destroyer were lost. The USN battleship WASHINGTON was unable to avoid the wreckage and was damaged by the PUNJABI's exploding depth charges. The French carrier BEARN was officially disarmed at Martinique. The British freighter MENELAUS escaped after an attack by the German armed merchant cruiser MICHEL. The U752 sank the Norwegian freighter BIDEVIND (4,956 tons). U752 survived until May 23, 1943. The U109 sank the Nicaraguan freighter WORDEN (555 tons) southeast of Cape

	Canaveral. U109 survived until May 4, 1943. The U69 sank the American sailing ship JAMES NEWSOM (671 tons). U69 survived until February 17, 1943. The U162 sank the Brazilian freighter PARNHYBA (6,692 tons). U162 survived until September 3rd.
1943	The German patrol boat V-1241 was sunk off Terschelling by British MTBs. The U107 sank the British freighter PORT VICTOR (12,411 tons). U107 survived until August 18, 1944. The U515 sank the British freighters CLAN MACPHERSON (6,940 tons) and CITY OF SINGAPORE (6,555 tons) and the Belgian freighter MOKAMBO (4,996 tons). U515 survived until April 9, 1944. The U182 sank the Greek freighter ADELFOTIS (5,838 tons). U182 survived until May 16th.
1944	The U181 sank the British freighter JANETA (5,312 tons). U181 survived the war. The U277 was sunk by aircraft from the Royal Navy escort carrier FENCER southwest of Bear Island.

North America

1896	General Mark Wayne Clark was born at Madison Barracks in New York. He graduated 110th in his 1917 West Point class of 139. He was wounded while serving as a Captain during WWI. On November 13, 1942 he became the Armys youngest Lieutenant General at the age of forty-six. On December 12th, he assumed command of the 5th Army in Italy. On December 12, 1944, he replaced British General Alexander as commander of the 15th Army Group. He was promoted to four-star rank at the age of 48 on March 10, 1945. In April 1952, he replaced Ridgeway as United Nations Supreme Commander in Korea. He retired on October 31, 1953. He died on April 17, 1984 in Charleston, South Carolina. General Joseph Lawton Collins was born in Algiers, Louisiana. He graduated 35th in his 1917 West Point class of 139. On December 14, 1941, he became Chief of Staff of the Hawaiian Department. In May of 1942, he assumed command of the 25th "Tropic Lightning" Division. It was while commanding that unit on Guadalcanal that he acquired his nickname "Lightning Joe". On January 19, 1944, he was named as commander of the 7th Corps in Europe. He, along with Troy Middleton, was considered by the Germans to be the best Corps commanders on the Allied side. On August 16, 1949 he was named as Army Chief of Staff. He retired in 1956 and died on September 12, 1987.
1937	FDR signed the Neutrality Act.
1943	The American freighter JOHN MORGAN and the tanker MONTANA collided off Norfolk, Virginia. The JOHN MORGAN exploded and sank. The MONTANA caught fire and was beached. The escort carrier CORAL SEA was launched. She was renamed the ANZIO in 1944 to make her

1944   FDR approved the partitioning plan for post-war Germany as proposed by the EAC (See January 14th).
1965   The destroyer CALDWELL was stricken.
1966   The destroyer KENDRICK was expended. The destroyer GREGORY was stricken and became the static training ship "INDOCTRINATOR". The destroyer JOHN D. HENLEY was stricken. The destroyer CHARLES F. HUGHES was stricken and would be expended as a target in March 1969.
1968   The destroyer MADISON was stricken and would be expended as a target the next year. The destroyer BAILEY was stricken and was later expended as a target. The destroyers PAUL HAMILTON, WILEY, IZARD and HALFORD were stricken. The destroyer YOUNG was sold for scrap. The USN submarine ARCHERFISH was decommissioned and would be expended later in the year off San Diego.
1973   The USN submarine TORSK was dedicated as a memorial in Baltimore, Maryland. She had established a record 11,884 dives during her 29-year career.
1988   Richard Woliver died in Austin, Texas. He had won a Distinguished Service Cross while flying a 330th Bomb Group B29 over Japan in 1945.
2010   German test pilot Paul Rudolf Poitz, age 99, died in Bridgeport, Connecticut. He had served as chief test pilot for the Me-163 rocket fighter and had made the aircraft's first powered flight.

South America
1941   The carrier YORKTOWN suffered minor damage when she hit the side of the Miraflores Lock while on a night-time transit of the Panama Canal.

Pacific
1942   The USN submarine TRITON sank the CALCUTTA MARU (5,338 tons). The USN submarine GRENADIER accidentally sank the Soviet freighter ANGARSTROI 90 miles off Nagasaki, Japan. USN Captain Forrest Sherman assumed command of the carrier WASP. In November 1949 he would be named as Chief of Naval Operations. An IJN force (commanded by Shima) left Rabaul, New Britain for the invasion of Tulagi Island in the Solomons. The USN carriers LEXINGTON and YORKTOWN rendezvoused in the Coral Sea. Six USAAF P39 "Airacobras" crash-landed near Bamaga, Australia. One was recovered in 1971 and two were recovered in 1972.
1943   The USN submarine POGY sank the KEISHAN MARU (1,434 tons). A USN PBY rescued 8 survivors from the American freighter PHOEBE A.

HEARST which had been sunk the previous day by I-19. The American 11th Air Force attacked Japanese-held Kiska in the Aleutians.

1944   The USN battleships ALABAMA and SOUTH DAKOTA, along with five other battleships, eleven destroyers and carrier aircraft bombarded Ponape in the Carolines. American forces took Kamti, New Guinea.

1945   The USN submarine BOWFIN sank the CHOWA MARU (2,719 tons). The Australian 9th Division landed on Tarakan Island, northeast of Borneo.

China-Burma-India

1942   Japanese forces cut the Burma-China supply route. The Japanese took Mandalay in Burma.

May 2nd

Western Europe

1933   S.S. and S.A. troops occupied all trade union headquarters throughout Germany.

1935   France and Russia signed a 5-year alliance.

1940   German forces reached Andalsnes in southern Norway. 5,400 Allied troops were evacuated from Namsos in central Norway. Thirty-six Royal Air Force bombers attacked Norwegian airfields. Twenty-six Royal Air Force bombers dropped mines in the Baltic.

1941   Twenty-five Royal Air Force "Blenheims" attacked targets from France to Norway. The German patrol boat V808 was sunk off Borkum by the Royal Air Force. The Luftwaffe attacked Liverpool, Britain. Ninety-five Royal Air Force bombers attacked Hamburg and lost three aircraft. Three people were killed in the raid. Twenty-three Royal Air Force bombers attacked Emden, Germany and lost one "Wellington".

1942   Ninety-six Royal Air Force bombers dropped mines from Brittany to Germany and lost two "Manchesters".

1943   Thirty-one Royal Air Force bombers attacked targets in Holland and France. Victor Lutze, Ernst Rohm's successor as Chief of the S.A., died in a car wreck. Norwegian ace Marius Ericksen (9 victories) was shot down and captured while flying with the Royal Air Force.

1944   The American 9th Air Force attacked transportation targets in France. Fifty American 8th Air Force B24s dropped 197 tons of bombs on Pas de Calais V-1 rocket sites. They were escorted by 102 8th Air Force fighters. The German 2nd S.S. Panzer Division burned several houses in Montpezat-de-Quercy, France after being fired upon. Twenty-nine Royal Air Force "Mosquitoes" attacked targets in Germany.

1945 The city of Berlin surrendered to Soviet forces commanded by Marshals Koniev and Zhukov. I.S. Koniev died in 1973 and Georgi Zhukov in 1974. The US Army's 13th Division crossed the Inn at Brannau, (Hitler's birth-place). The American and British governments agreed on a French occupation zone. 393 American 8th Air Force bombers dropped 765 tons of food on Holland. The U1007 and the steamer FLORIDA (5,542 tons) were sunk off Wismak by Royal Air Force "Typhoons". The U2359, the gun ferry SAT-16 and the minesweeper M-293 were sunk in the Kattegat by Royal Air Force "Mosquitos". The German patrol boat V-2001 was sunk in the Baltic by Allied aircraft. The U8, U14, U17, U60, U61, U62, U71, U137, U139, U140, U141, U142, U148, U151, U152 and U552 were scuttled at Wilhelmshaven. The U120 was scuttled at Bremerhaven. The U121 was scuttled at Wesermunde. The U316, U2510, U2526, U2527 and U2528, U2531, U2535, U2536, U3002, U3016, U3018, U3019, U3020, U3021, U3516, U3517, U3521 and U3522 were scuttled at Travemunde. The U717 was scuttled at Flensburg. The U1308 was scuttled at Warnemunde. The U2327, U2370, U2371, U2501, U2504, U2505, U3004, U3052 and U3056 were scuttled at Hamburg. The U2332 was scuttled at Kiel. The U1406 and U1407 were scuttled at Cuxhaven. The U1407 was later salvaged and was recommissioned as the Royal Navy's METEORITE. The German minesweeper M-387 was scuttled at Lubeck. The British entered Lubeck and Wismar. This effectively cut Doenitz' Flensburg government off from the rest of Germany and also prevented Soviet forces from entering Denmark. The British 6th Airborne Division and the Soviet 70th Army met near Wismar. Canadian forces took Oldenburg. At Oberammergau, in southern Germany, the German rocket scientists Herbert Wagner and Werner von Braun were captured. With them was the commander of the research staff at Peenemunde, General Walter Dornberger. Nearly 200 important prisoners were being held by a group of S.S. troops in the village of Niederdorf in South Tyrol. The S.S. had orders to execute the prisoners to prevent their falling into Allied hands. This was prevented by the intervention of Wehrmacht troops under the command of Captain von Alvensleben. Among those saved were Leon Blum, the former French Prime Minister, Pastor Martin Niemoller, leader of the German Confessional Church, former Austrian Chancellor Kurt von Schuschnigg and his wife, various relatives of Count von Stauffenberg and the nephew of Soviet Foreign Minister Vyacheslav Molotov. A Luftwaffe Ju88 carrying former French Prime Minister Pierre Laval landed in Barcelona, Spain. He was attempting gain asylum, but was returned by the Spanish government, to American forces in Austria three months later aboard the same aircraft. Fifty-three Royal Air Force "Mosquitoes" attacked airfields in the Kiel area and lost one aircraft. 126 Royal Air Force "Mosquitoes" attacked Kiel and killed eighteen people. Eighty-nine Royal Air Force bombers flew diversionary missions in support of the attack and lost two "Halifaxes". These would be the last Bomber Command losses in the war. Only three of the sixteen crewmen aboard the two aircraft survived. Since January 1st, the Royal Air Force's Bomber Command had flown 62,824 sorties on which it had lost 100 aircraft and had dropped 181,740 tons of bombs. During the war, the total number of sorties flown was 387,416 on which had been lost 8,953 aircraft had been lost and 955,044 tons of bombs had been dropped. Including those lost in accidents, aircrew losses had totaled 55,500.

1969 Franz von Papen, Deputy Chancellor, and Ambassador to Austria, died in Obersasbach.

Eastern Europe

1942 At the Royal Navy heavy cruiser EDINBURGH (fifty-eight dead) was torpedoed by the German destroyer Z-24 and was scuttled at 0550 by the Royal Navy destroyer FORESIGHT. The German destroyer HERMANN SCHOEMANN was severely damaged by the Royal Navy destroyers FORESIGHT and FORESTER in the Barents Sea. She was later scuttled by the Z-24.

1943 Heavy fighting continued in the Kuban area.

1944 Spain withdrew its "Azul" Division that had been serving on a voluntary basis on the eastern front.

Mediterranean

1936 Italian forces entered Addis Ababa, Ethiopia.

1941 The Royal Navy destroyer JERSEY was sunk off Malta by a mine. The Allied evacuation of Greece was completed. Iraqi troops attacked British garrisons near the Persian Gulf and occupied Basra.

1942 The U74 was sunk by the Royal Navy destroyers WISHART and WRESTLER.

1943 USAAF B26s attacked Axis shipping off Cap Bon, Tunisia.

1944 The American 15th Air Force attacked rail targets in Italy. The U371 damaged the USN destroyer escort MENGES.

1945 The British destroyers KIMBERLEY and CATTERICK and the Greek destroyer KRITI attacked the island of Rhodes. The Italian submarine ARGO was scuttled at Monfalcone. The surrender of German forces in Italy became effective.

1950 Marshal Rodolfo Graziani was sentenced to nineteen years of solitary confinement by an Italian military court.

Atlantic

1941 The U201 sank the British tanker CAPULET (8,190 tons). U201 survived until February 17, 1943.

1942 The German destroyer SCHOEMANN was scuttled after an attack by the Royal Navy destroyers FORESIGHT and FORESTER. She had been damaged by the U456 on April 30th. The Royal Navy cruiser EDINBURGH sank in the Arctic Ocean. In 1981 a British salvage team would recover five tons of the Soviet gold she had been carrying as payment for American Lend/Lease. The Polish submarine JASTRAZAB (the ex-USN S-25) was sunk in error by the Norwegian destroyer ST. ALBANS and the Royal Navy minesweeper SEAGULL. The USN converted yacht CYTHERIA (602 tons) was sunk by the U402. Sixty-six of her crew died. The two survivors were rescued by U402 and were taken to Germany as prisoners. U402 survived until October 13, 1943. The U66 sank the Norwegian tanker SANDAR (7,624 tons). U66 survived until May 6, 1944. The USN sub chaser PC-490 rescued all fifty-two survivors from the American tanker MOBILOIL which had been sunk by U108.

1943 The U332 was sunk by Royal Australian Air Force No.461 Squadron in the Bay of Biscay.

1944 At 1636, the USN destroyer PARROTT collided with the freighter JOHN MORTON off Norfolk, Virginia. Six of her crewmen were killed in the accident. She was declared unfit for further service and decommissioned in Portsmouth on July 14th. She would be sold for scrap on April 5, 1947. The U674 and U959 were sunk by aircraft from the Royal Navy escort carrier FENCER off Narvik, Norway.

1945 The U979 sank the British trawler EBOR WYKE (348 tons).

1982 The Argentine light cruiser GENERAL BELGRANO (the ex-USN PHOENIX) was sunk by a Royal Navy submarine during the Falklands War.

North America

1916 The battleship OKLAHOMA was commissioned. She would be sunk during the Pearl Harbor attack of December 7, 1941.

1942 The submarine SUNFISH was launched at Mare Island. She was discarded in 1960.

1943 The destroyer HOPEWELL was launched. The USCG cutter CGC-58012 exploded off Manomet Point, Massachusetts.

1944 The American destroyer PARROTT was a constructive loss after colliding with the merchantship JOHN MORTON off Norfolk, Virginia.

1974 Admiral James Otto Richardson, Kimmel's predecessor as C-in-C Pacific Fleet, died. He had been replaced when he protested the transferring of the USN Pacific Fleet to Pearl Harbor from its original base at San Diego.

1983 Edward Bennett died. He had won a Medal of Honor in Germany in 1945.

South America
1990 Joseph Schwammberger, age 78, was deported from Argentina to West Germany for killing Jews during WWII.

Pacific
1942 The IJN aircraft tender MIZUHO (10,930 tons) was sunk off Honshu by the USN submarine DRUM. The IJN heavy cruiser TAKAO rescued her survivors. The USN submarine TROUT sank the UZAN MARU (5,019 tons) off Honshu. The USN gunboat MINDANAO was scuttled off Corregidor. USN Admiral Chester Nimitz inspected the defenses on Midway Atoll. He would leave the following day. The IJN Tulagi invasion force was sighted. The Australian garrison was evacuated from Tulagi. Aircraft from the USN carrier YORKTOWN attacked the Japanese submarine I-21 in the Coral Sea. Townsville, Australia was put on an invasion alert. Royal Australian Air Force "Spitfires" shot down five Japanese Naval Air Force fighters and one bomber over Darwin, while losing five aircraft.

1943 The USN submarine STINGRAY sank the TAMON MARU (8,156 tons). The USN submarine GAR sank the JIMBO MARU No.12 (192 tons). The USN submarine SEAL sank the GENEI MARU No.1 off Palau. The IJN submarine I-19 damaged the American freighter WILLIAM WILLIAMS (7,181 tons). The American 11th Air Force attacked Kiska in the Aleutians.

1944 The USN submarine TAUTOG sank the RYOYO MARU (5,973 tons). The USN submarine BLUEGILL sank the ASOSAN MARU (8,811 tons). The Royal Navy submarine TANTALUS sank the AMAGI MARU (3,165 tons).

1945 Hospital/Apprentice 1st Class Robert Bush and Private First-Class William Foster (posthumous), both of the 1st USMC Division, won a Medals of Honor on Okinawa. The American freighters EDMUND F. DICKENS and HENRY L. ABBOTT were damaged after hitting mines in Manila Bay. The IJN escort MIKURA was sunk in the Sea of Japan by a mine. The USN submarine RATON sank the TORYU MARU (1,992 tons). The IJN escort OGA was sunk by the USN submarine SPRINGER. The USN YMS-481 was sunk off Tarakan, Borneo by shore-fire. The US Army's Americal Division took Badiang on Negros.

1991 A Japanese torpedo was recovered from the bottom of Pearl Harbor where it had rested since December 7, 1941.

China-Burma-India
1942 The Japanese took Kutkai, Burma.

May 3rd

Western Europe

1922   The Allied ban on the building of civilian aircraft in Germany was lifted.

1937   An anarchist uprising in Spain was put down by the government with much bloodshed.

1938   The existence of the Royal Air Force's "Hurricane" fighter was made public. The Hawker-built aircraft had made its first flight on November 6, 1935.

1939   The Royal Navy battleship PRINCE OF WALES was launched. She would be sunk off Malaya by Japanese aircraft in December 1941.

1940   Ten Royal Air Force bombers dropped mines in the Baltic. The Luftwaffe dropped thirty-nine mines off Dunkirk, Calais and Boulogne in France. At 1008, the French destroyer BISON (100 dead) was damaged by the Luftwaffe off Namsos, Norway. She was later scuttled by the Royal Navy destroyer AFRIDI. At 1446, the AFRIDI was herself sunk by Luftwaffe aircraft.

1941   Twenty-one Royal Air Force "Blenheims" attacked coastal targets and lost two aircraft. The Luftwaffe attacked Liverpool and Merseyside in Britain. 101 Royal Air Force bombers attacked Koln, Germany. Eleven people were killed in the raid. Thirty-three Royal Air Force bombers attacked Brest, France.

1942   Six Royal Air Force "Bostons" attacked Dunkirk, France. The Luftwaffe attacked Exeter, Britain. Eighty-one Royal Air Force bombers attacked Hamburg, Germany and lost five aircraft. Seventy-seven people were killed in the raid.

1943   US Army General Jacob Devers was chosen to replace Frank Andrews as commander of American Forces in Europe (See Atlantic). Royal Air Force Debden was handed over to the USAAF. Eleven Royal Air Force "Venturas" attacked the Amsterdam Power Station. Only one aircraft survived to return to Britain. The mission commander, Squadron/Leader L. Trent, won a Victoria Cross. Six Royal Air Force "Bostons" attacked Ijmuiden, Holland and lost one aircraft. Three Royal Air Force P51 fighters flew into the 150' tall cliffs at St.Albans, all three pilots were lost. 118 American 8th Air Force P47s flew a sweep over Belgium.

1944   British General Montgomery's 21st Army Group headquarters requested that the Allied Air Forces attack the bridges leading into Normandy. Forty-seven American 8th Air Force B24s dropped 173 tons of bombs on Pas de Calais V-1 rocket sites. They were escorted by 101 8th Air Force fighters. The American 9th Air Force attacked rail targets in Belgium and France. 360 Royal Air Force bombers attacked Mailly-le-Camp, France and lost forty-two "Lancasters". Ninety-two Royal Air Force bombers attacked Montdidier, France and lost four "Lancasters". Five B17s from the USAAF's 422nd Bomb Squadron dropped 960,000 leaflets and had one aircraft damaged by a Luftwaffe night-fighter. The USAAF's 801st Bomb Group dispatched nine B24s on "Carpetbagger" missions.

1945 The Soviets met the American 1st and 9th and the British 2nd Armies on the Elbe River. At 1130, four German officers approached British Field Marshal Montgomery's headquarters at Wendisch Evern near Flensburg. They attempted to surrender three German armies that were fighting the Soviets. The offer was refused. The British Army's XII Corps took Hamburg, Germany. Fifty-nine ships, nineteen floating docks and nearly 600 small craft were sunk or had been scuttled in the harbor. The American 7th Army took Innsbruck, Austria. 125 Royal Air Force bombers dropped 174 tons of bombs on Kiel, Germany. The German sloop HAI, the torpedo boats T-8 and T-9 and the transport DER DEUTSCH were sunk in the raid. The German target ships BOLKOBURG, SWAKOPMUND and WEGA were sunk in an air-raid on Fehmarn. 395 American 8th Air Force B17s dropped 741 tons of food on Holland. The USAAF's 352nd Fighter Group (P51) flew the last of its 420 8th Air Force missions, having lost 118 aircraft. American 9th Air Force A26 "Invaders" flew their last mission in the European Theater of Operations. 130 of them attacked the Stod Ammon Plant in Czechoslovakia. The U3028, U3030, and U3032 were sunk in the Little Belt by Allied aircraft. Royal Air Force "Typhoons" sank the German steamers CAP ARCONA (27,561 tons), THIELBEK (2,815 tons), DEUTSCHLAND (21,046 tons), DWARSEE (552 tons) and ERNA GAULKE (400 tons) off Lubeck. The German steamers INSTER (4,713 tons), IRMTRAUD CORDS (2,814 tons) and WOLGAST (164 tons) were sunk off Kiel by Royal Air Force "Typhoons". Royal Air Force "Beaufighters" sank the German steamer PALLAS (627 tons) and the submarine U2524 in the Baltic. The last German resistance ended in Berlin. Ireland's Prime Minister Eamon de Valera became the only head of state to express condolences to a German Ambassador upon Hitler's death. The German pocket battleship ADMIRAL SCHEER and destroyer Z-43 were scuttled. British forces took Hamburg. 1,500 Allied prisoners of war were air-lifted from Germany to France. The German battleship SCHLEISEN hit a mine off Swinemunde and was scuttled two days later. The Luftwaffe blew up more than seventy Me262 jet fighters at Salzburg, just before American forces arrived at the airfield. Royal Canadian Air Force ace Flight/Lieutenant R. Audet (10 victories) was killed in action. The U2524 was scuttled in the Kattegat after an air-attack. The U3505 was sunk by Allied aircraft at Kiel. The U11, U52, U57, U58, U475, U903, U922,

U924, U958, U1027, U1031, U1205, U2519, U2520, U2539, U2543, U2545, U2546, U2548, U3010, U3029, U3031, U3038, U3039, U3040, U3507, U3518, U3530, UA (the ex-Turkish BATIRAY), UB (the ex-Royal Navy submarine SEAL captured in the Kattegat on May 5, 1940), UD-1 (the ex-Dutch 0-8), UD-2 (the ex-Dutch 0-12), UD-3 (the ex-Dutch 0-25) and UD-4 (the ex-Dutch 0-26) and the corvette F-3 were scuttled at Kiel. The U323 was scuttled at Nordenham. The U3524 was scuttled at Flensburg. The U339, U554 and U708 were scuttled at Wilhelmshaven. The U428 and the heavy cruiser HIPPER and torpedo boats T-8 and T-9 and the minelayer BRUMMER were scuttled in Kiel. The U704 was scuttled at Vegesack. The U822 and U828 were scuttled at Wesermunde. The U748 was scuttled at Rendsburg. The U794 and the destroyer Z-43 were scuttled in Geltinger Bay. The U929 was scuttled at Warnemunde. The German submarines U3011, U3012, U3013 and U3023, U3025, U3026, U3027, U3037, U3511 and U3513 were scuttled at Travemunde. The U3014 and U3024 were scuttled of Neustadt on the Baltic coast.

Eastern Europe
1939 The pro-West Soviet Foreign Minister Maxim Litvinov was replaced by Vyacheslav Molotov, indicating a change in foreign policy.
1942 The U251 sank the British freighter JUTLAND (6,153 tons).
1943 Soviet Air Force ace Lieutenant Peter Sgibnev (19 victories) was killed in action.
1945 The German transports SACHSENWALD and WESERTROM and the torpedo boats T-36 and T-108 evacuated 8,850 refugees from Hela to Germany.

Mediterranean
1941 British forces fail in an attack on Amba Alagi in East Africa. The Axis staged a victory parade in Athens. The Italian torpedo boat CANOPO was sunk in Tripoli by the Royal Air Force.
1943 The US 1st Armored Division broke through the German lines in Tunisia.
1944 The U852 was sunk off Somaliland by the Royal Air Force.
1945 The German torpedo boat TA-22 was scuttled off Trieste. The last seven operational German S-boats in the Mediterranean, the S-30, S-36, S-61, S-151, S-152, S-155 and S-156 left Pola en route to surrendering to the Allies at Ancona.

Atlantic
1940 The German armed merchant cruiser ATLANTIS took the British freighter SCIENTIST (6,199 tons).

1941 The U95 sank the Norwegian freighter TARANGER (4,873 tons). U95 survived until November 28th.
1942 The U455 sank the British tanker BRITISH WORKMAN (6,994 tons). U455 survived until April 6, 1944. The U506 sank the Nicaraguan freighter SAMA (567 tons). U506 survived until July 12, 1943. The U564 sank the British freighter OCEAN VENUS (7,174 tons). U564 survived until June 14, 1943. The U109 sank the Dutch freighter LAERTES (5,825 tons). U109 survived until May 4, 1943. The U125 sank the Dominican Republic freighter SAN RAFAEL (1,973 tons). U125 survived until May 6, 1943.
1943 The U439 and U659 were lost in a collision west of Cape Ortegal. The U43 sank the German blockade runner DOGGERBANK in error. U43 survived until July 30th. USAAF General Frank Andrews, commander of the American Forces in Europe, was killed in plane crash near Iceland.
1944 At 1200, the USN destroyer escort DONNELL was a constructive loss after an attack by the U765. Twenty-seven of her crew died. U765 survived until May 6th.

North America
1942 The destroyers MERVINE, QUICK, FLETCHER and RADFORD were launched. MERVINE was stricken in 1968, QUICK was stricken in 1972, FLETCHER was stricken in 1967 and RADFORD was stricken in 1969.
1943 The destroyer COLAHAN was launched. She was stricken in 1966 and expended as a target. The USN tanker NECHES was damaged when she ran aground off Cold Bay, Alaska.
1944 The escort carrier WINDHAM BAY was commissioned. She was scrapped in 1961.

Pacific
1942 Twelve Japanese ships arrived off Tulagi in the Solomons. They disembarked landing forces that landed on Tulagi and Florida Island. Royal Australian Air Force PBYs attacked the newly arrived Japanese on Tulagi. The USN submarine SPEARFISH evacuated twenty-five people from Corregidor in the Philippines. It was the last operation of its kind. Two PatWing-10 PBYs returned to Australia from Corregidor (See April 29th). The USN carriers LEXINGTON and YORKTOWN separated in the Coral Sea, with the YORKTOWN going to raid Tulagi. The USN light cruiser NASHVILLE left Pearl Harbor under orders to attack the Japanese fishing fleet off Kamchatka. USN submarines S-34 and S-35 were to assist.
1943 The American 11th Air Force attacked Kiska in the Aleutians.
1944 Admiral Soemu Toyoda replaced Admiral Mineichi Koga, who had been killed in a plane crash off the Philippines on March 31st, as

Commander-in-Chief of the IJN. The USN submarine TAUTOG sank the FUSHIMI MARU (4,935 tons). The USN submarine SAND LANCE sank the KENAN MARU (3,129 tons). The USN submarine FLASHER sank the TEISEN MARU (5,050 tons). The USN submarine TINOSA sank the TOYOHI MARU (6,436 tons).

1945 Japanese forces began a counter-offensive from the south on Okinawa. The USN submarine LOGARTO was sunk by the IJN minelayer HATSUTAKE. Her wreck was located in May 2005 by a British diver. The USN submarine SPRINGER sank the IJN escort CD-25. The USN destroyer LITTLE (30 of her crew died) and LSM-195 were sunk off Okinawa by Japanese kamikazes. The USN destroyer AARON WARD was hit by five kamikazes and was declared a constructive loss (45 of her crew died). She was scrapped in 1964. The US Army's 24th Division occupied Davao, Mindanao.

1963 Japanese Major General Sueki Kusaba died. He had been in charge of the balloon-bomb assault on America.

China-Burma-India

1942 Japanese forces took Monywa, Burma. The British invasion fleet destined for French-held Madagascar (See April 25th and 28th) was joined by the carrier INDOMITABLE and two destroyers.

1943 US Army General Joseph Stilwell (Chiang Kai-shek's Chief of Staff) received word that FDR had decided to provide air support for Chinese operations.

1944 14th Air Force B24s sank the Japanese freighter SHINGU MARU off Formosa. The British submarine TANTALUS sank the Japanese freighter AMAGI MARU off Point Blair.

1945 Indian troops occupied Rangoon. The British 33rd Corps took Prome, Burma.

May 4th

Western Europe

1940 Five Royal Air Force bombers dropped mines in Oslofjord in Norway.

1941 Twelve Royal Air Force "Blenheims" attacked German shipping. The Luftwaffe attacked Liverpool and Merseyside in Britain. Ninety-seven Royal Air Force bombers attacked German naval units at Brest, France.

1942 Six Royal Air Force "Bostons" attacked Le Havre, France. 121 Royal Air Force bombers attacked Stuttgart and lost one "Stirling". Twenty-five people were killed in the raid. Five Royal Air Force "Stirlings" attacked Pilsen, Czechoslovakia.

THE MONTH OF MAY

1943 Sixty-five American 8th Air Force B17s dropped 161.5 tons of bombs on the Ford and General Motors plants in Antwerp. American actor Clark Gable flew the mission with the 303rd Bomb Group. It was also the first P47-escorted mission. 117 8th Air Force P47s flew various missions over Continent and lost one aircraft due to engine failure. 596 Royal Air Force bombers attacked Dortmund in Germany and lost thirty-one aircraft. Seven more crashed after returning to Britain. 1,218 buildings were destroyed and 693 people, including 200 prisoners of war, were killed in the raid.

1944 The American 9th Air Force attacked Channel shore batteries. Forty American 8th Air Force B17s dropped 116 tons of bombs on the Bergen/Alkmar Airfield. 516 8th and 9th Air Force fighters provided support for the bombers and claimed nine victories for the loss of two P47s and one P51. The Royal Navy minesweeper ELGIN was a constructive loss after hitting a mine off Portland. Thirty-two Royal Air Force "Mosquitoes" attacked targets in Germany. Twenty Royal Air Force "Halifaxes" dropped mines off French ports.

1945 The American 7th Army took Salzburg, Austria. The US Army's 101st Airborne Division took Berchtesgaden and Obersalzburg in Bavaria. The 103rd Division of the American 7th Army met the 88th Division of the American 5th Army at the Brenner Pass on the Italian/Austrian border. The American 3rd Army took Pilsen, Czechoslovakia. At 1730, the same four German officers that had visited Montgomery's headquarters the previous day returned. One hour later they signed the surrender of all German forces facing the British. It would go into effect at 0800 the next morning. The German forces in Holland under Johannes Blaskowitz in northwestern Germany, under Ernst von Busch and in Denmark under G. von Lindemann surrendered. German Field Marshal Fedor von Bock was killed in an air-raid. German Field Marshal Ewald von Kleist was captured in Bavaria. Royal Air Force "Typhoons" sank the German steamer OSTWIND, the MTB S-103, the submarines U2521 and U904 and damaged the submarines U733 and U876 in the Southern Baltic. Royal Air Force "Beaufighters" sank the German minesweeper M-36 and the submarines U236, U2338, U2503 and U393 in the Baltic. Royal Air Force "Mosquitos" sank the German steamers ELSE HUGO STINNES (3,291 tons) and ERNST HUGO STINNES (3,295 tons) and the gunboat K-1 in the Kattegat. The German minesweepers M-301 and M-36 were sunk in the Kattegat by the Royal Air Force. The German minesweeper R-104 was sunk in the Kiel Canal. The German escort K-1 was sunk at Aarhus, Denmark by the Royal Air Force. The German freighter HECTOR (the ex-armed merchant cruiser ORION) was sunk at

Swinemunde by Soviet aircraft. The U2503 and U2338 were sunk in the Little Belt by the Royal Air Force. The U2521 was sunk in the Kattegat by Allied aircraft. Construction of the U4711 and U4712 was abandoned when they were damaged in an Allied air-attack. The U46 and U48 were scuttled at Neustadt. The U326 was scuttled at Schleimundung. The U267, U2517 and U2540 (later salvaged and recommissioned into the Bundesmarine as the WILHELM BAUER) were scuttled at Flensburg. The U721 and U746 were scuttled at Geltinger Bay. Admiral Karl Doenitz sent a signal to his U-boats to cease hostilities and return to base. A British task force consisting of three escort carriers, two cruisers and seven destroyers attacked German shipping west of Narvik, Norway and sank the submarine U711, the depot ship BLACK WATCH and a trawler.

Eastern Europe
1932   Russia and Estonia signed a non-aggression treaty.
1939   Vyacheslav Molotov replaced Maxim Litvinov as Soviet Foreign Minister.
1942   German positions on the southeast shore of the Crimea were shelled by Soviet destroyers.
1945   The German torpedo boat T-36 was sunk by the Soviet Air Force.
1994   USAAF veterans of the air attacks on the Ploesti oil refineries, returned to see their old targets and the prisoner of war camps where some of them were imprisoned.

Mediterranean
1941   The 29th Indian Division captured three important mountains near Amba Alagi in East Africa. The Italian torpedo boat GIUSEPPE LA FARINA was sunk by a mine. The Royal Navy minesweeper FERMOY was destroyed, while in a Malta dry-dock by the Luftwaffe.
1942   The German High Command issued a directive ordering the capture of Malta ("Operation Herkules"). Royal Air Force ace Norman MacQueen (eight victories) was killed in action over Malta. Axis aircraft attacked Alexandria, Egypt.
1943   At 0100, the Italian torpedo boat PERSEO (133 died) and a freighter were sunk by the Royal Navy destroyers PALADIN, PETARD and NUBIAN off Tunisia. The USN sub chaser PC-496 was sunk by a mine off Bizerte, Tunisia.
1944   The U371 sank the French destroyer escort SENEGALAIS.

Atlantic
1940   The U9 sank the British tanker SAN TIBURCIO (5,995 tons). U9 survived until August 20, 1944.

1941 The U38 sank the Swedish freighter JAPAN (5,230 tons). U38 survived the war.
1942 The U507 sank the American freighter NORLINDO (2,686 tons-5 dead). U507 survived until January 13, 1943. The U162 sank the American freighters EASTERN SWORD (3,785 tons-16 dead) and FLORENCE DOUGLAS (119 tons). U162 survived until September 3rd. The U125 sank the American freighter TUSCALOOSA CITY (5,687 tons). U125 survived until May 6, 1943.
1943 The U125 sank the British freighter LORIENT (4,737 tons). U125 survived until May 6, 1943. The U109 was sunk by the Royal Air Force's No.86 Squadron south of Ireland. U109 survived until May 4th. The U630 was sunk by Royal Canadian Air Force No.5 Squadron south of Greenland. The Portuguese fishing trawler ALBUFEIRA rescued 11 survivors from the American freighter JAMES W. DENVER which had been sunk on April 11th by U195.
1944 The U846 was sunk by the Royal Canadian Air Force's No.407 Squadron in the Bay of Biscay.
1945 The U979 damaged the British tanker EMPIRE UNITY (6,386 tons).

North America
1944 The escort carrier KWAJALEIN was launched. She was scrapped in Japan in 1961. In America all meats, except steaks, were taken off rationing.
1945 The LCT-1358 was wrecked at San Pedro, California. A USN PBY crashed into Wolf Ridge in Marin County, California. Nine of the eleven men aboard died.
1985 The Royal Canadian Navy corvette SACKVILLE was dedicated as a memorial in Halifax, Nova Scotia.

Pacific
1940 The IJN carrier SHINANO's keel was laid at Yokosuka. She was the sister ship of the super battleships YAMATO and MUSASHI.
1942 Japanese forces fired 16,000 artillery shells at American-held Corregidor Island in the Philippines. The USN submarine SPEARFISH evacuated sixteen officers, thirteen nurses and a female civilian from Corregidor. The USN minesweeper TANAGER was sunk off Corregidor by Japanese shore-fire. The USN carrier YORKTOWN attacked Japanese forces at Tulagi, Florida Island and Gavutu sinking the IJN minesweepers TAMA MARU, Wa-1 and Wa-2 and damaging the destroyer KIKUZUKI. The KIKUZUKI was beached and abandoned after the attack. Also damaged in the raid were the destroyer YUZUKI, minelayer OKINOSHIMA, transport AZUMASAN and the freighter KOZUI MARU. Three of

YORKTOWN's aircraft were lost with two of the pilots surviving crashes on Guadalcanal. The USN destroyer HAMMANN rescued both of them, but the third pilot and his gunner had ditched in the sea and a search by the destroyer PERKINS failed to locate him. The USN submarine TROUT sank the KONGOSAN MARU (2,119 tons) off Honshu. The USN submarine GREENLING sank the KINJOSAN MARU (3,262 tons) off Truk. The Japanese Port Moresby invasion force left Rabaul, New Britain.

1943 The USN submarine SEAL sank the SAN CLEMENTE MARU (7,354 tons). The American submarine SILVERSIDES laid mines in Steffen Strait between New Ireland and New Hanover. The American 11th Air Force attacked Attu in the Aleutians.

1944 Since the American invasion of Aitape, New Guinea, the Japanese have suffered 525 dead and the American forces have lost twenty. The IJN sub chaser SAPPORO MARU was sunk at Truk by USN aircraft. Royal Australian Air Force PBYs attacked Japanese shipping off Celebes. The USN submarine PARCHE sank the SHORYU MARU (6,475 tons) and the TAIYOKU MARU (5,244 tons). The USN submarine TINOSA sank the TAIBU MARU (6,440 tons). The USN submarine BANG sank the KINREI MARU (5,945 tons). The USN submarine TUNA sank the TAJIMA MARU (89 tons). The USN submarine PARGO sank the EIRYU MARU (758 tons).

1945 Japanese kamikazes sank the USN destroyers LUCE (126 of her crew died) and MORRISON (150 died), the destroyer-transport DICKERSON, the LSM-190 and the LSM-194 (13 died) off Okinawa. The USN escort carrier SANGAMON, the heavy cruiser BIRMINGHAM, and the destroyers HUDSON (no casualties) and SHEA also were hit by kamikazes off Okinawa. The Royal Navy carriers INDEFATIGABLE and FORMIDABLE were also hit. USMC Sergeant Elbert Kinser, of the 1st Division, won a posthumous Medal of Honor on Okinawa. The USN PGM-17 ran aground off Okinawa and was lost. The Royal Navy battleships HOWE and KING GEORGE V bombarded airfields on Miyako Island in the Ryukyu Group. The USN submarine TREPANG sank the IJN minelayer W-20. The USN submarine CERO sank the SHINPEN MARU (884 tons).

China-Burma-India

1942 Japanese forces took Bhamo, Burma. The American Volunteer Group abandoned its bases in Burma.

1943 The USAAF's 308th Bomb Group flew its first 14th Air Force mission. Ten American 10th Air Force B25s attacked the Maymo railyards in Burma. The Japanese began sending small units to disrupt traffic on the Burma Road.

May 5th

Western Europe

1880   British General Adrian Carton de Wiart was born in Brussels, Belgium. During the First World War, he won the Distinguished Service Order and the Victoria Cross. He headed the British military mission to Poland, but managed to escape captivity when the Germans invaded. He served in various assignments during the war. He died on June 5, 1963.

1883   British Field Marshal Archibald Wavell was born in Colchester. He would command the British forces in North Africa and later as Viceroy of India. He died on May 24, 1950.

1887   British aircraft designer Richard Fairey was born in London. He worked for two years at Short Brothers and then formed his own company in 1915. His most famous aircraft were the FOX fast bomber (1925), the SWORDFISH torpedo bomber, the GANNET (1954) and the DELTA (1956). He died on September 30, 1956.

1917   The Royal Navy light cruiser CURACAO was launched. She would be rammed and sunk by the RMS QUEEN MARY on October 2, 1942.

1933   Adolf Hitler banned mixed (Aryan-Jewish) marriages.

1937   The keel of the Royal Navy battleship DUKE OF YORK was laid.

1940   In Norway, German forces moved north from Trondheim. The Ministers of the Norwegian government arrived in London. They had been evacuated by the Royal Navy to prevent their capture by the invading German forces. The Royal Navy submarine SEAL was captured in the Kattegat by Luftwaffe Arado 196s. She had been damaged by a mine on the 1st. The Polish destroyer GROM was sunk by the Luftwaffe off Narvik, Norway.

1941   Eleven Royal Air Force bombers attacked shipping off France. Adolf Hitler visited with Admiral Gunter Lutjens and his staff aboard the battleship BISMARCK. The Luftwaffe attacked Liverpool, Britain and Belfast, Ireland. 141 Royal Air Force bombers attacked Mannheim. Four people were killed in the raid.

1942   The Royal Navy corvette AURICULA hit a mine in Courier Bay and foundered the next day. Seventy-seven Royal Air Force bombers attacked Stuttgart and lost four aircraft. No bombs fell within the city.

1943   Five Royal Air Force "Mosquitoes" attacked Brussels, Belgium. Twenty-one Royal Air Force "Stirlings" dropped mines off Denmark and lost one aircraft.

1944   Thirty-three American 8th Air Force B24s dropped seventy-six tons of bombs on V-1 rocket launching sites at Sottevast, France. Fifty-two 8th Air Force P51s provided escort for the bombers. Twenty-eight Royal Air

Force bombers dropped mines off French ports. Thirty Royal Air Force bombers dropped supplies to Resistance forces. The USAAF's 801st Bomb Group dispatched twenty-one B24s on "Carpetbagger" missions and lost one aircraft.

1945 Czech resistance forces attacked German forces in Prague. The US Army's 90th Division suffered seven killed in action in a firefight with German soldiers near Zhurt, Czechoslovakia. The American 3rd Army took Linz, Austria. The German Army Group "G" surrendered in Bavaria. Hans Frank, German Governor General of Poland, was captured. 402 American 8th Air Force bombers dropped 742 tons of food on Holland. A Luftwaffe Ju88 flew to Gormanstown, Eire from Grove, Denmark for internment rather than be captured by the British or the Soviets. The U2367 was lost in a collision with another U-boat in the Baltic. She was salvaged in 1956 and recommissioned in the Bundesmarine as the HECHT. The Royal Air Force sank the U534 and U2521 in the Kattegat and U579 in the Little Belt. British "Liberators" sank the U3523, U579, U534 and U2365 in the Kattegat. The U29, U30, U349, U351, U397, U733, U750, U827, U1025, U1056, U1204, U1207, U1303, U1304, U1306, U1405 U2333, U2346, U2347, U2349, U2352, U2357, U2358, U2360, U2362, U2364, U2366, U2368, U2369, U2507, U2522, U2525, U2541, U2551, U3015, U3022, U3033, U3034, U3044, U3510, U3526, U3529, U4701, U4702, U4703, U4704 and U4710 were scuttled at Flensburg. The U38, U3047, U3048, U3049, U3050 and U3051 were scuttled at Wesermunde. The U2544 was scuttled in the Kattegat. The U37 was scuttled at Eckernforde. The U370 was scuttled in Geltinger Bay. The U1016 was scuttled in the Great Belt.

1948 The Royal Navy battleship RESOLUTION was sold for scrap.
1964 James Grigg, British Secretary of War 1942-45, died in London.
1987 Royal Air Force ace Robert Stanford-Tuck (29 victories) died in Kent at the age of 70.
1988 A Luftwaffe Me163 "Komet" rocket fighter captured at Husum, Germany in 1945 was returned to Germany by Britain.

Eastern Europe
1934 Russia and Poland extended their non-aggression pact through 1945.
1942 The Soviets began an offensive towards Kharkov and Kursk.
1943 Soviet forces took Krymskaya and Neberjaisk. Luftwaffe ace Gunther Hannak (47 victories) became a prisoner of war.
1944 Soviets forces launched their final attack on Sebastopol. The Royal Air Force lost three of forty-three bombers over Ploesti, Rumania. 500 American 15th Air Force bombers attacked Ploesti, Rumania losing nineteen aircraft.

1945   Four German destroyers, five torpedo boats, three minesweepers and a training vessel evacuated 45,000 German refugees from Hela to Copenhagen.

Mediterranean
1942   The French submarine BEVEZIERS was sunk by Allied forces.
1943   The British 1st Division took Djebel Bou Aoukaz, Tunisia. The Italian minesweeper RD-18 was sunk by Allied aircraft.
1944   The U371 was sunk by the Royal Navy destroyer BLANKNEY and the USN destroyer escorts PRIDE and CAMPBELL off Algiers. At 0446, the USN destroyer escort FECHTELER was sunk off Oran by the U967. 186 of her crew survived. USAAF fighter-bombers destroyed the Pescara Dam in Italy.

Atlantic
1941   The U38 sank the British freighter QUEEN MAUD (4,976 tons). U38 was scuttled on May 3, 1945.
1942   The U507 sank the American tankers MUNGER T. BALL (5,104 tons-30 dead) and JOSEPH M. CUDAHY (6,950 tons-27 dead). U507 survived until January 13, 1943. The U106 sank the Canadian freighter LADY DRAKE (7,985 tons). U106 survived until August 2, 1943. The U103 sank the British freighter STANBANK (5,966 tons). U103 survived until April 15, 1945. The U108 sank the American freighter AFOUNDRIA (5,010 tons), eight miles off Haiti. U108 would survive the war. USN PBYs rescued ten survivors from the American tanker JOSEPH M. CUDAHY which had been sunk by U507. Twelve survivors from the American freighter EASTERN SWORD reached the shores of British Guiana. Their ship had been sunk by U162.
1943   The U129 sank the Panamanian tanker PANAMA (7,277 tons). U129 survived until she was scuttled in August 1944. The U264 sank the American freighter WEST MAXIMUS (5,561 tons-6 dead) and the British freighters HARPERLEY (4,586 tons) and HARBURY (5,081 tons). The U264 survived until February 19, 1944. The U123 sank the British freighter HOLMBURY (4,566 tons). U123 survived the war. The U638 sank the British freighter DOLIUS (5,507 tons). U638 survived until May 6, 1943. The U584 sank the American freighter WEST MADAKET (5,565 tons). U584 survived until October 31, 1943. The U628 sank the British freighter WENTWORTH (5,212 tons). U628 survived until July 3, 1943. The U266 sank the British freighters SELVISTAN (5,136 tons) and GHARINDA (5,306 tons) and the Norwegian freighter BONDE (1,570 tons). U266 survived until May 14, 1943. The U707 sank the British freighter NORTH BRITAIN (4,635 tons). U707 survived until November 11, 1943. The U358

sank the British freighter BRISTOL CITY (2,864 tons). U358 survived until May 5, 1943. The U192 was sunk by the Royal Navy corvette PINK. The USN destroyer escort ANDRES rescued 31 survivors from the U.S. Army transport ONEIDA which sank on May 3rd off the Virginia Capes.

1944 The U473 was sunk by the Royal Navy sloops STARLING, WREN, and WILDGOOSE, west of the Canaries.

1945 The U853 sank the American freighter BLACK POINT (5,353 tons-12 dead). BLACK POINT was the last American-flagged merchantship to be sunk by a German submarine during the war. U853 survived until the next day when she was sunk by the American destroyer escort ATHERTON and the frigate MOBERLEY.

North America

1938 The destroyers ROWAN and STACK were launched. ROWAN was lost September 10, 1943 and STACK was scuttled in 1948 after serving as a Bikini target in 1946.

1943 The submarine BATFISH was launched. She was still on active duty in 1962.

1944 The battleship CALIFORNIA left San Francisco, en route to the Marianas. It would be her first action since December 7, 1941.

1945 The American government announced that 400,000 men would remain in Germany as an occupation force after the war. Mrs. Elsie Mitchell and five neighborhood children were killed sixty-five miles northeast of Klamath Falls, Oregon by a Japanese balloon-bomb. It was one of 285 known to have reached North America.

1962 Nubuo Fujita visited Brookings, Oregon. He had flown aircraft from the IJN submarine I-25 and attacked Oregon on September 9th and 29th of 1942.

Pacific

1942 Japanese forces landed on Corregidor in the Philippines. The USN minesweeper PIGEON was sunk by a bomb off Corregidor. Her crew had won two Presidential Unit Citations, three Navy Crosses and eight Silver Stars. She was being used as a submarine rescue vessel at the time of her loss. The USN tugs GENESEE and VAGA were scuttled off Corregidor. The IJN submarine I-21 sank the American freighter JOHN ADAMS (7,180 tons-5 dead). The USN carriers LEXINGTON and YORKTOWN rendezvoused in the Coral Sea. The Japanese General Headquarters ordered the invasion of Midway and the Aleutians.

1943 USN and USAAF aircraft attacked Japanese shipping off Bougainville and sank the freighter SHINTOKU MARU. The USN submarine SAWFISH sank the HAKKAI MARU (2,921 tons). The USN submarine SNOOK sank the KINKO MARU (1,268 tons) and the DAIFUKU MARU (3,194 tons) off Formosa. The IJN submarine I-180 sank the Norwegian freighter FINGAL (2,137 tons). The American 11th Air Force attacked Attu in the Aleutians.

1944   The USN submarine POGY sank the SHIRANE MARU (2,825 tons). USN PT-247 was sunk off Bougainville by shore-fire. Japanese Admiral Soemu Toyoda was named as Commander-in-Chief of the Combined Fleet.

1945   USAAF B29s mined Tokyo Bay, Ise Bay and the Inland Sea and attacked Kure.

China-Burma-India

1932   Japanese troops began withdrawing from Shanghai after an armistice was signed.

1942   USAAF Brigadier General James Doolittle left China en route to America after his raid on the Japanese homeland in April. The American Volunteer Group shot down eight Japanese aircraft near Pao Shan and lost one of their own. Four American 10th Air Force B17s attacked Rangoon airfields. The first Japanese aircraft destroyed by a 10th Air Force fighter was a "Sally" bomber downed by Colonel Robert L. (author of "God Is My Co-Pilot") Scott, in a P40E over Lashio. British carrier aircraft attacked French airfields and shipping on and around Madagascar. They sank the French armed merchant cruiser BOUGAINVILLE. The French submarine BEVEZIERS was sunk escorting destroyers, but was later salvaged. British troops landed at Courrier Bay where the Royal Navy corvette AURICULA hit a mine. She sank the next day.

May 6th

Western Europe

1880   British Field Marshal Edmund Ironside was born in Edinburgh. He would serve as Chief of the Imperial General Staff from September 3, 1939 until May 27, 1941 and would die in 1959.

1898   Sudeten German leader Konrad Henlein was born. He committed suicide on May 10, 1945.

1932   A Soviet immigrant assassinated French President Paul Doumer.

1940   Twelve Royal Air Force bombers dropped mines in the Elbe estuary.

1941   Eighteen Royal Air Force "Blenheims" attacked German shipping and lost two aircraft. The Luftwaffe attacked Merseyside and Liverpool in Britain. 115 Royal Air Force bombers attacked Hamburg, Germany. Sixteen Royal Air Force "Wellingtons" attacked La Havre, France and lost one aircraft.

1942   Eighteen Royal Air Force "Boston" bombers attacked targets in France. Ninety-seven Royal Air Force bombers attacked Stuttgart, Germany and lost six aircraft. No bombs fell within the city. One Royal Air Force "Blenheim" was lost on an intruder flight.

1944   Seventy American 8th Air Force B24s dropped 261 tons of bombs on V-1 rocket launching sites at Siracourt and on the Pas de Calais in France. Ninety B17s also attempted to attack the same targets, but had to abort due to cloud cover over the area. The USAAF's 398th Bomb Group (B17) flew its first 8th Air Force mission. 185 8th and 9th Air Force fighters provided support for the bombers. 149 Royal Air Force bombers attacked Mantes-la-Jolie, France and lost three aircraft. Fifty-four French civilians were killed in the raid. Sixty-eight Royal Air Force bombers attacked Sable-sur-Sarthe, France. Fifty-two Royal Air Force "Lancasters" attacked Aubigne, France and lost one aircraft. Five B17s from the USAAF's 422nd Bomb Squadron dropped 3,220,000 leaflets on nineteen different locations in France and Belgium and had one aircraft badly damaged by Luftwaffe night-fighters. The USAAF's 801st Bomb Group dispatched twenty-two B24s on "Carpetbagger" missions.

1945   The U1008 and U2534 were sunk in the Kattegat by British "Liberators". The German MTB S-226 was scuttled in the Baltic after an air-attack. Portugal severed its relations with Germany. Brigadier General Robert Stack was the first US Army field grade officer to meet former Luftwaffe Commander Hermann Goering. He would later be reprimanded by Supreme Allied Commander General Dwight Eisenhower for shaking Goering's hand. 381 American 8th Air Force bombers dropped 691 tons of food on Holland. 19,500 Allied prisoners of war were airlifted from Germany to France. Soviet forces took Breslau. The US Army's 16th Armored Division took Pilsen, Czechoslovakia.

1953   German Field Marshal Erich von Manstein was released from prison. A British Sergeant and a Corporal were killed in the explosion of a British mine laid in 1940.

Eastern Europe

1933   A Soviet-Italian economic accord was signed.
1944   The American 15th Air Force attacked Ploesti and rail targets in Rumania.
1952   S.S. Lieutenant General Jurgen Stroop was executed in Warsaw, Poland.

Mediterranean

1941   The siege of the Royal Air Force base at Habbaniyah, Iraq was lifted. "Ultra" intercepts revealed that German High Command expected preparations for the invasion of Crete to be completed by the 17th. Axis aircraft attacked Malta.

1942   American forces began arriving in Liberia.
1943   The British begin their attack on Tunis. USAAF B17s attacked Trapani, Sicily. USAAF B24s attacked Reggio di Calabria, Italy. At 1830, the Italian destroyer escort TIFONE was a constructive loss after a USAAF attack off Tunis and was scuttled on May 7th.

Atlantic

1941   The U97 sank the British freighter CAMITO (6,833 tons) and the Italian tanker SANGRO (6,466 tons). U97 survived until June 16, 1943. The U103 sank the British freighters SURAT (5,529 tons) and DUNKWA (4,752 tons). U103 survived until April 15, 1945. The U556 sank the Faeroes trawler EMANUEL (166 tons). U556 survived until June 27th. The U105 sank the British freighter OAKDENE (4,255 tons). U105 survived until June 2, 1943.

1942   The American freighter AMAZONE (1,294 tons) and the tanker HALSEY (7.088 tons) were sunk by the U333 off Florida. U333 survived until July 31, 1944. The U507 sank the American bauxite carrier ALCOA PURITAN (6,759 tons) 100 miles south of Mobile, Alabama. U507 survived until January 13, 1943. The U108 sank the Latvian freighter ABGARA (4,422 tons). U108 survived until April 11, 1944. The U125 sank the American freighter GREEN ISLAND (1,946 tons) and the British freighter EMPIRE BUFFALO (6,404 tons). U125 survived until May 6, 1943. The USN gunboat SEMMES rammed and sank the British armed trawler SENATEUR DUHAMEL off North Carolina. The USN net tender MULBERRY rescued all forty-six survivors from the American freighter AFOUNDRIA which had been sunk by U108. The fishing boat OCEAN STAR rescued the last survivor from the American freighter EASTERN SWORD which had been sunk by U162. The steamer SAN BLAS rescued twenty-three survivors from the American tanker NORLINDA which had been sunk by U507.

1943   The U125 was sunk off Newfoundland by the Royal Navy destroyer VIDETTE. The U438 was sunk northeast of Newfoundland by the Royal Navy sloop PELICAN. The U531 was sunk northeast of Newfoundland by the Royal Navy destroyer ORIBI and the corvette SNOWFLAKE. The U638 was sunk northeast of Newfoundland by the Royal Navy corvette LOOSESTRIFE.

1944   The U129 sank the British freighter ANADYR (5,321 tons). U129 was scuttled in August 1944. The U66 was sunk off Cape Verde by aircraft from the USN escort carrier BLOCK ISLAND and the destroyer escort BUCKLEY. The U765 was sunk by aircraft from the Royal Navy escort carrier VINDEX and the frigates BICKERTON, BLIGH and AYLMER.

1945 The U853 was sunk off New York by the USN destroyer escort ATHERTON and the frigate MOBERLEY. The U881 was sunk south of Newfoundland by the USN destroyer FARQHUAR.

North America
1875 Admiral William Daniel Leahy, presidential chief of staff from 1942 until 1949, was born in Hampton, Iowa. He graduated 35th in his 1897 Annapolis class of 47. In 1937 he was appointed as Chief of Naval Operations. He retired on August 1, 1939. He became governor of Puerto Rico on June 6, 1939. He arrived in Vichy France on January 5, 1941 as the American ambassador. He stayed there until May 1, 1942. He was named as FDR's chief of staff on July 6, 1942 and remained in that post until March 25, 1949 under Truman. He died on July 20, 1959 at Bethesda, Maryland.
1890 Admiral Charles Lockwood was born in Virginia. He graduated 136th in his 1912 Annapolis class of 156. On May 26, 1942 he replaced Captain John Wilkes as Commander Submarines Southwest Pacific. In February 1943 he assumed command of all American submarine forces in the Pacific. He retired on September 1, 1947 as a vice-admiral. He died on June 6, 1967.
1937 The destroyers PATTERSON and JARVIS were launched. PATTERSON was scrapped in 1947 and JARVIS was lost August 9, 1942.
1941 The first flight of the Republic-built P47B "Thunderbolt" took place.
1942 Sugar was rationed in America.
1956 The battleship WISCONSIN collided with the destroyer EATON off Norfolk, Virginia. The destroyer's commander, Commander Richard Varley, was court-martialed.
1974 The destroyers TAUSSIG, LOFBERG, JOHN W. THOMPSON, JOHN A. BOLE and LYMAN K. SWENSON were sold to Taiwan.
2010 Lieutenant Commander Willian Thayer died at the age of 90. He had scored 6 aerial victories while flying the F4F "Wildcat" in the Pacific.
2014 USN ace Robert Kinkaid died at the age of 97 in Berkeley, California. He had been credited with 5 aerial victories while flying Corsairs in the Pacific.

Pacific
1941 The American Philippine Department Air Force was activated.
1942 The 16,000 Allied troops on Corregidor Island in Manila Bay surrendered. The USN minesweeper FINCH was sunk at Corregidor by Japanese artillery. She was salvaged by the Japanese and recommissioned as P-103, which was sunk by American aircraft on January 12, 1945. The USN minesweeper QUAIL and the gunboats OAHU and LUZON were

scuttled off Corregidor. QUAIL's Captain, Lieutenant Commander Merrill, took seventeen of her crew and took a 38-foot liberty launch and sailed for Australia on an epic 31-day voyage. The USN gunboat LUZON was scuttled at Corregidor. She was salvaged by the Japanese and recommissioned as the KARATSU and was sunk on February 3, 1945. The USN gunboat OAHU was scuttled at Corregidor. The USN submarine SKIPJACK sank the KANAN MARU (2,567 tons) off Indochina. The USN submarine TRITON sank the TAIEI MARU (2,208 tons) and the TAIGEN MARU (5,665 tons) off Formosa. The IJN submarine I-21 sank the Greek freighter CHLOE (4,641 tons). The IJN light carrier SHOHO was sighted in the Coral Sea and attacked by USAAF B17s.

1943 The USN submarine GAR sank the KOTOKU MARU (164 tons). The American 11th Air Force attacked Attu in the Aleutians.

1944 The IJN heavy cruiser HAGURO was sunk in the Malacca Straits by Royal Navy destroyers. The USN submarine CREVALLE sank the NISSHIN MARU (16,801 tons). The USN submarine SPEARFISH sank the TOYOURA MARU (2,510 tons). The USN submarine GURNARD sank the ADEN MARU (5,823 tons), the AMATSUSAN MARU (6,886 tons) and the TAIJIMA MARU (6,995 tons).

1945 The USN submarine HAMMERHEAD sank the KINREI MARU (867 tons).

China-Burma-India

1942 The French sloop D'ENTRECASTEAUX was sunk off Madagascar by aircraft from the Royal Navy carrier INDOMITABLE and the destroyer LAFOREY. Three American 10th Air Force B17s attacked Rangoon, Burma. Chinese troops took Maymo, Burma. The Japanese took Wanting, Burma.

1944 Chinese and American forces unsuccessfully attacked Ritpong, Burma. Captain J. Randle, of the Norfolk Regiment, won a posthumous Victoria Cross at Kohima, Burma.

1945 British forces took Pegu, Burma.

May 7th

Western Europe

1892 German General Hermann Breith was born. He commanded the 5th Panzer Brigade, the 3rd Panzer Division and the 3rd Panzer Corps. He died on September 3, 1964.

1915 Luftwaffe ace Johannes Wiese (133 victories) was born in Brelau. He survived the war.

1919 The terms of the Versailles Treaty were published Berlin.
1940 After a vote of confidence of 281 to 200 in the House of Commons, the resignation of Neville Chamberlain as British Prime Minister was assured. Nine Royal Air Force bombers attempted to attack Stavanger airfield in Norway.
1941 Sixteen Royal Air Force "Blenheims" attacked German shipping and lost one aircraft. The first Royal Air Force B17 unit, No.90 Squadron, was activated at Royal Air Force Watton, Norfolk. The Luftwaffe attacked Liverpool and Merseyside in Britain. Eighty-nine Royal Air Force bombers attacked German naval units at Brest, France. Fifteen Royal Air Force "Wellingtons" attacked St. Nazaire, France and lost one aircraft.
1942 Twelve Royal Air Force "Bostons" attacked targets in Holland. Eighty-one Royal Air Force bombers dropped mines in the Baltic and lost two aircraft.
1943 Six Royal Air Force B25 "Mitchells" attacked Boulogne, France. 104 American 8th Air Force P47s flew sweeps over Belgium.
1944 Eight American 9th Air Force P47 fighter-bombers destroyed a 650-foot-long railway bridge over the Seine, near Vernon. 553 American 8th Air Force B17s dropped 1,345 tons of bombs on Berlin and lost eight aircraft. 312 8th Air Force B24s dropped 858 tons of bombs on Munster and Osnabruck in Germany and lost aircraft. 754 8th Air Force fighters provided support for the bombers and lost two P38s, one P47 and one P51. The 486th Bomb Group (B24) and 487th Bomb Group (B24) sent twenty-nine aircraft to bomb the Liege marshalling yards on their first 8th Air Force mission and dropped eighty-four tons of bombs. They were escorted by seventy-five 8th Air Force fighters. Ninety-nine Royal Air Force bombers attacked Nantes, France and lost one "Lancaster". Sixty-four Royal Air Force bombers attacked St. Valery, France. Sixty-two Royal Air Force bombers attacked Salbris, France and lost seven "Lancasters". Sixty-one Royal Air Force bombers attacked Tours, France and lost two aircraft. Fifty-five Royal Air Force bombers attacked Rennes, France. Three B17s from the USAAF's 422nd Bomb Squadron dropped 1,600,000 leaflets on sixteen targets in France. The USAAF's 801st Bomb Group dispatched fourteen B24s on "Carpetbagger" missions.
1945 The last ground combat in Western Europe took place near Volary, Czechoslovakia, when a patrol from the US Armys 5th Division was ambushed, suffering one killed and three wounded. The last shot fired in the European Theater of Operations was credited to Private First-Class Dominic Mozzetta, of the US Army's 97th Division, when he shot at a sniper that evening. Arthur Seyss-Inquart, Reich Commissioner of the Netherlands, was arrested in Hamburg. General Alfred Jodl and Admiral Freideburg signed the surrender of Germany at Rheims. Canadian, Polish

and British troops occupied Emden, Wilhelmshaven and Cuxhaven. 229 American 8th Air Force bombers dropped 423 tons of food on Holland. The 356th Fighter Group (P51) flew the last of its 413 8th Air Force missions, having lost 122 aircraft. The last aircraft lost by the 8th Air Force was a 95th Bomb Group B17G flying out of Framlingham. The Norwegian minesweeper NYMS-382 was sunk in the Irish Sea by the U1023. Belgian King Leopold III was liberated at Strobl by American troops. The German minesweeper M-22 was scuttled in the Kiel Canal. The German MTBs S-301 and S-191 sank after colliding in Fehmarnsund.

Eastern Europe
1944 Soviet forces attacked Sevastopol. The American 15th Air Force attacked rail and aircraft targets in Rumania.

Mediterranean
1941 General Quinlan assumed command of the British forces in Iraq. The Royal Navy minesweeper STOKE was sunk in Tobruk, Libya by the Luftwaffe. An artillery duel between the Allied forces trapped around the port and the Axis troops that surrounded them took place at Tobruk.
1943 The US Army's 2nd Corps took Bizerta, Tunisia and British forces took Tunis. The German destroyer ZG-3 (the ex-Greek GEORGIOS) was scuttled at Tunis. The French destroyer L'AUDACIEUX was sunk at Bizerta by Allied aircraft.

Atlantic
1941 The German weather ship MUNCHEN was captured northeast of Iceland by the Royal Navy destroyer SOMALI. Aboard the MUNCHEN was an intact "Enigma" coding machine and a book containing naval codes. The German armed merchant cruiser PINGUIN took the tanker BRITISH EMPEROR (3,663 tons). The U94 sank the British freighter IXION (10,263 tons) and the Norwegian freighter EASTERN STAR (5,658 tons). U94 survived until August 28, 1943. The Italian submarine TAZZOLI sank the Norwegian freighter FERNLANE (4,310 tons).
1942 The U162 sank the Norwegian freighter FRANK SEAMANS (4,271 tons). U162 survived until September 3rd. The US Coast Guard cutter CALYPSO rescued thirteen survivors from the PIPESTONE COUNTY and the US Coast Guard cutter BOUTWELL rescued another thirteen. The British freighter FORT QU'APPELLE rescued all twenty-two survivors from the American freighter GREEN ISLAND which had been sunk by U125.
1943 The U89 sank the Greek freighter LACONIKOS (3,803 tons). U89 survived until May 14th. The U447 was sunk west of Gibraltar by the Royal Air Force's No.233 Squadron. The U465 was sunk in Bay of Biscay by the

Royal Air Force's No.10 Squadron. The U663 was sunk in Bay of Biscay by the Royal Air Force's No.58 Squadron. The American freighter SAMUEL JORDAN KIRKWOOD (7,191 tons) was sunk off Ascension Island by the U195. U195 survived the war.

1944 At 0435, the Royal Canadian Navy frigate VALLEYFIELD was sunk off Cape Race by the U548. 121 of her crew died. Her thirty-eight survivors were rescued by the Royal Canadian Navy GIFFARD. U548 survived until April 30, 1945.

1945 The U2336 sank the Norwegian freighter SNELAND I (1,791 tons) and the British freighter AVONDALE PARK (2,878 tons) off Scotland. The U1023 sank the Norwegian minesweeper MS-382 off Lyme Bay, Britain. The U320 was damaged west of Bergen, Norway by a Royal Air Force No.210 Squadron PBY and would finally sink on the 9th. It was the last U-boat "kill" of the war by Allied forces. During the war Germany had built 1,162 submarines, of which 784 were lost, 156 surrendered and 220 were scuttled by their crews. Two others sailed to Argentina where they were interned. Of 40,900 personnel who served aboard them, 25,870 were killed and more than 5,000 were captured. German U-boats sank 175 warships and 2,452 merchant ships. The Royal Air Force's Coastal Command had lost 1,777 aircraft and 1,965 men during the Atlantic campaign.

North America

1942 The destroyers HARRISON and JOHN RODGERS were launched. They were both sold to Mexico in 1970.

1944 The submarines SEA OWL and BLUEBACK were launched. BLUEBACK was transferred to the Turkish Navy in 1958 and SEA OWL was still on active duty in 1963.

1953 Escaped German prisoner of war, Harry Girth, surrendered to authorities in New York.

1975 George Baker, creator of the comic strip character "Sad Sack", died.

1988 George Burns died of a heart attack. He had been one of the photographers assigned to take pictures of the famous flag raising on Iwo Jima in 1945.

Pacific

1940 FDR ordered the Pacific Fleet to remain in Hawaiian waters indefinitely. It had originally been planned as a temporary situation after which the Fleet would have returned to San Diego.

1942 At 0630, USN Admiral Frank Fletcher detached Task Force 44 (commanded by RN Admiral John Crace), which consisted of three cruisers and one destroyer, to block the Japanese Port Moresby invasion force. Task Force 44 was later attacked by Japanese aircraft. The USN destroyer

FARRAGUT was damaged by friendly fire during the attack. Task Force 44 was then attacked by USAAF B26s. At 0945, Task Force 17 (commanded by Fletcher), consisting of the carrier YORKTOWN, two cruisers and five destroyers, attacked the Japanese invasion force (commanded by Marusige), consisting of twelve transports. At 1057, USN carrier aircraft attacked the Japanese Striking Force (commanded by Takagi), consisting of the carriers SHOKAKU and ZUIKAKU, two heavy cruisers and six destroyers. The SHOKAKU was damaged by two bombs. At 1100, Task Force 11 (commanded by Fitch), consisting of the carrier LEXINGTON, two cruisers and five destroyers, attacked the Japanese covering group (commanded by Goto), consisting of the light carrier SHOHO and four heavy cruisers. At 1110, SHOHO was hit by twelve bombs and up to seven torpedoes and sank in ten minutes. At 1115, the Japanese Naval Air Force attacked the USN fleet. The LEXINGTON was hit by two bombs. At 1130, the USN destroyer SIMS (14 survivors) was sunk and the tanker NEOSHO (179 dead) was damaged by the Japanese Naval Air Force. USN Chief Watertender Oscar Peterson, of the NEOSHO, won a posthumous Medal of Honor. US Army General Jonathan Wainwright won a Medal of Honor for his actions while serving as Commander of Allied forces in the Philippines. Japanese forces took Hollandia, New Guinea.

1943   The USN light cruisers HONOLULU, NASHVILLE, and ST. LOUIS and four destroyers bombarded Munda. The USN submarine WAHOO sank the TOMAN MARU No.5 (5,260 tons). The USN submarine SNOOK sank the TOSEI MARU (4,363 tons) and the SHINSEI MARU No.3 (1,258 tons). The destroyer-minesweepers BREESE, GAMBLE and PREBLE laid a minefield across the Blackett Straits in the Kula Gulf. They were escorted by the USN destroyers STRONG, CHEVALIER, TAYLOR and O'BANNON. The USN battleship WEST VIRGINIA left Pearl Harbor, en route to Puget Sound in Washington to repair damage suffered during the December 7, 1941 attack.

1944   The USN submarine BURRFISH sank the tanker ROSSBACH (5,894 tons). The US Army's 40th Division took the Cape Hopkins airfield on New Britain.

1945   USMC Captain John Fardy and Private Dale Hansen, of the 1st Division, won posthumous Medals of Honor on Okinawa. The crew of the Royal Canadian Navy light cruiser UGANDA voted 605 to 300 to return home, as per a Canadian government decree that only volunteers would serve in the Pacific Theater of Operations. The IJN minelayer NUWASHIMA was sunk by USN carriers. The IJN minesweeper W-29 was sunk west of Honshu by a mine.

China-Burma-India

1942 The French submarine LE HEROS was sunk while attacking the British invasion fleet off Madagascar. A seaplane from the Japanese submarine I-30 flew over Aden.

1943 Japanese forces began an offensive near Buthidaung, Burma. The IJN submarine I-27 sank the Dutch freighter BERAKIT (6,608 tons).

1944 Chinese and American forces surrounded Ritpong, Burma.

May 8th

Western Europe

1937 German fighter pilot and future ace Adolf Galland arrived at El Ferrol, Spain, to assume command of the Kondor Legion's 3rd Staffel.

1940 The Belgian embassy in Berlin informed their government that the Germans were drafting an ultimatum and were increasing their forces on the border.

1941 Six Royal Air Force "Blenheims" attacked German shipping off Norway and lost one aircraft. The Luftwaffe attacked London. The Royal Navy battleship PRINCE OF WALES completed her acceptance trials. She would be sunk off Malaya in December 1941 by Japanese aircraft. 188 Royal Air Force bombers attacked Hamburg, Germany and lost four aircraft. 185 people were killed in the raid. 133 Royal Air Force bombers attacked Bremen, Germany and lost five aircraft. The only fatalities on the ground were two Allied prisoners of war. Twenty-seven Royal Air Force "Blenheims" attacked the Kiel Canal in Germany and the city of Bremerhaven. One Royal Air Force "Wellington" was lost over Berlin.

1942 Six Royal Air Force "Bostons" attacked Dieppe, France. 193 Royal Air Force bombers attacked Warnemunde, Germany and lost nineteen aircraft.

1944 Allied Supreme Commander US Army General Dwight Eisenhower designated June 5th as D-Day (the invasion of northern France). 742 American 8th American Air Force bombers dropped 1,851 tons of bombs on Berlin, Brandenburg, Magdeburg, and Brunswick in Germany and lost twenty-five B17s and eleven B24s. 729 8th and 9th Air Force fighters provided support for the bombers and claimed fifty-five victories for the loss of four P38s, four P47s and five P51s. Luftwaffe ace Leopold Munster (95 victories) was killed in a collision over Hildesheim with an 8th Air Force B17. Ninety-two 8th Air Force B17s dropped 238 tons of bombs on V-1 rocket sites at Glacerie and Sottevast in France. Fifty-seven 8th Air Force B24s dropped 164 tons of bombs on the marshalling yards in Brussels. Ninety-seven 8th Air Force P47s provided support for the bombers. The American 9th Air Force attacked bridges over the Seine River. 123 Royal Air Force bombers attacked Haine-St-Pierre, France and lost nine aircraft. Sixty-four Royal Air Force bombers attacked Brest, France and lost one "Lancaster". Thirty-nine Royal Air Force bombers attacked Morsalines, France and lost one "Halifax". Thirty-nine Royal Air Force bombers attacked Berneval, France. Thirty-eight Royal Air Force bombers attacked Cap Griz Nez, France. Three B17s from the USAAF's 422nd Bomb Squadron dropped 1,600,000 leaflets on ten different targets in France. The USAAF's 801st Bomb Group dispatched fifteen B24s on "Carpetbagger" missions.

1945   V-E (Victory in Europe) Day. Twelve USAAF 306th Bombardment Group B17s dropped leaflets on Germany. Lieutenant Robert Little, USAAF 12th Tactical Recon (F6C), scored the last USAAF victory in the European Theater of Operations, a Luftwaffe Fw190 over the Danube. Since its first mission on August 17, 1942, the American 8th Air Force had flown 330,523 sorties, dropped 686,406 tons of bombs, 2,807 tons of leaflets and had lost 5,855 aircraft and 41,125 personnel on combat operations. Total aircraft losses by type were: B17-4,118, B24-1,560, P47-705, P38-356 and P51-1,749. 8th Air Force personnel had won a total of fourteen Medals of Honor during the war. An explosion of German ordnance killed eight GIs of the US Army's 26th Division in Pernek, Czechoslovakia. American ground casualties in the European Theater Operations were 177,549 killed in action, 472,742 wounded in action and 151,920 evacuated for combat exhaustion. The U2365 was scuttled in the Skagerrak after an attack by Allied aircraft. She was salvaged in 1956 and recommissioned into the Bundesmarine as the HAI. The German minesweeper R-88 was scuttled in the Kiel Canal. The U37 and U2538 were scuttled off Sonderburg. The U3503 was scuttled in the Kattegat after an attack by Allied aircraft. The U995 surrendered at Trondheim, Norway. She was scrapped as the Norwegian KAURA in 1963.

Eastern Europe

1940   Semyon Timoshenko was named as Soviet Commissar for Defense.

1942   The Soviet transport KUBAN was sunk by the Luftwaffe. German forces began an offensive towards Kerch in the Crimea.

1944   Soviet forces continued their attack against Sevastopol. Hitler granted permission for a retreat from the Crimea. The German patrol boat V-1701 was sunk by Soviet aircraft in the Baltic.

1945   The Germans and the Soviets signed a surrender document at Karlhorst, near Berlin. Luftwaffe ace Erich Hartmann scored the last of his 352 victories, a Soviet Yak-7 fighter. He was captured by the US Army's 90th Division at Pisek, Czechoslovakia upon landing and eventually turned over to the Soviets. Seven German destroyers and five torpedo boats evacuated 20,000 German refugees to the west from Hela. Later in the day, the German freighters WESERBERG and evacuated a further 5,730. Sixty-five German small craft left Libau for the west. Aboard were 14,400 refugees. Sixty-one German small craft left Windau with 11,300 troops and headed west. In all, 142,000 people were safely moved to the west from the area between January 25th and May 8th.

Mediterranean
1941 The British launched an offensive to relieve Tobruk, Libya.
1942 The Royal Navy submarine OLYMPUS was sunk off Malta by a mine. Nine members of her 98-man crew survived. Her wreck was not located until 2008. The French submarine MONGE was sunk by the Royal Navy.
1943 Italian frogmen attacked Allied shipping at Gibraltar, damaging the American freighter PAT HARRISON. One of her crew was killed.
1945 The U485 surrendered at Gibraltar. The British forcibly repatriated 185 Soviet Russians at Rimini, Italy.

Atlantic
1940 The British transport ORAMA was sunk off Narvik, Norway by the German heavy cruiser ADMIRAL HIPPER.
1941 The U97 sank the British freighter RAMILLIES (4,553 tons). U97 survived until June 16, 1943.
1942 The U507 sank the Honduran freighter ONTARIO (3,099 tons) and the Norwegian freighter TORNY (2,424 tons). U507 survived until January 13, 1943. The American freighter OHIOAN (6,078 tons-17 dead) was sunk by the U564. U564 survived until June 14, 1943. The U136 sank the Canadian freighter MIDRED PAULINE (300 tons) off Nova Scotia. U136 survived until July 11th. The fishing boat IRENE AND MAY rescued survivors from the American freighter PIPESTONE COUNTY which had been sunk by U576.
1945 The American freighter HORACE BINNEY was a constructive loss after hitting a mine off Flushing, Belgium.

North America
1884 President Harry Truman was born in Lamar, Missouri near Independence. He died on December 26, 1972 at the age of eighty-eight.
1926 The first successful test of the USN magnetic torpedo exploder took place. The USN submarine L-8 was expended in the test.
1937 The light cruiser SAVANNAH (awarded three battle stars during the war) was launched. She was scrapped in Baltimore in 1960.
1942 The destroyer GILLISPIE was launched. She was stricken in 1971.

1943   The destroyer STEMBEL was launched. She was sold to Argentina in 1961.
1944   The carrier TICONDEROGA was commissioned. She was stricken in 1973. The destroyer GREGORY was launched. She was stricken in 1966 and used as a training ship.
1945   A riot took place in Halifax, Nova Scotia. It began with service personnel celebrating the end of the war in Europe. It ended with 564 business' damaged and 94 servicemen and 117 civilians arrested.
1960   The USN escort carrier SANTREE was sold for scrap. She had participated in the sinking of three U-boats during the war.
1973   USMC General Archer Vandegrift died in Bethesda, Maryland. He had commanded the USMC forces on Guadalcanal and had later served as Commandant of the Marine Corps.

Pacific

1942   The Japanese launched attacks on Mindanao in the Philippines. In the Coral Sea the Japanese Naval Air Force attacked USN forces. At 1118, the USN carrier LEXINGTON was hit by an aircraft torpedo. At 1120, she was hit by another one. At 1247, gasoline fumes that had been trapped below decks exploded. At 1600, the engine rooms were abandoned. At 1705, abandon ship was ordered. The USN destroyers HAMMANN and MORRIS rescued wounded survivors. The HAMMANN would be sunk the very next month while performing the same function for the carrier YORKTOWN during the "Battle of Midway". At 1730, an ammunition magazine exploded. At 1807, another major explosion occurred. At 1830, her commanding officer, Frederick Sherman, abandoned ship. 216 of her crew died in the action. At 1940, the USN destroyer PHELPS fired torpedoes into the floating hulk. At 2000, she sank. The USN carrier YORKTOWN was damaged in the same battle. USN Lieutenant (jg) William Hall and Lieutenant John Powers (posthumous) won Medals of Honor while flying SBD dive-bombers over the Coral Sea. USN Lieutenant Milton Ricketts, of the carrier YORKTOWN, won a posthumous Medal of Honor. The USN submarine SKIPJACK sank the BUJUN MARU (4,804 tons) off Indochina. The USN submarine GRENADIER sank the TAIYO MARU (14,457 tons) off Kyushu. The USN light cruiser NASHVILLE ran aground off Midway. The damage suffered in the incident postponed her mission against the Japanese fishing fleet off Kamchatka.
1943   The IJN destroyer KURISHIO was sunk by three mines off Rendova. The IJN destroyer KAGERO was damaged in the same minefield and was later sunk by aircraft. The IJN destroyer OYASHIO was sunk and the destroyer MICHISHIO was damaged by aircraft, while assisting the first two vessels. 5th Air Force B25s attacked Madang Harbor, New Guinea

and sank the Japanese freighters TOMIOKA MARU and SUMIDA MARU. 5th Air Force ace Captain Thomas Lynch shot down a Japanese "Hamp" fighter near Saidor, New Guinea. The IJN battleship MUTSU was sunk by an accidental explosion in Hiroshima Bay. The USN battleship WASHINGTON arrived at Pearl Harbor from action in the Solomons. The Royal Navy carrier VICTORIOUS departed Pearl Harbor, en route to operations in the South Pacific.

1944 American forces reinforced their perimeter at Aitape, New Guinea. The USN submarine TAUTOG sank the MIYAZAKI MARU (3,943 tons).

1945 The USN aircraft tender ST. GEORGE and the Royal Navy carrier VICTORIOUS were hit by kamikazes off Okinawa. Private First-Class Anthony Krotiak, of the 37th Division, won a posthumous Medal of Honor on Luzon. The USN submarine BOWFIN sank the DAITO MARU No.3 (880 tons).

China-Burma-India

1941 The German armed merchant cruiser PINGUIN was sunk in the Indian Ocean by the Royal Navy heavy cruiser CORNWALL. The dead included 292 German crewmen and 155 British prisoners who were aboard her.

1942 Japanese forces took Myitkyina, Akyab and Bhamo in Burma. The French submarine MONGE was sunk while attacking the British invasion fleet off Madagascar.

1944 The Chinese 30th Division attacked Ritpong, Burma but was beaten back. By this date there were 130 USAAF B29s operating in India.

May 9th

Western Europe

1940 The Belgian Army was placed on alert. The German minesweeper M-134 was sunk by the Royal Air Force's No.254 Squadron at Bergen, Norway. Thirty-one Royal Air Force bombers dropped mines in the Baltic. Since April 9th the Royal Air Force's Bomber Command had flown 931 sorties on which they lost thirty-six aircraft and had dropped 198 tons of bombs.

1941 Thirteen Royal Air Force "Blenheims" attacked German shipping and lost one aircraft. 146 Royal Air Force bombers attacked Mannheim and Ludwigshafen in Germany and lost one "Whitley" and one "Wellington". Sixty-four people were killed in the two raids.

1942 Twelve Royal Air Force "Bostons" attacked targets in Belgium. The German minesweeper M-533 was lost in a collision with the minesweeper R-45 off Boulogne. Twenty Royal Air Force bombers dropped mines in the Baltic. The German minesweepers M-533 and R-45 collided off Boulogne,

France and were lost. The German minesweeper EIDER was a constructive loss after hitting a mine off Heligoland. The German pocket battleship ADMIRAL SCHEER, the tanker DITHMARSCHEN and the torpedo boats T-5 and T-7 were transferred from Trondheim to Narvik in Norway.

1943   A Luftwaffe Ju88 night-fighter landed at Dyce, Scotland. Twenty-one Royal Air Force "Stirlings" dropped mines off the French coast.

1944   The American 9th Air Force bombers attacked Channel shore batteries and Seine River bridges. The USAAF's 322nd Bomb Group B26 "Mild and Bitter" became the first Allied bomber to complete 100 missions in the European Theater of Operations. 802 American 8th Air Force bombers dropped 1,678 tons of bombs on marshalling yards and airfields in France and lost four B24s and two B17s. 668 8th and 9th Air Force fighters provided support for the bombers and claimed four victories for the loss of one P38 and six P51s. This marked the beginning of the aerial campaign to disrupt German defenses in preparation for the invasion. The US Armys 101st Airborne Division had a full-scale D-Day rehearsal at Berkshire Downs. During the exercise 436 men were injured. 414 Royal Air Force bombers attacked German coastal batteries along the Channel coast and lost one "Lancaster". The USAAF's 801st Bomb Group dispatched thirteen B24s on "Carpetbagger" missions. Sixty-four Royal Air Force bombers attacked an aircraft engine factory at Gennevilliers, France and lost five "Lancasters". Forty-three Royal Air Force bombers attacked Annecy, France. Three B17s from the USAAF's 422nd Bomb Squadron dropped 1,340,000 leaflets on four targets in Holland and three in Belgium.

1945   The German forces on the Channel Islands surrendered. The ceremony took place aboard the Royal Navy destroyer BULLDOG. The occupation had lasted 1,774 days. The German garrisons in St. Nazaire, Lorient and La Rochelle in France surrendered. The Royal Navy minesweeper PROMPT was a constructive loss after hitting a mine off Ostend, Belgium. Vidkun Quisling surrendered to Norwegian police and was executed on the 24th of October. The German heavy cruiser PRINZ EUGEN and light cruiser NURNBERG surrendered at Copenhagen. The U2538 was sunk by mine off Denmark. The U249 surrendered at Portland, Britain. Soviet forces took Prague.

1965   The Dachau Concentration Camp Museum was opened.

Eastern Europe

1942   The Soviets began an offensive at Kharkov. Between this date and the 1st of the month, the German Navy laid 1,915 mines off the Baltic States.

1944   The Soviets took Sevastopol. They now controlled all the Crimea and the Ukraine.

Mediterranean

1941 The Royal Air Force attacked Derna. The British increased their pressure on Amba Alagi in East Africa.

1942 The Royal Navy carrier EAGLE and the USN carrier WASP launched sixty-four "Spitfires" for Malta in "Operation Bowery". Four aircraft were lost en route to the island.

1943 At 1100, the Axis forces in northeast Tunisia surrendered. The USAAF attacked Palermo on Sicily. Allied Supreme Commander US Army General Dwight Eisenhower issued orders for the aerial bombardment of the island of Pantelleria to begin.

1944 Allied convoy UGS.40 passed through the Straits of Gibraltar. It was made up of sixty-five merchant ships escorted by Task Force 60 (commanded by Sowell). Task Force 60 consisted of one USCG cutter, four American destroyers, eight American destroyer escorts, one British anti-aircraft cruiser, a French destroyer escort and two American minesweepers. The USN PC-558 was sunk off Palermo, Sicily by the U230.

1945 German forces on the islands of Milos, Piscopi, Leros, Simi, Kos and Western Crete surrendered.

1994 The Italian authorities signed extradition papers for S.S. Captain Erich Priebke, age 80, who was living in Argentina. Priebke had admitted to being involved in the massacre of 355 Italian civilians in 1944.

Atlantic

1940 The Royal Navy destroyer KELLY (commanded by Lord Mountbatten) was torpedoed off Holland by the German S-31. The French submarine DORIS was sunk in the North Sea by the U9. U9 survived until August 20, 1944.

1941 The U110 sank the British freighters ESMOND (4,976 tons) and BANGOR HEAD (2,609 tons). She was then damaged and captured by the Royal Navy destroyers BULLDOG and BROADWAY and the corvette AUBRETIA. Aboard was an intact "Enigma" code machine. Her commander was Fritz Lemp, who had sunk the passenger liner ATHENIA on the first day of the war. He and fourteen of his crew were shot and killed during the operation. She sank while under tow. The U201 sank the British freighter GREGALIA (5,802 tons). U201 survived until February 17, 1943. The Italian submarine TAZZOLI sank the Norwegian tanker ALFRED OLSEN (8,817 tons). The U103 sank the British freighter CITY OF WINCHESTER (7,120 tons). U103 survived until April 15, 1945.

1942 The US Coast Guard cutter ICARUS sank the U352 south of Cape Hatteras and rescued thirty-two survivors. The U162 sank the Canadian freighter MONT LOUIS (1,905 tons). U162 survived until September 3rd. The U564 sank the Panamanian tanker LUBRAFOL (7,138 tons). U564 survived

	until June 14, 1943. The U125 sank the Canadian tanker CALGAROLITE (11,941 tons). U125 survived until May 6, 1943. The American government issued an ultimatum to Admiral Georges Robert, Vichy commander of the French West Indies, to relinquish control of the islands.
1943	The U123 sank the British freighter KANBE (6,244 tons). U123 survived the war. The U515 sank the Norwegian freighter CORNEVILLE (4,544 tons). U515 survived until April 9, 1944. A USN VP-63 PBY rescued four survivors from the British freighter MELBOURNE STAR that had been sunk 38 days before. The USN light cruiser MARBLEHEAD rescued the crew of a crashed USAAF B26.
1945	The U963 was wrecked off Lisbon.

North America

1882	American industrialist Henry Kaiser was born in Canajoharie, New York. He was responsible for building almost one third of all American merchant ships launched between 1940 and 1945, a total of 1,460. He was also a major producer of aluminum, magnesium, and steel during the war. He died in Honolulu on August 24, 1967.
1892	General Brehon "Bill" Somerville was born in Little Rock, Arkansas. He graduated 6th in his 1914 West Point class of 107. He commanded the Army's Service Forces from 1942 until the end of the war. He died on February 13, 1955.
1936	The submarine PERCH was launched. She was lost on March 3, 1942.
1943	The submarine ROBALO was launched. She was lost on July 26, 1944.
1944	The escort carrier COMMENCEMENT BAY was launched. She was stricken in 1971.
1945	The U1228 surrendered at Portsmouth, Virginia.
1947	The DMS (destroyer minesweeper) LAMBERTON was scrapped at Terminal Island.
1966	The US Coast Guard cutter NIKE was sold.
1994	USAAF Chief of Staff General Henry Arnold's personal DC-3 left Oakland, California, en route to the 50th anniversary ceremonies in Normandy.
2010	Inventor Edward G. Uhl died at the age of 92 at an assisted living facility in Easton, Maryland of heart failure. He had co-designed, along with Colonel Leslie A. Skinner, the M-1 Rocket Launcher which became better known as the "Bazooka" during World War II.

Pacific

| 1942 | American troops landed on the Galapagos Islands. |
| 1943 | The USN submarine WAHOO sank the TAKAO MARU (3,204 tons) and the JINMU MARU (1,912 tons). The USN submarine GAR sank the ASO MARU (703 tons). |

1945 The Royal Navy carriers FORMIDABLE and VICTORIOUS were hit by Japanese kamikazes off Okinawa. The USN destroyer escorts OBERRENDER (eight of her crew died) and ENGLAND (thirty-four died) were constructive losses after kamikaze attacks off Okinawa. USMC Platoon Sergeant Joseph Julian, of the 5th Division, won a posthumous Medal of Honor on Iwo Jima.

1994 The "Victory" ship LANE VICTORY was forced to abandon her trip to the 50th anniversary ceremonies in Normandy. She had suffered severe oil leaks while en route to the Panama Canal from California.

China-Burma-India

1941 Japan and Vichy signed a treaty concerning access into Indo-China.

1942 The IJN armed merchant cruisers AIKOKU MARU and HOKOKU MARU took the Dutch tanker GENOTA (7,986 tons) off Madagascar. Six American 10th Air Force B17s attacked Rangoon, Burma.

1944 The Japanese broke out of the encircled village of Ritpong, Burma.

1945 American prisoners of war that had been captured on Wake Island in 1942 were moved from Shanghai to Pusan, Korea. The 82nd West African Division took Sandoway, Burma.

May 10th

Western Europe

1890 General Alfred Jodl was born in Wurzburg, Bavaria. He would become the Chief of the Operations Staff of the German Armed Forces. He would be executed in 1946 after the Nuremburg War Crimes Trials.

1933 The Nazis burned books at Berlin's Humboldt University.

1939 Hitler ordered the German Navy to prepare for a war against British and French merchant shipping.

1940 Shortly after midnight, the Luftwaffe began attacking Allied airfields. At 0535, German airborne forces attacked bridges at Dordrecht, Rotterdam, and Moerdijk in Holland. At about the same time German ground forces began crossing the borders of Belgium, Luxembourg, and Holland. Eleven German gliders landed on top of the Belgian Fort Eben Emael which contained two 120mm and sixteen 75mm cannon. Its main function was to guard the Albert Canal and was considered to be the strongest fort in the world. It would surrender the next day. At 0730, French and British troops moved into Belgium. The Dutch destroyer VAN GALEN was sunk at Rotterdam by the Luftwaffe. Three Luftwaffe He111s accidentally bombed the German town of Freiburg, killing fifty-seven civilians. The Luftwaffe lost 304 aircraft in the day's operations. Luftwaffe ace Guenther

Rall scored the first of his 275 victories, a French Air Force P36 fighter over Diedenhoven. A Swiss Air Force Me109 damaged a Luftwaffe He111 near Altenheim, Switzerland. The Royal Air Force sent three fighter squadrons, Nos.3, 79 and 501, to reinforce the six already in France. Another, No.504, would be sent two days later. German forces moving north from Trondheim in central Norway took Mosjoen to the north. Neville Chamberlain resigned and was replaced by Winston Churchill as Britain's Prime Minister.

1941 Hitler's deputy, Rudolf Hess, took off on his unauthorized flight to Scotland. The Luftwaffe attacked London, damaging Parliament, Westminster Abbey, and the British Museum. 1,436 were killed in the raid, which was the last major attack London would suffer for almost three years. 119 Royal Air Force bombers attacked Hamburg and lost four aircraft. Thirty-one people were killed in the raid. Twenty-three Royal Air Force bombers attacked Berlin and lost three aircraft.

1942 The Royal Air Force flew its first P51 "Mustang" mission, a recon to Berck-sur-Mer. The German armed merchant cruiser STIER was commissioned.

1943 General Jacob Devers officially replaced Frank Andrews as Commander of American Forces in Europe. Andrews had died in a plane crash.

1944 The American 15th Air Force lost twenty-eight bombers and three escorting fighters over Weiner Neustadt, Austria. The American 9th Air Force attacked radar sites on the Channel coast and Seine River bridges. Royal Air Force Air Marshal Trafford Leigh-Mallory ordered his Allied Expeditionary Air Force to attack bridges on the Meuse River and the Albert Canal. 506 Royal Air Force bombers attacked rail targets in France and Belgium and lost thirteen aircraft. Fifty-eight Belgian civilians were killed in a raid on Ghent. Three B17s from the USAAF's 422nd Bomb Squadron dropped 1,800,000 leaflets on eleven targets in Belgium. The USAAF's 801st Bomb Group dispatched thirteen B24s on "Carpetbagger" missions.

1945 German forces in Dunkirk, France surrendered to a Czech Armored brigade. The German garrisons in Lorient and St. Nazaire in France surrendered to the US Army's 66th Division. German General Heinz Guderian was captured in Tyrol by the American 7th Army. Richard Gluecks, German Inspector of Concentration Camps, committed suicide at Flensburg and the German Governor of Moravia and Bohemia, Konrad Heenlein, committed suicide in an Allied internment camp. USAAF General Carl Spaatz interviewed former Luftwaffe Commander Hermann Goering. The U1105, U1009 and U1305 surrendered at Loch Eriboll, Scotland. U1058 surrendered at Lough Foyle. U825 surrendered at Portland. U1023 surrendered at Weymouth. U532 surrendered at Liverpool. U510 surrendered at St. Nazaire. The U310 surrendered at

Trondheim, Norway. Norwegian and British troops landed Oslo, Norway. They were commanded by Robert Urquhart, who had commanded the British airborne forces at Arnhem in 1944 during "Operation Market-Garden". Urquhart died in 1988. A Royal Air Force transport plane carrying British occupation troops to Norway crashed near Oslo killing all twenty-four aboard.

Mediterranean
1942 The German S-31 was sunk by a mine off Malta. The USN carrier RANGER launched sixty-eight USAAF P40s off Accra, Gold Coast. She had transported them from Quonset Point, Rhode Island.
1943 The US Army's 6th Armored Division took Hammam Lif, Tunisia. USAAF B26s attacked Axis shipping off Sicily. Forty-six USAAF B17s attacked Bo Rizzo, Sicily. Thirty-two USAAF B25s attacked the island of Pantelleria.

Atlantic
1940 The Royal Navy heavy cruiser BERWICK landed Royal Marines at Reykjavik, Iceland. They arrested the German Consul, confiscated U-boat parts and dismantled a weather station. The German armed merchant cruiser ATLANTIS took the Norwegian freighter TIRRANA (7,230 tons) and laid ninety-two mines off the coast of South Africa.
1941 The U556 sank the British freighter EMPIRE CARIBOU (4,861 tons) and the Belgian freighter GAND (5,086 tons). U556 survived until June 27th.
1942 The U333 sank the British freighter CLAN SKENE (5,214 tons). U333 survived until July 31, 1944. The U588 sank the British freighter KITTY'S BROCK (4,031 tons). U588 survived until July 31st.
1944 The USN destroyer escort ALGER rescued ten survivors from the British freighter JANETTA.

North America
1944 James Forrestal replaced Frank Knox as Secretary of the Navy. The escort carrier ADMIRALTY ISLANDS was launched. She was scrapped in 1947.
1959 Escaped German prisoner of war Kurt Rossmeisl surrendered in Cincinnati, Ohio.
1968 The destroyer IRWIN was sold to Brazil.
1971 The RMS QUEEN MARY was opened as a hotel and convention center in Long Beach, California.

Pacific
1942 Organized Allied resistance ended in the Philippines. The planned Japanese invasion of Port Moresby, New Guinea was cancelled. A

floatplane from the IJN KIMIKAWA MARU took photos of Adak in the Aleutians. A USN PBY disappeared off Dutch Harbor in the Aleutians.

1943   The USN submarine PLUNGER sank the TATSUTAKE MARU (7,068 tons). The USN destroyers SICARD and MACDONOUGH were damaged in a collision off the Aleutians.

1944   American forces took Marubian, New Guinea. The USN submarine SILVERSIDES sank the OKINAWA MARU (2,256 tons), the MIKAGE MARU No.18 (4,319 tons) and the CHOAN MARU No.2 (2,613 tons). The USN submarine COD sank the IJN destroyer KARUKAYA and the SHOHEI MARU (7,255 tons) off Luzon.

1945   Pharmacist's Mate 2nd Class William Halyburton won a posthumous Medal of Honor on Okinawa. The 108th Regimental Combat Team of the 40th Division landed at Macalajar Bay. An American 11th Air Force B25 was shot down over Paramushiro in the Kuriles. An 11th Air Force B24 and a B25 were interned in Russia.

1947   The USN battleship OKLAHOMA left Pearl Harbor under tow, en route to Oakland, California, and scrapping.

China-Burma-India

1944   The Chinese 116th and 190th Divisions crossed the Salween River.

1945   The Japanese heavy cruiser HAGURO and destroyer KAMIKAZE left Singapore en route to evacuating the garrisons in the Andamans and the Nicobars. They were sighted in the Malacca Straits by the British submarines STATESMAN and SUBTLE. After an abortive attack by aircraft from the British escort carriers HUNTER, KHEDIVE, SHAH and EMPEROR, the Japanese ships returned to port.

May 11th

Western Europe

1940   At 0530, the Germans opened their first bridge across the Albert Canal near the Belgian Fort Eben Emael. About six hours later, the Fort itself surrendered. German forces reached the Afsluit Canal in Holland. Twenty-three Royal Air Force bombers attacked German troop concentrations in the Maastricht area and lost two "Blenheims". The British War Cabinet was formed. British Prime Minister Winston Churchill authorized Royal Air Force bombing attacks on Germany. Thirty-six Royal Air Force bombers attacked Munchen-Gladbach, killing four civilians, including an Englishwoman. It was the first raid on a German town. They lost two "Hampdens" and one "Whitley". The Dutch liners VEENDAM (15,450 tons) and STATENDAM (28,291 tons) were sunk at Rotterdam by the Luftwaffe.

1941 Rudolf Hess bailed out of his Me-110 over Scotland. He had been Hitler's protégé and hoped, with his unauthorized flight in a Me110, to instigate peace talks between Germany and Britain. French Admiral Jean Darlan and Adolf Hitler met at Obersalzburg. Ninety-two Royal Air Force bombers attacked Hamburg and lost three "Wellingtons". Eleven people were killed in the raid. Eighty-one Royal Air Force bombers attacked Bremen, Germany and lost one "Hampden". Eight people were killed in the raid.

1942 The American transport ANDES arrived in Liverpool, Britain. Aboard were 1,850 members of the American 8th Air Force. They were the first members of that unit to arrive in Britain.

1943 Six Royal Air Force "Mitchells" attacked Boulogne, France. 128 American 8th Air Force P47s attempted to fly a sweep in the vicinity of Dunkirk, France but the mission was cancelled due to bad weather.

1944 254 American 8th Air Force B24s dropped 752 tons of bombs on French airfields and railyards and lost eight bombers (three of the lost B24s landed in Switzerland). The 492nd Bomb Group (B24) flew its first 8th Air Force mission. Lieutenant Colonel Bernie Lay, commander of the USAAF's 487th Bomb Group (B24 then B17), was shot down and captured. He would later write the screen-play for the movie "12 O'clock High". 536 8th Air Force fighters provided support for the bombers and claimed ten victories for the loss of two P47s and three P51s. 547 8th Air Force B17s dropped 1,559 tons of bombs on marshalling yards in Germany, France, Belgium, and Luxembourg and lost eight bombers. 471 8th and 9th Air Force fighters provided support for the bombers and claimed one victory for the loss of four P51s. The American 9th Air Force attacked French airfields. Luftwaffe ace Walter Osau (123 victories) was killed in action by USAAF P38s near Aachen, Germany. 198 Royal Air Force bombers attacked Bourg-Leopold, France and lost five "Lancasters". 135 Royal Air Force bombers attacked Boulogne, France and lost two "Halifaxes". 128 civilians were killed in the raid. 132 Royal Air Force bombers attacked Hasselt, France and lost five "Lancasters". 110 Royal Air Force bombers attacked Louvain, France and lost four "Lancasters". Fifty-nine Royal Air Force bombers attacked Trouville, France. Fifty-nine Royal Air Force bombers attacked Colline Beaumont, France. Four B17s from the USAAF's 422nd Bomb Squadron dropped 2,400,000 leaflets on targets in Denmark. The USAAF's 801st Bomb Group dispatched four B24s on "Carpetbagger" missions.

1945 Schoerner's German Army Group "Center", surrendered east of Prague. Fighting between German and Soviet forces continued east of Pilsen, Czechoslovakia. American and Soviet troops met at Pilsen. The German Governor of Norway, Josef Terboven, committed suicide. The U826 surrendered at Loch Eriboll. U293 surrendered at Loch Ailsh.

1987   The war crimes trial of German war criminal Klaus "The Butcher of Lyon" Barbie began in France.

Eastern Europe
1942   The Germans recaptured Feodosiya.

Mediterranean
1941   The Royal Navy submarine RORQUAL laid a minefield in the Gulf of Salonika.
1942   The British destroyers JERVIS, JACKEL, KIPLING and LIVELY departed from Alexandria to intercept a German/Italian convoy that was en route to Benghazi. They were sighted south of Crete by a German aircraft. At 1645, the LIVELY (76 dead) was sunk by the Luftwaffe 100 miles northeast of Tobruk, Libya. At 2007, the JACKAL was damaged by the Luftwaffe sixty miles north of Mersa Matruh. She was scuttled the next day by the JERVIS. The KIPLING was sunk in the same attack.
1943   Organized Axis resistance in Tunisia ended. USAAF B24s attacked Catania, Sicily. Twenty-six USAAF B26s also attacked Catania, losing one aircraft.
1944   The Allies began an offensive against the German 10th Army along the Garigliano River (the "Gustav Line"). At 2300, 2,000 cannon opened fire on German positions. At 2345, Allied infantry attacked. Sixty-two Luftwaffe aircraft attacked Convoy UGS.40 (see May 9th). No ships are lost, but the Germans sacrificed nineteen aircraft in the attempt. The British destroyer BICESTER bombarded targets near Ardea, south of Rome.

Atlantic
1940   The U9 sank the Estonian freighter VIIU (1,908 tons) and the British freighter TRINGA (1,930 tons). U9 survived until August 20, 1944. Allied troops occupied the Dutch oil installations on Curacao and Aruba Islands in the Caribbean.
1941   The U103 sank the British freighter CITY OF SHANGHAI (5,828 tons). U103 survived until April 15, 1945.
1942   The U502 sank the British freighter CAPE OF GOOD HOPE (4,963 tons). U502 survived until July 5th.
1943   The U402 sank the British freighter ANTIGONE (4,545 tons) and the Norwegian freighter GRADO (3,082 tons). U402 survived until October 13th. The U456 and U403 sank the British freighter FORT CONCORD (7,138 tons). U456 survived until May 13th and U403 survived until August 17th. The U528 was sunk by the Royal Navy sloop FLEETWOOD southwest of Ireland.

1944   The U129 sank the British freighter EMPIRE HEATH (6,643 tons). U129 was scuttled in August 1944.
1945   A Royal Air Force No.172 Squadron "Wellington" bomber attacked a German U-boat in the North Sea.

North America
1891   US Secretary of the Treasury Henry Morgenthau was born in New York City. He died on February 6, 1967.
1939   The USN ordered the Curtiss XSB2C "Helldiver" dive-bomber.
1942   The Zionist Congress met in Washington D.C. to discuss forming a Jewish state in Palestine.
1943   Winston Churchill and his party of nearly 100 arrived in New York aboard the RMS QUEEN MARY for the "Trident Conference", also aboard several thousand Axis prisoners of war.
1945   The U873 surrendered at Portsmouth, Virginia.
1963   The USN battleship WEST VIRGINIA's mainmast was dedicated as a memorial on the West Virginia University campus.
1975   The destroyer BELL was expended as a target.
1984   USAAF Staff Sergeant Maynard Smith died in St. Petersburg, Florida. He had won a Medal of Honor over St. Nazaire in 1943.
1986   US Army Staff Sergeant Gerry Kisters died. He had won a Medal of Honor on Sicily.
1995   The USN carrier HORNET was towed from Hunters Point, San Francisco across the bay to Alameda Naval Air Station. She was to be put on public display until October 15, 1995, when she was scheduled to be towed back to Hunters Point. From there she was to be sent to Japan to be scrapped.
2010   USAF fighter ace Colonel Walker "Bud" Mahurin died at the age of 91 from complications of a stroke while at his home in Newport Beach, California. He had scored 20 aerial victories during World War II while flying P47s in Europe and P51s in the Pacific. Later, during the Korean War, he would shoot down 3 more while flying the F86 "Sabre" jet. Captain Ralph Rosen died at the age of 90 in McLean, Virginia. He had scored 6 aerial victories while flying the F6F "Hellcat" in the Pacific.

Pacific
1942   The drifting hulk of the USN tanker NEOSHO was sighted in the Coral Sea by a USN patrol plane. Within the hour the USN destroyer HENLEY was alongside and removing her survivors and the fourteen surviving crewmembers of the sunken USN destroyer SIMS. Both vessels had been attacked earlier by Japanese aircraft. HENLEY then sank the NEOSHO with a torpedo and gunfire. The USN submarine S-42 sank the

IJN minelayer OKINOSHIMA off New Britain. The Japanese freighter ORIDONO MARU was sunk by a mine off Java.

1943 The USN submarine PLUNGER sank the KINAI MARU (8,360 tons). The USN submarine GRAYBACK sank the YODOGAWA MARU (6,441 tons). The US Armys 7th Division landed on Attu Island in the Aleutians. USN forces supporting the operation included the light cruisers RALEIGH, RICHMOND, DETROIT and SANTA FE, as well as five destroyers. Two VC-21 F4Fs "Wildcats" ditched off Attu during the operation. The pilots were rescued by the USN destroyers MONAGHAN and AYLWIN.

1944 The USN submarine STURGEON sank the SEIRYU MARU (1,904 tons). The USN submarine SAND LANCE sank the MITAKESAN MARU (4,441 tons). The USN submarine RASHER sank the CHOI MARU (1,074 tons). The USN submarine CREVALLE evacuated 40 people from Negros in the Philippines.

1945 The USN carriers BUNKER HILL and ENTERPRISE were hit by kamikazes. The USN destroyers HUGH W. HADLEY (29 of her crew died) and EVANS (30 died) were declared constructive losses after kamikaze attacks. Both were sold for scrap in 1947. The US Coast Guard FS-255 was torpedoed off Mindanao and sunk. USAAF B29s attacked Konan, Japan. Private John McKinney, of the 33rd Division, won a Medal of Honor on Luzon. Captain Seymour Terry, of the 96th Division, won a posthumous Medal of Honor on Okinawa. The Australian 6th Division took Wewak, New Guinea. 11th Air Force B24s sank the Japanese freighter AITOKU MARU in the Kuriles.

China-Burma-India

1939 11,300 Bargut tribesmen, assisted by their Japanese advisors, made a raid into Soviet-controlled Mongolia.

1943 The U181 sank the British freighter TINHOW (5,232 tons). The U196 sank the British freighter NAILSEA MEADOW (4,962 tons).

May 12th

Western Europe

1882 German diplomat Ernst von Weizsaeker was born in Stuttgart. He died on August 4, 1954.

1890 German General Kurt Student was born. He commanded the German parachute forces during the war. He died in 1978.

1892 German Field Marshal Ferdinand Schoerner was born in Munich. He died on July 6, 1973 in Munich.

1936 The first flight of the Luftwaffe's twin-engine Me110 fighter took place.

1937   The Royal Navy heavy cruiser MANCHESTER was launched. She was sunk on August 13, 1942.
1938   Portugal recognized Francisco Franco's Spanish government.
1940   The Belgians reinforced their front-line troops. The Germans reached the Meuse River. Royal Air Force Flying Officer Donald Garland and his observer Sergeant Thomas Gray won posthumous Victoria Crosses for an attack on the bridges over the Meuse River at Maastricht in which all five attacking "Battle" bombers were lost. Forty-two Royal Air Force bombers attacked bridges in France, losing eleven "Blenheims". Twelve Royal Air Force bombers attacked road junctions near the German border. Luftwaffe Captain Adolf Galland scored the first of his 104 victories, a Royal Air Force "Hurricane" near Liege. The Luftwaffe dropped thirty-two mines off Belgian and Dutch ports. The Dutch gunboat FRISO was scuttled at Ijsselmeer after a Luftwaffe attack. The Royal Air Force's No.264 Squadron flew the first combat mission with the Boulton Paul "Defiant". Two battalions of the French Foreign Legion landed at Bjerkvik, Norway.
1941   105 Royal Air Force bombers attacked Mannheim, Cologne, and Ludwigshafen in Germany. 100 people were killed in the raid on Cologne.
1943   The American 94th and 95th Bomb Groups (B17) flew their first 8th Air Force missions. The target was the St. Omer airfield in France. 572 Royal Air Force bombers attacked Duisburg, Germany and lost thirty-four aircraft. 1,596 buildings were destroyed and 237 people were killed in the raid.
1944   American 9th Air Force B26s attacked Channel shore batteries and the bridges at Liege, Belgium. 814 American 8th Air Force bombers dropped 1,687 tons of bombs on industrial targets in Germany losing forty-three B17s and three B24s. 735 8th Air Force fighters provided support for the bombers and claimed sixty-six victories for the loss of four P47s and three P51s. Luftwaffe ace Guenther Rall (275 victories) was shot down near Berlin by a USAAF P47. Germany offered Switzerland twelve Me109s in exchange for an interned Me110 (See April 28th). When the Swiss refused, the same deal was offered if they destroyed the aircraft. Royal Air Force night-fighter ace Bob Braham (29 victories) was shot down off Denmark and rescued by the Royal Navy. The German minesweeper M-372 was sunk off Swinemunde by the Soviet Air Force. The Swedish Defense Staff announced that it was going to investigate the crash of a "flying torpedo" (a German V-2) that had come down at Brosarp, Sweden. 120 Royal Air Force bombers attacked Louvain, France and lost five aircraft. 160 civilians were killed in the raid. 111 Royal Air Force bombers attacked Hasselt, France and lost seven aircraft. Twenty-two Royal Air Force "Mosquitoes" dropped mines near the Kiel Canal and lost one aircraft. Five B17s from

the USAAF's 422nd Bomb Squadron dropped 1,740,000 leaflets on targets in Denmark.
1945 British forces officially liberated the island of Guernsey in the English Channel. German S.S. General Sepp Dietrich was captured. American 8th Air Force B17s began evacuating prisoners of war from Stalag Luft I near Barth which would be in the Soviet Zone of occupation. The U802 surrendered at Loch Eriboll.
1946 The Royal Navy escort carrier CHASER was transferred to the USN.
1964 The movie "633 Squadron" began filming at Bovingdon Airfield in East Anglia.

Eastern Europe
1926 Marshal Josef Pilsudski established a military dictatorship in Poland.
1942 The Germans began an offensive in the Crimea.
1944 The last German troops were evacuated from the Crimea. The Soviets took Sevastopol.

Mediterranean
1936 Italy announced its intention of withdrawing from the League of Nations.
1938 Benito Mussolini ordered his Foreign Minister, Count Ciano, to check with Berlin on the possibilities of a 3-power pact with Japan.
1941 The Allied "Tiger" convoy reached Alexandria, Egypt. The cargo consisted of 238 tanks and forty-three "Hurricane" fighters for the British forces fighting in Egypt. The Luftwaffe began operations from Syrian and Iraqi airfields. The Royal Navy gunboat LADYBIRD (625 tons and launched in 1916) was sunk off Libya by the Luftwaffe.
1943 German General Hans von Arnim surrendered 130,000 Germans and 180,000 Italians of the DAK in Tunisia. Since June 10, 1940 the Axis had lost 97,500 men, 7,600 aircraft, 6,200 cannon, 2,550 tanks, 70,000 vehicles and 624 ships in the Theater. USAAF B26s attacked Palermo, Marsal and Catania on Sicily.
1944 At 0300, Moroccan forces took Monte Faito, Italy. Polish forces almost reached the Cassino Abbey, but were driven back. French Admiral Edmond Derrien was sentenced to life in prison for collaboration by an Algiers court. The Allies crossed the Rapido and Garigliano Rivers in Italy. Luftwaffe Ju88s attacked the American 12th Air Force bases on Corsica destroying twenty-three aircraft. 2nd Lieutenant Charles Shea, of the 88th Division, won a Medal of Honor near Mount Damiano. Kamal Ram, of the 3/8th Punjab Regiment, and Captain R. Wakeford, of the Hampshire Regiment, won Victoria Crosses at Cassino in Italy. The American 15th Air Force attacked rail, aircraft and troop targets in Italy.

Atlantic

1942 The U124 sank the British freighters EMPIRE DELL (catapult-armed merchantman-7,065 tons), CRISTALES (5,389 tons) and LLANOVER (4,959 tons) and the Greek freighter MOUNT PARNES (4,371 tons). U124 survived until April 2, 1943. The U94 sank the Panamanian freighter COCLE (5,630 tons). U94 survived until August 28th. The U553 sank the British freighter NICOYA (5,364 tons). U553 survived until January 28, 1943. The U68 sank the Norwegian tanker LISE (6,826 tons). The U558 sank the Royal Navy trawler BEDFORDSHIRE. U558 survived until July 20, 1943. The U507 sank the American tanker VIRGINIA (10,731 tons- 26 dead). U507 survived until January 13, 1943. The US Coast Guard cutter SPENCER rescued fifty-two survivors from the freighters MOUNT PARNES and CRISTALES. The Soviet submarine K-23 was sunk by German surface craft off Oskafjord, Norway. Vichy French Admiral Georges Robert agreed to immobilize French ships in West Indies ports that were under his jurisdiction.

1943 The U221 sank the Norwegian tanker SANDANGER (9,432 tons). U221 survived until September 27th. The U603 sank the Norwegian freighter BRAND (4,819 tons). U603 survived until March 1, 1944. The U186 was sunk by the Royal Navy destroyer HESPERUS north of the Azores. Brazilian fishermen rescued the sole survivor of the Italian submarine ARCHIMEDE, which had been sunk by a USN PBY on April 15th. The "Fido" (an Allied airborne acoustic torpedo) was used for the first time.

1945 The last Murmansk convoy (JW-67) left Clyde, Scotland. The U234 surrendered to USN forces. Aboard was General Kessler who was to have been the new German Air Attaché to Tokyo.

North America

1938 The carrier ENTERPRISE was commissioned. She was scrapped in 1958.
1941 Japanese Ambassador Nomura presented a proposal for a "just peace in the Pacific" to Secretary of State Cordell Hull. The submarine DRUM was launched. She was still on active duty in 1962.
1942 The battleship MASSACHUSETTS was commissioned. She would be preserved as a memorial in her namesake state. The destroyer PARKER was launched. She was stricken in 1971.
1943 The Trident Conference in Washington D.C. began formal planning for the invasion of Italy. The escort carrier CORREGIDOR was launched. She was scrapped in New Orleans in 1960.
1944 A Southern Pacific train was hit by US Army artillery fire near San Luis Obispo, California. Miss Vertie Bea Loggins, seriously wounded in the incident, was awarded $5,000 in damages on October 24, 1945.

1945   The U889 surrendered at St. John's, Newfoundland. The carrier TARAWA was launched. She was stricken in 1967. The destroyer-transport SCHLEY was sold for scrap.
1959   The B24 "Strawberry Bitch" was flown from Davis-Monthan Air Force Base in Arizona to the USAF Museum at Wright-Patterson in Ohio.
1970   The destroyer HAYNESWORTH was sold to Taiwan.
1972   The light cruiser WILKES-BARRE was expended off Florida in explosives experiments off Florida.
2010   Colonel Jerry Collinsworth died at the age 90 in Phoenix, Arizona. He had scored 6 aerial victories while flying the "Spitfire" in the Mediterranean Theater.

Pacific
1930   The IJN heavy cruiser TAKAO was launched. She was declared a constructive loss on July 31, 1945.
1942   The USN submarine S-44 sank the IJN repair ship SHOEI MARU (5,644 tons) off Cape St. George.
1943   The USN submarine GUDGEON sank the SUMATRA MARU (5,861 tons). The IJN submarine I-180 damaged the Australian freighters ORMISTON (5,832 tons) and CARADALE (1,881 tons). The USN submarine STEELHEAD laid mines off Erimo Saki, Japan. The IJN submarine I-30 was sunk by the USN destroyer FRAZIER off Attu in the Aleutians after attempting to attack the battleship PENNSYLVANIA. A USN force of cruisers and destroyers (commanded by Ainsworth) bombarded Munda and Vila in the Solomons. A turret explosion aboard the USN light cruiser NASHVILLE killed eighteen and wounded seventeen.
1944   Heavy fighting continued around Hollandia and Aitape on New Guinea. The USN submarine TAUTOG sank the BANEI MARU No.2 (1,186 tons). The Japanese transport KASUMI MARU was sunk by a mine in the Strait of Malacca.
1945   The USN battleship NEW MEXICO was hit by a Japanese kamikaze, fifty-five of her crew died. Corporal J.B. Mackey, of the Australian Pioneer Battalion, won a posthumous Victoria Cross on North Borneo. The US Armys 108th Regiment took Del Monte Airfield on Mindanao. The USN submarine RATON sank the REKIZAN MARU (1,311 tons).

China-Burma-India
1942   The American Volunteer Group strafed Hanoi's airfields, destroying fifteen Japanese aircraft and losing one.
1943   The Indian 26th Division evacuated Maungdaw, Burma. U195 damaged the American freighter CAPE NEDDICK (6,797 tons).

1944 The Allied advance was stopped near Tingkrukawng, Burma by Japanese forces.

May 13th

Western Europe
1900 German General Karl Wolff was born on Darmstadt. He died in 1975.
1940 The Germans crossed the Meuse River near Sedan, France. German forces took Liege and reached Rotterdam. Twelve Royal Air Force bombers attacked road junctions on the German border. Brian Horrocks, later to command British Army's XXX Corps, took command of the 2nd Battalion of the Middlesex Regiment at Louvain, Belgium. The British advanced from Harstad towards Narvik in Norway. French troops landed ten miles north of Narvik, Norway. The British House of Commons gave Prime Minister Winston Churchill a 318-0 vote of confidence. Churchill made his "...blood and toil and tears and sweat" speech in the House of Commons. The British War Cabinet decided to send thirty-two more "Hurricane" fighters to France. Holland's Queen Wilhelmina was evacuated aboard the Royal Navy destroyer HEREWARD. The Dutch government was evacuated aboard the Royal Navy destroyer WINDSOR. The Dutch steamer PHRONTIS (6,181 tons) carried 900 German prisoners of war to Britain.
1941 Forty-four Royal Air Force "Blenheims" attacked German shipping and lost two aircraft. Martin Bormann assumed many of Rudolf Hess' former duties as a result of Hess' flight to Scotland (See May 11th). German agent Karl Richter was captured in Hertfordshire, Britain and was executed seven months later.
1942 Four Royal Air Force "Wellingtons" attacked Mulheim, Germany. At 0404, the German torpedo boat ILTIS was sunk off Boulogne, France by the Royal Navy's MTB-221. Thirty-four of her crew died. At 0409, the German torpedo boat SEEADLER was sunk off Boulogne by the Royal Navy's MTB-219. Eighty-four of her crew died.
1943 Eighteen Royal Air Force bombers attacked targets in France and lost one B25 "Mitchell". Twelve USAAF B26s attacked a generating plant at Ijmuiden, Holland. The American 8th Air Force's 3rd Division (B17) was activated. It would join the 1st (B17) and the 2nd (B24) that were already operating with that unit. Eighty-eight 8th Air Force B17s dropped 218 tons of bombs on the Meaulte airfield in France and lost three aircraft. Thirty-one 8th Air Force B17s dropped seventy-three tons of bombs on the St. Omer/Longuenesse airfield in France and lost one aircraft. 442 Royal Air Force bombers attacked Bochum, Germany and lost twenty-four aircraft.

394 buildings were destroyed and 302 people were killed in the raid. 168 Royal Air Force bombers attacked Pilsen, Czechoslovakia and lost nine aircraft. Twelve Royal Air Force "Mosquitoes" attacked Berlin and lost one aircraft.

1944   American 9th Air Force B26s attacked Abbeville airfields and Channel shore-batteries. 691 American 8th Air Force bombers dropped 1,833 tons of bombs on Stettin, Straslund, Tutow and Osnabruck in Germany and lost eleven B17s and one B24. 1,107 8th and 9th Air Force fighters escorted the bombers and claimed seventy-three victories for the loss of nine aircraft (one P51 landed in Sweden).

1945   A British naval force entered Oslo, Norway. Aboard the cruiser DEVONSHIRE was Norwegian Crown Prince Olaf. The U956 surrendered at Loch Eriboll.

1948   The Royal Navy battleship RESOLUTION was sold for scrap.

1981   A memorial to the American 8th Air Force's 390th Bomb Group (B17) was dedicated at Framlingham.

Mediterranean

1941   The British failed to relieve Tobruk, Libya. The Royal Navy submarine UNDAUNTED was sunk by Italian surface craft off Tripoli.

1942   The Luftwaffe attacked Malta.

1943   The Italian submarine MOCENIGO was sunk at Cagliari, Sardinia during a raid by 107 USAAF B17s. The Royal Navy cruiser ORION bombarded Pantelleria. USAAF B24s attacked Augusta, Sicily.

1944   The British 4th Division expanded its bridgehead over the Rapido River. The 2nd Moroccan Division took Monte Girofano and Monte Maio. The 4th Moroccan and 3rd Algerian Divisions took Castelforte and Damiano, after they broke through the "Gustav Line". The US Army's 88th Division took Santa Maria Infante. The American 15th Air Force attacked rail targets in Italy. Polish attacks on Monte Cassino were repulsed. The German minesweeper R-215 was sunk by Allied fighter-bombers off Chiavari.

Atlantic

1941   The Royal Navy armed merchant cruiser SALOPIAN (10,549 tons) was sunk by the U98. U98 survived until November 19, 1942. The U105 sank the British freighter BENVRACKLE (6,434 tons). U105 survived until June 2, 1943. The U111 sank the British freighter SOMERSBY (5,170 tons). U111 survived until October 4th.

1942   The U162 sank the American tanker ESSO HOUSTON (7,699 tons-1 dead). U162 survived until September 3rd. The U128 sank the British freighter DENPARK (3,491 tons). U128 survived until May 17, 1943.

The U94 sank the British freighter BATNA (4,399 tons) and the Swedish freighter TOLKEN (4,471 tons). U94 survived until August 28th. The U156 sank the Dutch freighter KOENJIT (4,551 tons) and the British freighter CITY OF MELBOURNE (6,630 tons). U156 survived until March 8, 1943. The U69 sank the American freighter NORLANTIC (2,606 tons-3 dead). U69 survived until February 17, 1943. The U506 sank the SS GULFPENN (8,862 tons-13 dead). U506 survived until July 12, 1943.

1943 The U176 sank the American tanker NICKELINER (2,249 tons) and the Cuban tanker MAMBI (1,983 tons). U176 survived until May 15th. The U456 was sunk by the Royal Navy frigate LAGAN and the Royal Canadian Navy corvette DRUMHELLER.

1944 The IJN submarine Ro-501, built in Germany as the U1224, was sunk the USN destroyer escort ROBINSON.

North America

1940 Igor Sikorsky's VS-300 helicopter made its first flight at Stratford, Connecticut.

1942 The US Material Command signed a contract for wooden framed "Waco" gliders. This was in the event of a shortage of steel tubing which was used in the original design.

1943 The USN battleship IDAHO and the destroyer PHELPS silenced Japanese shore batteries on Attu.

1945 The U1228 surrendered at Portsmouth, Virginia. U858 surrendered in the Delaware estuary.

Pacific

1940 German mines were discovered in the waters off Cape Agulhas, Australia.

1942 The USN submarine DRUM sank the SHONAN MARU (5,356 tons) off Honshu. RAAF "Hudsons" attacked Japanese shipping off Ambon in the East Indies and sank TAIFOKU MARU and damaged the gunboat TAIKO MARU. Japanese Naval Air Force ace Toshiaki Honda (15 victories) was killed in action over Port Moresby, New Guinea by USAAF P39s. The Japanese freighter NAGASAKI MARU was sunk off Nagasaki by a Japanese-laid mine.

1943 The American 13th Air Force attacked Kahili and Ballale airfields. USN TF-18 (commanded by Ainsworth) bombarded Munda and Vila in the Solomons. The light cruiser NASHVILLE and the destroyers CHEVALIER and NICHOLAS were all damaged by gun mount explosions.

1944 The USN submarine POGY sank the AWA MARU (4,532 tons).

1945 The USN destroyer BACHE (41 of her crew died) and the destroyer escort BRIGHT were hit by Japanese kamikazes. USN carriers attacked Kyushu.

The USN submarine BAYA sank the YOSEI MARU (2,594 tons) and the SHOSEI MARU No.15 (43 tons). The USN submarine PLAICE sank the NISSHIN MARU (111 tons). The USN submarine CERO sank the SHINNAN MARU (1,025 tons).

China-Burma-India

1943   The Royal Air Force attacked Maungdaw, Burma.
1944   Allied troops attempted to bypass Japanese forces at Tingkrukawng, Burma.
1945   Lachiman Gurung, of the 4/8th Gurkha Rifles, won a Victoria Cross in Burma. The 82nd West African Division took Gwa, Burma.

May 14th

Western Europe

1880   German Field Marshal Wilhelm List was born in Oberkirchberg. He would die in 1971.
1893   British airman William Sholto Douglas was born in Scotland. During WWI, he won a Military Cross and Distinguished Flying Cross. After the war he became a civilian pilot for the Handley Page Company, but by 1920 he had grown bored with civilian life and returned to the Royal Air Force. By 1938, he was an air vice marshal and served as Deputy Chief of Air Staff. During the "Battle of Britain" he was one of the severest critics of Dowding's tactics. He succeeded Dowding as Commander of Fighter Command on November 25, 1940. At the end of 1942, he was sent to the Mediterranean to serve as Tedder's deputy in the Middle East Air Force. Three months later he assumed command of that unit. By the time of the Normandy invasion, he was in command of Coastal Command and commander of the British Expeditionary Air Forces. In 1946, he promoted to Marshal of the Royal Air Force. In June of that year he replaced Bernard Montgomery as commander of British forces in Europe. He retired in 1948. He died on October 29, 1969.
1939   The first flight of the Royal Air Forces Short "Stirling" bomber took place.
1940   During the day, the Luftwaffe fighters flew 814 sorties over the Western Front on which they shot down ninety Allied aircraft. At 1330, the Luftwaffe attacked Rotterdam, Holland killing 900 people and destroying 25,000 buildings. The Belgian liner VILLE DE BRUGES (13,869 tons-the former American PRESIDENT HARDING) was sunk in the Scheldt by the Luftwaffe. The Dutch gunboat JOHAN MAURITS VAN NASSAU was sunk off Callantsoog by the Luftwaffe. The Dutch gunboat BRINIO was scuttled at Ijsselmeer after being damaged in an air raid. The Dutch

destroyers TJERK HIDDES and GERARD CALLENBURGH were scuttled at Rotterdam. The HIDDES was scrapped and the CALLENBURGH was salvaged by the Germans and renamed ZH-1 (See June 9, 1944). The Dutch steamer TEXELSTROOM (1,617 tons) carried 300 German prisoners of war to Britain. Allied bombers attacked German bridges over the Meuse near Sedan; eighty-five aircraft were lost. Thirty Royal Air Force bombers attacked communications targets in Germany and Holland, losing one "Hampden". Twenty-two Royal Air Force bombers dropped mines in the Baltic. French Premier, Paul Reynard, informed the British that the Germans had broken through the Allied lines south of Sedan, France and then requested another ten fighter squadrons from the Royal Air Force. A BBC broadcast called for information on all private boats of between 60 and 100 feet in length in preparation for an evacuation of the Allied Expeditionary Force from the area around Dunkirk, France. German forces took Mo-I-Rana in northern Norway. The British government appealed for Local Defense Volunteers (Home Guard).

1941 The French police arrested 3,700 Jews in Paris. A bomb was thrown at a German officer's club in Amsterdam, Holland.

1942 The Royal Air Force sank the German minesweepers M-26 and M-256 off Normandy. The German minesweeping trawler M-1307 was sunk by a mine off Esbjerg. The 689th Quartermaster Company, of the American 8th Air Force, arrived in Monmouth, Britain. They were the second group of men from that unit to land in Britain.

1943 At 0340, the German minesweeper M-8 was sunk off the Hook of Holland by the Royal Navy's MTB-232. 126 American 8th Air Force B17s and B24s dropped 291 tons of bombs on Kiel, Germany and lost three B17s and five B24s. The 44th Bomb Group (B24) received a Distinguished Unit Citation for this mission which was also the first mission for the 92nd Bomb Group (B17) since October 9, 1942. Luftwaffe ace Friedrich Rupp (53 victories) was killed in action over Germany. Thirty-eight 8th Air Force B17s dropped eighty-six tons of bombs on Antwerp, Belgium and lost one aircraft. Thirty-four 8th Air Force B17s dropped seventy-five tons of bombs on Courtrai, France and lost two aircraft. It was the first mission for the 96th and 351st Bomb Groups. American film actor Clark Gable flew with the 351st on the mission. Twelve American 322nd Squadron B26s attacked the Velsen Generating Plant in Ijmuiden, Holland and lost one aircraft. It was the first 8th Air Force operation for the type. 118 8th Air Force P47s escorted the Antwerp raid and lost one aircraft. Five Royal Air Force "Wellingtons" dropped leaflets over France.

1944 Forty-one Royal Air Force "Mosquitoes" attacked targets in Germany. The U1234 was lost in a collision with the tug ANTON in the Baltic.

1945   The German S-boat tender CARL PETERS and TFA-3 (the ex-Danish torpedo boat DRAGEN) were sunk by mines in the Baltic. The U764 and U1010 surrendered at Loch Eriboll. U244, U516 and U1231 surrendered at Lough Foyle. U485 and U541 surrendered at Gibraltar. U2336 surrendered at Dundee. Luftwaffe "Stuka" ace Hans Rudel was flown to London for interrogation. Wolfgang Luth, Germanys second highest scoring U-boat ace, was killed when he failed to answer a sentry's challenge outside Doenitz' headquarters in Flensburg, Germany.
1950   Royal Air Force ace Wing Commander R. Harries (20 victories) died in an aircraft accident.
1957   German S.S. General Sepp Dietrich was sentenced to eighteen months for his part in the May 30, 1934 S.A. purge.
1978   A monument to American 8th Air Force veterans was dedicated at Steeple Morden Airfield in Britain.
1983   Hermann Goering's yacht CARIN II was impounded by German police in connection with the "Hitler Diaries" fraud of 1980-83.

Eastern Europe
1942   The Soviet destroyer DZERHINSKI was sunk at Sevastopol by a mine. The Soviet transport MORYAK was sunk at Rostov by the Luftwaffe. Luftwaffe ace Hermann Graf became the 7th fighter pilot to reach 100 aerial victories.
1945   150,000 German troops surrendered in East Prussia. Another 180,000 surrendered in northern Latvia.

Mediterranean
1941   The Luftwaffe's Fliegerkorps VIII increased its attacks on the island of Crete. Since January 16th, sixty-two German, fifteen Italian and thirty-two British aircraft had been shot down over the island. Luftwaffe ace Sophus Baagoe (14 victories) was killed in action over Crete. Two Royal Air Force P40s and three "Blenheims" attacked the Luftwaffe airfields at Palmyra. It was the first combat for the P40.
1942   The Greek freighter MOUNT OLYMPOS (6,692 tons) and the Norwegian freighter HAV were sunk by mines.
1943   Forty-six USAAF B17s attacked Civitavecchia, Italy.
1944   The British 78th Division crossed the Rapido River and established a bridgehead. First Lieutenant Robert Wauch, of the 85th Division, won a posthumous Medal of Honor near Tremensucli, Italy. The U616 damaged the American tanker G.S. WALDEN (10,627 tons) and the British freighter FORT FIDLER (7,127 tons). U616 was then sunk by USN destroyers NIELDS, CLEAVES, ELLYSON, HILARY P. JONES, RODMAN,

HAMBLETON, MACOMB and EMMONS. The American 12th Air Force dropped 503 tons of bombs on airfields. The American 15th Air Force attacked rail and aircraft targets in Italy. 15th Air Force P38 ace Robert Seidman (5 victories) was killed in action over Villaorba, Italy.

Atlantic

1940   The armed merchant cruiser ORION rendezvoused with the German tanker WINNETOU for refueling.

1941   The German armed merchant cruiser ATLANTIS took the British freighter RABAUL (5,618 tons).

1942   The Royal Navy light cruiser TRINIDAD was damaged by one of her own torpedoes in the Barents Sea and was later scuttled, 81 of her crew died. The U506 sank the American tanker DAVID MCKELVEY (6,821 tons- 17 dead). U506 survived until July 12, 1943. The U162 sank the British tanker BRITISH COLONY (6,917 tons). U162 survived until September 3rd. The U155 sank the Belgian freighter BRABANT (2,483 tons). U155 survived the war. The U564 sank the Mexican tanker PORTRERO DEL LLANO (4,000 tons). U564 survived until June 14, 1943. The US Coast Guard cutters NIKE rescued nine survivors and TUCKAHOE rescued another nine from the tanker PORTRERO DEL LLANO. The U125 sank the Honduran freighter COMAYAGUA (2,493 tons). U125 survived until May 6, 1943. The U213 laid mines off St. John's, Newfoundland. The Norwegian tanker HAVPRINS rescued eighteen survivors from the American tanker ESSO HOUSTON which had been sunk by U162. The Norwegian freighter NORSOL rescued two survivors from the American freighter DAVID MCKELVY which had been sunk by U506.

1943   The U89 was sunk by the Royal Navy escort carrier BITER, the destroyer BROADWAY and the frigate LAGAN. The U266 was sunk by the Royal Air Force's No.86 Squadron southwest of Eire. The U657 was sunk by USN's VP-48 southwest of Iceland.

1944   The Royal Air Force sank the German minesweeper M-435.

North America

1882   Admiral Husband Kimmel was born in Henderson, Kentucky. He graduated 13th in his 1904 Annapolis class of 62. He was promoted to rear admiral in 1937. On February 1, 1941 he was promoted over thirty-two more senior officers to become CINCPAC. He was replaced in that position by Chester Nimitz ten days after the Japanese attack on Pear Harbor on December 7th. He died on May 14, 1968 in Groton, Connecticut.

1938   The destroyers MAYRANT and TRIPPE were launched. They were scuttled in 1948, after being used as targets at the Bikini A-bomb tests in 1946.

1942   In seventeen Eastern states, motorists were restricted to three gallons of gasoline a week for "non-essential" use of their vehicles. The first flight of the "Waco" glider took place.
1944   The escort carrier LUNGA POINT was commissioned. She was scrapped in 1960. The submarines MORAY and RONCADOR were launched. They were both still on active duty in 1962.
1945   The U805 and U234 surrendered at Portsmouth, Virginia.
1954   The U505 began a 3,000-mile tow trip from Portsmouth, Virginia up the St. Lawrence Seaway to Chicago.
1968   Admiral Husband E. Kimmel, Pacific Fleet Commander at Pearl Harbor on December 7, 1941, died.

Pacific
1942   The US Army's 32nd Division arrived in Australia.
1943   Thirteen USAAF B25s attacked Gasmata Airfield on New Guinea. One USAAF B24 and three USN F4Fs were shot down over Attu in the Aleutians. USMC TBFs sank the Japanese freighter HOUN MARU off Tonolei, Bougainville. The USN minesweeper DASH rescued 25 survivors from the American freighter PHOEBE A. HEARST on April 30th by I-19. A USN F4F ditched off Attu and the pilot was rescued by the USN destroyer AYLWIN. The IJN submarine I-177 sank the Australian hospital ship CENTAUR (3,222 tons-268 dead).
1944   The Japanese began retreating towards Rabaul on New Britain. The American 7th Air Force dropped 240 tons on Jaluit in the Marshalls. The USN submarine BONEFISH sank the IJN destroyer INAZUMI off Tawi Tawi, Borneo. The USN submarine BOWFIN sank the MIYAMA MARU (4,667 tons). The USN submarine ASPRO sank the BISAN MARU (4,500 tons). The USN submarine SAND LANCE sank the KOHO MARU (4,291 tons).
1945   472 USAAF B29s dropped 2,515 tons of bombs on Nagoya, burning out 3.6 square miles of the city. The USN carrier ENTERPRISE was hit by a kamikaze. Private First-Class James Diamond, of the 24th Division, won a posthumous Medal of Honor on Mindanao. USMC Corporal Louis Hauge, of the 1st Division, won a posthumous Medal of Honor on Okinawa. The Australian 6th Division landed at Wewak, New Guinea and captured the airfield there. The USN submarine SAND LANCE sank the YOSHINO MARU (220 tons).
1998   An American expedition (See North America-April 13th) located the wreck of the USN aircraft carrier YORKTOWN off Midway Atoll northwest of Hawaii.

China-Burma-India

1939 Two companies of Japanese regulars made a raid into Mongolia.
1941 Allied reinforcements arrived in Singapore.
1942 Japanese forces took Kalewa, Burma.

May 15th

Western Europe

1920 The Royal Navy battlecruiser HOOD was commissioned. She would be sunk in May of 1941 by the German battleship BISMARCK and heavy cruiser PRINZ EUGEN.

1940 At 0930, the Dutch Army Commander, General Winkelman, signed a surrender document. During the campaign, Dutch Army casualties were 2,100 killed and 2,700 wounded. The Germans broke through the Allied lines between Namur and Louvian. The Royal Navy destroyer VALENTINE was damaged in the Scheldt and beached to provide anti/aircraft support for Allied forces. The German panzers were halted in France, by order of Adolf Hitler himself. Ninety-nine Royal Air Force bombers attacked the Ruhr area of Germany with no losses. Twenty-four Royal Air Force bombers attacked communication targets in Belgium, losing three "Blenheims". Allied forces were landed at Bodo in northern Norway. They were to stop German units moving north from Trondheim from reaching the embattled town of Narvik. British Prime Minister Churchill drafted his first message to FDR concerning the loan of forty to fifty USN destroyers. He would raise the question again on July 11th.

1941 Twenty Royal Air Force "Blenheims" attacked German shipping and lost two aircraft. The first flights of the Royal Air Force's "Mosquito" and the Gloster jet interceptor E28/39 took place. 101 Royal Air Force bombers attacked Hannover, Germany and lost three aircraft. One Royal Air Force "Manchester" was lost over Berlin.

1942 Fifty Royal Air Force bombers dropped mines in the Baltic and lost four aircraft.

1943 Thirty-six Royal Air Force bombers attacked targets in France. Seventy-six American 8th Air Force B17s dropped 186 tons of bombs on Heligoland and Wangerooge Isle and lost five aircraft. Fifty-nine 8th Air Force B17s dropped 137 tons of bombs on Emden, Germany and lost one aircraft. 116 8th Air Force P47s flew sweeps over Holland and lost one aircraft to engine failure.

1944 SHAEF (Supreme Headquarters Allied Expeditionary Force) made their last presentation of the D-Day plans at St. Paul's School in Kensington. A Luftwaffe KG-200 B17 was shot down. KG-200 was a Luftwaffe unit that specialized in flying captured Allied aircraft and testing new types for the Luftwaffe. 128 American 8th Air Force B17s and B24s dropped 485 tons of bombs on the Siracourt and Mimoyecques V-1 rocket launching sites in France. 104 8th Air Force P51s provided support for the bombers and lost one aircraft. Forty-three Royal Air Force "Mosquitoes" attacked targets in France and Germany. Forty-three Royal Air Force bombers dropped mines and lost three "Lancasters". Three B17s from the USAAF's 422nd Bomb Squadron dropped 1,100,000 leaflets on ten different targets in France and Belgium. The USAAF's 801st Bomb Group dispatched five B24s on "Carpetbagger" missions.

1945   German Field Marshal Albert Kesselring was captured near Berchtesgaden by the US Army's 101st Airborne Division.

1954   German General Heinz Guderian died in Fussen.

1959   The proto-type of the Royal Air Force's "Mosquito" was put on display at the Mosquito Museum at Salisbury Hall in St. Albans north of London.

2010   A memorial was dedicated at Castle Douglas, Kirkcudbrightshire to Royal Air Force Squadron Leader Patrick Gifford. He was the first RAF pilot to shoot down a German bomber during the war. It occurred on October 16, 1939 when, while flying a "Spitfire" near Prestonpans, East Lothian, he downed one of 12 aircraft which had attacked Royal Navy units in the Firth of Forth. Gifford would later die over Belgium on May 16, 1940 while flying a "Hurricane".

Eastern Europe

1941   This was the original date for the German invasion of Russia. But it would be postponed until June 20th due to German intervention in the Mediterranean Theater. Soviet Marshal Zhukov presented a plan for a pre-emptive strike against Germany, but it was rejected by Stalin.

1942   Luftwaffe "Stuka" dive-bombers attacked Murmansk sinking the American freighter YAKA (6,187 tons) and damaging the Soviet submarine SHCH-403. German forces retook Kerch. Soviet casualties at Kerch were 176,000.

1944   The first of 380,000 Hungarian Jews were sent to the concentration camp at Auschwitz.

1945   150,000 German troops surrendered near Slovenigradesk, Yugoslavia.

Mediterranean

1941   The Luftwaffe began attacking the island of Crete. "Ultra" intercepts revealed that the German invasion of Crete had been postponed from the 17th to the 19th of the month. British forces began offensive to retake Halfaya Pass on the Egyptian-Libyan border.

1942   The Luftwaffe attacked Malta.
1943   The German trawler UJ-2213 was sunk fifteen miles south of Nice, France by the British submarine SICKLE. USAAF B26s attacked Cagliari, Sicily.
1944   The Germans began evacuating their "Gustav Line" in Italy. The French 1st Motorized Division took San Giorgio, Italy. The U731 was sunk off Tangiers by the Royal Navy sloop KILMARNOCK and trawler BLACKFLY. The British cruiser DIDO bombarded targets around the Gulf of Gaeta.

Atlantic
1940   The Luftwaffe sank the transport CHROBY off Norway.
1941   The U43 sank the French sailing ship NOTRE DAME DU CHATELET (488 tons). U43 survived until July 30, 1943. The U105 sank the British freighter BENEVENUE (5,920 tons). U105 survived until June 2, 1943.
1942   A Royal Air Force No.407 Squadron "Hudson" sank the German trawler V-2002 in the North Sea. The U156 sank the Norwegian freighter SILJESTAD (4,301 tons) and the Yugoslavian freighter KUPA (4,382 tons). U156 survived until March 8, 1943.
1943   The U105 sank the Greek freighter MAROUSSIO LOGOTHETIS (4,669 tons). U105 survived until June 2, 1943. The U607 sank the Irish freighter IRISH OAK (5,589 tons). U607 survived until July 13th. The U176 was sunk by the Cuban sub chaser CS-13 north of Havana. The U463 was sunk by the Royal Air Force's No.58 Squadron southwest of the Scillies. The U753 was lost in the North Atlantic.
1945   The U234 surrendered to the US Coast Guard cutter FORSYTH.

North America
1887   Admiral John Hoover was born in Ohio. He graduated 73rd in his 1906 Annapolis class of 86. At the beginning of the war, he commanded the Caribbean Sea Frontier. In 1942 he was promoted to vice-admiral and commanded the land-based air operations in the Gilberts, Marshalls, and Marianas. By the end of the war, he was in command of the Forward Areas of the Pacific. He retired on July 1, 1948. He died on December 2, 1970 in Bethesda, Maryland.
1937   The destroyer WARRINGTON was launched. She was lost September 13, 1944.
1940   The salvaged submarine SQUALIS was recommissioned as SAILFISH. She had been lost the previous year in a training accident. As the SAILFISH she was scrapped in 1948.
1941   American forces moved into Argentia, Nova Scotia. The battleship WASHINGTON was commissioned. She was scrapped in 1961.

Year	Event

1942 Gasoline (three gallons per week) and bicycles were rationed in America. The red ball center of the national insigne on USAAF aircraft was eliminated. It had resulted in some confusion with the red "meatball" used on Japanese aircraft. USAAF "Pursuit" units were reclassified as "Fighter" units. The escort carrier CORE and the light cruiser MOBILE (awarded eleven battle stars during the war) were launched. CORE was converted into a merchant ship in 1959 and MOBILE was scrapped in Portland, Oregon in 1960.

1943 The "Trident Conference" began in Washington D.C.

1945 A Japanese balloon-bomb was found near Kelvington, Saskatchewan.

1952 The USN destroyer escort BRONSTEIN was sold to Uruguay. She had participated in the sinking of three U-boats.

1957 The destroyers CAPP and DAVID W. TAYLOR were sold to Spain.

1959 Major Douglas Radney retired. He had flown on the "Doolittle Raid".

1976 USN historian Admiral Samuel Elliott Morison died in Boston, Massachusetts. He had been responsible for writing the USN's official history of World War II.

1992 USN Admiral Harold Miller died. He had been Pacific Fleet Commander Admiral Chester Nimitz' publicity aide during the war.

2004 USAAF Colonel Robert Morgan died as a result of injuries sustained in a fall while leaving an air show in April. He had been the pilot of the B17 "Memphis Belle", the first B17 to complete 25 missions in the ETO. He later flew missions in the PTO in B29s.

2012 USAAF Lieutenant Colonel Donald Bryan died in Adel, Georgia at the age of 90. He had been credited with 13 aerial victories over Europe while flying P47s and P51s.

Pacific

1932 Japan's Prime Minister Tsuyoshi Inukai was assassinated by the military.

1942 In Honolulu, a cryptanalyst team led by Lieutenant Commander Joseph J. Rochefort broke a top-secret Japanese naval code. It eventually gave them the information that the Japanese would be leaving the Home Islands on May 20th with the purpose of attacking Midway and the Aleutians some time after May 24th. The USN submarine TUNA sank the TOYOHARA MARU (805 tons) off Korea.

1943 The USN submarine GAR sank the MEIKAI MARU (3,179 tons) and the INDUS MARU (4,361 tons). The US Army's 7th Division continued its attack at Massacre Bay on Attu in the Aleutians. 7th Air Force B24s attacked Wake Island. An American 11th Air Force B24 was shot down over Japanese-held Attu.

1944 The USN submarine ASPRO sank the JOKUJA MARU (6,440 tons).

1945   USMC Major Henry Courtney, of the 6th Division, won a posthumous Medal of Honor on Okinawa. Private E. Kenna, of the Australian 4th Infantry Battalion, won a Victoria Cross on New Guinea. An American 11th Air Force B24 was interned in Russia. The USN submarine HAMMERHEAD sank the TOTTORI MARU (5,978 tons). The USN submarine Sea POACHER sank the UME MARU No.56 (100 tons). The USN submarine SHAD sank the MAKO MARU (1,398 tons).

China-Burma-India
1943   Seven American 10th Air Force B24s attacked Lashio, Burma. The Royal Air Force attacked Akyab, Burma.
1945   The Japanese heavy cruiser HAGURO and the destroyer KAMIKAZE left Singapore in a second attempt to evacuate the garrisons in the Andamans and the Nicobars. The first had been made on the 10th. They were sighted by an aircraft from the British escort carrier SHAH. During the night, HAGURO was sunk off Penang by the Royal Navy destroyers SAUMEREZ, VENUS, VIGILANT, VIRAGO and VERULAM. The SAUMEREZ was damaged during the action. The KAMIKAZE escaped with slight damage. Aircraft from the British escort carriers HUNTER and KHEDIVE attacked the Andaman Islands.

May 16th

Western Europe
1892   German General Dietrich von Saucken was born.
1940   The German forces were sixty miles east of Sedan, France. British Prime Minister Winston Churchill arrived in Paris to meet with Reynaud, the French Premier. Twenty-one Royal Air Force bombers attacked targets in Germany and lost one "Wellington". Churchill authorized the transfer of four more British fighter squadrons to France. The French Air Force reported that it had lost 500 of its 650 operational fighters. Second Lieutenant R. Annard, of the Durham Light Infantry, won a Victoria Cross in Belgium.
1941   Eight Royal Air Force "Blenheims" attacked German shipping off Norway and lost one aircraft. Ninety-three Royal Air Force bombers attacked Cologne, Germany and lost one "Whitley".
1942   Fourteen Royal Air Force bombers dropped mines in the Baltic.
1943   Seventeen Royal Air Force bombers attacked targets in France. 114 American 8th Air Force P47s flew a sweep over the Dunkirk area of France claiming two victories and losing one of their own. At 2050, nineteen "Lancasters" carrying specially-built 6,500-pound bombs of the Royal

Air Force's No.617 Squadron took off for their "Dam Buster's Raid" on the Ruhr valley dams. The commander of the force was 25-year-old Wing Commander Guy Gibson. Gibson had flown 172 missions and had been awarded a Distinguished Service Order and Bar as well as a Distinguished Flying Cross. The aircraft were divided into three formations. The first was composed of nine aircraft and were to attack the Mohne Dam. When that dam was breached, any with their bombs still aboard were to proceed to the Eder Dam. The second formation of five aircraft was to bomb the Sorpe Dam. A third formation was to serve as a mobile reserve. At 2235, the first of the bombers crossed the Dutch coast. Two were damaged by German anti-aircraft fire and forced to return to base without dropping their bombs. Of the remaining seventeen, five were shot down before reaching their targets. The surviving twelve sent five aircraft to the Mohne Dam, three to the Eder, two to the Sorpe and one to the Schwelme Dam. The first two were breached and the third was damaged. Three more "Lancasters" were lost after they had bombed the dams. 1,294 people were killed by the flood waters. 749 of the dead were slave laborers and prisoners. Of the 133 air-crew involved, fifty-six were killed or captured. Wing Commander Guy Gibson won a Victoria Cross and thirty-four other members of the force were also decorated for bravery. A major fire at the Spanish naval base at El Ferrol severely damaged the light cruisers MIGUEL DE CERVANTES, GALICIA and MENDES NUNEZ and the destroyers ALSEDO and LAZAGA.

1944 Twenty-nine Royal Air Force "Mosquitoes" attacked Berlin. The German trawler UJ-1210 was sunk off Lille Egge, Norway by Allied aircraft.

1945 Robert Ley, Nazi Labor Minister, was captured near Berchtesgaden. German commando Otto Skorzeny surrendered to American forces in Bavaria. The U255 surrendered at Lough Foyle. U776 surrendered at Portland. U287 was sunk in the Elbe River by a mine.

1946 Seventy-three Germans accused of war crimes during the "Battle of the Bulge" were tried at Dachau (See June 11th).

Eastern Europe

1934 Russia and Czechoslovakia signed a mutual assistance pact.

1942 The Germans took 170,000 prisoners, 3,800 vehicles, 1,100 cannon, 320 aircraft and 250 tanks at Kerch in the Crimea.

1943 Armed resistance in the Warsaw Ghetto ended.

1945 Luftwaffe ace Erich Hartmann (352 victories) and his entire command, including women and children were turned over to the Soviets by Allied High Command.

Mediterranean

1941 The last British reinforcements reached Crete. Three Luftwaffe He111s attacked the Royal Air Force base at Habbaniya, Iraq. The Italian garrison at Amba Alagi in East Africa surrendered. The German High Command ordered Rommel to leave the siege of Tobruk to the Italians and continue his operations around Sollum.

1942 Axis aircraft attacked British-held Malta.

1944 The last German positions in the "Gustav Line" were eliminated. Moroccan forces took Monte Petrella and Monte Revole. Royal Air Force "Wellington" bombers attacked the Piombino and San Stefano harbors in Italy. Private F. Jefferson, of the Lancashire Fusiliers, won a Victoria Cross at Cassino. French forces took Monte Petrella and Monte Revole in Italy.

Atlantic

1941 Iceland severed relations with German-occupied Denmark and became an independent country. The U105 sank the British freighter RODNEY STAR (11,083 tons). U105 survived until June 2, 1943.

1942 The U507 sank the Honduran freighter AMAPALA (4,148 tons). U507 survived until January 13, 1943. The U751 sank the American freighter NICARAO (1,445 tons-8 dead). U751 survived until July 17th. Three survivors from the American tanker T.C. MCCOBB landed ashore at Surinam, Dutch Guiana. The MCCOBB had been sunk by the Italian submarine PIETRO CALVI. The USN destroyer TARBELL rescued twenty-three survivors from the American freighter LAMMONT DU PONT which had been sunk by U125. The American tanker ESSO AUGUSTA rescued thirty-one survivors from the American freighter NICARAO which had been sunk by U751. The Dutch schooners INDIA and MISSISSIPPI rescued survivors from the American freighter NORLANTIC which had been sunk by U69.

1943 The U182 was sunk by the USN destroyer MACKENZIE north of Tristan da Cunha. The Italian submarine TAZZOLI was sunk by aircraft in the Bay of Biscay. The Spanish sailing ship JUAN rescued 18 survivors from the American freighter JAMES W. DENVER which had been sunk on April 11th by U195.

1944 The U240 was sunk by the Royal Air Force's No.330 Squadron west of Trondheim, Norway.

North America

1892 General Manton Eddy was born. On August 9, 1942, he assumed command of the 9th Infantry Division. On August 20, 1944, he took command of the 12th Corps in Normandy. On January 20, 1948, he was promoted to lieutenant general. He commanded the 7th Army in Europe from 1950 until he retired on March 31, 1953.

1940   The destroyers CHARLES F. HUGHES and MONSSEN were launched. CHARLES F. HUGHES was stricken in 1968 and expended as a target. MONSSEN was lost November 13, 1943.

1944   The escort carrier BOUGAINVILLE was launched. She was scrapped in Japan in 1960. A USN blimp crashed at Lakehurst, New Jersey and was destroyed.

1945   The U190 surrendered at St. John's, Newfoundland.

1946   The destroyer-minelayer BREESE was sold for scrap.

1947   The destroyer MOFFETT was sold for scrap.

1964   The US Coast Guard cutter BOUTWELL was sold.

Pacific

1941   Britain stopped rubber shipments from Malaya to Japan.

1942   The USN submarine TAUTOG sank the GOYO MARU (8,469 tons) off Truk. Her first torpedo had made a circular run which forced the submarine to go deep to avoid it. She then resumed her attack. The IJN submarine I-29 damaged the Soviet freighter UELEN (5,135 tons).

1943   The US Army's 7th Division continued its attack on Attu in the Aleutians. The USN destroyer STRONG shot down three Japanese bombers that attacked American shipping off Guadalcanal. The American freighter WILLIAM K. VANDERBILT (7,181 tons-1 dead) was sunk off New Caledonia by the IJN submarine I-19. The American tanker CITIES SERVICE BOSTON was wrecked off Bass Point, Australia. Four Australians died while rescuing the crew.

1944   Fighting continued on Bougainville. The IJN submarine I-176 was sunk by the USN destroyers FRANKS and HAGGARD.

1945   Sergeant Joseph Muller, of the 77th Division, won a posthumous Medal of Honor on Okinawa. The USN escort carrier SHIPLEY BAY was damaged in a collision with the tanker CACHE off Okinawa. 457 USAAF B29s dropped 3,609 tons of bombs on Nagoya, destroying 3.8 square miles of the city. The USN submarine HAWKBILL sank the IJN minelayer HATSUTAKE, which had sunk the USN submarine LOGARTO on the 3rd. The USN submarine RATON sank the EIJU MARU (2,456 tons). Dutch forces landed on Tarakan Island.

China-Burma-India

1940   The Italian submarine GALILEI sank the Norwegian tanker JAMES STOVE (8,215 tons).

1943   The Royal Air Force attacked the Narigna Road Bridge in Burma.

1945 The US Air Force ended its mining offensive in China. Since October 16, 1943 the 14th Air Force had flown 255 sorties and dropped 976 mines, while the 20th Air Force had flown 22 sorties and dropped 263 mines.

May 17th

Western Europe

1937 A new Loyalist government in Spain was formed under Juan Negrin.
1940 The German 6th Army (commanded by Reichenau) took Brussels, Belgium. Italian dictator Benito Mussolini declared that the Germans would never reach Paris. Royal Air Force Sergeant Gareth Nowell, of No.87 Squadron, scored his 12th victory in a week. He was awarded a Distinguished Flying Medal and Bar. Eleven of twelve Royal Air Force "Blenheim" bombers were lost in an attack in France. The surviving aircraft crash-landed on landing at its base at Watton, Britain. 130 Royal Air Force bombers attacked targets in Germany and Belgium with no losses. Forty-seven Germans were killed in the raids. Swiss fighters shot down a Luftwaffe He111 bomber near Lighieres, Switzerland.
1941 Ninety-five Royal Air Force bombers attacked Cologne, Germany and lost two aircraft. Twenty people were killed in the raid. Seventy Royal Air Force bombers attacked Kiel, Germany and killed five people.
1942 Twelve Royal Air Force "Bostons" attacked Boulogne, France. Sixty Royal Air Force bombers dropped mines in the Baltic and lost seven aircraft. Twenty-seven Royal Air Force bombers attacked Boulogne, France and lost one "Wellington".
1943 118 American 8th Air Force B17s dropped 289.5 tons of bombs on Lorient, France and lost six aircraft. Thirty-four 8th Air Force B24s dropped 85.5 tons of bombs on Bordeaux, France and lost one aircraft. The 8th Air Force B17 "Memphis Belle" flew the last of its twenty-five missions (See North America-1987). Ten of eleven 8th Air Force 322nd Bomb Group B26s were lost when they attempted to attack Haarlem and Ijmuiden in Holland. The only survivor had aborted before reaching the target area. Thirteen 8th Air Force P47s flew sweeps over the Brittany coast of France. At 1630, the German minesweeper M-414 was sunk off Texel by the Royal Air Force. Six Royal Air Force bombers dropped mines off La Pallice, France and lost one "Stirling".
1944 Luftwaffe Lieutenant Johnen's Me110 was destroyed by German and Swiss authorities at Dubdendorf Airfield in Zurich (See April 28th).
1957 Hans Funk, Minister of Economics, was released from Spandau Prison.
1993 Cunard Captain John Treasure Jones, age 87, died. He had commanded the RMS LAURENTIC when she was sunk by a German U-boat in November 1940. He had also been the last commander of the RMS QUEEN MARY.

Eastern Europe
1942 The Germans began a counter-offensive at Kharkov.
1944 The American 15th Air Force attacked troop concentrations in Yugoslavia.

Mediterranean
1940 General Maxime Weygand, the French Commander-in-Chief Mid-East, received orders to assume command of forces in France.
1941 The last Royal Air Force "Gladiators" and "Hurricanes" were evacuated from Crete to Egypt. The Germans completed their preparations for the invasion of Crete. The original date of May 18th was changed to the 20th. The Italian Air Force arrived in Iraq to assist the Iraqi Air Force in their attacks on the British.
1942 Axis aircraft attacked Malta. Royal Air Force ace Flying Officer P.A. Nash (12 victories) was killed in action over Malta. The German S-34 was sunk by a shore battery on Malta.
1944 Polish forces took Sant' Angelo Hill, near Monte Cassino. Field Marshal Albert Kesselring ordered all German troops off Monte Cassino. The American 15th Air Force B24s attacked San Stefano and Piombino harbors in Italy. The French took Esperia and Monte Faggeta in Italy.

Atlantic
1941 The U107 sank the Dutch tanker MARISA (8,029 tons). U107 survived until August 18, 1944.
1942 The U155 sank the British tanker SAN VICTORIO (8,136 tons) and the American freighter CHALLENGER (7,667 tons-8 dead). U155 survived the war. The U588 sank the Norwegian freighter SKOTTLAND (2,117 tons). U588 survived until July 31st. The U135 sank the British freighter FORT QU'APPELLE (7,127 tons). U135 survived until July 15, 1943. The U103 sank the American freighter RUTH LYKES (2,612 tons-6 dead). U103 survived until April 15, 1945. The U506 sank the American tanker GULFOIL (5,189 tons-21 dead). The U653 sank the British freighter PEISANDER (6,225 tons) off Bermuda. U653 survived until March 15, 1944. The U156 sank the British freighter BARRDALE (5,072 tons). U156 survived until March 8, 1943. The U432 sank the American trawler FOAM (324 tons-1 dead). U432 survived until March 11, 1943. The USN destroyers HAMBLETON and ELLYSON were damaged in a collision. Twenty-three survivors from the American tanker ESSO HOUSTON landed at St. Vincent, British Windward Islands in the Caribbean. Their ship had been sunk by U162. The Norwegian freighter SOMERVILLE rescued twenty-seven survivors from the American freighter RUTH LYKES which had been sunk by U103.

1943 The U657 sank the British freighter AYMERIC (5,196 tons). The U128 was sunk by the USN destroyers JOUETT and MOFFETT. The U640 was sunk by the Royal Navy frigate SWALE off Greenland. The U646 was sunk by the Royal Air Force's No.269 Squadron south of Iceland.

South America
1940 The Venezuelan government ordered the crews of the German freighters DURAZZO (1,153 tons) and SESTROSIS (3,978 tons) to dismantle their engines while they were at anchor in Maracaibo. This was done to prevent incidents in the Pan American Security Zone.

North America
1942 The destroyers FRANKFORD and STRONG and the submarine GUNNEL were launched. STRONG was lost on July 5, 1943 and GUNNEL was discarded in 1959.
1945 The U873 surrendered at Portsmouth, Virginia.
1987 A formation of seven B17 "Flying Fortress'" overflew Memphis, Tennessee as part of the dedication ceremony of the "Memphis Belle" Museum.
1991 The USN submarine tender FULTON was decommissioned. She had been commissioned September 12, 1941.

Pacific
1942 The USN submarine TAUTOG sank the IJN submarine I-28 north of Rabaul. The USN submarine TRITON sank the IJN submarine I-164 off Kyushu. The USN submarine SKIPJACK sank the TAZAN MARU (5,477 tons) off Siam. The USN submarine GRAMPUS was damaged off Truk by IJN gunfire. The USN submarine SILVERSIDES damaged the transport TOTTORI MARU and the freighter THAMES MARU off Honshu. The USN battleship WEST VIRGINIA was raised from the bottom of Pearl Harbor and towed into dry-dock to repair damage suffered in the December 7th attack. USN Captain Homer N. Wallin, who oversaw the salvage, was awarded a Distinguished Service Medal.
1943 American forces continued their attacks on Attu in the Aleutians. The USN submarine GRAYBACK sank the ENGLAND MARU (5,829 tons). The IJN submarine I-25 sank the American tanker H.M. STOREY (10,793 tons). The USN minesweeper DASH rescued 56 survivors from the American freighter WILLIAM K. VANDERBILT which had been sunk the previous day by I-19.
1944 American forces landed at Arare, New Guinea. The USN submarine SAND LANCE sank the TAIKOKU MARU (2,633 tons) and the FUKKO MARU (3,834 tons). The USN submarine TUNNY sank the NICHIWA

MARU (4,955 tons). The USN carrier SARATOGA and the Royal Navy carrier ILLUSTRIOUS attacked Surabaya, Java, destroying ten ships and twelve aircraft, while losing one aircraft. Later that night USAAF B24s attacked Surabaya, Java. USAAF ace Major Thomas McGuire shot down a Japanese "Oscar" over Noemfoor Island.

1945   US Army General Simon Bolivar Buckner assumed command of American Land Forces on Okinawa and Admiral Hill relieved Admiral Turner as commander of Task Force 51 off-shore. USMC Lieutenant Robert M. Wilhide was shot down and killed by American anti/aircraft fire near the island of Ie Shima. The USN destroyer DOUGLAS H. FOX (9 of her crew died) was hit by a Japanese kamikaze off Okinawa. The US Armys 43rd Division took the Ipoh Dam on Luzon. The USN carrier TICONDEROGA attacked Taroa and Maloelap in the Marshalls. The USN submarine SHAD sank the CHOZAN MARU (3,938 tons).

1947   The USN battleship OKLAHOMA sank while under tow 500 miles northwest of Hawaii. She had been sunk in the December 7, 1941 Japanese attack on Pearl Harbor and was salvaged.

China-Burma-India

1942   The American Volunteer Group attacked the rail station at Lao Kay, losing one aircraft.

1943   The Royal Air Force attacked Bume, Burma. The U198 sank the British freighter NORTHMOOR (4,392 tons).

1944   The Allies took Myitkyina Airfield in Burma.

May 18th

Western Europe

1939   The Royal Navy light cruiser HERMIONE was launched. She was sunk on June 16, 1942.

1940   The Germans took Antwerp in Belgium and St. Quentin and Cambrai in France. Luftwaffe ace Wolf Wilke (162 victories) was captured. Thirteen Royal Air Force bombers attacked German troop concentrations and lost three "Blenheims". Sixty Royal Air Force bombers attacked targets in Belgium and Germany and lost one "Whitley". France ordered 480 A20 "Havoc" bombers from America. Paul Reynaud appointed Phillippe Petain as Frances Vice-Premier. Artur Seyss-Inquart was appointed German Reich Commissar for Holland. The Norwegian torpedo boat TROLL was captured at Floro by the Germans. The Royal Navy's light cruiser EFFINGHAM (launched in 1925) ran aground off Narvik, Norway and was scuttled on the 21st. The Royal Navy battleship RESOLUTION was damaged by the Luftwaffe off Norway. Tyler Kent, a clerk at the American embassy in London, was arrested on charges of for spying for the Germans. He had actually been collecting hundreds of confidential communications between FDR and Churchill and had intended to present them to the isolationist Congress in the U.S.

1943 Thirteen Royal Air Force "Bostons" attacked Abbeville, France. At 0100, the German minesweeper M-345 was sunk off Gravelines by the Royal Air Force. Curtiss LeMay assumed command the 102nd Wing, American 8th Air Force. He would become USAF Chief of Staff during the 1960's. 100 American 8th Air Force P47s flew sweeps over France and Belgium claiming one victory and losing a 4th Fighter Group aircraft. 8th Air Force ace Duane Beeson (eventually 28 victories) scored his first, a Luftwaffe Me109 over Belgium. Seventeen Royal Air Force bombers dropped mines off the Biscay ports.

1944 German Field Marshal Gerd von Rundstedt was named as Commander-in-Chief in the West. German radar sites on the Channel coast were bombed by Allied aircraft.

1949 The Royal Navy battleship ROYAL SOVEREIGN was sold for scrap.

1987 German doctors Aquilin Ulrich, age 73, and Heinrich Bunke, age 72, were convicted in Frankfurt, Germany of killing 15,000 handicapped persons during Hitlers Euthanasia Program of 1940-41 and sentenced to 4-years each.

1992 80-year-old Josef Schwammberger (See May 2, 1990 and June 27, 1991) was convicted of war crimes by a Stuttgart court. He had commanded forced-labor camps during the war.

Eastern Europe

1941 The German battleship BISMARCK and heavy cruiser PRINZ EUGEN left Gdynia, Poland en route to the Atlantic.

1942 The Soviet submarine ShCh-205 sank the Turkish freighter DUATEPE.

1944 The American 15th Air Force attacked the oil refineries at Ploesti, Rumania losing fourteen bombers. The 15th Air Force also attacked rail targets in Yugoslavia.

Mediterranean

1941 Royal Navy Petty Officer A. Sephton won a posthumous Victoria Cross off Crete.

1943 The U414 sank the British freighters EMPIRE EVE (5,979 tons) and FORT ANNE (7,134 tons). The Italian minesweeper RD-38 was sunk.

1944 At 1030, the flag of the Polish 12th Regiment was raised over Monte Cassino in Italy and signified capture of that position.

Atlantic

1940 The German armed merchant cruiser ORION took the freighter TROPIC SEA (5,781 tons).

1941 The Royal Navy heavy cruiser SUFFOLK, which was patrolling the Denmark Strait, was warned to expect contact with German shipping (the battleship BISMARCK and heavy cruiser PRINZ EUGEN) within 48 hours. The U107 sank the British freighter PIAKO (8,286 tons). U107 survived until August 18, 1944.

1942 The U162 sank the British tanker BETH (6,852 tons). U162 survived until September 3rd. The U125 sank the American tanker MERCURY SUN (8,893 tons-6 dead) and freighter WILLIAM SALMAN (2,616 tons). U125 survived until May 6, 1943. The U558 sank the Dutch freighter FAUNA (1,254 tons). U558 survived until July 20, 1943. The U156 sank the American freighter QUAKER CITY (4,961 tons-11 dead). U156 survived until March 8, 1943. The British freighter HORORATA rescued the last survivor from the American freighter ALCOA GUIDE which had been sunk by U123. Seventeen survivors from the American fishing trawler FOAM reached the Sambro Lightship off Nova Scotia. The FOAM had been sunk by U432. The American tanker BENJAMIN BREWSTER rescued nineteen survivors from the American tanker GULFOIL which had been sunk by U506.

1944 The Dutch MTB AREND was sunk off Boulogne by a mine. The U241 was sunk by the Royal Air Force's No.210 Squadron northeast of the Faeroes.

North America

1912 The battleship TEXAS was launched. She would be preserved as a memorial in her namesake state after serving in both World Wars.

1940 FDR informed British Prime Minister Winston Churchill that the loan of USN destroyers to the Royal Navy (See May 15th) would require congressional approval. The destroyer NIBLACK was launched. She was stricken in 1968.

1945 The escort carrier POINT CRUZ was launched. She was scrapped in 1971.

1956 The IX-PRAIRIE STATE (the ex-battleship ILLINOIS) was sold for scrap in Baltimore.

1973 The destroyer HARLAN R. DICKSON was sold for scrap.

Pacific

1912 The IJN battleship KONGO was launched. She was sunk on November 21, 1944 by the USN submarine SEALION.

1943 American forces continued their attacks on Attu in the Aleutians. Seven USAAF B25s and eleven RAAF "Beaufighters" attacked Japanese shipping and installations at Lae, New Guinea. The USN submarine POLLACK sank the TERUSHIMA MARU (3,110 tons).

1944 The American 6th Army announced that it had secured the Admiralties. American losses were 326 dead and those of the Japanese were 3,280. The US 163rd Regimental Combat Team landed on Insoemoar Island off New Guinea and took Wakde airfield. The USN submarine PUFFER sank the SHINRYU MARU (3,181 tons).

1945 The USMC 6th Division secured most of "Sugar Loaf Hill" on Okinawa. The USN destroyer LONGSHAW was wrecked off Okinawa and was then destroyed by Japanese shore-fire, seventy-seven of her crew died. She had been awarded nine battle stars during her career. The American transport SIMS was hit by a Japanese kamikaze.

China-Burma-India

1943 The Japanese began an offensive across the Yangtze. Seven American 10th Air Force B24s attacked Prome, Burma and thirteen B24s attacked Minbu. The Royal Air Force attacked Satyogya Creek in Burma.

1944 The Chinese attacked Myitkyina, Burma.

1945 Chinese forces occupied Foochow, China.

May 19th

Western Europe

1920 The Royal Navy light cruiser EMERALD was launched. She was scrapped in 1948.

1931 The German pocket battleship DEUTSCHLAND was launched. She was scuttled on May 4, 1945. Her name would later be changed to LUTZOW. This was done by order of Adolf Hitler himself. He was concerned that the loss of a ship named in honor of the country might have an adverse effect on moral.

1940 General Maxime Weygand (died in 1965) replaced General Maurice Gamelin (died in 1958) as Commander-in-Chief French Army. French Colonel Charles de Gaulle led his 4th Armored Division in a counter-attack and came within one mile of German General Heinz Guderian's headquarters. The German 6th Army reached the Scheldt Estuary. The Royal Navy destroyer WHITLEY was beached after being damaged by the Luftwaffe off Nieuport, France and was later scuttled by the Royal Navy destroyer KEITH. Seventy-eight Royal Air Force bombers attacked targets in France, Germany and Belgium and lost two "Whitleys". The Royal Air Force began sending its fighter and recon units back to Britain from France. Of the 250 "Hurricanes" fighters that had been sent to

France, only sixty-six would return to Britain. Churchill decided to send no more fighter aircraft to France. Of the 261 that the Royal Air Force had already sent to France, only sixty-one returned. During the months of May and June the Royal Air Force would lose 432 fighters, 25% of its fighter strength.

1941 The German battleship BISMARCK and heavy cruiser PRINZ EUGEN left Kiel, Germany for Norway.

1942 197 Royal Air Force bombers attacked Mannheim, Germany and lost eleven aircraft. Two people were killed in the raid. Sixty-five Royal Air Force bombers attacked St. Nazaire, France and lost one "Wellington".

1943 The USN's Task Force 61 (consisting of the battleships ALABAMA and SOUTH DAKOTA and five destroyers) arrived at Scapa Flow for duty with the Royal Navy's Home Fleet. 103 American 8th Air Force B17s dropped 237 tons of bombs on Kiel, Germany and lost six aircraft. Fifty-five 8th Air Force B17s dropped 134 tons of bombs on Flensburg, Germany. Six Royal Air Force "Mosquitoes" attacked Berlin.

1944 818 American 8th Air Force bombers dropped 1,889 tons of bombs on Brunswick, Berlin and Kiel in Germany and lost sixteen B17s and twelve B24s (one of the lost B17s landed in Sweden). 700 8th Air Force fighters provided support for the bombers and claimed seventy-seven victories for the loss of four P38s, four P47s and eleven P51s. American 9th Air Force B26s and A20s attacked shore-batteries on the Channel coast. The U1015 was lost in a collision with U1014 west of Pillau. 143 Royal Air Force bombers attacked Boulogne, France and killed thirty-three civilians. 118 Royal Air Force "Lancasters" attacked Orleans, France and lost one aircraft. 121 Royal Air Force bombers attacked Amiens, France and lost one "Lancaster". 117 Royal Air Force bombers attacked Tours, France. 116 Royal Air Force bombers attacked Le Mans, France and lost two "Lancasters". Fifty-eight Royal Air Force bombers attacked Le Clipon, France. Sixty-three Royal Air Force bombers attacked Merville, France. Forty-four Royal Air Force bombers attacked Mont Couple, France and lost one "Lancaster".

1945 The U278, U294, U295, U312, U313, U318, U363, U427, U481, U668, U716, U968, U992, and U997 surrendered at Narvik, Norway.

1993 A WWII vintage "Lancaster" bomber and modern "Tornadoes" of the Royal Air Force's No.617 "Dambusters" Squadron made a series of passes over the Derwent Dam in Britain. The area had been used for training for the 1943 "Dambuster's Mission". Present for the ceremony were the three surviving pilots of the actual flight, American Joe McCarthy, New Zealander Les Munro, and Canadian Ken Brown. Also present was actor Richard Todd who had portrayed mission commander Guy Gibson in the 1954 movie "The Dambusters".

Eastern Europe

1942 The Germans completed the capture of the Kerch peninsula in the Crimea capturing 100,000. Luftwaffe ace Gordon Gollob became the 10th to reach 100 victories.

1944 The German minesweeper M-3121 was sunk in the Baltic by Soviet aircraft.

Mediterranean

1941 Churchill decided to replace Archibald Wavell with Claude Auchinleck as Commander-in-Chief in the Mid-East, but would wait until a less active time on the front. "Ultra" intercepts revealed that the German invasion of Crete would be postponed until the 20th. The last seven Royal Air Force fighters on Crete, four "Hurricanes" and three "Gladiators", were evacuated to Egypt. Sergeant N.G. Leaky, of the 6th King's African Rifles, won a posthumous Victoria Cross in Abyssinia.

1942 The Royal Navy carriers ARGUS and EAGLE launched seventeen "Spitfires" for Malta in "Operation L.B.".

1942 German aircraft attacked Oran, Algeria and damaged the American freighters SAMUEL GRIFFEN and LUTHER MARTIN.

1944 The US 5th Army's 85th Division reached Gaeta, Italy and was only forty-five miles from the surrounded Allied beach-head at Anzio. The U453 sank the British freighter FORT MISSANABLE (7,174 tons). She was the last ship sunk by a U-boat in the theater. The U960 was sunk by the USN destroyers LUDLOW and NIBLACK northwest of Algiers. The American 15th Air Force attacked rail, oil and shipping targets in Italy. The German minelayer KEHRWIEDER (ex-Italian COTRONE) was sunk at La Spezia by aircraft.

Atlantic

1940 The U37 sank the Swedish freighter FRISELL (5,066 tons). U37 survived the war.

1941 The U96 sank the British freighter EMPIRE RIDGE (2,922 tons). U96 survived until March 30, 1945.

1942 The Italian submarine CAPPELLINI sank the Swedish freighter TISNAREN (5,747 tons). The U506 sank the American freighter HEREDIA (4,732 tons-35 dead). U506 survived until July 12, 1943. The U751 sank the American freighter ISABELA (3,110 tons-3 dead). U751 survived until July 17th. The U103 sank the American freighter OGONTZ (5,037 tons-19 dead). U103 survived until April 15, 1945. The last three survivors from the trawler FOAM were rescued by the Canadian corvette HALIFAX. The FOAM had been sunk by U432. The American steamer

HOWARD rescued twenty-nine survivors from the American tanker MERCURY SUN which had been sunk by U125. The Latvian freighter KEGUMS rescued twenty-two survivors from the American freighter WILLIAM J. SALMAN which had been sunk by U125.

1943 The U161 sank the Canadian sailing ship ANGELUS (255 tons). U161 survived until September 27th. The U209 was sunk by the Royal Navy frigates JED and SENNEN south of Greenland. The U273 was sunk by the Royal Navy destroyers DUNCAN and VIDETTE southwest of Iceland. The U381 was sunk by the Royal Navy destroyer DUNCAN and the corvette SNOWFLAKE southeast of Greenland. The U954 was sunk by the Royal Air Force's No.120 Squadron. Aboard the U954 was Lieutenant Peter Doenitz who was the youngest son, age 20, of the Grand Admiral.

North America

1888 General William Hood Simpson was born in Weatherford, Texas. He graduated 101st in his 1909 West Point class of 103. He was promoted to lieutenant general on October 13, 1943. He took the advance cadre of the 8th Army to Britain. On May 22, 1944 that unit was redesignated the 9th Army to prevent confusion with the British 8th Army. The 9th became operational on September 5th as part of the 12th US Army Group. Its first assignment was the capture of the ports on the Brittany coast of France. It was then assigned to the northern flank of the American Armies. Simpson retired on November 30, 1946. He died on August 15, 1980 in San Antonio.

1943 The first flight of the XB38, a B17 bomber equipped with Allison engines, took place.

1944 The submarine SPOT was launched at Mare Island. She was transferred to the Chilean Navy. James Forrestal became Secretary of the Navy.

1966 The US Coast Guard cutter FREDERICK LEE was sold.

1974 The destroyer INGERSOLL was expended as a target.

2010 Anton Geiser, age 85, was deported for concealing his past as a concentration camp guard during the war.

Pacific

1941 By the 23rd of the month, the battleships MISSISSIPPI, IDAHO and NEW MEXICO, the cruisers SAVANNAH, BROOKLYN, NASHVILLE and PHILADELPHIA and the destroyers LANG, STERETT, WILSON, WINSLOW, WAINWRIGHT, STACK, MORRIS, BUCK and ROE would be transferred to the Atlantic.

1942 The USN light cruiser NASHVILLE left Midway en route to the western Aleutians and her continuing effort to attack the Japanese fishing fleet off Kamchatka. A seaplane from the IJN submarine I-21 flew over Suva, Fiji.

1943 American forces continued their attacks on Attu in the Aleutians. The USN submarine GAR sank the ASUKA MARU (37 tons) in the Makassar Strait. Nine Japanese bombers attacked Guadalcanal, losing two aircraft.

1944 Fighting continued on Insoemoar Island off New Guinea. The USN submarine SKATE sank the MEISHO MARU (31 tons). USN Task Group 58.6 (commanded by Montgomery) attacked Marcus Island. Piloting one of the F6F "Hellcats" on the mission was former Hollywood film actor Lieutenant Wayne Morris. USAAF ace Major Thomas McGuire shot down a Japanese "Tojo" fighter over New Guinea.

1945 The US Army's I Corps secured the area around the Ipoh Dam on Luzon. Two American 11th Air Force B25s were shot down over Paramushiro in the Kuriles and another was interned in Russia. American destroyers bombarded Paramushiro.

China-Burma-India

1942 "Doolittle Raider" Corporal Leland Faktor was buried near Wan Tsuen, China.

1943 The Royal Air Force attacked Kyautaw, Burma.

1945 The British submarine TERRAPIN was a constructive loss after being attacked by Japanese anti-submarine vessels.

May 20th

Western Europe

1932 Englebert Dollfuss was appointed as Austrian Chancellor.

1940 Forty-one of seventy-one Royal Air Force "Battle" bombers, which attacked German pontoon bridges at Sedan, were shot down. Forty-seven Royal Air Force bombers attacked German troop concentrations and lost no aircraft. Seventy-seven Royal Air Force bombers attacked targets in France and lost three "Whitleys" and one "Wellington". At 0900, the German 1st Panzer Division (commanded by Guderian) took Amiens, France. At 1900, the 2nd Panzer Division took Abbeville, France. At 2000, a battalion of the German 1st Panzer Division reached the Channel at Noyelles, France. Nine German S-boats attacked targets along the Belgian coast.

1941 The British Admiralty received a telegram from its Naval Attaché in Stockholm, Captain Denham, stating that two large German warships (the battleship BISMARCK and the heavy cruiser PRINZ EUGEN) had passed through the Kattegat into the North Sea. Germany released 100,000 French prisoners of war.

1943	Two Royal Air Force "Mosquitoes" attacked Tergnier, France. A Luftwaffe Fw190 landed in error at the Royal Air Force base at Manston. Twenty-three Royal Air Force bombers dropped mines off the Biscay ports. 115 American 8th Air Force P47s flew sweeps over Holland and lost one aircraft.
1944	288 American 8th Air Force B17s and B24s dropped 774 tons of bombs on airfields at Villacoublay, Reims and Orly in France, losing two B17s. 657 8th Air Force fighters provided support for the bombers and claimed three victories for the loss of one P38, one P47 and two P51s. A B17 crashed on take-off at Podington (92nd Bomb Group). It caused two others to collide, killing twenty-one and closing the runway for seventy-two hours. The American 9th Air Force attacked airfields and rail targets in France. Thirty Royal Air Force "Mosquitoes" attacked Dusseldorf, Germany.
1945	Former Luftwaffe commander Hermann Goering checked into the "Ashcan" interrogation center, the Palace Hotel in Mondorf, Luxembourg. The U953 surrendered at Trondheim, Norway. The U963 was scuttled off Nazare, Portugal after her mining mission off Portland, Britain was cancelled.

Eastern Europe

1881	Polish General Wladyslaw Sikorski was born in Tyszowce. He died on July 4, 1943 in a plane crash.
1944	A V-2 rocket crashed in Poland and was dismantled and shipped by air to Britain on 25 July.

Mediterranean

1941	On this date, the Allied garrison of the island of Crete numbered about 42,000 men. At 0530, the Luftwaffe attacked Crete in preparation for the airborne attack. At 0715, a second air attack began. After the second raid ended, the first airborne troops arrived in 493 Ju52s and 70 gliders. British anti/aircraft fire managed to shoot down only seven Ju52s. By evening of the first day, the British were still in control of the islands three airfields. The island was defended by 42,000 Allied troops. Captain Walter Gericke commanded the 4th Battalion of the 1st Regiment during the attack. He would survive to become commander of West Germany's Parachute Division in NATO. The Royal Navy minesweeper WIDNES was sunk in Suda Bay, Crete. The Germans salvaged her and she was recommissioned as the UJ-2109 (See October 17, 1943). The Italian torpedo boat CURATONE was sunk by a mine off Greece. The Luftwaffe attacked Malta.
1942	The U431 sank the British tanker EOCENE (4,216 tons). U432 survived until March 11, 1943.

1943   USAAF B26s attacked airfields on Sardinia. The Royal Navy minesweeper FANTOME was a constructive loss after hitting a mine off Cap Bon.
1944   The German minesweeper R-190 was sunk in the Strait of Otranto by Allied aircraft.
1945   Anti-French riots took place in Beirut, Lebanon.
1948   Royal Canadian Air Force ace Flight Lieutenant George "Screwball" Beurling (31 victories) died in a plane crash. His "Norseman" crashed at Urke Airport in Rome while on a ferry flight to Israel. He was 27 years old.

Atlantic

1941   The Italian submarine OTARIA sank the British freighter STARCROSS (4,662 tons). The U94 sank the British freighters HARPAGUS (5,173 tons), NORMAN MONARCH (4,718 tons) and the Norwegian tanker PEDERSEN (6,128 tons). U94 survived until August 28, 1942. The U556 sank the British tanker BRITISH SECURITY (8,470 tons) and freighter DARLINGTON COURT (4,974 tons). U556 survived until June 27th. The U103 sank the Egyptian freighter RADAMES (3,575 tons). U103 survived until April 15, 1945. The U111 sank the British freighter COCKAPONSET (5,995 tons). U111 survived until October 4th. The U98 sank the British freighter ROTHERMERE (5,356 tons). U98 survived until November 19, 1942. The U138 sank the British freighter JAVANESE PRINCE (8,593 tons). U138 survived until June 18th. The U109 sank the British freighter MARCONI (7,402 tons). U109 survived until May 4, 1943.
1942   The German armed merchant cruiser MICHEL took the Norwegian freighter KATTEGAT (4,245 tons). The U158 sank the British tanker DARINA (8,113 tons). U158 survived until June 30th. The U155 sank the Panamanian tanker SYLVAN ARROW (7,797 tons). U155 survived the war. The U108 sank the Norwegian tanker NORLAND (8,134 tons). U108 survived until April 11, 1944. The American freighter GEORGE CALVERT (7,191 tons-3 dead) was sunk off Cuba by the U753. The U506 sank the American tanker HALO (6,986 tons-39 dead). The USN YP-387 was lost in a collision off Delaware. The American tanker ESSO DOVER rescued twenty-two survivors from the freighter OGONTZ which had been sunk by U103.
1943   The U197 sank the Dutch tanker BENAKAT (4,763 tons). The U258 was sunk by the Royal Air Force's No.120 Squadron.

North America

1918   The battleship NEW MEXICO was commissioned. She was scrapped in November 1947.
1941   FDR created the Office of Civil Defense. Its first Director was New York Mayor Fiorello La Guardia.

1943 The USN's 10th Fleet was established under the direct control of Chief of Naval Operations Admiral Ernest King. Its purpose was to conduct the battle against the German submarines in the Atlantic. The carrier BUNKER HILL was commissioned. She was stricken in 1966.
1944 The escort carrier BISMARCK SEA was commissioned. She was sunk on February 21, 1945.
1945 A Japanese balloon-bomb was found near Chilliwack, British Columbia.
1949 Captain Alvin Jensen died when his Banshee jet lost a wing over Patuxtent, Maryland. He had been awarded a Navy Cross for destroying twenty-four Japanese aircraft on Bougainville.
1976 Admiral Royal Ingersoll, commander of the Atlantic Fleet, died at Bethesda, Maryland.
1978 A dormitory building dedicated at Chanute Air Force Base in memory of Corporal Leland Faktor. He had died on the "Doolittle Raid" of April 1942.
1998 Lester Marsh died in San Diego, California. He had been credited with 5 aerial victories while flying P51s in Europe.

Pacific
1942 USAAF ace Thomas Lynch (20 victories) scored his first, 2 Japanese "Zeros" over New Guinea. The IJN changed the numbering system for their fleet submarines by adding 100 to the individual boat numbers (i.e. I-73 became I-173). The USAAF's Air Force South Pacific Area was established.
1943 The USN submarine POLLACK sank the BANGKOK MARU (5,351 tons) off Jaluit. USN TBFs mined the waters near Buin, New Georgia. American forces continued their attacks on Attu. USN Commander-in-Chief-Pacific Admiral Chester Nimitz recommended that Kiska Island, in the Aleutians, be retaken.
1944 The USN submarine SILVERSIDES sank the IJN gunboat SHOSEI MARU (998 tons) off Saipan. The USN submarine BLUEGILL sank the MIYAURA MARU (1,856 tons). The USN submarine ANGLER sank the OTORI MARU (2,105 tons). A group of USN carriers (commanded by Montgomery) attacked Marcus Island. Allied forces secured Wadke Island off New Guinea. American losses were 53 and the Japanese lost 759.
1945 The USN destroyer THATCHER, the destroyer escort JOHN C. BUTLER (3 wounded) and the LST-808 were hit by Japanese kamikazes off Okinawa. Three USAAF 504th Bombard Group B29s were destroyed when the mines they were carrying exploded before take-off on Saipan. The advance party of the USAAF 509th Composite Group (A-bomb) arrived on Tinian. The USN submarine CERO sank the SEKI MARU No.5 (377 tons).

China-Burma-India

1943 Eight American 10th Air Force B24s attacked Allanmyo, Burma. The Royal Air Force attacked Akyab, Burma. The U181 sank the Swedish freighter SICILLIA (1,633 tons). U181 survived the war.

1944 14th Air Force B24s attacked Japanese shipping south of Hong Kong and sank the freighter SHINJU MARU.

May 21st

Western Europe

1893 British Air Marshal Charles Portal was born. He died on April 22, 1971 of cancer.

1916 Luftwaffe ace Wilhelm Batz (237 victories) was born in Bamberg. He survived the war.

1935 Hitler appointed Reich Defense Minister Werner von Blomberg as Commander-in-Chief of all three of Germany's armed forces.

1940 The French 3rd Light Mechanized Division and the British 6th Durham Light Infantry counter-attacked the German 7th Panzer and "Totenkopf" Divisions near Arras, France. They lost forty-six tanks and destroyed twenty. More than 100 German prisoners of war from the "Totenkopf" Division "disappeared" while under the control of the 6th Durham Light Infantry. Warrant Officer G. Gristock, of the Royal Norfolk Regiment, won a Victoria Cross in France. Lance/Corporal H. Nicholls, of the Grenadier Guards, won a Victoria Cross in Belgium. Fifty-seven Royal Air Force bombers attacked targets in France and lost three "Blenheims". 124 Royal Air Force bombers attacked German rail targets and lost five aircraft. At 0100, the French destroyer L'ADROIT was sunk off Dunkirk by the Luftwaffe. The German Navy Commander, Admiral Erich Raeder, had a conference with Hitler concerning the invasion of Britain. General Gaston Billotte, commander of French Army Group 1 in northern France, was injured in a car wreck. He died two days later.

1941 Forty-five Royal Air Force "Blenheims" attacked coastal targets and lost two aircraft. The German battleship BISMARCK and heavy cruiser PRINZ EUGEN were sighted in Bergenfjord, Norway by a Royal Air Force photo recon unit "Spitfire". The Royal Navy battleship PRINCE OF WALES, the battlecruiser HOOD and six destroyers left Scapa Flow to intercept them before they could enter the convoy lanes in the Atlantic.

1942 Forty-eight Royal Air Force bombers dropped mines off French ports.

1943 Four Royal Air Force "Mosquitoes" attacked Orleans, France and lost one aircraft. Seventy-seven American 8th Air Force B17s dropped 193 tons of bombs Wilhelmshaven, Germany and lost seven aircraft. Forty-six 8th Air Force B17s dropped 111 tons of bombs on Emden, Germany and lost five aircraft. 105 8th Air Force P47s flew a sweep over Belgium and lost three 4th Fighter Group aircraft. 104 Royal Air Force bombers dropped mines off the Biscay ports and lost four aircraft.

1944 124 American 8th Air Force B17s and B24s dropped 459 tons of bombs on V-1 rocket launching sites at Mimoyecques and Siracourt in France. They were supported by forty-eight 8th Air Force P47s. The first "Chattanooga Choo-Choo" mission was flown when 1,263 USAAF fighters went train-busting in Germany and France, losing eight P38s, four P47s and fifteen P51s. USAAF B26s attacked Abbeville, France. 532 Royal Air Force bombers attacked Duisburg, Germany and lost twenty-nine "Lancasters". 124 people were killed in the raid. 107 Royal Air Force bombers dropped mines in the Baltic and lost three "Lancasters". Luftwaffe night-fighter ace Prince Sayn-zu-Wittgenstein (83 victories) was killed by a "Mosquito" night-fighter near Schoenhausen. Luftwaffe night-fighter ace Manfred Meurer (65 victories) died when his He219 collided with a Royal Air Force bomber near Magdeburg.

1945 Heinrich Himmler, Commander of the Gestapo, and the Waffen S.S., was captured near Bremervorde by the British. He would commit suicide soon after his identity was discovered. The last of the wooden barracks at the Belsen Concentration Camp were burned down with flame throwers.

1948 The Swiss received nine P51Ds from the USAAF in Germany.

1961 Luftwaffe ace Josef "Pips" Priller (101 victories) died in Augsburg of a heart attack, at age 45.

Mediterranean

1941 A German seaborne invasion of Crete was repulsed. At 1250, the Royal Navy destroyer JUNO (launched in 1939) was sunk and the light cruiser AJAX was damaged off Crete by Italian aircraft. The Germans gained control of Maleme Airfield on Crete. The Italian destroyer CARLO MIRABELLO and gunboat MATTEUCI and the German transports MARBURG (7,564 tons) and KYBFELS (7,764 tons) were sunk in the Aegean Sea by mines laid by the Royal Navy minelayer ABDIEL. The Royal Navy carriers ARK ROYAL and FURIOUS launched forty-eight "Hurricanes" for Malta in "Operation Splice", two aircraft were lost.

1942 Hitler decided not to invade Malta until he had taken Egypt.

1943 The Italian submarine GORGO was sunk by the USN destroyer NIELDS. The U303 was sunk by the Royal Navy submarine SICKLE south of Toulon, France. USAAF B26s attacked airfields on Sardinia.

1944 The U453 was sunk by the Royal Navy destroyers TERMAGANT, TENACIOUS and LIDDESDALE. A battalion of the US Army's 85th Division landed near Sperlonga. The US Army's 88th Division took Monte Calvo and Cima del Monte, Italy.

Atlantic

1939 Survivors of the Egyptian transport ZAMZAM, which had been sunk on April 16th by the German armed merchant cruiser ATLANTIS, arrived at St. Jean-de-Luz, France aboard the freighter DRESDEN.

1941 The U93 sank the Dutch tanker ELUSA (6,235 tons). U93 survived until January 15, 1942. The freighter ROBIN MOOR became the first American ship sunk by a U-boat (the U69), after she had been stopped and identified. The U69 sank the British freighter TEWKESBURY (4,601 tons). U69 survived until February 17, 1943.

1942 The U159 sank the British freighter NEW BRUNSWICK (6,529 tons) and tanker MONTENOL (2,646 tons). U159 survived until July 15, 1943. The U106 sank the Mexican tanker FAJA DE ORO (6,067 tons). U106 survived until August 2, 1943. The U103 sank the American freighters CLARE (3,372 tons) and ELIZABETH (4,727 tons-6 dead). U103 survived until April 15, 1945. The U69 sank the Canadian freighter TORONDOC (1,927 tons). U69 survived until February 17, 1943. The U156 sank the Dominican Republic freighter PRESIDENTE TRUJILLO (1,668 tons). U156 survived until March 8, 1943. The American freighter PLOW CITY (3,282 tons-1 dead) was sunk by the U588. U588 survived until July 31st. The US Coast Guard cutter NEMESIS rescued twenty-eight survivors from the FAJA DE ORO and the US Coast Guard cutter AIVIK rescued forty-two from the steamer SVEND FOYNE.

North America

1932 The heavy cruiser PORTLAND (awarded sixteen battle stars and a Navy Unit Commendation during the war) was launched. She was scrapped in Panama City in December 1959.

1935 The submarine SHARK was launched. She was lost on February 11, 1942.

1936 The heavy cruiser VINCENNES (awarded two battle stars during the war) was launched. She was lost August 9, 1942.

1942 The first flight of the P61 "Black Widow" night fighter took place. The USN submarine HADDO was launched; she would be commanded by Chester Nimitz Jr., the Admiral's son. She was stricken in 1959.

1943 The first flight of the B17G model of the "Flying Fortress" took place.

1944 The submarine BOARFISH was launched. She was transferred to the Turkish Navy in 1948.

1980 American Liberty ship JEREMIAH O'BRIEN arrived at her berth at Fort Mason, San Francisco to become a memorial.

2009 USN Lieutenant Commander Robert Thomas, age 87, died in New London, New Hampshire. He had scored 5 victories while flying the F6F in the Pacific.

2013   Medal of Honor recipient Technical Sergeant Vernon McGarity, age 91, died of cancer in Memphis, Tennessee. He had received the awar for actions outde of Krinkelt, Belgium in December of 1944 while serving with the 99th Infantry Division.

Pacific

1942   The USN destroyer HELM rescued four survivors from the tanker NEOSHO which had been damaged by Japanese aircraft on May 7th. Admiral R. Theobold's North Pacific Force (five cruisers and four destroyers) left Pearl Harbor, en route to the Aleutians.

1943   American forces continued their attacks on Attu in the Aleutians. The American 5th Air Force B17 "Honikuu Okole" was shot down over Rabaul, New Britain. One crewman survived and hid with natives in the area until rescued nine months later. IJN Admiral Isoroku Yamamoto's ashes were returned to Tokyo aboard the battleship YAMATO. He had been killed by USAAF P38s over the Solomons. USN TBFs mined the waters near Buin, New Georgia. The Japanese Imperial General Headquarters decided to evacuate Kiska Island in the Aleutians.

1944   The USN tanker NECHES II was damaged off California by a mine. The USN LSTs 39, 43, 69, 179, 353 and 480, three LCTs, seventeen LVTs and eight 155mm cannon were destroyed in an ammo-loading accident in the West Loch of Pearl Harbor. Also damaged were LSTs 205 and 225. 163 men died and 396 were wounded. The USN submarine RAY sank the TEMPEI MARU (6,097 tons). The USN submarine POLLACK sank the IJN destroyer ASANAGI off Chichi Jima. The USN submarine PICUDA sank the IJN gunboat HASHIDATE. The Royal Navy submarine SEA ROVER sank the KOSHO MARU (1,365 tons). The American airfield on Wakde Island became operational. The American 5th Air Force attacked Noemfoor Island.

1945   Private First Class Desmond Doss, of the 77th Division, won a Medal of Honor on Okinawa. The US Army's 31st Division took Malaybalay, Mindanao. The IJN minesweeper W-34 was sunk in the Java Sea by the USN submarine CHUB. Two USAAF P39 "Airacobras" were abandoned at Tadji, New Guinea. One was recovered in 1967 and the other in 1972.

1951   The USN battleship NEW JERSEY was hit by shore-fire off Wonsan, Korea (one dead). It was the only combat loss of her career.

China-Burma-India

1943   The Royal Air Force attacked Akyab, Burma.

May 22nd

Western Europe

1892   German General Hans Gollnick was born. He commanded the 36th Panzer Grenadier Division, the 46th Panzer Corps and the 28th Corps on the Eastern Front.

1939   Britain and Portugal signed a treaty.

1940   Fifty-nine Royal Air Force bombers attacked targets in France and lost three "Blenheims". Forty-seven Royal Air Force bombers attacked targets in France, Belgium and Holland. The Royal Air Force evacuated its last airfield in France (at Merville). The Germans surrounded Calais on the Channel coast. The first member of the British Parliament killed in action was Ronald Cartland. Parliament passed the "Emergency Powers Defense Bill" giving the government unlimited powers.

1941   Sixteen Royal Air Force "Blenheims" attacked German shipping. The German battleship BISMARCK and heavy cruiser PRINZ EUGEN were attacked in Bergenfjord in Norway by six Royal Air Force "Whitleys" and six "Hudsons". No hits were scored. The German ships then left their anchorage and headed into the North Sea. The Royal Navy battleship PRINCE OF WALES, the battlecruiser HOOD and six destroyers were ordered to a position south of Iceland in case the BISMARCK and the heavy cruiser PRINZ EUGEN attempted to break out into the Atlantic. At 2245, the Royal Navy battleship KING GEORGE V, the carrier VICTORIOUS and eleven cruisers and destroyers left Scapa Flow to assist the forces already at sea searching for the German warships. The Dutch minelayer NAUTILUS was lost in a collision in the Humber Estuary.

1942   Eight German saboteurs left their training facility at Quentz Lake, near Brandenburg, and went on a 2-day binge in Paris. Their names were: Georg Dasch, Ernst Burger, Edward Kerling, Richard Quirin, Heinrich Heinke, Hermann Neubauer, Werner Thiel and Herbert Haupt (See May 26th and 28th and June 13th and 17th). Thirty-one Royal Air Force bombers dropped mines in the Baltic.

1943   Luftwaffe ace Adolf Galland made his first flight in a Me262 jet fighter while at Lechfield near Augsburg in southern Germany. USAAF General Curtis LeMay was awarded a Royal Air Force Distinguished Flying Cross. Seven Royal Air Force "Mosquitoes" attacked Nantes, France. Six American 8th Air Force P47s flew patrols over the Channel.

1944   289 American 8th Air Force B17s dropped 623 tons of bombs on Kiel, Germany and lost five aircraft. 568 8th Air Force fighters provided support for the bombers and claimed twenty-two victories for the loss of three P38s, three P47s and one P51. The P51 that was lost had been damaged by a P38 and was forced to land in Sweden where it was interned. The 8th Air Force received its 77th and last installation in Britain from the Royal Air Force when it assumed control of North Pickenham. The American 9th Air Force attacked Pointe du Hoc in Normandy and airfields in France. Luftwaffe Lieutenant Johnen's crew (See April 28th) was released after three days of interrogation by the Gestapo. The American 3rd Army's Finance Section received 3,760,000 French francs in "Invasion Money". The German minesweeper M-515 was sunk in the Baltic by a mine. 375 Royal Air Force bombers attacked Dortmund, Germany and lost eighteen "Lancasters". 858 buildings were destroyed and 361 people, including twenty-six Allied prisoners of war, were killed in the raid. 235 Royal Air Force bombers attacked Brunswick, Germany and lost thirteen "Lancasters". There were no casualties in the city. 133 Royal Air Force bombers attacked Le Mans, France and lost one "Halifax". 128 Royal Air Force bombers attacked Orleans, France and lost one "Halifax". Four B17s from the USAAF's 422nd Bomb Squadron dropped 320,000 leaflets on targets in Holland. The USAAF's 801st Bomb Group dispatched twelve B24s on "Carpetbagger" missions.

1945 The German Army's highest-ranking intelligence officer, Reinhard Gehlen, surrendered north of Darmstadt. He would later work with the Americans against the Soviets. American forces began shipping 400 tons of German rocket equipment from Nordhausen, Germany to Cherbourg, France. It was to be shipped to America.

1946 Karl-Hermann Frank, Minister of State for the Czechoslovakian "Protectorate", was executed in Prague in front of 5,000 spectators.

1949 Nazi music composer Hans Pfitzner died in Salzburg.

Eastern Europe

1942 Luftwaffe ace Hans Stretlow (68 victories) shot himself rather than be captured after he was shot down.

1943 170 Luftwaffe aircraft attacked Kursk.

Mediterranean

1941 In operations off Crete the Luftwaffe sank the Royal Navy destroyer GREYHOUND at 1351, the Royal Navy heavy cruiser GLOUCESTER at 1550 and the Royal Navy heavy cruiser FIJI at 2015. The Royal Navy battleships VALIANT and WARSPITE and the cruisers NAIAD and CARLISLE were damaged by the Luftwaffe north of Crete. The Royal Navy heavy cruiser YORK (See March 26, 1941) was scuttled in Suda Bay, Crete. Anzac General Freyberg ordered his forces on Crete to retreat. The Royal Air Force attacked Benghazi.

1943   Royal Air Force "Spitfires" and South African Air Force P40s shot down fourteen Luftwaffe Me323 "Gigant" transports and seven fighter escorts off Cap Bon, Tunisia. Allied aircraft attacked Sicily and Sardinia.
1944   The American 15th Air Force attacked shipping and rail targets in Italy.

Atlantic
1941   At 2245, the Royal Navy's main fleet left Scapa Flow to search for the German battleship BISMARCK. The Royal Navy heavy cruiser EDINBURGH took the German trawler MUNCHEN. The U111 sank British freighter BARNBY (4,813 tons). U111 survived until October 4th. The U103 sank the British tanker BRITISH GRENADIER (6,857 tons). U103 survived until April 15, 1945.
1942   The U158 sank the British freighter F.B. BAIRD (1,758 tons). U158 survived until June 30th. The USN destroyer BLAKELEY rescued seven survivors from the American freighter QUAKER CITY which had been sunk by U156.
1943   The U569 was sunk by the USN escort carrier BOGUE.

North America
1885   Admiral Richmond Kelly Turner was born in Portland, Oregon. He graduated 5th in his 1908 Annapolis class of 201. In 1927, at the age of forty-two, he received his naval aviator's wings. He was promoted to captain in 1935. In October 1940 he became Director of War Plans under the Chief of Naval Operations Admiral Stark. In that position, he was responsible for the evaluation and dissemination of military intelligence and should have been held accountable for the warnings or lack thereof to the naval commanders in the Pacific prior to the Japanese attacks of December 1941. In July 1942, he assumed command of Amphibious Forces South Pacific. He would hold similar positions throughout the war. He retired on June 30, 1947 and died on February 12, 1961. He was buried beneath a regulation headstone at the Golden Gate Cemetery in San Bruno, south of San Francisco. Lying nearby are Admirals Nimitz, Lockwood, and Spruance, also under regulation headstones.
1915   Cartoonist George Baker was born in Lowell, Massachusetts. He would gain fame as the creator of the "Sad Sack" character in the military magazine "Yank". He would die on May 7, 1975 in Los Angeles.
1939   The destroyer BUCK was launched. She was lost on October 9, 1943.
1941   FDR ordered three battleships and one carrier from the Pacific Fleet to reinforce the Atlantic Fleet. He also ordered the USMC to relieve the British forces on Iceland.
1942   The escort carriers ALTAMAHA and BARNES were launched. ALTAMAHA was scrapped in 1961 and BARNES in 1960.

1943   The light carrier LANGLEY was launched. She was scrapped in 1964. The destroyer CAPERTON was launched. She was stricken in 1974.
1944   The escort carrier MATANIKAU was launched. She was scrapped in Japan in 1960. The destroyer LITTLE was launched. She was lost May 3, 1945. The 9th Army headquarters was activated at Fort Sam Houston, Texas.
1945   It was announced that Britain had received over $12 billion in Lend-Lease while Russia received over $8 billion.
1947   The USN submarine rescue vessel MALLARD was scuttled.
1949   Secretary of the Navy James V. Forrestal committed suicide by jumping from the 19th floor of the Bethesda Naval Hospital. He had been diagnosed with paranoia and believed, among other things, that Israeli agents were following him. Years later the Israeli government would confirm that they indeed did have agents investigating him.
1978   Admiral Aubrey W. Fitch, age 94, died in Newcastle, Maine. He had commanded carriers during the Coral Sea and Guadalcanal campaigns.
2012   USN ace William Davis died in Santa Barbara at the age of 91. He had been credited with 7 aerial victories while flying F6F "Hellcats" off the LEXINGTON. He had also been awarded a Navy Cross for his part in sinking the IJN carrier ZUIKAKU.

South America
1942   Mexico declared war on the Axis.

Pacific
1942   400,000 tons of aviation fuel was accidentally destroyed during a demolition drill on Midway. The USN submarine TAUTOG damaged the transport SANKO MARU of Truk. The USN submarine SILVERSIDES damaged the transport ASAHISAN MARU off Honshu.
1943   American forces continued their ground attacks on Attu in the Aleutians. Japanese Air Force "Bettys" attacked the USN light cruiser CHARLESTON and destroyer PHELPS off Attu.
1944   The USN destroyer escort ENGLAND sank the IJN submarine Ro-106. USN destroyers bombarded Wake Island. The USN submarine PICUDA sank the IJN gunboat HASHIDATE in the South China Sea. The USN submarine POLLACK sank the IJN destroyer ASANAGI northwest of Chichi Jima. The Royal Navy submarine SEA ROVER sank the KOSHO MARU (1,365 tons). Charles Lindbergh flew a combat mission in an F4U "Corsair" from Green Island against Rabaul, New Britain.
1945   The US Army's 24th Division reached Tambongan, Mindanao. The US Army's 31st Division took Kalasungay, Mindanao. The US Army's 7th Division took Yonabaru, Okinawa. The USN destroyer-transport BARRY was a constructive loss after an air-attack off Okinawa.

China-Burma-India

1939 The Soviets attacked Japanese forces in Mongolia.
1940 The Italian submarine TORRICELLI sank the Royal Navy destroyer KHARTOUM and damaged the Royal Navy sloop SHOREHAM north of Perim.
1942 The American Volunteer Group attacked Salween losing one aircraft.
1944 The British submarine SEA ROVER sank the IJN gunboat KOSHO MARU off Malaya.
1945 Royal Canadian Air Force ace Sub/Lieutenant W.T. Klersy (14 victories) was killed in action.

May 23rd

Western Europe

1896 German General Felix Steiner was born. He died on May 17, 1966 in Munich.
1898 Nazi proconsul to Norway Joseph Terboven was born in Essen. He committed suicide on May 8, 1945.
1900 Hans Frank, future German Governor General of Poland, was born in Karlsruhe. He was executed for war crimes on October 16, 1946.
1928 The German light cruiser KÖLN was launched. She survived the war and was scrapped in 1946.
1939 Hitler informed his military commanders of his plans to attack Poland.
1940 German General Gerd von Rundstedt ordered his Army "Group A" to stop its advance towards Dunkirk. Lieutenant C. Furness, of the Welch Guards, won a posthumous Victoria Cross in France. At 0030, the French destroyer JAGUAR was beached off Dunkirk after being damaged by the German S-21 and S-23, 13 of her crew died. She was later destroyed by the Luftwaffe. At 0830, the French destroyer CHACAL was sunk off Pas de Calais by the Luftwaffe, there were twenty-one survivors. At 1812, the French destroyer ORAGE was damaged off Boulogne by the Luftwaffe, twenty-eight died. She sank at 0330 the next day. Royal Navy destroyers evacuated 4,368 troops from Boulogne, France. In the first combat between Royal Air Force "Spitfires" and Luftwaffe Me109s, the two Royal Air Force pilots involved, Alan Deere and Johnny Allen, scored one destroyed and one damaged. Sixteen Royal Air Force bombers attacked targets near Arras, France, losing three "Blenheims". Royal Air Force ace Robert Tuck (29 aerial victories) scored his first three, a Me109 and two Me110s. Royal Air Force Squadron Leader Roger Bushell, commander of No.92 Squadron, was shot down on the same mission. He would later be one of the leaders of the "Great Escape" from Stalag Luft III (See March

	24, 1944) and was one of fifty escapees that were executed after being recaptured. 122 Royal Air Force bombers attacked targets in Germany and Holland losing two "Hampdens" and one "Whitley".
1942	The German trawler V-1808 was sunk by a mine off Hoofden.
1943	Twelve Royal Air Force "Venturas" attacked Zeebrugge, Holland. The U441 left her base at Brest, France. She was the first of the "flak traps". Armed with two 20mm quads and a 37mm cannon, it was hoped that she could defend herself from Allied aircraft while crossing the Bay of Biscay on the surface. Six American 8th Air Force P47s flew patrols over the Channel. 826 Royal Air Force bombers attacked Dortmund, Germany and lost thirty-eight aircraft. Almost 2,000 buildings were destroyed and 599 people were killed in the raid. The town had been hit so hard that it would be another year before the Royal Air Force bothered to return. Fifteen Royal Air Force bombers dropped leaflets over France and lost one "Wellington".
1944	814 American 8th Air Force bombers dropped 2,283 tons of bombs on marshalling yards and airfields in France and lost two B17s and one B24. 562 8th Air Force fighters provided support for the bombers. Seventy-five 8th Air Force P51s attacked and destroyed a rail bridge in Hasselt, Belgium. A Luftwaffe intruder destroyed an 8th Air Force 385th Bomb Group B17 at Great Ashfield in Britain. Forty-six Royal Air Force "Mosquitoes" attacked targets in France and Germany. Four B17s from the USAAF's 422nd Bomb Squadron dropped 928,000 leaflets on Belgium and Holland. The USAAF's 801st Bomb Group dispatched seven B24s on "Carpetbagger" missions.
1945	Hitler's successor, Admiral Karl Doenitz, and his cabinet were arrested in Flensburg and sent to Bad Mondorf, Luxembourg to await trial. German Gestapo and Waffen S.S. Commander Heinrich Himmler committed suicide at Luneburg after being captured by British forces. Admiral Hans von Friedeburg, Doenitz' successor as Commander-in-Chief of the German Navy, committed suicide in Murwik.
1967	Ernst Niekisch, leader of the National Bolshevists in Weimar, died.
1994	The "Liberty" ship JEREMIAH O'BRIEN arrived at Portsmouth, Britain after a voyage from San Francisco. It took 35-days and spanned 8,000 miles. She was scheduled to take part in the 50th Anniversary ceremonies in Normandy.

Mediterranean

1941	Royal Air Force "Hurricane" fighters attacked German positions on Crete. The first Luftwaffe fighters landed at Maleme airfield on Crete. At 0755, the Royal Navy destroyers KELLY and KASHMIR were sunk off Crete by aircraft. The Royal Navy destroyer KIPLING rescued 279 survivors from

the two ships. King George II of Greece was evacuated from Crete by the Royal Navy destroyer DECOY.

1943   The Italian submarine LEONARDO DA VINCI was sunk by the Royal Navy destroyers ACTIVE and NESS.

1944   The Allied break-out began at Anzio, Italy. 335 Italians civilians were killed in the Ardeatine Caves in Rome by S.S. troops. 2nd Lieutenant Van Barfoot, of the 45th Division, won a Medal of Honor near Carano, Italy. 2nd Lieutenant Ernest Dervishian and Staff Sergeant George Hall, of the 34th Division, won Medals of Honor near Anzio. Private First-Class John Dutko (posthumous) and Private First-Class Patrick Kessler, of the 3rd Division, won Medals of Honor near Ponte Rotto, Italy. 2nd Lieutenant Thomas Fowler, of the 1st Armored Division, won a posthumous Medal of Honor near Carano, Italy. The American 15th Air Force attacked rail targets in Italy.

Atlantic

1940   The U9 sank the German tanker FAULBAUMS (3,256 tons), which had been captured by the British. U9 survived until August 20, 1944.

1941   At 1200, the German battleship BISMARCK and heavy cruiser PRINZ EUGEN entered the Denmark Strait. At 1922, they were sighted by the Royal Navy heavy cruisers SUFFOLK and NORFOLK. At 2000, Royal Navy Admiral Lancelot E. Holland commanding his force that consisted of the battleship PRINCE OF WALES, the battle cruiser HOOD and six destroyers south of Iceland ordered his ships to increase speed to 27 knots to intercept the German ships. At 2030, the BISMARCK fired at the NORFOLK. At 2400, the British cruisers lost contact. The U38 sank the Dutch freighter BERHALA (6,622 tons). U38 survived the war.

1942   The U432 sank the British freighter ZURICHMOOR (4,455 tons). U432 survived until March 11, 1943. The U588 sank the British freighter MARGOT (4,545 tons). U588 survived until July 31st. The U103 sank the American tanker SAMUEL Q. BROWN (6,625 tons-7 dead). U103 survived until April 15, 1945. The U155 sank the Panamanian freighter WATSONVILLE (2,220 tons). U155 survived the war.

1943   The U752 was sunk by aircraft from the Royal Navy escort carrier ARCHER.

1944   The Royal Navy submarine SCEPTRE sank the German iron-ore ship BALDUR in Spanish territorial waters near Castro Urdiales.

North America

1921   The light cruiser CINCINNATI (awarded one battle star during the war) was launched. She was scrapped in 1946.

1939   The submarine SQUALUS was lost in a training accident. Her commander, Francis Naquin, would be aboard the battleship CALIFORNIA at Pearl Harbor serving as her engineering officer on December 7, 1941. He would retire as a Rear Admiral and would die in 1989. USN Chief Bosun's Mate Orson Crandall, Torpedo 1st Class John Mihalowski and Chief Machinist Mate William Badders won Medals of Honor for their efforts at the sight of the SQUALUS sinking. The submarine would be salvaged and recommissioned as the SAILFISH and would have a distinguished career in WWII.

1943   The battleship NEW JERSEY was commissioned. The submarine DORADO was launched. She was lost on October 12, 1943. A B17, serial number 42-30620, crashed in Yellowstone Park while en route from Marysville, California to Lewiston, Montana. Ten of the eleven men aboard died. The wreckage was recovered in 1988, after a devastating forest fire in the park.

1946   The destroyer STEWART was expended. The destroyer-transport CROSBY and destroyer MAURY were sold for scrap.

1966   The "Liberty" ship ISAAC VAN ZANDT was scuttled off the coast of Washington with 400 tons of munitions aboard.

1972   The destroyer HERNDON was expended as a target.

1979   Lieutenant General Earl Barnes, age 76, died of emphysema in McLean, Virginia. He had commanded the 13th Fighter Command in the South Pacific.

2009   Charles Donald Albury, age 88, died in Orlando, Florida. He had been the co-pilot of the B29 "Bock's Car" when it dropped the atomic bomb on Nagasaki, Japan on August 12, 1945.

Pacific

1942   A single USAAF B26 attacked Lae, New Guinea shooting down one of fifteen attacking Japanese "Zeros". The USN YP-277 was sunk by a mine off French Frigate Shoals. A seaplane from the IJN submarine I-29 flew over Sydney, Australia.

1943   American forces continued their attacks on Attu in the Aleutians. American 11th Air Force P38s shot down nine Japanese "Betty" bombers over Attu, while losing two aircraft. The USN's first PT-tender, the gunboat NIAGARA, was sunk in the Solomons by the Japanese Naval Air Force. The IJN heavy cruiser MOGAMI was damaged in a collision with the tanker TOA MARU in Tokyo Bay.

1944   USN destroyers bombarded Wotje Island. USN Task Group 58.3 (commanded by Montgomery) attacked Wake Island. The USN destroyer escort ENGLAND sank the IJN submarine Ro-104. The USN submarine

RAY sank the TAIJUN MARU (2,825 tons). The USN submarine RATON sank the KOSHIN MARU (168 tons). The USN submarine LAPON sank the WALES MARU (6,586 tons). 5th Air Force A-20s attacked Biak, New Guinea.

1945 The USMC 6th Division took Naha, Okinawa. The port of Yokohama was closed due to the USN blockade. Staff Sergeant John Sjogren, of the 40th Division, won a Medal of Honor near San Jose Hacienda on Negros. 500 USAAF B29s fire-bombed Tokyo and destroyed 5.3 square miles of the city.

China-Burma-India

1940 The Italian submarine GALVANI sank the Royal Indian Navy patrol craft PATHAN in the Gulf of Oman.

1942 US Army General Joseph Stilwell arrived in Dimapur, India, after retreating 400 miles through Burmese jungle.

May 24th

Western Europe

1940 The German 10th Panzer Division attacked Calais, France. They were attacked by sixty-nine Royal Air Force bombers. The German 2nd Panzer Division attacked Boulogne, France. German forces attacked Tournai, France. 5,000 Allied troops were evacuated from Boulogne. Fifty-nine Royal Air Force bombers attacked targets in Germany. The Allies agreed to capture Narvik, Norway, destroy it and then evacuate. The Norwegian government was not told of the decision.

1941 Twenty-three Royal Air Force "Blenheims" attacked shipping and lost one aircraft.

1942 The German heavy cruiser LUTZOW, the tanker DITHMARSCHEN and the torpedo boat T-7 were transferred from Trondheim to Narvik in Norway.

1944 The American 9th Air Force attacked Channel shore-batteries. The American 15th Air Force attacked Vienna, Austria. 400 American 8th Air Force B24s dropped 1,200 tons of bombs on French airfields. 464 8th Air Force B17s dropped 1,081 tons of bombs on Berlin losing thirty-three bombers. 602 8th Air Force fighters provided support for the bombers and claimed thirty-three victories for the loss of one P38, one P47 and eight P51s. 194 8th Air Force fighters attacked rail bridges in France and lost three P51s. At 0030, the German torpedo boat GREIF was damaged by the Royal Air Force off Normandy and was later scuttled. At 0240, the German minesweeper M-39 was sunk off Dunkirk, France by the

Royal Navy MTBs 354 and 361. 442 Royal Air Force bombers attacked Aachen, Germany and lost twenty-five aircraft. 207 people were killed in the Aachen. Another fifty-two died in Eilendorf, a nearby village. Sixty-three Royal Air Force bombers attacked Eindhoven, Holland. 224 Royal Air Force bombers attacked coastal batteries along the Channel coast. Fifty-one Royal Air Force bombers attacked Antwerp. Four B17s from the USAAF's 422nd Bomb Squadron dropped 2,540,000 leaflets on targets in France and Belgium. The USAAF's 801st Bomb Group dispatched three B24s on "Carpetbagger" missions.

1945 Robert von Greim, Hermann Goering's successor as Commander-in-Chief of the Luftwaffe, committed suicide in Salzburg Prison.

1950 British Field Marshal Archibald Wavell died. He had commanded the British forces in North Africa.

1993 Sir Mark Pizey, age 93, died. He had commanded 6 destroyers in an attempt to stop the Germans "Channel Dash" in 1942.

Eastern Europe

1942 The Soviet freighter SEROV was sunk by the Luftwaffe.

1943 Heavy fighting took place along the entire Eastern Front.

Mediterranean

1870 South African Field Marshal Jan Smuts was born in Riebeck West. He served as Prime Minister during the war and he died on September 11, 1950.

1941 Royal Navy Lieutenant Commander M.D. Wanklyn, the commander of the submarine UPHOLDER, won a Victoria Cross for sinking the Italian liner CONTE ROSSO (17,879 tons).

1942 Axis aircraft attacked Malta.

1943 USAAF B26s attacked shipping off Pantelleria and airfields on Sardinia.

1944 Sergeant Sylvester Antolak and Private James Mills (posthumous), of the 3rd Division, won Medals of Honor near Cisterna di Littoria. Major J. Mahoney, of the Canadian Westminster Regiment, won a Victoria Cross at Cassino. A group of American PT-boats attacked German naval force off Italy. They sank the UJ-2223 (ex-Italian MARANGONE) and badly damaged the UJ-2222 (ex-Italian TUFFETO).

Atlantic

1940 The U37 sank the Greek freighter KYMA (3,994 tons). U37 survived the war.

1941 At 0247, the Royal Navy heavy cruiser SUFFOLK regained contact with the German battleship BISMARCK and heavy cruiser PRINZ EUGEN in the Denmark Strait. At 0535, the Royal Navy's battleship PRINCE OF WALES and battlecruiser HOOD sighted the German ships at seventeen miles. At 0552, the British opened fire. At 0601, HOOD was sunk by fire from the BISMARCK and the PRINZ EUGEN, killing all but three of her 1,419-man crew. The Royal Navy destroyer ELECTRA rescued the three survivors two hours after the battle. At 0605, the commander of the PRINCE OF WALES, Captain John Leach, ordered a withdrawal. The PRINCE OF WALES had damaged the BISMARCK with 3 14" hits, while suffering four 15" and three 8" hits herself. After receiving damage reports, the German commanders decided to abandon their mission of attacking Allied convoys and return to port. At 1816, the PRINZ EUGEN was detached from the BISMARCK and ordered to make her own way to a French port. During her maneuvers to cover the departure of the PRINZ EUGEN, the BISMARCK fired upon the SUFFOLK and was fired at in turn by the PRINCE OF WALES. No damage was suffered by either party in the exchange. The decision was made by German Admiral Gunter Lutjens, aboard the BISMARCK, to make for Brest rather than St. Nazaire. USN VP-52 PBYs based at Argentia began searching for BISMARCK. The German armed merchant cruiser ATLANTIS took the British freighter TRAFALGAR (4,530 tons). The U103 sank the Greek freighter MARIONGA (4,236 tons). U103 survived until April 15, 1945.

1942 The U103 sank the Dutch freighter HECTOR (1,828 tons). U103 survived until April 15, 1945. The U502 sank the Brazilian freighter GONCALVES DIAS (4,996 tons). U502 survived until July 5th. The steamer MARPESIA rescued two survivors from the American freighter NORLANTIC which had been sunk by U69. The USN destroyer GOFF rescued forty-eight survivors from the American tanker SAMUEL Q. BROWN which had been sunk by U103. Fifteen survivors from the American freighter QUAKER CITY reached Barbados. Their ship had been sunk by U156.

1943 The U441 (See Western Europe-May 23rd) shot down a Royal Air Force "Sunderland", but was forced to return to Brest because of damage sustained during the action. U441 survived until June 18, 1944. German Admiral Karl Doenitz ordered his U-boats to withdraw from the North Atlantic until counter-measures to Allied defensive tactics could be devised.

1944 The U476 was sunk by the Royal Air Force's No.210 Squadron northwest of Trondheim, Norway. The U675 was sunk by the Royal Air Force's No.4 (Operational Training Unit) west of Aalsund.

1945 The U979 ran aground on Amrum Island and was lost.

North America

1927 Lieutenant James Doolittle performed the first outside loop, while flying a Curtiss P-18. He would command the 8th Air Force during WWII.

1943 The US Chiefs of Staff approved the plan for the recapture of Kiska in the Aleutians.

1961 The battleship WASHINGTON (for $757,000) and the battlecruiser GUAM were sold for scrap.

1965 USMC General Thomas Holcomb, Commandant of the Corps November 1936 until December 1943, died in New Castle, Delaware.

2009 USAAF Lieutenant Robert Booth, age 85, died in California. He had scored 8 victories in the European Theater while flying P47s and P51s. USAAF Lieutenant Colonel Carl Luksic, age 87, died in Panama City, Florida. He had scored 8.5 victories in Europe while flying P51s.

Pacific

1942 The USN submarine POMPANO sank the fishing trawler KOTOKU MARU. A seaplane from the IJN submarine I-21 flew over Auckland, New Zealand.

1943 American forces continued their attacks on Attu in the Aleutians. The USN PTs 165 and 173 were lost when the tanker STANVAC MANILA (10,169 tons), which was transporting them, was sunk the IJN submarine I-17, 100 miles south of Noumea, New Caledonia.

1944 USN carriers (commanded by Montgomery) attacked Wake Island. Ten American 5th Air Force A20 "Havoc" bombers attacked Noemfoor Island, destroying ten Japanese aircraft. Charles Lindbergh flew an F4U "Corsair" from Green Island on a mission over New Ireland. The IJN escorts MATSUWA and IKI were sunk by the USN submarine RATON in the South China Sea. The USN submarine LAPON sank the BIZEN MARU (4,667 tons). The USN submarine GURNARD sank the TATEKAWA MARU (10,009 tons).

1945 The USN destroyers GUEST and STORMES and the destroyer escort COLES were hit by Japanese kamikazes. 520 USAAF B29s dropped 3,646 tons of bombs on Tokyo.

China-Burma-India

1942 The American Volunteer Group attacked Salween.

1943 The Royal Air Force attacked Udaung, Burma.

1944 The Japanese 18th Division defeated an American/Chinese force at Charpate, Burma. The Japanese transport TAICHI MARU was lost in a collision off Chinhai, China.

May 25th

Western Europe

1932 President Paul von Hindenburg asked Franz von Papen to form a new German government.

1940 The German 2nd Panzer Division took Boulogne, France. The Belgian Armys front was pierced. Forty-two Royal Air Force bombers attacked targets in France and lost four "Blenheims". The Luftwaffe was ordered to attack British shipping in the Channel. The Royal Navy destroyer WESSEX was sunk off Calais, France by the Luftwaffe. 103 Royal Air Force bombers attacked targets in France and Belgium, losing two "Hampdens" and one "Wellington".

1941 Thirty Royal Air Force "Blenheims" attacked German shipping and lost four aircraft. Forty-eight Royal Air Force "Hampdens" dropped mines off Brest and St. Nazaire in France.

1943 Twelve Royal Air Force B25 "Mitchells" attacked Abbeville, France and lost two aircraft. 116 American 8th Air Fighters flew sweeps over Belgium. 759 Royal Air Force bombers attacked Dusseldorf, Germany and lost twenty-seven aircraft. Thirty people were killed in the raid.

1944 Fifty-four American 8th Air Force bombers used H2X radar to locate their shore battery targets on the Channel coast. 326 8th Air Force bombers dropped 2,166 tons of bombs on marshalling yards, airfields and artillery positions in France and Belgium and lost two B24s and two B17s. 604 8th Air Force fighters provided support for the bombers and claimed sixteen victories for the loss of nine P38s and three P51s. The American 15th Air Force attacked railyards in Toulon and Lyon.

1965 Geoffrey de Havilland, designer of the "Mosquito", died.

1981 The American 8th Air Force 100th Bomb Group Memorial Museum was dedicated at Thorpes Abbotts in Norfolk.

2010 New Zealand ace Peter Hall died in England at the age of 88. He had scored 8 aerial victories while flying the "Mosquito".

Eastern Europe

1889 American aircraft designer Igor Sikorsky was born in Kiev. He escaped the Russian revolution and eventually made his way to America. He died in 1972.

1943 The Soviet submarine ShCh-408 was sunk by German surface craft.

1944 German commandoes attempted to capture Tito in Yugoslavia. Randolph Churchill, the son of the British Minister, narrowly escaped with Tito during the raid. The American 15th Air Force attacked troop concentrations in Yugoslavia.

1945 Harry Hopkins arrived in Moscow as Truman's envoy to confer with Stalin concerning problems that had arisen earlier in the month at the United Nations Conference in San Francisco.

Mediterranean

1940 Luftwaffe "Stuka" dive-bombers damaged the Royal Navy carrier FORMIDABLE.

1941 The Germans begin to take the offensive on Crete. German airborne commander Kurt Student arrived on Crete. At 1600, the Royal Navy sloop GRIMSBY and the freighter HELKA were sunk north of Tobruk by the Luftwaffe. The French sloop MENLIERE was stranded and lost off Corsica.

1943 The U414 was sunk by the Royal Navy corvette VETCH north of Oran. USAAF B26s attacked Pantelleria Island. At 1130, the Italian GROPPO was attacked at Messina by the USAAF B24s and B17s and sank at 1430.

1944 Allied forces from Anzio linked up with the American 5th Army at Terracinna. The Italian submarine BEILUL was sunk by the Royal Air Force. The US Army's 3rd Division took Cisterna and Cori in Italy. The British took Aquino, Italy. The American 15th Air Force attacked rail targets in Italy. The ex-Italian submarine BEILUL, the incomplete German submarine UIT-4 (ex-Italian R-7), the midget submarine UIT-18 (ex-Italian CM-2) and the corvette UJ204 (ex-Italian EURIDICE) were sunk at Monfalcone, Italy.

Atlantic

1941 At 0020, Royal Navy carrier VICTORIOUS "Swordfish" torpedo planes damaged the German battleship BISMARCK with one torpedo hit, killing 1 and wounding 6, but causing no serious damage to the ship. Six escorting "Fulmar" fighters were lost in the operation. En route to the BISMARCK, they had almost attacked the US Coast Guard cutter MODOC. The flight commander, Lieutenant Commander Eugene Esmonde, would later win a posthumous Victoria Cross during the "Channel Dash". At 0131, the PRINCE OF WALES and the BISMARCK exchanged gunfire with neither side suffering any hits. At 0316, the BISMARCK broke contact with the Royal Navy battleship PRINCE OF WALES and the heavy cruisers SUFFOLK and NORFOLK that had been shadowing her. The U103 sank the Dutch freighter WANGI WANGI (7,789 tons). U103 survived until April 15, 1945.

1942 The USN destroyer BLAKELY entered Fort du France, Martinique with torpedo damage inflicted by the U156. U156 survived until March 8, 1943. The Luftwaffe damaged the American freighter CARLTON off Norway.

The U558 sank the American freighter BEATRICE (3,451 tons-1 dead). U558 survived until July 20, 1943. The U593 sank the Panamanian tanker PERSEPHONE (8,426 tons), US Coast Guard No.882 rescued 12 survivors and the US Coast Guard cutter GENERAL GREENE rescued 18 from the steamer PEYSANDER. U593 survived until December 13, 1943. The Mexican freighter OAXACA rescued three survivors from the American tanker HALO which had been sunk by U506.

1943 The U467 was sunk by the USN's VP-84.
1944 The U990 was sunk by Royal Air Force's No.59 Squadron.

North America

1883 General Lesley McNair was born in Verndale, Minnesota. He graduated 11th in his 1904 West Point class of 124. He was promoted to brigadier general on October 1, 1918. After the war he reverted to his permanent rank of major. On April 6, 1939 he again was promoted to the rank of brigadier general. On June 9, 1941 he was promoted to lieutenant general. On March 9, 1942 he was named as Commander US Ground Forces. In June 1944 he was sent to Europe as commander of the 1st Army Group, a decoy unit formed to deceive the Germans into believing that the Allies were going to attack the Pas de Calais in France. He was killed on July 25, 1944 in Normandy by American bombs while observing an upcoming attack by American ground forces.

1897 Lord William Beaverbrook was born in Maple, Ontario. On May 14, 1940 he was named as Britain's Minister of Aircraft Production. He died of cancer on June 6, 1964.

1931 David R. Davis patented his "Fluid Foil" wing, which would be used on the B24 "Liberator".

1939 The submarine SEALION was launched. She was lost on December 25, 1941.

1940 The destroyer GWIN was launched. She was lost July 13, 1943.

1943 The "Trident Conference" ended in Washington D.C.

1947 The Governor of Utah declared Peter Tomich an honorary citizen of the state. Tomich had won a posthumous Medal of Honor aboard the target ship UTAH during the Pearl Harbor attack. He had no relatives, so his medal was placed in a permanent memorial to Utah's war dead.

2011 Medal of Honor recipient Paul Wiedorfer died at the age of 89. He had received it for actions on December 25, 1944 in Belgium.

Pacific

1942 The Japanese 2nd Carrier Force departed from Ominato, Hokkaido en route to attacking Dutch Harbor in the Aleutians. It included the carriers JUNYO and RYUJO, the heavy cruisers MAYA and TAKAO, the destroyers AKEBONO, SAZANAMI and USHIO and the tanker TEIYO MARU. The USN submarine POMPANO sank the TOKYO MARU (902 tons) off Okinawa. The IJN repair ship ASAHI was sunk by the USN submarine SALMON. The USN submarine TAUTOG sank the SHOKA MARU (4,467 tons) off Ulithi. The USN submarine DRUM sank the KITAKATA MARU (2,380 tons) off Honshu. The USN submarine PERMIT damaged the transport SENKO MARU Makassar Strait. The USN light cruiser ST. LOUIS landed USMC reinforcements at Midway. A seaplane from the IJN submarine I-9 flew over Kiska and Amchitka in the Aleutians.

1943 American forces continued their attacks on Attu in the Aleutians.

1944 American forces crossed the Tirfoam River in New Guinea. The USN submarine FLYING FISH sank the TAITO MARU (4,466 tons) and the OSAKA MARU (3,740 tons). Charles Lindbergh flew a combat mission against New Ireland in an F4U flying from Green Island.

1945 564 USAAF B29s attacked Tokyo, losing twenty-six aircraft. They destroyed 16.8 square miles of the city. Sixty-four American prisoners of war were also killed during the raid. Three USAAF B32 "Dominator" bombers arrived in the Philippines for combat evaluation. The type had been built as insurance against the possibility of operational failure by Boeings B29 "Superfortress". The USN destroyer-minesweeper BUTLER, the destroyer-transports BARRY and ROPER, the minesweeper SPECTACLE (11 died) were constructive losses after Japanese air attacks. The destroyer-transport BATES (21 died) and LSM-135 sank after air-attacks off Okinawa. The USN destroyers COWELL (2 wounded) and STORMES (21 died) were hit by Japanese kamikazes. The USN submarine BLENNY sank the KAIRYU MARU (81 tons). The Royal Navy submarine TRENCHANT sank the IJN minesweeper Wa-105. The Royal Navy submarine THOROUGH sank the NITTEI MARU (1,000 tons). Royal Navy carriers attacked Okinawa.

1948 The USN heavy cruiser SALT LAKE CITY was expended as a target 130 miles off southern California, after the Bikini Tests.

May 26th

Western Europe

1903 German diplomat Otto Abetz was born. He would serve as the Reich's ambassador to France and was sentenced to twenty years for war crimes. He died on May 5, 1958 in a car wreck. There was some question as to whether it was an accident or not.

1934 Reich Defense Minister, Werner von Blomberg, ordered that no soldier could be a Free Mason.
1936 Blomberg ordered that politically unreliable soldiers should be reported to the Gestapo.
1938 Britain began stock-piling food in preparation for war.
1940 At 1900, the British Admiralty instructed the Royal Navy headquarters at Dover (Vice-Admiral B.H. Ramsay), Britain to begin "Operation Dynamo" (the evacuation of the British Expeditionary Force from France by sea). At this time, it was hoped that 45,000 troops could be saved over a period of two days. The packet MONA'S ISLE became the first vessel to rescue British troops from Dunkirk (1,420). Thirty-four Royal Air Force bombers attacked German positions near Dunkirk. British Prime Minister Winston Churchill decided that the British garrison at Calais would not be evacuated. The Calais commander, Brigadier General Claude Nicholson, later died in a prisoner of war camp. The Royal Navy anti/aircraft light cruiser CURLEW was sunk off Narvik, Norway by the Luftwaffe. Forty-three Royal Air Force bombers attacked targets in France, Belgium and Holland.
1941 Twenty-eight Royal Air Force "Hampdens" dropped mines off Brest, France.
1942 Britain and Russia signed a 20-year mutual aid pact. A group of four German saboteurs led by Edward Kerling boarded the submarine U584 at Lorient, France en route to America. Four Royal Air Force "Lancasters" dropped mines in the Baltic.
1943 122 American 8th Air Force fighters flew sweeps over Holland.
1944 The USAAF's 479th Fighter Group (P38 then converted to the P51) flew its first 8th Air Force mission, a fighter sweep over Holland. The 479th was the 15th and last 8th Air Force fighter group to become operational. The American 9th Air Force attacked Seine River Bridges losing four aircraft. The American 15th Air Force attacked Toulon and Lyon railyards in France. Thirty Royal Air Force "Mosquitoes" attacked targets in France and Germany and lost two aircraft.
1945 The American 9th Army discovered a 14-ton cache of reports and papers concerning the V-2 rocket program at Dornten in the Harz Mountains of Germany. The Royal Navy carrier FURIOUS was designated as an explosives target ship. She was scrapped 1948-54.
1990 A memorial was dedicated at the Royal Air Force base at Watton.

Eastern Europe
1942 A Russian offensive against Kharkov began. It ended on the 26th in defeat. Russia and Britain signed a 20-year mutual aid pact. The U703 sank the American freighter SYROS (6,191 tons).

1944 Seventy-four Royal Air Force bombers attacked the oil installations at Ploesti, Rumania, losing one aircraft. The American 15th Air Force attacked troop concentrations in Yugoslavia.

Mediterranean
1941 General Freyberg, the Commander-in-Chief of the Allied Forces on the island of Crete, requested the evacuation of his remaining forces. Italian frogman attempted to attack shipping in Gibraltar. The Luftwaffe damaged the Royal Navy carrier FORMIDABLE and destroyer NUBIAN off Crete. The Italian Navy laid two minefields east of Malta. Malta-based Royal Air Force aircraft attacked an Italian convoy en route to Tripoli and damaged two ships.
1942 The German DAK attacked the British "Gazala Line".
1943 Allied aircraft attacked Sicily, Sardinia and Pantelleria.
1944 The US Army's 3rd Division took Artena, Italy. First Lieutenant Beryl Newman, of the 34th Division, won a Medal of Honor near Cisterna, Italy. French forces took Siserno and Amaseno. The Canadians took Ceprano.

Atlantic
1941 At 1036, the German battleship BISMARCK was sighted 690 miles from Brest by a Royal Air Force PBY "Catalina" co-piloted by USN Ensign Leonard Smith. At 1430, fourteen Royal Navy carrier ARK ROYAL aircraft attacked the Royal Navy heavy cruiser SHEFFIELD in error, scoring no hits. At 2225, an attack by fifteen "Swordfish" torpedo planes hit the BISMARCK with two torpedoes. One of them jammed the battleship's rudder and thus sealed her doom. Four of the aircraft were wrecked upon returning to their carrier. The US Coast Guard cutter GENERAL GREENE rescued thirty-nine survivors from the steamer MARCONI. The Dutch gunboat VAN KINSBERGEN took the Vichy French steamer WINNEPEG (8,379 tons) east of Martinique.
1942 The U103 sank the American freighter ALCOA CARRIER (5,588 tons). U103 survived until April 15, 1945. The American tanker CARRABULLE (5,030 tons-22 dead) was sunk by the U106. U106 survived until August 2, 1943. The USN yacht SAPPHIRE rescued thirty survivors from the American freighter PLOW CITY which had been sunk on May 21st by U588.
1943 The U436 was sunk by the Royal Navy frigate TEST and corvette HYDRABAD, west of Cape Ortegal.
1954 An explosion aboard the USN carrier BENNINGTON caused the deaths of approximately 150 of her crew.

North America

1895 Admiral John Wilkes was born in Charlotte, North Carolina. On December 7, 1941 he was in command of Submarine Division 14. He then served as Commander Submarines Southwest Pacific until replaced on May 26, 1942 by Charles Lockwood. He then took command of the light cruiser BIRMINGHAM and remained in command until he was promoted to rear admiral and named as Commander US Ports and Bases, France on June 26, 1944. From May 1945 until December 1945, he commanded Amphibious Forces Pacific Fleet. He retired on June 30, 1951 as a vice-admiral and died on July 20, 1957 in Bethesda, Maryland.

1943 The escort carrier MISSION BAY was launched. She was scrapped in 1960. The USN YMS-328 was commissioned in Seattle. In May 1961, actor John Wayne would buy her and rename her "WILD GOOSE". The USN gunboat CHARLESTON bombarded Japanese positions on Attu.

1944 The American government announced the termination of its contract for F4Us with Brewster Aircraft Corporation. The action was taken because of the poor quality of the aircraft produced by the company.

1945 A fire at Ladd Field in Fairbanks, Alaska destroyed $500,000 in equipment.

1988 Blytheville Air Force Base in Arkansas was renamed in honor of USAAF General Ira Eaker.

1998 The USN officially gave the carrier HORNET to the 500-person volunteer organization that had saved the ship from the scrapper in 1995. The ceremony took place in San Francisco.

2012 USAAF Major Robert Curtis died in Lexington, MA. He had been credited with 14 aerial victories over the Mediterranean and had been awarded a Distinguished Service Cross.

Pacific

1932 IJN Admiral Saito became Japan's Premier.

1942 The USN's Task Force 17 arrived at Pearl Harbor from the South Pacific. It had been recalled to participate in the defense of Midway against the upcoming Japanese attack. The Japanese 1st Carrier Fleet departed from the Inland Sea en route to attacking Midway. The freighter KITTYHAWK arrived at Midway with reinforcements consisting of twelve 3" cannon, three F4F "Wildcat" fighters and nineteen SBD "Dauntless" dive-bombers. The USN submarine SALMON sank the Japanese repair ship ASAHI off Indochina. A seaplane from the IJN submarine I-9 flew over Kiska in the Aleutians.

1943 American forces continued their attacks on Attu in the Aleutians. Private Joe Martinez, of the 7th Division, won a posthumous Medal of Honor on Attu. The USN submarine TROUT landed agents on Basilan Island in the Philippines. The USN submarine WHALE sank the SHOEI MARU (3,580 tons). The USN submarine SAURY sank the KAGI MARU (2,356 tons). The USN submarine POGY sank the TAINAN MARU (1,989 tons). The PALEMBANG MARU (5,256 tons) was damaged by a mine laid by the USN submarine TROUT.

1944   USN destroyers bombarded Mili Atoll in the Marshalls. The IJN submarine Ro-108 was sunk by the USN destroyer escort ENGLAND. The USN submarine CABRILLA sank the SANYO MARU (8,360 tons). The USN submarine TAMBOR sank the CHIYO MARU (657 tons). Charles Lindbergh flew an F4U from Emirau Island on a patrol over Kavieng, New Ireland.

1945   USAAF B29s dropped 3,252 tons of bombs on Tokyo. American 5th Air Force B25s attacked oil targets on Formosa. The USN submarine BILLFISH sank the KOTOBUKI MARU No.7 (991 tons).

China-Burma-India

1944   The Japanese recaptured Namkwi, near Myitkyina. Japanese forces attacked "Merrill's Marauders" near Myitkyina, Burma.

1945   Chinese forces took Nanning, China.

May 27th

Western Europe

1879   German lawyer Hans Lammers was born. He was Chief of the Reich Chancellery from 1933. He presided over cabinet meetings in Hitler's absence. He was sentenced to twenty years at the Nuremburg Trials, but was released on December 16, 1952. He died on January 4, 1962 in Dusseldorf.

1940   7,669 Allied soldiers were evacuated from Dunkirk, France. The British coasters YEWDALE and SEQUACITY and the French transport COTE D'AZUR were sunk off Dunkirk by the Luftwaffe. Forty-eight Royal Air Force bombers attacked German forces around Dunkirk losing two "Blenheims". The Royal Air Force lost fourteen fighters and shot down eighteen Luftwaffe aircraft over Dunkirk. Ninety British prisoners of war of the Norfolk Regiment were shot after being captured by the "Totenkopf" Division at Le-Cornet-Malo, France. The German forces resumed their advance on the port of Dunkirk. The British garrison at Calais, France surrendered. Thirty-eight Royal Air Force "Lysanders" dropped 864 grenades and 22,000 rounds of ammunition into Calais, unaware that it had already surrendered to the Germans. The Allies attacked Narvik, Norway. Sir John Dill replaced Sir Edmund Ironside as Commander Imperial General Staff. 120 Royal Air Force bombers attacked targets in Germany.

1941 Sixty-four Royal Air Force bombers attacked Cologne, Germany and killed eleven people. One Royal Air Force "Hampden" was lost on a minelaying mission off Brest, France.

1942 Reinhard Heydrich, Head of the Reich Main Security Office and Deputy Reich Protector of Bohemia and Moravia, was attacked by Czech Resistance in Prague and mortally wounded. He would die from his wounds on June 4th. 1,112 Jews were shipped from Paris to the concentration camp at Auschwitz. Only nineteen are known to have survived the war.

1943 Fourteen Royal Air Force "Mosquitoes" attacked Jena, Germany and lost five aircraft. 111 American 8th Air Force P47s flew sweeps over Belgium. A bomb-loading accident at Alconbury destroyed four USAAF 95th Bomb Group B17s, damaged eleven others and killed nineteen men. 518 Royal Air Force bombers attacked Essen, Germany and lost twenty-three aircraft. 488 buildings were destroyed and 196 people were killed in the raid. Ten nearby towns were also hit in the attack. Twenty-three Royal Air Force bombers dropped mines off Denmark and lost one "Stirling". The King and Queen of Britain visited the Royal Air Force's No.617 Squadron at their base at Scrampton near Lincoln. The unit had attacked the dams in the Ruhr Valley of Germany on May 16th in what has become known as the "Dambuster's Raid".

1944 930 American 8th Air Force bombers dropped 2,302 tons of bombs on German industrial targets and the marshalling yards at Strasbourg, France losing nineteen B17s and five B24s. One of the lost B17s landed in Switzerland. 710 8th Air Force fighters provided support for the bombers and claimed forty-four victories for the loss of one P38 and six P51s. The American 15th Air Force attacked Lyon and Toulon railyards in France. The American 9th Air Force attacked bridges over the Seine River in France. Twenty-four 8th Air Force P47s attacked a German convoy off Holland and sank two barges. 331 Royal Air Force bombers attacked Bourg-Leopold, France and lost ten aircraft. 170 Royal Air Force bombers attacked Aachen, Germany and lost twelve "Lancasters". 167 people died in the raid. 104 Royal Air Force bombers attacked Nantes, France and lost one "Lancaster". Eighty-three Royal Air Force bombers attacked Rennes, France. 272 Royal Air Force bombers attacked coastal batteries along the Channel coast and lost two aircraft.

1958 The Royal Navy battleship HOWE was sold for scrap. Her ship's bell was donated to St. Giles Cathedral in Edinburgh, Scotland.

2010 Vandals desecrated ninety-five German military graves at the Guebwiller Franco-German Cemetery in the Alsace region of France.

Eastern Europe
1942   The Soviet Navy delivered 3,017 reinforcements and 340 tons of supplies to the besieged city of Sevastopol on the Black Sea.
1943   The first British liaison officers were parachuted into Yugoslavia.

Mediterranean
1941   British Field Marshal Archibald Wavell authorized the evacuation of Crete. The Germans took Canea, Crete. The Royal Navy battleship BARHAM was bombed off Crete.
1942   The DAK had 560 tanks and the British 8th Army had 994 in North Africa.
1943   The French destroyer LEOPARD (launched in 1927) ran aground northeast of Benghazi, Libya and was lost.
1944   In Italy the US Army's 3rd Division took Artena, the French forces took Amaseno, Castro dei Volsci and Monte Siserno and the Canadians took Ceprano. American PT-boats sank the German UJ-2210.

Atlantic
1940   The U37 sank the British freighter SHEAF MEAD (5,008 tons) and the Argentine freighter URUGUAY (3,425 tons). U37 survived the war.
1941   The Royal Navy destroyers COSSACK, MAORI, ZULU and SIKH and the Polish destroyer PIORUN attacked the German battleship BISMARCK causing no damage. At 0815, the Royal Navy heavy cruiser NORFOLK sighted the BISMARCK and retreated out of range. At 0847, the Royal Navy battleships RODNEY and KING GEORGE V opened fire on the German battleship. At 0854, the NORFOLK joined the fight. At 0903, the Royal Navy heavy cruiser DORCHESTER began firing. By 1000, the BISMARCK could no longer return fire. At 1015, the British battleships broke off the action. At 1040, the BISMARCK capsized. She had been sunk due to combination of British fire and German scuttling charges. 110 BISMARCK survivors were rescued by the Royal Navy heavy cruiser DORSETSHIRE and destroyer MAORI. The U74 saved three more survivors and the German weather ship SACHSENWALD saved two more. Fifty-two Royal Air Force "Wellingtons" and twelve "Stirlings" flew searches for the German heavy cruiser PRINZ EUGEN in the Atlantic. The Royal Navy carrier ARK ROYAL was attacked by two Luftwaffe He111s. The U107 sank the British freighter COLONIAL (5,108 tons). U107 survived until August 18, 1944. The first Royal Navy CAM (catapult armed merchantman) the MICHAEL E., put to sea.
1942   The catapult-armed merchantman EMPIRE LAWRENCE was sunk off Norway by the Luftwaffe. The Luftwaffe sank the freighters ALAMAR (5,688 tons), MORMACSUL (three dead), CITY OF JOLIET and EMPIRE

PURCELL off Norway. The U578 sank the Dutch freighter POLYPHEMUS (6,269 tons). U578 survived until August 10th. The U172 sank the British tanker ATHELKNIGHT (8,940 tons). U172 survived until December 13, 1943. The U753 sank the Norwegian tanker HAMLET (6,578 tons). U753 survived until May 15, 1943. The British tanker ORINA rescued two survivors from the American tanker HALO which had been sunk on May 20th by U506.

1943 The U154 sank the American tanker JOHN WORTHINGTON (8,166 tons). U154 survived until July 3, 1944.

1944 The U292 was sunk west of Trondheim, Norway by the Royal Air Force's No.59 Squadron.

1945 The American merchantship JOHN WOOLMAN was damaged off Dunkirk by a mine.

North America

1880 American diplomat Joseph Grew was born in Boston. He was ambassador to Tokyo 1932-42. In 1944, he became Under Secretary of State. He retired in 1945 and died in 1965.

1885 Admiral Richmond Kelly Turner was born in Portland, Oregon. He would command many of the amphibious operations in the Pacific during the war.

1888 Admiral Frederick Sherman was born in Port Huron, Michigan. He graduated 24th in his 1910 Annapolis class of 131. In 1936, at the age of forty-eight, he qualified as an aviator. In June 1940, he assumed command of the carrier LEXINGTON. On April 3, 1942, he was promoted to rear admiral. After losing the LEXINGTON on May 8, 1942, he served for a short time on the staff of the Chief of Naval Operations. In November, he returned to the Pacific to take command of Task Force 16. After serving as commander of Carrier Division 2, he was sent home for a rest from March until August 1944. He then returned to combat as commander of Task Group 38.3/58.3. In July 1945, he was promoted to vice admiral and given command of the First Carrier Task Force. He retired on March 1, 1947 as a four-star admiral. He died on July 27, 1957 from a heart attack.

1937 The destroyers HELM and BLUE were launched. HELM was scrapped in 1947 and BLUE was lost on August 22, 1942.

1941 Allied convoy HX-129 left Halifax, Nova Scotia. It was the first convoy to be escorted all the way across the Atlantic. FDR declared a state of "unlimited national emergency".

1942 The North Pacific Force (nine vessels commanded by Theobald) arrived at Kodiak, Alaska. The USN destroyer tender PRAIRIE caught fire and burned for five hours in Argentia harbor, two of her crew died.

1944 The escort carrier ATTU was launched. She was scrapped in 1949.

1947 Evans Carlson (commander of the USMC Raiders) died in Portland, Oregon.
1974 The destroyer CHARLES J. BADGER was sold to Chile.
1992 USN Captain Donald K. Ross, age 81, died of a heart attack in Port Orchard, Washington. He had won a Medal of Honor while serving as Chief Engineer aboard the battleship NEVADA at Pearl Harbor on December 7th.
2002 Henry Potter, age 83, died in Austin, Texas. He had served as navigator on Jimmy Doolittle's bomber on the famous raid of April 18, 1942 on the Japanese Home Islands. He retired from the Air Force in 1970.
2010 USN Lieutenant John Finn died at the age of 100 at his ranch near Live Oak Springs, near San Diego. He had been the oldest living recipient of the Medal of Honor. He had been awarded the Medal for his actions at the Kaneohe Naval Air Station on December 7, 1941 while serving as a Chief Petty Officer. He was promoted to ensign after the attack and served as a limited duty officer for the rest of the war due to wounds suffered on December 7th.

Pacific
1942 IJN Admiral Nagumo's First Mobile Force, Carrier Strike Force left Hashirajima en route to Midway. It included the carriers AKAGI, KAGA, HIRYU and SORYU, the battleship KIRISHIMA and the heavy cruisers MIKUMA, MOGAMI, CHIKUMA and TONE. The USN carrier YORKTOWN, with the heavy cruisers PORTLAND and ASTORIA and six destroyers left Pearl Harbor en route to Midway. The US Army's "Americal" Division was organized in New Caledonia. A seaplane from the IJN submarine I-25 flew over Kodiak, Alaska.
1943 American forces took Fish Hook Ridge on Attu in the Aleutians. The USN submarine FINBACK sank the KOCHI MARU (2,910 tons). Allied aircraft attacked Lae, New Guinea.
1944 The US Army's 41st Division landed on Biak Island, northwest of New Guinea. The USN PT-339 was scuttled near Pur Pur, New Guinea. Charles Lindbergh flew an F4U from Emirau Island on a mission over Kavieng, New Ireland and later that night went on a patrol aboard a USN PT boat. The USN submarine LAPON fired two torpedoes at the USN submarine RATON, thinking that she was an IJN submarine.
1945 The US Army's 25th Division took Santa Fe, Luzon. The USMC 6th Division captured Naha, Okinawa. It was the largest city on Okinawa. The USN destroyer FORREST was a constructive loss after an air-attack off Okinawa. Eight of her crew died. The USN destroyers ANTHONY (no casualties) and BRAINE (50 of her crew died) were hit by kamikazes.

The American freighter MARY LIVERMORE was the last "Liberty" ship damaged by the Japanese when she was hit by a kamikaze off Okinawa. The USN submarine TIGRONE sank the YAWATA MARU No.3 (19 tons). The USN submarine TENCH sank the KINEI MARU (100 tons). The IJN submarine I-367 damaged the USN destroyer escort GILLIGAN.

1972   A memorial to the men who died aboard the target ship UTAH during the Pearl Harbor attack was dedicated on Ford Island.

China-Burma-India

1942   The American Volunteer Group ("Flying Tigers") attacked Lungling.
1943   Gaje Ghale, of the 5th Royal Gurkha Rifles, won a Victoria Cross in Burma. The Royal Air Force attacked Yegyanbyin, Burma.
1944   Chinese/American forces are involved in heavy fighting south of Charpate, Burma.

May 28th

Western Europe

1884   Czechoslovakian statesman Eduard Benes was born. In 1918, he was co-founder of Czechoslovakia with Thomas Masaryk. On December 18, 1935 he succeeded Masaryk as President. He resigned five days after being sold out by the Allies in the Munich Agreement of September 30, 1938. He then fled to Britain. On July 21, 1940 he formed a provisional government in London. He tried to form a coalition government after the war but resigned on June 6, 1948. He either committed suicide or was murdered on September 3, 1948.
1892   German S.S. General Sepp Dietrich was born in Hawangen. He would command the 6th S.S. Panzer Army during the "Battle of the Bulge". He would die in Ludwigsburg on April 21, 1966.
1937   Neville Chamberlain became Britain's Prime Minister.
1940   The Belgian Army surrendered to the Germans. 17,804 Allied troops were evacuated from Dunkirk, France. The British ferry QUEEN OF THE CHANNEL was sunk off Dunkirk by the Luftwaffe. The steamer ABOUKIR was sunk off Ostend, Belgium by a German S-boat, aboard were the last British refugees from Belgium. Ninety-five Royal Air Force bombers attacked German positions around Dunkirk and lost one "Blenheim" and one "Whitley". French General Charles de Gaulle's 4th Armored Division counter-attacked at Abbeville, France. Eighty British prisoners of war were shot at Wormhoudte by the German S.S. "Leibstandarte" Division. French and Norwegian forces took Narvik in

northern Norway. The Luftwaffe damaged the Royal Navy light cruiser CAIRO, the Royal Navy's flagship of the Narvik operation.

1941 Seven Royal Air Force "Blenheims" attacked German shipping off the Elbe River in the Baltic and lost one aircraft. Fourteen Royal Air Force "Whitleys" attacked the battleship TIRPITZ in Kiel, Germany and lost one aircraft.

1942 A group of four German saboteurs, led by Georg Dasch, boarded submarine U202 at Lorient, France en route to their assignments in America.

1943 Twelve Royal Air Force "Venturas" attacked Zeebrugge, Holland and lost one aircraft. Thirty-four Royal Air Force bombers dropped mines off the French coast. 120 American 8th Air Force P47s flew sweeps over France and Belgium.

1944 1,283 American 8th Air Force bombers attacked synthetic oil plants and targets of opportunity in Germany, losing thirty-six B17s and six B24s. Fifty-nine of the B17s flew the first GB-1 glide bomb mission. The target was the marshalling yards in Cologne, Germany. The attack was unsuccessful. 697 8th Air Force fighters provided support for the bombers and claimed twenty-seven victories for the loss of four P47s and five P51s. The American 9th Air Force attacked Namur, Belgium, and the Seine River bridges. 126 Royal Air Force bombers attacked Angers, France and lost one "Lancaster". 254 French civilians were killed in the raid. 201 Royal Air Force bombers attacked coastal batteries along the Channel coast and lost one "Lancaster".

1945 2,749 Cossacks were forcibly repatriated to the Soviets at Linz, Austria. William Joyce, Lord Haw Haw, was arrested in Flensburg, Germany.

Eastern Europe

1942 The Germans took 239,306 prisoners, 2,026 cannon and 1,249 tanks near Kharkov. The Soviet Navy shelled land targets near Sevastopol.

1943 German 6th Army Commander, Friedrich von Paulus and other generals that had been captured at Stalingrad, made an anti-German broadcast on Soviet radio.

1944 The American 15th Air Force attacked troop concentrations in Yugoslavia.

Mediterranean

1941 The British began evacuating their forces on Crete using the harbor at Sphakia on the southern coast. The operation would last until June 2nd. The Royal Navy light cruiser AJAX and destroyer IMPERIAL were damaged by aircraft. Sergeant A. Hulme, of the 23rd New Zealand Battalion, won a Victoria Cross on Crete. The Royal Navy destroyers NAPIER, NIZAM, KELVIN, and KANDAHAR evacuated more than 1,000 men from Crete.

1942   The U568 was sunk by the Royal Navy destroyers HERO, HURWORTH and ERIDGE north of Tobruk, Libya.
1943   At 1230, the Italian corvette FR-52 was sunk at Livorno, Italy. At 1300, the torpedo boats ANTARES and ANGELO BASSINI were damaged in the same action. Twenty-four USAAF B17s attacked Leghorn, Italy. USAAF B26s attacked Decimomannu.
1944   Heavy fighting took place along the entire front. The Germans abandoned Arce. The American 15th Air Force attacked Genoa. The German minelayer VALLELUNGA was sunk during the action.

Atlantic

1940   The U37 sank the French freighter BRAZZA (10,387 tons) and trawler JULIEN. U37 survived the war.
1941   The Royal Navy destroyers MASHONA and TARTAR were attacked by the Luftwaffe which was searching for the Royal Navy force that had sunk the German battleship BISMARCK. The MASHONA was sunk with the loss of 45 of her 250 crew. The German supply ship LECH (3,290 tons) was scuttled to prevent her capture by the Royal Navy. The U107 sank the Greek freighter PAPALEMOS (3,748 tons). U107 survived until August 18, 1944.
1942   The German minesweeper TINDEFJELL and the patrol trawler V-1103 were sunk by aircraft and mines off Ameland. The U506 sank the British freighter YORKMOOR (4,457 tons). U506 survived until July 12, 1943. The U502 sank the American freighter ALCOA PILGRIM (6,759 tons-31 dead). U502 survived until July 5th. The U106 sank the British freighter MENTOR (7,383 tons). U106 survived until August 2, 1943. The U155 sank the American freighter JACK (2,622 tons-39 dead). U155 survived the war. The U103 sank the American tanker NEW JERSEY (6,414 tons). U103 survived until April 15, 1945. The Italian submarine BARBARIGO sank the British freighter CHARLBURY (4,836 tons). The USN submarine GRUNION rescued sixteen survivors from the torpedoed American freighter JACK.
1943   The U304 was sunk by the Royal Air Force's No.120 Squadron south of Greenland. The U755 was sunk by the Royal Air Force's No.608 Squadron northwest of Majorca, Spain.
1945   Convoying was discontinued in the Atlantic and Arctic Oceans. In those areas, 2,575 Allied and neutral ships and 781 German U-boats had been sunk.

North America

1941   The Japanese whaler NISSHIN MARU entered San Francisco and had its code books seized by US Customs officials. They were copied and returned. This overzealous action resulted in the Japanese changing their codes which meant that the American military lost an important intelligence source. They had already broken the codes and would thus have to start from square one and attempt to break the new ones.

1943 The light carrier COWPENS was commissioned. She was scrapped in 1961. The destroyer TINGEY and the submarine ARCHERFISH were launched. TINGEY was stricken in 1965 and expended as a target and ARCHERFISH was still on active duty in 1960.

1944 The submarines LAGARTO and CHARR were launched. LOGARTO was lost on May 3, 1945 and CHARR was stricken in 1971.

1945 A Japanese balloon-bomb was found near High River, Alberta.

1946 B29 bomber production was stopped at Boeing's Renton, Washington plant.

1992 Michael Schmidt, age 69, agreed to be deported for concealing his past as a guard at Sachsenhausen Concentration Camp, north of Berlin, during WWII.

1994 A memorial was dedicated at Westover Air Force Base, Massachusetts. It was in memory of the 15,130 who died in USAAF training accidents during the war.

Pacific

1942 The Japanese First Fleet, Main Body (commanded by Yamamoto) left Japan. It was to supply Nagumo with distant support for his assault on Midway and the USN fleet. The Japanese Second Fleet, Escort Force (Tanaka) left Saipan en route to Midway. It included fifteen transports and was the actual Midway invasion force. The Japanese Second Fleet, Occupation Support Force (Kurita) left Guam en route to Midway. At 1130, USN Admiral Raymond Spruance left Pearl Harbor, en route to Midway with the carriers HORNET and ENTERPRISE, the heavy cruisers PENSACOLA, NEW ORLEANS, NORTHAMPTON, MINNEAPOLIS and VINCENNES, the anti/aircraft light cruiser ATLANTA, the destroyers HAMMANN, HUGHES, MORRIS, ANDERSON, RUSSELL, and GWIN and two tankers. The main Japanese invasion force left Japan en route to Midway. The USN submarine SALMON sank the GANGES MARU (4,382 tons) in the South China Sea. American forces occupied Espiritu Santo. Japanese forces conducted their initial scouting of Guadalcanal for an airfield location.

1943 Surviving Japanese forces on Attu were restricted to the Chicagof Harbor area. The USN submarine S-41 sank the Japanese barkentine SEIKI MARU (1,036 tons). The USN submarine SAURY sank the AKATSUKI MARU (10,216 tons).

1944 The Royal Navy submarine TEMPLAR sank the TYOKAI MARU (2,658 tons). The USN submarine PERMIT was attacked off Truk by

USN aircraft. The Japanese counter-attacked on Biak Island. The USN destroyer STOCKTON was damaged by shore-fire off Biak.

1945   The USN destroyer-minesweeper DREXLER was sunk (158 of her crew died) and the destroyer-transport LOY was damaged (15 died) by Japanese kamikazes. The DREXLER had been commissioned only six months before. Two USAAF B32 "Dominators", "Hobo Queen II" and "The Lady is Fresh", attacked Antatet, Luzon. It was the first action for the type. The USN submarine RAY sank the BIKO MARU (144 tons).

China-Burma-India

1939   The Japanese attacked Soviets in Mongolia.
1943   The U177 sank the American freighter AGWIMONTE (6,679 tons) and the Norwegian tanker STORAAS (7,886 tons). U177 survived until February 6, 1944.
1945   Convoying was discontinued in the Indian Ocean.

May 29th

Western Europe

1919   The Royal Navy light cruiser DURBAN was launched. She was scuttled as a breakwater on June 9, 1944.
1934   Jan Masaryk was re-elected as President of Czechoslovakia.
1940   47,310 Allied troops were rescued from Dunkirk, France. At 0045, the Royal Navy destroyer WAKEFUL (650 dead) was sunk off Dunkirk by the German S-30. At 0240, the Royal Navy destroyer GRAFTON was damaged off Dunkirk by the U62 while rescuing survivors from the WAKEFUL. At 0430 she was scuttled by the Royal Navy destroyer IVANHOE. The Royal Navy destroyer GRENADE was severely damaged by a Luftwaffe air attack in Dunkirk harbor and later exploded. The minesweeper WAVERLY, the trawlers CALVI and FENNALA, the ferry GRACIE FIELDS, the steamers CLAN MACALISTER, NORMANIA and LORINA and the paddle-wheeler CRESTED EAGLE were sunk in or near Dunkirk by the Luftwaffe. The Royal Navy destroyers GALLANT, JAGUAR, GREYHOUND, INTREPID, SALADIN, WOLFHOUND, the sloop BIDEFORD, and the French destroyer MISTRAL were damaged by the Luftwaffe. The Royal Navy destroyers MACKAY and MONTROSE were lost in a collision. Sixty-six Royal Air Force bombers attacked German positions around Dunkirk, France. The Germans took Ypres and Lille in France and Ostend in Belgium. Hitler met with his commanders at Cambrai, France and informed them that he had decided to use the panzers to attack the French forces to the south rather than the British at Dunkirk.

1942 A Royal Air Force "Mosquito" night-fighter scored the first victory for the type. Seventy-seven Royal Air Force bombers attacked Paris/Gennevilliers and lost five aircraft. They missed their factory target and killed thirty-four French civilians in the surrounding area. Thirty-one Royal Air Force bombers attacked Cherbourg, France. Twenty-one Royal Air Force bombers dropped mines in the Baltic and lost one "Stirling".

1943 Twelve Royal Air Force "Venturas" attacked Caen, France. 147 American 8th Air Force B17s dropped 277 tons of bombs on the submarine installations at St. Nazaire, France and lost eight aircraft. It was the first action for the YB-40, eight of which took part. The YB-40 was a B17 modified to carry extra ammunition and armament. It was supposed to act as an escort for the bomber formations. This was the first 8th Air Force mission for the 379th Bomb Group. Thirty-four 8th Air Force B24s dropped ninety-nine tons of bombs on La Pallice, France. This was the last mission for the 44th Bomb Group before it was transferred to North Africa. Fifty-seven 8th Air Force B17s dropped 132 tons of bombs on the Rennes Naval Storage Depot in France and lost six aircraft. 131 8th Air Force P47s flew escort missions. 719 Royal Air Force bombers attacked Wuppertal, Germany and lost thirty-three aircraft. 1,000 acres of the city were destroyed and 3,400 people were killed in the raid.

1944 888 American 8th Air Force bombers dropped 2,054 tons of bombs on synthetic oil plants and aircraft factories in Germany, losing seventeen B24s and seventeen B17s (two of the lost B17s-one was "Shoo-Shoo-Shoo Baby"-and six of the B24s landed in Sweden). 673 8th Air Force fighters provided support for the bombers and claimed fifty-five victories for the loss of four P47s and six P51s. After completing their escort mission, the fighters went on "Chattanooga Choo-Choo" (train-hunting) missions to Germany and Poland. The American 9th Air Force attacked the Seine River bridges. The American 15th Air Force attacked Vienna, Austria losing eighteen bombers. Royal Air Force Group/Captain James Stagg, Allied Supreme Commander General Dwight Eisenhower's weather man, predicted that there would be fair weather for an invasion of France during the first week of June. Royal Air Force Air Marshal Trafford Leigh-Mallory, commander of the Allied Expeditionary Forces Air Force, sent a message to Eisenhower stating that the airborne operations for D-Day should be cancelled because of possibly extreme casualties among the paratroops. Forty-six Royal Air Force "Mosquitoes" attacked targets in Germany and Holland. The USAAF's 801st Bomb Group dispatched twenty-three B24s on "Carpetbagger" missions and lost one aircraft.

1945 Two USAAF 4th Fighter Group pilots died in the crash of their P51s while flying them to Speke Air Depot near Liverpool for storage.

Eastern Europe

1942 Luftwaffe ace Erwin Fleig (66 victories) was captured by Soviet forces.

1944 The American 15th Air Force attacked troop concentrations in Yugoslavia.

Mediterranean

1941 A Royal Navy force consisting of the cruisers AJAX, ORION and DIDO and the destroyers HOTSPUR, DECOY, KIMBERLEY, HEREWARD, JACKEL and IMPERIAL left Alexandria, Egypt en route to Crete. At 0350, the IMPERIAL (launched in 1937) was damaged off Crete by the Luftwaffe and was scuttled by the HOTSPUR. At 0625, the HEREWARD (launched in 1936) was sunk south of Crete by the Luftwaffe. The DIDO, ORION and PERTH and the DECOY and KELVIN were damaged by aircraft. 60 "Stukas" attacked British positions Tobruk.

1942 The Italian destroyer PESSAGNO was sunk by the Royal Navy submarine TURBULENT.

1944 Captain William Galt, of the 34th Division, won a posthumous Medal of Honor at Villa Crocetta, Italy.

Atlantic

1937 The German pocket battleship DEUTSCHLAND was damaged off Spain by Loyalist aircraft, thirty-two died.

1940 The U37 sank the French freighter MARIE JOSE (2,477 tons) and the British tanker TELENA (7,406 tons). U37 survived the war. The Royal Navy destroyer GRAFTON was sunk by a mine.

1941 The German weatherships AUGUST WREIDT and HEINRICH FREESE were scuttled to prevent their capture by the Royal Navy. The U557 sank the British freighter EMPIRE STORM (7,290 tons). U557 survived until December 16th. The U38 sank the British freighter TABARISTAN (6,251 tons). U38 survived the war.

1942 The U156 sank the British freighter NORMAN PRINCE (1,913 tons). U156 survived until March 8, 1943. The U107 sank the British freighter WESTERN HEAD (2,599 tons). U107 survived until August 18, 1943. The U504 sank the British freighter ALLISTER (1,597 tons). U504 survived until July 30, 1943. The USN destroyer TATTNALL rescued twenty-six survivors from the American tanker NEW JERSEY which had been sunk on May 28th by U103. The USN net tender MULBERRY rescued six survivors from the British freighter WESTERN HEAD which had been sunk the previous day by U107.

1944 At 2045, the USN escort carrier BLOCK ISLAND (6 dead) was sunk by the U549, which was then sunk by the USN destroyer escorts ELMORE and AHERNS. The USN destroyer escort BARR was damaged in the action.

The BLOCK ISLAND had participated in the sinking of four U-boats before her loss.

North America

1940   The first flight of the F4U "Corsair" fighter took place.
1941   The destroyers SIMS, ANDERSON, HUGHES and HAMMANN were transferred from San Diego to the east coast. An arrangement for the training of 8,000 Royal Air Force pilots and navigators at American bases was begun. The Royal Air Force ordered 417 Lockheed "Hudson" patrol bombers and the Royal Australian Air Force ordered fifty-two.
1943   The third XB29 was almost lost on a test flight. After landing it was discovered that the control cables had been reversed and thus made the aircraft almost uncontrollable. The situation was remedied and the airplane flew flawlessly the next day. The destroyers ALBERT W. GRANT and BRYANT were launched. ALBERT W. GRANT was stricken in 1971 and BRYANT was stricken in 1968.
1945   A Japanese balloon-bomb was found near Chilanko River, British Columbia.

Pacific

1918   The IJN light cruiser TATSUTA was launched. She was sunk on March 13, 1944.
1922   The IJN light cruiser KINU was launched. She sunk on October 6, 1944.
1942   The USN submarine SWORDFISH sank the TATSUFUKU MARU (1,946 tons). The IJN Aleutian invasion force left Ominato. The first Royal Australian Air Force raid on Tulagi took place. Four USAAF B26 "Marauder" bombers and twelve USN PBY "Catalina" patrol planes landed at Midway to reinforce its defenses. The USN seaplane tender THORNTON relieved the minelayer PREBLE on station at French Frigate Shoals. The IJN submarine I-123 arrived there and found the two vessels occupying what it had planned to use as a refueling stop for IJN seaplanes en route to reconnoitering Pearl Harbor. The operation had to be cancelled thus depriving the Japanese the departure of main units of the USN en route to Midway. USN and RAAF "Catalinas" attacked Japanese installations at Tulagi.
1943   The USN submarine SCAMP sank the KAMIKAWA MARU (6,853 tons). The USN submarine TAMBOR sank the EISHO MARU (2,846 tons). The IJN submarine I-178 was sunk by the USN SC-669. The Japanese made their last counter-attacks on Attu in the Aleutians.
1944   The Japanese counter-attacked on Biak Island. It was the first major tank battle in the Pacific Theater. Charles Lindbergh flew an F4U "Corsair" from Emirau Island on a bombing mission over Kavieng, New Ireland.

	The USN submarine SILVERSIDES sank the SHOKEN MARU (1,942 tons) and the HORAIZAN MARU (1,998 tons).
1945	The USN submarine STERLET sank the KURETAKE MARU (1,924 tons) and the TENRYO MARU (2,231 tons). 450 USAAF B29s attacked Yokohama, destroying 6.9 square miles of the city, and losing five aircraft. The USN destroyer SHUBRICK was a constructive loss after an air-attack off Okinawa, thirty-two of her crew died. Ozawa replaced Toyoda as commander of the Japanese Combined Fleet.
1958	The USN submarine STICKLEBACK was rammed and sunk by the USN destroyer SILVERSTEIN off Honolulu. Her 82-man crew was saved.
2002	The wreckage of President John Kennedy's PT109 was reportedly located in Blackett Strait in the Solomons by Robert Ballard. Ballard had previously found the positions of the German battleship BISMARCK and the British liner TITANIC, as well as several other historic wrecks.

China-Burma-India

1942	An aircraft from the IJN submarine I-10 flew a recon over Diego Suarez, Madagascar.
1943	The U198 sank the British freighter HOPETARN (5,231 tons).

May 30th

Western Europe

1881	German General Georg von Kuechler was born near Hanau. He died on May 25, 1968.
1930	France evacuated the German Rhineland five years ahead of schedule.
1933	The League of Nations condemned Germany's treatment of Jews.
1940	53,823 Allied troops were evacuated from Dunkirk, France. The French destroyer BOURRASQUE (16 dead) was sunk north of Nieuport, France in a French minefield. The Royal Navy destroyers ANTHONY, SABRE and WORCESTER were damaged by the Luftwaffe. Forty-four Royal Air Force bombers attacked targets around Dunkirk. Forty-six Royal Air Force bombers attacked targets around Dunkirk and in Germany. Allied and German forces fought a battle near Bodo in northern Norway. The Germans were attempting to reach the embattled town of Narvik. The Allies lost the battle and were evacuated the next day.
1941	Twelve Royal Air Force "Blenheims" attacked German shipping.
1942	1,047 Royal Air Force bombers were dispatched for a raid on Cologne, Germany. Of these, 868 dropped bombs on the city. Flying Officer L. Manser won a posthumous Victoria Cross while flying a "Manchester" on the mission. The Royal Air Force lost a total of forty-one bombers in

the operation, which was the most up to this point in the war. Fifty-six Royal Air Force "Blenheims" attacked Luftwaffe airfields in support of the raid on Cologne and lost two aircraft. Since February 23rd, the Royal Air Forces Bomber Command had flown 8,571 sorties on which it had dropped 9,253 tons of bombs and had lost 313 aircraft. The Royal Navy heavy cruiser ROYALIST was launched. She was scrapped in 1968.

1943 The British submarine UNTAMED was lost during a training exercise off Campbeltown, Britain. She was later raised and renamed VITALITY. Twenty-seven Royal Air Force bombers dropped mines off the Biscay ports.

1944 Nazi Party Secretary Martin Bormann sent a circular to all Nazi leaders demanding that downed Allied airmen be executed without trial. 919 American 8th Air Force bombers dropped 2,500 tons of bombs on aircraft industry targets in Germany and marshalling yards in France and Belgium and lost nine B17s and three B24s. The 489th Bomb Group (B24) flew its first 8th Air Force mission. 672 8th Air Force fighters provided support for the bombers and claimed fifty-seven victories for the loss of one P47 and eight P51s. Ninety-eight 8th Air Force P47s and P38s attacked railroad bridges in northwestern France and lost one P47. The American 15th Air Force attacked aircraft targets in Austria. The Luftwaffe attacked troop concentrations near Falmouth, Britain causing casualties in a US Army ordnance company. Eisenhower was visited by Leigh-Mallory, who expanded on his message of the 29th regarding the cancellation of the airborne assault phase of D-Day. The American 9th Air Force attacked Seine River bridges. A Soviet crew commissioned the Royal Navy battleship ROYAL SOVEREIGN into the Soviet Navy as the ARKHANGELSK. Fifty-four Royal Air Force bombers attacked coastal batteries near Boulogne, France.

1981 Hermine Braunsteiner Ryan, a female guard supervisor at Ravensbruck and Majdanek Concentration Camps, was sentenced to life imprisonment in Dusseldorf, after being extradited from America.

1986 A Royal Air Force "Wellington" bomber which had crashed in Scotland on October 23, 1940 was unearthed near Lossiemouth, Britain.

Eastern Europe
1942 The Soviet Navy shelled land targets near Sevastopol.
1944 The American 15th Air Force attacked Zagreb, Yugoslavia. The Germans counter-attacked in Rumania.

Mediterranean
1940 Italian dictator Benito Mussolini decided to enter the war on June 5th.

1941 The Germans took Retimo and Heraklion on Crete. 2nd Lieutenant C. Upham, of the New Zealand 20th Battalion, won a Victoria Cross on Crete. He would win a second V.C. in North Africa. The Allied commander on Crete, General Freyberg, was evacuated from the island. The Royal Navy destroyers NAPIER and NIZAM evacuated 1,500 men from Crete.
1943 British Prime Minister Winston Churchill and Free French Forces leader Charles de Gaulle arrived in Algiers.
1944 The British 8th Army took Arce. Luftwaffe aircraft sank the NORDEFLINGE (2,873 tons).
1945 French aircraft attacked Damascus, Syria. The Teheran government asked the Allies to remove their troops from Iran.

Atlantic
1940 The U101 sank the British freighter STANHALL (4,831 tons). U101 survived the war.
1941 The Spanish cruiser CANARIAS made a search of the area where the German battleship BISMARCK had gone down but found no survivors. Of BISMARCK's 2,206-man crew, only 115 had been saved. The U106 sank the British freighter SILVERYEW (6,373 tons). U106 survived until August 2, 1943. The Italian submarine MARCONI sank the British tanker CAIRNDALE (8,129 tons). The U38 sank the British freighter EMPIRE PROTECTOR (6,181 tons). U38 survived the war.
1942 The U155 sank the Norwegian freighter BAGHDAD (2,161 tons). U155 survived the war. The U404 sank the American freighter ALCOA SHIPPER (5,491 tons-7 dead). U404 survived until July 28, 1943. Thirty-five survivors from the American freighter ALCOA CARRIER which had been sunk on May 25th by U103 were rescued by a USN patrol plane and a Cuban gunboat.
1943 The American freighter FLORA MACDONALD (7,177 tons-7 dead) was a constructive loss off Sierra Leone after an attack by the U126. U126 survived until July 3rd.

North America
1931 The USN heavy cruiser LOUISVILLE rescued 497 people from the steamer HARVARD which had run aground at Point Arguello, California.
1942 The first F-model of the B17 "Flying Fortress" was built. The submarine RUNNER was launched. She was discarded in 1963.
1943 The submarines HACKLEBACK and DEVILFISH were launched. Both were still on active duty in 1962. A major waterfront fire occurred in Seattle, Washington.
1947 This was the date that the battleship OKLAHOMA was to have arrived at Oakland, California for scrapping. She had sunk en route (See May 17th).

1962   Admiral Patrick Bellinger, commander of PatWing 2 and had sent the "Air-raid Pearl Harbor, this is no drill" message, died in Clifton Forge, Virginia.

1986   A memorial to four chaplains who had died aboard transport DORCHESTER (See February 3, 1943) was dedicated at Leetsdale, Pennsylvania.

1999   William Lawley, age 78, died in Montgomery, Alabama of pneumonia. He had won the Medal of Honor on February 20, 1944 while flying a B17 bomber over Leipzig, Germany.

2001   Canadian Denis Whitaker died in Oakville, Ontario at the age of eighty-six. As a captain, he had won a Distinguished Service Order at Dieppe in August 1942. He would win another before the end of the war and would retire as a brigadier general.

South America

1978   Gustav Wagner, Deputy Commandant at Sobibor Concentration Camp, was arrested outside Sao Paulo, Brazil (See June 22, 1979).

Pacific

1942   USN Admiral Frank Fletcher left Pearl Harbor with the carrier YORKTOWN en route to Midway. The USN submarine POMPANO sank the ATSUTA MARU (7,983 tons) in the East China Sea. The USN battleship WEST VIRGINIA was raised from the bottom of Pearl Harbor where she had been since the attack of December 7th.

1943   Organized Japanese resistance on Attu, in the Aleutians, ended. The USN submarine SAURY sank the SHOKO MARU (5,385 tons). The TAKAMISAN MARU (1,932 tons) and the HAKOSAKI MARU (3,948 tons) were sunk by mines. The USN submarine STEELHEAD laid mines off Erimo Saki, Japan. The American 11th Air Force attacked Kiska in the Aleutians.

1944   The USN submarine RASHER sank the ANSHU MARU (2,601 tons). The USN submarine POMPON sank the SHIGA MARU (742 tons). The USN submarine GUITARRO sank the SHISEN MARU (2,201 tons). Charles Lindbergh flew an F4U "Corsair" from Emirau Island on a bombing mission over Kavieng, New Ireland.

1945   American forces reached Shuri on Okinawa. The USN escort carrier ANZIO sank the IJN submarine I-136. The USN submarine BLENNY sank the HOKOKU MARU (520 tons).

1962   The ARIZONA Memorial was dedicated at Pearl Harbor.

China-Burma-India

1942 The Royal Navy battleship RAMILLIES was damaged and the tanker BRITISH LOYALTY (6,993 tons) was sunk at Diego Suarez, Madagascar by IJN midget submarines launched by the submarines I-20 and I-16.

May 31st

Western Europe

1892 German politician Gregor Strasser was born. He was murdered on June 30, 1934 during the "Night of the Long Knives".

1927 The Royal Navy heavy cruiser CANBERRA was launched. She would be sunk off Guadalcanal in August 1942 by the IJN.

1937 Five German warships and the Luftwaffe attacked Almeria, Spain in retaliation for a Loyalist attack on the pocket battleship DEUTSCHLAND.

1938 Germany and Denmark signed a non-aggression pact.

1939 The Royal Navy heavy cruiser FIJI was launched. She was sunk on May 22, 1941.

1940 In France, Lord John Gort turned over command of the British Expeditionary Force to General Harold Alexander. 68,014 Allied troops were evacuated from Dunkirk on the French coast. Captain H. Ervine-Andrews, of the East Lancaster Regiment, won a Victoria Cross at Dunkirk. At 0125, the French destroyer CYCLONE was damaged by the German S-24 off Dunkirk. At 0145, the French destroyer SIROCO (659 dead) was sunk off Dunkirk by the German S-23 and S-26. The Royal Navy destroyers EXPRESS, HARVESTER, ICARUS, IMPULSIVE, MALCOLM, SCIMITAR and the minesweeper HEBE were damaged by the Luftwaffe. Due to excessive losses, the British Admiralty decided to withdraw all modern destroyers from the Dunkirk operation. 126 Royal Air Force bombers attacked targets around Dunkirk and lost two "Wellingtons".

1941 British civilian air-raid casualties for the last two months were 11,459 dead and 12,107 wounded.

1942 The Luftwaffe attacked Canterbury, Britain. The first operation by the Royal Air Forces "Mosquito" bomber took place when five aircraft flew a photo recon mission to Cologne, Germany to check the damage inflicted by the previous night's raid. One of the aircraft was lost and the crew's bodies were buried in Antwerp, Belgium. British civilian air-raid casualties for the month were 399 killed and 425 wounded.

1943 Fifty-four Royal Air Force bombers attacked targets in Holland, France and Belgium and lost one "Mitchell". 110 American 8th Air Force P47s flew sweeps over France. The 8th Air Force's P47 "Thunderbolt" fighters began flying missions to a distance of 200 miles with the assistance of external fuel tanks.

1944 Allied troops began boarding ships for the D-Day invasion. 356 American 8th Air Force bombers dropped 1,022 tons of bombs on marshalling yards and aircraft industry targets in Germany and rail targets in France and Belgium losing one B17. The 490th Bomb Group (B24 then converted to the B17) flew its first 8th Air Force mission. 682 8th Air Force fighters provided support for the bombers and claimed four victories for the loss of one P47 and two P51s. 116 8th Air Force fighters dropped fifty tons of bombs on the German airfields at Gutersloh and Rheine/Hopstein. The American 9th Air Force attacked Seine River bridges. The German minesweeper M-13 was sunk by a mine in the Gironde estuary. 219 Royal Air Force bombers attacked Trappes, France and lost four aircraft. 129 Royal Air Force bombers attacked Au Fevre, France. 115 Royal Air Force bombers attacked Mont Couple, France. 115 Royal Air Force bombers attacked Tergnier, France and lost two "Lancasters". Eighty-six Royal Air Force bombers attacked Saumer, France. The USAAF's 801st Bomb Group dispatched twenty-two B24s on "Carpetbagger" missions.

1945 Odilo Globocnik committed suicide when he was arrested by the British at Weissensee. He had been in charge of exterminating Polish Jews. The British government awarded twenty-four Victoria Crosses in the month of May during the war.

1960 Walther Funk, Nazi Minister of Economic Affairs, died in Dusseldorf.

1992 A memorial to Arthur "Bomber" Harris was dedicated in London. Harris had died in 1984 at the age of 91.

Eastern Europe

1899 Soviet Air Force General Fyodor Falaleyev was born. He died on August 12, 1955.

1944 The Germans continued their counter-attacks in Rumania. 460 American 15th Air Force bombers attacked the oil refineries at Ploesti, Rumania.

Mediterranean

1941 The Allied forces on Crete surrendered. The Royal Navy's cruiser PHOEBE, minelayer ABDIEL, and destroyers JACKEL, KIMBERLEY and HOTSPUR evacuated 4,000 men from Crete. The Royal Navy's destroyer NAPIER was damaged off Crete by the Luftwaffe. The pro-Allied Regent in Iraq was re-instated. The Italian torpedo boat PLEIADI was sunk by Italian Air Force in error, off Tobruk, Libya.

1943 The Royal Navy cruiser ORION and the destroyers PETARD and TROUBRIDGE and USAAF B26 bombers bombarded the Italian defenses on Pantelleria.

1944 Allied forces were ordered to attack the Alban Hills behind Anzio. Private Furman Smith, of the 34th Division, won a posthumous Medal of Honor near Lanuvio, Italy. The US Army's 36th Division took Velletri. The British took Sora and Frosinone in Italy.

1945 Fighting broke out between Syrian and French forces. London informed Free French leader Charles de Gaulle that it would intervene if necessary.

Atlantic

1940 The Axis sank 288,461 tons of Allied and neutral shipping in May and lost 1 German U-boat. The U101 sank the British freighter ORANGEMOOR (5,775 tons). U101 survived the war. The U13 was sunk by the Royal Navy sloop WESTON. U13 survived until May 31st.

1941 The Axis sank 522,042 tons of Allied and neutral shipping in May and lost one U-boat. The German submarine U38 sank the Norwegian freighter RINDA (6,029 tons). U38 survived the war. The U106 sank the British freighter CLAN MACDOUGALL (6,843 tons). U106 survived until August 2, 1943. The U107 sank the British freighter SIRE (5,664 tons). U107 survived until August 18, 1944. The U147 sank the British freighter GRAVELINES (2,491 tons). U147 survived until June 2nd.

1942 The Axis sank 705,050 tons of Allied and neutral shipping in May and lost three German U-boats. The U506 sank the British freighter FRED GREEN (2,292 tons). U506 survived until July 12, 1943. The U432 sank the Canadian freighter LIVERPOOL PACKET (1,188 tons). U432 survived until March 11, 1943. The Italian submarine CAPPELLINI sank the British tanker DINSDALE (8,214 tons). The USN submarine GRUNNION rescued survivors from the U.S. Army freighter JACK which had been sunk by the U155.

1943 The Axis sank 299,428 tons of Allied and neutral shipping in May and lost forty-one German U-boats. U440 was sunk by the Royal Air Force's No.201 Squadron, west of Cape Ortegal. The U563 was sunk by the Royal Air Force's Nos.58 and 228 Squadrons and the Royal Australian Air Force's No.10 Squadron northwest of Brest, France. The USN light cruisers MILWAUKEE and OMAHA were damaged in a collision off Brazil.

1944 The Axis sank 27,297 tons of Allied and neutral shipping in May and lost 23 German U-boats. The U289 was sunk by the Royal Navy destroyer MILNE in the Arctic Ocean.

1945 The Axis sank 17,198 tons of Allied and neutral shipping in May and lost fourteen German U-boats.

North America

1940 The destroyers WILKES and NICHOLSON were launched. The WILKES was stricken in 1970 and NICHOLSON was transferred to Italy in 1951.

1941   Major General George Brett was named Chief of US Army Air Corps.
1942   The destroyer CAPPS was launched. She was sold to Spain in 1957.
1945   The last of 18,188 B24 "Liberators" was built. The American government awarded 36 Medals of Honor in the month of May during the war.
2006   Donald Rudolph died in Grand Rapids, Minnesota at the age of 85. He had won a Medal of Honor on February 5, 1945 for actions on Luzon.

Pacific

1920   The IJN battleship MUTSU was launched. She exploded and sank in Nagasaki harbor on June 8, 1943.
1934   The IJN heavy cruiser MIKUMA was launched. She was sunk on June 6, 1942.
1942   The Allies sank 96,565 tons of Japanese shipping (22 ships) in May. Sydney, Australia was attacked by IJN midget submarines launched from the submarines I-22, I-24 and I-27. The Royal Australian Navy barge KUTTABUL was sunk and the Dutch submarine K-IX was a constrictive loss after the attack. All three Japanese midgets were lost. The USN submarine POLLACK sank the IJN sub chaser No.5 SHUNSEI MARU. USN Captain Marc Mitscher was promoted to Rear Admiral.
1943   The Allies sank 131,440 tons of Japanese shipping (35 ships) in May. The USN submarine POLLACK sank the SHUNSEI MARU (92 tons). The American 11th Air Force attacked Kiska in the Aleutians.
1944   The Allies sank 129,846 tons of Japanese shipping (37 ships) in May. The USN destroyer escort ENGLAND sank the IJN submarine Ro-105. The IJN escort ISHIGAKI and the HOKUYO MARU (1,590 tons) were sunk off the Kuriles by the USN submarine HERRING. The USN submarine BARB sank the MADRAS MARU (3,802 tons) and the KOTO MARU (1,053 tons). The American freighter HENRY BERGH was lost when she ran aground off San Francisco.
1945   The Allies sank 211,536 tons of Japanese shipping (116 ships) in May. Private First-Class Clarence Craft, of the 96th Division, won a Medal of Honor on Okinawa.
1992   In commemoration of an IJN midget submarine attack on Sydney, Australia 50 years before, all the city lights were turned out.

China-Burma-India

1933   The Truce of Tangku was signed, ending fighting between China and Japan.
1939   The Soviets warned the Japanese against further aggression in Mongolia.
1942   A seaplane from the IJN submarine I-10 flew over Diego Suarez, Madagascar.

CHAPTER 6

THE MONTH OF JUNE

June 1st

Western Europe
1914 Luftwaffe ace Herbert Ihlefeld (130 victories) was born in Pinnow. He survived the war.
1932 Franz von Papen formed a new German government that totally excluded the Nazi Party.
1937 The keel of the Royal Navy battleship HOWE was laid. She was scrapped in 1957.
1939 The first flight of the Luftwaffe's Fw190 fighter took place.
1940 64,429 Allied troops were evacuated from Dunkirk. At 0800, the Royal Navy destroyer KEITH (36 dead) was damaged off Dunkirk by the Luftwaffe. She sank at 0940. At 0800, the Royal Navy destroyer BASILISK was damaged by the Luftwaffe. She was scuttled at 1200 by the Royal Navy destroyer WHITEHALL. At 0845, the Royal Navy minesweeper SKIPJACK (270 dead) was sunk by the Luftwaffe. At 0906, the Royal Navy destroyer HAVANT (8 dead) was damaged by the Luftwaffe. She sank at 1015. At 0950, the British tug ST. ABBS (100 dead) was sunk by the Luftwaffe. At 1030, the French destroyer FOUDROYANT was sunk by the Luftwaffe, 220 were rescued. At 1330, the Royal Navy gunboat MOSQUITO was sunk by the Luftwaffe. Charles Lightoller rescued 130 men from Dunkirk aboard his yacht the SUNDOWNER. He had been Second Officer aboard the RMS TITANIC when that ship sank in 1912. The British steamers BRIGHTON QUEEN, SCOTIA and the trawlers ARGYLLSHIRE and DORADO and the French steamers PAPIN, VENUS and MOUSAILLON were sunk by the Luftwaffe. The Royal Navy destroyers IVANHOE, VENOMOUS, VIMY, VIVACIOUS, WHITEHALL and the sloops BIDEFORD and KINGFISHER were damaged by the Luftwaffe. Fifty-six Royal Air Force bombers attacked targets around Dunkirk. The Germans breached the British lines at Bergues, near Dunkirk. The Allies informed the Norwegian government that they were evacuating Norwegian ports. The Swiss Air Force shot down two Luftwaffe aircraft that strayed over the border. Forty-one Royal Air Force bombers attacked targets around

	Dunkirk and in Germany. The British liner ORFORD (20,043 tons) was sunk at Marseilles by the Luftwaffe.
1941	The German heavy cruiser PRINZ EUGEN arrived at Brest, having cruised 7,000 miles, and refueled from tankers twice since leaving battleship BISMARCK in the North Atlantic.
1942	One of two Royal Air Force "Mosquitoes" that flew a recon mission over Köln, Germany was lost. The Luftwaffe attacked Canterbury, Britain. Jews in France and Holland were ordered to wear the Star of David. Food riots took place in Paris. 956 Royal Air Force bombers attacked Essen, Germany and lost thirty-one bombers. Only fifteen people were killed in Essen, Germany, but 150 more were killed in surrounding cities and villages. Forty-eight Royal Air Force "Blenheims" attacked Luftwaffe airfields in support of the raid and lost three aircraft.
1943	Forty-three Royal Air Force bombers dropped mines off the Continental coast.
1944	At 2100, Germans intercepted the BBC broadcast of the first coded message warning the French Resistance that D-day was eminent. 109 Royal Air Force bombers attacked Ferme D'urville, France. Fifty-eight Royal Air Force bombers attacked Saumer, France. The USAAF's 801st Bomb Group dispatched twenty-two B24s on "Carpetbagger" missions. The German minesweeper ATLAS was sunk off Alesund, Norway.
1945	Royal Air Force Flight/Sergeant G. Thompson, of No.9 Squadron, won a posthumous Victoria Cross over the Dortmund-Ems Canal.
2010	Three German bomb disposal experts were killed in the explosion of a WWII bomb in the city of Gottingen.

Eastern Europe

1941	Moscow received a description of the strategy the Germans would use in their invasion. The source was Richard Sorge, correspondent for the Frankfurter Zeitung in Tokyo and a Soviet spy.
1942	The Soviet Navy delivered supplies to the besieged city of Sevastopol on the Black Sea. German "Stuka" dive-bombers sank the British freighter EMPIRE STARLIGHT off Murmansk. Hitler flew to Poltava to inspect the German Army Group "South".
1943	The Soviet submarine ShCh-406 was sunk by German surface craft.
1946	The Rumanian Premier, Ion Antonescu, and three of his aides were executed by automatic rifle fire.

Mediterranean

1941	The battle for Crete ended. The Allies had lost 16,583 men, while the Germans lost 3,714. At 0920, the Royal Navy light cruiser CALCUTTA

was sunk eighty-five miles northwest of Alexandria by the Luftwaffe. At this time the comparative serviceable naval strengths of Britain and Italy in the Mediterranean were: Battleships-Italy four and Britain two, Cruisers-Italy nineteen and Britain eight, Destroyers-Italy fifty and Britain thirteen and Submarines-Italy 108 and Britain twelve. Numbers of aircraft for the two countries were 313 for Italy and 205 for Britain. British forces entered Baghdad, Iran.

1942 The Axis took 3,000 prisoners, 101 tanks and 124 cannons at Gazala.

1943 The USAAF dropped 141 tons of bombs on Pantelleria. The island was also shelled by the British cruiser PENELOPE and the destroyers PALADIN and PETARD. During the action, the PENELOPE was hit by counter-fire. The British destroyer JERVIS and the Greek destroyer VASILSSA OLGA sank the Italian torpedo boat CASTORE as well as a steamer off Cape Spartivento.

1944 The US Army's 36th Division took Velletri. German Field Marshal Albert Kesselring ordered his forces to retreat from the "Gustav Line" to the "Gothic Line" in Italy.

1962 Adolf Eichmann was hung in Israel. He had been Chief of the Jewish Office of the Gestapo during the war.

Atlantic

1940 The U37 sank the Greek freighter IOANNA (950 tons). U37 survived the war. The U58 sank the British freighter ASTRONOMER (8,401 tons). U58 survived the war.

1941 The U105 sank the British freighter SCOTTISH MONARCH (4,719 tons). U105 survived until June 2, 1943. The U204 sank the Icelandic trawler HOLMSTEINN (16 tons). U204 survived until October 19th. The U107 sank the British freighter ALFRED JONES (5,013 tons). U107 survived until August 18, 1944. The Italian submarine MARCONI sank the Portuguese trawler EXPORTADOR I (318 tons).

1942 The U107 sank the Panamanian freighter BUSHRANGER (4,536 tons). U107 survived until August 18, 1944. The U566 sank the British freighter WESTMORELAND (8,967 tons). U566 survived until June 27th. The U404 sank the American freighter WEST NOTUS (5,492 tons-4 dead). U404 survived until July 28, 1943. The U106 sank the American freighter HAMPTON ROADS (2,689 tons-5 dead). U106 survived until August 2, 1943. The U156 sank the Brazilian freighter ALEGRETE ((5,970 tons). U156 survived until March 8, 1943. The USN light cruiser OMAHA rescued survivors from the British freighter CHARLBURY which had been sunk by the Italian submarine BARBARIGO. The USN destroyers LUDLOW and BERNADOU rescued survivors from the British freighter

FRED W. GREEN which had been sunk the previous day by U506. The Norwegian freighter MARGRETHE BAKKE rescued twenty-five survivors from the American freighter ALCOA SHIPPER which had been sunk on May 30th by U404. The USN destroyer BIDDLE rescued fifteen survivors from the American tanker NEW JERSEY which had been sunk on May 28th by U103.

1943 The BOAC flight 777, a DC-3, was shot down over the Bay of Biscay by a Luftwaffe Ju88. All seventeen aboard died, including the British actor, Leslie Howard. The U119 laid sixty-six mines off Halifax, Nova Scotia. U119 survived until June 24th. The U202 was sunk by the Royal Navy sloop STARLING south of Greenland. The U418 was sunk by the Royal Air Force's No.236 Squadron in the Bay of Biscay. The American freighter MORGAN was lost in a collision with the American tanker MONTANA off the Virginia Capes.

North America

1934 The heavy cruiser ASTORIA was commissioned. She would be sunk in the "Battle of Savo Island" in August 1942.
1939 The destroyers MORRIS and WAINWRIGHT were launched. MORRIS was scrapped in 1947 and WAINWRIGHT was scuttled in 1948 after serving as a Bikini test target.
1940 The battleship WASHINGTON was launched. She was scrapped in 1961.
1942 The submarine GURNARD was launched. She was discarded in 1960.
1943 The first B29 unit (the 58th Bomb Wing-Very Heavy) was formed at Marietta, Georgia. Race riots in Detroit during the month of June killed thirty-four people and injured almost 700 people. Property damage was estimated at $2 million. The US Miner's Union went on strike. The destroyer PICKING was launched. She was expended as a target in 1975.
1944 The escort carrier HOLLANDIA was commissioned. She was scrapped in 1960.
1962 The battleship ALABAMA was stricken. She would be preserved as a memorial in her namesake state.
1965 The destroyer MURRAY (launched in 1942) was stricken and was scrapped in 1966.
1967 The destroyer KIMBERLY was sold to Taiwan and renamed AN YANG.
1968 The destroyers BAILEY, KALK, STEVENSON and HUGHES were sold for scrap.
1970 The destroyer ERICSSON was stricken and later expended as a target. The destroyer TILLMAN was sold for scrap. The light carriers MONTEREY and SAN JACINTO were stricken.

1971	The destroyer-minesweeper HAMBLETON and the destroyers GRAYSON, FRANKFORT, BANCROFT, GHERARDI, FARENHOLT, BOYLE, MEADE and KEARNY were stricken.
1973	USMC ace Major General Marion Carl (18 victories) retired.
1975	The destroyer STODDARD was stricken.
1978	The USN fleet tug TAWAKONI was decommissioned and transferred to Taiwan. She had been commissioned September 15, 1944.
1985	Edgar Schmued, Chief Designer of the P51 "Mustang" and F86 "Sabre", died.
1996	Medal of Honor winner and USN ace David McCampbell (34 victories) died this month at his home in Lake Worth, Florida.

South America

1942	Mexico declared war on the Axis.

Pacific

1935	The IJN light carrier SHOHO was launched. She was sunk on May 8, 1942.
1939	The IJN carrier SHOKAKU was launched. She was sunk on June 19, 1944.
1942	Japanese Naval Air Force ace Gitaro Miyazaki (13 victories) was killed in action over Port Moresby, New Guinea. Royal Australian Air Force PBYs attacked Tulagi. Six TBF "Avengers", flown by pilots of the carrier HORNET's Torpedo Squadron 8, landed at Midway to reinforce its defenses.
1943	The USN submarine TRIGGER sank the NOBORIKAWA MARU (2,182 tons). The American 11th Air Force attacked Kiska in the Aleutians. The Royal Navy's heavy cruiser SHROPSHIRE was transferred to the Royal Australian Navy. This was done to replace the CANBERRA which had been lost on August 9, 1942 during the "Battle of Savo" off Guadalcanal.
1944	The USN submarine HERRING sank the IWAKI MARU (3,124 tons) and the HIBURI MARU (4,366 tons) off the Kuriles. The HERRING was then sunk by shore-fire. The USN submarine PINTADO sank the TOHO MARU (4,716 tons). The USN submarine NARWHAL landed 16 agents and 25 tons of supplies on Mindanao. The USN tug SHAHAKA sank after she collided with the floating drydock ABSD-2 which she was towing from California to Hawaii. The American forces on Biak Island resumed their offensive. The Japanese attacked American forces around Aitape, New Guinea.
1945	Twenty-seven USAAF P51s were lost over Iwo Jima in bad weather. USAAF B29s attacked Osaka, destroying 3.1 square miles of the city and losing ten aircraft. The Royal Navy submarine TIPTOE sank the TOBI MARU (982 tons).

China-Burma-India

1942 A seaplane from the IJN submarine I-10 flew over Diego Suarez, Madagascar.

1943 The U178 sank the Dutch freighter SALABANGKA (6,586 tons). U178 survived until August 20, 1944.

1944 The Chinese 22nd Division cut the Kamaing Road in Burma.

1962 Reverend Archie Mitchell (husband of Elsye-See May 5, 1945) was kidnapped by Viet Cong in Viet Nam. As of 1973 he was still missing.

June 2nd

Western Europe

1918 Luftwaffe ace Anton Hafner (204 victories) was born in Erbach. He died on July 17, 1944.

1932 Franz von Papen became Chancellor of Germany.

1940 26,256 Allied troops were evacuated from Dunkirk. The Royal Navy destroyers MALCOLM and SABRE were damaged by the Luftwaffe off Dunkirk. Twenty-four Royal Air Force bombers attacked targets around Dunkirk. The German armed merchant cruiser KOMET was commissioned. Forty-six Royal Air Force bombers attacked targets around Dunkirk and in Germany.

1941 Forty-four Royal Air Force "Blenheims" attacked German shipping and lost two aircraft. 150 Royal Air Force bombers attacked Dusseldorf, Germany and lost three aircraft. Five people were killed in the raid. Twenty-five Royal Air Force "Wellingtons" attacked Duisburg, Germany. Eleven Royal Air Force bombers attacked Berlin and lost one "Stirling".

1942 Six Royal Air Force "Bostons" attacked Dieppe, France and two "Mosquitoes" attacked Essen, Germany. The Royal Air Force's No.403 Squadron lost eight of twelve "Spitfires" on a sweep over France. The Germans killed 132 Czechs in reprisal for the May 27th attack on Reinhard Heydrich. 195 Royal Air Force bombers attacked Essen, Germany and lost fourteen aircraft. There were no casualties in the city. Luftwaffe night-fighter ace Heinz-Wolfgang Schnaufer scored the first of his 121 victories. Eleven Royal Air Force bombers dropped mines off French harbors and lost one "Hampden". The German trawler V-1510 sank when she ran into a submerged wreck off Dieppe, France.

1943 Thirty-five Royal Air Force bombers dropped mines off the Biscay ports. Four American 8th Air Force P47s flew patrols over the Channel.

1944 The German 15th Army was placed on alert in expectation of an Allied invasion. 805 American 8th Air Force B17s and B24s dropped 2,507 tons of bombs on V-1 rocket sites in the Pas de Calais in France. They were escorted by 341 8th Air Force fighters. 299 8th Air Force bombers dropped 841 tons of bombs on airfields and rail targets in France and lost two B17s and five B24s. The 491st Bomb Group (B24) flew its first 8th Air Force mission. They were escorted by 392 8th Air Force fighters. American 9th Air Force fighters flew a "Chattanooga Choo-Choo" mission to France. 9th Air Force bombers attacked bridges at Rouen, France. 128 Royal Air Force bombers attacked and lost six aircraft. 107 Royal Air Force bombers attacked Berneval, France. 271 Royal Air Force bombers attacked coastal batteries along the Channel coast. The USAAF's 801st Bomb Group dispatched eighteen B24s on "Carpetbagger" missions. The German patrol boat V-2004 was sunk off Ijmuiden by British MTBs. The German patrol boat V-1810 was sunk off Boulogne, France by aircraft.

1948 German S.S. Colonel Victor Brack, one of the top men in the Euthanasia Program, was hung at Landsberg Prison.

1993 A French court ordered that Paul Touvier, age 78, be tried for crimes against humanity. He had served as a collaborator with Lyon Gestapo chief Klaus "The Butcher" Barbie.

Eastern Europe

1940 In response to a request from Hitler, Benito Mussolini agreed to postpone Italy's entry into the war until June 10th.

1942 The Germans began a 5-day artillery bombardment of Sevastopol. The Soviet Navy delivered supplies to the besieged city of Sevastopol on the Black Sea.

1943 424 Luftwaffe aircraft attacked Kursk.

1944 The first "Shuttle Mission" involved 130 USAAF Air Force B17s and 70 P51s flying from Italy to Piryatin, Russia that bombed Debrecen, Hungary en route. The American 15th Air Force attacked rail targets in Rumania.

Mediterranean

1941 Sixty German "Stuka" dive-bombers attacked Tobruk, Libya.

1942 The U652 was sunk by the U81 after being damaged by the Royal Air Force. "HalPro" arrived in Fayid, Egypt. It consisted of a group of B24s en route to the Far East and the war in the Pacific. This was as Far East as it would go. It was commanded by Colonel Harry Halvorson and would become the core of the USAAF in the Mediterranean.

1943 The Royal Navy cruiser ORION and destroyers PALADIN and TROUBRIDGE bombarded the island of Pantelleria. The USAAF's 99th Fighter Squadron (Negro) flew its first mission, an escort to Pantelleria. USAAF B26s attacked Sardinia. At 0315, the Italian torpedo boat

CASTORE and two freighters were sunk by the Royal Navy destroyer JERVIS and the Greek destroyer VASILISSA OLGA.

1944 Allied forces advanced all along the Italian front. The US Army's 85th Division took Maschio d'Ariano, Monte Fiori and Monte Ceraso. The German TA-16 (the ex-Italian CASTELFIDARDO) and AE GERHARD were sunk at Heraklion, Crete by the Royal Air Force.

Atlantic

1940 The U101 sank the British freighter POLYCARP (3,577 tons). U101 survived the war.

1941 The British catapult-armed merchantman MICHAEL E. (7,628 tons-See May 27th) was sunk by the U108. U108 survived until April 11, 1944. The U147 was sunk by the Royal Navy destroyer WANDERER and corvette PERIWINKLE northwest of Ireland.

1942 The U558 sank the Dutch freighter TRITON (2,078 tons). U558 survived until July 20, 1943. The U553 sank the British freighter MATTAWIN (6,919 tons). U553 survived until January 28, 1943. The U158 sank the American freighter KNOXVILLE CITY (5,686 tons-two dead). U158 survived until June 30th. The U578 sank the Norwegian freighter BERGANGER (6,826 tons). U578 survived until August 10th. The Italian submarine LEONARDO DA VINCI sank the Panamanian sailing ship REINE MARIE STEWART (1,087 tons). The American freighter THOMAS NELSON rescued nine survivors from the American freighter ALCOA PILGRIM.

1943 The U105 was sunk by French aircraft off Dakar. The U521 was sunk by USN PC-565 southeast of Baltimore.

North America

1892 Admiral Carleton Wright was born in New Hampton, Iowa. He graduated 16th in his 1912 Annapolis class of 156. On May 15, 1942, he was promoted to rear admiral and given command of a cruiser division in the South Pacific. After various commands at sea and ashore, he was named as Commander of the 12th Naval District in San Francisco. He retired on October 1, 1948 as a vice-admiral and died on June 27, 1970 in Claremont, California.

1940 British businessman Arthur Purvis agreed to purchase from America, on behalf of the British government, munitions costing a total of $37,619,556.60.

1941 The escort carrier LONG ISLAND was commissioned at Newport News, Virginia. She had been converted from the C-3 type freighter

MORMACMAIL in just 69 working days. She was converted back into a merchant ship in 1949.

1943 A gasoline explosion aboard the battleship PENNSYLVANIA, while in Puget Sound, killed one of her crew. Canned milk was rationed in America.

1944 The escort carrier ROI was launched. She was scrapped in 1947. The last Vultee "Vengeance" dive-bomber was built in Nashville, Tennessee.

2006 Edward Dahlgren died in Caribou, Maine at the age of 90. He had won a Medal of Honor on February 11, 1945 at Oberhoffen, France.

Pacific

1942 The USN forces of Admirals Spruance and Fletcher rendezvoused 350 miles northeast of Midway. They include three carriers, seven heavy cruisers, one light cruiser, sixteen destroyers and two tankers. After refueling operations, the tankers were dispatched and the fleet prepared for battle. Twenty-five USN submarines were also located around Midway. The IJN submarine I-168 reported to IJN headquarters that there were no USN vessels in the vicinity of Midway. The Japanese Naval Air Force attacked Dutch Harbor in the Aleutians. The supporting naval force consisted of the carriers RYUJO and JUNYO, the cruisers TAKAO, MAYA, NACHI, KISO and TAMA, twelve destroyers, three transports, a tanker and several submarines. The American freighter COLDBROOK ran aground and was lost off Alaska.

1943 The USN submarine TAMBOR sank the EIKA MARU (1,248 tons).

1944 The US Army's 186th Regiment attacked on Biak. The USN submarine GUITARRO sank the IJN frigate AWAJI off Formosa. The USN submarine SHARK sank the CHIYO MARU (4,700 tons). Charles Lindbergh flew an F4U from Emirau Island on a bombing mission over Kavieng, New Ireland.

1945 The USN submarine TENCH sank the MIKAMISAN MARU (861 tons).

1969 The USN destroyer FRANK E. EVANS was a constructive loss after colliding with the Royal Australian Navy carrier MELBOURNE in the South China Sea. She was expended later in the year.

China-Burma-India

1939 General Georgi Zhukov was appointed as Commander-in-Chief of the Soviet forces in Mongolia.

1942 The Japanese freighter KOFUKU MARU was sunk by a mine off Rangoon, Burma.

1944 Allied forces laid siege to Myitkyina, Burma. The Chinese 36th Division took Kaitou, Burma.

June 3rd

Western Europe

1936 Haille Selassie, the Ethiopian Premier, arrived in Britain aboard the steamer ORFORD.

1937 Spanish rebel leader General Emilio Mola was killed in a plane crash.

1938 The British government ordered 600 "Hurricane" fighters.

1940 26,746 Allied troops were evacuated from Dunkirk. The Germans mounted a major attack against the Allied lines around Dunkirk. Eighteen Royal Air Force bombers attacked targets near Dunkirk. The British evacuated Narvik in Norway. Over the next two days, the Luftwaffe dropped more than 1,000 bombs on Paris, killing more than 250 and losing twenty-five aircraft. 142 Royal Air Force bombers attacked targets in Germany and lost two "Hampdens".

1942 Twelve Royal Air Force "Bostons" attacked Cherbourg and Le Havre in France. The "Leigh Light" was mounted on an aircraft for the first time (a "Wellington VIII"). It was a spot light used to locate German U-boats running on the surface at night. British commandoes raided the Boulogne-La Touquet coast of France. 170 Royal Air Force bombers attacked Bremen, Germany and lost eleven aircraft. Eighty-three people were killed in the raid.

1943 The Michelin Tire Works at Clermont-Ferrand were damaged by sabotage. Thirty-nine Royal Air Force bombers dropped mines off the Biscay ports and lost one "Wellington".

1944 534 American 8th Air Force bombers dropped 1,580 tons of bombs on Pas de Calais. They were escorted by 439 8th Air Force fighters that lost one P51 to mechanical failure. American 9th Air Force fighters flew a "Chattanooga Choo-Choo" (train-busting) mission to France and attacked bridges at Rouen, France. American Army Ground Commander General Omar Bradley boarded the USN heavy cruiser AUGUSTA in preparation for D-Day. D-Day was postponed from June 5th to the 6th. Nine members of the French Resistance were executed after an attack near Fibeac. American actor James Stewart was promoted to Lieutenant Colonel. 100 Royal Air Force bombers attacked Ferme-D'urville, France. 135 Royal Air Force bombers attacked coastal batteries along the Channel coast. The USAAF's 801st Bomb Group dispatched twenty-three B24s on "Carpetbagger" missions. A Luftwaffe Ju290 transport returned to the continent from Greenland. Aboard were twenty-six men who had been operating the "Bassgeiger" weather station on Greenland since August 1943.

1965 Karl Oberg, head of the S.S. and Police in Occupied France, died.

1970   Hjalmar Schacht, President of the Reichsbank until 1939, died in Munich.

Eastern Europe
1942   The Soviet Navy delivered 1,759 reinforcements and evacuated 1,998 wounded and 275 civilians. The American freighter STEEL WORKER (5,686 tons) was sunk by a mine in Murmansk.
1943   The Soviet Air Force attacked the German base at Orel. 168 Luftwaffe aircraft dropped 224 tons of bombs on the Molotov Tank Works in Gorki, losing five bombers.
1944   Heavy fighting took place in Rumania. The American 15th Air Force attacked Omis, Yugoslavia.

Mediterranean
1941   Royal Air Force "Marylands" attacked an Italian convoy off Tunisia and sank the freighters BEATRICE C. (6,132 tons) and MONTELLO (6,117 tons). The Italian Navy laid defensive minefields off Tripoli. The Luftwaffe attacked Tobruk, Libya.
1942   The Royal Air Force attacked Cagliari and St. Antioco Island near Sardinia. The Royal Navy carrier EAGLE launched thirty-one "Spitfires" for Malta in "Operation Style"; four aircraft were lost en route. The Royal Navy trawler CROCKER (303 tons) was lost.
1943   USAAF A20 "Havoc" bombers attacked Pantelleria. The German trawler UJ-2212 was sunk between Naples and Palermo by an aerial torpedo. The first meeting of the French Committee of National Liberation took place in Algiers. On May 15, 1944 its leader Charles DeGaulle, proclaimed that it was the provisional government of France and on October 23, 1944 it was recognized as such by the governments of Britain and the United States.
1944   The Allies took Albano, Lanuvio and Frascati in Italy. Hitler authorized a withdrawal from Rome. Private Herbert Christian and Private Elden Johnson, of the 3rd Division, won posthumous Medals of Honor near Valmontone, Italy. Sergeant M. Rogers, of the Wiltshire Regiment, won a Victoria Cross in Italy. A Royal Air Force C-47 evacuated twenty-two wounded Yugoslavian partisans to Italy. A Soviet aircraft evacuated Tito to Italy until the situation in Yugoslavia stabilized.
1945   French troops were withdrawn from Damascus and Beirut.

Atlantic
1940   The U37 sank the Finnish freighter SNABB (2,317 tons). U37 was scuttled on May 3, 1945.

1941   The German tanker BELCHEN (6,367 tons) was sunk between Greenland and Labrador by the Royal Navy cruisers AURORA and KENYA. The survivors were rescued by U93. The U48 sank the British tanker INVERSUIR (9,456 tons). U48 was scuttled on May 3, 1945. The U75 sank the Dutch freighter EIBERGEN (4,801 tons). U75 survived until December 28, 1941.

1942   The U172 sank the American freighter ILLINOIS (5,447 tons-31 dead). U172 survived until December 13, 1943. The U156 sank the British sailing ship LILLIAN (80 tons). U156 survived until March 8, 1943. The U126 sank the Norwegian tanker HOEGH GIANT (10,990 tons). U126 survived until July 3, 1943. The American tanker M.F. ELLIOTT (6,940 tons-13 dead) was sunk by the U502. U502 survived until July 5, 1942. The U404 sank the Swedish freighter ANNA (1,345 tons). U404 survived until July 28, 1943. The U432 sank the American trawlers AEOLUS (41 tons) and the BEN AND JOSEPHINE (102 tons). U432 would survive until March 11, 1943. The Greek steamer CONSTANINOS H rescued eighteen survivors from the American freighter WEST NOTUS which had been sunk on June 1st by U404.

1943   The U180 sank the Greek freighter BORIS (5,166 tons). U180 survived until August 22, 1944. The Panamanian freighter HALMA (2,937 tons) was sunk by a mine.

1945   The U1277 was scuttled west of Oporto.

North America

1920   The battleship TENNESSEE was commissioned. She was scrapped in 1959.

1940   The first allotments of munitions left American arsenals en route to the east coast for shipment to Britain.

1942   The destroyers HUDSON (stricken in 1972) and CHARRETTE (sold to Greece in 1959) were launched. The minesweeper BUNTING was lost in a collision in San Francisco Bay.

1945   The carrier LAKE CHAMPLAIN (stricken in 1969) was commissioned. Actor Jack Lemmon would serve as her Communications Officer.

1970   USMC General Ralph J. Mitchell, age 71, died in San Diego. He had served as commander of various Air Groups in the Pacific.

1998   USMC ace Major Harold Segal died in Scottsdale, Arizona. He had been credited with 10 aerial victories while flying Corsairs in the Pacific. He had also served as CMH winner James Swetts wingman.

Pacific

1937   Prince Konoye became Japan's Prime Minister.

1942 The Japanese Naval Air Force attacked Dutch Harbor in the Aleutians, damaging the freighter NORTHWESTERN. Two USN PBYs were shot down over the IJN Aleutian invasion force. At 0904, a USN PBY, piloted by Ensign Charles Eaton, sighted three IJN ships 470 miles west of Midway. At 0925, a PBY flown by Ensign Jack Reid sighted an IJN force 700 miles from Midway. At 1230, nine B17s (commanded by Lieutenant Colonel Walter Sweeney) took off from Midway to attack the IJN forces west of the island, but scored no hits. At 2115, 4 PBYs (commanded by Lieutenant W.L. Richards) left Midway to attack the IJN ships. They would score a hit on the tanker AKEBONO MARU, killing thirteen and wounding eleven of her crew. IJN Admiral Yamamoto, Combined Fleet Commander, received information that a USN carrier was near Midway, but couldn't inform the Midway invasion force commander, Admiral Nagumo, because of radio silence. The IJN submarine I-24 sank the Australian freighter IRON CHIEFTAIN (4,812 tons).

1943 Royal Australian Air Force PBYs attacked Babo Airfield in northern New Guinea.

1944 American forces continued their attack on Biak Island. Charles Lindbergh flew an F4U "Corsair" from Emirau Island on a bombing mission over Kavieng, New Ireland. The USN destroyer REID was damaged by Japanese aircraft off western New Guinea.

China-Burma-India

1897 Royal Air Force Marshal Sir John Slessor was born in Ranikhet, India. He died on July 12, 1979.

1943 The Royal Air Force attacked Buthidaung, Burma.

1942 Six USAAF B25s attacked Lashio. Doolittle Raid veterans Lieutenant Eugene McGurl-navigator, Staff Sergeant Omer Duquette and Sergeant Melvin Gardner-engineer/gunners, died in a plane crash in China.

1943 The IJN submarine I-27 sank the American freighter MONTANAN (4,898 tons).

1944 The Allied forces continued their offensive around Myitkyina, Burma.

June 4th

Western Europe

1935 Pierre Laval became French Premier.

1936 Socialist Leon Blum became French Premier.

1940 Fifty-seven Royal Air Force bombers attacked targets in Germany and lost one "Whitley". The Royal Navy destroyer SHIKARI, the last ship to leave Dunkirk, departed with 600 troops aboard at 0340. The Allies had evacuated 338,226 troops from Dunkirk, but had left 2,000 guns, 60,000 vehicles, 600,000 tons of supplies 76,000 tons of munitions. Eighty-five per cent of the British Expeditionary Force had been saved. The Royal Air Force had flown 3,561 sorties in support of the operation and had lost ninety-eight fighters. The Germans occupied Dunkirk. The dredge EMILE DESCHAMPS was sunk off Margate by a magnetic mine. She was the last of 243 vessels lost in "Operation Dynamo". The French government requested twenty Royal Air Force fighter squadrons. British Prime Minister Churchill made his "...fight on the beaches" speech. Britain at this time has less than 500 artillery pieces in the country. The Allies evacuated 4,700 troops from Norway.

1941 Fifty-four Royal Air Force "Blenheims" attacked German shipping and lost two aircraft. The former German Kaiser died in Doorn, Holland. Royal Air Force ace Johnny Curchin (9 victories) died when his aircraft collided with a Me109 over Dover.

1942 Twelve Royal Air Force "Bostons" attacked Boulogne and Dunkirk in France and lost one aircraft. Reinhard Heydrich died in Prague (See May 27th). German surface-to-surface rockets were test-fired by the submerged U511 in the Baltic. Thirty-five Royal Air Force bombers attacked targets in Holland and France.

1943 The German steamer ALTENFELS (8,132 tons) was sunk in Korsfjord, Norway by the Norwegian MTBs 620 and 626. Six American 8th Air Force P47s flew patrols over the Channel.

1944 Allied D-Day invasion convoys already at sea had to return due to bad weather. At 0400 the RN midget submarine X-23 arrived off the mouth of the Orne River and took up her position as a positon beacon for the upcoming landing by British troops the next day. She was commanded by 25-year-old RNVR Lieutenant George Honour. The X-20 took up a similar position at the other end of the British beaches. Both would have to spend an extra day in their locations due to the postponement of the landings until the 6th. Twenty-three Royal Canadian Air Force "Spitfires" destroyed the German radar station at Cap D'Antifer on the Channel coast. 509 American 8th Air Force B17s and B24s dropped 1,472 tons of bombs on coastal defenses on the Pas de Calais. They were escorted by 172 8th Air Force fighters that lost two P51s. 394 8th Air Force B17s and B24s dropped 1,080 tons of bombs on rail bridges and airfields in France. 412 8th Air Force fighters provided escort for the bombers and lost one P51. The American 9th Air Force attacked Pointe du Hoc in Normandy. 9th Air Force fighters flew a "Chattanooga Choo-Choo" (train hunting) mission to France and attacked bridges in Rouen. There were only 183

Luftwaffe day-fighters based in France. 259 Royal Air Force bombers attacked coastal batteries along the Channel coast.

1990 A P63C "Kingcobra" crashed near La Ferte Alais, France, killing the pilot.

Eastern Europe

1867 Finnish Field Marshal Carl Mannerheim was born. During WWI he was a lieutenant general commanding an army corps. In 1918, with the help of the Germans, he drove out the Soviets and won Finland's independence on October 18th. He was named to the Defense Council in 1931. Although Russia and Finland signed a non-aggression pact in 1932, work began on the "Mannerheim Defensive Line" across the Karelian Peninsula. Construction continued until the Soviet invasion on November 30, 1939. Finland held out until March 12, 1940 when she was forced to cede 16,200 square miles of her territory and 450,000 of her citizens. When Germany invaded Russia on June 22, 1941, Finland declared war on Russia and regained her lost territory but refused to advance past her previous borders. A truce with Russia was signed on September 4, 1944. Mannerheim resigned as president on March 4, 1946. He died on January 27, 1951 at the age of 83 in Lausanne, Switzerland.

1909 Finland's third-ranking ace, Eino Luukkanen, was born on the Karelian Isthmus. He would score fifty-four victories during the war.

1942 Hitler visited Marshal Mannerheim in Finland.

1943 128 Luftwaffe aircraft dropped 179 tons of bombs on the Molotov Tank Works in Gorki, losing two bombers.

1944 The American 15th Air Force attacked rail targets in Yugoslavia. At 0010, the German minesweeper M-37 was sunk by Soviet MTBs in the Gulf of Finland.

1945 The American merchantship NEW BERN VICTORY was damaged by a mine off Odessa in the Ukraine.

Mediterranean

1940 Fifty-four Italian submarines received orders to move to positions around the Mediterranean in preparation for war.

1941 The Pro-Allied government was re-established in Iraq.

1942 The British 8th Army counter-attacked at Bir-el-Harmat.

1943 Allied aircraft dropped 200 tons of bombs on Pantelleria. The Royal Navy bombarded it at the same time. The USN PC-496 was sunk off Bizerte by a mine.

1944 The American 15th Air Force attacked Genoa, Leghorn, Bologna, and Turin. At 1915, the US Army's 88th Division reached the Piazza Venezia in Rome.

Atlantic

1941 The Royal Navy armed merchant cruiser MARSDALE took the German tanker GEDANIA (8,923 tons). The German tanker ESSO HAMBURG (9,849 tons) was scuttled to prevent her capture by the Royal Navy. The U101 sank the British freighter TRECARRELL (5,271 tons). U101 survived the war. The British barge ROBERT HUGHES (2,879 tons) was sunk by a mine.

1942 The U159 sank the American freighter CITY OF ALMA (5,446 tons-29 dead). U159 survived until July 15, 1943. The U158 sank the Norwegian freighter NIDARNES (2,647 tons). U158 survived until June 30th. The German armed merchant cruiser STEIR took the steamer GEMSTONE (4,986 tons). A Royal Air Force Coastal Command "Wellington" scored the first success for the new ASV radar and the Leigh Light when it damaged the Italian submarine LUIGI TORELLI. The Swiss steamer SAENTIS rescued eighteen survivors from the American freighter WEST NOVUS which had been sunk on June 1st by U404. The USN destroyer TARBELL rescued thirty survivors from the American tanker M.F. ELLIOTT which was sunk on June 3rd by U502.

1943 The U308 was sunk by the Royal Navy submarine TRUCULENT north of the Faeroes. The U594 was sunk by the Royal Air Force's No.48 Squadron west of Gibraltar.

1944 The U505 was taken by the USN escort carrier GUADALCANAL and the destroyer escorts CHATELAIN, JENKS, and PILLSBURY. It is now on display in Chicago, Illinois. Lieutenant (jg) Albert David of the PILLSBURY won a Medal of Honor during the operation.

1945 The American freighter COLIN P. KELLY was a constructive loss after hitting a mine off Ostend, Belgium. A No.201 Squadron "Sunderland" flew the Royal Air Force's last anti-sub patrol of the war.

North America

1934 The carrier RANGER was commissioned. She was the first USN ship that was built as a carrier from the keel up. She would be scrapped in 1947.

1939 The US Coast Guard refused the steamer ST. LOUIS entry into American waters. Aboard the ship were 937 German-Jewish refugees. The episode became known as "The Voyage of the Damned". The ship returned to Europe and most of the refugees were trapped when Holland fell to the Germans in 1940.

1941 American film actor Wayne Morris was commissioned as an ensign in the USN. He had appeared in "Submarine O-1"(1937), "Valley of the Giants"(1938), "The Kid from Kokomo"(1939) and "Flight of Angels"(1940). He would have an extremely active career during the war and would score seven aerial victories in the Pacific. He was the nephew of Navy Commander David McCampbell who would score thirty-four victories and win the Medal of Honor in the Pacific.

1942 The destroyer HOBBY (stricken in 1971) was launched. She was stricken in 1971. Colonel Curtis LeMay assumed command of the 305th Bomb Group (B17) at Salt Lake City, Utah. He would command the 20th Air Force in the Pacific at the end of the war.

1943 The destroyer LONGSHAW was launched. She was lost on May 18, 1945.

1944 The submarines SABALO (preserved as a memorial in 1973) and SABLEFISH (scrapped in 1971) were launched. Ernest King presented Chester Nimitz with a Distinguished Service Medal at San Francisco aboard the battleship PENNSYLVANIA.

1965 The battleship MASSACHUSETTS was dedicated as a memorial.

1970 USMC General Clifton B. Cates, former commander of the 4th Division, died in Annapolis, Maryland.

1974 The destroyers COLLETT and MANSFIELD were sold to Argentina.

Pacific

1942 At 0430, a Japanese force consisting of thirty-six "Kates", thirty-six "Vals" and thirty-six "Zeros" left their carriers to attack American installations on Midway. At the same time, the USN carrier YORKTOWN launched a ten aircraft search group. At 0530, a PBY flown by Lieutenant Howard Ady reported IJN carriers 180 miles from Midway. Also, at 0530, Midways radar sighted the incoming Japanese air-raid. At 0600, the American forces on Midway launched an air attack against the IJN. One of the aircraft sent was USMC SBD BuNo 2106. It would be sent to the USN Museum in Pensacola, Florida in 1994 after being recovered from Lake Michigan, where it had been since a June 1943 training accident. By 0616, all of Midway's aircraft were airborne. At 0700, Nagumo ordered a second attack against the island. At 0710, six TBFs of the USN carrier HORNET's Torpedo Squadron 8 that were temporarily based on Midway, attacked the Japanese fleet scoring no hits and losing five aircraft. It was the first combat operations for the type. Four torpedo-carrying B26 "Marauders" attacked the IJN carriers scoring no hits and losing three aircraft. By 0715, the Japanese raid on Midway had ended. American losses were fifteen "Buffaloes", two "Wildcats" and eleven dead and eighteen wounded on the island. The Japanese lost eleven aircraft. At 0730, USN Task Force 16 (commanded by Spruance), consisting of the carriers ENTERPRISE and HORNET, six cruisers and nine destroyers, launched sixty-seven SBDs, twenty-nine TBDs and twenty F4Fs. At 0748, sixteen USMC "Vindicators" and "Dauntless' (commanded by Major Lofton Henderson) attacked losing eight aircraft and scoring no hits. Henderson Field on Guadalcanal would be named in his honor. At 0810, fifteen USAAF B17s (commanded by Sweeney) attacked scoring no hits and suffering no losses. At 0820, eleven USMC "Vindicators" (commanded by Major Benjamin Norris) attacked scoring no hits and losing two aircraft. At 0837, the IJN began recovering its Midway strike force. At 0906, USN Task Force 17 (commanded by Fletcher), consisting of the carrier YORKTOWN, two cruisers and five destroyers, launched twelve TBDs, seventeen SBDs and six F4Fs. At 0920, the HORNET's VT-8 sighted the IJN forces. At 0918, the IJN turned East-Northeast to intercept the USN task force. At 0925, fifteen TBDs from the HORNET attacked. At 0930, the ENTERPRISE's VT-6 attacked. At 1000, twelve TBDs and six F4Fs from the YORKTOWN attacked. At 1025, thirty-seven SBDs from the ENTERPRISE attacked the IJN carriers AKAGI and KAGA, while seventeen YORKTOWN SBDs attacked the IJN carrier SORYU. At 1100, the IJN carrier HIRYU launched eighteen "Vals" and six "Zeros". Three American aviators were rescued by IJN vessels after the attack. They were interrogated and then executed. At 1205, Task Force 17 was attacked by HIRYU aircraft. The YORKTOWN was hit by three bombs. She came to a complete stop twenty minutes later and Fletcher was forced to move his flag to the heavy cruiser ASTORIA. At 1331, IJN Combined Fleet commander Yamamoto ordered the light carriers RYUJO and JUNYO to leave the Aleutians and move to Midway to support the Midway operation. Also, at 1331, the HIRYU launched ten "Kates" and six "Zeros" to attack the USN forces. At 1340, the YORKTOWN was able to resume a speed of eighteen knots. At 1425, the YORKTOWN was again damaged by aircraft from the HIRYU. A YORKTOWN fighter landing aboard HORNET accidentally fired its machine guns, killing five and wounding twenty. One of those killed was Lieutenant Royal Ingersoll, the 29-year-old son of the USN Atlantic Fleet Commander. At 1500, the YORKTOWN was abandoned. At 1530, USN Task Force 16 launched twenty-four SBDs to attack the HIRYU. At 1610, the SORYU sank (718 died). At 1700, the HIRYU suffered four bomb hits. At 1925, the KAGA sank (800 of her crew died). USMC ace Marion Carl had scored the first of his eighteen victories, a "Zero" over Midway. He would later become the first Marine to land a jet aboard a carrier and would command the first USMC jet squadron and would retire as a general. The Japanese Naval Air Force attacked Dutch Harbor in the Aleutians. USAAF P40s shot down four "Vals" and lost one during the attack. IJN Petty/Officer Tadayoshi Koga crash-landed his "Zero" on Unalaska, in the Aleutians, after shooting down a PBY near Dutch Harbor. It was sighted and dismantled five weeks later. An American 11th Air Force B26 disappeared after attacking the IJN off the Aleutians. The Royal Navy submarine TRUSTY sank the TOYOHASHI MARU (7,031 tons). The IJN submarine I-27 sank the Australian freighter IRON CROWN (3,353 tons) and damaged the freighter BARWON (4,239 tons).

1943 The 11th Air Force attacked Kiska in the Aleutians.

1944 The USN submarine FLIER sank the HAKUSAN MARU (10,380 tons) off Iwo Jima. The USN submarine SHARK sank the KATSUKAWA MARU (6,886 tons). Japanese aircraft attacked Allied shipping off Biak, New Guinea and damaged the USN light cruisers PHOENIX and NASHVILLE. 5th Air Force A20s attacked Manokwari, New Guinea.

1945 The USN submarine BILLFISH sank the TAIU MARU (2,220 tons). The USN submarine TENCH sank the RYUJIN MARU (517 tons). Two USMC regiments landed on Oroku Peninsula on Okinawa.

1982 A memorial was dedicated at Dutch Harbor in the Aleutians. Present at the ceremony were six PBY pilots, one B26 pilot and the flight commanders of the IJN "Kates" and "Vals" who had participated in the 1942 attack.

1998 The sunken USN carrier YORKTOWN (See 1942) was filmed by a special submersible at a depth of more than three miles. The ship had been located the previous month by the same team, headed by Robert Ballard that had filmed the liner TITANIC, the German battleship BISMARCK and several Allied and Japanese warships that had been lost off Guadalcanal in 1942.

China-Burma-India

1943 The Royal Air Force attacked Akyab, Burma.

1944 The Chinese 28th Division took Lameng, Burma.

June 5th

Western Europe

1940 The Germans attacked the French defenses along the Somme and Aisne Rivers. French Premier Paul Reynaud sent FDR a telegram requesting aircraft. Charles de Gaulle became French Under Secretary of State for National Defense. Luftwaffe ace Werner Moelders (115 victories) was shot down near Compiegne, France and captured after scoring his 25th victory. Twenty-three Royal Air Force bombers attacked targets in France. Sweden asked for P36 fighters from America. Ninety-two Royal Air Force bombers attacked targets in France and Germany. Sixteen people were killed in the raid on Hamburg. The Allies evacuated 4,900 troops from Norway.

1941 Nine Royal Air Force "Blenheims" attacked German shipping.

The Month of June

1942 Twenty-four Royal Air Force "Bostons" attacked targets in Holland and France. 180 Royal Air Force bombers attacked Essen, Germany and lost twelve aircraft. Ten people were killed in the raid.
1943 Twelve Royal Air Force bombers dropped mines off the Atlantic coast.
1944 At 0415, Supreme Allied Commander General Dwight Eisenhower made the decision to invade Normandy on the morning of the 6th. The Germans intercepted a coded BBC message to the Resistance warning them that the invasion would begin within forty-eight hours. The German 15th Army was put on maximum alert in anticipation of an Allied invasion. 626 American 8th Air Force bombers dropped 1,896 tons of bombs on coastal defenses on the Pas de Calais and near Cherbourg and lost four B17s and two B24s. Royal Air Force "Typhoon" fighter-bombers destroyed the radar station at Cap-de-la-Hague on the Channel coast. Lieutenant Colonel Leon Vance, of the USAAF's 489th Bomb Group, won a Medal of Honor over Wimereaux, France. Vance was the Group Executive Officer and his was the only Medal of Honor won by a B24 crewman flying from Britain. He would disappear on his return flight to America. 124 of the 160 serviceable Luftwaffe day-fighters in France had been withdrawn from the coastal areas due to heavy Allied air attacks. Twelve Allied minesweepers cleared mines off the French coast. At 1815, the USN minesweeper OSPREY was sunk off thirty miles Normandy by a mine. Nine of her crew died. The American 3rd Army's Finance Section received 352,256,000 French francs in anticipation of its landing in France. At just after 2200, Allied paratroopers began taking off from Britain en route to Normandy. 1,012 Royal Air Force bombers attacked coastal batteries along the Normandy coast and lost three aircraft. Thirty-one Royal Air Force "Mosquitoes" attacked Osnabruck, Germany. The USAAF's 801st Bomb Group dispatched eleven B24s on "Carpetbagger" missions and lost one aircraft over Belgium. Since March 31st, the Royal Air Force's Bomber Command had flown 24,072 sorties on which it had dropped 75,748 tons of bombs and had lost 525 aircraft.
1945 The Allies assumed governmental powers in Germany. Reich Transport Minister, Julius Dorpmuller, died in Malente, Schleswig-Holstein.

Eastern Europe
1942 The Germans attacked Sevastopol. The Soviet Navy delivered supplies to the besieged city of Sevastopol on the Black Sea.

Mediterranean
1941 British reinforcements arrived on Cyprus.

1942 Sergeant Q. Smythe Royal, of the Natal Carbineers, won a Victoria Cross at Gazala. The British 8th Army suffered 6,000 casualties in "The Cauldron".
1943 The Italian submarine H-8 was sunk and the battleships ROMA and LITTORIA were damaged at La Spezia by 113 12th Air Force B17s. The Royal Navy cruiser NEWFOUNDLAND and destroyers PALADIN and TROUBRIDGE bombarded Pantelleria. USAAF B26 "Marauders" attacked the island of Pantelleria.
1944 The American 15th Air Force attacked Turin, Bologna, Leghorn, and Genoa.

Atlantic
1941 The German tanker EGERLAND (9,798 tons) was sunk by the Royal Navy's heavy cruiser LONDON and destroyer BRILLIANT. The U48 sank the British tanker WELLFIELD (6,054 tons). U48 survived the war.
1942 The U159 sank the Honduran freighter SALLY (150 tons). U159 survived until July 15, 1943. The Portuguese sailing ship MARIA DA GLORIA (270 tons) was lost. The Dutch freighter POSEIDON (1,928 tons) was lost. The U158 sank the American freighter VELMA LYKES (2,572 tons-15 dead). U158 survived until June 30th. The U172 sank the American freighter DELFINA (3,480 tons-4 dead). U172 survived until December 13, 1943. The U68 sank the American tanker L.J. DRAKE (6,693 tons) with all hands. U68 survived until April 10, 1944.
1943 The U217 was sunk by the USN escort carrier BOGUE.
1944 The U539 sank the Panamanian freighter PILLORY (1,517 tons). U539 survived the war. The U987 was sunk by the Royal Navy submarine SATYR west of Narvik, Norway.
1993 The wreck of the U1226 was discovered 4 miles off Cape Cod. She had been sunk on October 28, 1944.

North America
1942 America declared war on Rumania, Hungary, and Bulgaria. An ordnance plant explosion in Elmwood, Illinois killed forty-nine civilian workers. Vice Admiral William S. Pye took Task Force 1 (seven battleships and the escort carrier LONG ISLAND) out of San Francisco to protect the West Coast in case the Japanese broke through the American defenses around Midway.
1943 The escort carrier GUADALCANAL was launched. She was scrapped in Japan in 1960. The destroyer COGSWELL (sold to Turkey in 1969) was launched. Astronaut Alan Shepard would serve aboard her in the Pacific.
1945 The heavy cruiser TOLEDO was launched. She was stricken in 1974.

1946   The destroyers BABBITT and SCHENCK were sold for scrap. A rusty torpedo was discovered on the beach near the Golden Gate Bridge in San Francisco.
1959   The destroyer GUEST was sold to Brazil and renamed PARA.
1961   The destroyer BALDWIN was scuttled after running aground on the 16th of April.
2009   US Navy Pharmicist Mate 2nd Class George Wahlen died. He had been awarded the Medal of Honor on March 3, 1945 for his action while serving as a medic with the 5th Marine Division on Iwo Jima.

Pacific
1940   The Italian merchant ship REMO (9,780 tons) was seized by the authorities in the port of Fremantle, Australia.
1942   At 0120, the IJN submarine I-168 shelled the American installations on Midway. The IJN heavy cruisers MIKUMA and MOGAMI collided off Midway. Japanese forces landed on Attu in the Aleutians. USAAF 54th Fighter Squadron (P38) arrived at Umnak Airfield in the Aleutians. They would be the first P38s flown in a combat zone. At 0500, the IJN carrier AKAGI (263 dead) was torpedoed and sunk by IJN destroyers. At 0840, 6 USMC SBDs (commanded by Captain Marshall Tyler) and 6 "Vindicators" (commanded by Captain Richard Flemming) attacked the MOGAMI and MIKUMA. The MIKUMA was damaged when Flemming crashed his aircraft into her after turret. He won a posthumous Medal of Honor for his actions. Eight USAAF B17s attacked the MOGAMI scoring no hits. At 0900, the IJN carrier HIRYU (416 died) was sunk off Midway by the USN carrier ENTERPRISE aircraft. USAAF B26s attacked Lae, New Guinea.
1943   A portion of Yamamoto's ashes were buried in Hibiya Park in Tokyo. The rest were buried in Nagoya two days later. American aircraft attacked shipping off Buin, New Georgia losing one P40, two SBDs and two TBFs. The American 11th Air Force attacked Kiska in the Aleutians.
1944   American forces continued their attack on Biak Island. The USN submarine PUFFER sank the tankers ASHIZURI (7,951 tons) and TAKASAKI (4,465 tons). The USN submarine SHARK sank the TAMAHIME MARU (3,080 tons) and the TAKAOKA MARU (7,006 tons). The USN submarine NAUTILUS landed 90 tons of supplies on Mindanao. The Japanese Naval Air Force attacked the USAAF base on Wakde Island. Charles Lindbergh flew an F4U from Emirau Island on a bombing mission over Kavieng, New Ireland.
1945   Corporal Harry Harr, of the 31st Division, won a posthumous Medal of Honor near Maglamin, Mindanao. USAAF B29s destroyed 4.3 square miles of Kobe and lost eleven aircraft. The USN battleship MISSISSIPPI

was hit by a Japanese kamikaze off Okinawa. The only fatality was her Chaplain, Lieutenant Floyd Withrow. The USN heavy cruiser PITTSBURGH lost her bow in a typhoon.

China-Burma-India
1942 The IJN armed merchant cruisers HOKOKU MARU and AIKOKU MARU sank the freighter ELYSIA off Madagascar. The IJN submarine I-10 sank the Panamanian freighter ATLANTIC GULF (2,639 tons) and the American freighter MELVIN H. BAKER (4,999 tons). The IJN submarine I-20 sank the Panamanian freighter JOHNSTOWN (5,086 tons).
1943 The Royal Air Force attacked Buthidaung, Burma. The U198 sank the British freighter DUMRA (2,304 tons). U198 survived until August 12, 1944.
1944 Ninety-eight USAAF B29s flew the type's first operational mission when they attacked the railyards at Bangkok, Thailand. Fourteen of the bombers aborted due to various problems. The mission had been flown from bases in India. This had been done to preserve fuel supplies in China that had to be carried over the "Hump". Five aircraft were lost and only 18 bombs fell within the target area. The U183 sank the British freighter HELEN MOLLER (5,259 tons). U183 survived until April 23, 1945.
1945 Royal Air Force B24s attacked Suratthani, Siam.

June 6th

Western Europe
1939 The Royal Navy anti/aircraft light cruiser EURYALUS was launched. She was scrapped in 1959.
1940 German forces under General Hermann Hoth broke through the French lines near Amiens, France. Thirty-eight Royal Air Force bombers attacked targets in France and lost five "Blenheims". Royal Air Force ace Edgar J. Kain (17 victories and the Royal Air Force's first ace of the war) died while slow-rolling his "Hurricane" over his field at Echemines, France. The New Zealander was on his way back to Britain when he crashed. The Allies evacuated 5,100 troops from Norway. The German minesweeper M-11 was sunk in a minefield laid by the Royal Navy submarine NARWHAL off Norway. Forty-one Royal Air Force bombers attacked targets in France and Germany. Sixteen people were killed in the raid on Hamburg.
1941 Hitler issued the "Commissar Order" for the Eastern Front. It required the immediate execution of all Soviet officials when they were captured.

1942 233 Royal Air Force bombers attacked Essen, Germany and lost nine aircraft. Seventeen people were killed in the raid.

1944 The Allied invasion of Normandy (D-Day) took place. Overall command was held by Eisenhower, the land forces were commanded by Montgomery, the sea forces by Ramsay and the air forces by Tedder. Air activity in support of the invasion included 3,467 sorties by heavy bombers, 1,645 by medium bombers, 5,409 by fighters and 2,316 by transports. Convoys for the American "Utah" and "Omaha" beaches included sixteen attack transports, one LSD, 106 LSTs, one LSR, fifteen LCCs, ninety-three LCIs, 350 LCTs, thirty-four LCSs, ninety-four LCAs, 189 LCVPs, thirty-eight LCS(S)s, fifty-four LCPs, nine LCGs, eleven LCFs, fourteen LCT(R)s, two LCS(M)s and thirty-six LCS(S)s. Escorts for the incoming convoys included the American destroyers JEFFERS, GLENNON, BARTON, O'BRIEN, WALKE, LAFFEY, FRANKFORD, NELSON, MURPHY, PLUNKETT and MEREDITH, the American destroyer escorts BORUM, AMESBURY and BLESSMAN, the French corvettes ACONIT and RENONCULE, the French frigates L'AVENTURE and L'ESCARMOUCHE, the British destroyers VESPER and VIDETTE. The support force for "Utah" (commanded by Deyo) consisted of the American battleship NEVADA, the British monitor EREBUS, the American cruisers TUSCALOOSA and QUINCY, the British cruisers HAWKINS, BLACK HAWK and ENTERPRISE, the Dutch gunboat SOEMBA, the American destroyers HOBSON, FITCH, FORREST, CORRY, BUTLER, SHUBRICK, HERNDON and GHERARDI and the American escort destroyers BATES and RICH. The support force (commanded by Bryant) for "Omaha" consisted of the American battleships TEXAS and ARKANSAS, the British cruiser GLASGOW, the French cruisers MONTCALM and GEORGES LEYGUES, the American destroyers MCCOOK, MCCORMICK, DOYLE, BALDWIN, HARDING, SATTERLEE, THOMPSON and EMMONS and the British destroyers MELBREAK, TANATSIDE and TALYBONT. There would actually be fewer Allied troops landed in Normandy on D-Day than were landed in the first day of the invasion of the island of Sicily in the Mediterranean the year before. 23,250 troops were landed on "Utah" and 34,250 on "Omaha". The Eastern Naval Task Force (commanded by Vian) covered the British and Canadian "Gold", "Juno" and "Sword" beaches. 24,970 troops would land on "Gold", 21,400 on "Juno" and 28,845 on "Sword". The convoys for those beaches included thirty-seven LSIs, 130 LSTs, two LSRs, one LSD, eleven LCCs, 116 LCIs, thirty-nine LCI(S)s, 487 LCTs, sixty-six LCSs, 408 LCAs, seventy-three LCS(S)s, ninety LCPs, ten LCP(S)s, sixteen LCG(L)s, twenty-two LCT(R)s, fourteen LCS(L)s, twenty-four LCS(M)s, eighteen

LCFs, forty-five LCA(H)s and 103 LCTs with armament. The support force for "Gold" was commanded by Captain Longley-Cook and was comprised of the British cruisers ARGONAUT, ORION, AJAX and EMERALD, the Dutch gunboat FLORES, the British destroyers GRENVILLE, ULSTER, ULYSSES, UNDAUNTED, UNDINE, URANIA, URCHIN, URSA, CATTISTOCK, COTTESMORE, PYTCHLEY and JERVIS and the Polish destroyer KRAKOWIAK. The support force for "Juno" included the British cruisers BELFAST and DIADEM, the British destroyers FAULKNOR, FURY, KEMPENFELT, VENUS, VIGILANT, STEVENSTONE, the French destroyer LA COMBATTANTE, the Norwegian destroyer GLAISDALE and the Canadian destroyers ALGONQUIN and SIOUX. For "Sword" the support force consisted of the British battleships WARSPITE and RAMILLIES, the British monitor ROBERTS, the British cruisers MAURITIUS, ARETHUSA, FROBISHER and DANAE, the Polish cruiser DRAGON, the British destroyers SAURAMEZ, SCORPION, SCOURGE, SERAPIS, SWIFT, VERULAM, VIRAGO, MIDDLETON, EGLINTON and KELVIN, the Norwegian destroyers SVENNER and STORD, the Polish destroyer SLAZAK. A total of seven battleships, two monitors, twenty-three cruisers, three gunboats, 105 destroyers and 1,073 smaller craft were directly involved in the operation. The Germans in comparison had five torpedo boats, thirty-four S-boats, 163 minesweepers and ninety-nine patrol boats and gun carriers in roughly the same area. At 0015, Allied paratroops began landing in France. At 0020, British paratroops captured the bridge over the Caen Canal. At about 0100, the German headquarters at St. Lo received word that paratroopers had landed at various points around Normandy. At 0200, 100 Royal Air Force "Lancasters" began bombing the British invasion beaches. At 0230, the USN battleship NEVADA and the cruisers QUINCY and TUSCALOOSA and the Royal Navy cruiser BLACK PRINCE reached their firing positions off "Utah" beach. At 0300, Allied gliders began landing reinforcements. At 0303, Allied minesweepers completed their operations off the coast. At 0309, German radar spotted the Allied fleet. At 0430, 132 members of the US Army's 4th and 24th Cavalry Regiments became the first seaborne Allied troops to invade Hitlers "Fortress Europe" from the sea when they landed on the islands of Iles St. Marcouf, three miles off "Utah" beach. They lost thirteen men in minefields. At 0440, British paratroops took the Merville battery. Also, at 0440, the Norwegian destroyer SVENNER was sunk off "Sword" beach by the German torpedo boats MOWE, JAGUAR and T-28. Torpedoes passed between the British battleships WARSPITE and RAMILLIES. The German S-139 and S-140 were lost in minefields outside Cherbourg while attempting to sortie against the Allied invasion. German S-boats sank LST-715 and an LCT off St. Vaast. 1,114 8th Air Force B17s and B24s dropped 3,205 tons of bombs on the invasion beaches and the road junction at the town of Argentan behind the beaches and lost three B24s. At 0500, Hitler's staff at his headquarters at Berchtesgaden received word of the invasion but they were unwilling to wake him until more definite information was available. At 0535, German batteries began firing on the USN battleship NEVADA. At 0542, the US Coast Guard PC-1261 was sunk by a mine. At 0547, the USN LCT-597 was sunk by a mine. 0630 was H-Hour on the American invasion beaches of "Omaha" and "Utah". At 0640, the USN destroyer CORRY was sunk off "Utah" by a mine, twenty-two died. Her survivors were rescued by the destroyers FITCH and HOBSON. At 0645, the Royal Navy destroyer WRESTLER was a constructive loss after hitting a mine 20 miles northwest of Le Havre. She had participated in the sinking of two German U-boats earlier in the war. 0725 was H-Hour on the British beaches of "Gold", "Juno" and "Sword". 508 8th Air Force B17s and B24s dropped 1,647 tons of bombs on the city of Caen and areas behind the invasion beaches and lost one B24. The fighters of the 8th and 9th Air Forces flew 1,719 sorties over the area during the day and claimed thirty victories for the loss of twenty-five aircraft. At 1110, the US Army's 101st Airborne and 4th Infantry Divisions linked up behind "Utah" beach. At 1600, Hitler approved the deployment of two panzer divisions to the invasion area in Normandy. Private Carlton Barrett, of the 1st Division, won a Medal of Honor near St. Laurent-Sur-Mer. 1st Lieutenant Jimmie Monteith, of the 1st Division, won a posthumous Medal of Honor near Colleville-Sur-Mer. Brigadier General Theodore Roosevelt, of the 4th Division, won a Medal of Honor on "Utah". Sergeant/Major S. Hollis, of the Green Howards, won a Victoria Cross in Normandy. American film actor Art Carney was wounded on "Omaha" Beach. American film actor Glenn Ford directed a film crew as a USN Commander during the invasion. American film actor Robert Montgomery was aboard the USN destroyer O'BRIEN as Operations Officer. American author Louis L'Amour landed in Normandy as commander of a tank-destroyer. American author Ernest Hemingway landed with the 5th wave at Normandy. British actor Lieutenant Colonel David Niven served as liaison with the US Army's 1st Division. British actor Peter Ustinov served as his batman. Future US Attorney General Elliot Richardson won a Bronze Star and two Purple Hearts in Normandy. Strom Thurmond, future US Senator, was wounded while with the 82nd Airborne Division. American film actor Charles Durning served as an Army Ranger during the attack. British actor Richard Todd was one of the first British Airborne officers to land in Normandy. American author Cornelius Ryan jumped with the 101st Airborne Division. He would later write "The Longest Day", which was based on the invasion. American actor Jack Warden would have jumped with his unit, the 501st Regiment of the 101st Airborne Division, but he broke his leg in the last practice jump before D-Day. German General Wilhelm Falley, commander of the 91st Division, became the first general killed on D-Day when he was shot by 508th Regiment paratroops. The 82nd Airborne Division raised the same flag it had flown over Naples, over St. Mere Eglise. The USN LCIs 85, 91 and 92 were sunk off Normandy by mines. The USN LCI-93 was sunk by shell-fire off Normandy. The British freighter SAMBUT was sunk in Dover Straits by German shore-batteries. The German gun ferries AFs-62, 64, 67 and 72 were scuttled in various ports in the area of the invasion. The German minesweeper R-221 was sunk at Blainville by Allied aircraft. Major League baseball player Lawrence "Yogi" Berra was aboard the USN transport BAYFIELD off Normandy. British author WIlliam Golding ("Lord of the Flies") commanded a rocket-firing ship off Normandy. Douglas Kennedy, editor of "True" magazine, commanded the USN PT-500 off Normandy. 106 Allied vessels were lost during D-day. By D+ 30 the Allies would lose 917 vessels, 437 of which had been lost due to weather. The Luftwaffe flew 140 sorties over Normandy losing one Fw190 and four Ju88s, while the Allies flew 14,674 sorties, losing 113 aircraft. American 8th Air Force bombers flew 2,362 of these sorties, dropping 3,596 tons of bombs and losing only three aircraft. The three lost aircraft included a 487th Bomb Group B24 that was shot down and two 493rd Bomb Group B24s that collided over the Channel. 493rd Bomb Group (B24 then converted to the B17) was flying its first 8th Air Force mission. It was the last 8th Air Force Bomb Group to be activated during the war. National Football League coach Tom Landry of the Dallas "Cowboys" would serve as a co-pilot aboard one of its B17s. Lieutenant General James H. Doolittle, commander of the 8th Air Force, and Major General Earle Partridge, his deputy, flew two P38s over Normandy to observe bombing results. 1,065 Royal Air Force bombers attacked communication targets in France and lost eleven aircraft.

1968 Sir Miles Dempsey, commander of the British 2nd Army in Normandy, died.

1984 A memorial was dedicated to the USAAF's 448th Bomb Group (B24) at their old base at Seething in East Anglia.

Eastern Europe

1942 The Soviet Navy delivered supplies to the besieged city of Sevastopol on the Black Sea.

1943   154 Luftwaffe aircraft dropped 242 tons on Molotov tank works in Gorki, losing one aircraft.

1944   The American 15th Air Force attacked Ploesti, Rumania, and rail targets in Yugoslavia. 104 15th Air Force B17s and 42 P51s flying from Russia to Italy attacked Galatz Airfield in Rumania, losing two P51s (See June 2nd for the first part of the mission). The Ira Eaker-led force then returned to its Soviet bases. Former Polish Foreign Minister Josef Beck died in exile in Rumania.

1945   Harry Hopkins had his sixth and last meeting with Stalin concerning American-Soviet relations since arriving in Moscow on May 25th as President Truman's personal envoy.

Mediterranean

1941   The Royal Navy carriers ARK ROYAL and FURIOUS launched 44 "Hurricane" fighters for Malta in "Operation Rocket", 1 aircraft was lost.

1942   The Luftwaffe attacked Malta. Lieutenant Colonel H. Foote, of the Royal Tank Regiment, won a Victoria Cross at Gazala, Libya. The Royal Air Force attacked Messina, Italy.

1943   The USAAF flew its first operations with the A36 ("Mustang") dive-bomber, the target was on Sicily. Allied aircraft attacked Pantelleria.

1944   The French took Tivoli. The US Army's 1st Armored Division was twenty-five miles north of Rome.

Atlantic

1940   The Royal Navy armed merchant cruiser CARINTHIA (20,277 tons) was sunk by the U46 off Ireland, 4 died (See June 8th). U46 survived the war. The U48 sank the British freighter STANCOR (798 tons). U48 survived the war.

1941   The blockade runner ELBE (9,179 tons) was sunk near the Azores by aircraft from the Royal Navy carrier EAGLE. She had been en route from East Asia. The Italian submarine MARCONI sank the British freighter BARON LOVAT (3,395 tons) and the Swedish freighter TABERG (1,392 tons). The U106 sank the British freighter SACRAMENTO VALLEY (4,573 tons). U106 survived until August 2, 1943. The U43 sank the Dutch freighter YSELHAVEN (4,802 tons). U43 survived until July 30, 1943. The U48 sank the British freighter TREGARTHEN (5,201 tons). U48 survived the war.

1942   The U68 sank the Panamanian tanker C.O. STILLMAN (13,006 tons). U68 survived until April 10, 1944. The US Coast Guard cutter SEA CLOUD rescued eight survivors from the schooner MARIA DA GLORIA. As of 1980, SEA CLOUD was still operating as a cruise ship in the Caribbean.

The American freighter GEORGE CLYMER (7,176 tons) was taken by the German armed merchant cruiser MICHEL. The freighter STANVAC CALCUTTA (10,170 tons-14 dead) was taken by the German armed merchant cruiser STIER.

1944 The U373 was sunk off Brest, France by the Royal Air Force's No.224 Squadron.

North America

1903 Ernest King received his naval commission. He would serve as Chief of Naval Operations during the war.
1938 The submarine SARGO was launched. She was scrapped in 1947.
1941 It became legal for the American government to seize idle foreign (meaning Axis) ships in American ports.
1942 The escort carrier BLOCK ISLAND was launched. She was lost May 29, 1944. The US Army Newspaper "Yank" began publication.
1943 The submarine DARTER was launched. She was lost on October 24, 1944. Soft cheese was rationed in America.
1944 The destroyer ROOKS and the submarine SENNET (stricken in 1968) were launched. The ROOKS was sold to Chile in 1962. The first flight of the XP-58 "Chain-Lightning", an enlarged version of the P38, took place.
1954 A memorial hospital was officially opened in Nova Scotia to serve the inhabitants of the Burin Peninsula. It had been donated by the American government and dedicated to people of the area who had rescued the crews of two American ships that ran aground on February 18, 1942.
1972 The destroyer O'BANNON was sold for scrap. A plan to preserve her as a memorial had failed.
1994 A C53 "Skytrooper" (a modified C47) was dedicated at the McClellan Air Force Museum in Sacramento, California. The aircraft had transported members of the 101st Airborne Division to Normandy on the 6th and 7th of June 1944 while attached to the 72nd Troop Carrier Squadron. It also participated in operations over Holland and the Rhine River in Germany.
2001 A National D-Day Memorial was dedicated in Bedford, Virginia. Bedford had suffered what was the highest per capita loss of any American town during the invasion. Out of a population of 3,200, it had sent thirty-five men to serve in Company A, 116th Infantry Regiment. Of those, sixteen lost their lives on the beaches of Normandy.

South America

1945 Brazil declared war on Japan.
1986 Doctor Josef Mengele, The Auschwitz death camps "Angel of Death", was exhumed from his grave near Sao Paulo, Brazil.

Pacific

1942 IJN submarines bombarded the Naval Base at Sydney, Australia. An LB-30 "Liberator" carrying the 7th Air Force commander, Major General Clarence Tinker, disappeared off Midway while on a mission to Wake with three other aircraft. The remaining aircraft failed to locate their target due to bad weather. Six USAAF B17s attacked the USN submarine GRAYLING off Midway. Japanese forces landed on Kiska in the Aleutians.

1943 The USN submarine S-30 sank the NAGASHIGE MARU No.2 (30 tons) off the Kamchatka Peninsula. The USN submarine TAUTOG sank the SHINEI MARU (970 tons). USAAF P38s and P40s attacked Japanese positions on Choiseul.

1944 American forces continued their attack on Biak Island. October 1, 1945 was set as the date for the invasion of Japan. Task Force 58 left Majuro for the Marianas campaign. The USN submarine PINTADO sank the KASHIMASAN MARU (2,825 tons) and the HAVRE MARU (5,652 tons). The USN submarine RATON sank the IJN escort CD-15 off Indo-China. The USN submarine HARDER sank the IJN destroyer MINAZUKI off Celebes. Charles Lindbergh flew an F4U from Green Island on a mission over Rabaul, New Britain.

1945 Staff Sergeant Howard Woodford, of the 33rd Division, won a posthumous Medal of Honor on Luzon. The USN AOG SHEEPSCOT was lost in a storm off Iwo Jima. The USN destroyer-minelayer J. WILLIAM DITTER was a constructive loss after an air-raid off Okinawa and was scrapped in 1946.

China-Burma-India

1942 The IJN submarine I-16 sank the Yugoslavian freighter SUSAK (3,889 tons).

1943 The U198 sank the American freighter WILLIAM KING (7,176 tons). U198 survived until August 12, 1944.

1944 American 10th Air Force P38s attacked Japanese Air Force airfields at Meiktila and Heho. Air Force ace Lieutenant Colonel Levi Chase (12 victories) was killed in action.

June 7th

Western Europe

1935 The appointment of Pierre Laval as France's new Premier was announced. Stanley Baldwin became Britain's Prime Minister replacing Ramsay MacDonald.

1940   King Haakon of Norway was evacuated aboard the Royal Navy heavy cruiser DEVONSHIRE at Tromso and departed for Britain. The Allies evacuated 5,200 troops from Norway. The Germans took Montdidier, Noyon and Forges-les-Eaux in France.

1941   Twenty-two Royal Air Force "Blenheims" attacked German shipping and lost three aircraft. Thirty Royal Air Force bombers attacked the German heavy cruiser PRINZ EUGEN at Brest, France.

1942   Britain's King George VI inspected the USN battleship WASHINGTON at the Royal Navy's anchorage at Scapa Flow. Forty-three Royal Air Force bombers dropped mines off French ports.

1943   143 American 8th Air Force P47s flew a sweep over the Pas de Calais in France.

1944   King Leopold III of Belgium was sent to Germany as a prisoner. 401 American 8th Air Force B17s and B24s dropped 1,159 tons of bombs on tactical targets behind the invasion beaches in Normandy. 476 B17s and B24s dropped 1,172 tons of bombs on targets in France and lost one B17 and one B24. 820 8th Air Force fighters flew sorties over the beach-head and northern France and lost eight P51s. 653 8th Air Force fighter-bombers dropped 196 tons of bombs on French targets. The American 9th Air Force lost thirteen fighter-bombers over Normandy. A USAAF P47 strafed a 10-truck German convoy that was carrying US Army paratrooper prisoners of war in Normandy. All the trucks were destroyed and thirty prisoners of war were killed. The American 90th Infantry Division began landing on "Utah" beach. The American 2nd Infantry Division began landing on "Omaha" beach. Eisenhower and his naval deputy, British Admiral Ramsay, visited the assault beaches aboard the fast minelayer APOLLO. The USAAF's 487th Bomb Group lost four B24s over Britain to Luftwaffe intruders. The Allied forces in Normandy had yet to reach the objectives assigned to them for the first day of the invasion. The USN minesweeper TIDE was sunk off "Utah" beach by a mine. The American freighter FRANCIS C. HARRINGTON was damaged by a mine off Normandy. LSTs 376 and 314 were sunk by German S-boats. S-boats also sank LCI-105 and LCT-875. British forces took Port-en-Bessin and Bayeaux in Normandy. 337 Royal Air Force bombers attacked communication targets in France and lost twenty-eight aircraft. 122 Royal Air Force bombers attacked Foret de Cerisy and lost two "Lancasters". The USAAF's 801st Bomb Group dispatched fourteen B24s on "Carpetbagger" missions.

1950   British Field Marshal Archibald Wavell was buried at Winchester College. He had commanded the British forces in North Africa.

1959 The Freiburg State Prosecutor issued an arrest warrant for Josef Mengele, S.S. doctor at Auschwitz, then living in Buenos Aires, Argentina.
2010 Former RAF pilot Jack Harrison died at the age of 97. He was believed to be the last survivor of the "Great Escape" which took place at Stalag Luft III near the Polish border on March 24, 1944.

Eastern Europe

1942 German General Erich Manstein's 11th Army attacked Sevastopol in the Crimea. The Soviet Navy delivered supplies to Sevastopol.
1943 Twenty Luftwaffe aircraft dropped thirty-nine tons of bombs on the Molotov Tank Works in Gorki.

Mediterranean

1941 The Italian Air Force attacked British positions in Tobruk, Libya. The Royal Air Force attacked Italian forces in Benghazi and Derna in Libya.
1942 A British No.202 Squadron "Catalina" sank the Italian submarine VANIERO. The Italian submarine CORALLO sank the Turkish sailing ship HADY M'HAMMED (26 tons).
1943 Allied aircraft dropped 600 tons of bombs on the island of Pantelleria which was located between Sicily and the coast of North Africa.
1944 The American 15th Air Force attacked Bologna, Turin, Genoa, and Leghorn in Italy. The US Army's 43rd Division took the town of Civitavecchi, Italy.

Atlantic

1940 The U48 sank the British freighters FRANCES MASSEY (4,212 tons). U48 survived the war.
1941 The U38 sank the British freighter KINGSTON HILL (7,628 tons). U38 survived the war.
1942 The U107 sank the Honduran freighter CASTILLA (3,910 tons). U107 survived until August 18, 1944. The U653 sank the USN aircraft tender GANNET (840 tons). U653 survived until March 15, 1944. The U158 sank the Panamanian freighter HERMIS (5,234 tons). U158 survived until June 30th. The U159 sank the American freighter EDITH (3,382 tons-2 dead). U159 survived until July 15, 1943. The Italian submarine DA VINCI sank the British freighter CHILE (6,956 tons). The American tanker ESSO MONTPELIER rescued six survivors from the freighter ILLINOIS which had been sunk on June 1st by U172.
1944 The U955 was sunk in the Bay of Biscay by the Royal Air Force's No.201 Squadron. The U970 was sunk west of Bordeaux, France by the Royal Air Force's No.228 Squadron.

North America

1901 Ernest King graduated from Annapolis. He would serve as the Chief of Naval Operations during the war.

1941 The battleship SOUTH DAKOTA was launched. She was scrapped in 1962. The keel of the light cruiser SANTA FE was laid at Camden, New Jersey (See 1942).

1942 The light cruiser SANTA FE (scrapped in 1960) and the destroyer TAYLOR (sold to Italy in 1969) were launched.

1944 The escort carrier KWAJALEIN was commissioned. She was scrapped in 1961.

1949 President Harry Truman signed a bill which authorized $20,000 in payments to surviving relatives of the Mitchell incident (See June 15, 1945).

1964 "Doolittle Raider" Lieutenant Ross Wilder died.

1989 The USN submarine BLENNY was scuttled off Ocean City, Maryland as an artificial reef.

2011 Flying Tiger ace John Alison died at the age of 98. He had scored 6 aerial victories while serving with that unit in China.

2013 USAAF ace Lieutenant Colonel Donald McGee died at the age of 92 in Knoxville, Tennessee. He had been credited with 5 aerial victories while flying P39s and P38s in the Southwest pacific and 1 more while piloting a P47 in Europe.

Pacific

1942 Japanese forces landed on Kiska in the Aleutians. The only casualty was a 60-year-old American school teacher named Charles Foster Jones. On August 8, 1948 he was reburied at Fort Richardson (Plot A-Grave 2) near Anchorage, Alaska. The USN carrier YORKTOWN (19,000 tons) and destroyer HAMMANN (102 died) were sunk off Midway by the IJN submarine I-168. The USN submarine GRAYLING was attacked by USAAF B17s. The USN battleship CALIFORNIA left Pearl Harbor en route to Bremerton to repair damage suffered during the attack of December 7th. The American freighter COAST TRADER (3,286 tons-1 dead) was sunk off Cape Flattery, Washington by the IJN submarine I-26. The USN submarine GROUPER was attacked by USAAF B17s northwest of Midway.

1943 The Japanese lost 23 of 112 aircraft over the Russells, while shooting down 9 American aircraft. Japanese Naval Air Force ace Masuaki Endo (14 victories) died in a collision with a P40 during the action.

1944 The US Army's 162nd Regiment took Mokmer Airfield on Biak. Charles Lindbergh flew an F4U from Green Island on a mission over Rabaul,

New Britain. The USN submarine HARDER sank the IJN destroyer HAYANAMI east of Tawi Tawi, Borneo. The USN submarine WHALE sank the SHINROKU MARU (2,857 tons) off Chichi Jima.

1945 The USN destroyer ANTHONY was hit by a Japanese kamikaze off Okinawa. USMC Private Robert Mctureous, of the 6th Division, won a posthumous Medal of Honor on Okinawa. The US Army's I Corps took Bambang, Luzon. 400 B29s attacked the Osaka Army Arsenal and destroyed 2.2 square miles of the surrounding city. The USN submarine TENCH sank the HANSHIN MARU (92 tons). The USN submarine SHAD sank the AZUSA MARU (1,370 tons).

China-Burma-India

1943 The U181 sank the South African freighter HARRIER (193 tons). U181 survived the war.
1944 The Chinese 88th Division reached the outskirts of Lungling, Burma.

June 8th

Western Europe

1918 The Royal Navy carrier EAGLE was launched. She was sunk in the Mediterranean by a German U-boat in 1942.
1921 The Royal Navy light cruiser EFFINGHAM was launched. She was wrecked on May 17, 1940.
1937 The German heavy cruiser BLUCHER was launched. She was sunk on April 9, 1940.
1940 The Allies evacuated 4,600 troops from the area around Narvik in northern Norway. They had been fighting there since April 15th. A French Navy Farman-223.4 bomber named "Jules Verne" dropped two tons of bombs near Berlin. There were only seventy-two Royal Army tanks in Britain at that time. By August there would be 200 and by September there were 438.
1941 Thirty-seven Royal Air Force "Whitleys" attacked Dortmund, Germany.
1942 Twelve Royal Air Force "Bostons" attacked targets in Holland. 170 Royal Air Force bombers attacked Essen, Germany and lost nineteen aircraft. Thirteen people were killed in the raid.
1944 American and British forces linked up near Port-en-Bessin in Normandy. The US Army's 4th Division advanced towards Cherbourg, France. Technical/Sergeant Frank Peregory, of the 29th Division, won a posthumous Medal of Honor at Grandcampe, France. The British 7th Armored Division began landing on "Gold" beach. At 0152, the USN destroyer MEREDITH was damaged off "Utah" beach by a mine and

was bombed and was later sunk by the Luftwaffe on the 9th. She was the second destroyer named MEREDITH to be lost in the war. The first had been lost south of the Solomons in the South Pacific on October 25, 1942. The USN LST-499 was sunk off Normandy by a mine. At 0445, the Royal Navy frigate LAWFORD was sunk off "Juno" beach by the Luftwaffe. At 0830, the USN destroyer GLENNON was damaged off Normandy by a mine and was sunk by German artillery on the 10th. Twenty-five of her crew died in the explosion. At 0920, the USN destroyer escort RICH was sunk off Normandy by a mine, ninety-nine of her crew died. She had been attempting to assist the GLENNON. The American freighters ARTEMAS WARD, COURAGEOUS, GALVESTON, GEORGE W. CHILDS, GEORGE S. WASSON and BENJAMIN CONTEE, JAMES MARSHALL, JAMES IREDELL, VICTORY SWORD, WEST GRAMA, WEST HONAKER, WOLSCOX and MATT W. RANSOM were scuttled as "Gooseberry" breakwaters off Normandy. The No.144 Squadron became the first Royal Air Force unit to operate from French soil when its "Spitfires" arrived at St. Croix-sur-Mer in Normandy. US Army engineers opened an airfield behind "Omaha Beach". 724 American 8th Air Force bombers dropped 1,876 tons of bombs on French targets and lost one B17 and two B24s. 1,353 8th Air Force fighters flew 1,353 sorties over the invasion area. Allied aircraft attacked Toulon, France. 483 Royal Air Force bombers attacked communication targets in France and lost four aircraft.

1951 German S.S. General Otto Ohlendorf, commander of Einsatzgruppe "D", was hung at Landsberg Prison along with three other "E-gruppe" commanders and Oswald Pohl, Chief of S.S. Economic and Administrative Department.

1968 British inventor Barnes Wallis was knighted. He had designed the Royal Air Force's "Wellington" bomber as well as various bombs used during the war.

1973 Emmy Goering, Hermann's wife, died in Munich.

1993 Accused French war criminal Rene Bousquet, age 84, was shot to death in his Paris apartment. He had been awaiting trial on charges of transporting thousands of Jews to Germany.

Eastern Europe

1941 German forces began arriving in Finland for "Operation Barbarossa".

1944 The Soviets attacked Finnish positions on the Karelian Peninsula.

Mediterranean

1940 Over the next four nights the Italian Navy would lay almost 2,000 mines in the Sicilian Channel.

1941	Free French forces attacked Vichy-controlled Syria and Lebanon.
1942	The U83 sank the Egyptian sailing ship SAID (231 tons). U83 survived until March 4, 1943. At 2125, the Italian destroyer ANTONIOTTO USODIMARE was sunk in error by the Italian submarine ALAGI.
1943	The Royal Navy cruisers AURORA, EURYALUS, NEWFOUNDLAND, ORION and PENELOPE and destroyers JERVIS, LAFOREY, LOOKOUT, LOYAL, NUBIAN, TARTAR, TROUBRIDGE and WHADDON and the MTBs 73, 77 and 84 bombarded the island of Pantelleria. Allied aircraft dropped 700 tons of bombs on Pantelleria.
1944	The American 15th Air Force attacked the Pola submarine pens.

Atlantic

1940	The German battlecruiser SCHARNHORST was torpedoed by the Royal Navy destroyer ACASTA and 48 of her crew died. 1,515 British sailors died when the battlecruisers SCHARNHORST and GNEISENAU sank the Royal Navy carrier GLORIOUS (22,500 tons and launched in 1917 as a battlecruiser) and destroyers ACASTA and ARDENT off Norway. The Royal Navy armed merchant cruiser CARINTHIA sank after being torpedoed off Ulster, Northern Ireland by the U46 on the 6th. U46 survived the war.
1941	The U108 sank the British freighter BARON NAIRN (3,164 tons) and the Greek freighter DIRPHYS (4,240 tons). U108 survived until April 11, 1944. The U107 sank the British freighter ADDA (7,816 tons). U107 survived until August 18, 1944. The U103 sank the British freighter ELMDENE (4,853 tons). U103 survived until April 15, 1945. The U46 sank the British freighter TREVARRACK (5,270 tons). U46 survived the war. The U48 sank the Dutch tanker PENDRECHT (10,746 tons). U48 survived the war.
1942	The German minesweeper TARONGA was declared a constructive loss after an air-attack off Scharhorn. The U172 sank the American transport SICILIEN (1,654 tons-44 dead) off Haiti. U172 survived until December 13, 1943. The U504 sank the Honduran freighter TELA (3,901 tons) and the British freighter ROSENBORG (1,512 tons). U504 survived until July 30, 1943. The U128 sank the Norwegian tanker SOUTH AFRICA (9,234 tons). U128 survived until May 17, 1943. The U107 sank the American freighter SUWIED (3,249 tons-6 dead), and the US Coast Guard cutter NEMISIS rescued twenty-seven survivors. U107 survived until August 18, 1944. The U135 sank the Norwegian freighter PLEASANTVILLE (4,549 tons). U135 survived until July 15, 1943. The Brazilian tanker SANTA MARIA rescued two survivors from the American tanker M.F. ELLIOTT which had been sunk on June 3rd by U502. The two had been held briefly aboard the submarine as prisoners of war. The USCG cutter NEMISIS

rescued twenty-seven survivors from the American freighter SUWIED which had been sunk on June 7th by U107.

1943 The U758 ("a flak trap") was attacked by seven Allied aircraft. She destroyed one F4F and damaged a P51 and a "Lysander". U758 survived the war.

1944 The U373 and U629 were sunk off Brest, France by the Royal Air Force's No.224 Squadron.

1989 The wreck of the German battleship BISMARCK was located at a depth of 15,617 feet, by an expedition led by Robert Ballard. Ballard had also located the wreck of the RMS TITANIC on an earlier expedition.

North America

1944 The escort carrier MUNDA was launched. She was scrapped in Japan in 1960.

1945 A Japanese balloon-bomb was found near Mahogany Mountain, Oregon.

1973 A cannon shell that had been fired by the IJN submarine I-26 on June 20, 1942 was recovered near Estavan Point, Vancouver Island. Admiral Gerald Bogan, commander of the carrier Saratoga, Carrier Division 25, Task Group 58.4, Task Group 38.2, and Task Group 38.3, died.

Pacific

1942 The USN submarine tender FULTON arrived at Pearl Harbor with 2,025 carrier YORKTOWN survivors aboard. YORKTOWN had been sunk during the "Battle of Midway". Japanese Premier Tojo declared that the results of the Midway fiasco would be kept secret from the Japanese public. The IJN aircraft tender KAMIKAWA MARU arrived at Kiska, in the Aleutians, with twenty-four aircraft aboard. The Japanese began preliminary planning for the proposed airfield on the Lunga plain on Guadalcanal. "Doolittle Raiders" Hallmark, Meder, Farrow, Hite, DeShazer, Barr and Spaatz were sent from Tokyo to Nagasaki en route back to China. A member of Sorge's spy ring, Tokutaro Yasuda, was arrested.

1943 The Japanese High Command issued orders for the evacuation of Kiska in the Aleutians. The IJN battleship MUTSU exploded in Hiroshima Bay. The cause of the accident was assumed to be experimental 16" ammunition that was aboard. The USN submarine FINBACK sank the KAHOKU MARU (3,277 tons).

1944 The USN submarine HAKE sank the IJN destroyer KAZEGUMO off Davao. The USN submarine RASHER sank the tanker SHIOYA (7,905 tons). The IJN destroyer HARUSAME was sunk off New Guinea by the USAAF. The USN opened a PT boat base on one of the islets off

Biak Island. Heavy fighting continued on Biak Island. American forces counter-attacked near Aitape, New Guinea. The USN submarine HARDER rescued an Australian commando unit from Borneo. USAAF ace Colonel Charles MacDonald shot down a Japanese "Zeke" over New Guinea.

1945 The American 6th Army reached Magat, Luzon. The USN submarine COBIA sank the NANSHIN MARU No.22 (834 tons) and the transport HAKUSA (6,000 tons). The IJN heavy cruiser ASHIGARA was sunk in the Java Sea by the Royal Navy submarine TRENCHANT. The USN minesweeper SALUTE was sunk by a mine off Brunei. USN Hospital Apprentice 1st Class Fred Lester, of the 6th USMC Division, won a posthumous Medal of Honor on Okinawa. Ninety-three USAAF B29s made emergency landings on Iwo Jima after an attack on Osaka.

China-Burma-India
1942 The IJN submarine I-18 sank the Norwegian freighter WILFORD (2,158 tons). The IJN submarine I-16 sank the Greek freighter AGIOS GEORGIOS IV (4,847 tons). The IJN submarine I-10 sank the British freighter KING LUD (5,224 tons). The IJN submarine I-20 sank the Greek freighter CHRISTOS MARKETTOS (5,209 tons).

June 9th

Western Europe
1889 German Generals Hans-Karl von Esebeck and Hans von Boineburg-Lengsfeld were born.
1895 German General Kurt Zeitzler was born. He died on September 25, 1963.
1938 Britain announced that it would purchase 200 aircraft from the Lockheed and North American aircraft companies in America.
1940 The Germans took Rouen, Dieppe, and Compiegne in France. French forces along the Somme River were routed. The British 51st Highland Division surrendered in France. It was one of last British units in France. The Allies completed their withdrawal from Narvik, Norway. The Norwegian government ordered its forces to cease-fire at midnight.
1941 Eighteen Royal Air Force bombers attacked coastal targets and lost four aircraft.
1942 The Germans destroyed Lidice, Czechoslovakia in retaliation for the attack on Nazi leader Reinhard Heydrich. Fifty-four Royal Air Force bombers dropped mines in the Baltic. The RMS QUEEN ELIZABETH dropped anchor in the Firth of Clyde. Aboard was the ground contingent

of the USAAF's 97th Bomb Group (B17). It was the first such unit to arrive in Britain.

1943 The USAAF B17 "Memphis Belle" was sent back to America on a bond tour. She was the first American B17 to complete 25 missions over Europe. Eight Royal Air Force "Wellingtons" dropped leaflets over France and lost one aircraft.

1944 The French battleship COURBET, the Dutch heavy cruiser SUMATRA, the Royal Navy battleship CENTURION, light cruiser DURBAN (launched in 1921) and anti/aircraft auxiliary ALYNBANK were scuttled off Normandy as breakwaters. Also scuttled were fifty-three merchant ships. The USN LSTs-314 and 376 were sunk off Normandy by German MTBs. The German gun ferry AF-15 was sunk off Dieppe by Allied aircraft. At 1010, the USN destroyer MEREDITH (See June 8th) sank after being attacked by Luftwaffe bombers off Normandy. A French salvage company began scrapping her hulk on August 5, 1960. The German destroyer Z-28 was sunk at Sassnitz Roads by the Royal Air Force. Private First-Class Charles DeGlopper, of the 82nd Airborne Division, won a posthumous Medal of Honor at La Giere, Normandy. The British 51st Infantry Division began landing on "Juno" and "Sword" beaches. The German destroyers ZH-1 and Z-32 were sunk off Brittany by Royal Navy destroyers. The British lost the HURON and suffered severe damage to the TARTAR during the action. The German S-boats 180 and 190 were lost to mines while transferring from Flushing to Boulogne. The American 15th Air Force attacked Munich. A USAAF 460th Bomb Group B24 landed near Fussach, Germany and was captured. 401 Royal Air Force bombers attacked airfields in France and lost two "Halifaxes". 112 Royal Air Force bombers attacked Etampes, France and lost six "Lancasters". 133 French civilians were killed in the raid.

1950 Royal Admiral Sir Henry Harwood died. He had commanded the forces that forced the German pocket battleship GRAF SPEE to be scuttled in 1939 and had served as Commander-in-Chief of the Mediterranean in 1942.

Eastern Europe

1934 Russia, Poland, Czechoslovakia, and Rumania agreed to respect their common borders.

1943 The Soviet Air Force attacked German forces at Yaroslavi. The Luftwaffe sank forty-seven Soviet landing craft off the Caucasian coast.

1944 The Soviets began a major offensive against Finland. The Soviets had 450,000 men, 800 tanks and 2,000 aircraft against Finnish forces of 268,000 men, 110 tanks and 250 aircraft.

Mediterranean

1940 The Italian battleship ROMA was launched. She was sunk on September 9, 1943.

1941 The Allies occupied Tyre, Lebanon.

1942 The Royal Navy carrier EAGLE launched thirty-two "Spitfire" fighters for Malta in "Operation Salient". She was escorted by the cruisers CAIRO and CHARYBDIS, the destroyers PARTRIDGE, ITHURIEL, ANTELOPE, WISHART, WRESTLER, and WESTCOTT. The U83 sank the Palestinian sailing ship TYPHOON (175 tons). The Italian submarine ZAFFIRO was sunk by a British No.202 Squadron "Catalina". The Royal Air Force attacked Taranto, Italy.

1943 Twenty-one American 9th Air Force B24s attacked Gerbini, Sicily. Allied aircraft dropped 800 tons of bombs on Pantelleria. The Royal Navy bombarded Pantelleria. Aboard the Royal Navy light cruiser AURORA, during the action, were Supreme Allied Commander American General Dwight Eisenhower and his naval commander, Royal Navy Admiral Andrew Cunningham.

1944 The American 15th Air Force attacked Porto Marghero, Italy. The US Army's 34th Division took Tarquinia, Italy. The German torpedo boat TA-27 was damaged off Elba by the USAAF and sank on the 9th. The German hospital ship INNSBRUCK was sunk off Venice by Allied aircraft.

Atlantic

1940 The U46 sank the Finnish freighter MARGARETA (2,155 tons). U46 survived the war.

1941 The U46 sank the British freighter PHIDIAS (5,623 tons). U46 survived the war. The U101 sank the British freighter SILVERPALM (6,373 tons). U101 survived the war.

1942 The U502 sank the American tanker FRANKLIN K. LANE (6,589 tons-4 dead) and the Belgian freighter BRUXELLES (5,085 tons). U502 survived until July 5th. At 0215, the French corvette MIMOSA was sunk in North Atlantic by the U124. U124 survived until April 2, 1943.

North America

1939 The USN destroyer WARRINGTON arrived in Manhattan from Fort Hancock in New Jersey. Aboard were the King and Queen of England who were en route to FDR's residence in Hyde Park, New York. The WARRINGTON would be lost in a hurricane on September 13, 1944.

1941 The US Army adopted the new pattern helmet, although the 1917-model would be used well into 1942.

1942   USAAF Brigadier General James Doolittle was awarded the Medal of Honor in Washington D.C. for his Tokyo raid.
1943   The RMS SCYTHIA arrived in New York to repair torpedo damage suffered in Algiers the previous November.
1945   The heavy cruiser OREGON CITY was launched. She was stricken in 1970.
1969   The destroyer SAMUEL N. MOORE was sold to Taiwan.
1972   USMC Colonel John Smith committed suicide. He had won a Medal of Honor over Guadalcanal.

Pacific
1942   All formal Allied resistance in the Philippines ended. The Allies had suffered 140,000 casualties while trying to defend the islands. Japanese Naval Air Force ace Satoshi Yoshino (15 victories) was killed in action over New Guinea by P400s. USN Lieutenant Commander Lyndon Johnson, future American President, was awarded a Silver Star when the 19th Bomb Squadron B26 "Heckling Hare" in which he was riding, returned with engine trouble from a mission to Lae, New Guinea. No one else on the aircraft was cited. USAAF P39s shot down five Japanese "Zeros" near Morobe, New Guinea. The IJN submarine I-24 damaged the British freighter ORESTES (7,748 tons). USN submarine TROUT rescued two survivors from the IJN heavy cruiser MIKUMA which had been sunk on June 6th.
1943   The IJN tanker AKEBONO MARU was damaged by the USN submarine GREENLING.
1944   The USN submarine SWORDFISH sank the IJN destroyer MATSUKAZE off Chichi Jima. The USN submarine HARDER sank the IJN destroyer TANIKAZE. Charles Lindbergh flew an F4U from Green Island on a mission over Rabaul, New Britain. Two American 11th Air Force B25s were hit by Soviet anti/aircraft fire over Kamchatka. One crashed and the other was interned by the Soviets.
1945   Mandog, Mindanao was taken by the US Army's 24th Division. Japanese in the Cagayan Valley on Luzon were surrounded. The Japanese forces were trapped on the Okoku Peninsula on Okinawa. USAAF B29s attacked the Aichi plant in Nagoya and the Kawasaki plant in Akashi, Japan. The IJN escort CD-41 was sunk by the USN submarine SEA OWL. The USN submarine TENCH sank the SHINROKU MARU (2,857 tons). The USN submarine TINOSA sank the WAKATAMA MARU (2,211 tons). The USN submarine SEA DOG sank the SAGAWA MARU (1,186 tons) and the SHOYO MARU (2,211 tons). The USN submarine CREVALLE sank the HOKUTO MARU (2,215 tons).

China-Burma-India

1935   Japan demanded that China remove its troops from Peking and Tientsin.

June 10th

Western Europe

1926   A French-Rumanian treaty was signed.

1940   The Italians occupied Cannes and Nice in France. Over the next three days 11,059 British troops were evacuated from Le Havre, France. The last Norwegian forces surrendered to the German. The Royal Navy destroyers BULLDOG and BOADICEA were seriously damaged and the freighters BRITSUM, DALLAS CITY, DEUCALION and KOLGA were sunk by Luftwaffe "Stuka" dive-bombers in the Channel.

1941   The Royal Navy corvette PINTAIL was sunk by a mine off the Humber. 104 Royal Air Force bombers attacked German naval units at Brest, France.

1942   Twenty-three Royal Air Force "Bostons" attacked French airfields and lost one aircraft.

1943   Ninety-two American 8th Air Force P47s flew a sweep off the Dutch coast. Six Royal Air Force bombers dropped leaflets over France and lost one "Whitley".

1944   The American forces on "Omaha" and "Utah" beaches finally linked up. The US Army's 9th Division began landing on "Utah". Serving with the 9th Division was Major William C. Westmoreland, who would become US Army Chief of Staff in July 1968. The American 2nd Armored Division began landing on "Omaha" beach. The Allies had 325,000 men ashore in Normandy. 609 8th Air Force B17s and B24s dropped 1,407 tons of bombs on French targets, losing one B24. 8th Air Force fighters flew 1,491 sorties over the invasion area and claimed fourteen victories for the loss of twenty-two P47s and two P51s. The USN destroyer GLENNON (See June 8th) was sunk off Normandy by shore-batteries. The French destroyer MISTRAL was a constructive loss after being hit by German artillery three miles off Quineville in Normandy. The American freighter CHARLES MORGAN (8 dead) was sunk off "Utah" beach by the Luftwaffe. In an action off Cherbourg, the Germans lost the S-136 and the British lost MTB-448. In an action off Den Helder, the Germans lost the V-1314, V-2020 and V-2021 and the British lost the MTB-681. Staff Sergeant Arthur DeFranzo won a posthumous Medal of Honor near Goville, France. The German S.S. "Das Reich" Division destroyed the French town of Oradour-sur-Glane. Allied B25 "Mitchell" bombers and "Typhoon" fighter-bombers attacked the German Panzer Group "West" headquarters. The US Chiefs of Staff arrived in London. 432 Royal Air Force bombers attacked rail targets in France and lost eighteen aircraft. Thirty-two Royal Air Force "Mosquitoes" attacked Berlin and lost two aircraft.

1945 Marshal Georgi Zhukov presented the Soviet Order of Victory to Eisenhower and Montgomery in Frankfurt, Germany. They were the first foreigners to receive the jewel-encrusted medal valued at $100,000.

1950 A Luftwaffe Ju52 transport which had landed on the frozen Lake Hartvikvann near Narvik, Norway, April 13, 1940, was recovered from the bottom of the lake.

2001 The German government began paying 4.3 billion dollars in compensation to an estimated 1.5 million surviving Nazi-forced laborers from World War II.

Eastern Europe

1942 The Soviet destroyer SVOBODNY and transport ABKHAZIYA were sunk at Sevastopol by the Luftwaffe.

1944 Thirty-six American 15th Air Force P38s attacked Ploesti, Rumania losing twenty-three aircraft. The Soviets broke through the Finnish line at Valkcasaari, northeast of Leningrad.

Mediterranean

1940 Italy declared war on France and Britain. At this time the Italian Navy consisted of six battleships, seven heavy cruisers, twelve light cruisers, fifty-nine destroyers, sixty-seven torpedo boats and 116 submarines. The Italian freighter OLTERRA was scuttled at Gibraltar. She would later be used as a base for Italian "Pigs" (midget submarines). The USN heavy cruiser VINCENNES began loading $241,000,000 in French gold at Casablanca for evacuation to North America.

1941 Italy announced that it would occupy Greece.

1942 The U559 sank the Norwegian tanker ATHENE (4,681 tons) and damaged the British tanker BRAMBLELEAF (5,917 tons). The U431 sank the British freighter HAVRE (2,073 tons).

1944 The American 15th Air Force attacked rail and oil targets in Italy. New Zealand troops took Avezzano, Italy.

Atlantic

1940 The German armed merchant cruiser ATLANTIS took the steamer TIRRANNA (7,230 tons).

1941 The U204 sank the Belgian freighter MERCIER (7,886 tons). U204 survived until October 19th. The U108 sank the Norwegian freighter CHRISTIAN

KROHG (1,992 tons). U108 survived until April 11, 1944. The U552 sank the British freighter AINDERBY (4,860 tons). U552 survived the war.

1942   The U107 sank the American freighter MERRIMACK (2,606 tons-43 dead). U107 survived until August 18, 1944. The U94 sank the British freighters RAMSAY (4,855 tons) and EMPIRE CLOUGH (6,147 tons). U94 survived until August 28th. The U68 sank the British freighters SURREY (8,581 tons), PORT MONTREAL (5,882 tons) and ARDENVOHR (5,025 tons). U68 survived until April 10, 1944. The U129 sank the Norwegian freighter L.A. CHRISTENSEN (4,362 tons). U129 survived until August 1944. The Italian submarine DA VINCI sank the Dutch freighter ALIOTH (5,483 tons).

1943   The U66 sank the American tanker ESSO GETTYSBURG (10,173 tons-57 dead). U66 survived until May 6, 1944.

1944   The U821 was sunk off Brest, France by the Royal Air Force's Nos.208 and 246 Squadrons.

South America

1942   Reinforcements for the USN Pacific Fleet began passing through the Panama Canal. They included the carrier WASP, the battleship NORTH CAROLINA, the heavy cruiser QUINCY and the destroyers LANG, STERETT, STACK, WILSON, FARENHOLT, AARON WARD, LAFFEY and BUCHANAN.

North America

1936   Captain Patrick Bellinger assumed command of the carrier RANGER. He had been the pilot of the NC-1 on its trans-Atlantic flight and would send the "Air raid Pearl Harbor, this is no drill" message on December 7th.

1942   A full convoy system was finally organized in the Caribbean. The light cruiser SANTE FE was launched. She was scrapped in Portland, Oregon in 1960. The 21st Bomb Squadron (B24) arrived at Cold Harbor, Alaska.

1944   The escort carrier BLOCK ISLAND was launched. She was scrapped in Japan in 1960.

1946   An IJN torpedo washed ashore near the Golden Gate Bridge.

1949   The destroyers LANSDOWNE and LARDNER were sold to Turkey.

1961   Mildred Gillars, alias "Axis Sally" was paroled from the Federal Women's Reformatory in Alderson, West Virginia.

1968   The destroyer YARNELL was sold to Taiwan and renamed KUEN YANG.

2009   USAAF Colonel Ernest Bankey, age 88, died in Newbury Park, California. He had scored 10.5 victories while flying P38s and P51s in the European Theater.

Pacific

1942 The American 11th Air Force B24s attacked Kiska in the Aleutians losing one aircraft.

1943 The USN submarine TRIGGER damaged the IJN light carrier HIYO. The IJN tanker IRO was damaged by the USN submarine TINOSA. The IJN submarine I-9 was sunk by USN PC-487. USAAF Captain Thomas Lynch shot down a Japanese "Betty" over New Guinea. The American 11th Air Force attacked Kiska.

1944 Fighting continued on Biak Island. The American Saipan invasion force left Roi in the Kwajalein Atoll. The USN battleship PENNSYLVANIA and the destroyer-transport TALBOT collided in the Marianas. The Royal Navy submarine TANTALUS sank the HIYOSHI MARU (536 tons). The IJN submarine Ro-36 was sunk by the USN destroyer TAYLOR. The IJN submarine Ro-42 was sunk by the USN destroyer escort BANGUST.

1945 The USN destroyer WILLIAM D. PORTER was sunk off Okinawa by a Japanese kamikaze. She was the only USN ship sunk by kamikazes off Okinawa that did not suffer any fatalities among its crew. USN Lieutenant Richard McCool, commander of the LSC (L) 122, won a Medal of Honor off Okinawa. The USN submarine SPADEFISH sank the DAIGEN MARU No.2 (1,999 tons), the UNKAI MARU No.8 (1,293 tons) and the JINTSU MARU (985 tons). The IJN submarine I-122 was sunk by the USN submarine SKATE. The USN submarine FLYING FISH sank the TAGA MARU (2,220 tons). The USN submarine DACE sank the HAKUYO MARU (1,391 tons). The USN submarine CREVALLE sank the DAIKI MARU (2,217 tons). The USN submarine TENCH sank the SHOEI MARU No.6 (834 tons). The Australian 9th Division invaded Borneo. The American cruisers RICHMOND and CONCORD and five destroyers bombarded Matsuwa in the Kuriles.

China-Burma-India

1943 The Royal Air Force attacked Rathedaung, Burma.

1944 Chinese forces attacked Lungling, Burma.

1945 The Chinese took Wenchow.

June 11th

Western Europe

1933 The Austrian police began a crackdown on Nazis.

1937	Reginald Mitchell, the designer of the "Spitfire", died of cancer, at the age of forty-two.
1940	Paris was declared an open city. The Germans took Rheims, France. 3,321 Allied troops were evacuated from St. Valery, France. Fifteen "Skua" dive-bombers attacked the German battlecruiser SCHARNHORST at Trondheim, Norway and lost eight aircraft. Fifty-nine Royal Air Force bombers attacked targets in France and Germany and lost one "Hampden" and one "Whitley".
1941	Twenty-five Royal Air Force "Blenheims" attacked Bremerhaven, Germany and lost one aircraft. 300 Jews were arrested in Amsterdam, Holland for a May 14th attack on a German officer's club. Ninety-two Royal Air Force bombers attacked Dusseldorf and lost six "Wellingtons". Eighty Royal Air Force bombers attacked Duisburg, Germany and lost one "Whitley". Twenty-nine Royal Air Force bombers attacked Boulogne, France and lost two aircraft. A Royal Air Force "Hampden" was lost on a minelaying mission.
1942	Ninety-one Royal Air Force bombers dropped mines in the Baltic and lost four aircraft.
1943	218 American 8th Air Force B17s dropped 426 tons of bombs on Wilhelmshaven and Cuxhaven in Germany and lost eight aircraft. 8th Air Force P47s flew 275 sorties over Belgium and France. German Gestapo Chief Heinrich Himmler ordered the liquidation of all Jewish ghettoes. 783 Royal Air Force bombers attacked Dusseldorf, Germany and lost thirty-eight aircraft. 130 acres of the city were destroyed and 1,290 people were killed in the raid. Seventy-two Royal Air Force bombers attacked Munster, Germany and lost five aircraft. 132 buildings were destroyed and fifty-two people were killed in the raid.
1944	606 American 8th Air Force bombers dropped 1,611 tons of bombs on French targets and lost two B17s and one B24. 914 8th Air Force fighters flew patrols and fighter-bomber missions over northwest France. The US Army's 101st Airborne Division took Carentan, France. Lieutenant Colonel Robert Cole, of the 101st Airborne Division, won a posthumous Medal of Honor near Carentan. The British 49th Infantry Division began landing on "Gold beach. The USN tug PARTRIDGE and LST-496 were sunk off Normandy by German S-boats. LST-538 was also damaged during the action. At 0315, the Royal Navy destroyer escort HALSTED was a constructive loss after being attacked off Normandy by the German torpedo boats JAGUAR and MOWE. The German S-130 was severely damaged off Cherbourg by Allied aircraft. German S-boats attacked a convoy off the Isle of Wight and sank the freighters BRACKENFIELD (534 tons), ASHANTI (534 tons) and DUNGRANGE (621 tons). The American

freighters WEST CHESWALD and WEST NOHNO were scuttled off Normandy as breakwaters. 329 Royal Air Force bombers attacked rail targets in France and lost four aircraft.

Eastern Europe
1895 Soviet General Nikolay Bulganin was born. He died on February 24, 1975.
1937 Eight Soviet generals were executed signaling the start of the Purges in which more than 20,000 would die.
1942 The B24s of "HalPro" attacked oil installations at Ploesti, Rumania.
1944 The American 15th Air Force attacked Foscani Airfield in Rumania en route from Russia to Italy (See June 2nd and 6th). The 15th Air Force attacked oil targets in Rumania and rail targets in Yugoslavia.

Mediterranean
1940 The Italian Air Force made eight raids on Malta. There would be 3,340 more raids by Axis aircraft before the end of the war. The Italian Air Force attacked targets in Sudan and Aden. Eleven Royal Air Force "Whitley" bombers flying from Britain attacked Genoa and Turin, losing two aircraft. The Royal Air Force attacked the Italian airfield at El Adem in Cyrenica.
1942 The Axis took Bir Hacheim, Libya. The U83 sank the British sailing ship FAROUK (91 tons). U83 survived until March 4, 1943.
1943 The Italian forces on Pantelleria Island surrendered.
1944 The French took Montefiascone and Valetano. The British took Canalupo.

Atlantic
1940 The Luftwaffe sank the Royal Navy auxiliary VAN DYCK (13,241 tons) off Norway. The U48 sank the Greek freighter GOULANDRIS (3,598 tons). U48 survived the war. The U101 sank the Greek freighter MOUNT HYMETTUS (5,820 tons). U101 survived the war.
1941 The U79 sank the Norwegian freighter HAVTOR (1,524 tons). U79 survived until December 23rd.
1942 The U87 planted 10 mines in the waters off Boston, Massachusetts. The field remained undiscovered until after the war. U87 survived until March 4, 1943. The U373 planted 15 mines off Delaware Bay. U373 survived until June 8, 1944. The German armed merchant cruiser MICHEL took the British freighter LYLEPARK (5,186 tons). The U504 sank the Dutch freighter CRIJNSSEN (4,282 tons) and the American freighter AMERICAN (4,846 tons-4 dead). U504 survived until July 30, 1943. The U159 sank the British freighter FORT GOOD HOPE (7,130 tons). U159 survived until July 15, 1943. The USN gunboat ERIE rescued forty-six

survivors from the freighter FORT GOOD HOPE. The U455 sank the British tanker GEO. H. JONES (6,914 tons). U455 survived until April 6, 1944. The U157 sank the American tanker HAGAN (6,401 tons). U157 survived until June 13th. The U158 sank the Panamanian tanker SHEHERAZADE (13,476 tons). U158 survived until June 30th. The U94 sank the British freighter PONTYPRIDD (4,458 tons). U94 survived until August 28th.

1943   The U417 was sunk south of Iceland by the Royal Air Force's No.206 Squadron.

1944   The U980 was sunk northwest of Bergen, Norway by Royal Canadian Air Force's No.162 Squadron.

North America

1938   The destroyer ELLET was launched. She was scrapped in 1947.

1942   America extended Lend-Lease to Russia. Thirty-six survivors from the tanker F.W. ABRAMS (See June 10th) drifted ashore at Ocracoke, North Carolina.

1944   The battleship MISSOURI was commissioned.

1951   The destroyers NICHOLSON and WOODWORTH were sold to Italy.

2010   A B17 bomber known as the "Swamp Ghost" arrived at Long Beach, California aboard a ship from New Zealand. The aircraft had crash-landed in New Guinea on February 23, 1942 while returning from its first mission of the war, an attack on Rabaul, New Britain.

Pacific

1942   USN Admiral Raymond Spruance, en route to the North Pacific with the carriers HORNET and ENTERPRISE, six cruisers and ten destroyers, was recalled to Pearl Harbor. The American 11th Air Force attacked Kiska, damaging the IJN destroyer HIBIKI and losing one B24. The Japanese reconnoitered Amchitka in the Aleutians.

1943   Allied aircraft attacked Koepang, Timor. The USN submarine SILVERSIDES sank the HIDE MARU (5,256 tons). The USN submarine FINBACK sank the GENOA MARU (6,784 tons). The USN submarine S-30 sank the JINBU MARU (5,131 tons). The Royal Australian Navy minesweeper WALLERO was rammed and sunk off Fremantle by the freighter GILBERT COSTIN.

1944   Fighting continued on Biak Island. Fifteen carriers of USN Task Force 58 attacked Tinian and Saipan. USN Lieutenant Wayne Morris shot down a Japanese "Mavis" seaplane off Saipan. Before the war, Morris was a well-known film actor. The USN submarine REDFIN sank the ASANAGI MARU (5,141 tons). The USN submarine BARB sank the TOTEN MARU

(3,823 tons) and the CHIHAYA MARU (1,160 tons). The American 13th Air Force attacked Rabaul, New Britain.

1945 The USN submarine FLYING FISH sank the MEISEI MARU (1,893 tons). The USN submarine BOWFIN sank the SHINYO MARU No.3 (1,898 tons). The USN submarine CREVALLE sank the HAKUSAN MARU No.5 (2,211 tons). The USN submarine TIRANTE sank the HAKUJU MARU (2,220 tons). The USN submarine SEA DOG sank the KOFUKU MARU (753 tons). The USN LCS-122 was hit by a Japanese kamikaze off Okinawa.

China-Burma-India

1942 The IJN submarine I-20 sank the British freighter MAHRONDA (7,926 tons).
1943 The Royal Air Force attacked Akyab, Burma.
1945 Chinese forces took Ishan, China.

June 12th

Western Europe

1892 German Field Marshal Ferdinand Schoerner was born. He commanded Army Group "South" on the Eastern Front.
1897 British statesman Anthony Eden was born. He won the Military Cross during WWI. He became Secretary for Foreign Affairs 1931-34. In October 1935, he was named as Secretary of State for Foreign Affairs. He resigned on February 20, 1938 in protest of Prime Minister Neville Chamberlain's appeasement policy towards the Axis. On September 3, 1939, Chamberlain named him as Secretary for Dominions Affairs. When Churchill became Prime Minister, he named him as Secretary of State for War. In December, he became Foreign Secretary. He followed Churchill out of the government in July 1945. When Churchill returned to power in 1951, Eden again became Foreign Secretary. The failed attempt by Britain, France, and Israel to take control of the Suez Canal forced his resignation in January 1957. He died on January 14, 1977.
1908 The German commando, Otto Skorzeny, was born in Vienna. He would be responsible for the rescue of Mussolini after his arrest by Italian authorities. He died in 1967.
1929 Anne Frank was born in Frankfurt. Her father, Jewish businessman Otto, took his family to Amsterdam in 1933 to escape Nazi persecution. On July 5, 1942 13-year-old Anne and her sixteen-year-old sister Margot received orders to report to the S.S. Four days later, the family went into hiding. They would remain undetected until August 4, 1944, when the entire

families, except for Otto, were arrested. All those incarcerated would die before the end of the war. The house that they hid in is now a museum and her diary was published in 1947.

1940   46,000 Allied troops surrendered at St. Valery-en-Caux, France. The Germans took Chalons-sur-Marne, France. General Weygand ordered a general retreat by the French Army. Fifteen Royal Air Force bombers attacked targets in France and lost two "Hampdens".

1941   Ninety-one Royal Air Force "Hampdens" attacked Soest, Germany and lost two aircraft. Eighty-four Royal Air Force bombers attacked Schwerte, Germany and lost three "Whitleys". Eighty-three Royal Air Force "Wellingtons" attacked Hamm, Germany. Sixty-one Royal Air Force "Wellingtons" attacked Osnabruck, Germany and lost one aircraft. Royal Air Force "Beauforts" torpedoed the German pocket battleship LUTZOW (the former DEUTSCHLAND) in the Baltic. She would be out of action for six months.

1942   Four Royal Air Force "Wellingtons" attacked Essen, Germany. The German minesweeper M-4212 was sunk by a mine off Bayonne.

1943   The Luftwaffe's He219 night-fighter made its operational debut. Luftwaffe night-fighter ace Werner Streib (66 victories) shot down five bombers. He then died when he crashed on landing. Three Free French DB-7 bombers attacked Rouen, France. 503 Royal Air Force bombers attacked Bochum, Germany and lost twenty-four aircraft. 449 buildings were destroyed and 312 people were killed in the raid. American 8th Air Force P47s flew 140 sorties over France.

1944   The British MGB-17 was sunk by the German S-171. The German UJ-1401 and V-206 were scuttled at Caen. 1,277 American 8th Air Force bombers dropped 3,103 tons of bombs on French targets and lost six B17s and two B24s. 8th Air Force fighters flew 988 sorties over France and claimed twenty-seven victories for the loss of four P38s, nine P47s and three P51s. German General Erich Marcks, commander of the 84th Corps in Normandy, was killed by strafing fighters. All invasion beaches in Normandy were now linked up creating a 50-mile front. American forces took the German 210mm battery at St. Marcouf-Crisbecq near "Utah" beach. American PT-71 arrived off Normandy. Aboard were Generals Marshall, Eisenhower, Arnold, Bradley and Hodges and Admirals King, Stark, Kirk, Moon, and Wilkes. British Prime Minister Churchill arrived at Courseulles, Normandy. By this time, the Allies had landed 326,000 troops, 104,000 tons of supplies and 54,000 vehicles. The German 155th Flak Regiment fired the first operational V-1 rocket. 671 Royal Air Force bombers attacked communication targets in France and lost twenty-three aircraft. Royal Canadian Air Force Pilot Officer Andrew C. Mynarski, of No.419 Squadron, won a posthumous Victoria Cross over Cambrai, France. He was the only member of the Royal Canadian Air Force to win a Victoria Cross while serving with Bomber Command. In 1981 a memorial to his crew was dedicated near Guadiempre, France. 303 Royal Air Force bombers attacked Gelsenkirchen, Germany and lost seventeen aircraft. 270 people were killed in the raid. The USAAF's 801st Bomb Group dispatched sixteen B24s on "Carpetbagger" missions.

1952 Cardinal Michael von Faulhauber, Archbishop of Munich during WWII, died.
1969 Emmanuel Astier De La Vigerie died in Paris. During the war he had been a major resistance leader.
1973 Field Marshal Erich von Manstein died in Irschenhausen.

Eastern Europe
1940 Russia issued territorial demands to Latvia, Lithuania, and Estonia.
1942 The Soviet Navy delivered 3,300 reinforcements and supplies to the besieged city of Sevastopol on the Black Sea. The Soviet freighter SEVASTOPOL was sunk by the Luftwaffe. Twelve B24s of "HalPro" attacked oil installations at Ploesti, Rumania.

Mediterranean
1940 The Italian Air Force flew its first raid against southern France. At 0200, the Royal Navy light cruiser CALYPSO (4,180 tons and launched in 1917) was sunk south of Crete by the Italian submarine BAGNOLINI. The Italian submarines NEREIDE and NAIADE sank the Norwegian tanker ORKANGER (8,029 tons). The Royal Navy bombarded German-held Tobruk in Libya. The Royal Air Force attacked Turin and Genoa in Italy.
1941 Axis aircraft attacked Malta.
1942 At 0540, the Royal Navy destroyer escort GROVE was sunk by the U77 in the Gulf of Sollum. U77 survived until March 28, 1943. The British began a double convoy operation to resupply Malta. "Harpoon" would depart from Gibraltar and "Vigorous" would do the same from Alexandria. "Harpoon" would consist of five freighters and one tanker. Their close escort was made up of one cruiser, nine destroyers, four minesweepers and six gunboats. The long-range escort consisted of two carriers, one battleship, two cruisers and eight destroyers. "Vigorous" would consist of eleven freighters and two rescue ships. They would be escorted by twelve destroyers and four corvettes. At long-range they would have the support of eight cruisers and fourteen destroyers. During the day, "Vigorous" is attacked by the Luftwaffe. The steamer CITY OF CALCUTTA (8,063

tons) was damaged and forced to put into Tobruk. Major tank battles between the British and the Axis were fought near El Adem.

1943   The Italian island of Lampedusa surrendered. Britain's King George VI visited his troops in North Africa. A USAAF P38 landed in error at Capoterra, Italy and was captured. The U97 sank the Dutch freighter PALIMA (1,179 tons). U97 survived until June 16th.

Atlantic

1940   The U101 sank the British freighter EARLSPARK (5,250 tons). U101 survived the war. The U46 sank the British freighters BARBARA MARIE (4,223 tons) and WILLOWBANK (5,041 tons). U46 survived the war.

1941   The German tanker FRIEDRICH BREME (10,397 tons) was scuttled to prevent her capture by the Royal Navy. The U553 sank the British freighter SUSAN MAERSK (2,355 tons) and the Norwegian tanker RANELLA (5,590 tons). U553 survived until January 28, 1943. The U48 sank the British freighter EMPIRE DEW (7,005 tons). U48 survived the war.

1942   The U701 laid mines off Cape Henry, Virginia. The U124 sank the British freighter DARTFORD (4,093 tons). U124 survived until April 2, 1943. The U129 sank the British freighter HARDWICKE GRANGE (9,005 tons). U129 survived until August 1944. The U158 sank the American tanker CITIES SERVICES TOLEDO (8,192 tons-14 dead). U158 survived until June 30th. The USN gunboat ERIE rescued forty-six survivors from the British steamer FORT GOOD HOPE which had been sunk by U159. The USCG cutter NIKE rescued nineteen survivors from the Panamanian freighter BUSH RANGER which had been sunk on May 31st by U107.

1943   The U118 was sunk west of the Canaries by the USN escort carrier BOGUE. The USN submarine R-12 was lost in an accident off Key West. Forty-two of her crew died and five survived.

1944   The U490 was sunk by the USN escort carrier CROATIAN and the destroyer escorts INCH, FROST and HUSE.

North America

1887   Admiral Thomas Charles Hart was born in Davison, Michigan. He graduated 13th in his 1897 Annapolis class of 47. He was superintendent of Annapolis 1931-34. In June 1939, he was promoted to Admiral and assumed command of the Asiatic Fleet. He retired on June 30, 1942 and was elected as senator from Connecticut in 1945. He died at Sharon, Connecticut on July 4, 1971.

1893   General John Hodge was born. He assumed command of the Americal Division in the Southwest Pacific in May 1943. On April 9, 1944 he took over the 24th Corps and received his third star on June 6, 1945. He retired on June 30, 1953 as a four-star general. He died in 1963.

1916   The battleship PENNSYLVANIA was commissioned. She was expended on February 10, 1948 after participating in the Bikini A-bomb tests.

1937   The submarine SALMON was launched. She was scrapped in 1946.

1940   The Navy Department issued contracts for twenty-two new warships.

1941   Non-exempted United States Naval Reserve members were recalled to active duty.

1942   A group of four German saboteurs named Georg Dasch, Ernst Burger, Richard Quirin and Heinrich Heinick were landed by U202 at Amagansett Beach on Long Island (See June 17th, 19th and 27th, July 2nd, 8th and 31st and August 3rd and 8th). U202 survived until June 1, 1943. Canada and Russia resumed diplomatic relations after a 6-year break.

1943   The destroyer COTTEN was launched. She was stricken in 1974.

1958   8th Air Force ace John T. Godfrey (26 victories) died of "Lou Gehrigs Disease".

1989   The Victory ship LANE VICTORY arrived at her new home in Los Angeles, where she would be dedicated as a memorial to merchant sailors of WWII. She had been towed from Suisun Bay near San Francisco by the USN tug NARRAGANSETT.

Pacific

1940   The Italian merchant ship ROMOLO (9,780 tons) was scuttled by her crew when she was approached by the Royal Australian Navy armed merchant cruiser MANOORA southwest of the island of Nauru. All 129 of her crew and passengers were rescued and returned to Australia.

1942   The USN submarine SWORDFISH sank the BURMA MARU (4,585 tons) in the Gulf of Siam. The IJN submarine I-21 sank the Panamanian freighter GUATAMALA (5,527 tons). American 11th Air Force B24s attacked Kiska in the Aleutians and damaged the IJN destroyer HIBIKI.

1943   Thirty-one Japanese Naval Air Force aircraft were shot down over Guadalcanal and the Russells. American losses were six aircraft. USAAF B26s attacked Lae, New Guinea. The USN submarine TROUT landed a six-man US Army commando team at Labangen, Mindanao. USAAF ace Lieutenant Richard Bong shot down a Japanese "Oscar" over New Guinea.

1944   Fighting continued on Biak Island. The IJN gunboat OTORI was sunk by USN carriers west of Saipan. The USN destroyer KALK was damaged off western New Guinea by Japanese aircraft.

1945   The Visayan Islands were secured, by American forces. 835 Americans and 10,000 Japanese died in the operation. Two USAAF B32 "Dominators" attacked Basco Airfield on Batan Island. The USN submarine SEA DOG sank the SHINSEN MARU (887 tons). The USN submarine SKATE sank the YOZAN MARU (1,227 tons), the ZUIKO MARU (887 tons) and the KENJO MARU (3,142 tons). The USN submarine SPADEFISH sank the DAIDO MARU (69 tons). The USN submarine TINOSA sank the KEITO MARU (873 tons).

2011   New Zealand ace Geoff Fisken died at the age of 96. He had scored 11 aerial victories and had been the Commonwealth's most decorated pilot in the Pacific.

China-Burma-India

1942   The IJN armed merchant cruisers AIKOKU MARU and HOKOKU MARU sank the freighter HUAKARI in the Indian Ocean. The IJN submarine I-20 sank the Panamanian freighter HELLENIC TRADER (2,052 tons). The IJN submarine I-16 sank the Yugoslavian freighter SUPETAR (3,748 tons). The IJN submarine I-12 sank the British freighter CLIFTON HALL (5,063 tons).

1943   The Royal Air Force attacked Buthidaung, Burma.

1944   Ganju Lama, of the 7th Gurkha Rifles, won a Victoria Cross in Burma. The Royal Navy submarine STOIC sank the KAINAN MARU (1,134 tons) off Phuket, Siam.

June 13th

Western Europe

1940   163 Royal Air Force bombers attacked targets in France and lost one "Wellington". The Italian Air Force attacked French air bases at Fayence and Hyeres in southern France. Spain declared itself a non-belligerent in the war. The French battleship RICHELIEU ran her speed trials off Brest and achieved a speed of thirty-two knots. The German light cruiser NURNBURG arrived in Trondheim, Norway from Germany.

1941   110 Royal Air Force bombers attacked Brest, France. Forty-two Royal Air Force bombers attacked Schwerte, Germany.

1943   122 American 8th Air Force B17s dropped 304 tons of bombs on Bremen, Germany and lost four aircraft. Sixty 8th Air Force B17s dropped 119 tons of bombs on Kiel, Germany and lost twenty-two aircraft. USAAF Brigadier General Nathan B. Forrest became the first American general killed in action in the European Theater of Operations. He died while flying in a 95th Bomb Group B17 over Kiel. 8th Air Force P47s flew 140 sorties over France. Royal Air Force ace Wing Commander J. Ellis (13 victories) was shot down and captured. Royal Australian Air Force ace Flying Officer V.P. Brennan (10 victories) was killed in an accident. Thirteen Royal Air

Force "Mosquitoes" attacked targets in Germany. Thirty Royal Air Force bombers dropped mines off the Biscay ports and lost one "Wellington".

1944 At 0330, the first V-1 rockets fired at Britain were in a salvo of ten. The first to hit London was fired from near Amiens, France and impacted in Swanscombe, the second hit Cuckfield, the third hit Bethnal Green and the fourth hit Sevenoaks. The first Londoner killed by a V-1 was Shelter Warden Frederick Westgate. 5,863 more people would die before the V-1 attacks would end. By September 6th, more than 8,000 V-1s would be launched. A V-2 rocket fired from Peenemunde hit near Grasdala Garo, Sweden. British "Beaufighters" sank the German S-boats 178, 189 and 197. They also destroyed the R-97 which was attempting to assist the S-boats. Off Brittany, the Polish destroyer PIORUN and the British destroyer ASHANTI attacked a German convoy. They sank the M-83, 343, 412, 422 and 432. The PIORUN was also damaged during the action. The American 15th Air Force attacked the BMW plant in Munich, losing five B24s. 341 8th Air Force B17s and B24s dropped 798 tons of bombs on French targets and lost two B24s. 416 8th Air Force fighters flew sorties over France and claimed six victories for the loss of one P51, two P38s and one P47. American Generals Henry Arnold and George Marshall visited the 91st Bomb Group base at Bassingbourn. Obersturmfuhrer Michel Wittmann, of the German 501st S.S. Heavy Tank Battalion (MkVI), destroyed twenty-five vehicles of the British 7th Armored Division. He had been previously credited with 117 Russian tanks. The Germans counter-attacked at Carentan, France. The advance party of the USAAF's 354th Fighter Group (P51) arrived in Normandy. The Royal Navy battleship WARSPITE was damaged off Normandy by a mine. The Royal Navy destroyer BOADACEA was sunk off Portland by the Luftwaffe, twelve of her crew survived. Eleven "Mosquitoes" attacked targets in Germany. The USAAF's 801st Bomb Group dispatched six B24s on "Carpetbagger" missions.

1945 The U-boat tender DONAU and the torpedo recovery vessels TFA-1, 2, 5 and 6 were destroyed when an ammunition dump exploded.

1953 Luftwaffe ace Rudolf Rademacher (126 victories) died in a glider accident near Luneburg.

1960 Wilhelm Keppler, Hitler's personal advisor on economic affairs, died.

Eastern Europe

1942 The Soviet transport GRUZIYA (4,857 tons) was attacked by Italian torpedo boats while she was en route to Sevastopol with supplies and reinforcements. She made it to her destination only to be sunk the next day by the Luftwaffe.

Mediterranean

1940 The Royal Navy submarine ODIN was sunk in the Gulf of Taranto by the Italian destroyer STRALE.

1942 General Neil Ritchie, commander of the British 8th Army, ordered 300 tanks to attack Axis positions near El Adem. 230 were lost, and the action would lead to his eventual replacement by Bernard Montgomery.

1943 The Allies took Linosa Island. Twenty-four American 9th Air Force B24s attacked Gerbini, Sicily. USAAF B26s attacked Milo Airfield on Sicily.

1944 The American 15th Air Force attacked Porto Marghera.

Atlantic

1940 The U25 sank the Royal Navy armed merchant cruiser SCOTSTOUN (17,046 tons) north of Ireland. U25 survived until August 3rd. The Dutch submarine O-13 was lost in a North Sea minefield. The German armed merchant cruiser WIDDER took the British tanker BRITISH PETROL (6,891 tons). The British freighter EASTERN PRINCE, the first ship to carry munitions from America to Britain left Raritan, New York. Her cargo included 48 cannon, 12,000 rifles, 15,270 machine guns and 37,000,000 rounds of ammunition.

1941 The U77 sank the British freighter TRESILLIAN (4,743 tons). U77 survived until March 28, 1943. The Italian submarine BRIN sank the British freighter DJURDJURA (3,460 tons) and the Greek EIRINI KYRIAKIDES (3,781 tons). The U107 sank the Greek freighter PANDIAS (4,981 tons). U107 survived until August 18, 1944.

1942 The U159 sank the American transport SIXAOLA (4,693 tons) and the American freighter SOLON TURMAN (6,762 tons). U159 survived until July 15, 1943. The U157 was sunk in the Gulf of Mexico by the US Coast Guard cutter THETIS. The Italian submarine DA VINCI sank the British freighter CLAN MACQUARRIE (6,471 tons).

1943 The German trawler V-1109 was sunk in an air-attack southwest of Nieuwdiep. The US Coast Guard cutter ESCANABA was sunk by an explosion off Greenland. 101 of her 103-man crew died.

1944 The U715 was sunk north of the Faeroes by Royal Canadian Air Force No.162 Squadron.

North America

1940 US Naval Intelligence estimated that a combined coalition of the German, Italian and French fleets would outnumber a similar grouping of the USN and Royal Navy by one third. The battleship NORTH CAROLINA was launched.

1943 The destroyer PORTERFIELD was launched. She was expended in 1975.

1944 The escort carrier ADMIRALTY ISLANDS was commissioned. She was scrapped in 1947.
1946 The destroyers DENT and MAURY were sold for scrap.
1956 Admiral Charles Turner Joy, commander of the light cruiser LOUISVILLE and CruDiv-6, died. A destroyer named in his memory is now a memorial at Bremerton, Washington.
1960 An IJN midget submarine was found 4 miles from the mouth of Pearl Harbor. It is now on display at the IJN Naval Academy at Eta Jima.
1972 Admiral Felix Budwell Stump, commander of the carrier LEXINGTON II, CarDiv-24 and "Taffy 2" off Leyte, died in Bethesda, Maryland.
1990 General Isaac White, commander of the 2nd Armored Division in the European Theater of Operation 1944-45, died in San Francisco at the age of 89.

Pacific

1940 The German armed merchant cruiser ORION laid 222 mines off the New Zealand coast. Admiral William F. Halsey relieved Admiral Charles A. Blakley as Commander Aircraft Battle Force aboard the carrier YORKTOWN at Lahaina Roads, Maui.
1942 The American 11th Air Force attacked Kiska in the Aleutians.
1943 Allied aircraft attacked Humboldt Bay, New Guinea. The USN submarine GUARDFISH sank the SUZUYA MARU (897 tons). The USN submarine SARGO sank the KONAN MARU (5,226 tons). The IJN submarine I-31 was sunk off the Aleutians by the USN destroyer FRAZIER.
1944 The IJN submarine Ro-114 was sunk by the USN destroyers MELVIN and WADLEIGH. USN TF-58 commanded by Mitscher attacked shipping off the Marianas. USN Task Group 58.7, consisting of seven battleships and eleven destroyers and commanded by Admiral Willis Lee, bombarded Tinian and Saipan. The IJN First Mobile Fleet moved towards the Marianas. The IJN submarine I-33 was lost in a training accident in the Inland Sea. The USN submarine BARB sank the TAKASHIMA MARU (5,633 tons). The USN submarine NARWHAL bombarded Bula, Ceram. A USN task group (commanded by Small) consisting of two heavy cruisers, two light cruisers and nine destroyers bombarded Matsuwa in the Kuriles.
1945 The Oroku Peninsula on Okinawa was declared secure. The USN submarine BONEFISH sank the OSHIKASAN MARU (6,892 tons). The USN submarine SPADEFISH sank the Soviet freighter TRANSBALT (10,000 tons) in the Sea of Japan. The USN submarine BOWFIN sank the AKIURA MARU (887 tons). The USN submarine SKATE sank the SANJIN MARU (2,560 tons). The Australians took Brunei, Borneo. Two USAAF B32s attacked Koshun, Formosa.

China-Burma-India

1944 Heavy fighting took place around Myitkyina, Burma. Seventy-nine USAAF B29s began moving from India to bases in China. They were due to attack the Imperial Iron and Steel Works at Yawata, Japan on the 15th. It was to be the first time American aircraft had attacked the Japanese Home Islands since the "Doolittle Raid" in April of 1942.

June 14th

Western Europe

1901 German General Heinrich Schuldt was born. He died on March 24, 1944 in combat.

1931 German S.S. leader Heinrich Himmler and his future deputy Reinhard Heydrich met for the first time.

1933 Hitler's "Inspector of Austria", Theo Hibachi, was expelled from that country.

1940 The Germans occupied Paris. The Canadian Armys 1st Regiment landed at Brest on Frances Brittany coast. Sixty Royal Air Force bombers attacked targets in France and lost four "Blenheims". The French Army retreated to the Loire River. The French government moved from Tours to Bordeaux. The French battleship RICHELIEU returned to the port of Brest from her speed trials of the previous day and was attacked by the Luftwaffe. Eighty-eight Royal Air Force bombers attacked targets in France and Germany, losing one "Whitley".

1941 Thirty Royal Air Force "Blenheims" attacked coastal targets and lost one aircraft. Twenty-nine Royal Air Force "Hampdens" attacked Cologne, Germany and killed one person.

1943 203 Royal Air Force bombers attacked Oberhausen, Germany and lost seventeen "Lancasters". 267 buildings were destroyed and eighty-five people were killed in the raid. Twenty-nine Royal Air Force bombers dropped mines off the French coast and lost one "Stirling".

1944 The US Army's 2nd Armored Division landed in Normandy. The US Army's XIX Corps was activated. Charles de Gaulle visited the Normandy beachhead. 1,357 American 8th Air Force bombers dropped 2,922 tons of bombs on targets in France and the Low Countries and lost twelve B17s and two B24s. 8th Air Force fighters flew 751 sorties over France and claimed four victories for the loss of four P47s, three P38s and one P51. The German M-83 was sunk by British MTBs off Jersey. The American 15th Air Force attacked oil targets in Czechoslovakia. 337 Royal Air Force bombers attacked German troop concentrations in France. 330 Royal Air Force bombers attacked rail targets in France and lost four aircraft. The USAAF's

801st Bomb Group dispatched twenty B24s on "Carpetbagger" missions. The German minesweeper R-73 was sunk by a mine in the Baltic.
1945 Joachim von Ribbentrop, German Foreign Minister, was arrested in Hamburg.
1965 Carl (bomb-sight inventor) Norden died in Zurich, Switzerland.

Eastern Europe
1940 The USSR issued an ultimatum to Lithuania. On the 16th, it would do the same to Estonia and Latvia.
1942 The Soviet destroyer DZERZHINSKY was sunk by a mine.
1944 The Soviets advanced into the Karelian Isthmus. The American 15th Air Force attacked Budapest, Hungary. 15th Air Force ace Louis Benne (5 victories) was captured when his P38 was shot down near Petfurdo, Hungary.
1945 The American merchantship ATTLEBORO VICTORY was damaged by a mine in the Black Sea.

Mediterranean
1934 Hitler and Mussolini met for the first time in Venice.
1940 French heavy cruisers and destroyers bombarded Genoa and Vado, in Italy. The Italian submarine MACALLE (launched in 1936) was wrecked on a reef southeast of Port Sedan. The Royal Navy submarine GRAMPUS (launched in 1937) was sunk off Augusta, Sicily. The Royal Navy submarine ODIN was sunk in the Gulf of Taranto. The first Royal Air Force victory over North Africa was scored by Vernon Woodward, of the No.33 Squadron ("Gladiator"). Spain occupied the international zone of Tangier.
1941 British forces were within 25 miles of the Libyan border. The Italian Air Force attacked Alexandria, Egypt. The Royal Navy carriers ARK ROYAL and VICTORIOUS launched forty-eight "Hurricanes" for Malta in "Operation Tracer", three aircraft were lost.
1942 Italian torpedo planes attacked the British "Harpoon" convoy (See June 12th) sinking the British freighter TANIMBAR (8,619 tons) and damaging the heavy cruiser LIVERPOOL. The LIVERPOOL had to be towed back to Gibraltar. Forty Luftwaffe dive-bombers sank the Dutch freighter AGTERKERK (6,811 tons) and damaged the Royal Navy destroyer PRIMULA off Tobruk, Libya. They had been separated from the "Vigorous" convoy (see June 12th) due to engine trouble. Luftwaffe Ju88s sank the freighter BHUTAN (6,104 tons) with the main convoy and damaged the freighter POTARO (5,410 tons). During the evening, German S-boats attacked "Vigorous". They damaged the cruiser NEWCASTLE.

1943 The Royal Navy occupied Lampione Island in the Sicilian Channel.
1944 The Royal Navy submarine SICKLE was sunk by a mine. The German torpedo boats TA-26 and TA-30 were sunk off La Spezia by the USN PTs 552, 558 and 559. Staff Sergeant Homer Wise, of the 36th Division, won a Medal of Honor at Magliano, Italy. The South African 6th Armored Division took Orvieto, Italy.

Atlantic
1940 The U47 sank the British freighter BALMORAL WOOD (5,834 tons). U47 survived until March 7, 1941. The U101 sank the Greek freighter GEORGANDIS (3,557 tons). U101 survived the war. The U38 sank the Greek freighter MOUNT MYRTO (5,403 tons). U38 survived the war.
1941 The U751 sank the British freighter ST. LINDSAY (5,370 tons). U751 survived until July 17, 1942. The US Coast Guard cutter DUANE rescued forty-six survivors from the freighter TRESILLIAN.
1942 The German armed merchant cruiser THOR took the Dutch tanker OLIVIA (6,307 tons). The U172 sank the American freighter LEBORE (8,289 tons-1 dead) and the British sailing ship DUTCH PRINCESS (125 tons). U172 survived until December 13, 1943. The U504 sank the Latvian freighter REGENT (3,280 tons). U504 survived until July 30, 1943. The Colombian schooners ENVOY and ZAMORA rescued fifty-three survivors from the American freighter SOLON THURMAN which had been sunk on June 13th by U159.
1943 The U334 was sunk southwest of Iceland by the Royal Navy frigate JED and sloop PELICAN. The U564 was sunk northwest of Cape Ortegal by the Royal Air Force's No.10 Squadron.
1944 The U547 sank the Royal Navy trawler BIRDLIP (750 tons) and the French freighter SAINT BASILE (2,778 tons). U547 survived until November 1944.

North America
1938 The battleship WASHINGTON's keel was laid.
1940 FDR signs the "11% Naval Expansion Act". It increased the Navy's warship tonnage by 167,000 tons and the number of its aircraft to 4,500. The next day, he would increase the number of aircraft to 10,000.
1941 FDR froze Axis assets in America. The destroyers FORREST and FITCH were launched. FORREST was scrapped in 1946 and FITCH was stricken in 1971.
1942 The destroyer BALDWIN was launched. She was lost by grounding in 1961.

Pacific

1942 The American 11th Air Force attacked Kiska in the Aleutians. A USN PBY was shot down over Kiska. Advance units of the 1st USMC Division arrived in New Caledonia. The Japanese Imperial General Staff decided to invade New Caledonia and Fiji.

1943 USAAF B25s and USMC F4Us attacked Vila Airfield in the Solomons.

1944 The USN submarine GOLET was sunk by a mine. The USN submarine RASHER sank the KOAN MARU (3,183 tons). Fighting continued on Biak Island. Preliminary bombardment of Saipan and Tinian by seven battleships, eleven cruisers and twenty-six destroyers (commanded by Oldendorf and Ainsworth) began. The USN battleship CALIFORNIA was hit by shore-fire off Saipan and suffered one dead and nine wounded. Also damaged were the battleship TENNESSEE, heavy cruiser INDIANAPOLIS, light cruiser BIRMINGHAM and destroyer BRAINE. A Royal Navy force consisting of the carrier IMPLACABLE, the escort carrier RULER, the cruisers SWIFTSURE, NEWFOUNDLAND, HMCS UGANDA and HMNZS ACHILLES and the destroyers TERMAGANT, TROUBRIDGE, TENACIOUS, TERPSICHORE and TEASER began a two-day attack on Truk. The IJN destroyer SHIRATSUYU was sunk in a collision with the tanker SEIYO MARU off the Philippines.

1945 The US Army's XXIV Corps took Mount Yagu on Okinawa. An Royal Navy fleet consisting of the carrier IMPLACABLE, escort carrier RULER, the cruisers NEWFOUNDLAND, ACHILLES, UGANDA and SWIFTSURE and the destroyers TERMAGANT, TROUBRIDGE, TEASER, TERPSICHORE and TENACIOUS attacked Truk. The USN submarine SPADEFISH sank the SEIZAN MARU (2,018 tons). The USN submarine SEA DEVIL sank the WAKAMIYASAN MARU (2,211 tons).

China-Burma-India

1943 The American 14th Air Force headquarters was established at Kweilin, in southern China. The Royal Air Force attacked Akyab, Burma.

1944 Heavy fighting took place around Myitkyina, Burma. The Japanese took Liuyang, China.

June 15th

Western Europe

1894 British Admiral Philip Vian was born in London. He died on May 27, 1968.

1936   The first flight of the Royal Air Force's "Lysander" took place.

1937   A submarine attack on the German light cruiser LEIPZIG, as well as another on the 18th, resulted in Germany and Italy withdrawing from the international patrol.

1940   The Germans took Strasbourg and Verdun in France. Between this date and the 20th, almost 145,000 British troops were evacuated from France. The Canadian Army's 1st Regiment began withdrawing towards the port of Brest. They had arrived from Britain the previous day with little or no knowledge of the location of the German forces in the area. When they did acquire that knowledge, they were forced to turn their trains around and attempt an evacuation from the Continent. Twelve Royal Air Force bombers attacked targets in France and lost two "Blenheims". The Italian Air Force attacked French air bases at Cvers Pierre-Feu and Cannet de Maures. The French Admiralty ordered the battleships JEAN BART and RICHELIEU to prepare to move from Brest to a British-controlled port. The German armed merchant cruiser PINGUIN left Germany. The American liner WASHINGTON left Galway, Eire with 2,000 American civilians aboard. She was stopped en route to the America by a German U-boat, but was then allowed to continue after being identified.

1941   Twenty-three Royal Air Force "Blenheims" attacked German shipping and lost one aircraft. Ninety-one Royal Air Force bombers attacked Cologne, Germany and lost one "Hampden". One person was killed in the raid. Fifty-nine Royal Air Force bombers attacked Dusseldorf, Germany. Sixteen Royal Air Force bombers attacked Hannover, Germany.

1943   The first flight of the Luftwaffe's Arado 234V1 jet bomber took place. 155 American 8th Air Force B17s were recalled after taking off for missions over the continent. General Curtis LeMay assumed command of the USAAF's 4th Combat Wing, 8th Air Force. He would command the 20th Air Force in the Pacific by the end of the war. The German minesweeper M-483 was sunk in the Channel by the Royal Air Force. 222 Royal Air Force bombers attacked Cologne, Germany and lost fourteen "Lancasters". 147 people were killed in the raid. The German minesweeper M-483 was sunk south of Alderney by the Royal Air Force.

1944   American forces took Quineville and Goubesville in France. At 0045, 235 Royal Air Force bombers attacked Le Havre, France and lost one aircraft. They sank thirty-five small naval vessels, including the torpedo boats FALKE, JAGUAR and MOWE. This attack all but eliminated any threat that may have been posed to the Allied invasion by the German S-boats based there. At 0557, the German minesweeper M-103, the S-boat depot ship NACHTIGALL and a merchantman were sunk by Royal Air Force "Beaufighters" off the Ems Estuary. At 1145, the Royal Navy frigate

MOURNE was sunk in the English Channel by the U767. U767 survived until the 18th. At 1910, the Royal Navy escort BLACKWOOD was torpedoed off Portland by the U764 and foundered the next day. U764 survived the war. The USN LST-280 was sunk by the U621. U621 survived until August 18th. Royal Air Force "Beaufighters" sank the German transport COBURG (7,900 tons), the S-boat tender GUSTAV NACHTIGAL and the minesweeper M-103 in the North Sea. 244 V-1s rockets were fired at London, 144 crossed the English coast and seventy-three hit London. A No.605 Squadron "Mosquito" scored the Royal Air Force's first victory over a German V-1 rocket. 1,200 American 8th Air Force B17s and B24s dropped 3,259 tons of bombs on targets in France, Holland, Belgium, and Germany and lost two B17s. 742 8th Air Force fighters flew sorties over France and claimed five victories for the loss of three P38s and one P51. The American 15th Air Force's 325th Fighter Group (P51) attacked targets in southern France, losing seven aircraft. At 2300, 297 Royal Air Force "Halifaxes" and "Lancasters" attacked Boulogne, sinking twenty-seven small naval vessels, including the minesweepers M-402, M-507 and M-550. They lost one "Halifax" in the raid. 227 Royal Air Force bombers attacked German supply and fuel storage areas in France. 224 Royal Air Force bombers attacked rail targets in France and lost eleven aircraft. Thirty-one Royal Air Force "Mosquitoes" attacked Gelsenkirchen, Germany and lost one aircraft.

1945 The American 9th Army's area and personnel were transferred to the 7th Army.

1967 British Field Marshal Harold Alexander died. He had commanded the Allied Forces in the Mediterranean Theater of Operations.

Eastern Europe

1940 The Lithuanian minesweeper PREZIDENT SMETONA was seized by the Soviets and renamed the KORALL. The Soviet submarine M-95 was sunk by a mine.

1941 Moscow received the date of the upcoming German invasion from Soviet spy Richard Sorge, in Tokyo.

1942 The Soviet Navy delivered 3,855 reinforcements to Sevastopol and evacuated 3,000 wounded and civilians.

1943 The Soviet minesweeper ZASHCHITNIK was sunk by the U24 in the Black Sea. U24 survived until September 10, 1944.

1944 The Soviets broke through the Finnish "VT Line" of resistance and forced them to retreat to their "VKT Line".

Mediterranean

1940 The French submarine MORSE was sunk by a mine off Sfax. The Italian submarine MACALLE ran aground and was lost off Port Sudan.

1942 The British forces in North Africa, commanded by Field Marshal Alexander Wavell, launched "Operation Battleaxe" in an attempt to relieve the besieged Australian 6th Division at Tobruk, Libya. Ninety-one tanks were lost in the battle which was won by the Axis. This would lead to Wavell losing his command on the 21st and being sent to India. He would be replaced by General Sir Claude Auchinleck. German S-boats continued their attacks against the British "Vigorous" convoy from Alexandria. At 0525, the Royal Navy destroyer HASTY (launched in 1936) was damaged by the German S-55 and was later scuttled. At 0700, the Royal Navy destroyer BEDOUIN was damaged by the Italian cruisers MONTECUCCOLI and DI SAVOIA and was later sunk by aircraft. The Italian Navy also damaged the destroyer PARTRIDGE. They had been escorting the "Harpoon" convoy from Gibraltar. The freighters CHANT (5,601 tons and 3 dead) and BURDWAN (5,601 tons) and the tanker KENTUCKY (9,308 tons) were sunk off the island of Pantelleria by German "Stukas". At 1010, the Italian heavy cruiser TRENTO was sunk off Crete by the Royal Navy submarine UMBRA. At 1525, the Royal Navy destroyer escort AIRDALE was damaged by the Luftwaffe and was later scuttled by Royal Navy ALDENHAM and HURWORTH. At 1806, the Royal Navy destroyer NESTOR damaged by the Luftwaffe and was later scuttled. The U431 sank the Royal Navy LCT-119. U431 survived until October 30, 1943. Seven B24s of "HalPro" attacked Italian fleet units off Taranto. During the action they shot down one Luftwaffe Me109. It was the first USAAF aerial victory in either the Mediterranean or European Theaters of Operation. The British abandoned Gazala.

1943 The U97 sank the British tanker ATHELMONARCH (8,995 tons). U97 survived until June 16th.

1944 The American 5th Army reached the Ombrone River.

Atlantic

1940 The U38 sank the Norwegian tanker ITALIA (9,973 tons) and the Danish freighter ERIK BOYE (2,238 tons). U38 survived the war. The Royal Navy armed merchant cruiser ANDANIA (13,950 tons) was torpedoed off Reykjavik, Iceland by the German submarine U-A. She sank the next day.

1941 The German supply ship LOTHRINGEN was captured off South Africa by the Royal Navy cruiser DUNEDIN.

1942 The U161 sank the American freighter SCOTTSBURG (8,001 tons-6 dead). U161 survived until September 27, 1943. The U552 sank the British freighters ETRIB (1,943 tons), CITY OF OXFORD (2,759 tons),

THURSO (2,436 tons) and PELAYO (1,346 tons) and the Norwegian tanker SLEMDAL (7,374 tons). U552 survived the war. The U502 sank the Panamanian freighter COLD HARBOR (5,010 tons). U502 survived until July 5th. The U126 sank the Dominican Republic sailing ship NUEVA ALTA GRACIA (30 tons). U126 survived until July 3, 1943. The American tankers ROBERT TUTTLE (11,000 tons) and ESSO AUGUSTA (11,237 tons), the USN destroyer BAINBRIDGE and the Royal Navy trawler KINGSTON CEYLONITE were sunk off Hampton Roads, Virginia by mines that had been laid by the U701. U701 survived until July 7th. The Italian submarine ARCHIMEDE sank the Panamanian freighter CARDINA (5,586 tons). The U172 sank the Norwegian freighter BENNESTVET (2,438 tons). U172 survived until December 13, 1943. The U502 sank the American freighter WEST HARDAWAY (5,702 tons). U502 survived until July 5th. The U68 sank the Portuguese tanker FRIMAIRE (9,242 tons). U68 survived until April 10, 1944. The USN destroyer BORIE rescued nine survivors from the American freighter MERRIMACK which had been sunk on June 9th by U107. The American freighter KAHUKU rescued forty-six survivors from the freighter SCOTTSBURG sunk by U161 and seventeen from the steamer COLD HARBOR that was sunk by U502. She was then torpedoed by U126. The USN gunboat ERIE rescued twenty-three survivors from the American bulk carrier LEBORE which had been sunk the previous day by U172.

1943 The German armed merchant cruiser MICHEL took the steamer HOEGH SILVERDAWN (7,715 tons).

1944 The U860 was sunk by the USN escort carrier SOLOMONS.

North America

1942 The escort carrier COPAHEE was commissioned. She was scrapped in 1961. The destroyer BOYLE (stricken in 1971) was launched.

1964 Colonel Ross Wilder retired. He had flown on the "Doolittle Raid".

1971 The destroyer INGRAHAM was sold to Greece.

1973 The carrier RANDOLPH was stricken. Major General David Jones retired. He had flown on the "Doolittle Raid".

1975 The carrier ESSEX was stricken.

2013 USN ace Captain Walter Harman died at the age of 93 in Escondido, California. He had been credited with 6 aerial victories while flying F6Fs off the USN ENTERPRISE in the Pacific.

Pacific

1892 British Air Chief Marshal Keith Park was born in Thames, New Zealand. During WWI, he was wounded twice while serving as an artillery officer. He transferred to the Royal Flying Corps in 1918. In April 1940 he commanded the No.11 Fighter Group during the Dunkirk evacuation. He would command that unit until after he had helped win the "Battle of Britain". He was then sent to the Mediterranean where he led various units until January 1944 when he became Supreme Commander of Air in the Middle East. From February 1945, he was Commander-in-Chief of Air in Southeast Asia. He retired in 1946 and died in 1975.

1927 The IJN heavy cruiser NACHI was launched. She survived until November 5, 1944.

1940 The Royal Australian Navy armed merchant cruiser MANOORA rescued the 31-man crew and 160 passengers of the American merchant ship ADMIRAL WILEY (3,514 tons) which had run aground off Kitava Island in the Trobriands.

1942 The USN submarine SEAWOLF sank the IJN gunboat NANPO MARU (1,206 tons) off Corregidor. The USN carrier HORNET returned to Pearl Harbor from the "Battle of Midway".

1943 The USN submarine GUNNEL sank the KOYO MARU (6,426 tons). The USN submarine TROUT sank the SANRAKU MARU (3,000 tons). The USN submarine SAILFISH sank the SHINJU MARU (3,617 tons). USN "Ventura" bombers attacked Japanese-held Kiska in the Aleutians.

1944 The Japanese counter-attacked with tanks on Biak Island. At 0545, the USN began bombarding Saipan. At 0840, the USMC 2nd and 4th Divisions landed on Saipan. One of the staff officers with the 2nd Division was Lieutenant Colonel Wallace Greene, who would become USMC Commandant in January 1964. There were 17,600 Japanese troops on the island. The USN battleship TENNESSEE was hit by Japanese artillery located on Saipan. IJN carriers were sighted moving through the San Bernadino Straits towards the American operations in the Marianas. The IJN submarine I-184 was sunk by aircraft from the USN escort carrier SUWANNEE. The USN submarine SWORDFISH sank the KANSEISHI MARU (4,804 tons). The American 13th Air Force was transferred from the South Pacific Command to the Southwest Pacific Command and combined with the 5th Air Force to form the Far East Air Forces under General George Kenney. USN ace Paul Henderson (5 victories) was killed in action over the Philippine Sea. The USN escort carrier FANSHAW BAY was hit by a bomb off Saipan, 14 of her crew died. USN aircraft attacked Iwo Jima. USN carriers (commanded by Clark and Harrill) attacked the Bonin and Volcano Islands. Forty-seven USAAF B29s made their first attack on Japan from bases in China and inflicted minor damage on the Yawata Steel Works on Kyushu and lost seven aircraft.

1945 American forces took Mount Yuza on Okinawa. USAAF B29s destroyed 2.4 square miles of Osaka, Japan. The USN submarine SEA DOG sank the KOAN MARU (661 tons).

China-Burma-India

1943 The Royal Air Force attacked Muangdaw and Akyab in Burma.

1944 Heavy fighting continued around Myitkyina, Burma. The U198 sank the South African freighter COLUMBINE (3,268 tons). U198 survived until August 12th.

1945 The four remaining "Doolittle Raiders" in Japanese captivity were transferred to Peking Prison.

June 16th

Western Europe

1912 German ace Gordon Gollob was born in Vienna. He scored 150 victories and on January 15, 1945 was named as General of Fighters.

1932 A 2-month-old ban on Nazi storm troopers was lifted by the new von Papen government in Germany.

1936 For the first time in its history, Germany's police force was unified.

1940 Britain offered France a union of their Empires. Paul Reynaud resigned as French Premier. The Germans took Dijon, France and crossed the Rhine at Colmar. A 9-man German sabotage team was arrested in Switzerland. They were to have attacked the Swiss airfields at Payerne and Dubendorf. The British freighter BROOMPARK loaded 400lbs. of "heavy water" at Bassens, France and departed for Britain. It had been moved earlier from Norway. The French submarine MORSE was sunk by a mine.

1941 Twenty-five Royal Air Force bombers attacked shipping and lost three aircraft. Dutch Resistance leader Lodewijck Van Hamel was shot by the German Gestapo. 105 Royal Air Force bombers attacked Cologne, Germany and lost three aircraft. Nineteen people were killed in the raid. Seventy-two Royal Air Force bombers attacked Dusseldorf, Germany and killed four people. Thirty-eight Royal Air Force "Wellingtons" attacked Duisburg, Germany and lost one aircraft.

1942 106 Royal Air Force bombers attacked Essen, Germany and lost eight aircraft. One person was injured in the raid.

1944 313 American 8th Air Force B17s and B24s dropped 893 tons of bombs on French airfields and V-1 rocket sites and lost one B17. 620 8th Air Force fighters provided support for the bombers and also attacked ground targets in the invasion area and claimed one victory for the loss of three P38s. 658 American 15th Air Force bombers and 290 fighter escorts attacked the Kragen oil refinery in Vienna, losing fourteen bombers and six escorting fighters. The US Army's VII Corps reached the Douve River. German Lieutenant General Witt, commander of the 12th S.S. Panzer Division, was killed by naval gunfire in Normandy. Britain's King George VI visited

Normandy. 405 Royal Air Force bombers attacked V-1 rocket launching sites in France. 321 Royal Air Force bombers attacked Sterkrade/Holten and lost thirty-one aircraft.
1945 The Belgian government resigned in protest over the return of King Leopold III.

Eastern Europe
1894 Soviet Marshal Fyodor Tolbukhin was born. He died on October 17, 1949.

Mediterranean
1940 The Royal Navy submarine ORPHEUS was sunk off Tobruk by the Italian destroyer TURBINE. The Royal Navy submarine GRAMPUS was sunk off Syracuse by the Italian torpedo boats POLLUCE, CIRCE and CLEO. The Italian submarine GALILEI sank the Norwegian tanker JAMES STOVE (8,215 tons). Fourteen Royal Air Force bombers attacked Genoa, Italy and suffered no losses.
1941 At 0300, the French destroyer CHEVALIER PAUL was sunk off Syria by Royal Navy aircraft.
1942 At 0100, the Polish destroyer escort KUJAWIAK was sunk east of Malta by a mine. She was escorting the British "Harpoon" convoy from Gibraltar. The destroyer MATCHLESS, the minesweeper HEBE and the freighter ORARI (10,350 tons) were also damaged in the same minefield. At 0127, the Royal Navy light cruiser HERMIONE was sunk off Crete by the U205. U205 survived until February 17, 1943. Italian aircraft damaged the British cruiser BIRMINGHAM and the destroyer AIRDALE.
1943 The U97 was sunk off Haifa by the Royal Australian Air Force. U97 survived until June 16th. The Royal Air Force attacked Naples.
1944 Royal Air Force "Wellington" bombers attacked Porto Ferraio, Italy. The Italian tanker GIULIANA was sunk in the Gulf of Quarnarno by the French destroyers LE FANTASQUE and LE TERRIBLE.

Atlantic
1937 Britain and France arranged for the Non-Intervention Patrol off Spain to be protected.
1940 The U101 sank the British freighter WELLINGTON STAR (13,212 tons). U101 survived the war. The German armed merchant cruiser ORION took the steamer NOTOU (2,489 tons). At 0025, the Royal Navy armed merchant cruiser ANDANIA was damaged southeast of Iceland by the UA (the ex-Turkish submarine BATIRAY). The USN destroyer BORIE rescued survivors from the freighter MERRIMAC. The RMS FRANCONIA was damaged off Brittany by the Luftwaffe.

1942 The US Coast Guard cutter CHEROKEE (5,896 tons-86 dead) and the British freighter PORT NICHOLSON (8,402 tons) were sunk by the U87. U87 survived until March 4, 1943. The US Coast Guard cutter ESCANABA rescued twenty-two survivors. The USN gunboat ERIE and destroyer TATTNALL rescued survivors from the freighter LEBORE. Among those rescued were forty-nine survivors from the Dutch steamer CRIJNSSEN who had rescued by the LEBORE when their ship had been sunk on June 11th by U504. The LEBORE herself had been sunk on June 14th by U172. The U126 sank the American freighters ARKANSAN (6,997 tons-4 dead) and KAHUKU (6,062 tons-18 dead). U126 survived until July 3, 1943. The U67 sank the Nicaraguan freighter MANAGUA (2,220 tons). U67 survived until July 16, 1943. The USN sub chaser PC-460 rescued forty-two survivors from the American steamer SIXAOLA which had been sunk on June 12th by U159. The USN stores ship PASTORES rescued thirty-six survivors from the American freighter ARKANSAN which had been sunk the previous day by U126.

North America

1940 The US Congress passed a Naval Expansion Bill that increased the Navy's tonnage from 1,557,840 tons to 1,724,000 tons. British envoy Arthur Purvis and his French counterpart, Bloch Laine, agreed to transfer Frances $600,000,000 worth of American military contracts to Britain.
1941 FDR closed the German Consulates in America.
1942 USAAF Chief of Staff General Henry Arnold issued orders that a route to be used for ferrying aircraft through Alaska to the Soviet Union be established.
1945 The B29 "Enola Gay" came off the assembly line in Omaha, Nebraska. She would later drop the atomic bomb on Hiroshima.
1959 The destroyer CHARRETTE was sold to Greece.
1964 The battleship ALABAMA was presented to the state of Alabama as a memorial.
1977 Werner von Braun died of cancer in Alexandria, Virginia. The former German rocket scientist had been instrumental in the American space program.
2007 The remains of Army Private Lawrence Burkett were returned to his family. He had died on December 11, 1944 while with the 90th Division near Dillingen, Germany. His remains had been located earlier in the month by Joint POW/MIA Accounting Command team. As of this date, there were still more than 78,000 members of the US military still missing from World War II.

Pacific

1941 The American government formally protested Japanese over flights of the US-controlled island of Guam.

1942 The USMC 1st Division commander, Major General Alexander Vandergrift, met with the South Pacific commander Vice Admiral Robert Ghormley in Auckland, New Zealand. It was at this meeting that Vandergrift first heard of the proposed invasion of Guadalcanal, which was to take place in just five weeks. The American freighter COLDBROOK was wrecked on Middleton Island, off Alaska.

1943 118 Japanese Naval Air Force aircraft attacked Allied shipping off Guadalcanal and the Russells, damaging the USN freighter CELANO and an LST, and losing ninety-seven aircraft while downing one P40, three F4Fs and one F4U. Japanese Naval Air Force ace Yoshio Oki (17 victories) was killed in action over the Russell Islands. American 13th Air Force ace Murray Shubin (11 victories) shot down five Japanese aircraft in one day. Captain Jay Zeamer and 2nd Lieutenant Joseph Sarnoski, of the 43rd Bomb Group (B17), won Medals of Honor over Buka. They were pilot and bombardier aboard the same B17. A USN TBF "Avenger" was shot down over the Northern Solomons. The 3-man crew would not be rescued until 148 days later. The IJN submarine I-174 sank the American freighter PORTMAR (5,551 tons) and damaged the USN LST-469. The USN battleship OKLAHOMA was righted at Pearl Harbor. She had capsized during the attack of December 7, 1941.

1944 USMC Gunnery Sergeant Robert McCard, of the 4th Division, won a posthumous Medal of Honor on Saipan. Fighting continued Biak Island. USAAF ace Major Thomas McGuire shot down a Japanese "Sonya" and an "Oscar" near Jefman, New Guinea. A USN force commanded by Ainsworth bombarded Guam. The IJN submarine Ro-44 was sunk by the USN destroyer escort HASTINGS. The USN submarine BLUEFISH sank the NANSHIN MARU (1,422 tons). The USN submarine BREAM sank the YUKI MARU (5,704 tons).

1945 The USN destroyer TWIGGS was sunk by an aircraft torpedo, 153 of her crew died. The Royal Navy bombarded Japanese-held Truk. An American 11th Air Force B24 was shot down off Paramushiro in the Kuriles. The USN submarine PIRANHA sank the EISO MARU (6,890 tons). The Royal Navy submarine TACITURN sank the IJN submarine chaser Cha-105.

China-Burma-India

1943 The IJN submarine I-37 sank the British tanker SAN ERNESTO (8,078 tons).

1944 The Chinese took Kamaing and Chiaotou in Burma. The Japanese began their offensive against Changsha, China.

June 17th

Western Europe

1888   German General Heinz Guderian was born in Kulm, East Prussia. He would serve as Chief of the Wehrmacht General Staff. He would die on May 14, 1954.

1900   Nazi Martin Bormann was born in Halberstadt. He would become Nazi Party Secretary after the departure of Rudolf Hess and would die in 1945 when the Soviets took Berlin.

1925   The Arms Traffic Convention was convened by the League of Nations. A major result was the Geneva Protocol, prohibiting the use of poison gas, which America did not sign.

1940   The French liner CHAMPLAIN was sunk by an acoustic mine. The RMS LANCASTRIA was sunk off St. Nazaire, France by the Luftwaffe, 3,000 died. The Canadian Army's 1st Regiment arrived at Plymouth after being evacuated from Brest. 139 Royal Air Force bombers attacked targets in Germany, losing two "Whitleys". Six people were killed in the raid on Cologne. Germany's Kaiser Wilhelm sent Hitler a telegram of congratulations, from his residence in Doorn, Holland. Hitler ignored it. The Germans took Pontarlier, France, near the Swiss border.

1941   Twenty-three Royal Air Force "Blenheims" attacked Bethune, France. None of the bombers was lost, but ten of their escorting fighters were. Seventy-six Royal Air Force bombers attacked Cologne, Germany and lost one "Whitley". Fifty-seven Royal Air Force "Wellingtons" attacked Dusseldorf, Germany. Twenty-six Royal Air Force "Wellingtons" attacked Duisburg, Germany.

1942   British Prime Minister Churchill and the Chief of the Imperial General Staff General Alan Brooke left Britain for America. Twenty-seven Royal Air Force bombers attacked St. Nazaire, France. Forty-six Royal Air Force bombers dropped mines in the Baltic and off the French port of St. Nazaire.

1943   The BBC warned French civilians to stay away from factories operating for the Nazis. Seven Royal Air Force "Mosquitoes" attacked targets in Germany. 137 American 8th Air Force P47s flew a sweep over Belgium.

1944   232 American 8th Air Force B17s and B24s dropped 582 tons of bombs on French airfields and lost two B17s. 582 8th Air Force fighters provided support for the bombers and claimed six victories for the loss of one P51 and four P38s. 274 8th Air Force B24s dropped 704 tons of bombs on French airfields and lost one aircraft. 317 8th Air Force fighters provided support for the bombers and lost one P51 and two P38s. An 8th Air Force "Carpetbagger" was shot down over West Eaton in Britain by a Luftwaffe intruder. The US Army's 9th Division launched an attack against the town of Carteret on the Contentin Peninsula. Hitler flew to France to meet with his commanders in the West, Rommel, and Rundstedt. A major storm hit the Normandy coast; it would last until the 21st. The German minesweeper M-546 was sunk off Boulogne by the Royal Canadian Air Force. 317 Royal Air Force bombers attacked rail targets in France and lost one "Lancaster". 114 Royal Air Force bombers attacked V-1 rocket launching sites in France.

1963 British Field Marshal Alan Brooke died at Ferney Close, Hampshire. He had been Chief of the Imperial General Staff during the war.

Eastern Europe
1942 The Germans took Fort Siberia outside Sevastopol.

Mediterranean
1940 The Royal Navy's "Force H" was established at Gibraltar. It consisted of the carrier ARK ROYAL the battlecruiser HOOD. It would be reinforced by the battleships VALIANT and RESOLUTION and placed under the command of Vice-Admiral Sir James Somerville. It also included the light cruiser ARETHUSA and the destroyers FAULKNOR, FOXHOUND, FEARLESS, ESCAPADE, FORESTER, FORESIGHT and ESCORT. Admiral Sir Andrew Cunningham, Commander of the Royal Navy's Mediterranean Fleet, was informed that in case of a separate peace by France the French fleet was to be seized or sunk. The Italian submarine PROVANO (launched in 1938) was rammed and sunk by the French corvette LA CURIEUSE off Oran. The Italian Air Force attacked Borga Airfield on Corsica.
1942 "Ash Wednesday" in Cairo took place as the British burned records and documents in preparation for the DAK's arrival.
1943 The British freighter YOMA (8,131 tons) was lost.
1944 The French landed on the island of Elbe.

Atlantic
1940 The U46 sank the Greek freighter ELPIS (3,651 tons). U46 survived the war.
1941 The Royal Navy armed merchant cruiser PRETORIA CASTLE took the Vichy French steamer DESIRADE (9,645 tons) east of the Antilles. The U43 sank the British freighter CATHERINE (2,727 tons). U43 survived until July 30, 1943. The German armed merchant cruiser ATLANTIS took the steamer TOTTENHAM (4,640 tons).

1942   The American collier SANTORE (7,117 tons) was sunk off Hampton Roads by a mine laid by the U701, 3 of her crew died. U701 survived until July 7th. At 2005, the Royal Navy destroyer escort WILD SWAN was damaged by the Luftwaffe, and then at 2305, she collided with a Spanish fishing boat off Ireland and sank. The U158 sank the Panamanian freighter SAN BLAS (3,601 tons) and the Norwegian tanker MOIRA (1,560 tons). U158 survived until June 30th.

1943   The German armed merchant cruiser MICHEL took the steamer FERNCASTLE (9,940 tons).

1944   The U423 was sunk north of the Faeroes by the Royal Air Force's No.333 Squadron. The American freighter MAURICE Tracy was lost in a collision with the freighter JESSE BILLINGSLEY.

North America

1936   The destroyer LAMSON was launched. She was expended as a target at Bikini in 1946.

1939   The destroyer HUGHES was launched. She was scuttled in 1948 after serving as a Bikini target in 1946.

1940   The USAAC had just fifty-six B17 "Flying Fortress" bombers in its inventory. Chief of Naval Operations, Admiral Harold R. Stark, asked for $4 billion to build a "Two-Ocean Navy".

1941   The first flight of the Brewster "Buccaneer" dive-bomber took place.

1942   The U584 landed four German agents at Ponte Vedra Beach, Florida. U584 survived until October 31, 1943.

1943   The light carrier MONTEREY was commissioned; future President Gerald Ford would serve aboard as Assistant Navigation Officer. MONTEREY was stricken in 1970.

1944   The battlecruiser ALASKA was commissioned. She was scrapped in 1961.

1946   The destroyer DAHLGREN was sold for scrap.

1992   Jacob Beser, the only man to have flown both A-bomb missions in WWII, died of cancer. He had served as radar operator.

Pacific

1939   The IJN light cruiser KATORI was launched. She was sunk on February 17, 1944.

1943   The USN submarine DRUM sank the MYOKO MARU (5,086 tons). The USN SC-740 ran aground on the Great Barrier Reef and was lost.

1944   The USN submarine HAKE sank the KINSHU MARU (5,591 tons). The USN submarine FLOUNDER sank the NIHONKAI MARU (2,683 tons). The IJN submarine Ro-117 was sunk by USN aircraft. The US Army's 27th Division landed on Saipan.

1945 American forces gained ground on Kunishi Ridge on Okinawa. The USN battleship WEST VIRGINIA was bombed off Okinawa. The IJN minelayer EIJO MARU was sunk by the USN submarine SPADEFISH.

China-Burma-India
1943 The Royal Air Force attacked Buyhidaung, Burma.

June 18th

Western Europe
1884 Edouard Daladier, French Prime Minister 1938-40, was born in Carpentaras. He died in 1970.
1935 The Anglo-German Naval Agreement was signed. It gave Germany a submarine force equal to Britain's and a total naval force not to exceed 35% of the Royal Navy.
1937 Bilbao, Spain was captured by Nationalist forces.
1940 Six Royal Air Force "Blenheims" attacked German units near Cherbourg, France. The French Admiralty ordered the ships of the French Navy to sail to various French colonies. At 1235, the French tug PROVENCAL was sunk at Brest, France by a mine. 30,630 Allied troops were evacuated from Cherbourg, France. The Germans took Cherbourg, Caen, Rennes, Le Mans, Nevers, Colmar, and Briare in France. 21,474 Allied troops were evacuated from St. Malo and 32,584 from Brest in France. The French sloop VAUQUOIS was damaged off Brest by a mine. The French destroyer CYCLONE and sloop ETOURDI were scuttled at Brest. The French sloop ENSEIGNE HENRI was scuttled at Lorient, France. The French battleship RICHELIEU left Brest en route to Dakar in North Africa. The German minesweeper M-5 was sunk off Norway by a mine laid by the Royal Navy submarine PORPOISE. Irish President Eamon De Valera announced that Eire would resist any invasion. Sixty-nine Royal Air Force bombers attacked targets in Germany, losing two "Whitleys" and one "Wellington". The raid on Hamburg killed one person. The German minesweeper M-1802 was sunk by a mine off Norway. Hitler and Mussolini met in Munich.
1941 100 Royal Air Force bombers attacked Bremen, Germany and lost six aircraft. Sixty-five Royal Air Force bombers attacked Brest, France.
1942 USAAF General Carl Spaatz assumed command of the 8th Air Force. Sixty-five Royal Air Force bombers dropped mines off Lorient, France.
1944 Fifty-eight American 8th Air Force B24s dropped 220 tons of bombs on V-1 rocket sites near Watten, France. 1,160 8th Air Force bombers attacked targets in Germany and lost seven B17s and four B24s (one of the B24s

landed in Sweden). This was the first 8th Air Force mission directed against strategic targets since D-Day. The objectives of the raid were oil refineries near Hamburg, Bremen and Misburg and Luftwaffe control centers at Fassberg and Stade. An 8th Air Force B24 "Carpetbagger" was shot down over France. A V-1 rocket impacted near Buckingham Palace in London, killing 121. The 500th German V-1 was fired at Britain. The British "Operation Goodwood" began near Caen. American forces reached Barneville on the west coast of the Contentin Peninsula cutting the Peninsula off from the rest of France. The Royal Navy destroyer QUAIL sank after hitting a mine three days before. At 0200, the German minesweeper M-133 was damaged in the Channel by the Royal Navy MTBs 727 and 748 and scuttled on August 6th. Nine Royal Air Force "Mosquitoes" attacked V-1 sites at Watten, near St. Omer, France.

1945 British citizen William Joyce (Lord Haw Haw) was put on trial for treason in London.

1968 General Nikolaus von Falkenhorst, the German Commander-in-Chief in Norway, died in Holzminden.

1971 German Field Marshal Wilhelm List, commander of Army Group "A" until dismissed on September 10, 1942, died in Garmisch.

Eastern Europe

1940 The Soviets broke through the Finnish "Mannerheim Line".

1942 The Soviet MTB tender BIELOSTOK was sunk off Sevastopol by the Luftwaffe. The Germans took Forts Gorki, Gepeu, Molotov, Cheica, Volga and Urals outside Sevastopol, leaving only one to defend the city.

1944 The German UJ-316 was sunk in the Black Sea by a mine.

1962 Soviet General Aleksei Antonov died at the age of 66 and was buried in the Kremlin Wall.

Mediterranean

1941 The Royal Air Force attacked Benghazi, Libya.

Atlantic

1940 The U28 sank the Finnish freighter SARMATIA (2,417 tons). U28 survived until March 1944. The U32 sank the Norwegian freighter ALTAIR (1,522 tons) and the Spanish trawlers SALVORA and FAROONS. U32 survived until October 30th.

1941 The U552 sank the British freighter NORFOLK (10,948 tons). U552 survived the war. The U138 was sunk by the Royal Navy destroyers FAULKNOR, FEARLESS, FORESTER and FOXHOUND.

1942 The U159 sank the Dutch freighter FLORA (1,417 tons). U159 survived until July 15, 1943. The U172 sank the American tanker MOTOREX

(1,958 tons). U172 survived until December 13, 1943. The U129 sank the American freighter MILLINOCKET (3,274 tons-11 dead). U129 survived until August 1944. The U124 sank the American freighter SEATTLE SPIRIT (5,627 tons-4 dead). U124 survived until April 2, 1943. The U502 sank the American freighter TILLIE LYKES (2,572 tons), with all hands. U502 survived until July 5th.

1944   The Royal Navy submarine SICKLE was sunk by a mine. The U441 was sunk northwest of Brest by the Royal Air Force's No.304 (Polish) Squadron. The U767 was sunk southwest of the island of Guernsey by the Royal Navy destroyers INCONSTANT, FAME and HAVELOCK.

North America

1942   The first air units of the 8th Air Force received orders to fly to Presque Isle in Maine, in preparation for movement to Britain. Bernard Robinson became the first Black to be commissioned in the USN.

1943   The submarine BURRFISH was launched. She was transferred to the Canadian Navy in 1961. Staff Sergeant Clifford W. Wherley of Elmwood, Illinois was honorably discharged. He had won four Air Medals as a B26 gunner in the Mediterranean. He was 16-years old.

1944   The escort carrier BOUGAINVILLE was commissioned. She was scrapped in 1960. The submarines LAMPREY and CHUB were launched. CHUB was transferred to the Turkish Navy in 1948 and LAMPREY went to Argentina in 1960.

1945   A Japanese balloon-bomb was found near Anchorage, Alaska. USMC ace Major Bob Fraser (6 victories) was killed on a training flight near Santa Barbara, California.

1980   Lieutenant General Henry Speise died in Laguna Beach, California. During the war he had served as Deputy Chief Ordnance Officer in the European Theater of Operations.

1990   A P51D crashed at Carver County Airport, Minnesota, killing two.

1994   The Travis Air Force Base Museum in California dedicated the B29 "Miss America '62", which had flown out of North Field on Tinian during the war. Members of the original crew attended the ceremony.

Pacific

1940   The RMS NIAGARA (13,415 tons) was sunk 60 miles off Auckland, New Zealand by a mine laid by the German armed merchant cruiser ORION. NIAGARA had 590 gold ingots aboard.

1942   Nine American 11th Air Force B24s attacked Kiska in the Aleutians sinking the freighter NISSAN MARU (6,537 tons).

1944   The USMC took Aslito Airfield on Saipan. American forces on Biak Island received reinforcements. USN Task Force 58 rendezvoused west of Saipan to meet the IJN. Japanese aircraft located the American fleet. The Royal Navy submarine STORM sank the EIKO MARU (3,011 tons). The USN PTs 63 and 107 were destroyed by fire in Hamburg Bay, Emirau Island.

1945 General Simon Buckner, commander American Ground Forces on Okinawa, was killed by Japanese artillery fire. He would eventually be replaced by General Joseph Stilwell. The USN submarine BONEFISH was sunk in the Sea of Japan by IJN surface craft. The USN submarine TINOSA sank the WAKAE MARU. The USN submarine DENTUDA sank the HEIWA MARU (88 tons) and the REIKO MARU (88 tons). The USN submarine APOGEN sank the HAKUAI MARU (2,636 tons) and the KUSUNOKI MARU No.2. The USN YMS-50 was sunk off Balikpapan by a mine. Australian forces took Tutong, Borneo. Japanese resistance ended on Mindanao. A USAAF B32 "Dominator" attacked Hainan Island in the Gulf of Tonkin.

China-Burma-India

1943 Archibald Wavell was appointed Viceroy of India and Claude Auchinleck as Commander-in-Chief. Both men had previously commanded the British forces in North Africa.

1944 The Japanese took Chang-Sha, China.

June 19th

Western Europe

1933 The Nazi Party was outlawed in Austria.

1940 The incomplete French battleship JEAN BART left St. Nazaire, France for Casablanca in North Africa. She was hit by a Luftwaffe bomb as she left port. The French liner LAFAYETTE was sunk by a mine in the Gironde Estuary. The German S-19 and S-26 sank the British freighter ROSEBURN (3,103 tons) off Dungeness. 57,525 Allied troops were evacuated from Nantes and St. Nazaire in France. Thirty Royal Air Force "Blenheims" attacked airfields near Amiens and Rouen in France, losing no aircraft. The Germans took Brest, Nantes, St. Nazaire, and Saumec in France. 108 students from the flying school in Morlaix, France left Brittany for Britain aboard a fishing boat in the hope of joining the Free French air force. Sweden stated that it would allow German troops to pass through its territory en route to Norway. Royal Air Force ace Adolf "Sailor" Malan shot down two Luftwaffe He111s, the first of his thirty-two victories. 112 Royal Air Force bombers attacked targets in Germany, losing one "Whitley" and one "Wellington". One person died in the raid on Hamburg and six more in Munster.

1941 Thirty-six Royal Air Force bombers attacked Le Havre, France. Germany closed the American embassies in that country. Twenty-eight Royal Air Force "Wellingtons" attacked Köln, Germany and lost one aircraft. Twenty Royal Air Force "Whitleys" attacked Dusseldorf, Germany and lost one aircraft. The German and Italian governments requested the closure of American consulates.

1942 The development of the German V-1 rocket began at Peenemunde, Germany. 194 Royal Air Force bombers attacked Emden, Germany and lost nine aircraft. There were no casualties in the city.

1943 290 Royal Air Force bombers attacked Le Creusot, France and lost two "Halifaxes". Twelve Royal Air Force "Lancasters" dropped mines off the Gironde estuary in France and lost one "Lancaster". The German trawler UJ-1708 was sunk by a British submarine off Norway. The German minesweeper R-41 was sunk in the English Channel by a British MTB.

1944 The USN LST-523 was sunk off Normandy by a mine. American forces took Valognes and Montebourg, and began their final assault on Cherbourg. 774 American 8th Air Force bombers dropped 1,675 tons of bombs on V-1 rocket sites and airfields in France and lost seven B17s and one B24. The 452nd Bomb Group B17 "Dog Breath" was interned in Spain. 715 8th Air Force fighters provided support for the bombers and lost sixteen aircraft. Twenty-one Royal Air Force bombers attacked V-1 launching sites at Watten, France.

1969 The German aircraft designer Siegfried Gunter died. He had designed most of the Heinkel aircraft built between the years of 1930 and 1945.

1981 British General Richard O'Connor died in Scotland.

1995 Royal Air Force ace Group Captain Peter Townsend (11 victories), died of cancer at age 80.

Eastern Europe

1942 The Soviet submarine ShCh-214 was sunk by the Italian MTB Mas571. Luftwaffe ace Helmut Belser (36 victories) died in an accident.

1944 The Soviet freighter PESTEL (1,850 tons) was sunk by the U20 in the Black Sea. U20 survived until September 10, 1944. At 0230, the German torpedo boat T-31 was sunk in the Gulf of Finland by Soviet MTBs, 105 died.

Mediterranean

1940 The South African Air Force attacked the Italian Air Force base at Yavello in Ethiopia. The Italian submarine GALELEI (launched in 1934) was captured by Royal Navy trawler MOONSTONE and was placed in Royal Navy service as the P-711. The Royal Navy submarine ORPHEUS was sunk by Italian surface craft.

1941 Italy closed the American embassies in that country.
1944 The French took Elbe Island.

Atlantic
1940 The U48 sank the Norwegian freighter TUDOR (6,607 tons), the British freighters BARON LOUDON (3,164 tons) and BRITISH MONARCH (5,661 tons). U48 survived until May 3, 1945. The U52 sank the British freighter THE MONARCH (824 tons) and the Belgian freighter VILLE DE NAMUR (7,463 tons). U52 survived until May 1945. The U32 sank the Yugoslavian freighter LABUD (5,334 tons). U32 survived until October 30th. The U28 sank the Greek freighter GEORGANDIS (3,443 tons). U28 survived until March 1944.
1942 The German armed merchant cruiser THOR took the Norwegian tanker HERBORG (7,892 tons). The U701 sank the US Coast Guard YP-389. U701 survived until July 7, 1942. The U159 sank the Yugoslavian freighter ANTE MATKOVIC (2,710 tons). U159 survived until July 15, 1943. The U161 sank the American sailing ship CHEERIO (35 tons). U161 survived until September 27, 1943. The US Coast Guard No.459 rescued nine survivors from the CHEERIO.

North America
1915 The battleship ARIZONA was launched. She would be sunk at Pearl Harbor on December 7, 1941. She still rests on the bottom of that port.
1935 The heavy cruiser QUINCY (awarded one battle star during the war) was launched. She was lost August 9, 1942 in the "Battle of Savo Island".
1942 The US Army Chief of Staff, General George Marshal, sent a highly critical letter to USN Commander-in-Chief Admiral Ernest King regarding the failure to properly protect shipping along the east coast of America and in the Caribbean. The light cruiser SANTA FE (awarded thirteen battle stars and a Navy Unit Commendation during the war) was launched. She was scrapped in 1959. Georg Dasch, the leader of a group of German saboteurs that had landed on Long Island on the 13th, called the FBI and informed them of his identity. He was arrested the same day. He then proceeded to tell them of the landing of four other agents in Florida and the planned attacks on aluminum plants, transportation, power supplies and civilian moral that were to occur over the next two years.
1943 The light cruiser HOUSTON (awarded three battle stars during the war) was launched. She was scrapped in Baltimore in 1960.
1990 Melvin Mayfield died. He had won the last Medal of Honor awarded in WWII. It was awarded for actions in the Philippines on July 29, 1945.

Pacific

1936 The IJN light carrier ZUIHO was launched. She survived until October 25, 1944.

1942 A Japanese survey party began laying out an airfield on Guadalcanal. USAAF 5th Air Force B17s attacked Rabaul, New Britain and damaged the IJN water carrier WAYO MARU. The USN seaplane tender BALLARD rescued thirty-five survivors from the IJN carrier HIRYU which had been sunk on June 5th. The USN submarine S-27 ran aground and was lost on Amchitka in the Aleutians, the crew was rescued by USN PBYs with no casualties. The IJN submarine I-9 attacked the US Army transport GENERAL GORGAS in the Gulf of Alaska. The American 11th Air Force attacked Kiska in the Aleutians. USN Admiral Robert Ghormley assumed command of the South Pacific Area with his headquarters in Auckland, New Zealand.

1943 The USN submarine SCULPIN sank the MIYASHO MARU No.1 (79 tons) and the SAGAMI MARU (135 tons). The USN submarine GUNNEL sank the TOKIWA MARU (6,971 tons) and the HONG KONG MARU (2,797 tons) and damaged the IJN minelayer TSUBAME. The USN submarine GROWLER sank the MIYADONO MARU (5,196 tons).

1944 Heavy fighting continued on Saipan. At 0900, the IJN carrier TAIHO (29,300 tons) was torpedoed northwest of Yap by the USN submarine ALBACORE. She sank at 1706 with the loss of 1,650 of her crew. At 1220, the IJN carrier SHOKAKU (29,800 tons) was damaged north of Yap in the Philippine Sea by the USN submarine CAVALLA. She exploded and sank at 1510. The USN battleship SOUTH DAKOTA was bombed. A USN PBM from the aircraft tender POCOMOKE was attacked by two USN F6F "Hellcats" off Saipan and suffered one dead and two wounded. The "Marianas Turkey Shoot" took place over the Philippine Sea with the Japanese losing 301 aircraft and the Americans losing fifteen and suffering minor damage to four ships. USN Commander David McCampbell, Commander Air Group-15, won a Medal of Honor over the Philippine Sea. USN ace Charles Brewer (6.5 victories) was killed in action over the Philippine Sea. Future US President George Bush ditched his TBM "Avenger" off Guam and was rescued by the USN destroyer C.K. BRONSON. Fighting continued on Biak Island.

1945 The US Army's I Corps took Ilagan on Luzon in the Philippines. Eight captured American airmen were executed in Japan. Technical/Sergeant John Meagher, of the 77th Division, won a Medal of Honor on Okinawa. Three USAAF B32 "Dominators" attacked bridges on Formosa. The USN submarine CABEZON sank the ZAOSAN MARU (2,631 tons). The USN submarine SEA DOG sank the KOKAI MARU (1,272 tons) and the

SHINEI MARU No.3 (958 tons). The USN submarine BONEFISH sank the KONZAN MARU (5,488 tons).

1947 IJN Admiral Sakaibara, who had ordered the execution of nearly 100 American civilian construction workers on Wake Island after the air-raids of October 6th and 7th, 1943, was executed.

China-Burma-India

1943 The IJN submarine I-37 sank the American freighter HENRY KNOX (7,176 tons-26 dead).

1944 The Chinese took Kutung, Burma. The U181 sank the Dutch freighter GAROET (7,118 tons). U181 survived the war.

June 20th

Western Europe

1914 German submarine commander Albrecht Brandi was born. During the war he commanded U617 and the U967. He sank 115,000 tons of shipping including three cruisers and twelve destroyers. He survived the war and died in Köln on January 6, 1966.

1936 The Royal Navy light cruiser GLASGOW was launched. She was scrapped in 1958.

1938 The Luftwaffe's Focke-Achgelis Fa-61 helicopter was flown a distance of 143 miles.

1939 The Luftwaffe's Heinkel He-176 rocket plane made its first flight.

1940 Hitler and the German Navy Commander Erich Raeder had a conference concerning the invasion of Britain. At 1430, a French delegation left the temporary French capital at Bordeaux. Their mission was to determine Germany's terms for an end to the conflict. Forty-seven Royal Air Force bombers attacked Luftwaffe airfields in France and Holland and suffered no losses. The Germans took Vichy and Lyons in France. 450,000 Italian troops attacked positions in the Maritime Alps held by 185,000 French soldiers. By the time the armistice on the 25th, the Italians had reached the French defenses, but had failed to break through at any point. Royal Air Force Flight/Lieutenant Bufton and Corporal Mackie confirmed the existence of "Knickbein", while flying an Avro "Anson" over Britain. It was a Luftwaffe directional beam 400-500 yards wide. Fifty-six Royal Air Force bombers attacked targets in Germany and lost one "Hampden" and one "Whitley".

1941 115 Royal Air Force bombers attacked Kiel, Germany and lost two "Wellingtons".

1942 Twelve Royal Air Force "Bostons" attacked Le Havre, France. 185 Royal Air Force bombers attacked Emden, Germany and lost eight aircraft. One person was injured in the raid.
1943 127 American 8th Air Force P47s flew sweeps over France and Holland. A Luftwaffe Fw190 landed in error at the Royal Air Force base at Manston. Sixty Royal Air Force "Lancasters" attacked Friedrichshaven, Germany. Forty-four people were killed in the raid.
1944 355 American 8th Air Force bombers dropped 877 tons of bombs on Pas de Calais V-1 rocket sites and lost two B24s. 1,252 8th Air Force bombers dropped 3,029 tons of bombs on oil and industrial targets in Germany and lost forty-eight aircraft (20 of which landed in Sweden). 1,111 8th and 9th Air Force fighters provided support for the bombers and attacked ground targets and lost two P47s, four P38s and two P51s. A V-1 hit the Guard's Chapel in London killing 119. American forces were within 15 miles of Cherbourg, France. Twenty Royal Air Force bombers attacked V-1 launching sites at Wizernes, France. The USAAF's 801st Bomb Group dispatched twenty-five B24s on "Carpetbagger" missions.
1945 The Normandie-Nieman Air, which had flown with the Soviet Air Force during the war, arrived in Paris with forty Yak-3 fighters.
1959 A monument was dedicated at Ljungbyhed, Sweden to two crewmen who died in the crash of their USAAF 392nd Bomb Group B24 on this date in 1944.

Eastern Europe
1940 The Latvian minesweeper VIRSAITIS was seized at Libau by the Soviets.
1942 The Soviet Navy delivered 845 reinforcements and 293 tons of ammunition to Sevastopol. The Germans took Fort Lenin outside Sevastopol.
1944 The German T-31 was sunk by Soviet MTBs. A USAAF 448th Bomb Group B24 landed northwest of Stettin, Poland and was captured. The Soviets took Viipuri near Leningrad. The Soviets broke through the Finnish "VKT Line".
1946 Arthur Greisler, Gauleiter of Warthgau, Poland, was hung in Poznan, Poland.

Mediterranean
1940 The Italian submarine DIAMANTE (launched in 1933) was sunk by the Royal Navy submarine PARTHIAN. France asked Italy for an armistice.
1941 The Italian submarine ONDINA sank the Turkish freighter REFAH (3,805 tons).
1942 The Axis attacked Tobruk, Libya.

1943 USAAF A36 "Apache" fighter-bombers occupied airfields on Pantelleria Island. Britain's King George VI arrived in Malta aboard the cruiser AURORA, escorted by the destroyers LOOKOUT, JERVIS, NUBIAN and ESKIMO.
1944 The Italian liner ROMA was hit by five bombs while undergoing carrier conversion at Genoa. The British took Perugia, Italy. American PT-boats sank the German torpedo boat TA-25.

Atlantic
1940 The U122 sank the British freighter EMPIRE CONVEYOR (5,911 tons). U122 survived until June 21st. The U38 sank the Swedish freighter TILIA GORTHON (1,776 tons). U38 survived until May 1945. The U48 sank the Dutch tanker MOERDRECHT (7,493 tons). U48 survived until May 3, 1945. The U30 sank the British freighter OTTERPOOL (4,876 tons). U30 survived until May 5, 1945. The German battlecruiser GNEISENAU was torpedoed by the Royal Navy submarine CLYDE. The Dutch submarine O-13 was sunk in error by the Polish submarine WILK.
1941 The U123 sank the Portuguese freighter GANDA (4,333 tons). U123 survived until August 19, 1944. The USN battleship TEXAS was nearly attacked by the U203 after being tracked for 140 miles. U203 survived until April 25, 1943.
1943 The U388 was sunk south of Greenland by USN VP-84.

North America
1888 Admiral Royal Ingersoll was born in Washington D.C. He graduated 4th in his 1905 Annapolis class of 114. He was promoted to rear admiral in 1938 and vice-admiral on January 1, 1942 when he assumed command of the Atlantic Fleet. In July 1942 he was promoted to admiral. He retired on August 1, 1946 and died on May 20, 1976 in Bethesda, Maryland.
1924 Audie Murphy was born near Kingston, Texas. He would be the highest decorated American serviceman during the WWII.
1930 Future Chief of Naval Operations Ernest King assumed command of the carrier LEXINGTON.
1934 The heavy cruiser MINNEAPOLIS was commissioned. She was scrapped in 1960.
1935 The submarine PORPOISE was launched. She was scrapped in 1957.
1939 The personnel strength of the United States Marine Corps stood at 19,432. During the war, that number would increase to 125,162. Members of the USMC would be awarded eighty Medals of Honor (48 posthumous) and 957 Navy Crosses. The USMC would suffer 91,718 casualties during the war.

1941   The United States Army Air Corps was reorganized as the United States Army Air Force. During the war, it would number 2,411,294 personnel and suffer 115,382 battle casualties. The USN submarine O-9 sank off New London. All thirty-three aboard were lost.

1942   The IJN submarine I-26 bombarded Estevan Point on Vancouver, British Columbia. The American military in Alaska confiscated 46 commercial airliners for an airlift.

1943   Race riots in Detroit killed twenty-five Blacks and nine Whites. The destroyers DORTCH and GATLING and the submarines ROCK and FLASHER were launched. The DORTCH was sold to Argentina in 1961 and FLASHER was scrapped in 1963.

1945   The personnel strength of the US Navy stood at 3,383,196. During the war, the USN had accepted 74,896 vessels ranging from battleships to yard craft.

1947   The destroyer ELLIS was sold for scrap.

1959   The incomplete battlecruiser HAWAII was sold for scrap.

1961   The destroyer HAILEY was sold to Brazil.

1962   General John DeWitt, commander of the American west coast 1941-43, died in Washington D.C.

2009   USMC Colonel Kenneth Reusser, age 89, died in Clackamas, Oregon. He had received 59 medals during his 27-year military career, including two Navy Crosses. He was awarded one during World War II and another during the Korean War. He had completed a total of 253 combat sorties in 3 different wars. He was finally forced into retirement by injuries suffered when his helicopter was shot down in 1968 during a rescue mission.

Pacific

1942   The Japanese began burning the Kunai grass on the Lunga plain on Guadalcanal in preparation for the construction of the airfield which would induce the Allies into invading the island. The USN staged a controlled test of its MkXIV torpedo in Hawaii, it ran eleven feet deeper than set. This was the US Navy's primary submarine weapon and had several other faults and defects. This failure of the Navy saved the Japanese countless ships and caused physical losses as well as severe moral problems for the Navy itself. The IJN submarine I-25 damaged the British freighter FORT CAMOSUN (7,126 tons) off Cape Flattery.

1943   The American 6th Army (commanded by Krueger) established its headquarters at Milne Bay, New Guinea. The USN submarine TAUTOG sank the MEITEN MARU (4,474 tons). The USN submarine SEAWOLF sank the SHOJIN MARU (4,739 tons). Japanese Naval Air Force aircraft attacked Darwin, losing fourteen aircraft. Two Royal Australian Air Force

"Spitfires" were shot down during the action. USN "Ventura" bombers attacked Kiska in the Aleutians.

1944 Heavy fighting continued on both Saipan and Biak Island. At 1845, the IJN light carrier HIYO was damaged north of Yap in the Philippine Sea by USN light carrier BELLEAU WOOD aircraft. She sank at 2030. The IJN carrier ZUIKAKU, the light carrier CHIYODA, the battleship HARUNA, the heavy cruiser MAYA and two tankers were damaged by USN carrier aircraft. The IJN submarine I-185 was sunk by the USN destroyer NEWCOMB and destroyer-minesweeper CHANDLER. A TBM, from the USN escort carrier SUWANNEE, was shot down by USN anti-aircraft fire. The USN destroyer PHELPS was damaged by shore-fire off Saipan. The USN submarine NARWHAL landed 4 agents and supplies on Panay in the Philippines and evacuated 14. The USN submarine HAKE sank the HIBI MARU (5,875 tons).

1945 The USN carriers LEXINGTON, HANCOCK and COWPENS attacked Wake Island. The Australians landed at Lutong, Sarawak. Two USAAF B32 "Dominators" attacked Formosa. The USN submarine TINOSA sank the KAISEI MARU (880 tons) and the TAITO MARU (2,726 tons). The NANSHIN MARU was sunk by a mine.

China-Burma-India

1944 The Chinese took Watien, Burma. American Vice-President Henry Wallace met with Chaing Kai-shek in Chungking.

1945 Aircraft from the British escort carriers STALKER, KHEDIVE and AMEER attacked Japanese airfields in Northern Sumatra and shipping in the Malacca Straits.

June 21st

Western Europe

1884 British General Claude Auchinleck was born in Ulster. He would command the British forces in North Africa.

1887 British General Hastings Ismay was born. He died in 1965.

1890 German General Eduard Dietl was born. He led the invasion of Narvik, Norway in 1940. He then commanded German forces in Finland and Lapland. He and his corps commanders were killed in a plane crash on June 23, 1944 while returning from a conference with Hitler at the Berghof.

1919 The German Imperial High Seas Fleet was scuttled at Scapa Flow.

1933 The first flight of the Royal Navy's "Walrus" seaplane took place.

1937   Leon Blum resigned as French Premier and was replaced by Camille Chautemps.
1940   At 1530, a German delegation consisting of Hitler, Goering, Hess, Ribbentrop, Keitel and Raeder met with representatives of the French government to discuss the surrender of France. The meeting took place in the same railway carriage that had been used to accept Germany's surrender at the end of WWI. The negotiations would continue until the next day. Luftwaffe ace Adolf Galland was shot down northeast of Boulogne. 105 Royal Air Force bombers attacked targets in Germany and Holland and lost one "Hampden" and one "Wellington". The German S-21 and S-32 were sunk by mines off Boulogne, France.
1941   Twenty-three Royal Air Force "Blenheims" attacked St. Omer airfield in France and lost one aircraft. Sixty-eight Royal Air Force "Wellingtons" attacked Koln, Germany. Fifty-six Royal Air Force bombers attacked Dusseldorf, Germany. A Royal Air Force "Manchester" was shot down in error by a Royal Air Force fighter.
1942   Twelve Royal Air Force "Bostons" attacked Dunkirk, France. Fifty-six Royal Air Force bombers dropped mines off St. Nazaire, France and lost one "Wellington".
1943   The BBC warned Belgian civilians to stay away from factories operating for the Nazis. 705 Royal Air Force bombers attacked Krefeld, Germany and lost forty-four aircraft. 1,056 people were killed in the raid.
1944   1,110 American 8th Air Force bombers dropped 2,315 tons of bombs on industrial targets in Germany and lost seventeen B17s and nineteen B24s (thirteen bombers landed in Sweden). 188 of the B17s involved, continued on to bases in Russia (See Eastern Europe). 1,269 8th and 9th Air Force fighters provided support for the bombers and claimed twenty victories for the loss of four P38s, three P47s and two P51s. At 1045, the Royal Navy destroyer FURY hit a mine off "Sword Beach" in Normandy and drifted ashore at 2300 where she became a total loss. The USN CGs-83415 and 83471 foundered off Normandy. 322 Royal Air Force bombers attacked V-1 rocket sites in France. 139 Royal Air Force bombers attacked Wesseling, Germany and lost thirty-seven aircraft. 312 Royal Air Force bombers attacked Schloven/Buer, Germany and lost eight "Lancasters". The USAAF's 801st Bomb Group dispatched twenty-one B24s on "Carpetbagger" missions.
1951   Nazi physicist Johannes Stark died in Traunstein.

Eastern Europe

1944   The German minesweeper M-538 was a constructive loss after an attack by the Soviet Air Force. The American steamer ALCOA CADET (4,823 tons) was sunk by a mine off Murmansk. The Luftwaffe attacked the Soviet air base at Poltava and destroyed forty-four B17s that had landed there earlier in the day and damaged twenty-six more (See Western Europe).

Mediterranean
1941   Free French forces occupied Damascus, Syria.
1942   The Germans took Tobruk, Libya and 32,220 prisoners. American actor David Wayne was listed as killed in action while serving as a volunteer ambulance driver, but he escaped to British lines. German S-boats attacked Allied shipping off Tobruk sinking the South African minesweeper PARKTOWN, six landing craft, two motor launches and a militarized yacht. The S-58 was badly damaged during the action. The U561 laid a minefield off Port Said. At 0100, the Italian destroyer STRALE ran aground near Cape Bon, Tunisia and was destroyed on August 8th by the Royal Navy submarine TURBULENT. "HalPro" B24s attacked Benghazi, Libya. The commander of the DAK, General Erwin Rommel, was promoted to Field Marshal.
1943   American 9th Air Force B24s attacked San Giovanni, Italy. USAAF B26s attacked airfields on Sicily. The U73 sank the British freighter BRINKBURN (1,598 tons). U73 survived until December 16, 1943.
1944   Sixty-five Royal Air Force bombers attacked the Ventimiglia railyards in Italy. At 0230, the German torpedo boat TA-25 (the ex-Italian ARDITO) was sunk by USN PT-boats. 107 of her crew were rescued.

Atlantic
1940   The U52 sank the Finnish freighter HILDA (1,144 tons). U52 survived until May 1945. The U65 sank the French freighter CHAMPLAIN (28,124 tons). U65 survived until April 28, 1941. The U28 sank the British freighter PRUNELLA (4,443 tons). U28 survived until March 1944. The U43 sank the British tanker YARRAVILLE (8,627 tons). U43 survived until July 30, 1943. The U38 sank the Belgian freighter LUXEMBOURG (5,809 tons). U38 survived until May 1945. The U47 sank the British tanker SAN FERNANDO (13,056 tons). U47 survived until March 7, 1941. The U122 was lost in the North Sea.
1942   The British submarine P-514 (ex-USN R-19) was lost in a collision with the minesweeper GEORGIAN off Cape Race. The U128 sank the American freighter WEST IRA (5,681 tons-1 dead). U128 survived until May 17, 1943. The Luftwaffe sank the American freighter ALCOA CADET (1 dead) off Norway.
1943   The U513 sank the Swedish freighter VENEZIA (1,673 tons). U513 survived until July 19th.

North America

1890 USAAF General Lewis Hyde Brereton was born in Pittsburgh, Pa. He graduated from Annapolis on June 2, 1911, 56th in a class of 193. At the time, the Navy had more ensigns than it needed and the Army was short of second lieutenants, so he was allowed to accept an Army commission. In 1913 he won his wings. He would command the Far East Air Force, the 9th Air Force and the 1st Allied Airborne Army during the war. He died on July 20, 1967.

1934 The first landing by an aircraft aboard the USN carrier RANGER took place.

1939 The destroyer ROE and the submarine SEARAVEN were launched. ROE was scrapped in 1947 and SEARAVEN was expended as a target on September 11, 1948.

1941 The American government requested the closure of Italian consulates.

1942 FDR and Churchill met at the White House to discuss the "Torch" (North African) landings. The IJN submarine I-25 bombarded Ft. Stevens, Oregon. The destroyers JENKINS and LAVALLETTE and the submarine HADDO were launched. JENKINS was stricken in 1979; LAVALLETTE was stricken in 1974 and HADDO was scrapped in 1960.

1945 A Japanese balloon-bomb was found near Tampico, Washington.

1946 The destroyer-transport KANE was sold for scrap.

1958 Admiral Robert Ghormley died at Bethesda. He had commanded the American Forces in the South Pacific in 1942.

Pacific

1942 The USN submarine S-44 sank the IJN gunboat KEIJO MARU (2,626 tons) off Gavutu in the Solomons. A USN "Catalina" rescued the two-man crew of a TBD from the ENTERPRISE. They had ditched their aircraft 360 miles north of Midway on June 4th. They were the last survivors of the "Battle of Midway" to be rescued.

1943 The USMC 4th Raider Battalion landed at Segi Point, New Georgia. They were landed by the destroyer-transports SCHLEY, CROSBY, DENT and WATERS. USAAF ace Captain George Welch shot down two Japanese "Zekes" over Lae, New Guinea; he had scored his first aerial victories over Oahu on December 7, 1941.

1944 Heavy fighting continued on Saipan and Biak Islands. Aircraft from the USN escort carrier WHITE PLAINS sank the Japanese freighter SHOUN MARU off Saipan. The USN submarine BLUEFISH sank the KANAN MARU (3,280 tons).

1945 Okinawa was declared secure after a battle that lasted eighty-one days and cost 17,427 American and 130,000 Japanese military and 42,000 civilian dead. 10,755 Japanese were taken prisoner. USN losses were 36 ships sunk and 368 damaged. The American forces also lost 763 aircraft. The USN LSM-59 was sunk and aircraft tender CURTISS was damaged by Japanese kamikazes. The USN destroyer-transport BARRY (See May 22nd) was sunk by kamikazes while serving as a decoy, the LSM-59 was also lost. USAAF Major George Laven became the last P38 ace when he shot down a Japanese "Emily" over Formosa. The USN submarine PARCHE sank the HIZEN MARU (947 tons).

June 22nd

Western Europe

1892   German Luftwaffe General Robert von Greim was born. During WWI, he scored 28 aerial victories. In April 1935, he became the Luftwaffe's Inspector of Fighters and Dive-bombers and in 1939 he assumed command of Fliegerkorps V. From February 1943, he commanded Luftflotte 6 on the Eastern Front. On April 24, 1945, while in Munich, he was ordered to report to Berlin. On the 26th, he and Hanna Reitsch landed a light plane on a Berlin street. He was wounded during the landing and was resting in bed when Hitler walked into his room and announced that he was the new commander of the Luftwaffe with the rank of Field Marshal. On the 28th, he and Reitsch flew another airplane out of the doomed city. He was captured by American troops and committed suicide on May 24, 1945 while in a Salzburg prison.

1940   At 1830, the French signed the armistice ending the war with Germany. Eighteen Royal Air Force bombers attacked airfields in France and suffered no losses. The Italians occupied Menton, France. The Free French corvette LA BASTIASE was sunk off West Hartlepool by a mine.

1941   Seventy Royal Air Force bombers attacked Bremen, Germany and lost two aircraft. Twenty-seven Royal Air Force bombers attacked Wilhelmshaven, Germany. The nearest bomb fell two miles away from the city. A Royal Air Force B17 broke up in a storm over Catterick, Yorkshire. The sole survivor was Flight/Lieutenant (later Air vice Marshal) William K. Stewart. The U48 returned to Kiel, Germany from what was to be her last war patrol. During her wartime cruises, she had sunk one sloop and fifty-four merchant ships totaling 322,378 tons and had damaged two more of 11,024 tons. She was thus the most successful submarine of the war. She would survive as a training boat until March 8, 1945 when she was scuttled at Neustadt, Germany.

1942   Twelve Royal Air Force "Bostons" attacked Dunkirk, France. The Royal Navy battleship ANSON was commissioned. 227 Royal Air Force bombers attacked Emden, Germany and lost six aircraft. Six people were killed in the raid.

1943 183 American 8th Air Force B17s dropped 422 tons of bombs on Huls, Germany and lost sixteen aircraft, one of which was the only YB-40 to be lost in combat. Thirty-nine 8th Air Force B17s dropped ninety-five tons of bombs on Antwerp, Belgium and lost four aircraft. It was the first 8th Air Force mission for the 381st and 384th Bomb Groups. 136 8th Air Force P47s flew as escorts for the Antwerp raid. The 100th Bomb Group (B17) also flew its first 8th Air Force mission on this day, a diversion flight over the North Sea. 557 Royal Air Force bombers attacked Mulheim, Germany and lost thirty-five aircraft. 578 people were killed in the raid.

1944 At 1240, American forces began their final assault on Cherbourg, France. Danish saboteurs destroyed a rifle factory in Copenhagen. 217 American 8th Air Force B17s and B24s dropped 594 tons of bombs on V-1 rocket launching sites on the Pas de Calais of France. 922 8th Air Force bombers dropped 2,441 tons of bombs on industrial targets and airfields in France and lost five B17s and two B24s. 311 American 9th Air Force bombers attacked Cherbourg, France. 234 Royal Air Force bombers attacked V-1 rocket sites in France and lost one "Halifax". 221 Royal Air Force bombers attacked rail targets in France and lost eight aircraft.

1948 The Soviets instituted a rail and road blockade of Berlin.

1976 The French Communist journal "L'Humanite" published a report that Joachim Peiper, the S.S. commander at the Malmedy massacre, was living in Traves, France. He was killed there in a gun-battle on July 14th ("Bastille Day").

Eastern Europe

1941 "Operation Barbarossa" (the German invasion of Russia) began at 0315 with a barrage of more than 7,000 artillery pieces. Germany contributed 152 divisions and 2 brigades, Finland 16 divisions and 3 brigades, Rumania 13 divisions and 9 brigades and Hungary 4 brigades to the offensive that covered a 500-mile-long front along the Bug River. The Soviets had the equivalent of 158 divisions in the area of the attack. An hour earlier, the Luftwaffe had dropped mines in the Black Sea and the Baltic. By noon, more than 1,000 Soviet aircraft had been destroyed. The German Army Group "Center" attacked north of the Pripet Marshes. Wolfgang Schellmann, Kommodore of JG-27, collided with a Soviet Air Force I-16 fighter and was captured. He was shot two days later by the NKVD (the Soviet Secret Police). The Soviet Navy began laying defensive minefields off its major ports in the Black Sea. The Luftwaffe dropped 27 mines off Kronstadt. The German S-44 sank the Soviet patrol boat

MO-238 off Hango. German S-boats laid a minefield in the Irben Strait. On this date Russia had the world's largest submarine fleet with 139 vessels commissioned. By the end of the war, they would sink a total of only 292,000 tons of German shipping, as compared to Germany's total of 14.5 million tons, America's 5.5 million and Britain's 1.8 million. Much of the disparity in tonnage sunk can be attributed to the diverse theaters of operation as well as the differences between the submarine fleets.

1942 The last Soviet fortress guarding the city of Sevastopol was taken by the Germans.

1944 Joachim von Ribbentrop, Germany's Foreign Minister, arrived in Helsinki to try and persuade the Finns not to surrender to the Soviets. The Soviets began their summer offensive against the German Army Group "Center" with 146 infantry divisions and 43 tank brigades.

Mediterranean

1940 At 1700, the French battleship JEAN BART arrived in Casablanca from St. Nazaire, France. The Italian submarine CAPPONI sank the Swedish freighter ELGO (1,888 tons) north of Sfax. The Italian submarine EVANGELISTA TORRICELLI (launched in 1934) was sunk by the Royal Navy destroyers SHOREHAM, KANDAHAR, and KINGSTON. The Royal Navy destroyer KHARTOUM was lost in an accident in the Red Sea.

1941 Archibald Wavell was informed that he would be replaced as British commander in North Africa.

1942 The German 90th Light Division crossed the border into Egypt.

1943 The USN LST-387 and the Royal Navy LST-333 were sunk off Algeria by the U593. U593 survived until December 13th.

1944 580 American 15th Air Force bombers dropped 1,400 tons of bombs on various Italian transportation targets. The Italian light cruiser BOLZANO was sunk by Royal Navy "Chariots" (midget submarines) at La Spezia.

1945 The American freighter PIERRE GIBAULT was damaged by a mine off Kytheria, Greece and declared a constructive loss. She suffered four dead and five wounded.

Atlantic

1940 The U38 sank the Greek freighter NEION (5,154 tons). U38 survived until May 1945. The U32 sank the Norwegian tanker ELI KNUDSEN (9,026 tons). U32 survived until October 30th. The U65 sank the Dutch freighter BERENICE (1,177 tons). U65 survived until April 28, 1941. The U30 sank the Norwegian freighter RANDSFJORD (3,999 tons). U30 survived until May 5, 1945.

1941 The U141 sank the Swedish freighter CALABRIA (1,277 tons). U141 survived until May 1945. The U77 sank the British freighter ARAKAKA (2,379 tons). U77 survived until March 28, 1943. The German armed merchant cruiser ATLANTIS took the steamer BALZAC (5,372 tons).

1942 The U202 sank the Argentine freighter RIO TERCERO (4,864 tons). U202 survived until June 1, 1943. The U159 sank the American tanker E.J. SADLER (9,639 tons). U159 survived until July 15, 1943.

1943 The U572 sank the French tanker LOT (4,220 tons). U572 survived until August 3rd.

North America

1944 The Ninth Army headquarters group left New York for Europe aboard the RMS QUEEN ELIZABETH. The GI Bill of Rights was signed into law.

South America

1979 The Brazilian Supreme Court refused a West German extradition request for Gustav Wagner, the former Deputy Commandant at Sobibor Concentration Camp. It had also refused similar requests from Israel, Austria and Poland.

Pacific

1943 American forces occupied Woodlark Island, 95 miles southeast of New Guinea. The US Army's 43rd Division reinforced USMC forces on Segi Point, New Georgia. The IJN submarine I-174 sank the American freighters OURAY and ROBERT LINCOLN south of Guadalcanal. The USN SC-751 ran aground off Western Australia and was lost. The IJN submarine I-7 was sunk in the Aleutians by the USN destroyer MONAGHAN.

1944 American aircraft began using the Mokmer airfield on Biak Island, but fighting continued around the area. The 2nd USMC Division began a northward attack on Saipan. Forty-four USAAF P47s were catapulted from the USN escort carrier NATOMA BAY for operations on Saipan. The USN battleship MARYLAND was torpedoed by Japanese aircraft off Saipan, two of her crew died. The Japanese took Tuguearao, Luzon from Philippine guerrillas. The USN submarine BATFISH sank the NAGARAGAWA MARU (887 tons).

1945 Two USAAF B32s attacked Formosa. The IJN submarine I-36 damaged the USN LST-513.

China-Burma-India

1944 The British relieved Imphal, India.

June 23rd

Western Europe

1899   Hitler's personal interpreter Paul Schmidt was born in Berlin. He died on April 21, 1970 in Munich.

1937   Germany and Italy withdrew from the Non-Intervention Patrol off Spain.

1940   Pierre Laval was named Vice-Premier of France. Maxime Weygand formally ousted Charles de Gaulle from the French government. A French delegation left for Rome to negotiate an armistice with Italy. After an assault that had lasted three days, the Italian "Assietta" Division a small fort at Chenaillet that was held by a 19-man French force. Twenty-six Royal Air Force bombers attacked targets in Germany and lost three "Blenheims". The French Air Force shot scored its last aerial victory (a Luftwaffe Hs126-recon). Seventy-nine Royal Air Force bombers attacked targets in Germany and suffered no losses.

1941   Thirty-nine Royal Air Force "Blenheims" attacked coastal targets and lost two aircraft. Sixty-two Royal Air Force bombers attacked Koln, Germany and lost one "Wellington". Forty-one Royal Air Force bombers attacked Dusseldorf, Germany. Twenty-six Royal Air Force bombers attacked Kiel, Germany and killed one person.

1942   Eighteen Royal Air Force "Bostons" attacked targets in France. A Luftwaffe Fw190 fighter landed in error at the Royal Air Force base at Pembry. Fifty-two Royal Air Force bombers dropped mines off French ports and lost two "Wellingtons".

1943   172 American 8th Air Force B17s and eight YB-40s took off to attack French targets, but were recalled due to bad weather. While preparing for the mission, a 381st Bomb Group B17 exploded and killed twenty-three people on the ground. The Portuguese government formed a new fighter unit with eighteen P39 "Airacobras" which had lost their way on various ferry flights from Britain to Gibraltar and had landed in Portugal. It was to be named the "Esquadrilha OK".

1944   At 2300, the Royal Navy light cruiser SCYLLA was declared a constructive loss after hitting a mine off "Sword" beach in Normandy. The US Army's VII Corps penetrated the outer defenses of Cherbourg on the Contentin Peninsula in Normandy. Second Lieutenant John Butts, of the 9th Division, won a posthumous Medal of Honor in Normandy. The British took Ste. Honorine, France. 410 American 8th Air Force bombers dropped 1,012 tons of bombs on V-1 rocket sites and airfields in France and lost one B17 and six B24s. 310 8th Air Force fighters provided support for the bombers and dropped ninety-one tons of bombs on targets near Paris and lost one P51 and two P38s. 412 Royal Air Force bombers attacked V-1 launching sites in France and lost five "Lancasters". 207 Royal Air Force bombers attacked rail targets in France and lost two "Lancasters". The USAAF's 801st Bomb Group dispatched twenty-one B24s on "Carpetbagger" missions.

Eastern Europe

1941 The Germans crossed the River Bug in Poland. The Soviet Air Force lost 500 aircraft and the Luftwaffe lost twelve. The commander of the Soviet "Red Bomber Group", Lieutenant General Kopets, committed suicide. Hungary declared war on Russia. The Soviet destroyer GNEVNY was sunk by a mine in the eastern Baltic. The cruiser MAKSIM GORKI and the destroyer GORDY were damaged in the same minefield. The U144 sank the Soviet submarine M-78. U144 survived until August 9th.

1942 The Soviet Navy delivered supplies to Sevastopol.

1943 The Soviet freighter LENINGRAD (1,783 tons) was sunk by the U18 in the Black Sea. U18 survived until September 10, 1944.

1944 761 American 15th Air Force attacked oil installations at Ploesti, losing five bombers. Second Lieutenant David Kingsley, of the 97th Bomb Group (B17), won a posthumous Medal of Honor on the mission. Major Herschel Green, of the 52nd Fighter Group (P51), scored his 15th victory, a Me109. Heavy fighting took place between the Pripet Marsh and Dvina. The Soviets surrounded German forces at Vitebsk, Orsha, Mogilev and Bobruisk. The German UJ-307 and UJ-2306 were sunk in the Black Sea by mines.

Mediterranean

1934 The Italians entered Durazzo, Ethiopia forcing the Ethiopian government to grant concessions to Mussolini.

1940 The Italian submarine TORRECELLI was sunk by the Royal Navy destroyers KANDAHAR, KHARTOUM, KINGSTON, and the sloop SHOREHAM. The KHARTOUM was lost during the action. The French delegation arrived in Rome to sign an armistice. The French battleship RICHELIEU arrived in Dakar from Brest.

1941 An Axis convoy reached Italy from Tripoli having endured air attacks from Malta for the past three days. The British reached Palmyra, Syria.

1942 The British submarines THRASHER and TURBULENT spent the next two days attacking an Italian three-ship convoy. They sank two ships of 1,480 tons and one of 1,085 tons.

1943 Fifty-two Royal Air Force "Lancasters" attacked La Spezia.

1944 The British XIII Corps entered Chiusi.

Atlantic

1941 The German freighter ALSTERTOR was scuttled off Spain when she was trapped by Royal Navy destroyers and aircraft.

1942 The U67 sank the American tanker RAWLEIGH WARNER (3,664 tons), with all hands. U67 survived until July 16, 1943. The U128 sank the Norwegian tanker ANDREA BROVIG (10,173 tons). U128 survived until May 17, 1943. The U172 sank the Colombian sailing ship RESOLUTE (35 tons). U172 survived until December 13, 1943. The U158 sank the US Army freighter MAJOR GENERAL HENRY GIBBINS (5,766 tons). U158 survived until June 30th. The U84 sank the Norwegian freighter TORVANGER (6,568 tons). U84 survived until August 24, 1943. The U68 sank the Panamanian tanker ARRIAGA (2,469 tons). U68 survived until April 10, 1944.

North America

1937 The USAAC issued a contract to Lockheed for the XP38 (proto-type of the "Lightning").

1941 The US Secretary of the Interior Harold Ickes urged FDR to embargo oil destined for Japan. Future 8th Air Force ace Duane Beeson (24 victories) enlisted in Royal Canadian Air Force.

1942 The submarines SAWFISH and POGY were launched. SAWFISH was discarded in 1960 and POGY was discarded in 1959.

1943 The heavy cruiser QUINCY (awarded four battle stars during the war) was launched. She was stricken in 1973.

1963 George Turner died. He had been the oldest enlisted man to win a Medal of Honor in WWII (Europe-1945).

1990 A P51D crashed at Dyess Air Force Base, Texas, killing the pilot.

South America

1944 Britain and America resumed relations with Bolivia.

Pacific

1942 The USN minelayer OGLALA was refloated at Pearl Harbor. She had capsized during the December 7th attack.

1943 The USN submarine HARDER sank the SAGARA MARU (1,189 tons). The USN freighters DEIMOS (7,440 tons) and ALUDRA (7,440 tons) were sunk off San Christobal by the IJN submarine Ro-103. America forces occupied Kiriwina Island, ninety-five miles southeast of New Guinea. 5th Air Force B24s attacked Makassar and damaged the IJN light cruiser KINU.

1944   American forces made an unsuccessful attack up Mount Tapotchau on Saipan. Forty-four USAAF P47 "Thunderbolts" were catapulted from the USN escort carrier MANILA BAY for Saipan. USN Lieutenant Wayne Morris shot down a Japanese "Zero" over Saipan. Before the war Morris had been a well-known film actor. The crew of a Navy SB2c was rescued by a PBM flying boat. They had gone down during the night attack on the Japanese fleet on June 20th. Corporal Sukanaivalu Sefanaia, of the Fiji Military Forces, won a posthumous Victoria Cross on Bougainville. American forces continued mopping up operations on Biak.

1945   US Army General Joseph Stilwell relieved USMC General Roy Geiger as commander of the 10th Army on Okinawa. Geiger had served as temporary commander since the death of General Simon Buckner. The USN submarine HARDHEAD sank the IJN sub chaser Chas-113 and 23. The USN submarine TIRANTE sank the ANTUNG MARU No.293 (132 tons).

China-Burma-India

1940   At 0100, the Royal Indian Navy sloop PATHAN (5 dead) was torpedoed off Bombay by the Italian submarine GALVANI and was scuttled the next day by the Royal Navy sloop FALMOUTH. The next day, GALVANI (launched in 1938) was sunk by the FALMOUTH.

1944   Captain M. Allmand (posthumous) and Tulbahadur Pun, of the 6th Gurkha Rifles, won Victoria Cross' in Burma.

June 24th

Western Europe

1940   The French Air Force sent eleven Leo-45 bombers against German pontoon bridges located between Moirans and Grenoble, two days after signing the armistice. Eight Royal Air Force bombers attacked Dutch airfields and suffered no losses. British Commandoes made a raid near Boulogne, France. 103 Royal Air Force bombers attacked targets in Germany and lost no aircraft. The German S-36 sank the British ALBUERA (3,477 tons).

1941   Fifty-four Royal Air Force bombers attacked Köln, Germany. Forty-eight Royal Air Force bombers attacked Kiel, Germany and lost one "Wellington". Thirty-one Royal Air Force bombers attacked Dusseldorf, Germany. One Royal Air Force "Wellington" was lost and another was shot down by British anti-aircraft fire off Harwich.

1942   US Army General Dwight Eisenhower assumed command of the American Forces in Britain. Twenty-one Royal Air Force bombers attacked St. Nazaire, France.

1943   630 Royal Air Force bombers attacked Wupertal and lost thirty-four aircraft. 1,800 people were killed in the raid. 128 American 8th Air Force P47s flew sweeps over France and Holland.
1944   Fighting continued in Cherbourg, France. 286 American 8th Air Force bombers dropped 767 tons of bombs on Wesermunde and Bremen in Germany losing one B17. The minesweeper R-141 was lost in the raid on Wesermunde. 532 8th Air Force bombers dropped 1,335 tons of bombs on French targets losing six bombers and one escorting fighter. 275 American 9th Air Force B26s attacked German positions in Cherbourg, France. At 0735, the Royal Navy destroyer SWIFT was sunk by a mine off "Sword" Beach in Normandy. The Royal Navy minesweeper LORD AUSTIN and two freighters were sunk off Normandy by mines. The Norwegian destroyer GLAISDALE, the French frigate LA SURPRISE, a British minesweeper and a freighter were constructive losses after hitting mines off Normandy. Allied aircraft bombed the US Army's 30th Division in Normandy, killing twenty-five. 321 Royal Air Force bombers attacked V-1 rocket launching sites in France and lost one "Lancaster".
1953   Winston Churchill suffered a stroke while serving as British Prime Minister. Luftwaffe ace Gunther von Maltzahn (68 victories) died.
1970   The French battleship JEAN BART was scrapped at La Seyne, France.

Eastern Europe
1941   The Soviet XII Armored Corps counter-attacked the German Army Group "North" with 100 tanks. The attack was repulsed with heavy losses. A battle involving more than 4,000 tanks took place near Lutsk Dubno. The Germans took Vilnyus and Kaunus in Lithuania. The Soviet destroyer LENIN was scuttled at Libau to avoid capture. The Soviet submarine M-78 was sunk by the U144. U144 survived until August 9th. The Soviet submarine S-3 was sunk by German surface craft. The Soviet minesweeper SHKIV was sunk by a mine in the eastern Baltic.
1942   The Soviet Navy delivered supplies to the besieged city of Sevastopol. The Royal Navy minesweeper GOSSAMER was sunk in Kola Inlet with the loss of twenty-three men.
1944   377 American 15th Air Force attacked oil installations in Ploesti losing fourteen bombers.

Mediterranean
1940   At the Villa Olgiata, near Rome, the French delegation signed an armistice with the Italians.
1941   The Royal Navy sloop AUCKLAND was sunk off Tobruk, Libya by Italian aircraft. The Royal Australian Navy PARRAMATTA rescued 162 survivors.

1942	The Italian submarine ZAFFIRO was sunk by the Royal Navy submarine ULTIMATUM.
1943	The Royal Air Force attacked Italian naval installations at La Spezia.
1944	At 2200, the Croat torpedo boat T-7 was damaged in the Adriatic by the Royal Navy MGBs 662 and 659 and the MTB 670 and was beached.
1970	The French battleship JEAN BART left Toulon, France to be scrapped at La Seyne.

Atlantic

1940	The U47 sank the Panamanian freighter CATHERINE (1,885 tons). U47 survived until March 7, 1941.
1941	The U203 sank the Norwegian freighter SOLOY (4,402 tons) and the Dutch freighter SCHIE (1,967 tons). U203 survived until April 25, 1943. The U371 sank the Norwegian freighter VIGRID (4,765 tons). U371 survived until May 4, 1944. The U651 sank the British freighter BROCKLEY HILL (5,279 tons). U651 survived until June 29th.
1942	German Admiral Karl Doenitz ordered his U-boats not to surface in the Bay of Biscay except to recharge their batteries. This was due to the intensive Allied aerial activity in the area. The U156 sank the British freighter WILLIMANTIC (4,558 tons). U156 survived until March 8, 1943. The U404 sank the Yugoslavian freighter LJUBICA MATKOVIC (3,289 tons). U404 survived until July 28, 1943. A U373-laid mine sank the USN tug JOHN R. WILLIAMS (14 dead). The U373 survived until June 8, 1944.
1943	The U119 was sunk southwest of Iceland by the Royal Navy sloop STARLING. U194 was sunk southwest of Iceland by the Royal Air Force's No.120 Squadron. The U200 was sunk southwest of Iceland by USN VP-84. The U449 was sunk northwest of Cape Ortegal by the Royal Navy sloops WOODPECKER, WREN, KITE, and WILDGOOSE.
1944	The U1225 was sunk northwest of Bergen, Norway by the Royal Canadian Air Force's No.162 Squadron (PBY). The pilot of the aircraft, Flight/Lieutenant Hornell, won a posthumous Victoria Cross for the attack. The U971 was sunk by the Royal Navy destroyers ESKIMO and HAIDA.

North America

1939	The USAAC ordered sixty-three A20 "Havoc" bombers.
1941	FDR pledged aid for Russia in her fight against Germany.
1942	The destroyers STEVENS (stricken in 1971) and BELL (expended in 1972) were launched.
1944	The Soviet freighter ILYICH capsized at Portland, Oregon. The escort carrier MATANIKAU was commissioned. She was scrapped in 1960.

1945   Japanese balloon-bombs were found near Hailey and Gilmore in Idaho.
1969   The destroyer BEALE was expended as a target.
1988   Mildred Gillars, "Axis Sally", died at age 87 in Columbus, Ohio. She had served 12 years of a 10-to-30-year sentence for treason before being released in 1961.
1995   The USN repair ship JASON was decommissioned. She had been commissioned on June 19, 1944.

Pacific

1941   The IJN light carrier HIYO was launched. She was lost on June 20, 1944.
1944   Fighting continued on the island of Biak. General Ralph Smith, commander of the US Army's 27th Division on Saipan, was relieved for inefficiency by the landing force commander USMC General Holland Smith and was replaced by General Sanderford Jarmen. American actor Lee Marvin was seriously wounded while serving with the USMC's 4th Division on Saipan. Japanese aircraft attacked American shipping off Saipan. USN carriers attacked Iwo Jima and Chichi Jima. Japanese Naval Air Force ace Sadao Yamaguchi (12 victories) was killed in the action over Iwo Jima. The USN submarine GROUPER sank the KUMANOSAN MARU (2,857 tons) and the NANMEI MARU No.6 (834 tons). The USN submarine REDFIN sank the ASO MARU (3,028 tons). The USN submarine TANG sank the TAMAHOKO MARU (6,780 tons), the KENNICHI MARU (1,937 tons), the NASUSAN MARU (4,399 tons) and the TAINAN MARU (3,175 tons). A USN PBM seaplane was shot down when it failed to identify itself to USN Destroyer Divisions 92 and 104. USN PT-193 was lost when she ran aground off western New Guinea.
1945   The USN submarine TIRANTE sank the ANTUNG MARU No.284 (132 tons).

China-Burma-India

1943   The IJN submarine I-27 sank the British tanker BRITISH VENTURE (4,696 tons).
1945   A USAAF B32, flying from the Philippines, attacked Macao, China.

June 25th

Western Europe

1880   French General Charles Huntzinger was born.
1900   British Lord Louis Mountbatten was born. He was killed on August 27, 1979 when an Irish Republican Army bomb exploded aboard his fishing boat.

The Month of June

1940 The Luftwaffe attacked the Royal Air Force base at Debden. Twenty-five Royal Air Force bombers attacked targets in Holland and lost no aircraft. The Germans reached Roman, France. The 220,000 French troops holding the defenses of the Maginot Line ceased fighting but refused to leave their positions until they received written orders from French Army Commander, General Weygand. At 0135, the German-Italian-French armistice took effect. During the battle for Western Europe, the French had suffered 92,000 dead, the British 3,500, the Dutch 2,900, the Belgians 7,500, and the Germans 27,000. At 2215, the Royal Canadian Navy destroyer FRASER was lost in a collision with the Royal Navy light cruiser CALCUTTA of the Gironde Estuary in France. Forty-seven Canadians and nineteen British sailors died in the incident. Forty-eight Royal Air Force bombers attacked targets in Holland and Germany and lost no aircraft. Since May 10th, the Royal Air Force had flown 5,085 bomber sorties on which it had dropped 3,492 tons of bombs and lost 145 aircraft. The German patrol boat M-1107 was sunk off Norway.

1941 Twenty-four Royal Air Force "Blenheims" attacked Luftwaffe airfields in France and lost one aircraft. Sixty-four Royal Air Force bombers attacked Bremen, Germany and lost one "Wellington". Forty-seven Royal Air Force bombers attacked Kiel and Hamburg and lost one "Hampden".

1942 1,067 Royal Air Force bombers attacked Bremen, Germany and lost forty-eight aircraft. Eighty-five people were killed in the raid. Fifty-six Royal Air Force bombers attacked Luftwaffe airfields in support of the raid and lost two "Blenheims". Luftwaffe aircraft attacked the new the Bomber Command base at Polebrook.

1943 British Foreign Minister Anthony Eden visited the USAAF's 44th Bomb Group (B24) at its base at Shipdham. 149 American 8th Air Force B17s dropped 363 tons of bombs on targets off Holland and lost fifteen aircraft. Eighteen 8th Air Force B17s dropped forty tons of bombs on a convoy off Belgium and lost three aircraft (all from the 100th BG). It was the first combat mission for the 100th Bomb Group. 130 8th Air Force P47s flew escort missions over the North Sea. 473 Royal Air Force bombers attacked Gelsenkirchen, Germany and lost thirty aircraft. Only twenty-one people were killed in the target area, but the town of Solingen thirty miles away had twenty-one killed. Thirty-three Royal Air Force bombers dropped mines off the Atlantic coast and lost one "Lancaster".

1944 929 American 8th Air Force bombers dropped 2,133 tons of bombs on airfields, transformer stations and an oil dump and lost seven B24s and six B17s. 471 8th Air Force fighters provided support for the bombers and claimed twenty-two victories for the loss of two P51s. The American 15th Air Force attacked oil targets in Southern France. The first operations for the Luftwaffe's "Mistletoe" (a tandem Fw190 and Ju88) took place. The target was the Allied invasion fleet off Normandy. The USN battleships TEXAS and NEVADA, the heavy cruiser TUSCALOOSA, the light cruiser QUINCY, the destroyers BARTON, O'BRIEN, PLUNKETT, HOBSON and LAFFEY and the Royal Navy light cruisers ENTERPRISE and GLASGOW bombarded the area around Cherbourg, France. The TEXAS and the BARTON were hit by counter-fire. Corporal John Kelly and First Lieutenant Carlos Ogden, of the 79th Division, won Medals of Honor at Fort Du Roule in Cherbourg. The US Army's 30th Division was bombed for the second consecutive day by the American 8th Air Force, 111 soldiers died. The U269 was sunk in the English Channel by the Royal Navy frigate BICKERTON. The U1191 was sunk in the English Channel by the Royal Navy frigates AFFLECK and BALFOUR. 323 Royal Air Force bombers attacked V-1 rocket launching sites in France and lost one "Halifax". The USAAF's 801st Bomb Group dispatched twenty-four B24s on "Carpetbagger" (resistance resupply) missions.

Eastern Europe
1941   The Soviet Air Force attacked Finland. Finland declared war on Russia. The Soviet minesweeper SHKIV was sunk by a mine.
1942   The Soviet Navy delivered supplies to the besieged city of Sevastopol.
1944   Five German divisions were surrounded at Vitebsk.

Mediterranean
1940   The first Italian troop convoy left Naples for Tripoli. It consisted of the transports ESPERIA (11,398 tons) and VICTORIA (13,098 tons). They carried 1,727 troops and were escorted by the armed merchant cruiser RAMB II and the torpedo boats ORSA and PROCIONE.
1942   "HalPro" B24s attacked Benghazi, Libya. The Commander of British Forces in North Africa, General Sir Claude Auchinleck, assumed personal command of the British 8th Army, relieving Lieutenant General Neil Ritchie.
1943   Allied aircraft attacked Sicily.
1944   The German torpedo boat TA-22 (the ex-Italian GIUSEPPE MISSORI) was a constructive loss after a USAAF attack off Trieste. The French destroyer BISON was rammed in Toulon harbor by a German submarine and sank. The US Army's 36th Division took Piombino, Italy.

Atlantic
1940   The U51 sank the British freighter WINDSORWOOD (5,395 tons) and tanker SARANAC (12,049 tons). U51 survived until August 20th.

1941 The U77 sank the Greek freighter ANNA BULGARIS (4,603 tons). U77 survived until March 28, 1943. The U108 sank the Greek freighter ELLINICO (3,059 tons). U108 survived until April 11, 1944. The French submarine SOFFLEUR was sunk by the Royal Navy submarine PARTHIAN. The Royal Navy heavy cruiser NIGERIA took the German trawler LAUENBURG.

1942 The U404 sank the American freighter MANUELA (4,772 tons-2 dead) and the Panamanian freighter NORDAL (3,845 tons). U404 survived until July 28, 1943. The U153 sank the British freighter ANGLO CANADIAN (5,268 tons). U153 survived until July 13th. The British trawler BROMELIA was lost off Iceland. The Luftwaffe sank the Royal Navy minesweeper GOSSAMER off Murmansk.

1944 The Royal Navy frigate GOODSON was a constructive loss after an attack off Portland, Britain by the U984. U984 survived until August 20th.

North America

1886 General Henry Harley "Hap" Arnold was born in Gladwyne, Pa. He would serve as USAAF Chief of Staff during the war.

1942 The destroyer CHAMPLIN (stricken in 1971) was launched.

1943 The destroyer STOCKHAM (stricken in 1975) and the submarine SAND LANCE were launched. SAND LANCE was transferred to Brazil in 1963.

1944 The submarine BRILL was launched. She was transferred to the Turkish Navy in 1948.

1956 Former Chief of Naval Operations Admiral Ernest King died in Portsmouth, New Hampshire.

1959 The heavy cruiser TUSCALOOSA was sold for scrap.

1967 The destroyer-transport LIDDLE was sold for scrap.

1990 William A. Shomo died in Warren, Pa. He had won a Medal of Honor in 1945 for shooting down seven Japanese aircraft over the Lingayen Gulf.

Pacific

1941 Richard Sorge reported to Moscow that Japan intended moving into Indo-China.

1942 The USN minelayer OGLALA sank at Pearl Harbor having been raised from the bottom on the 23rd. American diplomats sailed from Japan to be exchanged in Portuguese East Africa. The American 11th Air Force attacked Kiska in the Aleutians. The USN submarine NAUTILUS sank the IJN destroyer YAMAKAZE 60 miles southeast of Yokosuka, Japan. The USN submarine GROUPER damaged the Japanese tanker No.3 TONAN MARU east of the Ryukyus. USN PBYs attacked Tulagi. The USN carrier SARATOGA delivered twenty-five USAAF P40s and eighteen

USMC SBDs to Midway to replace the severe aircraft losses suffered by the island's defenses during the battle earlier in the month.
1943 The USN submarine SAILFISH sank the IBURI MARU (3,291 tons).
1944 The Japanese retreated on the island of Biak. American forces reached the summit of Mount Tapotchau on Saipan. USMC Private First-Class Harold Epperson, of the 2nd Division, won a posthumous Medal of Honor on Saipan. The USN submarine BASHAW sank the YAMAMIYA MARU (6,440 tons). The USN submarine JACK sank the SAN PEDRO MARU (7,268 tons). The USN PT-193 was scuttled off Noemfoor Island.
1945 The Australians secured the Miri oilfields on Borneo. The US Army's 37th Division took Tuguegarao, Luzon.

China-Burma-India
1944 The Japanese defeated the Chinese 261st Regiment near Lunling, Burma.
1950 RB17Gs of the USAF 6204th Photo Mapping Flight, flying from Clark Field in the Philippines, flew a recon mission over Korea.

June 26th

Western Europe
1898 German aircraft designer Wilhelm "Willy" Messerschmitt was born in Frankfurt-am-Main. He died of pneumonia in Munich on September 15, 1978 at the age of 80.
1917 Luftwaffe ace Ludwig Franzisket (43 victories) was born in Dusseldorf. He survived the war.
1940 120 Royal Air Force bombers attacked targets in Germany, Holland and Belgium, losing one "Blenheim" and three "Hampdens".
1941 Fifty-one Royal Air Force bombers attacked Cologne, Germany and lost one "Wellington". Forty-four Royal Air Force bombers attacked Dusseldorf, Germany and lost one "Wellington". Forty-one Royal Air Force bombers attacked Kiel, Germany and lost two "Manchesters".
1942 Twelve Royal Air Force "Bostons" attacked the port of Le Havre, France. Twenty-nine Royal Air Force bombers dropped mines off Lorient and St. Nazaire in France.
1943 Fifty-six American 8th Air Force B17s dropped 130 tons of bombs on French airfields and lost five aircraft. The USAAF's 384th Bomb Groups B17, "Flak Dancer", landed near Laon, France and was captured. 130 8th Air Force P47s flew missions over France and lost five 56th Fighter Group aircraft. Sixteen Royal Air Force "Wellingtons" dropped mines off the Biscay ports and lost one aircraft. Seven Royal Air Force "Mosquitoes"

	attacked targets in Germany. COSSAC selected Normandy as the most desirable location for an invasion of Northwest France in 1944.
1944	550 American 15th Air Force bombers attacked oil targets in Austria, losing eleven bombers. The Royal Navy battleship RODNEY shelled Caen, France. The British "Operation Epsom" began near Caen. The US Army's 9th Division captured General Karl von Schlieben, German commander of Cherbourg, France and Admiral Walther Hennecke, commander of the Cherbourg Naval Arsenal. The US Army's 69th Division took Fort du Roule in Cherbourg. The Royal Navy frigate GOODSON (the ex-USN GEORGE) was a constructive loss after being torpedoed by the U984 off Cherbourg. Thirty-five Royal Air Force "Mosquitoes" attacked Gottingen, Germany and lost one aircraft.
1949	Royal Canadian Air Force ace D. Gordon (11 victories) died.

Eastern Europe

1940	Russia demanded that Rumania cede to Bessarabia part of Bukovina within 48 hours.
1941	A major tank battle took place outside Minsk. German commandoes, dressed as Soviets, took an important bridge at Daugaupils, Latvia. The Soviet destroyer MOSKVA was sunk by a mine off Constanta, Rumania. The U149 sank the Soviet submarine M-101. U149 survived the war.
1942	The Soviet submarine S-32 was sunk by the Luftwaffe. The Soviet destroyer BEZUPRECHNY was sunk by the Luftwaffe. The Soviet Navy delivered supplies to the besieged city of Sevastopol.
1943	The Soviet destroyer MOSKVA was sunk by a mine.
1944	The Soviets took Vitebsk and 80,000 prisoners. Seventy-two 8th Air Force B17s and 103 P51s dropped 104 tons of bombs on Drohobyz, Hungary flying while flying from Russia to Italy. A USAAF P38, flying from Poltava, was shot down by Soviet fighters.

Mediterranean

1940	Hitler urged Mussolini to attack towards the Suez Canal.
1941	Mussolini reviewed the "Torino" Division, which was scheduled to go to Russia.
1942	"HalPro" B24s attacked Tobruk, Libya.
1943	The U81 sank the Greek freighter MICHALIOS (3,742 tons) and the Syrian sailing ship TOUFIC ALLAH (75 tons). U81 survived until January 9, 1944. 100 Axis aircraft attacked an Allied convoy off Cap Bon, Tunisia causing no serious damage and losing six aircraft.
1944	The Italian heavy cruiser GORIZIA was sunk at La Spezia by Italian "Pigs".

Atlantic

1940 The German submarine UA sank the Norwegian freighter CRUX (3,828 tons). The U29 sank the Greek freighter DIMITRIS (5,254 tons). U29 survived until May 5, 1945. The German armed merchant cruiser WIDDER took the steamer KROSSFONN (9,323 tons).

1941 The German armed merchant cruiser KORMORAN took the Yugoslavian freighter VELEBIT (4,153 tons) and the Australian freighter MAREEBA (3,472 tons).

1942 The U203 sank the British freighter PUTNEY HILL (5,216 tons). U203 survived until April 25, 1943. The U107 sank the Dutch freighter JAGERSFONTEIN (10,083 tons). U107 survived until August 18, 1944. The U203 sank the Brazilian freighter PEDRINHAS (3,666 tons). U203 survived until April 25, 1943. Germany announced that it would commence unrestricted submarine warfare off the American coast.

1944 The U317 was sunk north of the Shetlands by the Royal Air Force's No.86 Squadron. The U719 was sunk northwest of Ireland by the Royal Navy destroyer BULLDOG.

North America

1898 USMC Colonel Lewis Burwell "Chesty" Puller was born in West Point, Va.

1942 The first fifteen B17Es of the 8th Air Force arrived at Goose Bay, Labrador en route to Britain. After refueling, they left later the same day for Bluie West 1, on the southwest coast of Greenland. The first flight of the F6F "Hellcat" took place.

1944 The submarines THREADFIN (sold to Turkey in 1973) and PIPER (stricken in 1970) were launched.

1945 The United Nations Charter was signed in San Francisco. A fire at Ladd Field, Alaska caused $230,000 in damage and killed 1.

1969 The destroyer CONWAY was expended as a target.

Pacific

1941 The IJN carrier JUNYO was launched. She was scrapped in 1947.

1942 Three American 7th Air Force LB30s (an export version of the B24) attacked Wake from Midway. It was their second attempt (See June 6th). A Royal Australian Air Force PBY was attacked and damaged by a USN F4F.

1943 The USN submarine JACK sank the TOYO MARU (4,163 tons) and the SHOZAN MARU (5,859 tons).

1944 The Royal Navy submarine TRUCULENT sank the HARUGIKU MARU (3,040 tons). 150 Japanese infantry attacked Aslito Airfield on Saipan and destroyed one P47. A USN squadron (Small) consisting of the cruisers CHESTER, PENSACOLA and CONCORD and the destroyers PICKING,

WICKES, SPROSTON, YOUNG, WILLIAM D. PORTER, ISHERWOOD, KIMBERLY, LUCE, and CHARLES J. BADGER bombarded the Kuriles.

1945 USAAF B29s began night attacks on Japans oil refineries. The USN submarine SEA ROBIN was attacked by a USAAF B29. The IJN destroyer ENOKI was sunk in the Inland Sea by a mine. The USN YMS-39 and YMS-365 were sunk off Balikpapan by a mine. The USN submarine PARCHE sank the KAMITSU MARU (2,721 tons) and the EIKAN MARU (2,721 tons).

China-Burma-India

1942 Brigadier General Earl L. Naiden assumed command of the American 10th Air Force.

1944 Chinese and Indian troops took Mogaung, Burma. Agansing Rai and Netrabahadur Thapa (posthumous), of the 2/5th Royal Gurkha Rifles, won a Victoria Cross' at Imphal, Burma. The Japanese took the American 14th Air Force base at Hengyang, China.

1945 The Chinese took Liuchow Airfield.

June 27th

Western Europe

1940 Britain announced that it was imposing a naval blockade from North Cape in Norway to the Spanish border. The Germans reached St. Jean-de-Luz, France on the Spanish border. 120 Royal Air Force bombers attacked targets along the Channel coast, Holland and in Germany, losing one "Blenheim" and one "Hampden".

1941 Twenty-three Royal Air Force "Blenheims" attacked Lille, France. Royal Air Force ace John Mungo-Park (12 victories) was killed in action over St. Omer, France. 108 Royal Air Force bombers attacked the ports of Bremen and Hamburg in Germany and lost fourteen aircraft. They killed seven people in Hamburg. Twenty-eight Royal Air Force "Hampdens" attacked the U-boat yards at Vegesack, Germany. The German blockade runner REGENSBURG (8,068 tons) arrived in Bordeaux, France from East Asia.

1942 144 Royal Air Force bombers attacked Bremen, Germany and lost nine aircraft. Seven people were killed in the raid. The commander of the 2nd Canadian Infantry Division, Major General J.H. Roberts, briefed his staff on the upcoming raid on Dieppe, France.

1943 Thirty Royal Air Force bombers dropped mines and lost one "Lancaster".

1944 218 American 8th Air Force bombers dropped 565 tons of bombs on V-1 rocket sites at Pas de Calais, France and lost five B24s. The 8th Air Force's Intelligence Chief, Brigadier General Arthur Vanaman, became the first American general captured by the Germans, when the 379th Bomb Group B17 he was aboard was damaged by anti/aircraft fire over St. Martin L'Hortier. After the war, Vanaman would revert to his permanent rank of Colonel and would eventually be promoted to major general in 1948. He died in 1987. 360 8th Air Force fighters flew sorties over France and claimed seventeen victories for the loss of two P51s and three P38s. US Army General Lawton Collins, the commander of the VII Corps, returned the city of Cherbourg to French civil control. The German forces in the dock area of Cherbourg surrendered. At 1515, the Royal Navy corvette PINK was declared a constructive loss after an attack by U988 off Normandy. A Luftwaffe KG200 B17 was shot down. 104 Royal Air Force bombers attacked V-1 rocket launching sites at Mimoyecques, France. 721 Royal Air Force bombers attacked V-1 sites in France and lost three "Lancasters". 214 Royal Air Force bombers attacked rail targets in France and lost four "Lancasters". The USAAF's 801st Bomb Group dispatched sixteen B24s on "Carpetbagger" missions. An 801st Bomb Group B24 was shot down by a Luftwaffe intruder while on a training flight over Eaton Socon, Britain.

1980 Walter Dornberger, age 84, died in West Germany. He had supervised the development of the V-2 rocket during WWII (he had been born in Giessen).

1991 German S.S. Lieutenant Josef Schwammberger, age 79, went to trial in Stuttgart for the murder of 3,377 persons during WWII, including fifty by his own hand.

2001 The wreck of the Royal Navy's destroyer EXMOUTH was located off the coast of Scotland. She had been sunk by the German U22 on January 21, 1940 with the loss of her entire 189-man crew.

Eastern Europe

1891 Soviet aircraft designer Vladimar Petlyakov was born. He died on January 12, 1942 in a plane crash.

1941 German forces arrived at Minsk, the capital of White Russia. 290,000 Soviet troops were surrounded west of Minsk. Hungary declared war on Russia. A British delegation arrived in Moscow for economic and military talks. The Soviet freighter MARTA was sunk by the Luftwaffe.

1942 The Germans took Sevastopol, although resistance did not end until July 3rd.

1944 The Soviets took Orsha. 35,000 Germans were captured near Vitebsk. 331 American 15th Air Force attacked rail targets in Yugoslavia, Poland, and Hungary.

Mediterranean

1940　The Italian submarine CONSOLE GENERALE LIUZZI (launched in 1939) was sunk southeast of Crete by the Royal Navy destroyers DEFENDER, DAINTY, DECOY, and ILEX. The Royal Navy submarine ORPHEUS (launched in 1930) was sunk between Malta and Alexandria.

1941　The Italian submarine GLAUCO was scuttled after action with the Royal Navy destroyer WISHART. The Italian submarine SALPA was sunk by the Royal Navy submarine TRIUMPH. The Royal Navy carrier ARK ROYAL launched 22 "Hurricanes" for Malta in "Operation Railway I", 1 aircraft was lost.

1942　The Axis surrounded Mersa Matruh, Egypt. Private A. Wakenshaw, of the Durham Light Infantry, won a posthumous Victoria Cross at Mersa Matruh, Egypt.

1943　The U73 damaged the British tanker ABBEYDALE (8,299 tons). U73 survived until December 16th.

Atlantic

1940　The U47 sank the Dutch tanker LETICIA (2,580 tons) and the Norwegian freighter LENDA (4,005 tons). U47 survived until March 7, 1941.

1941　The Italian submarine GLAUCO was sunk west of Gibraltar by the Royal Navy WISHART. The U69 sank the British freighters EMPIRE ABILITY (7,603 tons) and RIVER LUGAR (5,423 tons). U69 survived until February 17, 1943. The U564 sank the Dutch freighter MAASDAM (8,812 tons) and the British freighter MALAYA II (8,651 tons). U564 survived until June 14, 1943. The U123 sank the British freighter P.L.M.22 (5,646 tons) and the Dutch freighter OBERON (1,996 tons). U123 survived the war. The U556 was sunk southwest of Iceland by the Royal Navy corvettes NASTURTIUM, CELANDINE and GLADIOLUS.

1942　Allied Convoy PQ-17 left Reykjavik, Iceland for the port of Archangel in northern Russia. It was composed of thirty-five freighters. They included twenty-two American, eight British, two Russian, two Panamanian and one Dutch. They were escorted by six destroyers, four corvettes, four trawlers, three minesweepers, two submarines and two anti/aircraft auxiliaries. Long-range escort consisted of the Royal Navy carrier VICTORIOUS, the battleship DUKE OF YORK, the USN battleship WASHINGTON, six heavy cruisers and seventeen destroyers. The U129 sank the Mexican tankers TUXPAM (7,008 tons) and LAS CHOAPAS (2,005 tons). U129 survived until August 1944. The U126 sank the Norwegian tanker LEIV EIRIKSSON (9,952 tons). U126 survived until July 3, 1943. The U404 sank the Norwegian freighter MOLDANGER (6,827 tons). U404 survived until July 28, 1943. The U128 sank the American freighter POLYBIUS

(7,041 tons-10 dead). U128 survived until May 17, 1943. The U153 sank the American freighter POTLATCH (6,085 tons-8 dead). U153 survived until July 13th.

North America
1940 The US Secretary of State, Cordell Hull, received a list of Britain's requested military supplies. The battleship IOWA's keel was laid.
1941 The USAAF contracted for the XP63 "King Cobra".
1942 USAAF Commanding General Henry "Hap" Arnold awarded Distinguished Flying Crosses to 23 of the "Doolittle Raiders" in a ceremony at Bolling Field near Washington D.C. The FBI arrested German agents Herbert Haupt and Hermann Neubauer at the Sheridan Hotel in Chicago, Illinois. The two had landed on a Florida beach on the 17th with 2 others and were the last of 8 such agents to be captured. P38s of the 8th Air Forces 1st Fighter Group began their ferry flight to Britain. The escort carrier BRETON was launched. She was converted into a merchant ship in 1959. The destroyer MACKENZIE was launched. She was stricken in 1971. The US Army freighter MATAGALPA (the ex-USN destroyer OSBORNE) was lost due to a fire.
1943 The first flight of the YB29 "Superfortress" took place. Fourteen of them would be built to continue the preliminary testing begun by the 3 original XB29s.
1945 A Japanese balloon-bomb was found near Dease Lake, British Columbia. The escort carrier MINDORO was launched. She was scrapped in Hong Kong in 1960. The USN battleships WASHINGTON and NORTH CAROLINA were placed in reserve.
1946 There were 5,660 surplus military aircraft in storage at Walnut Ridge, Arkansas.
1976 USN Admiral Wade McCluskey died in Bethesda at age 75. He had won a Navy Cross during the "Battle of Midway".
2005 Robert Galer died. He had won a Medal of Honor for actions over Guadalcanal in August of 1942.
2009 USMC Colonel John Ruhsam, age 86, died in Sun City, Florida. During the war he had flown F4U "Corsairs" and had been credited with seven aerial victories and had received the Navy Cross.

Pacific
1940 Japan proclaimed a "Greater East Asia Co-Prosperity Sphere".
1942 The USN submarine NAUTILUS sank the MUSASHI MARU (227 tons). Royal Australian Air Force PBYs attacked Japanese positions at Lae and Salamaua on New Guinea. The USN minelayer OGLALA was refloated

1944   at Pearl Harbor. She had capsized during the December 7th attack. A USAAF P38 fighter was lost over Unalaska in the Aleutians.
1944   Fighting continued on Saipan. The USN submarine SEAHORSE sank the tanker MEDAN MARU (5,135 tons). Charles Lindbergh made his first flight with the 475th Fighter Group (P38), a mission along the New Guinea coast.
1945   Organized Japanese resistance ended on Luzon, although isolated pockets of Japanese troops would hold out until the end of the war. The USN submarine BLUEBACK sank the IJN sub chaser Cha-2. The IJN submarine I-165 was sunk by USN aircraft.

China-Burma-India
1939   Thirty Japanese Air Force aircraft attacked Soviet targets in Mongolia.
1943   The U511 sank the American freighter SEBASTIAN CERMANO (7,194 tons-5 dead) in the Indian Ocean. U511 survived the war.
1950   An F82 "Twin-Mustang" scored the first USAF victory in the Korean War, a Yak over Seoul.

June 28th

Western Europe
1883   French politician Pierre Laval was born.
1913   Luftwaffe ace Walter Osau (123 victories) was born in Farnewinkel. He was killed on May 11, 1944.
1919   The Treaty of Versailles was signed in the Hall of Mirrors. The Royal Navy light cruiser CAPETOWN was launched.
1935   Germany commissioned the U1, its first submarine since 1918. U1 survived until April 16, 1940.
1939   The Royal Air Force's Women's Auxiliary Air Force was formed.
1940   Germany informed the French government that the French Fleet would be interned in French ports. The British government recognized Charles de Gaulle as leader of the Free French forces. Britain de-militarized and evacuated the Channel Islands. Twenty Royal Air Force bombers attacked Merville, France. The Luftwaffe attacked Jersey and Guernsey later in the day killing forty-four civilians. 108 Royal Air Force bombers attacked targets in Germany and Holland. A Do17 scored the Luftwaffe's first night-fighter victory in German air-space.
1941   A Royal Air Force "Stirling" was lost over the Baltic. Luftwaffe ace Wilhelm Balthasar (40 victories) died in the crash of his Me109. He was buried in Abbeville Cemetery next to his father who had died in WWI. Thirty-four Royal Air Force "Hampdens" dropped mines in the Baltic.

1942 The Royal Navy left its anchorage at Scapa Flow to escort convoy PQ-17 from Iceland to Russia. Fourteen Royal Air Force bombers attacked St. Nazaire, France and lost one "Stirling".

1943 158 American 8th Air Force B17s dropped 300 tons of bombs on St. Nazaire, France and lost eight aircraft. 130 8th Air Force P47s escorted them to their target. Forty-three 8th Air Force B17s dropped 103 tons of bombs on the Beaumont-le-Roger airfield in France. 608 Royal Air Force bombers attacked Cologne, Germany and lost twenty-five aircraft. 6,417 buildings were destroyed and 4,377 people were killed in the raid.

1944 The last German positions in Cherbourg, France surrendered. The Germans began retreating near St. Lo, France. The Vichy Minister of Propaganda, Philippe Henriot, was assassinated in Paris. The American freighter CHARLES ELIOT was sunk off Normandy by a mine. The German torpedo boat KONDOR was scuttled at Le Havre, France. The American 9th Army headquarters arrived at Gourock, Scotland. 684 American 8th Air Force bombers dropped 1,554 tons of bombs on the Saarbrucken marshalling yards and airfields, supply dumps, bridges and oil depots in France and lost one B17 and one B24. 569 8th Air Force fighters flew sorties over France and claimed one victory for the loss of one P47 and one P51. 110 Royal Air Force bombers attacked V-1 rocket sites at Wizernes, France. 230 Royal Air Force bombers attacked rail targets in France and lost twenty aircraft. The USAAF's 801st Bomb Group dispatched eighteen B24s on "Carpetbagger" missions.

1971 Franz Stangl, German commander at Treblinka Concentration Camp, died in Dusseldorf Prison.

2010 Former S.S. sergeant Adolf Storms died in Duisburg, Germany at the age of 90. He had been awaiting trial for the murder of at least 57 people during the war. He had been listed as the 4th most wanted Nazi war criminal. He was discovered the previous November while working as a train station manager.

Eastern Europe

1940 The Soviets occupied Bessarabia and northern Bucovina in Rumania.

1941 3,800 Jews were executed by Germans in Kaunus, Lithuania. Soviet Major General A.A. Korobkov, commander of the 4th Army, was shot for cowardice. The Germans attacked east of Kursk. The Germans took Minsk. Albania declared war on Russia.

1942 The Soviet destroyer TASHKENT was sunk by the Luftwaffe. The Germans began their summer offensive east of Kursk.

1944 200 American 15th Air Force attacked oil targets in Rumania and Bulgaria. Walther Model replaced Ernst von Busch as commander of German Army Group "Center". The Soviets took Petrozavodsk.
1945 A "National Unity Government" was formed in Poland.

Mediterranean

1940 Italian General Italo Balbo was killed by Italian anti/aircraft fire over Tobruk, Libya. The Italian ARGONAUTA (launched in 1931) became the first submarine sunk by aircraft (a Sunderland) in WWII. At 2015, the Italian destroyer ESPERO (launched in 1928) was sunk by the Royal Navy cruisers ORION, NEPTUNE, LIVERPOOL and GLOUCESTER and the Royal Australian Navy cruiser SYDNEY.
1942 The British broke out of Mersa Matruh, Egypt. The US Military Attaché in Cairo changed his code, thus depriving Rommel of one of his sources of information. USAAF General Lewis Brereton arrived in Heliopolis, Egypt to assume command of the Mid-East Air Force (later renamed the 9th Air Force). The U97 sank the British freighter ZEALAND (1,433 tons) and the Greek freighter MEMAS (1,755 tons). U97 survived until June 16, 1943.
1943 Ninety-seven USAAF B17s dropped 261 tons of bombs on Leghorn, Italy. The Royal Air Force attacked Messina, Italy. The Italian light cruiser BARI was sunk at Livorno by the USAAF.

Atlantic

1940 The U30 sank the British freighter LLANARTH (5,053 tons). U30 survived until May 5, 1945.
1941 The U146 sank the Finnish freighter PLUTO (3,496 tons). U146 survived until May 1945. The Italian submarine DA VINCI sank the British tanker AURIS (8,030 tons). The German weather ship LAUENBERG was captured by the Royal Navy.
1942 The U701 sank the American tanker WILLIAM ROCKEFELLER (14,054 tons), the US Coast Guard No.460 rescued fifty survivors, as well as twenty-five from the tanker C.O. STILLMAN. U701 survived until July 7th. The U203 sank the American freighter SAM HOUSTON (7,176 tons-5 dead) off the Virgin Islands. U203 survived until April 25, 1943. The U332 sank the American freighter RAPHAEL SEMMES (6,027 tons-nineteen dead). U332 survived until May 2, 1943. The U505 sank the American freighter SEA THRUSH (5,447 tons). U505 was captured on June 4, 1944. She is now on display in Chicago, Illinois.
1943 The U172 sank the British freighter VERNON CITY (4,748 tons). U172 survived until December 13th.

1944   The U988 sank the British freighter MAID OF ORLEANS (2,385 tons). U988 survived until June 29th.

North America
1890   American Admiral William Blandy was born. In 1913, he graduated first in his Annapolis class of fifty-nine in 1913. He commanded amphibious and carrier groups in the Pacific during the capture of Kwajalein, Saipan and Iwo Jima. He also commanded the assault on Kerama Retto. He directed the atomic bomb tests at Bikini Atoll in 1946 and commanded the Atlantic Fleet from February 1947 until he retired on February 1, 1950. He died on January 12, 1954 at St. Albans Hospital in New York.
1891   USAAF General Carl Spaatz was born in Boyertown, Pennsylvania. He graduated 57th in his 1914 West Point class of 107. In 1916 he became one of the Army's first twenty-six aviators. During WWI he shot down three German aircraft and was awarded a Distinguished Service Cross. In 1927 Major Spaatz won a Distinguished Flying Cross when he and his co-pilot Captain Ira Eaker set a record when they stayed aloft for over 150 hours. In 1940 Colonel Spaatz went to Britain to serve as an observer during the "Battle of Britain". In July 1941 he became Deputy Commander of the USAAF. He activated the 8th Air Force on January 28, 1942 and took it to Britain. He later established the Northwest African Air Force in Algiers. After that he served as Deputy Commander of the Mediterranean Allied Air Forces. On December 22, 1943 he was named as commander of the US Strategic Air Forces in Europe. On March 11, 1945 he was promoted to four-star rank. He would move to the Pacific and direct the final air assault on Japan. He would serve as the first Chief of Staff of the independent USAF. He died on July 14, 1974 at the age of eighty-three.
1894   Admiral Arthur Struble was born in Portland, Oregon. He graduated 12th in his 1915 Annapolis class of 179. After several staff assignments he assumed command of the 9th Amphibious Group in the Pacific. He played a major part in landings in the Philippines. He retired on July 1, 1956 and died on May 1, 1983 in Chevy Chase, Maryland.
1942   The destroyers HARDING and DEHAVEN were launched. The HARDING was scrapped in 1947 and DEHAVEN was lost on February 1, 1943.
1943   The destroyer INGERSOLL was launched. She was stricken in 1970.
1961   The American "Liberty" ship MELVILLE FULLER was sunk by the USN submarine CUTLASS in torpedo tests.
1971   The destroyer HOBBY was expended as a target.

Pacific

1942 The USN submarine STINGRAY sank the IJN gunboat SAIKYO MARU (1,296 tons) north of Yap in the Carolines. The USN submarine NAUTILUS was damaged by depth charges off Honshu. USN PBYs attacked Tulagi.

1943 The USN submarine TUNNY sank the SHOTOKU MARU (1,964 tons). Eight Japanese bombers and six fighters were shot down over Darwin, Australia, for the loss of seven "Spitfires".

1944 Fighting continued on Biak and Saipan. The IJN escort No.24 was sunk west of Iwo Jima by the USN submarine ARCHERFISH. The USN submarine PARGO sank the YAMAGIKU MARU (5,236 tons). The USN submarine SEALION sank the SANSEI MARU (2,386 tons).

1945 General Douglas MacArthur announced that Luzon had been secured. Private L. Starcevitch, of the Australian 43rd Infantry Battalion, won a Victoria Cross on North Borneo. Eleven American airmen were executed in Japan.

China-Burma-India

1942 The IJN submarine I-10 sank the British freighter QUEEN VICTORIA (4,937 tons).

1943 The IJN submarine I-27 sank the Norwegian freighter DAH PU (1,974 tons).

1944 The Japanese took Hengyang, China.

June 29th

Western Europe

1880 German General Ludwig Beck was born in Biebrich, near Wiesbaden. He would serve as the Chief of Staff for the Armed Forces (OKW) from 1935 until 1938 when he was relieved by Hitler. He was executed on July 21, 1944 for his part in the July 20th conspiracy.

1936 The German battlecruiser SCHARNHORST was launched. She would be sunk on November 26, 1943.

1940 The French government decided to move from Bordeaux to Vichy. Twelve Royal Air Force bombers attacked Abbeville airfield in France. Eighty-three Royal Air Force bombers attacked targets in Germany and Holland losing two "Hampdens" and one "Whitley".

1941 106 Royal Air Force bombers attacked Bremen, Germany and lost seven aircraft. Twenty-eight Royal Air Force bombers attacked Hamburg, Germany and lost six aircraft. Eight people were killed in the raid on Hamburg, Germany.

1942 Captain Charles Kegelman, of the 15th Bomb Squadron, led the first USAAF crew to bomb occupied Europe when they flew one of twelve Royal Air Force A20 "Bostons" which attacked the Hazelbrouck railyards in Belgium. The aircraft belonged to the No.226 Squadron based at Swanton Morley. 253 Royal Air Force bombers attacked the port of Bremen, Germany and lost eleven aircraft.

1943 Seventy-six American 8th Air Force B17s dropped 181 tons of bombs on Le Mans, France. 148 8th Air Force B17s failed to drop their bombs on Villacoubay and Tricqueville in France due to cloud cover over the target. Sixteen Royal Air Force "Wellingtons" dropped mines off the Biscay ports and lost one aircraft.

1944 In Normandy, Friedrich Dollman was replaced as commander of the German 7th Army by SS general Paul Hausser and Geyr von Schweppenburg was replaced by Heinrich Eberbach as commander of Panzer Group "West". Dollman died of a heart attack within hours of his dismissal. 705 American 8th Air Force bombers dropped 1,775 tons of bombs on synthetic oil plants, bearing factories and aircraft assembly plants in Germany and lost six B17s and nine B24s. 678 8th and 9th Air Force fighters provided escort for the bombers and claimed fifty victories for the loss of three P51s. The American freighters JAMES FARRELL (7,176 tons), H.G. BLAISDAL (7,176 tons) and JOHN TREUTLEN (7,198 tons) were constructive losses after an attack by the U984 in the English Channel. U984 survived until August 20th. The U988 sank the British freighter EMPIRE PORTIA (7,058 tons) in the English Channel. U988 was then sunk by the Royal Navy frigates ESSINGTON, DUCKWORTH, DOMETT and COOK. The British stopped their "Operation Epsom" near Caen, France. Rommel and Rundstedt arrived at the Berghof to meet with Hitler. 305 Royal Air Force bombers attacked V-1 rocket launching sites in France and lost five aircraft.

Eastern Europe

1906 Soviet General Ivan Chernyakovsky was born. He was killed in Poland on February 18, 1945.

1941 The Germans attacked towards Murmansk from Norway and came within thirty-five miles of the city. Stalin declared that cowardice and the spreading of panic or rumors was to be punishable by death.

1944 The Soviets took Bobruisk.

Mediterranean

1940 The Italian submarine RUBINO (launched in 1933) was sunk by a Royal Air Force "Sunderland" west of Crete. The Royal Navy destroyers

VOYAGER, DAINTY, DECOY, DEFENDER, and ILEX sank the Italian submarine UEBI SCEBELI (launched in 1938). By this date, the Italian Navy had lost ten of the seventeen submarines with which it had started the war.

1941 The Royal Navy destroyer WATERHEN was damaged by "Stukas" and sank the next day.

1942 Italian dictator Benito Mussolini arrived in North Africa to participate in a planned victory parade in Cairo. "HalPro" lost a B24 over Tobruk. The Germans were within fifteen miles of El Alamein. The Axis took Mersa Matruh, Egypt. At 1120, the Italian sloop DIANA was sunk northwest of Tobruk by the Royal Navy submarine THRESHER.

1944 The British destroyers TENACIOUS, TERPSICORE and TUMULT bombarded German positions near Valona.

Atlantic

1940 The U51 sank the British freighter EDGEHILL (4,724 tons). U51 survived until August 20th. The U47 sank the British freighter EMPIRE TOUCAN (4,421 tons). U47 survived until March 7, 1941.

1941 The U103 sank the Italian freighter ERNANI (6,619 tons). U103 survived until April 15, 1945. The U651 sank the British freighter GRAYBURN (6,342 tons) south of Iceland. U651 was then sunk by the Royal Navy destroyers MALCOMB and SCIMITAR and corvettes VIOLET, SPEEDWELL and ARABIS. The U66 sank the Greek freighters GOULANDRIS (4,375 tons) and VERGOTTI (5,686 tons). U66 survived until May 6, 1944. The U123 sank the British freighter RIO AZUI (4,088 tons). U123 survived until August 19, 1944. The U564 sank the Icelandic freighter HEKLA (1,215 tons). U564 survived until June 14, 1943.

1942 The U126 sank the Canadian sailing ship MONA MARIE (126 tons). U126 survived until July 3, 1943. The U158 sank the Latvian freighter EVERALDA (3,950 tons). U158 survived until June 30th. The British tanker EMPIRE MICA (8,032 tons) was sunk off Florida by the U67. U67 survived until July 16, 1943. The U754 sank the British freighter WAIWERA (12,435 tons). U754 survived until July 31st. The American freighter THOMAS MCKEAN (7,191 tons-5 dead) was sunk off Puerto Rico by the U505. U505 was captured later in the war and is now on display in Chicago, Illinois. The U153 sank the American freighter RUTH (4,833 tons-31 dead). U153 survived until July 13th.

North America

1922 The light cruiser DETROIT (awarded six battle stars during the war) was launched. She was scrapped in Baltimore in 1946.

1944 The carrier RANDOLPH was launched. She was stricken in 1973.

1945 German POWs who had admitted to Soviet citizenship rioted at Fort Dix, New Jersey when they were informed that they were to be repatriated back to the Soviet Union.

1998 USMC ace Marion Carl (18.5 victories) was shot to death in his Roseburg, Oregon home by a burglar. He had set the worlds speed record of 651 miles per hour on August 25, 1947 and had established an altitude record of 83,235 feet in 1953. He later would fly U-2 missions over China and would command the 2nd Marine Air Wing during the Vietnam War. He had retired in 1973 with 13,000 flying hours.

Pacific

1942 The USN minelayer OGLALA sank again during salvage operations at Pearl Harbor (the third time). She had been sunk originally on December 7, 1942 during the Japanese attack.

1943 USN Task Unit 36.2.1 consisting of four cruisers and four destroyers and commanded by Aaron S. Merrill bombarded Vila on Kolombangara and Buin on Bougainville.

1944 The USN submarine FLASHER sank the NIHO MARU (6,079 tons). The USN submarine GROWLER sank the KATORI MARU (1,920 tons). The USN submarine STURGEON sank the TOYAMA MARU (7,089 tons). The USN submarine DARTER sank the IJN minelayer TSUGARU west of Morotai.

China-Burma-India

1944 The IJN submarine I-8 sank the British freighter NELLORE (6,942 tons).

June 30th

Western Europe

1884 German General Franz Halder was born in Wurzburg. He would serve as Chief of the Army General Staff from 1938 until 1942 when he was relieved by Hitler. He was imprisoned in connection with the July 20th conspiracy. He was detained by the Allies after the war as a prisoner of war and wasn't released until his birthday in 1947. He died on April 2, 1972.

1934 The "Night of the Long Knives" occurred when the leaders of the German S.A. were massacred. Hitler had ordered the action to placate the Wehrmacht which had become concerned with the size of Ernst Rohm's private army. The German pocket battleship GRAF SPEE was launched. She would be scuttled on December 17, 1939.

1936	Ethiopian Premier Haile Selassie addressed the League of Nations on Italian aggression in Ethiopia. The French Fascist Party was outlawed.
1937	British observers were pulled off the Portuguese border in response to Germany and Italy withdrawing from the Neutrality Patrol off Spain.
1940	The Germans landed on Jersey and Guernsey Islands in the English Channel. Eighteen Royal Air Force bombers attacked targets in France and lost three "Blenheims". Luftwaffe commander Hermann Goering issued orders for the first phase of the Battle of Britain. The Luftwaffe was to gain control of the air over the English Channel. Eighty-eight Royal Air Force bombers attacked targets in Germany.
1941	Twenty-eight Royal Air Force bombers attacked targets in Germany and lost two aircraft. The Vichy government broke relations with Russia. Germany suspended the "Battle of Britain" in view of new commitments in the east. Sixty-four Royal Air Force bombers attacked targets in the Ruhr and lost four aircraft.
1942	Adolf Eichmann arrived in Paris with orders from Heinrich Himmler to deport all French Jews. 300 British civilians were killed and 337 were wounded in air-raids in Britain in June.
1944	The US Army's 9th Division attacked German positions on Cap-de-la-Hague. A general strike was called in Copenhagen, Denmark and lasted until July 4th. The Allies had landed 630,000 men, 600,000 tons of supplies and 177,000 vehicles in Normandy since the 6th. 1,935 British civilians were killed and 5,906 were wounded in air-raids in June. 135 American 8th Air Force bombers dropped 317 tons of bombs on airfields in France and Belgium. 305 8th Air Force fighters flew sorties over France and Belgium and claimed four victories for the loss of one P38. 8th Air Force fighters flew 25,402 sorties during the month-the highest monthly total of the war. 266 Royal Air Force bombers attacked German troop concentrations at Villers-Bocage, France and lost two aircraft. 107 Royal Air Force bombers attacked V-1 rocket launching sites at Oisemont, France. 118 Royal Air Force bombers attacked Vierzon, France and lost fourteen aircraft.
1945	The British government awarded fifteen Victoria Crosses in the month of June during the war.
1988	A Luftwaffe 2,200 lbs. bomb was unearthed and defused near the Tower of London.

Eastern Europe

1941	General D.G. Pavlov, commander of the Soviet Western Front, and his staff were recalled to Moscow and executed for the collapse of the Front. The Germans took Bobryusk. The German losses for the operation so far were 8,886 men.

1942   The Soviet Headquarters ordered the evacuation of the Sevastopol area. It could only be carried out on a small scale before the Germans took the city. The Germans began an offensive south of Kharkov.

1944   The American 15th Air Force attacked airfields in Yugoslavia and Hungary.

Mediterranean

1941   The Royal Navy gunboat CRICKET was a constructive loss after a Luftwaffe attack east of Mersa Matruh.

1942   The Axis reached El Alamein, fifty-seven miles from Alexandria. The U372 sank the Royal Navy submarine tender MEDWAY (14,650 tons). U372 survived until August 4th.

1943   The U453 damaged the British freighter OLIGARCH (6,894 tons). U453 survived until May 21, 1944.

Atlantic

1940   The Axis sank 585,496 tons of Allied and neutral shipping in June and lost one German U-boat. The U102 sank the Norwegian freighter BELMOIRA (3,214 tons) and the Estonian freighter MERKUR (1,291 tons). U102 survived until August 21st. The U26 sank the Greek freighter GOULANDRIS (6,701 tons). U26 survived until July 3rd. The U47 sank the Greek freighter KYRIAKIDES (4,201 tons). U47 survived until March 7, 1941. The U43 sank the British freighter AVELONA STAR (13,376 tons). U43 survived until July 30, 1943.

1941   The Axis sank 432,025 tons of Allied and neutral shipping in June and lost four German U-boats. The Royal Navy cruiser DUNEDIN captured the Vichy French steamer VILLE DE TAMATAVE. The U66 sank the British freighter ST. ANSELM (5,614 tons). U66 survived until May 6, 1944.

1942   The Axis sank 834,196 tons of Allied and neutral shipping in June and lost two German U-boats. The Italian submarine MOROSINI sank the Dutch freighter TYSA (5,327 tons). The U458 sank the Norwegian freighter MOSFRUIT (2,714 tons). U458 survived until August 22, 1943. The USN minesweeper COURIER rescued thirty survivors from the American freighter SAM HOUSTON which had been sunk on June 28th by U203. The USN gunboat SURPRISE rescued survivors from the American freighter SEA THRUSH which had been sunk on June 28th by U505.

1943   The Axis sank 123,825 tons of Allied and neutral shipping in June and lost seventeen German U-boats. The Vichy ships that had been interned at Martinique and Guadeloupe were turned over to the Free French. They were the carrier BEARN, the cruisers JEANNE DE ARC and EMILE BERTIN along with several smaller vessels.

1944 The Axis sank 104,084 tons of Allied and neutral shipping in June and lost twenty-two German U-boats.

North America
1942 A USN XPBS-1 seaplane carrying Pacific Fleet Commander Admiral Chester Nimitz crashed while landing at Alameda Naval Air Station in San Francisco. The submarine TUNNY was launched at Mare Island. She was expended in 1969. The USN minesweeper HORNBILL was sunk in a collision with the lumber schooner ESTHER JOHNSON in San Francisco Bay.
1943 The destroyer HALSEY POWELL (sold to Korea in 1968) was launched.
1944 America broke relations with Finland. The US Coast Guard No.83421 was sunk in a collision with the USN SC-1330 off Miami.
1945 The heavy cruiser ALBANY was launched. She was still in service in 1980. The American government awarded twenty-eight Medals of Honor in the month of June during the war.
1946 The carrier BUNKER HILL received a Presidential Unit Citation for actions between November 11, 1943 and May 11, 1945.
1947 The light cruiser AMSTERDAM was decommissioned. She was sold for scrap in 1971.
1957 Major Jacob Eierman retired. He had flown on the "Doolittle Raid".
1961 Curtis LeMay was sworn in as USAF Chief of Staff. He had commanded the 20th Air Force during the war.
1962 Brigadier General Leslie Smith (7 victories while with the 56th Fighter Group 8th Air Force) retired from the California Air National Guard. Lieutenant Colonel Edgar McElroy retired. He had flown on the "Doolittle Raid".
2012 USMC ace Fred Gutt died in Seattle, Washington at the age of 92. He had been credited with 8 aerial victories while flying with VMF-223 in the Pacific.

Pacific
1942 The Allies sank 32,379 tons of Japanese shipping (8 ships) in June. The USN submarine PLUNGER sank the UNKAI MARU No.5 (3,282 tons) off Shanghai. Royal Australian Air Force PBY "Catalinas" attacked Lae, New Guinea.
1943 The Allies sank 109,115 tons of Japanese shipping (28 ships) in June. The US Army's 43rd Division landed on Rendova and Vangunn Islands. The US Army's 6th Division landed on Woodlark and Kiriwina Islands. The USN attack transport MCCAWLEY was torpedoed and later sunk in error by USN PT boats off Rendova. The USN destroyer GWIN was hit by

shore-fire off Rendova, seven of her crew died. She was accompanied by the destroyers FARENHOLT, JENKINS, RADFORD, and BUCHANAN in the operation. The Japanese Naval Air Force lost 101 aircraft over Rendova while downing fourteen American planes.

1944 The Allies sank 285,204 tons of Japanese shipping (75 ships) in June. The US Army's 27th Division took "Death Valley" and "Purple Heart Peak" on Saipan. Mopping up operations continued on Biak. American 13th Air Force B24s attacked Noemfoor Island. The USN submarine TANG sank the NIKKIN MARU (5,705 tons). The USN submarine JACK sank TSURUSHIMA MARU (4,645 tons) and the MATSUKAWA MARU (3,832 tons). The USN submarine PLAICE sank the HAYAKUFUKU MARU (986 tons).

1945 The Allies sank 196,180 tons of Japanese shipping (108 ships) in June. Luzon was declared secure, although there were still 23,000 Japanese troops on the island. Organized Japanese resistance ended on Okinawa. The IJN destroyer NARA was a constructive loss after hitting a mine in the Kuriles. The USN submarine LOGARTO sank the HOKUSHIN MARU (5,819 tons).

1969 The USN destroyer FRANK E. EVANS collided with the HMAS carrier MELBOURNE. Her stern was salvaged and expended as a target in October.

1989 The wreckage of a Japanese Air Force Ki46 "Dinah" was uncovered at Clark Field on Luzon.

China-Burma-India

1942 The IJN submarine I-20 sank the Norwegian freighter GOVIKEN (4,854 tons) and the British tanker STEAUA ROMANO (5,311 tons). The IJN submarine I-10 sank the American freighter EXPRESS (6,736 tons-13 dead).

1945 The Chinese took Chungchin.

www.ingramcontent.com/pod-product-compliance
Lightning Source LLC
LaVergne TN
LVHW091651070526
838199LV00050B/2140